THE CONCISE SANSKRIT-ENGLISH DICTIONARY

The Concise Sanskrit-English Dictionary

Compiled by

VASUDEO GOVIND APTE

MOTILAL BANARSIDASS PUBLISHERS
PRIVATE LIMITED • DELHI

12th Reprint: Delhi, 2014
Second Revised Edition: Bombay, 1933

ISBN: 978-81-208-0151-6 (Cloth)
ISBN: 978-81-208-0152-3 (Paper)

MOTILAL BANARSIDASS
41 U.A. Bungalow Road, Jawahar Nagar, Delhi 110 007
8 Mahalaxmi Chamber, 22 Bhulabhai Desai Road, Mumbai 400 026
203 Royapettah High Road, Mylapore, Chennai 600 004
236, 9th Main III Block, Jayanagar, Bengaluru 560 011
Sanas Plaza, 1302 Baji Rao Road, Pune 411 002
8 Camac Street, Kolkata 700 017
Ashok Rajpath, Patna 800 004
Chowk, Varanasi 221 001

Printed in India

by RP Jain at New Age Books Printing Unit,
A-44, Naraina Industrial Area, Phase I, New Delhi–110028
and published by JP Jain for Motilal Banarsidass Publishers (P) Ltd,
41 U.A. Bungalow Road, Jawahar Nagar, Delhi-110007

PREFACE TO THE FIRST EDITION

During the pretty long period that I was doing the work of a teacher in one of the largest high schools in the Bombay Presidency, I observed no need more keenly felt by High School and College students than that of a Sanskrit-English dictionary, which met all their requirements and was at once concise, cheap and handy. There are no doubt excellent lexicons in existence compiled by eminent scholars like the late Principal V. S. Apte and L. R. Vaidya, but their bulkiness and cost prohibit a large number of students from enjoying an advantage so necessary in their study of Sanskrit. Besides the long explanations and exhaustive meanings of words intermixed with quotations from standard works in Sanskrit literature, which form the chief merit of the two scholarly and invaluable works above referred to, embarrass rather than help the students who have limited intelligence and time at their disposal. There is, therefore, a crying need of a dictionary which supplies everything required by an ordinary student of Sanskrit in his school and college career and which is at the same time characterised by brevity and cheapness. These considerations form my apology for ushering into existence the present compilation, which, it is hoped, will serve the purpose for which it is intended.

Having the requirements of students constantly in view I have endeavoured in the present work to keep out all those Sanskrit words, which are hardly, if ever, used in ordinary text-books used by students and in order to secure compactness I had often recourse to eschewing all technicalities as well as words which even an ordinary intelligence and common sense told every student to be simple derivatives of some given word. Thus I have endeavoured to reduce the bulk of the dictionary without compromising its usefulness to students.

I can lay no pretensions to originality in the compilation of this work nor can I claim by any manner or means immunity from mistakes either of matter or of printing. I am indeed fully conscious of the several errors that have surreptiously crept both in compilation and printing. Nonetheless I venture to give this book into the hands of my young friends with full confidence that in spite of all its shortcomings it will serve to some extent to lighten their labours and to guide them along the path of their study of Sanskrit literature.

I cannot conclude this preface without acknowledging my indebtedness to the authors of works upon which I have freely drawn in the compilation of this dictionary. Lexicons compiled by eminent scholars like Monier Williams, H. H. Wilson, the late Principal V. S. Apte, the late Mr. L. R. Vaidya, Mr. Mādhav Chandrobá (author of the *Shabdaratnákar*) and similar works of Bengali scholars, such as the *Shabdakalpadruma* and the *Shabdarthamanjari* have rendered me invaluable help for which I cannot be too thankful to their authors.

Poona City, V. G. APTE
23rd, June 1912.

PREFACE TO THE SECOND EDITION

We have the pleasure to bring out a second and revised edition of this useful work.

1st, April 1933. Gopal Narayen & Co.

ABBREVIATIONS USED IN THIS BOOK

A. or Atm. . for Atmanepada.	*pl* ....Plural.
a..........Adjective.	*pp*. ....Past passive participle.
caus ......Causal.	*pron* ...... Pronoun.
Compar. ....Comparative	*sing*........Singular.
du........Dual.	*super* .....Superlative.
f..........Feminine.	U ....Ubhayapada viz. Par. and Atm.
gram ......Grammar.	*vi* ....Verb intransitive.
ind ....Indeclinable.	*vt* .... Verb transitive.
m ....Masculine.	
n ....Neuter.	
P..........Parasmaipada.	

INSTRUCTIONS

Words having the same meanings but having slight variations in their spellings are for the sake of brevity thus put together:—

को (कौ) शलिक = कोशलिक, कौशलिक

A new word formed by the mere addition of a letter or two is indicated by means of a dash before such addition. Thus कैवर्तं, (-क) = कैवर्तं, कैवर्तक; केश पक्ष (-पाश, हस्त) = केशपक्ष, केशहस्त.

THE CONCISE
SANSKRIT-ENGLISH DICTIONARY.

अ.

अ *ind.* A prefix meaning 'not', corresponding to *un* or *in* in English. Before a vowel it becomes अन्. *m* A name of Vishnu, also of Brahman (*n.*)

अंश् *vt.* 10 U. To divide; With वि-to break asunder; to deceive.

अंश *m* A share; a shoulder; a degree; the numerator of a fraction (in mathe.).

अंशक *m.* A part; a kinsman; *n.* A day.

अंशभाक् *m.* An heir.

अंशल *a.* Strong.

अंशहर (हारिन्) *a.* A sharer.

अंशांशि *ind.* Share by share.

अंशिन् *n* A sharer, a co-heir.

अंशु *m* A ray of light; dress.

अंशुक *n* Cloth, a robe, a leaf.

अंशुजाल *n.* A collection of ar

अंशुधर (-पति, बाण, मत्, मालिन्, हस्त) *m.* The sun.

अंशुल *a.* Radiant, splendid, *m.* A name of Chânakya.

अंस् *vt.* See अंश्.

अंस *m.* A shoulder.

अंसकूट *m.* A bull's hump.

अंसल *a.* Strong.

अंह् 10 U. To shine; to speak; I A. to go.

अंहति *f.* A gift; pain.

अंहिति (अंहिती) *f.* A gift.

अंहस् *n.* Sin.

अंह्रिप *m* A tree.

अंह्रिस्कंध *m.* The upper part of the sole of the foot.

अक् I. P. To go tortuously.

अक *n.* Sin; sorrow.

अकरणि *f.* Failure.

अकर्ण *m.* A snake; *a.* deaf.

अकर्तन् *m.* A dwarf.

अकर्मन् *a.* Idle *n.* an improper act.

अकर्मक *a.* Intransitive.

अकर्मभोग *m.* The liberation

of the soul from the fruits of action.

अकल *a.* Whole. *n.* The supreme soul.

अकलित *a.* Incomprehensible.

अकल्क *a.* Clear sinless.

अकल्का *f.* Moon-light.

अकल्प *a.* Uncontrolled; weak.

अकल्पित *a.* Natural.

अकल्य *a.* Unwell.

अकल्पसंध *a.* True to one's word.

अकस्मात् *ind.* Suddenly.

अकाण्ड *a.* Sudden.

अकाण्डे *ind.* Suddenly, causelessly. [ally.

अकामतः *ind.* Unintention-

अकाय *m.* A name of Râhu; the supreme soul.

अकारणम् *ind.* Causelessly.

अकारणोत्पन्नगुण *m.* Natural (not acquired) merit

अकार्य *n.* Wicked act.

अकाल *m.* Improper or unfavourable time.

अकाल्य *a.* Unseasonable.

अकिंचन *a.* Poor, destitute. *n.* That which is worth nothing.

अकिंचित्कर *a.* Innocent; powerless.

अकिंचिज्ज्ञ *a.* Altogether ignorant.

अकिल्बिष *a.* Sinless.

अकीर्ति *f.* Disgrace.

अकुण्ठ *a.* Not blunted, excessive [where.

अकुतस् *ind.* Not from any

अकुतोभय *a.* Secure.

अकुप्य *n.* Gold or silver; a base metal.

अकुल *a.* Low; baseborn.

अकुशल *a.* Unlucky; clumsy. *n.* misfortune.

अकूपार *m.* The sea; a tortoise; *a.* Unlimited.

अकूर्च *a.* not deceitful.

अकृच्छ्र *m* *n.* Facility. *a.* Free from difficulty.

अकृत *n.* An unheard of action.

अकृतार्थ *a.* Unsuccessful

अकृतज्ञ *a* Ungrateful.

अकृत-धी,-बुद्धि *a.* Ignorant.

अकृता *f.* A daughter not placed on a level with sons.

अकृत्य *n.* A crime.

अकेतु *a.* Unconscious.

अक्का *f.* A mother.

अक्त *n.* Oil; ointment

अक्त्र *n.* An armour.

अक्ष् *v. t.* 5 P. to pervade; to accumulate.

अक्ष *m.* A dice; a beam of a balance; an axis; a terrestrial latitude; a wheel; a car; a snake; a seed of which rosaries are made; the soul; sacred lore; a weight of 16 *mashas*; a lawsuit; an eye; a person born blind; *n*. An organ of sense; sea-salt.

अक्षकर्ण *m*. Hypotenuse.

अक्षकूट *m*. The pupil of the eye. [Vishnu.

अक्षज *m*. A diamond;

अक्षज्ञ *a*. Skilled in gambling.

अक्षदर्शक *m*. A judge.

अक्षदेवन *n*. Gambling.

अक्षद्यूत *n*. Gambling.

अक्षपटल *n* A law-court.

अक्षपाद *m*. The name of the founder of the Nyáya philosophy.

अक्षभार *m*. A cart-load.

अक्षमाला *f*. A rosary.

अक्षवती *f*. A game of dice.

अक्षवाट *m*. A gambling-house.

अक्षवाम *m*. An unfair gambler.

अक्षविद्या *f*. The art of dice.

अक्षत *a*. Uninjured, whole. *m. n*. An eunuch; (*pl.*) *yava* or rice grain.

अक्षतयोनि *i*. A virgin.

अक्षता *f*. A virgin.

अक्षय *a*. Undecaying.

अक्षय (अक्षत) तृतीया *f*. The third day of the bright half of Vaisâkha.

अक्षय्य *a*. Imperishable.

अक्षर *a*. Imperishable. *m*. 1 Siva; 2 Vishnu. *n*. A syllable, a vowel; final beatitude; Brahman (*n*.)

अक्षरचंचु(चुं)चु *m*. A writer.

अक्षरछंदस् *n*. A metre.

अक्षरजननी *f*. A pen.

अक्षरतूलिका *f*. A reed, a pen.

अक्षरन्यास (-संस्थान) *m*. Writing; the alphabet.

अक्षरमुख *m*. A scholar.

अक्षरशस् *ind*. Syllable by syllable.

अक्षरवर्जित *a*. Illiterate.

अक्षरशिक्षा *f*. The science of mystic syllables.

अक्षरि *f*. The rainy season.

अक्षांति *f*. Intolerance, malice.

अक्षारलवण *n* Natural salt.

अक्षावली *f*. A rosary.

अक्षावाप *m*. A gambler.

अक्षि *n*. The eye.

अक्षिकूटक *n*. The eye-ball.

अक्षिगत *a*. Seen, hated.

अक्षि(क्षी)व *n*. Sea-salt.

अक्षुण्ण *a*. Unbroken.

अक्षेत्र *n*. A bad field; a bad pupil.

अक्षेत्रविद् *a*. Destitute of spiritual knowledge.

अक्षोट *m*. A walnut tree.

अक्षौहिणी *f*. An army consisting of 21870 elephants, 21870 chariots,

65610 horses and 109350 foot.

अक्षण *n.* Time.

अखण्ड *a.* Entire, whole.

अखात *m.n.* A natural lake.

अखिल *a.* Complete, whole.

अग् *vi.* I P. (*pres.* अंगति) To go. I P. (*pres.* अगति) To move tortuously.

अग *m.* A mountain; a tree; a serpent; the sun.

अगति(ती)क *a.* Helpless.

अगद *m.* Health; medicine.

अगम *m.* A mountain; a tree.

अगम्य *a.* Inaccessible; unfit for sexual intercourse; difficult to understand.

अग(गु)रु *m. n.* A kind of sandal wood.

अगस्ति (स्त्य) *m.* Name of a sage, of a star, or of a plant.

अगाध *a.* unfathomable, incomprehensible. *m. n.* A deep hole or chasm.

अगार *n.* A house.

अगृह *m.* A hermit.

अगोचर *a* Imperceptible by the senses

अगोह्य *a.* Not to be concealed; bright

अग्नायी *f.* A name of of Svá-há, the wife of Agni; Treta or the second age of the Hindus.

अग्नि *m.* Fire; appetite; gold.

अग्निकण *m.* A spark of fire.

अग्निकाष्ठ *n.* Agallochum.

अग्निकुक्कुट *m.* Fire brand.

अग्निकुमार *m.* A name of Kârtikeya.

अग्निकेतु *m.* Smoke.

अग्निकोण *m.* The south-east.

अग्निक्रीडा *f.* Fire-work, illumination.

अग्निगर्भा *f.* The earth.

अग्निचित् *m.* A house-holder who has placed and consecrated sacrificial fire.

अग्निद *m.* An incendiary.

अग्निबाहु *m* Smoke.

अग्निभ *n.* Gold; the Plaeiades.

अग्निभु *n.* Water.

अग्निमांद्य *n.* Dyspepsia.

अग्निमुख *m.* A deity; a Brâhmana.

अग्निमुखी *f.* Kitchen.

अग्निवाह *m.* Smoke.

अग्निवीर्य *n.* Gold.

अग्निशिख *m.* A lamp; a rocket; an arrow; saffron.

अग्निष्टोम *m.* A kind of sacrifice.

अग्निसख (सहाय) *m.* Wind; smoke.

अग्निसात् *ind.* + कृ or भू *vt.* To consign to fire.

अग्निहोत्र *n*. Maintenance of sacred fire.

अग्निय *a*. Referring to fire.

अग्न्युत्पात *m*. A fiery meteor.

अग्र *a*. Foremost, best.

अग्रणी *m*. A leader.

अग्रदूत *m*. A harbinger.

अग्रनिरूपण *n* A prophecy.

अग्रपूजा *f*. The highest mark of reverence.

अग्रभुज् *a*. Voracious.

अग्रा *f*. Goal of ambition.

अग्रमांस *n*. The heart.

अग्रसंध्या *f*. Early dawn.

अग्रसर *a*. Taking the lead.

अग्रहायण *m*. Commencement of the year; the month of Mârgasîrsha.

अग्रहार *m*. A royal donation of lands to Brâhmanas.

अग्रतस् *ind*. In front of, before.

अग्रिम *a*. Foremost, elder.

अग्रे *ind*. In front, later on.

अग्रेसर *m*. A leader.

अग्रेसरिक *m*. A servant; a leader.

अग्र्य *a*. Chief. *m*. An elder brother *n*. The roof..

अघ् *vi*. I A. (*pres.* अंघते) To go. 10 P. to sin.

अघ *n*. Evil, sin, vice

अघमर्षण *n*. A prayer by Brâhmanas; *m*. name of the author of the prayer.

अघविष *m*. A snake.

अघशंसिन् *a*. Wicked.

अघर्म *a*. Cool

अघायु *a*. Malicious; sinful.

अघांशु *m*. The moon.

अघोरपथिन् (-मार्ग) *m*. A worshipper of Siva and Durgâ.

अघोष *a*. Hard-sounding.

अंक् *vt*. 10 P. To count; to mark.

अंक *m*. Mark; a stain; an act of a drama; proximity; a number; a book; a curve or bend.

अंकतन्त्र *n*. The science of numbers.

अंकपालि (पालिका) *f*. An embrace, a nurse.

अंकपाश *m*. Permutations and combinations (in Mathe.).

अंकपूरण *n*. Multiplication of numbers.

अंकलोप *m*. Subtraction.

अंकित *a*. Marked; stained.

अंकुट *m*. A key.

अंकु(कू)र *m*. A sprout; hair; blood.

अंकुरित *a*. Budded; arisen.

अंकुश *m*. *n*. A hook, a goad, a restraint.

अंकुशग्रह *m*. an elephant-driver.

अंकोलिका *f*. An embrace.

अंख् *v*. *i*. 10 P. To crawl; to check.

अंग् *vt.* 10 U. To mark; to go.

अंग *ind.* Indeed; to be sure *n.* A limb, a part; an expedient, *m. pl.* Name of the country about the modern Bhagalpur in Bengal or people living in it.

अंगांगि *ind.* Jointly or reciprocally.

अंगांगिभाव *m.* The relation of principal and subordinate.

अंगज *m.* A son; the god of love; passion; a disease. *n.* Blood; hair.

अंगजनुस् *m.* A son.

अंग-भू *m.* a son, the God of love.

अंगमर्ष *m.* Rheumatism.

अंगराग *m.* Scented unguent.

अंगरुह *n.* Hair.

अंगविक्षेप *m.* Jesticulation.

अंगविद्या Palmistry.

अंगण (न) *n.* A court.

अंगद् *m.* Name of son of Vāli, the monkey king of Kishkindhā. *n.* A bracelet worn on the upper arm.

अंगना *f.* A woman.

अंगस् *n.* A bird.

अंगसंस्कार *m.* Personal decoration.

अंगार (-क*m,m.n.* Charcoal. *m.* The planet Mars.

अंगारकमणि *m.* A coral.

अंगारिका *f.* The stalk of the sugarcane; a fire-pan.

अंगारिता *f.* A bud; a creeper

अंगिका *f.* A bodice or jacket.

अंगिन् *a.* Corporeal; chief.

अंगिरस् *m.* Name of a sage.

अंगीकरण *n.* Acceptance, promise.

अंगीकार *m. see* **अंगीकरण.**

अंगीकृ *vt.* 8 U. to accept; to agree.

अंगीकृति *f. see* **अंगीकरण.**

अंगु *m.* A hand (as in **अंगुष्ठ.**)

अंगुरि-री *f.* A finger.

अंगुरी(ली)य, **(-क)** *n.* A finger ring.

अंगुल *m.* A finger.

अंगुलि (-ली) *f.* A finger, the thumb.

अंगुलित्र (-त्राण) *n.* A finger-protector.

अंगुलिमुद्रा(-मुद्रिका) *f* A seal-ring.

अंगुलिक *m.n.* A finger-ring.

अंगुष्ठ *m* The thumb.

अंगुष्ठय *m.* The nail of the thumb.

अंगूष *m.* An arrow; an ichneumon.

अंघ् I A. to go; to hasten.

अंघस् *n.* Sin.

अंघ्रि *m.* A foot; the root of a tree.

अंघ्रिज *m.* A Sûdra
अंघ्रिप *m.* A tree.
अंघ्रिस्कंध *m.* The ankle.
अच् *vt.* 1U. (*pp.* अक्त) To speak indistinctly. 1 P. (*pp.* अञ्चित) To go; to honour. With अप to run away; उत् to go up; नि to bend down; परा to go back. परि to go about.
अचण्डी *f.* A tractable cow.
अच *a.* Immoveable. *m.* A mountain,; a pin or bolt *n.* Brahman (*n.*)
अचलकन्या *f.* Name of Párvati.
अचला *f.* The earth.
अचलाधिप *m.* The Himalayas.
अचिंत्य (अचिंतनीय) *a.* Inconceivable. *n* Name of Brahman (*n*).
अचित्र *a.* Indistinct.
अचिर *a.* Transitory, brief.
अचिर (-द्युति) -प्रभा -भास्, -रोचिस्) *f.* Lightning.
अचिरम् (अचिरेण, अचिराय, अचिरात्, अचिरस्य,) *ind.* Soon, shortly after.
अचेतन *a.* / **अचेतस्** *a.* Inanimate; lifeless; senseless.
अचैतन्य *n.* Unconsciousness.
अच्छ *a.* Clear, transparent, pure.
अच्छ (च्छा) / **अच्छम्** *ind.* Toward.
अच्छिद्र *a.* Faultless.
अच्छोद (अच्छ + उद्) *a.* Having clear water.
अच्युत *a.* Firm ; imperishable. *m.* A name of Vishnu or Krishna.
अज् *vt.* 1 P. (*pp.* वीत or अजित) To go ; to drive, *vi.* 10 U. (*pp.* अंजित) To shine.
अज *a.* Unborn. *m.* A he-goat; Brahman (*m*); Vishnu; Siva; Kāmadeva.
अजगर *m.* A large serpent that swallows a goat.
अजघन्य *a.* Not last, not the least
अजनि *f.* A path, a road.
अजननि *f.* Destruction.
अजन्य *n.* A portent, an omen.
अजबंधु *m.* A fool; one silly like a goat.
अजंभ *m.* A frog; the sun.
अजया *f.* Indian hemp or bhang ; Máyâ.
अजय्य *a.* Invincible.
अजर *a.* Undecaying ; *m.* A god.
अजर्य *n.* Friendship.
अजस्र *a.* Continual, perpetual.
अजस्रम् (अजस्रेण) *ind.* Ever, constantly.

अजा *f.* A she-goat; nature; Mâyá or illusion.

अजागलस्तन *m.* A term for a worthless person.

अजात *a.* Unborn

अजातव्यवहार *m.* A minor, a youth under sixteen.

अजातशत्रु *m.* A name of युधिष्ठिर.

अजानि (-क) *m.* Having no wife.

अजित *a.* Unconquered. *m.* A name of Siva ; or of Vishnu.

अजिन *n.* The hide of an antelope.

अजिर *n.* Court; air; a frog.

अजिह्म*a.* Straight, upright.

अजिह्मग *m.* An arrow.

अजिह्व *m.* A frog.

अजीर्ण *a.* Undigested. *n.* Indigestion, vigour.

अजीवनि *f.* Non-existence (used as an impreca· tion).

अज्युका *f.* A courtezan.

अज *n.* A shield.

अज्ञ *a.* Ignorant, stupid.

अज्ञात *a.* Unknown ; unconscious.

अज्ञातवास *a.* Remaining *incognito.*

अज्ञान *a.* Ignorant. *n.* Ignorance ; spiritual ignorance.

अञ्च् *vt.* 10 U. To unfold.

अञ्चति *m.* Wind ; fire.

अञ्चल *m. n.* End, border.

अञ्चित *a.* Curved, handsome, honoured.

अञ्ज् *vt.* 7 P (*pp.* अक्त) To anoint; to decorate; to glorify; to distinguish; to go. With अभि to anoint; to pollute. अभिवि to reveal; to make manifest. आ-to anoint; to extol वि to manifest; सम् to adorn.

अञ्जन *m.* A guardian element. *n.* A collyrium for eyelashes ; ink ; night.

अञ्जना *f.* Name of Hanumat's mother ; the process by which a suggested meaning is got at.

अञ्जलि *m.* The hollow of hands joined together ; (hence) a mode of supplication; a libation.

अञ्जलिबन्ध *m.* (-न *n.*) Salutation.

अञ्जस *a.*Straight, upright.

अञ्जसा *ind.* Truly, straight, soon.

अञ्जिष्ट *m.* The sun.

अंजीर *फा. n.* The fig-tree or its fruit.

अट् *vt.* 1. P. To roam or wander ; with परि to wander about.

अट *a.* Roaming, wandering.

अटल *a.*Firm;steady; solid.

अटवि–वी *f.* A wood, a forest

अटविक *m.* A wood-man, a forester.

अटा *f.* The habit of roaming or wandering, especially of a religious mendicant.

अट्ट् *vt.* 1.A. To transgress; 10 U. to slight.

अट्ट *a.*High;loud; frequent; dried. *m. n.* Top of a house;a tower;a market-palace; palatial building.

अट्टहास *m.* (-**हास्य** *n.*) Loud laughter.

अट्टालिका *f.* A lofty house.

अडन *n.* A shield.

अणक *a.* Small, insignificant.

अणि (-**णी**) *m.* A pin of the axle; a limit.

अणिमन् *m.*Minuteness;one of the eight Siddhis

अणिष्ठ *a.* Smallest.

अणीयस् *a.* Smaller.

अणु *a.* Small, atomic. *m.* An atom of matter; name of Siva.

अणुभा *f.* Lightning.

अणुमात्र(-**मात्रिक**) *a.* Having the size of an atom.

अणुरेणु *m. f.* Atomic dust.

अणुजाल *n.* The motes in a a sunbeam.

अण्ड *m. n.* An egg, the scrotum, an epithet of S'iva.

अण्डज *m.* A bird, a fish, a snake, a Brahman (*n.*).

अण्डीर *m.* A full man.

अत् *vt.* I. P. To go constantly,to walk,to bind.

अतट *m* A precipice.

अतदर्हम् *ind.*Undeservedly, unjustly.

अतन्द्र *a.* Unwearid, active.

अतन्द्रित *a.* Unwearied, energetic.

अतर्कितम् *ind.* Unexpectedly, suddenly.

अतस् *ind.* Therefore.

अतःपरम् *ind.* Henceforth, further on.

अतस *m.* Wind.

अतिकथा *f.*An exaggerated tale; idle speech.

अतिकल्यम् *ind.* Too early in the morning.

अतिकश *a.* Unmanageable (as a horse).

अतिकृच्छ्र *m.* Extreme pain; a kind of penance.

अतिक्रम् IU,4 P.To step beyond,to exceed, to neglect, to overcome,to lose.

अतिक्रम *m.* Breach of decorum or duty; trespass.

अतिगव *a.* A fool.

अतिचमू *a.* Victorious over armies.

अतिचर् 1 P. To transgress; to offend.

अतिछत्र *m.* A mushroom.

अतिजन *a.* Uninhabited.

अतिजीव् 1 P To survive.

अतितराम् *ind.* More higher, exceedingly.

अतितमाम् *ind.* Exceedingly.

अतिथि *m* A guest; the dead.

अतिथिक्रिया *f* Hospitality.

अतिदिश् 6 P. To transfer; to extend the application of.

अतिनिद्रम् *ind.* Past sleeping time.

अतिनौ *a* Disembarked.

अतिपात *m.* Passing away; neglect; befalling.

अतिप्रगे *ind.* In the early dawn.

अतिप्रबन्ध *m.* Unbroken continuity.

अतिप्रसंग *m* Excessive familiarity, impertinency.

अतिभू 1 P. To arise, to surpass.

अतिभूमि *f.* Last extremity, excess.

अतिमात्रम् *ind.* Exceedingly.

अतिमुक्त *a.* Entirely free from worldly desires.

अतिराजन् *m.* An excellent king.

अतिरात्र *m.* Dead of night.

अतिवह् *vt.* P. To spend; to endure, to avoid; to carry over.

अतिवेल *a.* Excessive.

अतिवेलम् *ind.* Excessively.

अतिव्याप्ति *f.* An overstretching of a rule.

अतिरिच् 7 U (Used in passive) to exceed.

अतिरिक्त *a.* Excessive, superfluous.

अतिरेक *m.* Excess; surplus.

अतिवर्तन *n.* A pardonable misdemeanour.

अतिवाद *m.* An unpleasant speech; exaggeration.

अतिविस्तर *m.* Prolixity; diffuseness.

अतिवृत *vt.* I A. to exceed; to offend; to overcome.

अतिशेष *m* Remainder.

अतिसन्धम् *ind.* In violation of an agreement.

अतिशय *a.* Pre-eminent, superior *n.* Excellence, superiority.

अतिशय (-शयेन) *ind.* Exceedingly.

अतिशयोक्ति *f.* Exaggeration; hyperbole.

अतिशी *vt* 2 A. To surpass; to annoy.

अतिश (शा) यिन् *a.* Abounding, excelling.

अतिसंधा *vt*. 3 U. To deceive; to injure.

अतिसंधान *n*. Cheating, fraud.

अतिसंध्या *f* The time about twilights.

अतिसर *m*. A leader.

अतिसर्ग *m*. A gift, dismissal

अतिसर्जन *n*. Liberality, killing.

अति(ती)सार *m*. Dysentery.

अतिसृज् 6 P. To grant, to dismiss, to forgive.

अतीत *a*. Gone, beyond past.

अतींद्रिय *a*. Imperceptible; *n* the supreme soul.

अतीव *ind*. Exceedingly, quite.

अतुल(-ल्य) *a*. Incomparable.

अत्ता (अत्ति) *f*. A mother; the mother-in-law of a woman; and elder sister.

अत्यन्त *a*. Excessive, perpetual.

अत्यन्ताभाव *m*. Absolute non-existence (in logic).

अत्यन्तिक *a*. Going fast, very near.

अत्यन्तीक *a*. Going too fast.

अत्यय *m*. Lapse; destruction; danger; guilt; absence.

अत्यायित *a*. Exceeded, outraged

अत्यर्थम् *ind*. Exceedingly.

अत्याकार *m*. Contempt.

अत्याचार *m*. Negligence; irreligious conduct.

अत्यारूढ *a* Grown to excess.

अत्याहित *m*. A great danger; a desperate act.

अत्र *ind*. Here; in this case.

अत्रभवत् *a*. Honorable, venerable.

अत्रत्य *a*. Local.

अत्रि *m*. The name of a great sage.

अत्रिजात *m*. The moon.

अथ *ind*. Now; hence; moreover; if; what; and; also.

अथ किम् *ind*. Assuredly; what else

अथ किमु *ind* How much more.

अथवा *ind*. Or.

अथापि *ind*. Moreover.

अथर्वन् *m n*. The fourth Veda.

अथर्वाण *n*. Ritual of the Atharvaveda.

अथो *ind*. Same as **अथ**.

अद् *vt*. 2 P, (*pp*. **जग्ध**) To eat; to destory.

अदत्ता *f*. An unmarried girl.

अदभ्र *a*. Much, plentiful.

अदर्शन *n*. Disappearance.

अदस् *pron*. That.

अदिति *f*. The mother of gods, a cow; the earth; speech.

अदृग् *a.* Blind.

अदृष्ट *a.* Invisible, unforeseen; *n.* destiny.

अदृष्टार्थ *a.* Metaphysical.

अदृष्टकर्मन् *a.* Inexperienced.

अदृष्टि *a.* Evil eye.

अदेव *a.* Impious.

अद्धा *ind.* Certainly, truly, manifestly.

अद्भुत *a.* Marvellous. *m.* One of the nine Rasas. *n.* Surprise, a prodigy.

अद्मनि *m* Fire.

अद्मर *a.* Gluttonous.

अद्य *ind.* To-day, now.

अद्यश्वीन *a.* Likely to happen to-day or to-morrow.

अद्यश्वीना *f.* A female near delivery.

अद्यतन (-तनीय) *a* Referring to to-day; modern.

अद्यापि *ind.* Even now, to this day.

अद्यावधि *ind.* From or till to-day.

अद्रि *m.* A mountain; a cloud; a tree; the sun.

अद्रिकीला *f.* The earth.

अद्रिसार *m.* The iron.

अद्रोह *m.* Mildness, moderation.

अद्वय *a.* Unique. *n.* Unity.

अद्वितीय *a.* Matchless;

अद्वैत *a.* Unique. *n.* Identity; the Vedantic doctrine of the identity of Brahman (*n.*) with the universe or with the soul.

अधम *a.* Lowest meanest.

अधमर्ण (-र्णिक) *m.* A debtor.

अधर *a.* Lower, vile; silenced. *m.* The lower lip.

अधरेण (अधरात्, अधरस्मात् and अधरतस्) *ind.* Below, beneath.

अधरीण *a.* Reproached, censured.

अधरेद्युस् *ind.* The day before yesterday; the other day.

अधर्म *m.* Irreligiousness.

अधवा *f.* A widow.

अधस् *ind.* Below, down, beneath.

अधश्चर *m.* A thief.

अधस्तन *a.* Lower.

अधस्तात् *ind.* See अधस्.

अधि *ind.* Above, over, besides.

अधिक *a.* More; peculiar to.

अधिकर्मन् *n.* Supervision, superintendence.

अधिकरण *n.* Place; support; a court of justice.

अधिकरणिक *m.* A judge.

अधिक्षिप्त *a* Censured.

अधिज्य *a.* Having the bowstring stretched.

अधिपति (-नाथ) *m.* A master, king.

अधिपत्नी *f*. A female sovereign or ruler.

अधिपुरु(रू)ष *m*. The supreme spirit.

अधियोग *m*. An auspicious conjunction of stars.

अधिरथ *m*. A charioteer.

अधिराज *m*. An emperor, a supreme ruler.

अधिरोहिणी *f* A ladder.

अधिरुह् I P. To ascend ; to string ; *a*. growing on.

अधिरूढ *a*. Mounted, ascended. *n*. the Universe.

अधिवचन *n*. A partial speech; an appellation.

अधिश्री *a*. Very beautiful ; very rich. [residence.

अधिवास *m*. An abode;

अधिष्ठातृ *a*. Presiding.

अधिष्ठान *n* Residence ; power ; benediction

अधि(धी)कार *m*. Government, ownership, title, a paragraph, charge, duty.

अधिकारिन् a. An officer.

अधिकृत *a*. Appointed.

अधिक्रम *m*. (-ण *n*.) An invasion, attack.

अधिक्षेप *m*. Abuse, dismissal.

अधिगत *a* Acquired; known.

अधिगम *m*. Acquisition ; knowledge.

अधित्यका *f*. A table-land.

अधिप *m*. A ruler, lord, head.

अधीति *n*. Perusal ; study.

अधीन *a*. Dependent.

अधीयान *m*. A student.

अधीर *a*. Impatient; excited

अधीवास *m*. A long coat or mantle.

अधीष्ट *n*. Honorary office or duty.

अधुना *ind*. Now ; at this time.

अधुनातन *a* Modern.

अधृष्ट *a*. Modest ; shy.

अधृष्य *a*. Invincible; proud

अधोंऽशुक *n*. An undergarment.

अधोऽक्षज *m*. Name of Vishnu

अधोधस् *ind*. Lower and lower.

अधोमुख *a*. Topsy turvy ; headlong.

अधोलम्ब *m*. A plummet.

अधोलोक *m*. The nether world.

अध्यक्ष *a*. Visible ; *n*. A president.

अध्ययन *n*. A study.

अध्यवसान *n*. Determination, effect.

अध्यवसाय *m*. Effort perseverence.

अध्यात्म (त्मिक) *a* Belonging to self.

अध्यात्मज्ञान *n*. Knowledge of the supreme spirit ; metaphysical knowledge.

अध्यात्मयोग *m*. Concentration of mind on the A'tman.

अध्यापक *m*. A preceptor ; a teacher.

अध्यापन *m*. Instructing espec'ally on sacred knowledge.

अध्याय *m*. Proper time for study ; chapter.

अध्यारोप *m*. False attribution or knowledge.

अध्यावाप *m*. Act of sowing seed.

अध्यास *m*.False attribution

अध्याहरण *n*. (-हार *m*.) Supplying an ellipsis.

अध्येषण *n*. (-णा *f*) Solicitation.

अध्रुव *a*. Uncertain, unstable.

अध्वन् *m*. A road; distance; time ; sky ;

अध्वगा *f* The Ganges.

अध्वनीन *m*. A traveller.

अध्वन्य *a*. Going fast. *m*. A traveller.

अध्वर *a*. Sound ; attentive; *m*. A sacrifice.

अध्वर्यु *n*. An officiating priest.

अध्वान्त *n*. Twilight.

अन् *vi*.2 P. 4 A. To breathe. With **प्र** to be alive.

अनकदुन्दुभि *m*. A name of Vasudeva, father of *Krishna*.

अनघ *a*. Sinless ; safe ; faultless.

अनंग *a*. Incorporeal, *m*. The god of love. *n*. Sky; the mine.

अनडुह *m*.(nom. ड्वान्-हौ-हः ; *f*, डुही or ड्वाही) An ox or bull

अनध्याय *m*. A holiday.

अनन्त *a*. Infinite ; *m*. Vishnu ; Shesha (king of serpents)

अनन्तपार *a*. Of boundless extent.

अनन्तर *a*. Near; immediate.

अनन्तरम् *ind* Afterwards (used with abl.).

अनन्तरीय *a*. Next in succession.

अनन्ता *f*. The Earth; Parvati.

अनन्य *a*. The same ;identical.

अनन्यगति (क) *a* Helpless.

अनन्यज *m*. God of love

अनपत्य *a* Childless.

अनपत्रप *a*. Shameless.

अनपाय *a*. Free from loss.

अनपायिन् *a*. Constant, steady.

अनपेक्ष *a*. Regardless ; absolute.

अनपेक्षम् *ind*. Regardlessly.

अनपेत *a* Possessed of (with the abl.); faithful to.

अनभिज्ञ *a* Ignorant ; unused to.

अनय *m*. Misfortune ; vice, gambling.

अनर्घ (-र्घ्य) *a*. Invaluable.

अनर्थ *m.* A worthless object, misfortune.

अनर्थक *a* Idle; fruitless.

अनर्ह *a.* Unworthy.

अनल *m* Fire, digestive power.

अनलस *a.* Diligent.

अनवकाश *a.* Uncalled for, inapplicable

अनवद्य *a.* Irreproachable, estimable.

अनवधानता *f.* Inadvertence.

अनवधि *a.* Unlimited, infinite.

अनवरत *a.* Incessant, uninterrupted.

अनवरतम् *ind.* Incessantly, uninterruptedly.

अनवस्कर *a.* Pure, clean.

अनवस्था *f.* Endlessness, an unsettled state ; incontinence.

अनवस्थान *a.* Unstable, fickle.

अनवेक्ष *a.* Regardless.

अनवेक्षम् *ind.* Regardlessly.

अनवेक्षण *n.* (-क्षा *f.*) Regardlessness.

अनशन *n.* Fasting, a fast.

अनश्वर *a.* Imperishable.

अनस् *n.* A cart ; a living being; birth.

अनसूया *f.* Name of the wife of the sage Atri.

अनाकाल *m.* Improper time; famine [composed

अनाकुल *a.* Undisturbed,

अनागस् *a.* Sinless ; innocent

अनाचार *m.* Bad or irreligious conduct.

अनातप *a.* Cool, free from heat.

अनाथ *a.* Poor, helpless.

अनादर *m.* Disregard, contempt.

अनादि *a.* Without any beginning

अनादीनव *a.* Faultless, defectless.

अनामय *n* Health.

अनामा (अनामिका) *f.* The ring-finger

अनायत(-त्त) *a.* Independent, uncontrolled.

अनायास *a.* Easy.

अनारतम् *ind.* Continually, eternally. [disease.

अनार्जव *n.* Crookedness,

अनार्तवा *f.* A girl who has not arrived at puberty.

अनार्य *m.* Other than an Arya ; *a.* Ignoble, unworthy.

अनावृष्टि *f.* Drought.

अनाश्रव *a.* Not listening to the advice of.

अनासादित *a* Not obtained; non-existent

अनास्था *f.* Disrespect, indifference.

अनाहत *a* Unimpaired.

अनाहार्य *a.* Not artificial not eatable.

अनित्य *a*. Uncertain, fugitive.

अनिभृत *a*. Bold; not private.

अनिमित्त *n*. An ill omen.

अनिमित्ततस् *ind*. Without a cause.

अनिमिष (-मेष) *a*. Unwinking; *m*. A god, a fish.

अनिरुक्त *a*. Unexplained.

अनिर्वचनीय *a*. Unutterable, indescribable.

अनिर्वृत *a*. Unhappy, discontented.

अनिल *m*. Wind; rheumatism.

अनिशम *ind*. Incessantly, constantly.

अनिष्ट *a*. Undesirable; ominous; *n*. Disadvantage; evil.

अनीक *m*. *n*. An army; battle; front row; splendour.

अनीकस्थ *m*. A warrior; a sentinel; a trumpet; a sign.

अनीकिनी *f*. An army.

अनीति *f*. Impropriety; injustice.

अनीश (-श्वर) *a*. Unchecked; unable; atheistical.

अनीश्वरवाद *m*. Atheism.

अनीश्वरवादिन् *m*. An atheist.

अनीहा *f*. Disregard; apathy.

अनु *ind*. After; along; subsequently.

अनुक *a*. Greedy, lustful.

अनुकथन *n* Discourse, conversation.

अनुकम्पन (-पा f.) *n*. Sympathy; compassion; tenderness.

अनुकम्प्य *a*. Swift, pitiable.

अनुकरण *n*. Imitation, resemblance.

अनुकरणीय } अनुकर्तव्य } *a*. Fit to be imitated.

अनुकर्ष *m*. (-ण *n*.) Attraction.

अनुकल्प *m*. An alternative or substitute.

अनुकांक्षा *f*. Desire, wish.

अनुकामीन *a*. One who goes as he pleases.

अनुकार *m*. Imitation, resemblance.

अनुकाल *a*. Opportune.

अनुकालम् *ind*. Opportunely.

अनुकीर्तन *n*. The act of proclaiming.

अनुकूल *a*. Favourable, friendly.

अनुकूलता *f*. Favour, conformity, good will.

अनुकृति *f*. Imitation, copy.

अनुक्रम *m*. Succession.

अनुक्रमण *n*. Proceeding in order, following.

अनुक्रमणी (-णिका) *f*. A table of contents.

अनुक्रिया *f*. Imitation, a subsequent rite.

अनुक्रोश *m*. Tenderness, compassion.

अनुक्षणम् *ind.* Prepetually, every instant.

अनुग *m.* A companion, a follower.

अनुगतिक *a.* Following, imitating.

अनुगम *m.* Following.

अनुगमन *n.* Post-cremation of a widow (Sati)

अनुगवीन *m* A cow-herd.

अनुगामिन् *m.* A companion a follower.

अनुगुण *a.* Congenial with, suitable to.

अनुगुणम् *ind.* Naturally, favourably.

अनुग्रह *m.* (–ग्र n) Favour, acceptance

अनुचर *m.* A companion, a follower.

अनुचित *a.* Improper, unusual.

अनुच्छित्ति *f.*(-च्छेद् *m.*)Non-extirpation, indestructibility.

अनुज (·जन्मन्) *m.* A younger brother.

अनुजा *f.* A younger sister.

अनुजात *a.* Born after.

अनुजीविन् *a.* Living by; dependent

अनुज्ञा *f.* Assent, permission.

अनुज्ञापक *m.* One who commands or enjoins.

अनुतर्ष *m.* Thirst, desire.

अनुताप *m.* Repentance.

अनुतिलम् *ind.* Very minutely.

अनुत्क *a.* Free from regret or anxiety.

अनुत्तम *a.* Unsurpassed.

अनुत्तर *a.* Principal, excellent;

अनुत्तरा *f.* The south.

अनुत्थान *n.* Want of exertion.

अनुदार *a.* Niggardly.

अनुदिनम् *ind* Every day.

अनुदिश् 6 P. To point out.

अनुदिशम् *ind.* In every quarter; in every direction.

अनुदेश *m.* Order, a rule.

अनुदर्शन *n.* Consideration, regard.

अनुद्वाह *m.* Celibacy.

अनुध्यान *n.* Meditation, religious contemplation.

अनुनय *m.* Conciliation; courtesy, discipline.

अनुनाद *m.* Echo. [humble.

अनुनायक *a.* Submissive,

अनुनासिक *a* Nasal.

अनुनीति *f.* See **अनुनय.**

अनुपकारिन् *a.* Ungrateful, worthless.

अनुपद् 4 A. To go after, to be attached to, to discover.

अनुपथम् *ind.* Along the road.

अनुपद *n.* A chorus, the burden of a song.

अनुपदम् *ind.* Step by step.

अनुपदवी *f.* A way.

अनुपदिन् *m.* A searcher.

अनुपाधि *n.* Guileless.

अनुपन्यास *m.* Doubt.

अनुपपत्ति *f.* Failure, inapplicability, adversity.

अनुपम *n.* Incomparable, excellent.

अनुपमर्दन *n* Non-refutation of a charge.

अनुपमेय *a.* Incomparable.

अनुपलब्धि *f.* Non-perception, non-recognition.

अनुपलम्भ *m.* Non-perception, want of apprehension.

अनुपशय *m.* Any aggravating thing.

अनुपस्थिति *f.* Absence, inability.

अनुपहत *n* A new garment not used before.

अनुपातक *n.* A heinous offence.

अनुपातम् *ind.* In succession.

अनुपान *n.* Drink taken with or after medicine.

अनुपूर्व *a.* Regular, orderly.

अनुपूर्वशस् *ind-* In regular order.

अनुपेत *a.* Not endowed with.

अनुप्रपातम् *ind.* Going in succession.

अनुप्रयोग *m* Repetition.

अनुप्रवेश *m.* Entrance.

अनुप्रसक्ति *f.* Close connection.

अनुप्रसादन *n.* Propitiation.

अनुप्रहरण *n.* Throwing into.

अनुप्रास *m.* Alliteration.

अनुप्लव *m.* A companion, a follower.

अनुबन्ध *m.* Connection, attachment, uninterrupted series, intention, pursuit, introductory reasons. [thought.

अनुबोध *m.* An after-

अनुभव *m.* Understanding, experience.

अनुभाव *m.* Authority, certainty, an outward manifestation of a feeling.

अनुभूति *f.* See अनुभव.

अनुभोग *m,* A grant of hereditary land in return for service.

अनुमति *f.* Assent, permission.

अनुमरण *n.* The cremation of a widow with the body of her husband.

अनुमान *n.* Conjecture.

अनुमापक *a.* Being the ground of inference.

अनुमिति *f.* A conclusion from given premises.

अनुमेय *a.* Inferable.

अनुमोद *m.* Pleasure arising from sympathy.

अनुमोदन *n*. Assent, acceptance.

अनुयातृ *m*. A follower, a companion.

अनुयात्रा *f*. Retinue, attendance.

अनुयात्रिक *m*. A follower.

अनुयायिन् *a*. Following.

अनुयोग *m*. A question, solicitation, censure, explanation.

अनुयोजन *n* A question

अनुरक्ति *f*. Affection, love, devotion.

अनुरति *f* Love, attachment.

अनुराग *m*. Love, attachment.

अनुरात्रम् *ind*. Every night.

अनु(नू)राधा *f*. The seventeenth Nakshatra.

अनुरूप *a*. Resembling; suitable.

अनुरूपम् *ind*. Conformably, agreeably to.

अनुरोध *m n*. Compliance; application.

अनुलाप *m*. Repetition; tautology.

अनुलेप *m*. Anointing; an unguent.

अनुलोम *a*. In natural direction.

अनुवंश *m*. A geneological table.

अनुवचन *n*. Repeating.

अनुवर्तन *n*. Compliance.

अनुवश *m*. Obedient.

अनुवाक *m*. A chapter of the Vedas.

अनुवाद *m*. Repetition; translation.

अनुवारम् *ind*. Repeatedly.

अनुविद्ध *a*. Surrounded, pierced, set (as a jewel)

अनुवृत्ति *f*. Following; complaisance; repetition.

अनुवेलम् *ind*. Constantly.

अनुवेश *m.n*. Entering after.

अनुवेशन *n*. See. अनुवेश.

अनुव्रत *a*. Devout, faithful.

अनुशय *m*. Repentance, intense enmity, close attachment.

अनुशासन *n*. Instruction, precept, explanation.

अनुशासिन् *a*. Instructor.

अनुशीलन *n*. Repeated and constant exercise.

अनुशोक *m*. Repentance, regret.

अनुशोचन *n*. Sorrow, repentance.

अनुश्रव *m*. Sacred tradition.

अनुषंग *m*. Connection, attachment, compassion.

अनुष्टुभ् *f*. A kind of metre.

अनुष्ठान *n*. A course of proceeding; performance, religious practice.

अनुष्ठापन *n*. The causing to perform an act.

अनुसंधान *n.* Inquiry, a plan.

अनुसमय *m.* Regular connection of words.

अनुसमापन *n.* Regular completion.

अनुसरण *n.* Following.

अनुसवनम् *ind* Every evening.

अनुसार *m.* Custom, consequence.

अनुसारणा *f.* Pursuit.

अनुसारिन् *a.* Following; prying into.

अनुस्कन्दम् *ind.* In succession.

अनुस्यूत *a.* Uninterrupted.

अनुस्वार *m.* The nasal sound

अनुहरण *n.* (-हार) *m.* Imitation, resemblance.

अनूचान *m.* One versed in the Vedas and Vedangas.

अनूढ *a.* Unmarried.

अनून *a.* Whole, not inferior.

अनूप *a.* Wet (land) *m.* A buffalo; an elephant; a frog.

अनृजु *a.* Not straight; [wicked

अनृण *a.* Free from debt.

अनृत *n* False-hood.

अनेक *a.* More than one.

अनेकान्तवाद *m.* Scepticism.

अनेकवचन *n.* The dual and plural numbers.

अनेकवारम् *ind.* Many times, frequently.

अनेकशस् *ind.* In various manners, frequently.

अनेनस *a.* Sinless, faultless.

अनेहस् *m.* (nom. sing. अनेहा) Time.

अनैक्य *n.* Plurality; anarchy.

अनो *ind.* No, not.

अनोकह *m.* A tree.

अनौजस्य *n.* Want of strength.

अन्त *a.* Lowest, last, handsome, *m.* End, limit, place in general; death; definite ascertainment; nearness, *n.* Nature, essence. *m n.* The last portion.

अन्तावसायिन् *m.* A barber; a Chandala.

अन्तवासिन् *m.* A pupil; Chandala.

अन्तक *m.* Death. [the end.

अन्तस् *ind.* From, on, at

अन्तर् *ind.* In the middle; within; between; in the interior of.

अन्तःकरण *n.* The mind; the thinking faculty.

अन्तर्गडु *a.* Unnecessary, unavailing.

अन्तर्गत *a.* Included in; interior, hidden, secret.

अन्तस्त्य *n.* Intestines, bowels.

अन्तःपट *m. n.* A screen of cloth held between two persons to be married.

अन्तःपुर *n.* The female apartment, especially of a king; or ladies living therein.

अन्तःपुराध्यक्ष (-रक्षक) *m.* A chamberlain.

अन्तर्ज्ञान *n.* Secret knowledge

अन्तर्दशा *f* The time when a particular planet exercises its influence over the destiny of man.

अन्तःपुरिक *m.* A superintendent of the women's apartments.

अन्तर्बाष्प *a.* One who has suppressed his tears.

अन्तर्मुख (-खी) *a.* Turned inward.

अन्तर्याम *m.* The suppression of the breath and voice.

अन्तर्लीन *a.* Inherent, latent.

अन्तर्वत्नी *f.* A pregnant woman.

अन्तर्वेदी *f* The Doab or district between the Gangá and the Yamunâ rivers.

अन्तःसत्त्वा *f.* A pregnant woman.

अन्तःस्थ *m.* A semi-vowel.

अन्तर्हित *a* Interposed; concealed.

अन्तर *a.* Interior, exterior, similar, related, dear. *n.* Period, term, space in general, an occasion, difference, a variety, a hole, a failing, the supreme soul, the mind.

अन्तरतस् *ind.* Internally.

अन्तरम् *ind.* In the middle, within.

अन्तरय (-राय) *m.* Obstacle, impediment.

अन्तरा *ind.* In the way, between;in the mean time; near.

अन्तराल *n.* Intermediate space or time.

अन्तरि(री)क्ष *n.* The atmosphere, sky.

अन्तरित *a* Intervening; screened, obstructed by.

अन्तरीप *n.* An Island.

अन्तरीय *n.* An under-garment

अन्तरे *ind.* Amidst, between

अन्तरेण *ind.* Between; without; with reference to.

अन्तर्धान *n.* Disappearance.

अन्तर्धि *m* Concealment.

अन्तिक *a.* Near, proximate.

अन्तिम *a.* Immediately following; final; last.

अन्ते *ind.* In the end; near.

अन्तेवास *m.* A pupil; a neighbour.

अन्तेवासिन् *m.* A pupil; a Chânda'a.

अन्त्य *a.* Last; lowest. *m.* A thousand billions.

अन्त्येष्टि *f.* Funeral ceremony.

अन्त्र *n.* Entrail, intestine.

अन्द् I P. To bind.

अन्दु (न्दू) *f.* A chain, a fetter. [waving.

अन्दोलन *n.* Swinging;

अन्ध् *vi.* 10 U. To make or become blind.

अन्ध *a.* Blind. *n.* Darkness;

अन्धकार *m. n.* Darkness.

अन्धतमस (-तामस,-तामिस्र) *n.* Pitchy darkness.

अन्धातमस *n.* Complete darkness.

अन्धक *a.* Blind.

अन्धस् *n.* Food.

अन्धिका *f.* Night; the blind man's buff.

अन्धु *m.* A well.

अन्ध्र *m. pl.* The name of a country (modern Telingana) and its people; a man of a mixed caste; a fowler.

अन्ध्रभृत्य *m. pl.* A dynasty of Andhra kings.

अन्न *m.* The sun. *n.* Food; boiled rice.

अन्नपूर्णा *f.* A form of दुर्गा.

अन्नप्राशन *n.* The ceremony of giving food to the new born child for the first time.

अन्नमयकोश (-ष) *m.* The material creation.

अन्य *pron.* Other; extraordinary. [ous.

अन्यग (-गामिन्) *a.* Adulter-

अन्यतम *a* Any one of many.

अन्यतर *a.* Either of two.

अन्यपुष्ट (-भृत) *m.* The Indian cuckoo.

अन्यपूर्वा *f* A remarried widow.

अन्यभृत् *m* A crow.

अन्यमनस् (-मनस्क,-मानस) *a.* Fickle, inattentive.

अन्यवाप *m.* The cuckoo.

अन्यक *m.* See अन्य.

अन्यत् *a.* Another; *ind.* Again; moreover.

अन्यतरद्युस् *ind.* On one of two sides.

अन्यतरेद्युस *ind.* On either of two days.

अन्यतस् *ind.* From another; on the other side; otherwise. [adversary.

अन्यतरत्य *m.* An enemy; an

अन्यत्र *ind.* Elsewhere; on another occasion.

अन्यथा *ind.* Differently, otherwise, on the contrary, untruly, wrongly.

अन्यथाकारम् *ind.* Doing otherwise, differently.

अन्यदा *ind* At another time or in another case.

अन्यदीय *a.* Belonging to another.

अन्यादृक्ष् (-श् or श) *a*. Of another kind; unusual.

अन्याय *m*. Injustice, impropriety; irregularity.

अन्याय्य *a*. Unlawful, improper.

अन्यून *a*. Entire, not deficient.

अन्योन्य *pron*. Each other, mutual. [ably.

अन्वक् *ind*. After; favour-

अन्वक्षम् *ind*. Afterwards; immediately.

अन्वञ्च् *a*. Following.

अन्वन् *a*. Following.

अन्वय *m*. Retinue, attendance, family; connection.

अन्वयज्ञ *m*. A geneologist.

अन्वयव्यतिरेक *m*. Positive and negative assertion.

अन्वर्थ *a*. Significant, appropriate

अन्ववाय *m*. Race, lineage.

अन्ववेक्षा *f*. Regard, consideration

अन्वहम् *ind*. Day after day, every day.

अन्वाजेकृ 8 P. To support.

अन्वादिष्ट *a*. Mentioned after; inferior.

अन्वादेश *m*. Repeated mention.

अन्वाधान *n*. Putting fuel on the sacred fire.

अन्वाधि *m*. A bail or deposit; repentance.

अन्वाधेय *n*. Woman's property.

अन्वारोहण *n*. A widow's ascending the funeral pile with the body of her husband. [sorrow.

अन्वासन *n*. Worship,

अन्वाहार्य *n*. The monthly s'raddha.

अन्वाहिक *a*. Daily.

अन्वाहित *n*. See अन्वाधेय.

अन्वि [न्वी] त *a*. In company with; having.

अन्विरति *a*. Won over; *n*. Food.

अन्वीक्षण *n*. [अन्वीक्षा *f*.] Investigation; searching.

अन्वेष *m* (अन्वेषण *n*) Seeking for.

अन्वेषणा *f*. See अन्वेष

अप् *f*. (only *pl*. nom. आपः] Water.

अप *ind*. From; away; badly.

अपकरण *n*. Doing wrong; ill-treating.

अपकर्मन् *n*. Paying off [as a debt].

अपकर्ष *m*. Decay, decline, degradation.

अपकर्षक *a*. Detracting.

अपक्रर्षण *m*. Drawing down; superseding.

अपकार *m*. [-कृति or क्रिया *f*.] Hurt, injury, a mean action.

अपकारक [अपकारिन्] *a.* Acting wrongly, injuring.

अपकृष्ट *a.* Low, inferior.

अपकौशली *f.* News, information. [gestion.

अपक्ति *f.* Immaturity; indi-

अपक्रम *m.* [-क्रमण *n.* क्राम *m.*] Retreating; irregular.

अपक्रोश *m.* Reviling, abusing.

अपक्ष *a.* Adverse.

अपक्षपात *m.* Impartiality.

अपक्षय *m.* Decline decay.

अपक्षेपण *n.* Casting away.

अपगम *m* [-गमन *n.*] Departure, elapse; disappearance.

अपगति *f.* A bad fate.

अपगर्जित *a.* Free from the thunder of a cloud.

अपगा *f.* A river.

अपघन *m.* A limb of the body, the whole body.

अपघात *m.* Warding off; a violent death; a fatal accident.

अपच *m.* A man who does not cook for himself; a bad cook [a term of abuse].

अपचय *m.* Decline.

अपचरित *n.* Fault; offence.

अपचार *m.* Departure, a failure, absence improper conduct.

अपचिति *f.* Worship, reverence, loss, expiation [of sin], expense.

अपच्छाय *a.* Shadowless; dim; *m.* A god.

अपच्छेद *m* Cutting off; interruption.

अपजय *m.* Defeat, overthrow.

अपटी *f.* A screen; a curtain.

अपटु *a.* Awkward, diseased.

अपण्डित *a.* Not learned.

अपण्य *a.* Unsaleable.

अपतर्पण *n* Fasting in sickness &c.].

अपतिक *a.* Without a husband or master.

अपत्नीक *a.* Without a wife.

अपत्य *n.* Offspring.

अपत्रपण *n.* Bashfulness, shame.

अपत्रपा *f.* Bashfulness.

अपत्रपिष्णु *a.* Bashful.

अपत्रस्त *a.* Afraid of.

अपथ्य *a* Unwholesome, obnoxious, bad, unlucky.

अपदक्षिणम् *ind.* On the left side.

अपदान *m.* Pure conduct; an accomplished work; an excellent work.

अपदार्थ *m.* Non-entity.

अपदेश *m* Stating, an argument; a pretext; a mark; place, reputation, deceit, refusal.

अपद्वार *n.* A side door.

अपध्यान *n* Evil thoughts.

अपध्वंस *m*. Degradation, disgraceful conduct.

अपनय *m*. Removing, refuting, bad conduct

अपनिद्र *a*. Sleepless.

अपनुत्ति *f*. (**अपनोद** *m*. **-न** *n*.) Removing, taking away.

अपप्रदान *n*. A bribe.

अपभ्रंश *m*. Falling away; a corrupt form of a word.

अपभूति *f*. Defeat [or anger.

अपमन्यु *a*. Free from grief

अपमान *m*. *n*. Disrespect.

अपमार्ग *m*. A side-way.

अपमार्जन *n*. Cleaning.

अपमूर्धन् *a*. Headless.

अपमृत्यु *m*. Accidental death

अपमृषित *a*. Obscure, unintelligible, unbearable.

अपयान *n*. Retreat flight.

अपर *a*. Posterior, later, western, other, different.

अपरति *f*. Cessation, dissatisfaction.

अपरव *m*. Contest, dispute.

अपरस्पर *a*. Continued, uninterrupted.

अपरा *f*. The West.

अपराक् *ind*. In front of.

अपराग *m*. Aversion, antipathy.

अपराग्नि *m.du*. The Southern and Western [**दक्षिण** & **गार्हपत्य**] fires.

अपराच् *a*. In front.

अपराजिष्णु [**अपराजेय**] *a*. Invincible.

अपराद्ध *a*. Sinned, missed.

अपराध *m*. Offence, transgression, fault.

अपरान्त [**-क**] *m*. Death; the Konkan, or its inhabitants.

अपराह्ण *m*. Afternoon.

अपरिग्रह *a*. Destitute.

अपरिच्छद *a*. Poor; without property.

अपरिपन्थिन् *a*. Not antagonistic.

अपरिसंख्यान *n*. Innumerableness, infinity. [behind.

अपरेण *ind*. In the West;

अपरेद्युस् *ind*. On the following day.

अपरेतरा *f*. The East.

अपरोक्ष *a*. Not invisible, not distant. [sence of.

अपरोक्षम् *ind*. In the pre-

अपरोध *m*. Exclusion; prohibition.

अपर्णा *f* A name of Párvati.

अपर्याप्त *a*. Insufficient; incompetent, unlimited.

अपर्याय *m* Want of order or method.

अपर्युषित *a*. Fresh; new.

अपलाप *m*. Denial of knowledge; evasion; concealing.

अपलाषिका *f*. Ardent desire.

अपलाषिन् *a*. Free from desires.

अपवन *n*. A park or grove.

अपवरण *n*. Covering.

अपवर्ग *m*. Completion; final beatitude;gift;exception.

अपवर्जन *n*. Abandoning; a gift; final beatitude.

अपवर्तन *n*. Removal; depriving one of.

अपवाद *m*. Refutation; exception; a scandal.

अपवाह *m*.(-न *n*.)Deduction.

अपविद्या *f*. Mâyà; illusion.

अपविद्ध *a*. Rejected, abject. *m* A son rejected by his natural parents and adopted by a stranger.

अपवृत्ति *f*. Cessation, end.

अपव्यय *m*. Prodigality.

अपशद *m*. See अपसद.

अपशंकम् *ind*. Fearlessly.

अपशब्द *m*. A corrupted word, a vulgar speech; censure.

अपशुच् *a*. Without sorrow.

अपश्चिम *a*. Not last.

अपसद *m*. A low man; an outcaste.

अपसर्जन *n*. Abandonment; gift; final deliverance.

अपसर *m*. A valid reason; departure; retreat.

अपसरण *n*. An outlet.

अपसर्प *m*. A spy.

अपसारण *n*. Removing; driving away; expelling.

अपस्मार *m*. Epilepsy.

अपहसित *n* A silly laughter.

अपहरण *n*. Taking away, stealing, robbing.

अपहार *m*. See अपहरण.

अपहीन *a*. Left abandoned.

अपह्नव *m*. Denial; concealment of knowledge.

अपह्नुति *f* See अपह्नव; a figure of speech.

अपह्रास *m*. Diminution, reduction.

अपाकरण *n*. Removal; payment.

अपाकर्मन् *n*. Payment, liquidation.

अपाकृति *f*. Emotion arising from fear &c.

अपांक्त *a*. An out-caste.

अपांक्तेय *a*. See अपांक्त.

अपांग *m*. The outer corner of the eye.

अपाच् *a*. Western; Southern.

अपाची The South or West.

अपाचीन *a*. Opposite; Western; Southern.

अपात्र *a*. Worthless.

अपाध्वन् *m*. A bad road.

अपान *m*. One of the five life-winds in the body.

अपाय *m*. Misfortune.

अपारण *a*. Distant, far.

अपार्ण *a*. Far. *ind*. Far.

अपार्थ [-क] *a*. Useless, unmeaning.

अपावरण *n*. Covering, concealment.

अपावर्तन *n.* Retreat.
अपाश्रय *a.* Helpless.
अपासु *a.* Lifeless. [likewise.
अपि *ind.* Moreover; also;
अपितृक or अपित्र्य*a.* Not ancestral; father-less.
अपिधान [पिधान] *n.* Covering, a cover.
अपिनद्ध [पिनद्ध] *a.* Tied on.
अपिहित *a.* Covered; concealed.
अपीति *f.* Destruction.
अपुंस्का *f.* Without a husband. [meal, &c.
अपूप *m.* A cake of flour,
अपूर्व *a.* Quite new; unparalleled. [tention.
अपेक्षण *n.* [अपेक्षा *f.*] At-
अपेक्षणीय *a.* To be desired.
अपेत *a.* Departed, lost; deprived of; contrary to.
अपोह *m.* Removal of doubt by means of reasoning; negative reasoning.
अपोहन*n* Reasoning faculty
अपौरुषेय *a.* Not being of human origin.
अप्य *a.* Watery.
अप्रकृत *a.* Irrelevant.
अप्रगम *a.* Going too fast.
अप्रतिकर *a.* Trusting; confidential. [helpless.
अप्रतिकार *a.* Irremediable,
अप्रतिघ *a.* Invincible; not to be warded off.
अप्रतिपक्ष *a.* Without an opponent; unlike.
अप्रतिपत्ति *f.* Neglect, omission, absence of mind.
अप्रतिभ *a.* Modest, dull.
अप्रतिम *a.* Unequalled.
अप्रतिरथ *a.* An unrivalled warrior.
अप्रतिरव *a.* Uncontested.
अप्रतिष्ठ *a.* Fluctuating, useless. [ness.
अप्रतिष्ठान *n.* Want of firm-
अप्रतिसंख्य *a.* Unobserved.
अप्रतिहत *a.* Unimpaired.
अप्रतीक *a.* Without parts or body.
अप्रतीत *a.* Unintelligible.
अप्रत्यक्ष *a.* Not visible, absent.
अप्रत्यय *a.* Having no confidence or knowledge.
अप्रदक्षिणम् *ind.* From the left to the right. [dinate.
अप्रधान *a.* Secondary, subor-
अप्रधृष्य *a.* Invincible.
अप्रमत्त *a.* Assiduous, vigilant; attentive.
अप्रमद *a.* Joyless, sad.
अप्रमा *f.* Incorrect knowledge.
अप्रमाण *a.* Immeasurable, unauthorized. *n.* A rule or authority which is not binding.
अप्रमेय*a.* Immeasurable, not

to be properly understood or ascertained.

अप्रयुक्त *a.* Wrongly used.

अप्रसंग *m.* Want of attachment or connection; inopportune time.

अप्रस्ताविक *a.* Irrelevent.

अप्रस्तुत *a.* Irrelevant, accidental, absurd.

अप्रस्तुतप्रशंसा *f.* Name of a figure of speech.

अप्रहत *a.* Unploughed.

अप्राकरणिक *a.* Irrelevant.

अप्राकृत *a.* Extraordinary, not original.

अप्सरस् *f.* [Generally pl.] Celestial nymph.

अप्सरा *f.* See **अप्सरस्**.

अफेन *n.* Opium. [sive.

अबद्धमुख *a.* Scurrilous, abusive.

अबला *a.* Weak, *f.* A woman

अबाध *a.* Unimpeded.

अबाल *a.* Youthful.

अबाह्य *a.* Familiar; internal.

अबिंधन *m.* Submarine fire.

अबुद्धि *f.* Ignorance foolishness.

अबुद्धिपूर्वम् [-पूर्वकम्] *ind.* Unconsciously.

अबुध-ध *a.* Foolish. *f.* (nom. sing. **अभुद्.**) Ignorance.

अब्ज *m.* The moon; the physician of gods; camphor. *n.* A lotus; one thousand millions, *m.n.* The conch. [Brahman.

अब्जभू [-भव, -योनि] *m.*

अब्जा *f.* A pearl-oyster.

अब्जिनी *f.* A multitude of lotus-flowers.

अब्द *m.* A cloud, a year.

अब्धि *m.* The ocean.

अब्धिज *m.* The moon.

अब्धिजा *f.* Spirituous liquor; Goddess Lakshmi.

अब्धिशयन *m.* Vishnu.

अब्धिसार *m.* A gem.

अब्रह्मण्य *a.* Not proper for a Brâhmana; disgraceful.

अभग *a.* Luckless, unfortunate. [Sin, sorrow.

अभद्र *a.* Inauspicious. *n.*

अभय *a.* Secure *n.* safety.

अभयदक्षिणा *f.* Promise of protection from danger.

अभयदान *n* Giving assurance of safety.

अभयपत्र *n.* A written document granting assurance of safety; 'a safe conduct'.

अभव *m.* Non-existence; end; final beatitude.

अभव्य *a.* Inauspicious, unhappy.

अभाव *m.* Non-existence, absence; destruction.

अभावना *f.* Non-perception.

अभावनीय *a.* Improbable.

अभि *ind.* Towards, to, for, against, on. [uptuous.

अभि[-भी]क *a.* Lustful, vol-

अभिकांक्षा *f.* Wish, desire.

अभिकाम *a.* Lustful; desiring for. [ful

अभिक्रतु *a.* Haughty; power-

अभिक्रम *m.* A courageous attack; a beginning.

अभिक्रांति *f.* See अभिक्रम.

अभिक्रोशक *m.* A reviler.

अभिख्या *f.* A name, a synonym; fame; look; beauty; proclaiming.

अभिख्यान *n.* Fame, notoriety, glory.

अभिगम(-न *n.*)*m.* Approaching; sexual intercourse.

अभिगम्य *a.* Accessible.

अभिगामिन् *a.* Approching; having sexual intercourse.

अभिगर्जन *n.* A tumult, an uproar. [tecting.

अभिगुप्ति *f.* Guarding, pro-

अभिग्रह *m.* Attack, robbing.

अभिघर्षण *n.* Friction.

अभिघात *m.* Striking, extirpation.

अभिघातिन् *m.* An enemy.

अभिघ्राण *n.* Smelling at or touching the forehead with the nose.

अभिचर् *m.* An attendant.

अभिचार *m.* Destructive charms or spells.

अभिचारिन् *m.* A magician.

अभिजन *m.* Family; noble descent; attendants.

अभिजात *a.* Well-born, learned, fruitless.

अभिजाति *f.* Noble descent.

अभिजय *m.* Complete victory

अभिजिघ्रण *n* See अभिघ्राण.

अभिजित् *m.* Vishnu. *f.* The twenty-second asterism.

अभिज्ञ *a* Knowing, clever.

अभिज्ञा *f.* Recognition.

अभिज्ञान *n* Recollection; a token of recognition.

अभितस् *ind.* In the presence of; towards; never; completely.

अभितराम् *ind.* Nearer to.

अभिताप *m* Extreme heat or

अभिताम्र *a* Deep red. [pain.

अभिदक्षिणम् *ind.* Towards the right.

अभिदर्शन *n.* Appearance.

अभिद्रव *m.* An attack. [sion.

अभिद्रोह *m.* Abuse, oppres-

अभिधर्षण *n.* Possession by an evil spirit.

अभिधा *f.* A name.

अभिधान *n.* A name, a word, a speech, a vocabulary.

अभिधानक *n.* A sound.

अभिधायक[-यिन] *a.* Naming.

अभिधावन *n.* Pursuit, attack.

अभिधेय *n.* Meaning.

अभिध्या *f.* [-न *n.*] Desire.

अभिनन्द *m.* [-न *n.*] Delighting, applauding.

अभिनम्र *a.* Bent, curved.

अभिनय *m.* Action, gesticulation.

अभिनव *a.* Quite new.

अभिनियुक्त *a.* Engaged in.

अभिनियोग *m.* Close attention.

अभिनिर्वृत्ति *f.* Completion, accomplishment. [tent

अभिनिविष्ट *a.* Resolute; in-

अभिनिवेश *m.* Devotion, love, resoluteness. [forth.

अभिनिष्क्रमण *n.* Going out or

अभिनिष्पत्ति *f.* Completion.

अभिनीत *a.* Represented [as a drama]; fit, friendly.

अभिनीति *f.* Friendship, gesture; patience.

अभिनेतृ *m.* An actor. [ture.

अभिपतन *n.* Arrival, depar-

अभिपत्ति *f.* Approaching, completion.

अभिपन्न *a.* Come near, seeking refuge afflicted, dead.

अभिपूर्वम् *ind.* Successively.

अभिप्राय *m.* Intention, opinion, implied sense.

अभिप्रेत *a.* Intended, implied.

अभिप्लव *m.* Affliction, inundation. [upon.

अभिप्रोक्षण *n.* Sprinkling

अभिभव *m.* Defeat, humiliation, contempt, prevalence.

अभिभाषण *n.* Addressing.

अभिभूति *f.* See **अभिभव.**

अभिमत *a.* Agreeable.

अभिमाति *f.* See **अभिमान.**

अभिमनस् *a.* Wishing for.

अभिमन्यु *m.* Name of a son of Arjuna by his wife Subhadrâ. [sion, war.

अभिमर्द *n.* Rubbing, inva-

अभिमर्दन *n.* Oppression, devastation of a country.

अभिमर्श [-र्ष] *m.* Touch, sexual intercourse, insult, offence.

अभिमाद *m.* Intoxication.

अभिमान *m.* Self-respect, pride, affection, solicitation.

अभिमुख *a.* Facing, approaching, friendly disposed.

अभिमुखता *f.* Presence, being favourable.

अभिमुखम् *ind.* In the direction of, in front of.

अभिमृष्ट *a.* Touched, rubbed.

अभिम्लान *a.* Quite withered.

अभियाचना [-याञ्चा] *f.* A solicitation.

अभियाति [-त] *m.* An enemy.

अभियान *n.* Approaching, attacking.

अभियुक्त *a.* Assaulted, assiduous, learned prosecuted

अभियोक्तृ *m.* An assailant, an enemy, accuser.

अभियोग *m.* Attack, battle, energetic effort, learning,

scholarship, close application, a charge.

अभिरक्षा *f*. Complete protection. [beautiful.

अभिराम *a*. Delightful,

अभिरुचि *f* Relish or taste, delight, a strong desire.

अभिरूप *m*. Pleasing; conformable to [pression.

अभिलाप *m*. Speech, ex-

अभिलाष *m*. Desire.

अभिलीन *a*. Adhering, embracing. [playful.

अभिलुलित *a*. Disturbed,

अभिवाद *m*. [-न]*n*. Addressing; salutation.

अभिवास *m*. Covering.

अभिविधि *m*. Complete comprehension or inclusion

अभिविनीत *a*. Well-behaved;

अभिविश्रुत *a*. Widely known. [crease.

अभिवृद्धि *f*. Growth, in-

अभिव्यक्त *a*. Revealed, made manifest, distinct.

अभिव्यक्ति *f*. Manifestation.

अभिव्यापक *a*. Comprehending.

अभिव्याप्ति See अभिविधि.

अभिव्याहरण *n*. [व्याहार *m*.] Pronouncing, speech.

अभिशंका *f*. Fear, doubt, anxiety. [lumny.

अभिश[-ष]स्ति *f*. Abuse, ca-

अभि (भी) शाप *m*. Charge, curse, calumny.

अभिशीत *a*. Cold.

अभिशोचन *n*. [-शोक *m*.] Intense grief or pain.

अभिषंग *m*. Defeat, calamity, attachment.

अभिषिक्त *a*. Sprinkled over, enthroned.

अभिषेक *m*. [-षेचन *n*.] Coronation, consecration by sprinkling water.

अभिष्टव *m*. Praise, eulogy.

अभिष्य [स्य] न्द *m*. Oozing, excess.

अभिष्वंग *m*. Love, devotion.

अभिसंश्रय *m*. Shelter.

अभिसंस्तव *m*. High praise.

अभिसन्धक *m*. A detractor.

अभिसन्धा *f*. Promise; deceit

अभिसन्धि *m*. Declaration; promise; purpose; implied sense; belief; opinion.

अभिसम्पात *m*. Concourse, war, curse. [association.

अभिसम्बन्ध *m*. Connection,

अभिसम्मुख *a*. Facing.

अभिसर *m*. A companion.

अभिसरण (-सर्पण) *n*. Approaching with hostile intention.

अभिसर्ग *m*. Creation.

अभिसर्जन *n*. Gift, killing.

अभिसायम् *ind* In the evening. [ment of lovers.

अभिसार *m* An appoint-

अभिसारिका (-सारिणी) *f.* A woman who meets her lover by appointment.
अभिसेवन *n.* Indulgence in.
अभिस्यन्द *m.* See अभिष्यन्द.
अभिहार *m.* Robbing; attack
अभिहास *m.* Laughter, sport
अभिहित *a.* Said, declared, named, fastened upon.
अभी *a.* Fearless. [fearless.
अभीक *a.* Lustful, anxious,
अभीक्ष्ण *a.* Frequent, perpetual, excessive.
अभीक्ष्णम् *ind.* Repeatedly, constantly, exceedingly.
अभीप्सित *a.* Wished, desired.
अभीर *m.* A cowherd.
अभीशु (-षु) *m.* A ray of light; a rein.
अभीष्ट *a.* Wished.
अभुग्न *a.* Straight, sound.
अभूतपूर्व *a.* Unprecedented.
अभूति *f.* Non-existence, nonentity. [object.
अभूमि *f.* An unfit place or
अभेद *m.* Close union, identity. [diamond.
अभेद्य *a.* Indivisible; *n.* A
अभोज्य *a.* Unfit for food.
अभ्यंग *m.* Rubbing the body with unctuous substances; an unguent.
अभ्यंजन *n.* Anointing; applying collyrium to the eye-lashes; an unguent.
अभ्यधिक *a.* Pre-eminent; exceeding.
अभ्यनुज्ञा *f.* (-न *n.*) Permission, consent, command; admission of an argument.
अभ्यन्तर *a.* Conversant with; intimate. *n.* interior; the mind.
अभ्यर्चन *n.* (-र्चा *f.*) Worship, reverence.
अभ्यर्ण *a.* Near, proximate.
अभ्यर्थना *f.* Request, solicitation.
अभ्यर्थिन् *a.* Soliciting.
अभ्यर्हणा *f.* Respect; worship. [suitable.
अभ्यर्हित *a.* Respected;
अभ्यवकर्षण *n.* Extracting.
अभ्यवकाश *m.* An open space.
अभ्यवस्कन्द *m.* An impetuous attack. [ing food.
अभ्यवहरण *n.* (-हार *m.*) Tak-
अभ्यवहार्य *n.* Food.
अभ्यसन *n.* Practice, study.
अभ्यसूयक *a.* Envious.
अभ्यसूया *f.* Calumny, envy
अभ्यस्त *a.* Repeated, studied. [complaint.
अभ्याख्यान *n.* A groundless
अभ्यागत *m.* A guest.
अभ्यागम *m.* Arrival, neighbourhood, battle, enmity.
अभ्याघात *m.* Assault attack.
अभ्यादान *a.* Beginning.
अभ्यावर्त *m.* Repetition.
अभ्यावृत्ति *f.* Repetition.

अभ्याश *a.* Near, proximate.

अभ्यास *m.* Repetition, study, habit. [tation.

अभ्यासयोग *m.* Deep medi-

अभ्याहार *m.* Robbery, conveying. [sprinkling.

अभ्युक्षण *n.* Consecration by

अभ्युचित *a.* Usual, customary. [perity.

अभ्युच्चय *m.* Increase, pros-

अभ्युत्थान *n.* Rising from one's seat to receive a guest, rise, elevation.

अभ्युत्पतन *n.* Assault.

अभ्युदय *m.* Rise; elevation.

अभ्युदाहरण *m.* An illustration of a thing by its reverse. [sunrise.

अभ्युदित *m.* One asleep at

अभ्युद्यत *a.* Approaching.

अभ्युन्नति *f.* Great prosperity

अभ्युपगम *m.* Approach, promise, admission.

अभ्युपपत्ति *f.* Defence, protection, consolation.

अभ्युपाय *m.* A good expedient. [ducement.

अभ्युपायन *n.* A bribe, in-

अभ्युपेत *a.* Accepted.

अभ्यूह *m.* Discussion, guess.

अभ्र *n.* A cloud ; sky.

अभ्रक *n.* Talc ; mica.

अभ्रंकष (-लिह) *a.* Touching the clouds ; very high. *m.* Wind.

अम् *ind.* Quickly ; a little.

अम *a.* Unripe. *m.* Sickness.

अमंगल (-ल्य) *a.* Inauspicious *n.* ill luck, evil.

अमण्ड *a.* Without decoration ; without froth.

अमति *f.* Unconsciousness.

अमनस् (-स्क) *a.* Inattentive; *m.* The supreme spirit. *n.* Inattention. [greatly.

अमनाक् *ind.* Not a little,

अमम *a.* Devoid of worldly attachment.

अममता *f.* Disinterestedness, indifference.

अमर *n.* Immortal imperishable. *m.* A god; gold; a pillar; name of a mountain ; the name of a lexicographher.

अमरावती *f.* The name of Indra's capital. [god.

अमर्त्य *a.* Immortal. *m.* A

अमर्याद *a.* Boundless, disrespectful, improper.

अमर्ष *m.* Anger, nonendurance, impetuosity.

अमर्षण *a.* Impatient, passionate.

अमर्षित *a.* Angry.

अमा *f.* The day of the new moon. *a.* Measureless. *ind.* Near; with.

अमात्य *m.* A minister.

अमात्र *a.* Boundless; not whole.

अमानना *f.* Insult, disrespect.
अमानिन् *a.* Modest, humble.
अमानुष *a.* Superhuman.
अमानुष्य *a.* See अमानुष.
अमाम (मा) सी See अमावास्या.
अमाव (वा) सी *f.* The same as अमावास्या.
अमाव (वा) स्या *f.* The new moonday.
अमित *a.* Boundless, infinite
अमित्र *m.* An enemy.
अमिथ्या *ind.* True.
अमुक *a.* Such a one, certain
अमुतस् *ind.* From there; from heaven; henceforth
अमुत्र *ind.* Here, there, in the other world.
अमुत्रत्य *a.* Belonging to a future state or world.
अमुथा *ind.* Thus, in this or that manner.
अमुष्यायण *a.* Of respectable birth.
अमूदृश् (-श,-क्ष) *a.* Like that of such form or kind.
अमूर्त *a.* Formless, incorporeal.
अमूल *a.* Unfounded.
अमूल्य *a.* Invaluable.
अमृत *a.* Immortal *m.* A god; Dhanvantari. *n.* Ambrosia; water; clarified butter; milk.
अमृतबन्धु *m.* The moon.
अमृताक्षर *a.* Immortal.
अमृतांशु *m.* The moon.
अमृतान्धस् *m.* A god, deity.
अमृताशन(-शी) *m.* A god.
अमृषा *ind.* Rightly, truly.
अमेदस्क *a.* Without fat, thin.
अमेधस् *a.* Foolish, idiotic.
अमेध्य *a.* Not fit for sacrifice, unholy. *n.* Excrement; an unlucky omen.
अमेय *a.* Immeasurable.
अमोघ *a.* Infallible.
अम्ब (-क) *n.* An eye.
अम्बर *n.* The sky, a garment.
अम्बरि (री) ष *m.n.* The sun; a name of Vishṇu, S'iva, as also of a king of the solar race.
अम्बा (अम्बिका, अम्बालिका) *f.* A mother; term of respect.
अम्बु *n.* Water.
अम्बुज *n.* A lotus; the thunderbolt of Indra; *m.* The moon, the *sarasa* bird, the conch, camphor.
अम्बुद *m.* A cloud.
अम्बुधर *m.* A cloud.
अम्बुधि *m.* The ocean.
अम्बुनिधि *m.* The ocean.
अम्बुप *m.* Varuna.
अम्बुभव *n.* A lotus.
अम्बुभृत् *m* A cloud; the ocean.
अम्बुमुच् *m* A cloud.
अम्बुराशि *m.* The ocean.
अम्बुरुह *m.* The lotus.
अम्बुरोहिणी *f.* A lotus.
अम्बुवाह(-वाहिन्) *m.* A cloud
अम्बुजासना *f.* Lakshmi.

अम्भ् *vi.* 1 A. To sound.
अम्भस् *n.* Water, the sky.
अम्भःसार *n.* A pearl.
अम्भःसू *m.* Smoke.
अम्भोज *m.* The moon; a crane; *n.* a lotus.
अम्भोजिनी *f.* A lotus-plant.
अम्भोद (**अम्भोधर**) *m.* A cloud.
अम्भोधि (**अम्भोनिधि, अम्भोराशि**) *m.* The ocean.
अम्भोरुह *n.* A lotus.
अम्मय *a.* Watery.
अम्र *m.* A mango-tree.
अम्ल *a.* Sour, acid. [ach.
अम्लपित *n.* Acidity of stom-
अम्ला *f.* The tamarind tree.
अम्लान *a.* Not withered, bright. *n.* A lotus
अम्लानि *f.* Vigour; freshness
अम्लिमन् *m* Sourness.
अय् *vt.* 1 A. To go with **अन्तर** to intervene; with **उत्** to rise; with **परा** or **पला** to retreat.
अय *m.* Good luck.
अयक्ष्म *n.* Healthiness.
अयथा *ind.* Unsuitably, *a.* Unlike; disproportioned.
अयथोचित *a.* Improper.
अयथातथ Unfit improper, useless. [uselessly.
अयथातथम् *ind.* Unsuitably;
अयथातथ्य *n.* Unsuitableness.
अयथार्थ *a.* Incorrect, improper. [improperly.
अयथावत् *ind.* Erroneously.

अयन *n.* Motion; the sun's path north and south of the equator (called respectively **उत्तरायण** and **दक्षिणायन**); rotation; the period of duration of each solstice.
अयनवृत्त *n.* The ecliptic.
अयनसंक्राति *f.* (**संक्रम**) Passage through the zodiac; the ecliptic.
अयशस् *n.* Dishonour.
अयशस्कर *a.* Disgraceful.
अयशस्य *a.* Disgraceful.
अयस् *n.* Iron, steel. *m.* Fire.
अयस्कान्त *m.* Loadstone.
अयाचित *a.* Unasked, unsolicited.
अयाचितवृत्ति *a.* Subsisting on alms obtained without begging.
अयाथार्थिक *a.* Improper, absurd, incongruous.
अयान्वित *a.* Fortunate; lucky.
अयि *ind.* A particle of encouragement, solicitation, interrogation, &c. corresponding to ho ! so ho !
अयुग *a.* Single. [gradually.
अयुगपद् *ind.* Not at once,
अयुगपद्भाव *m.* Successiveness.
अयुग्म *a.* Separate. [ness.
अयुग्मशर *m.* God of love.
अयुज् *a.* Odd.

अयुत *n.* Ten thousand.

अयुत *a.* Undisturbed; unconnected.

अये *ind.* An interjection showing anger, grief, surprise or fear.

अयोग *m.* Separation.

अयोगू *m.* A blacksmith.

अयोग्य *a.* Improper.

अयोग्र *n.* A pestle.

अयोध्या *f.* The capi al of Râma's kingdom.

अयोनि *a.* Without origin. *m.* Name of Brahman (*m*) or of Siva. [of Sîtâ.

अयोनिजा(सम्भवा)*f.* A name

अयोमुख *m.* An arrow.

अर *m.* The spoke or radius of a wheel;an angle.

अरघट्ट(-घट्टक) *m.* A wheel or machine for drawing water from a well.

अरंगिन् *a.* Passionless.

अरणि -णी *m. f. du.* Two pieces of wood used in kindling the sacred fire. *m. n.* The sun; fire.

अरण्य *m.* A forest.

अरण्यौकस् *m.* An anchorite.

अरण्यचन्द्रिका *f.* A useless ornament.

अरण्यपण्डित *m.* A fool.

अरण्यराज(-राजा) *m.* The lion or tiger. [wilderness.

अरण्यरुदित *n.* Crying in the

अरण्यश्वन् *n.* A wolf.

अरण्यक *n.* A forest.[forest.

अरण्यानी (नि) *f.* A large

अरति *f.* Dissatisfaction; anxiety; uneasiness.

अरत्नि *m.* The elbow, a fist.

अरंगम् 1. P To be present.

अरंगर *a.* Praising readily.

अरम *a.* Low, vile.

अरमति *f.* Splendour.

अरविन्द *n.* A blue or red lotus. [lotus-flowers.

अरविन्दिनी *f.* A collection of

अरसिक *a.* Devoid of taste.

अराग (अरागिन्) *a.* Cool, unimpasssioned.

अराजक *a.* Anarchical.

अराति *m.* An enemy.

अराल *a.* Crooked, curved.

अराला *f.* A Courtezan.

अरि *m.* An enemy, a wheel of a carriage.

अरित्र *n.* A rudder.

अरिष्ट *m.* A crow; a heron; a woman's lying in chamber; evil; buttermilk.

अरिष्ट-गृह *n.* A lying-in chamber.

अरुचि *f.* Aversion.

अरुचिर *a* Disagreeable.

अरुज् *a.* Free from disease.

अरुण *a.* Ruddy, dumb. *m.* The sun;the name of the charioteer of the sun.

अरुणोदय *m.* Dawn.

अरुणोपल *m* A ruby.

अरुणसारथि *m.* An epithet of the sun.

अरुणित *a.* Reddened.

अरुणिमन् *m.* Redness. [ous.

अरुन्तुद *a.* Sharp, acrimoni-

अरुन्धती *f.* The wife of Vasistha; the morning star.

अरुष् *a.* Not angry, good-tempered.

अरुस् *m.n.* A sore or wound

अरे *ind.* An interjection of

अरेतस् *a* Seedless. [address.

अरोक *a.* Dim.

अरोग *a.* Healthy.

अर्क् 10 U. To heat; to praise.

अर्क *m.* The sun, a ray; fire; crystal; copper; the name of a plant. [sun.

अर्कमण्डल *n.* The disc of the

अर्गल *m.n.* A bolt for fastening a door; a bar; a wave.

अर्गला *f.* The same as **अर्गल**.

अर्गलिका *f.* A small bolt.

अर्घ् *v.i.* 1 P. To be worth.

अर्घ *m.* Value; price; an offering of various ingredients to a god or a Brâhmana.

अर्घ्य *a.* Valuable, venerable; *n.* A respectful offering to a god or a venerable person.

अर्च् 7 U. To praise, to worship, to salute. With **आभि** to worship. **प्र**-to worship.

अर्चक *a.* Worshipper.

अर्चन *n.* (**अर्चना** or **अर्चा** *f.*) Worship, homage.

अर्चि *f.* A flame.

अर्चिस् *n.* A flame; light.

अर्चिष्मत् *m.* Fire; the sun.

अर्ज् *v.t.* 1. P. To procure, to take up; With **उप** to procure.

अर्जुन *a.* White, clear; *m.* The white colour; a peacock; the only son of his mother; a name of the third Paṇḍava prince.

अर्णव *m.* The ocean.

अर्णस् *n.* Water. [bow.

अर्ति *f.* Pain; the end of a

अर्थ 10 A. To request, to wish. With **अभि** to beg, **अभिप्र**-to request, to desire. **प्र**-to request, to search; **प्रति**-to encounter; **सम्**-to consider, to corroborate **संप्र**-to beg.

अर्थ *m.* Meaning, purpose; money; use; affair; worldly prosperity.

अर्थकर (-**कृत्**) *a.* Yielding wealth.

अर्थकृत्य *n.* Execution of any business. [ing.

अर्थगौरव *a.* Depth of mean-

अर्थघ्न *a.* Extravagant, wasteful.

अर्थप्रयोग *m.* Usury.
अर्थबन्ध *m.* Composition.
अर्थवत् *a.* Significant.
अर्थवाद *m.* An explanatory remark, praise.
अर्थविद् *a.* Sagacious, wise.
अर्थविकल्प *m.* Deviation from truth;prevarication.
अर्थशास्त्र *n.* Science of polity, especially that of political economy.
अर्थसंस्थान *n* Treasury.
अर्थसिद्धि *f.* Success, fulfilment of one's desired object
अर्थना *f.* Request, entreaty.
अर्थात् *ind.* As a matter of course, in fact namely.
अर्थान्तरन्यास *m.* Name of a figure of speech.
अर्थालंकार *m.* A figure of speech dependent on sense and not on sound.
अर्थिक *m.* A watchman.
अर्थिन् *a.* Desirous of; *m.* A begger, a suitor, a complainant.
अर्द् 1. P. To ask for; to go; to kill, to hurt; with अति to fall upon, अभि-to afflict. 10 U. to kill.
अर्ध *a.* Half.
अर्धमौलि (-न्) *m.* S'iva
अर्धोदय *m.* The rising of the half moon.
अर्धचन्द्र *m.* The half moon; a half-moon-shaped arrow.
अर्धभास्कर *m.* Mid-day.
अर्धवीक्षण *n.* A side-look, a glance.
अर्धव्यास *m.* The radius of a circle.
अर्धिक *a.* Measuring a half.
अर्धिन् *a.* Entitled to a half.
अर्पण *n.* Delivering.
अर्बुद *m.* A hundred millions; a serpent; a cloud.
अर्भक *a.* Little; weak; *m.* A child, a fool.
अर्य *a.* Excellent. *m.* A master; a Vais'ya.
अर्यमन् *m.* The sun.
अर्वन् *m.* A horse.
अर्वती *f.* A mare;a procuress.
अर्वाक् *ind.* Before, behind.
अर्वाच् *a.* Following, subsequent.
अर्वाचीन *a.* Modern; later.
अर्ह् 1. P. To deserve, to be entitled to. 10. P. To worship.
अर्ह *a.* Worthy of respect, *m.* price.
अर्हण *n.* (-णा *f.*) Worship.
अर्हन्त *a.* Worthy. *m.* A Buddhist mendicant.
अर्हा *f.* Worship.
अर्हन्ती *f.* Veneration, homage.
अर्ह्य *a.* Worthy, respectable.
अलक *m. n.* Hair, a curl.

अलक्त *m*. The red resin of certain trees or its juice.

अलक्षण *a*. Inauspicious.

अलक्ष्य *a*. Invisible, unknown.

अलंकरण *n*. Decoration.

अलंकरिष्णु *a*. Fond of decoration.

अलंकर्मीण *a* Skilful, clever.

अलंकार *m*. An ornament; a figure of speech.

अलंकारशास्त्र *n* The science and art of rhetoric.

अलंकृति *f*. See अलंकार.

अलंक्रिया *f*. Adorning, ornamenting.

अलंधन *a*. Rich.

अलंभूष्णु *a*. Able, competent

अलम् *ind*. Enough, away with; greatly.

अलय *a*. Homeless, imperishable.

अलर्क *m*. A mad dog

अलवाल *n*. A basin for water at the foot of a tree; also आलबाल.

अलस (-क) *a*. Slow; languid.

अलात *n*. A fire-brand.

अलाबु (-बू) *f*. A kind of gourd.

अलार *n*. A door.

अलि *m*. A black bee, a scorpion; a liquor; a crow.

अलिक *n*. The forehead.

अलिन् *m*. A large black bee.

अलिनी *f*. A swarm of bees.

अलिन्द *m*. A terrace before a house-door.

अलीक *a*. Unpleasant; false.

अलीकिन् *a*. Disagreeable; false.

अलोकसामान्य *a*. Extraordinary.

अलोल *a*. Firm, free from desire.

अलौकिक *a*. Uncommon, peculiar to the sacred literature. [rare.

अल्प (-क) *a*, Small, little,

अल्पित *a* Diminished; degraded

अल्पिष्ठ *a*. Least, smallest.

अल्पीयस् *a*. Less, smaller.

अव् 1. P To protect, to like; with -अनु to encourage. -उद् to regard; to promote; -उप to cherish; -सम् to satisfy; to maintain.

अव *ind*. Away; down; off;

अवकट *a*. Opposite.

अवकर्तन *n*. Cutting off.

अवकर *m*. Dust, sweepings.

अवकलित *a*. Seen; known.

अवकाश *m*. Space, occasion, interval, footing, scope.

अवकीर्ण *a*. Scattered.

अवकुंचन *n*. Contraction.

अवकुण्ठन *n*. Investing, surrounding, attracting.

अवकृष्ट *a*. Removed; low.

अवक्लृप्ति *f*. Suitableness; possibility.

अवक्रन्दन *n*. Crying out.

अवक्रय *m*. Rent; tax; price.
अवक्रान्ति *f*. Descent approach. [sion.
अवक्रिया *f*. Neglect, omis-
अवक्रोश *m*. Abuse; a curse.
अवक्लेद *m*. Fetid discharge.
अवक्षय *m*. Decay, waste.
अवक्षेप *m*. (-ण *n*.) Censure.
अवखात *n*. A deep ditch.
अवगणन *n*. Disregard; insult
अवगति *f*. Perception, true knowledge.
अवगम *m*. See **अवगति**.
अवगाढ *a*. Immersed, low.
अवगाह *m*. (-न *n*.) Plunging bathing.
अवगीत *a*. Abused *n*. An evil report.
अवगुण *m*. Fault.
अवगुण्ठन *n*. A veil.
अवगुण्ठिका *f*. A veil; a curtain. [ing.
अवगूहन *n*. Hiding; embrac-
अवग्रह *m*. Drought; obstacle; a particular sign.
अवग्रहण *n*. Obstacle, disregard. [**अवग्रह**.
अवग्राह *m*. The same as;
अवघर्षण *n*. Rubbing.
अवघात *m*. Striking a blow.
अवघूर्णन *n*. Whirling round
अवघोषण *n*. (-णा *f*.) A proclamation. [smelling.
अवघ्राण *n*. The act of
अवच(-चा)य *m*. Gathering.
अवचनीय *a*. Not blameable; indecent.
अवचस्कर *a*. Silent.
अवचार *m*. A road; a field of action. [habited.
अवचित *a*. Gathered; in-
अवचूर्णन *n*. Pounding.
अवच्छद *m*. A cover.
अवच्छिन्न *a*. Cut off; divided.
अवच्छेद *m*. Part, limit.
अवच्छेदक *n*. A characteristic.
अवजय *m*. Victory.
अवज्ञा *f*. (-न *n*.) Disregard.
अवट *m*. A hole; a pit.
अवटि(-टी) *f*. A hole, a well.
अवतंस *m*. *n*. A garland; an ornament.
अवतंसक *m*. *n*. See **अवतंस**.
अवतमस *n*. Slight darkness.
अवतरण *m*. Descending; quotation; translation; an incarnation.
अवतरणिका *f*. An introduction.
अवताडन *n*. Treading, striking.
अवतान *m*. Stretching.
अवतार *m*. See **अवतरण**.
अवदंश *m*. A stimulant.
अवदात *a*. Clean; pure, white: beautiful meritorious.
अवदान *n*. A heroic deed.
अवदारण *n*. Tearing.
अवदाह *m*. Burning down.
अवदीर्ण *a*. Melted, fluid.
अवदोह *m*. Milk; milking.

अवद्य *a.* Low, faulty, disagreeable, *n.* A fault, sin, reproach.

अवधान *n.* Attention, devotion.

अवधारण *n.* Determination; affirmation.

अवधि *m.* A period of time.

अवधीरण(-णा) *n.* Disrespect.

अवधूत *a.* Shaken, insulted; *m.* An ascetic.

अवध्वंस *m.* Falling off; dust. [faction

अवन *n* Protection, satis-

अवनत *a.* Humble.

अवनति *f.* Humility.

अवनद्ध *a.* Fastened.

अवनम्र *a.* Bowed, bent.

अवनि (-नी) *f.* The earth.

अवनीचर *a.* Vagabond.

अवनीमण्डल *n.* The globe.

अवनेजन *n.* Washing, ablution.

अवन्ति (-उरी) or अवन्तिका *f.* Ujjayini, the capital of the Avantis.

अवपतन *n.* Alighting.

अवपात *m.* Falling down; a whole.

अवबोध *m.* Perception, knowledge.

अवभास *m.* Light; false knowledge.

अवभुग्न *a.* Contracted, bent.

अवभृथ (-स्नान) *m.* Bathing after a sacrifice for the purpose of purification.

अवभ्र *m.* Abduction.

अवम *a.* Low, youngest.

अवमति *f.* Disregard.

अवमर्द *m.* Trampling; devastation.

अवमर्षण *m.* Impatience.

अवमर्ष *m.* Consideration.

अवमान *m.* Disrespect.

अवमानन *n* (-ना *f.*) Disrespect.

अवमोचन *n.* Setting at liberty.

अवयव *m.* A limb; a body; a portion.

अवयवशस् *ind.* Severally

अवर *a.* Inferior; Western.

अवरज *m.* A younger brother; a S'udra.

अवरजा *f.* A younger sister.

अवरशैल *m.* The Western mountain over which the sun sets. [tion.

अवरति *f.* Cessation, relaxa-

अवरार्ध *m.* The minimum; the last half.

अवरावर *a.* Lowest.

अवरीण *a.* Despised.

अवरुग्ण *a.* Torn; diseased.

अवरुद्धि *f.* Restraint.

अवरूप *a.* Deformed.

अवरोचक *m.* Want of appetite.

अवरोध *m.* (-न *n.*) Obstruction; a siege.

अवरोध (-धि)**क** *m.* A guard, n. A barrier, a fence.

अवरोधिका *f.* A female of the inner apartments.

अवरोह *m.* (-**ण** *n.*) Descent; heaven.

अवर्ण *m.* Stain, ill fame.

अवलक्ष *a.* White. *m.* The white colour.

अवलग्न *a.* Clinging to; hanging down *m.* the waist.

अवलम्ब *m.* (-**न** *n.*) A support.

अवलिप्त *a.* Proud.

अवलीढ *a.* Licked; surrounded.

अवलीन *a.* Clinging to.

अवलीला *f.* Sport, mirth, contempt.

अवलुण्ठन *n.* Wallowing; robbing.

अवलेप *m.* (-**न** *n.*) Smearing; pride.

अवलेह *m.* (-**हिका** *f*) Licking; an extract (of some drug)

अवलोक *m.* Sight.

अवलोकन *n.* (-**कित** *n.*) A look, an eye

अवलोप *m.* Destruction.

अवलोम *a.* Favourable.

अववद (-**वाद**) *m.* Evil report; command

अवश *a.* Helpless.

अवशेष *m.* Remainder.

अवश्य (-**क**) *a.* Ungovernable; necessary.

अवश्यम् *ind.* Necessarily.

अवश्यंभाविन् *a.* Inevitable.

अवष्टब्ध *a.* Supported; haughty; near; obstructed.

अवष्टम्भ *m.* A support; pride; resoluteness; paralysis.

अव (**आव-**) **सथ** (-**थ्य**) *m.* A dwelling place; a school.

अवसन्न *a.* Ended, sad.

अवसर *m.* Occasion, scope; introduction; rain.

अवसर्ग *m.* Relaxation; independence.

अवसर्प *m.* A spy.

अवसाद *m.* Sinking, failure.

अवसान *n.* End; a limit.

अवसाय *n.* Conclusion.

अवसित *a.* Ended; known.

अवसेक *m.* Sprinkling.

अवसेचन *n.* Sprinkling.

अवस्कन्द *m.* (-**न** *n*) A camp. n. Assault.

अवस्तु *n.* The unreality of matter.

अवस्था *f.* State, circumstance, stage.

अवस्थान *n.* (-**स्थिति** *f.*) Place.

अवस्फूर्जित *n.* Thunder.

अवस्फोट *m.* Appearance.

अवस्यन्दन *n.* Trickling.

अवस्रंसन *n.* Falling off.

अवहार *m.* A thief; a shark.

अवहास *m.* A smile; a jest.

अवहेलन *n.* (-**ना** *f.* -**हेला** *f.*) Disrespect, disregard.

अवाक् *ind.* Downwards; Southwards.

अवाक्ष *a.* A guardian.

अवाग्र *a.* Stooping.

अवाच् *a.* Dumb; lower.

अवाची *f.* The south.

अवाचीन *a.* Southern

अवाच्य *a.* Improper to be uttered; bad; inexpressible.

अवाञ्चित *a.* Bent, low.

अवान्तर *a.* Situated between; secondary.

अवाप्ति *f.* Obtaining.

अवार *n.* This side.

अवारपार *m.* The ocean.

अवारपारीण *a.* Belonging to the ocean.

अविकत्थन *a.* Modest.

अविकल *a.* Full, entire.

अविकल्प *a.* Unchangeable. *m* Absence of doubt or option.

अविकृति *f.* Absence of change.

अविक्रिय *a.* Unchangeable

अविग्रह *a.* Bodiless.

अवितथ *n.* Truth.

अविदग्ध *a* Unlearned.

अविद्य *a.* Unlearned, foolish.

अविद्या *f.* Illusion; Máyà.

अविनय *m.* Rude behaviour.

अविनाभाव *m.* Inseparable connection.

अविनीत *a.* Rude, immodest.

अविमृष्य *a.* Undoubted.

अविरतम् *ind.* Eternally, continually.

अविरति *f.* Uninterruptedness.

अविरलम् *ind.* Closely.

अविविक्त *a.* Indiscriminate.

अविवेक *m.* Want of judgment or foresight.

अविश्रांत *a.* Untiring; ceaseless.

अविष *m.* The ocean; a king.

अविषा *f.* A river; the earth.

अविसंवादिन् *a.* Unfailing; agreeing.

अवृष्टि *f.* Drought.

अवेक्षण *n.* (-क्षा *f.*) Looking towards, attention, care.

अवेद्य *a.* Unknowable; unattainable.

अवेल *a.* Untimely; unlimited.

अवैध *a.* Irregular.

अव्यक्त *a.* Indistinct; *n.* The soul; the primary germ of Nature.

अव्यभि(-भी) चार *m.* Non-separation, fidelity.

अव्यय *a.* Imperishable, immutable. *m.* A name of Vishnu. *n.* An indeclinable.

अव्ययीभाव *m.* One of the four principal compounds in Sanskrit grammar.

अव्यलीक *a.* Agreeable, true.

अव्यवस्था *f.* Irregularity.

अव्यवहार्य *a.* Excommunicated.

अव्यवहित *a.* Immediate, direct.

अव्याकृत *a.* Not manifest.

अव्याज *a;* Guileless.

अव्यापार *m.* Cessation from work; not one's own business.

अव्याप्ति *f.* Inadequate extent of a proposition.

अव्याहत *a.* Unobstructed.

अव्युत्पन्न *a.* Not proficient in the grammar and idiom of a language.

अश् 5 A.(*pp.* अशित or अष्ट) To reach; to obtain; to pervade, With उप-to obtain. वि-to pervade, 9 P (*pp.* अशित) To eat, to enjoy. प्र-to eat, सम्-to eat, to enjoy.

अशना (-या) *f.* Hunger.

अशनि *m.* Indra; fire. *m. f.* A missile; the thunderbolt; a flash of lightning.

अशरण *a.* Helpless; forlorn.

अशिर *m.* Fire; the sun; a demon; wind.

अशिव *a.* Inauspicious. *n.* ill luck; mischief.

अशिष्ट *m.* Ill-bred; unrefined.

अशीत *a.* Hot.

अशीतकर *m.* The sun.

अशीति *num.* Eighty.

अशेष *a.* Whole, perfect.

अशौच *n.* Impurity, defilement.

अश्मन् *m.* Stone, thunderbolt.

अश्म *m. n.* Iron; sapphire.

अश्मन्त *n.* A fire-place; a field.

अश्रान्त *a.* Unwearied.

अश्रान्तम् *ind.* Continually.

अश्रीक (-ल) *a.* Unlucky; unprosperous.

अश्रु *n.* A tear.

अश्रेयस् *n.* Mischief, unhappiness.

अश्रौत *a.* Not sanctioned by the *S'ruti* or Vedas.

अश्लील *a.* Obscene.

अश्लेषा *f.* The ninth lunar mansion.

अश्व *m.* A horse.

अश्वतर *m.* (-री *f.*) A mule.

अश्वभा *f.* Lightning.

अश्वमेध *m.* A horse sacrifice.

अश्ववैद्य *m.* A farrier.

अश्वशाला *f.* A stable.

अश्वशाव *m.* A colt.

अश्वहृदय *n.* Skill in horsemanship.

अश्वत्थ *m.* The holy fig-tree.

अश्वस्तन *a.* Of today; making no provision for to-morrow.

अश्विन् *m.* A cavalier.

अश्विनी *f.* The first lunar mansion.

अश्वीय *a.* Relating to a horse.

अषाढ *m.* The same as आषाढ.

अष्टक *a.* Eightfold *n.* A chapter of the Rigveda; group of eight.

अष्टका *f*. The seventh, eighth or ninth day after full noon.

अष्टन् *num*. (always *pl*.nom. अष्ट or अष्टौ.) Eight.

अष्टकृत्वस् *ind*. Eight times.

अष्टकोण *n*. An octagon.

अष्टमूर्ति *m*. S'iva.

अष्टादशन् *num*. (always *pl*.) *a*. Eighteen.

अष्टापद *m*. A spider.

अष्टाविंशति *f*.Twenty-eight.

अष्टम *a*. Eighth.

अस् *vt*. or *vi*. 1. U To take, to shine, to go. *vi*. 2 P. To be, to suffice (with a dat.); WITH आविस्-to become manifest; प्रादुस्-to appear. *vt*. 4. P (*pp*.अस्त) To throw. WITH अति-to surpass; अधि-to attribute falsely. अप-to abandon अभि-to practise. -उद्-to throw up. उपनि-to trust; नि-to place down, to resign. निस्-to expel, to defeat. परा-to leave परि-to spread, to turn away; परिनि-to stretch. प्र to throw; वि-to separate, विनि to place; परि-to take wrongly; सम् to unite, to take jointly; सन्नि-to become an anchorite.

असंव्यवहित *a*. Immediate.

असंशयम् *ind*. Undoubtedly.

असंश्रव *a*. Out of hearing.

असंश्रावम् *ind*. Inaudibly.

असंस्कृत *a*. Not refined.

असंस्तुत *a*. Not familiar; strange.

असंस्थान *n*. (असंस्थिति *f*.) [Disorder.

असकृत् *ind*. Again and again.

असंकुल *m*. A broad road.

असंख्य (असंख्यात) *a*. innumerable.

असंगति *f*. Incongruity.

असत् *a*.Unreal, wrong bad, *n*. Nonentity, falsehood.

असत्क्रिया *f*.Bad treatment, inhospitableness.

असतायी *f*. Wickedness.

असती *f*. An unfaithful woman.

असत्य *a*. Untrue, *n*. False- [hood.

असत्यसंध *a*. Treacherous.

असदृश *a*. Unlike, improper.

असन्दिग्ध *a*. Certain.

असमबाण [-सायक] *m*. A name of Kamadeva.

असमंजस *a*. Unbecoming, nonsensical.

असमवायिन् *a*. Accidental, separable.

असमीक्ष्यकारिन् *a*. Acting considerately.

असंबद्ध *a*. Incoherent.

असंबाध *a*. Open, accessible.

असंभव *m*. Improbability.

असंभ(-भा)व्य *a*. Impossible; incomprehensible.[tural.

असंभृत *a*. Not artificial, na-

असंमोह *m*. True insight, composure.

असम्यच् *a*. Improper.

असाक्षात् *ind*. Invisibly, indirectly.

असाक्षिक *a*. Unattested.

असामान्य *a*. Peculiar; extraordinary. [proper.

असांप्रत *a*. Unbecoming, im-

असांप्रतम् *ind*. Improper, unbecoming. [fitable.

असार *a*. Worthless, unpro

असि *m*. A sword.

असिधाराव्रत *n*. The vow of standing on the edge of a sword; hence any difficult task.

असित *a*. Dark, *m*. The black colour; the planet Saturn.

असु *m*. *pl*. The five vital airs; animal life. *n*. Grief.

असुधारण *n*. Existence.

असुर *m*. Demon; the sun; an elephant.

असुस् *m*. An arrow.

असुहृद् *m*. An enemy.

असूय् *vi*. or *vt*. 1 U. To detract, to envy, to be angry with. With अभि to calumniate.

असूयक *m*. detractor.

असूया *f*. Envy, calumny.

असूयु *a*. Envious.

अस्खलित *a*. Fluent; unshak-

अस्त *m*. Setting. [en.

अस्तव्यस्त *a*. Confused.

अस्तमन *n*. (-य *m*.) Setting.

अस्तिकाय *m*. A predicament.

अस्तित्व *n*. Existence.

अस्तिनास्ति *ind*. Doubtfully.

अस्त्र *n*. A missile, weapon.

अस्त्रचिकित्सा *f*. Surgery.

अस्त्रागार *n*. An arsenal.

अस्थान *n*. A bad or improper place or occasion.

अस्थि *n*. A bone; the stone of a fruit.

अस्थिपंजर *m*. A skeleton.

अस्थिमालिन् *m*. A name of

अस्थिर *a*. Unsteady. [S'iva.

अस्फुट *a*. Indistinct.

अस्मद् *pron*. The first personal pronoun.

अस्मदीय *a*. Our, ours.

अस्मादृश् (-श) *a*. Like us.

अस्मार्त *a*. Illegal, not within memory.

अस्मिता *f*. Egotism.

अस्र *m*. Hair of the head.

अस्रकंठ *m*. An arrow.

अस्व *a*. Poor, indigent.

अस्वरम् *ind*. In a low tone.

अस्वर्ग्य *a*. Unheavenly.

अस्वाध्याय *m*. Interruption of study.

अह् *vt*. 1. A (*pp* अंहित) To go, 10 U. To shine.

अहंयु *a.* Proud, haughty.
अहन् *n.*(nom, **अहः**; **अहनी** or **अह्नी**; **अहानि**) Day-time, day and night together.
अहर्दिवस् *ind.* Daily.
अहर्निश *n.* Day and night.
अहम् *pron.* I [superiority.
अहमाग्रिका *f.* A contest for
अहमहमिका *f.* Rivalry.
अहंकार *m.*(**-कृति** *f.*)Egotism
अहंभद्र *n.* Self-conceit.
अहंभाव *m.* (**-मति** *f.* **-मान** *m*) Conceit, egotism.
अहल्या *a.* Unploughed. *f.* name of the wife of Gautama. [Indra.
अहल्याजार *m.* An epithet of
अहस्कर *m.* The sun.
अहह *ind.* Oh!, alas! hey-day! aha! [the sun.
अहि *m.* A snake, a cloud.
अहिनकुलिका *f.* Natural enmity (as between a snake and an ichneumon).
अहिफेन *n.* Opium.
अहिंस्र *a.* Harmless.
अहिंसा *f.* Harmlessness.
अहित *a.* Improper, disadvantageous; *m.* An enemy.
अहीर *m.* A cowherd.
अहे(-है)तुक *a.* Causeless, groundless.
अहो *ind.* A particle implying surprise, sorrow, compassion, &c.
अह्नाय *ind.* Instantly.
आ *ind.* Aye, true! (As a prefix) upto; near; toward; slightly.
आं (**आः**) *ind.* An interjection expressing the sense of 'oh', 'yes'; verily ho! 'I see it now,' determination, &c.
आकत्थन *a.* Boasting.
आकम्प *m.* (**-न** *n.*) Shaking.
आकर *m.* A mine. [ing.
आकर्णन *n.* Hearing; listen-
आकर्ष *m.* (**-णn.**) Attraction, fascination; a die, a touch-stone. [magnet.
आकर्षक *a.* Attractive, *n.* A
आकलन *n.* Seizing; inquiry; wish, standing; count-
आकल्प *m.* Ornament. [ing.
आकष *m.* A touch-stone.
आकस्मिक *a.* Unforeseen, sudden.
आकांक्षा *f.* Wish, inquiry;
आकार *m.* Form, appearance, countenance.
आकालिक *a.* Untimely, unseasonable.
आकालिकी *f.* Lightning.
आकाश *m.* *n.* Sky, atmosphere, light; ether; place.
आकाशकक्षा *f.* The horizon
आकाशगंगा *f.* The milky way.

आकाशभाषित *n.* A voice in the air.

आकाशयान *n.* An aeroplane

आकाशवर्त्मन् *n.* The sky.

आकाशवाणी *f.* Voice from heaven.

आकिंचन (-न्य) *n.* Poverty.

आकीर्ण *a.* Crowded, scattered. [contraction.

आकुञ्चन *n.* Compression,

आकुञ्चित *a.* Contracted.

आकुण्ठित *a.* Confounded, rash.

आकुल (आकुलित) *a.* Full of, agitated, irresolute, affected. [tracted.

आकूणित *a.* A little con-

आकूत *n.* Intention, wish.

आकृति *f.* Form, figure, ap pearance. [tation.

आकृष्टि *f.* Attraction, gravi-

आकेकर *a.* Half-shut (applied to eyes.)

आक्रन्द *m.* (-न *n.*) A cry of lamentation. [attacking.

आक्रम *m.* (-ण *n.*) Arriving;

आक्रान्ति *f.* Placing upon; overcoming; valour.

आक्रीड *m.n.* Sport, a pleasure; garden.

आक्रुष्ट *n.* A harsh sound.

आक्रोश *m.* (-न *n.*) A loud cry.

आक्रोड *m.* A walnut tree.

आक्लेद *m.* Sprinkling; moistening.

आक्षपण *n.* Fasting.

आक्षिक *a.* Relating to gambling.

आक्षीव *a.* Intoxicated;

आक्षेप *m.* Throwing off; reproach; a deposit; an inference.

आक्षोदन *n.* Hunting.

आख *m.* A spade, a hoe.

आखण्डल *m.* A name of Indra.

आखनिक *m.* A rat; a thief.

आखात *m.* A natural pond.

आखु *m.* A mouse; a miser.

आखेट(-क) *m.* Chase, hunt-

आख्या *f.* Name, title. [ing.

आख्यात *a.* Counted; made known; *n.* A verb.

आख्यान *a.* Allusion, a story. [fame; name.

आख्याति *f.* Publication;

आख्यानक *n.* A legend.

आख्यायक *m.* A messenger.

आख्यायिका *f.* A narrative.

आख्येय *a.* Proper to be told.

आगति *f.* Arrival, return.

आगन्तु *a.* Coming, external; *m.* A stranger.

आगन्तुक *a.* Incidental, *m.* An uninvited person; a stranger.

आगम *m.* Arrival, addition; origin, science, the Vedas

आगमवृद्ध *m.* A learned man

आगमन *n.* Approach.

आगस् *n.* Sin; offence, fault.

आगस्कृत *a.* Giving offence.
आगस्ती *f.* The South.
आगाध *a.* Unfathomable.
आगार *n.* A dwelling, a house. [fire.
आग्निक *a.* Belonging to a
आग्नेय *a.* Fiery; *m.* An epithet of Skanda.
आग्नेयी *f.* The south-east.
आग्रह *m.* Persistence; favour.
आग्रहायण *m.* A name of the month of **मार्गशीर्ष**.
आघट्टना *f.* Friction.
आघर्ष *m.* (-ण *n.*) Rubbing.
आघात *m.* Striking; a blow; a slaughter-house.
आघूर्णन *n.* Rolling; whirling.
आघोष *m.* Invocation.
आघोषणा *f.* A proclamation
आघ्राण *n.* Smelling; satisfaction, satiety.
आंग, आंगिक *a.* Bodily.
आचक्षुस् *m.* A learned man
आचम *m.* (-न *n.*) Sipping.
आचरण, आचरित *n.* Conduct
आचार *m.* Conduct; a custom
आचारवेदी *f.* The holy land of A'ryávarta.
आचार्य(-क) *m.* A preceptor.
आचार्यमिश्र *a.* Venerable, honourable.
आचार्या *f.* A spiritual preceptress.
आचार्यानी *f.* The wife of a spiritual preceptor.

आचूषण *n.* Suction.
आच्छाद *m.* (-न *n.*) Covering; a cloak.
आच्छेद *m.* (-न *n.*) Cutting off
आजनन *n.* High birth.
आजि *f.* A war, a battle.
आजीव *m.* (-न *n.*) Livelihood.
आजीविका *f.* Livelihood.
आज्य *n.* Clarified butter.
आज्यभुज् *m.* An epithet of Agni; a deity.
आज्ञप्ति *f.* Order, command.
आज्ञा *f.* Order, command.
आज्ञापत्र *n.* An edict, a written order.
आज्ञाभंग *m.* Disobedience, insubordination.
आज्ञापन *n.* Ordering, making known.
आञ्जन *n.* Ointment for the eyes; *m.* Name of Mârutî.
आञ्जनेय *m.* A name of Mârutî.
आटविक *m.* A forester.
आटीकर *m.* A. bull.
आटोप *m.* Puffing, pride
आडम्बर *m.* A show; noise; pride. [grain.
आढक *m. n.* Measure of
आढ्य *a.* Wealthy, rich.
आढ्यता *f.* Opulence.
आणव *n.* Exceeding minuteness.
आतंक *m.* Disease, agony, fear, doubt.

आतत *a.* Spread, stretched.
आततायिन् *a.* A desperado, a thief, a murderer.
आतप *m.* Heat, sunshine, light.
आतपत्र *n.* An umbrella.
आतपलंघन *n.* The sun stroke
आतपवारण *n.* An umbrella.
आतपात्यय *m* Sunset.
आतपादक *n.* A mirage.
आतर, आतार *m.* Fare for being ferried over a river, passage-money.
आतापि (यि) न् *m.* A kite.
आतिथेय *a.* Hospitable.
आतिथेयी *f.* Hospitality.
आतिथ्य *m.* A guest. *n.* Hospitality.
आतिरेक्य *n.* Excess.
आतिशय्य *n.* Abundance.
आतु *m.* A raft, a float.
आतुर *a.* Weak, affected by.
आतुरशाला *f.* An hospital.
आतुरसंन्यास *m.* A kind of **संन्यास** taken by a person when sick or grown hopeless of life.
आत्त (*pp.* of **दा** with **आ**) *a.* Taken, extracted.
आत्मकाम *a.* Loving one's self.
आत्मगतम् *ind.* Aside.
आत्मज *m.* A son.
आत्मजा *f.* A daughter.
आत्माराम *a.* Seeking spiritual knowledge.
आत्मजन्मन् *m.* A son.
आत्मजय *m.* Self-denial.
आत्मत्याग *m.* Self-sacrifice.
आत्मन् *m.* A soul, self; the supreme spirit, mind; courage; vitality; a son; natural disposition.
आत्मनिवेदन *n.* Offering oneself (as a living sacrifice to the deity).
आत्मनेपद *n.* One of the modes in which Sanskrit verbs are conjugated.
आत्मप्रभव *m.* A son; the god of love.
आत्मंभरि *a* Selfish, greedy.
आत्ममानिन् *a.* Proud.
आत्मयोनि *m* An epithet of Brahman, of Vishnu, and of S'iva. [composed.
आत्मवत् *a.* Self-possessed,
आत्मवत्ता *f.* Self-control.
आत्मवश *m.* Self-control.
आत्मविद्या *f.* Spiritual knowledge.
आत्मसंभव *m.* A son.
आत्मसंभवा *f.* A daughter.
आत्मसात् *ind.* One's own.
आत्मापहारक *m.* An impos- [tor.
आत्मीय *a.* One's own.
आत्मीन *a.* Belonging to self
आत्यन्तिक *a.* Infinite, abundant, absolute.
आत्ययिक *a.* Urgent; destructive.

आत्रेय *m.* A descendant of Atri.

आत्रेयी *f.* The wife of Atri.

आदर *m.* Reverence, attention, careful effort; desire.

आदर्श *m.* A mirror; the original manuscript; a model

आदर्शक *m.* A mirror.

आदर्शन *n.* Showing; a mirror

आदंश *m.* A bite; a tooth.

आदान *n.* Receiving, earning.

आदि *a.* First, principal, *m.* Commencement.

आदिपुरुष(-पूरुष) *m.* The supreme deity, an epithet of Vishnu or Krishna.

आदितेय *m.* A god.

आदित्य *m.* A god, the sun.

आदिम *a.* First prior.

आदीनव *m.* Distress; fault.

आदृत *a.* Honoured.

आदेवन *n.* Gambling; a die

आदेश *m.* Advice, instruction, information; a command.

आद्य *a.* First, pre-eminent.

आद्या *f.* A name of Durgá.

आद्योत *m.* Light. brilliance.

आद्यून *a.* Voracious, hungry.

आधर्षण *n.* Injuring; conviction of a crime; refutation

आधान *n.* Performing, providing, inspiring, creating.

आधार *m.* Support; a vessel or reservoir, embankment, a basin.

आधि *m.* Mental agony; misery, a curse.

आधिकरणिक *m.* A judge.

आधिक्य *n.* Excess, superiority.

आधिदैविक *a.* Caused by fate.

आधिपत्य *n.* Supremacy, duties of a king.

आधिभौतिक *a.* Caused by animals, material.

आधिराज्य *n.* Royalty.

आधुनिक *a.* Recent.

आध्मान *n.* Blowing, a bellows.

आध्यात्म *f.* Sorrowful recollection.

आध्यात्मिक *a.* Spiritual, holy

आध्यान *n* Anxiety; sorrowful recollection.

आध्यापक *m.* See अध्यापक.

आध्वनिक *a.* Way-faring.

आनक *m.* A military drum.

आनति *f.* Stooping, salutation, homage, reverence.

आनन *n.* Mouth, face.

आनन्तर्य *n.* Immediate proximity, absence of interval.

आनन्त्य *n.* Infinity, immortality.

आनन्द *m.* Happiness, joy, the supreme spirit.

आनन्दमय *a.* Blissful, happy.

आनंदमयकोश *m.* The innermost case of the body.

आनन्दन *a.* Pleasing.

आनर्त *m.* A theatre, a dancing-hall; a battle

आनुकूल्य *n.* Favourableness, suitableness, conformity.

आनुगत्य *n.* Acquaintance.

आनुग्रामिक *a.* Rural. [sion.

आनुपूर्वी *f.* Order, succes-

आनुमानिक *a.* Derived from inference.

आनुषंगिक *a.* Relative, analogous, implied.

आनूप *a.* Wet, marshy.

आनृण्य *n.* Acquittance of debt. [passion.

आनृशंस्य *n* Mildness; com-

आन्त *a.* Final, terminal.

आन्तर *a.* Internal, hidden.

आन्तरि (री) क्ष *a.* Heavenly. *n.* The firmament.

आन्दोल् *vt.* 10U. To swing.

आन्दोल *m.* A swing.

आन्दोलन *n.* Swinging.

आन्ध्य *n.* Blindness.

आन्ध्र *m.* (pl.) Modern Telagu country.

आन्वयिक *a.* Well-born; orderly.

आन्वाह्निक *a.* Daily. [physics.

आन्वीक्षिकी *f.* Logic, meta-

आप् *vt.* 5. P (*pp.* आप्तः *desid.* ईप्स्) to pervade; to suffer; With अनुप्र-to go to, to reach, अव-to obtain, to reach; परि-to be able; to be competent, to obtain; to reach, वि-to pervade, सम्-to finish.

आपगा *f.* A river a stream.

आपण *m.* A market, a shop.

आपणिक *a.* Merchantile.

आपतन *n.* Natural sequence.

आपत्ति *f.* Misfortune, an undesirable conclusion. [ty.

आपद् *f.* Misfortune, calami-

आपद्धर्म *m.* A practice not usually proper to the caste but allowable in time of distress.

आपद्ग्रस्त *a.* Involved in difficulties. [mity.

आपदा *f.* Misfortune, cala-

आपन्न *a.* Distressed.

आपन्नसत्त्वा *f.* A pregnant woman [afternoon.

आपराह्णिक *a.* Occuring in the

आपस् *n.* Water.

आपात An attack, the present moment, first sight.

आपाततः *ind.* At first sight.

आपाद *m.* Reward, remuneration.

आपान *n.* A drinking party.

आपालि *m.* A louse.

आपीड *m* A crest-jewel.

आपीन *a.* Stout, fat. *n.* An udder or teat.

आपूप्य *m.* Flour.
आपूर *m.* A flow, current.
आपूरण *n.* Filling.
आपृच्छा *f.* Converastion.
आप्त *p. p* Trusted, got, *m.* A friend, a relative.
आप्तवाच् *f.* The advice of a friend; authoritative word.
आप्ति *f.* Acquisition, fitness, completion
आप्यायन *n.* The act of making full or fat.
आप्लव (आप्लाव) *m.* Bathing.
आफूक *n.* Opium.
आबद्ध *a.* Bound.
आबन्ध *m* A tie or bond.
आबर्ह *m.* (-ण *n.*) The act of tearing out. [injury.
आबाध *m.*(-धा *f.*) Affliction,
आबिल *a.* Turbid; dirty.
आबुत्त *m.* A sister's husband
आबोधन *n.* Knowledge.
आब्दिक *a.* Annual.
आभरण *n.* Ornament.
आभा *f.* Light, splendour, colour, a reflection.
आभाष *m.* An introduction a preface.
आभाषण *n.* Addressing.
आभास *m.* Splendour; a reflection, phantom, fallacious appearance.
आभिजन *a.* Relating to birth. [birth; beauty.
आभिजात्य *n.* Nobility of
आभिधा *f.* The same as अभिधा.
आभिधानिक *m.* A lexicographer.
आभिमुख्य *n.* Direction towards; favourableness.
आभिक्ष्ण्य *n.* Continued repetition.
आभीर *m.* A cowherd.
आभील *n.* Physical pain. *a.* Fearful.
आभोग *m.* Expanse, circumference, enjoyment.
आभ्यन्तर *a.* Inner, interior.
आभ्यवहारिक *n.* An eatable.
आभ्यासिक *a.* Resulting from practice.
आभ्युदयिक *a.* Auspicious, important.
आम *a.* Raw, unbaked, undigested. *m.* Constipation.
आमञ्जु *a.* Lovely, charming
आमनस्य *n* Pain, sorrow.
आमन्त्रण *n.* Invitation, permission, conversation.
आमन्द्र *a.* Having a slightly deep tone.
आमय *m.* Disease, sickness.
आमरणान्त (-न्तिक) *a.* Lasting till death. [ing.
आमर्द *m* Crushing, squeez-
आमर्श *m.* Advice, counsel.
आमर्ष *m.* Anger; impatience
आमलक *m. f.* A kind of tree, or its fruit.
आमात्य *m.* A minister

आमानस्य *n.* Sorrow, anxiety

आमाशय *m.* The upper part of the belly.

आमिष *m. n.* Flesh, a bait; a bribe, a prey.

आमुख *n.* Commencement; a prelude.

आमुखम् *ind.* To the face.

आमुष्मिक *a.* Belonging to the next world.

आमुष्यायण *a.* Well-born; of high birth.

आमोचन *n.* Liberating.

आमोद *m.* Joy, perfume.

आमोदन *n.* Rejoicing, making fragrant. [studied.

आम्नात *a.* Remembered;

आम्नान *n.* Mention, study of sacred texts.

आम्नाय *m.* The Vedas.

आम्भसिक *m.* A fish.

आम्र *m.* The mango tree. *n.* The fruit of the mango tree.

आम्रेडन(-डित) *n.* Tautology

आम्ल *m.* [आम्लि(-म्ली)का *f.*] The tamarind tree, *n.* Sourness.

आय *m.* Arrival; income.

आयत *a.* Diffuse, prolix; long; restrained.

आयतन *n.* A resting place; a sanctuary.

आयति *f.* Length, futurity, dignity; work.

आयत्त *a.* Dependent.

आयत्ति *f.* Dependence; strength; expedient; steadiness of conduct; length. [ness.

आय(था)थातथ्य *n.* Unfit-

आयमन *n.* Length, extension.

आयस *a.* Made of iron.

आयान *n.* Arrival; natural temperament,

आयाम *m.* Stretching; restraint.

आयास *m.* Effort, fatigue.

आयुक्त *m.* An agent

आयुध *m. n.* A weapon.

आयुधागार *n.* An armory, arsenal.

आयुधिक *m.* A soldier.

आयुस् *n.* Life, vital power.

आयुष्मत् *a.* Long-lived; (a form of addressing a nobly born person).

आयुर्वेद *m* The science of medicine.

आयुष्य *a.* Giving long life.

आयोग *m.* Appointment.

आयोजन *n.* Effort, taking.

आयोधन *n.* War, field.

आरकूट *m. n.* Brass.

आरक्षक *m.* A watchman.

आराणि *m.* An eddy.

आरण्य *a.* Wild. *m. n.* A forest.

आरण्यक *a.* Wild; *m.* A forest, *n.* a class of religious and philosophical writings.

आराति *f.* Cessation; waving lights before an image.
आरब्धि *m.* Beginning.
आरभट *m.* A bold man.
आरम्भ *m.* (-ण *n.*) Work, beginning, haste; effort, posture.
आर (रा) व *m.* Sound.
आरात् *ind.* Far off; near.
आराति *m.* An enemy. [mate.
आरातिय *a.* Remote; proxi-
आराधन *n.* Propitiation.
आराधना *f.* Service.
आराम *m.* Delight, a garden.
आरामिक *m.* A gardener.
आरूढि *f.* Rise, elevation.
आरोग्य *n.* Good health.
आरोप *m.* Attributing the nature of one thing to another; imputation.
आरोपण *n.* Planting.
आरोह *m.* An ascent; a rider; pride; an elevation; waist.
आरोहण *n.* A stair-case.
आर्घ्य *n.* Wild honey.
आर्जव *n.* Straightness; uprightness.
आर्त *a.* Afflicted, sick. [al.
आर्तव *a.* Seasonal; menstru-
आर्ति *f.* Pain, agony.
आर्थिक *a.* Significant; rich.
आर्द्र *a.* Wet, fresh. [tion.
आर्द्रा *f.* Name of a constella-
आर्धिक *a.* Sharing half, relating to half.
आर्य *a.* Noble; respectable, *m.* Name of a race; a master.
आर्यावर्त *m.* A tract of land lying between the Himalaya and the Vindhya mountains.
आर्यगृह्य *a.* Respectable.
आर्यमिश्र *a.* Distinguished, respectable.
आर्या *f.* A name of Párvati; a respectable lady; a kind of metre.
आर्ष *a.* Relating or belonging to a Rishi; Vedic.
आलभन *n.* (आलंभ *m.*) Killing.
आलम्ब *m.* A support.
आलम्बन *n.* Supporting; a house; reason, base.
आलम्भ *m.* Killing.
आलय *m. n.* A house. [dog.
आलर्क *a.* Relating to a mad
आलवाल *n.* A basin for water round the root of a tree.
आलस *a.* Idle; lazy.
आलस्य *n.* Idleness; sloth.
आलात *n.* A fire-brand.
आलाप *m.* Speech; conversation; narration.
आलाबु (-बू) *f* A gourd.
आलि *m.* A bee; a scorpion. *f.* A woman's female friend.
आलिंगन *n.* An embrace.
आलिंद *m.* A terrace before a house.

आलिम्पन *n.* Plastering walls (with lime &c.).

आलु *m.* An owl; ebony. *f.* A pitcher. [ing.

आलेखन *n.* Painting; writ-

आलेखनी *f.* A brush; a pencil

आलेख्य *n.* A writing; a painting.

आलेप *m.* (-न *n.*) Smearing, plastering.

आलोक *m.* *n.* Sight, light.

आलोडन *n.* Agitating.

आलोल *a.* Agitated.

आवपन *n.* Sowing, seed.

आवरण *n.* A shield, covering; ignorance.

आवर्त *m.* A whirlpool, a crowded place.

आवर्तक *m.* Name of a form of cloud.

आवर्तन *n.* Turning.

आवालि (-ली) *f.* A row, a series, a dynasty.

आवलित *a.* Slightly turned.

आवश्यक *a.* Necessary.

आवसाति *f.* Midnight.

आवसथ *m.* *n.* A dwelling place, a village.

आवसथ्य *n.* A house. [ed.

आवासित *a* Decided, finish-

आवह *a.* Bringing. [seed.

आवाप *m.* Throwing, sowing

आवापन *n.* A loom.

आवाल *n.* A basin for water round the root of a tree.

आवास *m.* A house.

आवाहन *n.* Inviting; invoking a deity to be present.

आविर्भाव *m.* Manifestation, incarnation; presence.

आविल *a.* Turbid, impure, dim

आविष्करण *n.* (**आविष्कार** *m.*) Manifestation

आविष्ट *a* Possessed (as by an evil spirit). [dently.

आविस् *ind.* Openly, evi-

आवुक *m.* A father. [band.

आवुत्त *m.* A sister's hus-

आवृत्ति *f.* Return, repeti-

आवृष्टि *f.* A shower. [tion.

आवेग *m.* Hurry; agitation.

आवेदन *n.* Representation; a plaint.

आवेश *m.* Influence, demoniacal possession; pride; intentness.

आवेशन *n.* Entrance, passion; work-shop, a dwelling.

आवेष्टन *n* A wrapper, a wall.

आश *m.* Eating. [gination.

आशंसा *f.* Desire, hope, ima-

आशंसु *a.* Desirous, hopeful.

आशंका *f.* Fear, uncertainty.

आशय *m.* The mind, meaning, a seat, a reservoir.

आशा *f.* Desire, hope, a region

आशित *a.* Eaten. [demon.

आशिर *m.* Fire; the sun; a

आशिस् *f.* Prayer, a serpent's fang, blessing.

आशी *f.* A benediction; a serpent's fang.

आशीर्वाद *m.* Expression of a prayer or wish.

आशीर्वचन *n.* A blessing, a benediction.

आर्शाविष *m.* A snake.

आशु *a.* Fast. *ind.* Quickly.

आशुग *m.* An arrow.

आशुतोष *a.* Easily appeased.

आशोषण *n.* Drying.

आश्चर्य *a.* Marvellous *n.* A wonder, a marvel.

आश्म (-न) *a.* Stony.

आश्मिक *a.* Made of stone.

आश्यान *a.* Congealed.

आश्रम *m. n.* A hermitage. An order of the religious life of a Bráhman.

आश्रय *m* A resting place, an asylum; an authority.

आश्रयाश *m.* Fire.

आश्रयण *n.* Refuge, asylum.

आश्रव *a.* Compliant, obedient. *m.* Stream, fault.

आश्रित *a.* Having recourse to.

आश्रुत *a.* Promised.

आश्लेष *m.* An embrace, contact.

आश्वास *m.* Consolation.

आश्विक *m.* A cavalier.

आश्विन *m.* The name of a month.

आश्विनेय *m.* A name of Nakula and Sahadeva, the last two Pandava princes; the twin physicians of Gods (*du.*).

आषाढ *m.* Name of a Hindu month; a staff.

आस् *ind.* Ah! oh or similar expressions of anger, pain, or sorrow.

आस् *vt.* 2. A To sit down, to live, to let go. With अधि-to sit down, to occupy; अनु-to sit down after, to serve, to follow. उत्-to be careless or apathetic; to be inactive पर्युप-to wait upon; to surronnd; सम्-to sit down, समुप-to wait upon, to perform.

आस *m n.* A seat; a bow.

आसक्त *a.* Strongly attached to, continuous.

आसक्ति *f.* Strong attachment.

आसंग *m.* Association.

आसत्ति *f.* Intimate union, junction; gain.

आसन *n.* a seat, any peculiar mode of sitting.

आसन्न *a.* Near, imminent.

आसन्नकाल *m* Hour of death

आसव *m.* Distillation, spirituous liquor.

आसादन *n.* Attacking, attaining.

आसुर *a.* Belonging or relating to evil spirits; demoniacal. *m* A demon; one of the eight forms of marriage.

आसुरी *f.* Surgery; a female demon. [ing.

आसेक *m.* Wetting, water-

आसेचन *n.* See **आसेक.**

आसेध *m.* Arrest, custody.

आसेवन *n.* (**आसेवा** *f.*) Assiduous practice, repetition, intercourse.

आस्कन्द *m.* (-**न** *n.*) An attack, reproach.

आस्तर *m.* A covering.

आस्तरण *n.* A carpet, a bed.

आस्तिक *a.* One who believes in God and another world.

आस्तिक्य *n.* Belief in the existence of God and another world.

आस्था *f.* Consideration, care, hope; support; effort; an assembly.

आस्थान *n.* A place, an assembly.

आस्थित *pp.* Abiding; using; occupied; covered.

आस्पद *n.* Place, dignity, authority; business; object.

आस्पन्दन *n.* Trembling.

आस्फालन *n.* Striking against, stirring; arrogance.

आस्फोटन *n.* Blowing, contracting.

आस्य *n.* Mouth; opening.

आस्यन्दन *n.* Flowing; ooz-

आस्र *n.* Blood. [ing

आस्रप *m.* A demon.

आस्रव *m.* Discharge; pain.

आस्राव *m.* A wound; flow, discharge, pain.

आस्वाद *m.* Flavour, taste.

आहत *a.* Beaten, struck.

आहति *f.* (**आहनन** *n.*) A blow, a hit, multiplication.

आहरण *n.* Removing, performing; a dowry.

आहव *m.* A sacrifice.

आहवन *n.* A sacrifice.

आहवनीय *a.* To be offered; *m.* One of the three sacred fires.

आहार *m.* Taking food.

आहार्य *a.* Artificial; pursed. [potained.

आहित *a.* Placed, enter-

आहिताग्नि *m.* A Bráhmana who keeps sacred fire.

आहितुण्डिक *m.* A juggler, a snake-catcher.

आहुति *f.* An oblation offered to a deity.

आहूति *f.* Calling, invoking

आहो *ind.* What ! Yes ! Alas !

आहोस्वित *ind.* A particle implying doubt.

आह्न *n.* A series of days.

आह्निक *a.* Daily. *n.* Daily duties.

आल्हाद *m.* Joy, delight.

आल्हादन *n.* Gladdening.

आह्वय *m.* (-न *n.*) A name; appellation. [call.

आह्वान *n.* Challenge; a

आह्वायक *m.* A messenger.

इ.

इ *ind.* Even; indeed; very.

इ *vi* 2 P To go, With उत to rise. अभ्युत्-to prosper *vt.* 2. P. to go towards; अति-to excel, to spend time; to go beyond; अधि to remember, अनु-to follow; अन्वा-to follow, अंतर्-to intervene; अप-to depart, अभि-to get; to approach, अभ्या-to approach, अभ्युत्-to prosper, अभ्युप-to arrive, to accept, अभिप्र-to intend, अव-to know, आ-to come उत्-to rise, उप-to go, to attain, निर्-to set out, परा-to depart, परि-to go round, to surround, प्र-to depart life, प्रति-to trust, to be known; to be pleased; प्रत्युत् to go, receive, वि-to spend; to undergo a change, व्यति-to transgress, व्यप-to go away, विपरि-to change, सम्-to meet, समनु-to accompany, समव-to assemble, समा-to unite, समुत to collect, समुद-to obtain, संप्रति-to determine.

इक्षव *m.* The sugar-cane.

इक्षु (-र) *m.* The sugar-cane.

इक्षुविकार *m.* Sugar.

इक्ष्वाकु *m.* The celebrated ancestor of the solar kings of Ayodhyá or his descendant.

इख् *vt.* 1. P. (*pp.* एखित) To go *vt.* 1. P. (इंखित) to move. With प्र to move to and fro.

इग् *vt.* or *vi.* 1 P.(*pp*इंगित) To go, to move. [hint.

इंगित *n.* Intention, gesture,

इंगुद *m.* (-दी *f.*) Name of a

इच्छा *f.* Wish, desire. [tree.

इज्य *m.* Teacher; Brihaspati.

इज्या *f.* A sacrifice, a gift.

इडा (-ला) *f.* The earth; speech; a cow.

इतर *pron.* (*f.*-रा, *n.*-रत्) Another; low. [where.

इतरतः (इतरत्र) *ind.* Else-

इतरथा *ind.* In another way.

इतरेतर *pron.* Mutual.

इतरेद्युस *ind.* The other day.

इतस् *ind.* Hence, here.

इति *ind.* Thus, so. [tion.

इतिकर्तव्य *n.* Duty, obliga-

इतिकर्तव्यतामूढ *a.* Perplexed.

इतिमात्र *a.* Of such extent or quality.

इतिवृत्त *n.* An account.

इतिह *ind.* Thus indeed.

इतिहास *m*. History; legend; tradition.
इत्थम् *ind*. Thus
इत्थंभूत *a*. True, faithful
इत्यर्थ *m*. Substance.
इदम् *pron*. (*m*. अयम्, *f*. इयम्, *n*. इदम्,) This, the same.
इदानीम् *ind*. Now, in this case.
इदानीन्तन *a* Of the present moment, coeval.
इध्म *n* Fuel
इन *m*. The sun; a king.
इन्दिरा *f* An epithet of Lakshmi.
इंदि(दी)वर *n*. The blue lotus.
इन्दु *m*. The moon.
इंदुकान्त *m*. The moon stone.
इन्दुमती *f*. The full-moon day.
इदुमौलि (-शेखर) *m*. S'iva.
इन्दूर *m*. A rat, a mouse.
इन्द्र *m*. The king of Gods; Lord; best.
इन्द्रकोष *m*. A sofa; a platform.
इन्द्रचाप *m* *n*. A rainbow.
इन्द्रजाल *n*. Conjuring; jugglery; deception.
इन्द्रनील *m*. Sapphire.
इन्द्रावरज *m*. Vishnu.
इन्द्राणी *f*. The wife of Indra.
इन्द्रिय *n*. An organ of sense
इन्द्रियस्वाप *m* Unconsciousness, insensibility.
इन्ध् *v. i*. A 7 (*pp* इद्ध) To kindle, With सम्-to kindle.

इन्ध *m*. (-न *n*.) Fuel.
इभ *m*. An elephant.
इभ्य *a*. Wealthy *m*. A king; an elephant-driver.
इभ्या *f*. A female elephant
इयत् *a*. So much.
इयत्ता *f*. (-त्त्व *n*.) Standard.
इरम्मद *m*. Submarine fire; a flash of lightning
इरा *f*. The earth; water; speech.
इरावत् *m*. The ocean.
इव *ind*. Like, as if; nearly.
इष् *vt*. 1 U (*pp*. एषित) To go. With अनु-to follow. *vt*. 4. P (*pp* इषित) To go अनु-to search, प्र-to send *vt*. 6 P (*pp*. इष्ट) To wish अनु-to search, to try. अभि to desire. परि-to search, प्रति-to receive.
इषिर *m* Fire.
इषु *m*. *f*. An. arrow; five.
इषुधि *m*. *f*. A quiver.
इष्ट *p. p* Desired.
इष्टका *f*. Brick
इष्टि *f*. Sacrifice; desired object.
इष्टिका *f*. A brick.
इष्म (-ष्य) *m*. The spring.
इह *ind*. Here.

ई.

ई *vt*. or *vi*. 2. P. To go; to pervade; to desire; *vt*. 4 To go.
ईक्ष् *vt*. 1. A To look, with अधि-to suspect, अनु-to

inquire after, अप-to expect, to pay regard to, अभिवि-to look towards, अव-to look at, to consider, उत्-to look up to, to wait, उत्प्र-to conjecture, to expect उद्वि-to look up, उप-to overlook, निर्-to observe, परि-to examine, प्र-to look at, to wait, प्रति-to look in return, वि-to see व्यप-to mind, सम् to behold; to think, समव-to inspect; to consider, समुप-to neglect.

ईक्षण *n* A look.

ईक्षा *f.* Viewing, sight.

ईख् *vt.* or *vi.* 1.P (*pp.*ईंखित) To go, with प्र to tremble.

ईड् *vt.* 2. A To praise.

ईड्य *a.* Praiseworthy. [son.

ईति *f.* A calamity of the sea-

ईदृक्ष (-क्षी *f.*) } *a.* Such, of
ईदृश (-शी *f.*) } such a kind

ईप्सा *f.* Desire to obtain.

ईप्सित *a.* Desired.

ईप्सु *a.* Desirous to obtain.

ईर् *vt.* 1. P To go, to shake. *vt.* 2. A (*pp.* ईर्ण) To go; to move. With उत्-to rise. 10 U. To Pronounce, उद्-to utter, to put forth, -प्र to send.

ईर्ष्य् *vi.* 1. P To envy.

ईर्ष्यक *a* Envious.

ईर्ष्या (र्षा) लु *a.* Envious.

ईश् *vt.* 2. A to rule; to possess.

ईश *a.* Powerful, supreme. *m.* A lord.

ईशान *m.* A ruler, an epithet of S'iva or of Vishnu.

ईशानी *f.* An epithet of Durgá.

ईशिता *f.* (त्व *n.*) Supremacy, one of the eight *siddhis*.

ईश्वर *a.* Powerful; *m.* Master, lord; S'iva. [to see.

ईष् *vt.* 1 U To give, to kill:

ईषत् *ind.* Little.

ईषत्पुरुष *m.* A mean man.

ईषत्प्रलम्भ *a.* To be gained for little.

ईषा *f.* The pole of a carriage

ईषि (षी) का *f.* A painter's brush; an arrow.

ईषिर *m.* Fire.

ईह् *vi.* 1 A to desire; to aim at, With सम्-to desire.

ईहा *f.* Effort, desire.

उ

उ *m.* S'iva.

उक्त *a* Said, spoken.

उक्ति *f.* Speech, expression.

उक्थ *n* A name of the Sámaveda.

उक्ष् *vt.* 1. P To sprinkle, to wet, With अभि-to sprinkle with consecrated water; परि-to sprinkle around. प्र or सं प्र-to consecrate by sprinkling.

उक्षन् *m*. An ox or bull.
उक्षतर *m* A small bull.
उख् *vi*. I.P(*pp* ओखित or उंखित) To go, to move
उखा *f*. A cooking pan or pot
उख्य *a*. (-ख्या *f*.) Boiled in a pot.
उग्र *a*. Powerful, terrible, noble; sharp.
उच् *vt*. 4.P. To gather.
उचित *a*. Worthy; proper.
उच्च *a*. High, loud.
उच्चकैस् *ind*. High, above.
उच्चक्षुस् *a*. With the eyes raised up; blind.
उच्चंड *a*. Formidable, quick.
उच्चय *m*. Collection, prosperity.
उच्चलित *a*. Setting out.
उच्चाटन Expulsion; removal; extirpation.
उच्चार *m* Pronunciation, utterance; excrement, discharge.
उच्चारण *n* Articulation, pronunciation.
उच्चावच *a*. High and low.
अच्चूड (-ल) *m*. A banner.
उच्चैस् *ind*. Aloft high loud.
उच्चैःश्रवस् *m*. An epithet of the horse of Indra.
उच्छन्न *a*. Destroyed.
उच्छल *a*. Going up.
उच्छित्ति *f*. Extirpation.
उच्छिलींध्र *a*. Full of mushrooms.
उच्छिष्ट *n*. Remainder (especially of food.
उच्छीर्षक *n*. A pillow.
उच्छून *a*. Swollen.
उच्छृंखल *a*. Unbridled.
उच्छेद *m*.(-न *n*.) Extirpation.
उच्छेष *m*. Remainder
उच्छ्र(च्छ्रा)य *m*. Height, growth.
उच्छ्वसन *n* Breathing, sighing.
उच्छ्वसित *a*. Breathing; consoled. *n*. Life.
उच्छ्वास *m*. Breath, consolation, chapter of a book.
उछ् *vt*. 6. P. (*pp*. उष्ट) To bind, to finish.
उज्जयि (य) नी *f*. The capital of the Avantis.
उज्जिहान *a*. Rising.
उज्जृंभ *m*. Opening; blown.
उज्जृंभण *n*. Opening.
उज्ज्वल *c*. Splendid.
उज्ज्वलन *n*. Shining.
उज्झ् *vt*. 6 P (*pp* उज्झित) To abandon, to emit; With प्र- to abandon altogether, to avoid.
उञ्छ् *vt*. 6. P (*pp*. उञ्छित) To glean. With प्र- to wipe out.
उञ्छ (-न *n*.) *m*. Gleaning.
उट *m* Grass; leaves.
उटज *m*. *n*. A hermitage.
उडु *n*. *f*. A star, water.
उडु (डू) प *m*. *n*. A raft or boat.
उडुपति (-राज) *m*. The moon.

उड्डयन *n* Soaring.
उड्डीन *a.* Flying.
उत *ind.* Whether, or, either, it may be, else, and, also.
उत्क *a.* Desirous, anxious.
उत्कट *a* Abounding in, excessive, *m.* An elephant in rut.
उत्कंठ *a.* Anxious, eager.
उत्कंठा *f.* Longing, anxiety
उत्कर *m.* A heap; rubbish.
उत्कर्ष *m* Prosperity; excellence.
उत्कर्षण *n.* Pulling off.
उत्कलिका *f.* A bud; a wave; dalliance.
उत्कषण *n.* Ploughing.
उत्कीर्तन *n.* Proclaiming, praising.
उत्कुण *m.* A bug; a louse.
उत्कुल *n.* Dishonouring one's family.
उत्कृष्ट *a.* Tilled, excellent.
उत्कोच *m.* A bribe.
उत्कोचक *m.* The receiver of a bribe. [increase.
उत्क्रम *m.* Progressive
उत्क्रमण *n.* (उत्क्रान्ति *f*) Going up or out. [gression.
उत्क्राम *m* Surpassing; trans-
उत्क्रोश *m* Clamour.
उत्क्षिप्त *a.* Tossed up.
उत्क्षेपण *n.* Throwing upwards, lifting; vomiting.
उत्खचित *a.* Interwoven.
उत्खात *a.* Dug up, eradicated.
उत्खातिन् *a.* Uneven.
उत्त *a.* Wet, moist. [crest.
उत्तंस *m. n.* An ear-ring, a
उत्तट *a.* Overflowing. [lent
उत्तम *a.* Uppermost, excel-
उत्तमर्ण *m.* A creditor.
उत्तमा *f.* An excellent woman.
उत्तमांग *n.* The head.
उत्तमाह *m.* The last day.
उत्तंभ *m.* (-नन.) Upholding; stopping.
उत्तर *a.* Upper, northern, superior; *n.* An answer; the remainder.
उत्तरक्रिया *f.* Funeral rites.
उत्तरत्र *ind.* Subsequently.
उत्तरपक्ष *m.* A reply. [west
उत्तरपश्चिमा *f.* The north-
उत्तरपूर्वा *f.* The north-east.
उत्तरप्रत्युत्तर *n.* A discussion.
उत्तर-मीमांसा *f.* A school of Indian philosophy.
उत्तरंग *a* Ruffled by waves.
उत्तरम् *ind.* Above; after.
उत्तरा *f.* The north.
उत्तराधिकार *m.* Heirship.
उत्तरायण *n.* The progress of the sun to the North.
उत्तरीय *n.* An upper garment. [quent day.
उत्तरेद्युस् *ind.* On a subse-
उत्तरोत्तर *a.* Successive [ing.
उत्तर्जन *n.* Violent threaten-

उत्तान *a.* Stretched out; upright; open.

उत्ताप *m.* Great heat; affliction: excitement.

उत्तारक *m.* Deliverer.

उत्ताल *a.* Great, formidable

उत्तुंग *a* Lofty, high.

उत्तेजन *n* (-ना *f.*) excitement, sharpening an inducement.

उत्तोलन *n.* Lifting up.

उत्थान *n.* Standing up, exertion, origin.

उत्थापन *n.* Causing to rise; awakening. [or rising.

उत्थित *a.* Produced, risen

उत्पत्ति *f.* Birth, origin.

उत्पथ *m.* A wrong road.

उत्पथम् *ind.* Astray.

उत्पन्न *a.* Born, produced.

उत्पल *n.* The blue lotus, any water-lily.

उत्पाटन *n.* Eradicating.

उत्पात *m.* A jump, a portent, a calamity.

उत्पाद *m.* Birth. [Origin.

उत्पादक *m.* A father. *n.*

उत्पीड *m.* Foam.

उत्प्रेक्षा *f.* Indifference; a figure of speech; poetical fancy.

उत्प्लव *m* A jump, leap.

उत्प्लवा *f.* A boat. [spring.

उत्फाल *m.* A jump, a

उत्फुल्ल *a.* Blown, full, open.

उत्स *m.* A fountain.

उत्संग *m.* Embrace, the lap, the edge of a hill, the interior.

उत्संगित *a.* Associated.

उत्सन्न *a.* Decayed; ruined

उत्सर्ग *m.* Emission, giving up, gift, excretion; a general rule. [gift.

उत्सर्जन *n.* Abandoning;

उत्सव *m.* A festival, joy.

उत्सादन *n.* Destroying, ploughing, interrupting; rising.

उत्सारक *m.* A policeman.

उत्साह *m.* Energy, resolution, perseverance; power.

उत्सिक्त *a.* Proud, excessive. fickle.

उत्सुक *a.* Restless, eager.

उत्सूत्र *a.* Loose, irregular.

उत्सेक m. Sprinkling, overflow, pride.

उत्सेध m. Height, thickness.

उद् *ind.* A prefix implying 'superiority, seperation, publicity, expansion, pride, &.' [ward.

उदक् *ind.* Above, north-

उदक *n.* Water.

उदक(कि)ल *a.* Watery.

उदक्त *a.* Raised up. [excited

उदग्र *a.* High, large, fierce

उदच् *a.* Upper: Northern subsequent,

उदंचन *n.* A bucket.

उदन् *n*. Water.
उदधि *m*. The ocean, a cloud; a lake.
उदन्वत् *m*. The ocean. *m*. A cloud.
उदंत *m*. Intelligence; a pure and virtuous man.
उदंतक *m*. News, tiding.
उदंतिका *f*. Satisfaction.
उदन्या *f*. Thirst.
उदय *m*. Prosperity, rise, splendour.
उदर *n*. The belly, interior
उदरपिशाच *m*. A glutton.
उदरपूरम् *ind*. Till the belly is full.
उदरंभरि *a*. Gluttonous.
उदराधि *m*. The ocean.
उदरिक *a*. Having a large belly.
उदरिणी *f*. A pregnant woman.
उदरिल *a*. Fat, corpulent.
उदर्क *m*. Consequence, futurity.
उदर्चिस् *m*. Fire.
उदश्रु *a* Weeping.
उदात्त *a*. Elevated, generous. *m*. The accute accent.
उदान *m*. Breathing upwards
उदार *a*. Munificent, honest, eloquent large, beautiful.
उदारचरित *a*. Noble-minded.
उदास(-सीन) *a*. Indifferent.
उदाहरण *n*.(उदाहार *m*.) Opening of a speech, example, an illustration.
उदित *a*. Spoken, risen, born.
उदीची *f*. The north.
उदीचीन *a*. Northern.
उदीच्य *a*. Living in the north.
उदीरण *n*. Throwing uttering.
उदुंबर *m*. A kind of fig-tree.
उदूखल *n*. A mortar.
उदेजय *a*. Terrifying.
उद्गति *f*. Ascent.
उद्गंधि *a*. Fragrant.
उद्गम *m*. Appearance, a shoot
उद्गमनीय *n*. Bleached clothes.
उद्गाढ *a*. Excessive.
उद्गातृ *m*. A priest chanting the hymns of Sâmaveda at a sacrifice.
उद्गार *m*. Eructation; spittle. [a sound.
उद्गीर्ण *p. p*. Vomited.
उद्ग्राहित *a*. Excellent.
उद्ग्रीव *a*. One having the neck uplifted.
उद्घ *m* Excellence.
उद्घट्टन *n*. (-ना *f*.) Friction.
उद्घर्षण *n* Rubbing.
उद्घात *m*. Beginning; a wound; chapter.
उद्घोष *m*. General report.
उद्दंड *a*. Formidable
उद्दान *n*. Confinement, middle.
उद्दाम *a*. Free, proud, excessive.
उद्दिष्ट *a*. Mentioned, wished for.

उद्दीपन *n*. Exciting, illuminating.

उद्देश *m*. Illustration, inquiry, a brief statement, a motive.

उद्देश्य *n*. The subject of a sentence.

उद्द्योत *m*. Light; chapter.

उद्द्राव *m*. Flight, retreat.

उद्धत *a*. Raised; excessive; haughty.

उद्धरण *n*. Rescuing, eradication, final emancipation.

उद्धर्ष *m*. A festival, great joy; courage.

उद्धार *m*. Elevation; redemption; final beautitude; debt

उध्दृत *a*. Raised; delivered.

उध्दृति *f*. An extract; rescuing from sin.

उद्ध्मान *n*. A fire-place.

उद्बल *a*. Strong, powerful.

उद्बाहु *a*. Having the arms raised.

उद्बुद्ध *a*. Awakened.

उद्बोध *m*. (-न *n*.) Reminding, awakening.

उद्भट *a*. Excellent, magnanimous.

उद्भव *m*. Creation, source.

उद्भाव *m*. Production, magnanimity.

उद्भावन *n*. Thinking, production, neglect.

उद्भास *m*. Radiance.

उद्भासुर *a*. Radiant.

उद्भिद् *m*. A plant.

उद्भिद्विद्या *f*. Botany.

उद्भूत *a*. Born.

उद्भूति *f*. Generation, increase, prosperity.

उद्भेद *m*. Breaking out.

उद्यत *a*. Ready, engaged in.

उद्यम *m*. Effort.

उद्यान *n*. A pleasure-garden, a park.

उद्यापन *n*. Bringing to a conclusion.

उद्योग *m*. Effort, exertion, work.

उद्राव *m* A loud noise.

उद्रिक्त. *p.p*. Increased, distinct.

उद्रेक *m*. Excess, increase.

उद्वपन *n*. A gift, donation.

उद्वर्त *m*. A remainder, excess.

उद्वर्तन *n*. Turning from side to side.

उद्वह *m*. A son.

उद्वहन *n*. Carrying; marrying.

उद्वास *m* (-न *n*.) Banishment.

उद्वाह *m*. Marriage.

उद्विग्न *a*. Sorrowful, anxious.

उद्वीक्षण *n*. Looking upwards; sight, looking at.

उद्वृंहण *n*. Increase.

उद्वेग *m*. Agitation, anxiety.

उंदर (दु, दू,) रु } *m*. A rat, a mouse.

उन्नत *p.p*. Raised, high.

उन्नति *f*. Elevation, prosperity.

उन्नमन *n*. Raising, lifting up

उन्नयन *n* Making straight, discussion; inference.

उन्नम्र *a.* Erect, lofty.
उन्निद्र *a.* Sleepless.
उन्मत्त *a.* Insane, frantic.
उन्मद *a.* Mad;drunk.[mind.
उन्मनस्क *a.* Disturbed in
उन्मंथन *n.* Shaking, killing.
उन्मयूख *a.* Shining.
उन्माथ *m.* Torment; pain.
उन्माद *m.* Madness, bloom.
उन्मार्ग A wrong road; evil course.
उन्मिषित *a.* Opened, blown.
उन्मीन *n.* Winking.
उन्मील *m.* (-न *n.*) Opening the eyes; expanding.
उन्मुख *a.* Raising the face; expecting; prepared for.
उन्मुखर *a.* Noisy.
उन्मूलन *n.* Rooting out.
उन्मेष *m.* (-ण *n.*) Opening the eyes; flash.
उन्मोचन *n.* Unfastening.
उप *ind.* Towards, near, with, under, down, nearly, almost. subordinate to, in addition to, &c.
उपकंठ *n.* Neighbourhood.
उपकथा *f.* A short story.
उपकरण *n.* Instrument, apparatus. [port.
उपकर्णिका *f.* Rumour, re-
उपकर्तृ *a.* Obliging.
उपकार *m.* Favour, obligation.
उपकार्या *f.* A royal tent.
उपकुंभ *a.* Solitary, retired.
उपकुर्वाण *m.* A Bráhmana in a state of pupilage.
उपकुल्या *f.* A canal, ditch.
उपकृति *f.* Aid, favour.
उपक्रम *m* Advance., enterprise; commencement.
उपक्रमणिका *f.* An introduction; preface.
उपक्रिया *f.* Service favour.
उपक्रोश *m.* Censure, reproach. [tion.
उपक्षेप *m.* Mention accusa-
उपग *a.* Approaching.
उपगण *m.* An inferior class.
उपगत *p. p.* Acquired.
उपगम *m.* (-न *n.*) Approach, knowledge, attainment.
उपगु *m.* A cowherd.
उपगुरु *m.* An assistant teacher.
उपगूढ *n.* An embrace.
उपगूहन *n.* Hiding; embrace; surprise.
उपग्रह *m.* A minor planet, holy study.
उपग्राह *m.* A present.
उपग्राह्य *m. n.* A present.
उपघात *m.* Damage, injury; assault.
उपघोषण *n.* Proclaiming.
उपचक्षुस् *n.* An eye-glass.
उपचय *m.* Accumulation.
उपचार *m.* Attendance, courtesy, homage, an article of worship, a present, a request

उपचिति *f.* Accumulation.
उपच्छंदन *n.* Persuading.
उपजन *m.* Addition, birth, origin.
उपजल्पन (-ल्पित) *n.* Talk.
उपजाप *m.* Treason.
उपजीवन *n* Subsistence.
उपजीविका *f* Subsistence.
उपजीविन् *a.* Dependent.
उपजीव्य *m.* A patron.
उपज्ञा *f.* Self-acquired knowledge.
उपताप *m.* Heat, pain.
उपत्यका *f.* Land at the foot of a hill or mountain.
उपदंश *m.* The venereal disease.
उपदा *f.* A present.
उपदेश *m.* Instruction, advice.
उपद्रव *m.* Misfortune, trouble, violence.
उपधा *f.* Forgery, fraud, an expedient.
उपधातु *m.* A semi-metal.
उपधान *n.* A pillow, excellence.
उपधि *m.* Fraud, terror.
उपध्मान *n.* Breathing.
उपनत *a.* Befallen.
उपनगर *n.* A suburb.
उपनयन *n.* Investiture with the sacred thread.
उपनायक *m.* A character in a dramatic work next in importance to the hero; a paramour.
उपनिक्षेप or उपनिधान *n.* A deposit.
उपनिधि *m.* A deposit.
उपनिपात *m.* Sudden and unexpected attack or occurrence.
उपनिमंत्रण *n* Invitation.
उपनिवेशित *p. p.* Placed, established.
उपनिषद् *f.* A portion of the religious and philosophical literature of the Hindus.
उपनेतृ *a.* A preceptor.
उपन्यास *m.* Statement. suggestion.
उपपत्ति *f.* Cause, reasoning ascertainment: conclusion.
उपपद *n.* A prefix; a title; a degree.
उपपन्न *p. p.* Fit, proper.
उपपादन *n.* Demonstration.
उपप्रदान *n.* A tribute.
उपप्रलोभन *n.* A bribe, an inducement.
उपप्लव *m.* Unlucky accident, a calamity.
उपबंध *m.* Connection.
उपभोग *m.* Use,enjoyment.
उपमर्द *m.* Friction, reproach, refutation of a charge.
उपमा *f* Resemblance, a

figure of 'speech, the standard of comparison.

उपमान *n*. Comparison, the standard of comparison.

उपमेय *a*. The object of comparison.

उपयंतृ *m*. A bride-groom.

उपय (या) म *m*. Marriage, restraint.

उपयाचित *n*. A present promised to a deity for the fulfilment of a desired object. [utilty, fitness.

उपयोग *m*. Application,

उपरक्ष *m*. A body-guard.

उपरत *p. p.* Stopped, dead.

उपरति *f*. Cessation; death.

उपर (रा) म *m*. Death.

उपराग *m*. Colour; an eclipse; affliction.

उपरि *ind*. On, above, afterwards, besides.

उपरिष्टात *ind*. Over, above, afterwards.

उपरोध *m*. (–न *n*.) Obstruction, disturbance.

उपरोधक *n*. Private apartment.

उपल *m*. A precious stone.

उपलक्षण *n*. A distinctive mark.

उपलब्धि *f*. Gain, knowledge.

उपलंभ *m*. Acquisition comprehension. [taining.

उपलिप्सा *f*. Desire of ob-

उपवन *n* A grove, a garden.

उपवर्णन *n*. Minute description.

उपवास *m*. A fast.

उपवीत *n*. Investiture with the sacred thread; the sacred thread.

उपशम *m*. Assuagement, calmness. [pupil.

उपशिष्य *m*. The pupil of a

उपशोभन *n*. Adorning.

उपश्रुत *p. p.* Promised

उपश्लेष *m*. (-ण *n*.) Contact.

उपसंयम *m*. Restraint.

उपसंवाद *m*. An agreement.

उपसंहार *m*. Summing up, a *resume*, conclusion, a percration.

उपसंख्यान *n*. Addition.

उपसंग्रह *m* (-ण *n*.) Respectful salutation.

उपसत्ति *f*. Connection, worship; gift.

उपसदन *n* Becoming a pupil, neighbourhood.

उपसंभाषा *f*. Friendly persuasion.

उपसर *m* Pregnancy.

उपसर्ग *m*. Sickness, misfortune; portent; an eclipse; a preposition prefixed to roots.

उपसृष्ट *p.p.* Joined troubled, eclipsed. [ship.

उपसेवा *f*. Service, wor-

उपस्कर *m*. An ingredient,

condiment, furniture, an ornament, blame.

उपस्कार *m.* An ornament, a collection, a supplement, an ellipsis.

उपस्तरण *n.* A bed, anything spread out.

उपस्त्री *f.* A concubine.

उपस्थ *m.* The lap, *m. n.* The male or female organ of generation.

उपस्थान *n* Proximity, worshipping.

उपस्थिति *f.* Presence, remembrance, service.

उपहत *pp.* Censured, doomed, polluted.

उपहतक *a* Unfortunate.

उपहत्या *f.* Dazzling of the eyes.

उपहासित *n.* Satirical laughter.

उपहार (-क) *m* A present to a superior, an offering to a deity.

उपहास *m.* Ridicule.

उपह्वर *n.* Solitude.

उपांशु *ind.* Secretly.

उपाकरण *n* Preparation, commencement.

उपाकर्मन् *n* A ceremony performed before commencing to read the Veda after the monsoons.

उपाख्यान (-क) *n.* A short story.

उपागम *m* Approach, occurrence; promise.

उपाग्र *n.* The part next to the end or top.

उपांग *n.* A subdivision; any minor limb or member.

उपाजे *ind.* + कृ To support.

उपादान *n.* Taking, a material cause.

उपाधि *m.* Fraud, distinguishing property, a title.

उपाधिक *a.* Supernumerary.

उपाध्याय *m.* A spiritual teacher.

उपाध्याया (-यी) *f.* A female preceptor.

उपाध्यायानी *f.* The wife of a preceptor.

उपानह् *f.* A shoe.

उपांत *m* Proximity, border.

उपांत्य *a.* Last but one.

उपाय *m.* A remedy, an expedient.

उपायन *n.* Becoming a pupil; a gift or present.

उपारंभ *m.* Beginning.

उपार्जन *n.* Acquiring.

उपालंभ *m.* (-न *n.*) Taunt.

उपावर्तन *n.* Returning, revolving.

उपाश्रय *m.* Recourse, reliance.

उपासक *m.* A servant or worshipper; a S'udra.

उपासना *f.* Service worship.

उपाहार *m.* Light refreshment.

उपेक्षण *n* (-क्षा *f.*) Neglect, indifference.

उपेत *p. p.* Posessed of.

उपेंद्र *m.* Name of Visnu or Krishṇa.

उपोद्घात *m.* A preface; occasion, an apposite argument.

उपोषण (-षित) *n.* A fast.

उभ *pron.* (used in the dual only) Both.

उभय *pron.* (used in the singular and plural only) Both.

उभयचर *a.* Living in water and on land, amphibious.

उभयतस् *ind.* From both sides; in both cases or ways.

उभयत्र *ind.* In both cases.

उभये (य) द्युस् *ind.* On both days.

उमा *f.* A name of Párvati; splendour; tranquility.

उंब (बु) र *m.* A door-frame.

उरग, उरंग (-म) *m.* A snake.

उरण *m.* A ram, a sheep.

उरस् *n.* The breast.

उरःस्थल *n.* The bosom.

उरस्य *a.* Legitimate *m.* A son

उरु *a.* (*f.* रु or र्वी; *compar.* वरीयस् *super.* वरिष्ठ) Wide, great, large, much.

उर्णनाभ *m.* A spider.

उर्णा *f.* Wool.

उर्वरा *f.* Land; fertile soil.

उर्वशी *f.* Name of a nymph.

उर्वी *f.* The earth.

उलूक *m.* An owl.

उलूखल *n.* A wooden mortar.

उल्का *f.* A meteor, a flame.

उल्काधारिन् *a.* A torch-bearer

उल्ब (ल्व) ण *a* Thick. superfluous, clear.

उल्लंघन *n.* Transgression.

उल्लल *a.* Shaking, trembling.

उल्लसन *n.* Happiness.

उल्लाप *m.* A speech, taunt, hint.

उल्लास *m.* Happiness, joy, a chapter of a book.

उल्लासन *n.* Splendour.

उल्लीढ *a.* Polished.

उल्लुंठन *n.* Irony.

उल्लेख *m.* Allusion, scratching.

उल्लोल *m.* A large wave. *a.* Violently moving.

उशनस् *m* (nom. *sing* उशना; voc. *sing*. उशनन्, उशन उशनः) S'ukra, preceptor of the *Asuras*.

उशी (षी) र *m.* (-क *n.*) The fragrant root of a certain plant.

उष् *vt.* 1. P (*pp.* ओषित, उषित. उष्ट) To burn, to punish,

उषस् *f.* Morning light; dawn.

उषसी *f.* The evening twilight.

उषा *f.* Early morning; twilight.

उषित *a.* Dwelt; burnt.

उष्ट्र *m.* (fem. उष्ट्री or उष्ट्रिका) A camel, a buffalo: a bull.

उष्ण *a.* Hot,sharp,pungent, clever. *m. n.* Heat.

उष्ण-कर (गु, दीधिति,-रश्मि, -रुचि,-अंशु) *m.* The sun.

उष्णवाष्प *m.* Tears.

उष्णालु *a* Suffering from heat

उष्णिमन् *m.* Heat. [coronet.

उष्णीष *m. n.* A turban, a

उष्म(-क) *m.* Heat; the hot season; anger.

उष्मन् *m.* Heat, vapour, the hot season; the letters श्, ष्, स्, ह्.

उस्र *m.* A ray of light,a bull

उह् *v.t.* 1. P to hurt; With अप or व्यप- to surpass.

ऊ

ऊ *m.* Name of Śiva; a protector; the moon.

ऊढ (*pp.* of वह्) Carried; married. [ed.

ऊढा *f.* A girl who is married.

ऊढी *f.* Marriage.

ऊति *f.* Weaving, sewing; protection; enjoyment.

ऊधस् *n.* An udder.

ऊधन्य (-स्य) *n.* Milk.

ऊन *a.* Wanting, inferior.

ऊय् *vt.* 1. A (*pp.* ऊत) to weave.

ऊरु *m.* The thigh.

ऊर्ज् *f.* Strength. Food.

ऊर्ज *m.* Energy; life; the month of Kártika.

ऊर्जस् *n.* Vigour.

ऊर्जस्वल *a.* Strong.

ऊर्जास्विन् *a.* Powerful.

ऊर्जा *f.* Energy; strength.

ऊर्जिताश्रय *a.* Spirited.

ऊर्ण *n.* A wooolen cloth.

ऊर्णनाभ (-पट-नाभि) *m.* A spider.

ऊर्णा *f.* Wool.

ऊर्णायु *m-* A ram; a spider.

ऊर्णु *vt* 2. U. To Cover, With प्र–to cover.

ऊर्ध्व *a.* Rising upwards, upper.

ऊर्ध्वदेह *m.* A funeral ceremony.

ऊर्ध्वरेतस् *a.* One who lives in perpetual celibacy.

ऊर्ध्वश्वास *m.* Expiration.

ऊर्ध्वसानु *a.* Rising higher and higher.

ऊर्ध्वम् *ind.* Upwards: aloud: afterwards.

ऊर्ध्वक *m.* A kind of dram.

ऊर्मि *m. f.* A wave; a current; a row; a human infirmity; distress.

ऊर्वरा *f.* Fertile soil.

ऊलूक *m.* An owl.

ऊषर *m. n.* A barren spot with saline soil.

ऊष्म *m.* Heat; summer.

ऊष्मन् *n* See उष्मन्.

ऊह् *vt.* 1. A To conjuncture:

With अप-to remove; अपावि- to ward off; अभि-to guess; निर्वि-to achieve परिसम्-to sprinkle round. प्रति-to deny; वि or प्रतिवि-to arrange an army against. सम्-to assemble.

ऊह *m.* A conjecture; supplying an ellipsis; understanding.

ऊहिनी *f.* An assembly; a collection.

ऋ.

ऋ *vi.* 1. P. To go; with सम् (A)-to join *vt.* 5. P.(*pp.* ऋण) To hurt; to attack.

ऋक्थ *n.* Property left at death.

ऋक्थग्राह *m.* An inheritor.

ऋक्थहर(-हारिन्) *m.* An heir.

ऋक्थादान *n.* Inheritance.

ऋक्ष *m.* A bear; a star.

ऋक्संहिता *f.* The collection of the hymns of Rigveda.

ऋक्षर *m.* A thorn; a priest.

ऋग्वेद *m.* The first of the four Vedas.

ऋच् *vt.* or *vi.* 6 P.(*pp* अर्चित) To praise; to shine.

ऋच् *f.* Splendour; a verse of the Rigveda.

ऋच्छ् *vi.* 6. P. To become hard; to go.

ऋच्छका *f.* Wish, desire.

ऋज् *vi.* 1. A To go; to be strong, to acquire.

ऋजु *a.* Straight, honest.

ऋजुग *m.* An arrow.

ऋण *n.* Debt; a fort; water.

ऋणमत्कुण (-मार्गण) *m.* A security, a bail.

ऋणमुक्ति *f* (-मोक्ष*m.*-मोचन*n.*) Discharge from debt.

ऋणिक *m.* A debtor.

ऋणिन् *a.* One indebted to another.

ऋत *a.* Right, honest, worshipped.

ऋतंभर *m.* God, the upholder [of truth.

ऋतम् *ind.* Truly.

ऋतीया *f.* Reproach, censure.

ऋतु *m.* A season; menstruation; appointed time; light.

ऋतुमती *f.* A woman during [her courses.

ऋतुस्नाता *f.* A woman who has bathed after menstruation.

ऋते *ind.* Except.

ऋत्विज् *m.* A priest who officiates at a sacrifice.

ऋद्ध *a.* Prosperous *n.* Increase; distinct result.

ऋद्धि *f.* Increase; prosperity; supernatural power.

ऋध् *vt.* 4. 5. P.(*pp.* ऋद्ध) To prosper; to please. With सम्-to prosper.

ऋभु *m.* A deity, a divinity.

ऋभुक्ष (-क्षिन्) *m.* Indra; heaven.

ऋष् *vt.* 6. P. To go, to kill.

ऋषभ *m.* A bull; the best; the second of the seven notes of the gamut.

ऋषभध्वज *m.* S'iva.

ऋषभी *f.* A cow; a masculine woman; a widow.

ऋषि *m.* A sage; an anchorite.

ॠ.

ॠ *at.* 9. P. (*pp.* ईर्ण) To go, to move.

ए.

एक *pron.* One, singular, chief, true, excellent, same.

एककार्य *a.* A co-worker.

एकक *a.* Solitary.

एककालिक (-लीन) *a.* Contemporaneous.

एकचत्वारिंशत् *f.* Fortyone.

एकचर *a.* Alone.

एकचारिणी *f.* A loyal wife.

एकचेतस्, (-चित्त, -मनस्,) *a.* Unanimous

एकज *a.* Uniform. [S'udra.

एकजन्मन्, *m.* A king, a

एकजाति *m. f.* A S'udra.

एकतम *a.* One of many.

एकतर *a.* One of two.

एकतस् *ind.* From one side. Singly, one by one.

एकता *f.* Unity, identity.

एकतान *a.* Closely attentive to one thing. *n.* Harmony. [student.

एकतीर्थिन् *m.* A fellow-

एकत्र *ind.* In one place.

एकत्रिंशत् *f.* Thirtyone.

एकदण्डिन् *a.* One of an order of sannyasins.

एकदा *ind.* At once; once upon a time. [Ganes'a.

एकदंष्ट्र *m.* A name of

एकधा *ind.* Singly; together; at once; sometimes.

एकपक्ष *m.* An associate.

एकपत्नी *f.* A faithful wife.

एकपदे *ind.* Suddenly.

एकपदी *f.* A path.

एकल *a.* Solitary, alone.

एकवाक्यता *f.* Unanimity.

एकवारम्, (-वारे) *ind.* Only once. [warrior.

एकवीर *m.* A pre-eminent

एकशस् *ind.* One by one.

एकशेष *m.* A kind of *Dvandva* compound.

एकहायन *a.* One year old.

एकाकिन् *a.* Solitary, alone.

एकाक्ष *a.* One-eyed; *m.* A crow; God S'iva.

एकाग्र *a.* Closely attentive.

एकातपत्र *a.* Showing universal sovereignty.

एकान्त *m.* Solitude; monotheism. *a.* Invariable; excessive; absolute.

एकान्ततस्(**एकान्ते**or**एकान्तम्**) *ind.*Excessively;wholly.
एकान्तर *a.* Next but one.
एकान्तिक *a.* Final.
एकावली *f.*A single string of pearls.
एकीभाव *m.* Combination.
एकीय *a.* Belonging to the same party.
एकैक *a.* One by one; every one.
एकैकम् *ind.* Singly.
एकैकशस् *ind.* One by one.
एकोदरm.Brother or sister.
एज् *vi.*1.A. To shake; with **अप**–to drive away **उद्**– *vi.* 1. P. To shine.
एजनm.Trembling; shaking.
एड *a.* Deaf.
एडक *m.* A ram.
एण *m.* A kind of black antelope.
एत(*f.*एता,एनी)*a.*Of a variegated colour, *m.* A deer.
एतद् *pron.* This. *ind.* Thus, at this time.
एतदीय*a* Belonging to this.
एतर्हि *ind.*Now,at this time.
एतादृक्ष (-श,-श्) *a.*Such.
एतावत् *a.* So much. *ind.* So far.
एध् *vi.* 1 A To grow ; to prosper; to swell.
एध *m* Fuel.
एधस् *n.* Fuel.
एधा, *f.* Prosperity.
एनस् *n.* Sin; mischief,censure.
एनस्वत् (-स्विन्) *a.* Sinful.
एरण्ड *m.* Castor-oil plant.
एला *f.* A cardamom plant or its seed.
एव *ind.*Just, exactly,same, only, like, already; also.
एवम् *ind.* So; thus; yes.
एवंकारम् *ind.* In this manner.
एवंगत *a.*Being in this condition.
एवंगते Under these circumstances.
एवंगुण *a.* Of such qualities.
एवंप्राय *a.* Of such kind.
एवंभूत *a.* Such.
एवंविध *a.* Of such kind.
एष् *vi.*I A to go; **परि**-to seek.
एषणा (**एषा**) *f.* Desire.
एषणीय (**एष्य**) *a.* To be desired.

ऐ

ऐकध्यम् *ind.* At once.
ऐकपत्य *n.* Absolute power.
ऐकपद्य *n.* Unity of words.
ऐक्यभाव *n.* Singleness of purpose.
ऐकमत्य *n.* Unanimity.
ऐकश्रुत्य *n.* Monotony.
ऐकागारिक *m.* A thief.
ऐकाग्र्य *n.* Intentness on one object.
ऐकांग *m.* A soldier of the body-guard.
ऐकात्म्य *n.* Unity; identity.

ऐकाधिकरण्य *n.* Existence in the same subject; co-extension. [sive.

ऐकान्तिक *a.* Absolute, exclu-

ऐकार्थ्य *n.* Consistency in meaning; the sameness of purpose.

ऐकाहिक *a.* Lasting for one day; ephemeral.

ऐक्य *n.* Identity; unanimity; friendship. [sugar.

ऐक्षव ***n.*** Sugar. ***a.*** Made of

ऐक्ष्वाक ***m.*** A decendent of इक्ष्वाकु, king of Ayodhyâ.

ऐच्छिक *a.* Optional, arbitrary.

ऐतरेयिन् ***m.*** A reader of the Aitareya Bráhmana.

ऐतिहासिक *a.* Historical; legendary. ***m.*** An historian.

ऐतिह्य *n.* Traditional instruction; a kind of proof.

ऐदंपर्य ***n.*** Substance; scope.

ऐनस *n.* Sin.

ऐन्दव *a.* Lunar.

ऐन्द्र *a.* Belonging to Indra.

ऐन्द्रजालिक *a.* Deceptive, magical; ***m.*** A juggler.

ऐन्द्रिय ***a.*** Perceptible to the senses; sensual.

ऐन्द्री *f.* East; S'achi; misfortune.

ऐरावण (-त) ***m.*** Indra's elephant.

ऐरावती *f.* Lightning. [vas.

ऐल ***m.*** Mars; King Purura-

ऐश *a.* Divine; regal.

ऐशानी *f.* The North-east.

ऐश्वर *a.* Majestic; powerful.

ऐश्वर्य ***n.*** Power; supremacy.

ऐषमस् ***ind.*** In this year.

ऐष्टिक ***a.*** Sacrificial.

ऐहिक *a.* Worldly; temporal.

ओ

ओ ***ind.*** A vocative particle.

ओक ***m.*** A house; a refuge.

ओकस् ***n.*** A house; an asylum; pleasure.

ओख् *vt. vi.* 1 P. To adorn; to be dry. [titude.

ओघ, ***m.*** Current; flood; mul-

ओज् *vi.* 10. U. To be strong.

ओज *a.* Odd, uneven.

ओजस् ***n.*** Vigour, lustre; vitality; water; an elaborate form of style.

ओजस्वत् (-स्विन्) Strong; vigorous, powerful, bright.

ओजिष्ठ *a.* (Super. of उग्र) Most strong; vehement.

ओत ***a.*** Woven.

ओतप्रोत ***a.*** Extending in all directions.

ओतु ***m. f.*** A cat.

ओदन ***m.*** Boiled rice.

ओधस् *n.* An udder.

ओम् ***ind.*** The sacred syllable (***om***).

—

ओंकार *m.* The sacred and mystic syllable (*om*).

ओल (-ल्ल) *a.* Wet, damp.[up.

ओलण्ड् *vt.* 1 P. 10 To throw

ओष *m.* Combustion.

ओषधि (-धी) *f.* A herb; a medicinal plant.

ओषधि(धी)पति *m.* A physician; the moon.

ओषधीश *m.* The moon.

ओष्ठ *m.* A lip.

ओष्ठपल्लव *m n.* A tender lip.

ओष्ठपुट *n.* The cavity made by opening the lips.

ओष्ण *a.* A little warm.

औ.

औचिती *f.* (-त्य*n.*)Propriety.

औजसिक *a.* Energetic, vigorous.

औजस्य *n.* Vigour of life.

औज्ज्वल्य *n.* Brightness.

औत्कंठ्य *n.* Desire; anxiety.

औत्तर *a.* Northern. [ral.

औत्पत्तिक *a.* Inborn, natu-

औत्पात (-तिक) *a.* Portentous. *n.* A portent.

औत्सङ्गिक *a.* Borne on the hips. [ral.

औत्सर्गिक *a.* General, natu-

औत्सुक्य *n.* Anxiety, zeal.

औदक *a.* Watery.

औदनिक *m.* A cook.

औदरिक *a.* Gluttonous

औदर्य *a.* Being in the womb.

औदार्य *n.* Generosity, excellence; depth of meaning. [apathy;loneliness

औदासीन्य *n.* Indifference,

औद्धत्य *n.* Arrogance, boldness. [marriage.

औद्वाहिक *a.* Relating to

औन्नत्य *n.* Height; elevation.

औपकार्य *n.* A residence.

औपग्रस्ति(हि)क *m.* An eclipse.

औपचारिक *a.* Metaphorical; figurative; secondary.

औपदेशिक *a.* Living by teaching. [heresy.

औपधर्म्य *n.* A false doctrine;

औपधिक *a.* Deceitful.

औपनिषद *a.* Scriptural.

औपपत्तिक *a.* Ready;proper; theoretical.[comparison.

औपमिक *a.* Serving for a

औपम्य *n.* Similarity; a simile. [means remedy.

औपयिक *a* Right, *n.* A

औपराजिक *a.* Belonging to a viceroy.

औपरिष्ट *a.* Produced above.

औपरोधिक *a.* Opposing.

औपल *a.* Made of stone.

औपवस्त *n.* Fasting; a fast.

औपवस्त्र *n.* Food suitable for a fast.

औपवास्य *n* Fasting [tary.

औपसंख्यानिक *a* Supplemen-

औपसर्गिक *a.* Able to harm, portentous.[fornication.

औपस्थिक *a.* Living by

औपस्थ्य *n*. Co-habitation.
औपहारिक *n*. An offering.
औपाधिक *a*. Conditional.
औपाध्यायक *a*. Obtained from an Upádhyáya.
औम (-क) *a*. Flaxen. [pent.
औरग *a*. Relating to a ser-
औरस (-स्य) *a. m* A legitimate son.
और्ण (और्णिक) *a*. Woolen.
और्ध्वकालिक *a*. Relating to a later time. [mony.
और्ध्वदेह *n*. A funeral cere-
और्ध्वदेहिक *a*. Funeral.
और्वर *a*. Earthly.
औल्वण्य *n* Excess.
औशीर *n*. A bed, a seat; a fan or *chowri*; root of fragrant grass or an unguent made therefrom.
औषध *n*. A herb; a drug; a mineral. cinal herb.
औषधि(-धी) *f*. A herb; a medi-
औषर (-क) *n*. Rock-salt.
औषसी *f*. Day break.
औष्ठ *a*. Lip-shaped.
औष्ठ्य *a*. Labial. [warmth.
औष्ण (-ष्ण्य, -ष्म्य) *n*. Heat.

क.

क *m*. Brahman(*m*.)Vishnu; Cupid; fire; air; the god of death; the sun; the soul; a king; a peacock; a bird; the mind; body; time; a cloud; a word; hair. *n*. Happiness, water, Head.
कंस *m. n*. A cup; a particular measure; bell-metal. *m* Name of a king of Mathurá.
ककर्दु *m*. Destruction.
ककुंजल *m*. The *Chátaka* bird.
ककुद् *f*. (-द *m. n.*) A peak, chief, head, the hump, an ensign.
ककुद्मत्(-द्मिन्) *m*. A buffalo with a hump on his shoulders, a mountain.
ककुद्मती *f*. The hip and loins. [the loins.
ककुंदर *n*. The cavities of
ककुभ् *f*. A peak, a direction; beauty.
कक्खट *a*. Hard, laughing.
कक्ष *m*. A hiding place; an arm-pit; a side; grass; a dry wood; buffalo; a gate; the harem. *n*. Sin; a star.
कक्षप *m*. A tortoise
कक्षशाय (-शायु) *m*. A dog.
कक्षा (-क्ष्या) *f*. An elephant's girth; a woman's girdle; the wrist; a courtyard, an apartment; similarity; the arm-pit; the end of the lower garment brought up behind and tucked into the waistband; the waist; an upper garment; emulation.

कक्षा(क्ष्या)न्तर *n.* A private apartment.

कख्या *f.* An enclosure.

कंक *m.* A heron; an epithet of Yama; a Kshatriya; A name assumed by युधिष्ठिर.

कंकपत्र (-पत्रिन्) *m.* An arrow furnished with the feathers of a heron.

कंकट (–क) *m.* A defensive armour.

कंकण *m. n.* A bracelet, a string tied round the wrist. *m.* Water-spray.

कंकणी (–णीका) *f.* A small bell.

कंकत *m. n.* } A comb, a
कंकतिका *f.* } hair-comb.

कंकाल *m. n.* A skeleton.

कंकालय *m.* The body.

कच् *vt.* 1. P. To sound. *vt.* or *vi.* 1. U. To bind.

कच *m.* Hair, a scar; the hem of a garment; name of a son of Brihaspati.

कचग्रह *m.* Seizing by the hair.

कचपक्ष (-पाश -हस्त) *m* Thick or ornamented hair.

कचाकचि *nd.* Pulling each other's hair in a fight.

कच्चर *a* Dirty, wicked.

कच्चित् *ind.* A particle of interrogation or of joy.

कच्छ *m. n.* The hem of a garment. *m.* A border; a particular part of the tortoise. [toise.

कच्छप *m.* A turtle, a tor-

कच्छभू *f.* Marshy ground.

कच्छ(च्छा)टिका, कच्छाटी. *f.* The end of a lower garment tucked into the waistband.

कच्छु (-च्छू) *f* Itch, scab.

कच्छुर *a.* Scabby; unchaste.

कज्जल *m.* A cloud. *n.* Lamp-black, collyrium.

कंचार *m.* The sun.

कंचुक *m.* A dress fitting close to the upper part of the body; armour; a bodice.

कंचुकिन् *a. m.* A chamberlain, a debauchee.

कंचुलिका *f.* A bodice.

कञ्ज *m.* Hair, a lotus.

कंज(जा)र *m.* The belly; an elephant; the sun.

कट *m.* The temples of an elephant; mat; hip; a corpse; an arrow; a custom; a cemetery; excess.

कटंकट *m.* Fire; gold.

कटक *m. n.* A string; a bracelet; the link of a chain; a mat; side or ridge of a mountain, table-land; an army.

कटमालिनी *f.* Wine.

कटाह *m.* A frying pan, a turtle's shell, a well.

कटाक्ष *m.* A glance.
कटि (-टी) *f.* The hip, the buttocks.
कटितट *n.* The loins.
कटिप्रोथ *m.* The buttocks.
कटिशृंखला *f.* A girdle of small bells. [band.
कटिसूत्र *n.* A female waist-
कटिका *f.* The hip.
कटीर *m. n.* A cave; the cavity of the loins.
कटीरक *n.* The posteriors.
कटु (-क) *a.* Pungent, acrid, sharp, strong-scented, bitter, disagreeable.
कटुकीट (-क) *m.* A gnat.
कटोदक *n.* Water for funeral libation.
कटोर *n* An earthen vessel.
कठ् *vt.* 1. P. 10. U. (*pp.* कंठित) To miss; *vi.* 1. A To be anxious.
कठर *a.* Hard.
कठिका *f.* Chalk. [ble;cruel.
कठिन *a.* Hard, stiff, inflexi-
कठिनता *f.* (-त्वं *n.*) Hardness.
कठोर *a.* Hard, sharp, hard-hearted, full-grown.
कड् *vi.* or *vt.* 1. U. To be proud; to unhusk.
कड *a.* Dumb, ignorant.
कडंग(क)र *m.* Straw.
कडंग(क)रीय *a.* To be fed with straw.
कडं(लं)ब *m.* Stem.

कण् *vt.* or *vi.* 1. P. To sound; *vi.* 10, P. To wink.
कण *m.* A grain, spray, atom.
कणशस् *ind.* Little by little.
कणिक *m.* (-का *f*) A grain; an ear of corn.
कणिश *m.n.* An ear of corn.
कंटक *m.n.* A thorn; a sting, a finger-nail; horripilation; a source of vexation; a bamboo; a workshop.
कंटकित *a.* Thorny.
कंटकिन् *a.* Thorny, vexatious.
कंठ *m. n.* The throat, neck, the voice, immediate proximity.
कण्ठगत *a.* On the point of departing.
कण्ठतस् *ind.* From the throat; explicitly.
कन्टनीडक *m.* A kite.
कण्ठनीलक *m.* A torch.
कण्ठभूषा *f.* A short necklace.
कण्ठमणि *m.* A dear or beloved object. [tulation.
कण्ठशोष *m* Fruitles expos-
कंठाल *m.* A boat; spade; war; a camel. [string.
कंठिका *f.* A necklace of one
कंठी *f.* Neck, a necklace.
कण्ठीरव *m.* A lion; an elephant in rut; explicit mention.
कंठील *m.* A camel.
कंठ्य *a.* Guttural.

कंडन *n.* Threshing; chaff.
कंडनी *f.* A pestle.
कंडरा *f.* Sinew.
कंडु *m.* (-डू *f.*) Itching.
कंडूय् *vt.* or *vi.* 1. U To scratch. [Scratching.
कंडूति (-या) *f.* (**कण्डूयन** *n.*)
कंडूयनी *f.* A brush for rubbing.
कंडूल *a.* Itchy. [a camel.
कंडोल *m.* A basket; a safe;
कण्व *m.* The name of a sage. [of many.
कतम *pron.* Who or which
कतर *pron.* Who or which of two.
कति *pron.* How many.
कति (-अपि, -चन, -चित्) Several; some. [times.
कतिकृत्वस् *ind.* How many
कतिधा *ind.* How often; in how many places or parts. [eral.
कतिपय *pron.* Some sev-
कतिविध *a.* Of how many kinds. [a time.
कतिशस् *ind.* How many at
कत्थ् *vt.* or *vi.* 1. A. To boast, to celebrate, to praise, to abuse. With वि-to boast; to disparage.
कत्थन *n.*(-ना *f.*) Boasting.
कथ् *vt.* or *vi.* 10. U. To tell, to describe, to converse.
कथक *m. a.* A story-teller.
कथन *n.* Narration, relation.
कथम् *ind.* How, whence, in what way.
कथम् with **इव वा नाम, नु** or **स्विद्** How indeed! [how.
कथंचन In every way, some-
कथंचित् (-चिदपि, -अपि) On any account, somehow, with great difficulty.
कथंकथिक *m.* An inquisitive person. [manner.
कथंकारम् *ind.* How, in what
कथंता *f.* What manner.
कथंप्रमाण *a.* Of what measure.
कथंभूत *a.* Of what nature.
कथा *f.* Allusion, conversation; a tale, a fable, prose composition.
कथान्तर *n.* The course of conversation.
कथाछल *n.* The device of a fable; giving a false account. [part of a story.
कथानक *n* A small tale.
कथापीठ *n.* The introductory
कथाप्रबंध *m.* A tale, a fiction.
कथाप्रसंग *m* The course of conversation.
कथाविपर्यास *m* Changing the course of a story.
कथाशेष *a.* Dead.
कथित *a.* Told, expressed.
कथितपद *n.* Tautology.
कद् *vt.* or *vi.* 1. P To grieve; to call. *vi.* 4 A. To be confused.

कद् *ind.* A particle expressive of badness, littleness, &c. [ing.

कदर्थ *a.* Useless; unmean-

कदर्थित *a.* Despised, insignificant. *m.* A miser.

कदर्य *a.* Miserly.

कदाकार *a.* Ill-formed, ugly.

कदाचार *a.* Wicked.

कदुष्ण *a.* Tepid.

कदक *n.* A canopy.

कदन *n.* Destruction.

कदंब (-क) *m.* A particular plant; turmeric. *n.* A multitude.

कदम्बकोरकन्याय *m.* The maxim denoting simultaneous rise or action.

कदर *m.* An iron goad; a saw. *n.* Coagulated milk.

कदल (-क, or कदली *f.*) *m.* The plantain tree.

कदा *ind.* When.

कदापि *ind.* Now and then, some times, at some time.

कदाचन *ind.* At some time.

कदाचित् *ind.* Once upon a time.

कद्रु (-द्रू) *a.* Tawny.

कनक *n.* Gold.

कनकमय *a.* Golden.

कनन *a.* One-eyed.

कनिष्ट *a.* (*super.* of अल्प or युवन्) The smallest, the youngest.

कनिष्ठिका *f.* The little finger.

कनीनिका or कनीनी *f.* The pupil of the eye; the little finger.

कनीयस् *a.* (*comp.* of अल्प or युवन्) Smaller; younger.

कंतु *m.* The heart; Kamadeva.

कंथा *f.* A patched garment.

कंद *m. n.* A bulbous root; *m.* A cloud.

कंदमूल *a.* A radish.

कंदर *m.n.* A cave, a valley.

कंदरा *f.* A cave, a valley.

कंदर्प *m.* Love; cupid.

कंदर्पज्वर *m.* Passion, desire.

कंदर्पदहन *m.* God S'iva.

कंदल *m. n.* The cheek; a portent; a new shoot.

कंदली *f.* The plantain tree.

कंदलीकुसुम *n.* A mushroom.

कंदुक *m n.* A ball for playing with.

कंधर *m.* The neck, a cloud.

कंधरा *f.* The neck. [neck.

कंधि *m.* The ocean. *f.* The

कन्यका *f.* A girl ten years old; a virgin.

कन्यकाछल *m.* Seduction.

कन्यस *a.* Younger.

कन्या *f.* An unmarried girl ten years old; a woman in general; the sign *Virgo*.

कन्यागत *n.* The position of a planet in the sign *Virgo*.

कन्याधन *n.* Dowry [*Virgo.*
कन्याराशि *m.* The sign
कन्यिका *f.* A virgin.
कपट *m. n.* Fraud, deceit.
कपटप्रबंध *m.* A fraudulent contrivance.
कपटिक *m.* A rogue.
कपर्द (-क,) *m.* A cowrie; braided hair of S'iva.
कपर्दिका *f.* A small shell (used as a coin.)
कपाट *m. n.* A door; the leaf of a door.
कपाल *m. n.* The skull; a beggar's bowl.
कपालपाणि (-भृत,-मालिन्,-शिरस्) *m.* An epithet of S'iva
कपालिन् *a.* Wearing skulls. *m.* An epithet of S'iva.
कपि *m.* An ape, a monkey, an elephant.
कपिकेतन (-ध्वज) *m.* An epithet of Arjuna.
कपिंजल*m.*The *Chátaka* bird
कपित्थ *m.* The wood-apple-tree or its fruit. [fire.
कपिल *a.* Tawny; *m.* a dog;
कपिलद्युति *m.* The sun.
कपिलधारा *f.* The Ganges.
कपिला *f.* A brown cow.
कपिश *a.* Brown; dark-red.
कपूय *a.* Mean, worthless.
कपोत *m.* A pigeon; a bird.
कपोतक *m.* A small pigeon. *n.* Antimony.
कपोतपालिका (-पाली) *f.* A pigeon house.
कपोतसार *n.* Antimony.
कपोतहस्त*m.* Folding hands.
कपोल *m.* A cheek.
कपोलफलक *m.* The cheeks.
कपोलभित्ति *f.* The temples and cheeks. [foam.
कफ *m.* Phlegm, watery
कफक्षय *m.* Pulmonary consumption. [matic.
कफल or कफेलु *a.* Phleg-
कबंध*m.n.*A headless trunk. *m.* Ráhu; the belly; a comet. *n.* Water.
कबरी *f.* A braid of hair.
कम् *vi.* 1. A (*pp.* कामित or कांत; *pres.* कामयते) To desire, to love; नि or प्र- to desire excessively.
कमठ *m.* A tortoise, a bamboo; a water-jar.
कमंडलु *m. n.* A water-pot used by an ascetic.
कमन *a.* Lovely. *n.* Desire. *m.* The god of love.
कमनीय *a.* Desirable, beautiful.
कमर *a.* Lustful.
कमल *n.* A lotus; water; copper; a medicament.
कमलज (-भव,-योनि,-संभव)*m.* A name of Brahman(*m*).
कमला *f.* An epithet of Lakshmi; an excellent woman.

कमलासन *m.* An epithet of Brahman (*m.*)

कमलिनी *f.* An assemblage of lotuses; a lotus plant.

कमा *f.* Beauty.

कमितृ *a.* Lustful.

कम्प् *vi.*1 A (*pp.*कंपित pres. कंपते) To shake, to tremble. With अनु-to pity, to take compassion on; आ-to shake gently, प्र or वि-to shake, to tremble.

कंप *m.*(-पा *f.*-नn.-ता *f.*) Shaking, tremor.

कंपाक *m.* Wind.

कंबर *a.* Variegated. [ter.

कंबल *m.* A blanket. *n.* Wa-

कंबलिका *f.* A small blanket. [spoon.

कंबि (-बी) *f.* A ladle; a

कंबु *a.* Variegated. *m. n.* A conch, a shell, *m.* The neck; an elephant; a bracelet.

कंबुग्रीवा *f.* A neck marked with three lines like a shell.

कंबू *m.* A thief; a bracelet.

कंबोज *m. pl.* The name of a country and its inhabitants.

कर *m.* A hand, a ray of light, the trunk of an elephant; hail; a tax, a tribute.

करकंटक *m. n.* A nail.

कर-कमल (-पंकज,-पद्म) *n.* A lotus-like hand, a beautiful hand.

कराकिसलय *m. n.* A tender hand, a finger.

करग्रह *m.* (-ग्रहण *n*) Taking the hand in marriage; levying a tax. [collector.

करग्राह *m.* A husband; a tax-

करज *m.* finger-nail.

करजाल *n.* A stream of light.

करतल *m.* The palm of the hand.

करतलामलक *n.* An expression used to signify ease and vividity.

करताली (-लिका) *f.* Clapping of the hands.

करपत्र *n.* A saw.

करपल्लव *m.* A tender hand; a finger. [sword; a cudgel.

करपाल *m.* (पालिका *f.*) A

करपीडन *n.* Marriage.

करपुट *m.* The hands joined and hollowed.

करबाल (वाल) *m.* A sword; a finger nail [tribute.

करभार *m.* An excessive

कररुह *m.* A finger-nail.

करका *f.* Hail.

करंक *m.* A skeleton; the skull; a small box.

करट *m.* An elephant's cheek; a crow; atheist.

करटक *m.* A crow.

करटिन् *m.* An elephant.

करण *n*. An act; an organ of sense; the body; an instrument; a cause; a bond; a division of the day. [ket; a sword.

करंड *m*. A bee-hive; a bas-

करंडिका, करंडी *f*. A basket.

करभ *m*. The back of the hand from the wrist to the root of the fingers; a young elephant; a young camel.

करभोरू *f*. A lady with thighs resembling the back of the forearm or the trunk of an elephant.

करभिन् *m*. An elephant

करंब(-बित) *a*. Intermingled.

करंभ (-ब) *m*. Mud.

कराल *a*. Dreadful. [phant.

करिणी *f*. A female ele-

करीर *m*. A shoot; a thorny plant without leaves; a water-jar.

करीष *m. n*. Dry cow-dung.

करुण *a*. Tender, pitiable.

करुणा *f*. Compassion, pity.

करुणात्मन् *a*. Kind

करुणार्द्र *a*. Tender-hearted.

करेणु *m*. An elephant. *f*. A female elephant.

कर्क *m*. A crab.

कर्कट (-क) *m*. A crab.

कर्कर *a*. Hard, firm. *m*. A broken piece of skull.

कर्कश *a* Cruel, muscular; incomprehensible; unfaithful; desperate.

कर्कोट (-क) *m*. One of the eight principal cobras.

कर्ण् *vt*. 10 U To pierce, With आ or समा-to hear, to listen to.

कर्ण *m*. The ear; the helm or rudder; the hypotenuse; name of a renowned hero in the Mahâbhârata.

कर्णगोचर *a*. Audible.

कर्णग्राह *m*. A helmsman.

कर्णजप *m*. An informer.

कर्णधार *m*. A helmsman, a pilot. [hearing.

कर्णपथ *m*. The range of

कर्णपरंपरा *f*. Hearsay.

कर्णपाश *m*. A beautiful ear.

कर्णपूर *m*. An ear-ring.

कर्णश्रव *a*. Audible, loud. [ear.

कर्णाकर्णि *ind*. From ear to

कर्णिक *m*. A steersman.

कर्णिका *f*. An ear-ring; the middle finger; a fruit-stock.

कर्णिन् *m*. An Ass; an arrow.

कर्णोपकर्णिका *f*. A rumour.

कर्त् 10 P. To slacken.

कर्तन *n*. Cutting, spinning.

कर्तनी *f*. Scissors.

कर्तरिका or **कर्तरी** *f*. A knife; a small sword; scissors.

कर्तव्य *a*. Duty, task.

कर्तृ *m* The supreme spirit; a doer; an agent.

कर्त्री *f.* A knife; scissors.
कर्द (-ट, -म) *m.* Mud, sin.
कर्पट *m. n.* An old garment.
कर्पर *m.* A frying-pan; a piece of a broken jar.
कर्पास *m. n.* Cotton.
कर्पूर *m. n.* Camphor.
कर्फर *m.* A mirror.
कर्बु (-र) *a.* Variegated.
कर्मन् *n.* Action, moral duty; performance of religious rites; object; fate.
कर्मकर *m.* A hired labourer.
कर्मकांड *m. n.* That department of the Vedas which relates to ceremonial acts and sacrificial rites.
कर्मकार *m.* An artisan.
कर्मक्षेत्र *n.* The land of religious acts.
कर्मत्याग *m* Abandonment of worldly duties or ceremonial rites. [pound.
कर्मधारय *m.* Name of a com-
कर्मपाक *m.* (-फल *n.*) Reward for actions done in a former life
कर्मबंध *m.* (-न *n.*) Confinement to repeated birth.
कर्मभू, (-भूमि) *f.* Ploughed ground.
कर्मयुग *n.* The Kaliyuga.
कर्मयोग *m.* Performance of action.
कर्मवश *m.* Fate considered as the inevitable consequence of actions done in a former life.
कर्मशाला *f.* A workshop.
कर्मसचिव *m.* A minister.
कर्मठ *a.* Skilful clever.
कर्मण्य *a* Skilful, clever.
कर्माजीव *m.* An artisan.
कर्मात्मन् *a.* Active.
कर्मान्त *m.* Work; a cultivated land; a barn.
कर्मान्तर *n.* Contrariety of action; a penance. [san.
कर्मिन् *m.* A doer; an arti-
कर्मिष्ठ *a.* Skilled in business.
कर्मीर *a.* Variegated.
कर्मेंद्रिय *n.* An organ of action. [prowess.
कर्मोदार *n.* Magnanimity;
कर्ष *m.* A furrow, a trench. *m n.* A weight equal to sixteen *mashas.*
कर्षक *m.* A husbandman.
कर्षण *n.* Drawing; ploughing; emaciation.
कर्हिचित् *ind.* At any time.
कल् *vt.* or *vi.* 1. A To count; to sound. *vt.* 10. U. To count, to hold, to assume, to undergo, to know, to regard, to go. With आ-to take hold of, to know, to take notice of; परि-to know, to understand, to consider, to regard; to re-

member; वि-to maim, सम्-to sum up, *vt*.10. U. to impel

कल *a*. Sweet and indistinct.

कलकल *m*. A confused noise.

कलंक *m*. A spot, the rust of iron; a stain.

कलत्र *n*. A wife, the hip.

कलधौत, *n*. Gold; silver.

कलन *n*. A spot, fault; grasping, apprehension.

कलना *f*. Seizing apprehension; wearing.

कलभ *m*. A young elephant.

कलम *m*. A pen; a thief.

कलरव *m*. A low sweet tone.

कलहंस *m*. A swan; the supreme soul.

कलल *m*. *n*. The foetus.

कलश (-स) *m*. *n*. A pitcher.

कलशी (-सी) *f*. A pitcher.

कलह *m*. *n*. Quarrel, war, violence.

कलहप्रिय *m*. An epithet of Nárada *a*. Quarrelsome

कला *f*. A small part; a digit of the moon; interest; a division of time; an art.

कलाधर (-निधि,-पूर्ण,-भृत,-वत) *m*. The moon.

कलाद (-क) *m* A goldsmith.

कलाप *m*. A collection; an ornament; an arrow; a peacock's tail.

कलापक *n*. A series of four stanzas.

कलापिन् *m*. A peacock, the Indian cuckoo.

कलापिनी *f*. The night.

कलालाप *m*. A sweet humming sound.

कलि *m*. The fourth or the iron age of the world; quarrel, war, a bud.

कलि (-का) *f*. A bud; a digit of the moon.

कलिंद *m*. Name of a mountain; the sun.

कलिन्दकन्या(-जा,-तनया,-नंदिनी) *f*. The river Yamuná.

कलिल *a*. Full of; mixed. *n*. Profusion.

कलुष *a*. Turbid, foul, dark, choked, wicked, incompetent.

कलेवर *m*. *n*. The body.

कल्क *m*. *n*. A viscous sediment; hypocricy; sin; incense; levigated powder. *a*. Sinful; wicked.

कल्कि (-न्) *m*. The tenth and last incarnation of Vishnu.

कल्प *a*. Practicable, proper, able. *m* A sacred precept, a proceeding, universal destruction; a day of Brahman (*m*.); a resolve; one of the six *Vedángas*; a prescribed rule; first duty.

कल्पक *m*. A rite; a barber.

कल्पक्षय *m*. The end of the world.

कल्पान्त *m*. Universal destruction.

कल्पतरु (-द्रुम,-पादप,-वृक्ष) *m*. A wish-yielding tree.

कल्पना *f.* Arranging; decorating; fabrication; composition; invention; a fancy, an image formed in the mind; a contrivance; imagination.

कल्पनी *f.* Scissors.

कल्पलता (-तिका) *f.* A creeper granting all desires.

कल्पित *a.* Imagined.

कल्मष *a.* Sinful; dirty. *m.n.* Stain, sin.

कल्माष *a.* Variegated; *m.* A mixture of black and white.

कल्य *a.* Sound, healthy, ready, clever; auspicious. *n.* Dawn, to-morrow; congratulation.

कल्यजाग्धि *f.* Breakfast. [fle.

कल्यवर्त *m.* Breakfast; a tri-

कल्या *f.* Spirituous liquor.

कल्याण *a.* Beautiful propitious, good, *n.* Good fortune; virtue; a festival; gold.

कल्याणि *f.* A cow.

कल्पाश *m.* Break-fast.

कल्ल *a.* Deaf. [enemy; joy.

कल्लोल *m.* A large wave, an

कल्लोलिनी *f.* A river.

कव् *vt.* 1. A to praise; to describe, to paint

कवक *m.* A mouthful. *n.* A mushroom. [charm.

कवच *m. n.* An armour a

कव (ब) र *a.* Mixed, intermingled; acidity. *m.* A braid of hair.

कव (ब) री *f.* A braid of hair.

कवल *m.n.* A mouthful.

कवलित *a.* Eaten; seized.

कवाट *n.* The panel of a door.

कवि *a.* Omniscient, wise. *m.* A wise man, a poet, a name of S'ukra (the preceptor of demons); Vàlmîki (the first poet); the sun.

कविता *f.* Poetry; a poem.

कवोष्ण *a.* Tepid.

कव्य *n.* An oblation of food to deceased ancestors.

कव्यवाह् (-वाह, -वाहन) *m.* Fire.

कश *m.* A whip. [ging.

कशा (-षा) *f.* A whip; flog-

कशिपु *m* Food and clothing.

कश्मल *a.* Foul, dishonourable, *n.* Sin; depression.

कश्मीरज *m. n.* Saffron.

कश्यप *m.* A tortoise; name of a Rishi [to destroy.

कष् *vt.* 1. P To test, to rub,

कष *a.* Rubbing. *m.* A touchstone.

कषाय *a.* Astringent; fragrant; dark-red, brown; improper, dirty. *m. n.* Astringent flavour; the red colour; a decoction.

कषायित *a.* Tinged.

कषेरुका *f.* The back-bone.

कष्ट *a.* Bad; difficult, painful. *n*. Evil, difficulty, misery, suffering, uneasiness. *ind*. Alas!

कस् *vt*. 1. P to approach. With वि or प्र-to open, to expand. निस्-to take out; to expel. *vt*. 2. A to go; to destroy.

कस्तु(स्तू)रिका *f*. Musk.

कस्तुरी *f*. Musk. [deer.

कस्तुरीमृग *m*. The musk-

कस्मात् *ind*. On what account

कांस्य *n*. Bell-metal.

कांस्यकार *m*. A brazier.

काक *m*. A crow, a contemptible or impudent person; dipping the head only while bathing; a sectarial mark.

काकतालीय *n*. An accident.

काकतालीयम् *ind*. Accidentally.

काकदंत *m*. Anything impossible or not existing.

काकगवेषण *n*. Any useless and unprofitable task.

काकनिद्रा *f*. A light slumber.

काकपक्ष (-क) *m*. Side-locks of hair. [omission.

काकपद *n*. The sign of

काकपुच्छ (-पुष्ट) *m*. The Indian cuckoo.

काकपेय *a*. Shallow.

काकलि(-ली) *f*. A low and sweet tone.

काकु *f*. Change of the voice in different emotions; murmuring. [ककुत्स्थ.

काकुत्स्थ *m*. A descendant of

काकोदर *m*. A snake.

काकोल *m*. A raven, a snake.

काकोलूकीय *n*. Natural enmity (as between a crow and an owl.)

काक्ष *m*. A glance.

कांक्ष् *vt*. 1. P or A. To desire. With अभि (आ, वि, or समा) to long for. प्रत्या-to lie in wait for.

कांक्षा *f*. Wish, inclination.

कांक्षिन् *a*. Wishing for.

काच *m*. Glass; a loop, an eye-disease.

काचमणि *m*. Crystal. [water.

काजल *n*. A little or bad

कांचन *a*. Golden; made of gold. *n*. Gold; brilliancy; wealth.

कांची *f*. A girdle; name of an ancient city in the south of India.

काठिन (-न्य) *n*. Hardness.

काण *a*. One-eyed, blind.

काणेली *f*. An unchaste or unmarried woman.

काणेलीमातृ *m*. A term of reproach.

कांड *m*. n. A section; a division or chapter of a book; a stem; a bundle; an arrow; water; a cane; opportunity; private place. *a*. Vile, bad, sinful (at the end of compounds only.

कांडपृष्ठ *m.* A soldier; an adopted son (a term of reproach.)

कांडीर *m.* An archer; a term of reproach.[fused.

कातर *a.* Timid, afraid, con-

कातर्य *n.* Cowardice.

कात्यायनी *f.* An elderly widow; a name of Párvatí.

कादंबरी *f.* A spirituous liquor; the goddess of learning; a female cuckoo.

कादंबिनी *f.* A row of clouds.

कादाचित्क *a.* Incidental.

काद्रवेय *m.* A species of snake

कानन *n.* A forest, a home.

कानिष्ठिक *n.* The little finger.

कानीन *m.* The son of an unmarried woman; a name of व्यास or कर्ण.

कांत *a.* Loved, dear; pleasing, beautiful. *m.* A lover; a husband; the moon; the spring; a precious stone.

कांता *f.* A mistress, a wife.

कांतार *m. n.* A large forest; a bad road; a hole.

कांति *f.* Loveliness, beauty; brilliancy.

कान्दविक *m.* A baker.

कान्दिशीक *a.* Fugitive.

कापट्य *n.* Wickedness; fraud.

कापथ *m.* A bad road.

कापाल (-लिक) *m.* A member of the S'aiva sect characterized by carrying skulls as ornaments and eating and drinking from them.

कापालिन् *m.* S'iva.

कापुरुष *m.* A contemptible man, a coward, a wretch.

कापोत *a.* Grey.

काम *m.* Wish, affection, lust, the god of love. *n.* Object of desire.

काम, कामिन् *a.* Following the dictates of passion.

कामकार *m.* Voluntary action; influence of desire.

कामकूट *m.* The paramour of a harlot.

कामक्रीडा *f.* Amorous sport.

कामगति *a.* Able to go to any desired place.

कामचर (-चार) *a.* Moving unrestrained; *m.* Wilful action.

कामतस् *ind.* Of one's own accord, intentionally, at will.

कामद *a.* Fulfilling a desire.

कामद (-दुघ) *a.* Granting a desired object.

कामदुघा, (-दुह, -धेनु) *f.* A heavenly cow yielding all desires. [cuckoo.

कामदूती *f.* The female

कामपत्नी *f.* Rati, wife of the god of love.

कामरूप *a.* Taking any shape at will; beautiful.
कामरेखा(-लेखा) *f.* A harlot.
कामलता *f.* Membrum virile.
कामलोल *a.* Overcome with passion.
कामवल्लभा *f.* Moonlight.
कामवश *m.* Subjection to love.
कामवृत्त *a.* Licentious.
कामवृत्ति *a.* Independent.
कामसख *m.* The spring.[sire.
कामसू *a.* Fulfilling any de-
कामना *f.* Desire, wish.
कामनीय *n.* Beauty.
कामम् *ind.* At will, well, indeed, really, undoubtedly, surely, willingly, freely.
कामयमान, (**कामयान, कामायितृ**) *a.* Lustful.
कामातुर (or **कामार्त**) *a.* Affected by love.
कामात्मन् *a.* Enamoured.
कामारि *m.* A name of S'iva.
कामार्थिन् *a.* Amorous.
कामिनी *f.* A woman or a lovely woman.
कामुक *a.* Lustful. *m.* A lover; a sparrow.
कामुका *f.* A woman desirous of wealth, &c.
कामुकी *f.* A lustful woman.
कामेश्वर *m.* A name of Kuber.
काम्य *a.* Desirable, lovely, agreeable, optional.
काम्यकर्मन् *n.* A rite performed for some particular object with a view to its future fruition.
काम्यमरण *n.* Suicide, voluntary death.
काम्यव्रत A voluntary vow.
काम्या *f.* Wish, intention.
काय *m. n.* The body, assemblage, a home, capital, a mark; natural temperament.
कायस्थ *m.* The supreme spirit; the writer-caste; proceeding from a **क्षत्रिय** father and a **शूद्र** mother.
कायस्थी *f.* The wife of a **कायस्थ.**
काय(यि)क *a.* Bodily, corporeal.
कायिका *f.* Interest.
कार *a.* (At the end of a compound) Making, doing. *m.* Act, action, effort, determination; power, a tax.
कारका *a.* (Often at the end of compounds) Making, creating, an agent. *n.* The relation of a noun to the verb or to other words governing it in a sentence; syntax
कारकहेतु *m.* The active cause.
कारण *n.* A cause, means, motive, proof, element.
कारणवादिन् *m.* A plaintiff.
कारणशरीर *n.* The causal frame (in **Vedanta phil.**)

कारणा *f.* Pain, agony.
कारणिक *a.* A judge.
कारंडव *m.* A sort of duck.
कारव *m.* A crow.
कारा *f.* Imprisonment, jail; pain; a female messenger.
कारागार *n.* A jail.
कारागृह *n.* A gaol.
कारिका *f.* An actress, a business, a memorial verse or verses; torture; interest.
कारीष *n.* A heap of dried cow-dung.
कारु *a.* An artist. *m.* The artist of the gods.
कारुज *m.* A piece of mechanism; an ant-hill; froth.
कारुणिक *a.* Compassionate.
कारुण्य *n.* Compassion.
कार्कश्य *n.* Sternness.
कार्तस्वर *n.* Gold.
कार्तान्तिक *m.* An astrologer; a fortune-teller.
कार्तिक *m.* Name of a month; a name of Skanda.
कार्तिकेय *m.* Skanda.
कार्त्स्न्य *n* Totality, entirety.
कार्दम *a.* Muddy.
कार्पट *m.* A petitioner, a candidate; a rag.
कार्पटिक *m.* A pilgrim; an experienced man.
कार्पण्य *n.* Poverty, compassion niggardliness.
कार्पास (कार्पासिक) *a.* Made of cotton.
कार्मण *n.* Magic, witchcraft.
कार्मिक *a.* Manufactured, embroidered.
कार्मुक *n.* A bow, a bamboo.
कार्य *n* Duty, work occupation, want, conduct, a lawsuit, an effect, purpose.
कार्यकर *a.* Efficacious. [officer.
कार्यचिंतक *m.* An executive
कार्यच्युत *a.* Out of work.
कार्यतस् *ind.* Consequently, necessarily.
कार्यपुट *m.* A mad eccentric man; an idler.
कार्यप्रेष्य *m.* A messenger.
कार्यवस्तु *n.* An aim.
कार्याकार्यविचार *m.* Discussion as to the propriety or otherwise of a thing.
कार्यार्थ *m.* A purpose.
कार्याधिप *m.* The superintendent of a work. [duty.
कार्योद्धार *m.* Discharge of a
कार्ष *m.* A husbandman.
कार्षापण *m.* *n.* A coin or weight of different values.
कार्षिक *m.* See **कार्षापण**.
कार्ष्ण *a.* Black.
कार्ष्णि *m.* God of love.
काल *a.* Black, *m.* Time; proper time; God of death; destiny; the plant Saturn; poison. *n.* Iron.
कालकंज *n.* A blue lotus.
कालकटंकट *m.* A name of S'iva.

कालकंठ *m*. A peacock; a sparrow; S'iva. [tune.
कालकर्णिका(-कर्णी) *f*. Misfor-
कालकर्मन् *n*. Death.
कालकील *m*. Noise. [son.
कालकूट *m*. *n*. A deadly poi-
कालक्रम *m*. Course of time.
कालक्षेप *m*. Loss of time.
कालखंजन(-खंड)*n*. The liver.
कालग्रंथि *m*. A year.
कालचक्र *n*. The wheel of time; the vicissitudes of life. [cock.
कालज्ञ *m*. An astrologer; a
कालधर्म(-धर्मन्) *m*. The line of conduct suitable to any particular time.
कालनियोग*m*. Fate destiny.
कालनिरूपण *n*. Chronology.
कालपाश*m*.The noose of यम.
कालपृष्ठ *n*. A species of antelope; a bow.
कालयाप *m*. (-न *n*.) Procrastination; delay.
कालयोग *m*. Fate, destiny.
कालविप्रकर्ष *m*. Prolongation of time. [terest.
कालवृद्धि *f*. Periodical in-
कालसदृश *a*. Opportune.
कालशेय *n*. Buttermilk.
काला *f*. An epithet of Durgâ.
कालागरु *m* A kind of sandal tree. [antelope.
कालाजिन *n*. Hide of a black
कालातिरेक *m*. Delay.
कालात्यय *m*. Lapse of time.
कालान्तर *m*. Interval; another time. [delay.
कालान्तरक्षम *a*. Able to bear
कालाप *m* A serpent's hood.
कालावधि*m*. Appointed time
कालेक *a*. Seasonable.
कालिका *f*. Durga; black colour; ink; a female crow; a dark cloud; wine. [nâ.
कालिंदी *f*. The river Yamu-
कालिमन् *m*. Blackness.
कालिय *m*. Name of a large serpent inhabiting the Yamunâ.
काली *f*. Ink; Parvati; a row of black clouds; night.
कालीन *a*. Belonging to a particular time.
कालुष्य *n*. Foulness [terfeit.
काल्पनिक*a*.Fictitious, coun-
काल्य *a*. Timely, agreeable.
कावेर *m*. Saffron.
कावेरि *f*. Turmeric; a courtezan; a river in the south of India.
काव्य *a*. Prophetic; inspired; poetical. *m*. S'ukra, the preceptor of demons *n*. a poem; happiness; inspiration.
काव्या *f*. Understanding, intelligence.
काव्यार्थ *m*. Poetic idea.
काश् *vi*. 1. A To shine; with प्र-to be visible; *vt*. to dis-

close; to shine; to proclaim; to look like; प्रति- to shine in opposition. वि-to open up; सम्-to appear like; निस्-to open; to banish; *vi.* 4. A. To shine to be visible.

काश (-स) *m.n.* A species of grass.

काशि *f.* The modern Benares.

काशिन् *a.* Shining.

काश्मीरजन्मन् *n.* Saffron.

काश्यप Name of a celebrated sage.

काश्यपी *f.* The earth.

काष *m.* Rubbing.

काषाय *a.* Red.

काष्ठ *n.* Fuel, wood.

काष्ठभारिक *m.* A wood-carrier.

काष्ठमय *a.* Wooden.

काष्ठमठी *f.* A funeral pile.

काष्ठमल्ल *m.* A bier.

काष्ठा *f.* The path of wind and clouds; a quarter; direction; last limit; climax

कास् *vi.* 1. A To cough.

कास *m.*(-सा *f.*)Cough, catarrh

कासार *m. n.* A pond, a pool.

कासृति *f.* A by-way.

काहल *a.* Dry; mischievous; large. *m.* A cat; a cock. *n.* Indistinct speech.

काहला *f.* A large drum.

काहली *f.* A young woman.

किंशुक *m.* A kind of tree or its blossom.

किकि *m.* The cocoanut tree; the *chât*a*ka* bird.

किंकणी, किंकिणिका, किंक्रिणी, किंकिणीका *f.* A small bell.

किंकर *m.* A servant; a slave.

किंकरा *f.* A female servant.

किंकरी *f.* The wife of a servant.

किंकर्तव्यता(-कार्यता) *f.* Perplexity; a difficult situation.

किंक्षण *a.* A lazy fellow.

किंकिर *m.* A horse; the Indian cuckoo; a large black bee.

किंकिरात *m.* A parrot; the Indian cuckoo; the god of love.

किंकिल *ind.* What a pity!

किंजल *n.*(-स्क *m*) The blossom.

किट्ट (-क) *n.* Secretion, dirt.

किण *m.* A corn, a scar.

किण्व *n.* Sin.

कित *vt.* or *vi.* 1. P. To cure; to doubt. (*pres.*. चिकित्सति to live; to desire.

कितव *m.* A rogue, a liar, a mad person.

किम् *ind.* (a substitute for कु used only at the beginning of compounds and expressing defect or deterioration.)

किन्नर *m.* A mythical being with a human figure and the head of a horse.

किन्नरी *f.* A female Kinnar; a kind of lute.

किम् *pron* (nom. *sing.* कः *m.* का *f* किम् *n.*) Who, what.

किञ्च *ind.* Moreover

किञ्चित् (-मपि, -ञ्चिदपि, -ञ्चन) A certain thing, &c.

किञ्चिज्ज्ञ *a.* A smatterer.

किमपि To some extent, indescribably; much more.

किम् *ind.* Why; किमपि (किंचित्) a little; somewhat.

किञ्चिन्मात्र *ind.* Only a little.

किमर्थ *a.* Having what motive.

किमर्थम् *ind.* Why, wherefore.

किमिति *ind* Why, indeed.

किमिव *ind.* What possibly.

किमुत *ind.* Why, how much less.

किंतर्हि *ind.* How then, but, however.

किंतु *ind.* But, yet, nevertheless.

किंनिमित्त *a.* Having what cause or reason.

किंनिमित्तम् *ind.* Why, wherefore.

किंनु *ind.* Whether, much more, much less, what indeed.

किंनु खलु *ind.* How possibly, why indeed, can it be that.

किंपच (-पचान) *a.* Miserly, niggardly.

किंपुनर् *ind.* How much more; how much less.

किंभूत *a.* Of what nature.

किंव्रत् *a.* Poor; mean.

किंवदंति (-ती) *f.* Rumour.

किंवराटक *m.* A spend-thrift.

किंवा *ind.* A particle of interrogation: whether, or.

किंस्वित् *ind.* Whether, how.

कियत् *a.* How great, how far, how much, some, a little.

कियत्कालम् *ind.* How long; some little time.

कियच्चिरम् *ind.* How long.

कियद्दूरम् *ind.* A little way, how far.

किरण *m.* A ray or beam.

किरात *m.* A mountain tribe; a savage; a dwarf.

किरि *m.* A hog; a cloud.

किरीट *m. n.* A diadem.

किरीटिन् *m.* A name of Arjuna.

किर्मीर *a.* Variegated. *m.* Name of a Rákshasa.

किल *ind.* Verily; indeed, as they say.

किलकिल *m.* A sound, a cry expressing joy.

किल्बिष *n.* Sin, fault, disease.

किशलय *m. n.* A sprout.

किशोर *m.* A youth below fifteen; a colt; the sun.

किशोरी *f.* A maiden, a young woman.

किसल (-य) *m. n.* A sprout.

कीकट *a.* Poor, miserly; *m.* a horse; modern Bihar.

कीचक *m.* A hollow bamboo; name of the commander-in-chief of King Viráṭa.

कीट *m.* A worm; an insect, a miserable thing.

कीटज *n.* Silk.

कीटक *m.* A worm.

कीदृक्ष (-श, -श्) *a.* Of what sort.

कीर *m.* A parrot.

कीर्ण *a.* Strewn, scattered covered, injured.

कीर्तन *n.* Telling, narrating.

कीर्तना *f.* Narration; fame.

कीर्ति *f.* Fame, glory, good name, favour, dirt, extension, lustre.

कीर्तिभाज् *a.* Famous, celebrated.

कील् *vt.* 1. P. To fix.

कील *m.* A wedge, a lance; a post, a flame.

कीलक *m.* A wedge, a pillar.

कीलिका *f.* The pin of an axle.

कु *f.* The earth; the base of a triangle; *ind.* Bad.

कु *vi.* 1. A (*pres.* कवते) To sound. *vi* 6. A (pres कुवते) To moan, to groan. *vi.* 2. P. (*pres.* कौति) To hum.

कुकूल *m. n.* Chaff, a fire made of chaff. *n.* A ditch; an armour.

कुक्कुट *m.* A cock, a firebrand; a spark.

कुक्कुटि (-टी) *f.* Hypocrisy.

कुक्कुटी *f.* A hen.

कुक्कुभ *m.* A cock; varnish.

कुक्कुर *m.* A dog.

कुक्ष *m.* The belly.

कुक्षि *m.* The belly, the womb, the interior, a cave, the sheath of a sword.

कुक्षिंभरि *a.* Voracious.

कुकुम *n.* Saffron.

कुच् *vt.* or *vi.* 6. P. To sound; to go; to polish; to contract; to impede; to write; with सम् to be contracted, *vt.* P. to lessen; to shrink, to contract; आ or वि-to contract.

कुच *m.* The female breast.

कुचतट *n.* (-तटी *f.*) A female breast.

कुचाग्र *n.* A nipple.

कुचर *a* Going slowly.

कुज्झटि (-टी,) कुज्झटिका *f.* A fog.

कुंचिका *f.* A key.

कुंचित *a.* Contracted, bent.

कुंज् 1 P. To murmur.

कुंज *m. n.* A bower, an arebour, ivory

कुंजकुटीर *m.* A bower.

कुंजभन, कुंजभिल *m.* A thief who breaks into a house.

कुंजर *m.* An elephant; anything pre-eminent or excellent.

कुट् *vt.* 6. P. To curve, *vi.* 4. P. To break asunder.

कुट *m. n.* A jar. *m.* A fort, a hammer.

कुटंक *m.* A roof.

कुटर *m* The post round which the string of the churning stick passes.

कुटल *n.* A roof, a thatch.

कुटिर *n.* A cottage, a hut.

कुटिल *a.* Crooked.

कुटी *f.* A curve ; a cottage.

कुटीर (-क) *m. n.* A hut, cottage [Kinsman.

कुटुंब(-क) *n.* A family. *m. n.*

कुटुंबिक(-न्) *m.* A householder.

कुटुंबिनी *f.* The wife of a householder. [blame.

कुट्ट् *vt.* 10 U To cut, to

कुट्ट (-ट्टि) नी *f.* A procuress ; a go-between.

कुठारिक *m.* A wood-cutter

कुठारिका *f.* A small axe.

कुडव (-प) *m.* A measure of grain. [bud.

कुड्मल *m.* An opening

कुड्य *n.* A wall.

कुण् *vt.* 6. P. To support, to sound ; 10 P. To advice.

कुणप *m n.* A dead body, *m.* A spear; a foul smell.

कुंठ् *vt.* or *vi.* 1. P. (*pp.* कुंठित) To be lame, to be dull.

कुंठ *a.* Blunt; stupid; weak.

कुंठित *a.* Blunted, stupid.

कुंड *m. n.* A basin; a pool.

कुंडल *m. n.* An ear-ring.

कुंडलिन् *a.* Circular. *m.* A snake, a peacock.

कुंडिका *f.* A pitcher. [S'iva.

कुंडिन् *m.* An epithet of

कुंडिर *m.* A man.

कुंडोध्नी *f.* A cow with a full udder ; a woman with a full bosom.

कुतप *m.* A Bráhmana ; the sun; fire; a guest; an ox.

कुतस् *ind.* From where, where else, how, much more, much less. [try.

कुतर्क *m.* A fallacy, sophis-

कुतीर्थ *n.* A bad teacher.

कुतुक *n.* Desire, curiosity, eagerness. [sity.

कुतूहल *n.* Eagerness; curio-

कुत्र *ind.* Where:

कुत्राचित् Somewhere.

कुत्स् *vt* 10. A. To abuse.

कुत्सन *n.* कुत्सा *f.* Abuse, contempt ; reproach.

कुत्सित *a.* Despised, contemptible ; low ; mean.

कुथ् *v.* 4 P. To stink.

कुद्दार (-ल,-क) *m.* A spade.

कुनक *m.* A crow.

कुंत *m.* A lance, a barbed dart, an insect; passion.

कुंतल *m.* The hair; plough.

कुंथ् *vi.* 9.P. To suffer pain.

कुंद *m. n.* A kind of jasmine.

कुंदु *m.* A rat, a mouse.

कुधी *a.* Foolish ; wicked.

कुप् *vi.* 4. P To be angry; to gather strength. अति- (परि, प्र, सम्) to be angry.

कुपिंद *m.* A weaver.

कुपूय *a.* Despised, mean.

कुप्य *n.* A base metal. [wealth

कुबे (वे) र *m.* The god of

कुब्ज *a.* Humpbacked.

कुभृत् *m.* A mountain.

कुमार *m.* A son, a youth, a boy below five; Kártikeya; Agni; a prince.

कुमारक *m.* A child, the pupil of the eye.

कुमारिका, (कुमारी) *f.* A young girl from 10 to 12 years old; a maiden, a daughter; an epithet of Durgá.

कुमुद् *a.* Unkind, avaricious. *n.* The white water-lily; the red lotus.

कुमुद *m. n.* The white water-lily; red lotus. *n.* Silver. *m.* Vishnu; camphor.

कुमुदनाथ (-पति, -बंधु, -बांधव, -सुहृद्) *m.* The moon.

कुमुदिनी *f.* A place abounding in lotuses; the water-lily.

कुमुद्वती *f.* A pond filled with lotuses.

कुंभ *m.* A pitcher; a particular sign of the zodiac; a certain practice of Yoga (also कुंभक); the frontal globe on the forehead of an elephant; the paramour of a harlot.

कुंभकार *m.* A potter.

कुंभज (-जन्मन्, -योनि. -संभव) *m.* An epithet of Agastya, of Drona, as also of Vasistha.

कुंभा *f.* A harlot. [harlot.

कुंभिका *f.* A small pot; a

कुंभिन् *m.* An elephant; a crocodile; a fish

कुंभिल *m.* A thief who breaks into a house; a plagiarist; a wife's brother

कुंभी *f.* A small water-jar.

कुंभीपाक *m.* (*sing* or *pl.*) A particular hell.

कुंभीर *m.* A shark.

कुंभीरक, कुंभील, कुंभीलक *m.* A thief; crocodile.

कुरंग (-म) *m.* A deer.

कुरंगनाभि *f.* Musk.

कुरट *m.* A shoe-maker.

कुररी *f.* A female osprey.

कुरव (-ब) or -क *m.* A species of amaranth.

कुरुक्षेत्र *n.* The extensive plain near Delhi.

कुरुल *m.* A lock of hair on the forehead. [mirror.

कुरुविंद *m. n.* A ruby. *n.* a

कुर्कुट *m.* A cock; rubbish.

कुर्कुर *m.* A dog.

कुल *n.* A family; multitude; a house; noble descent.

कुलक *a.* Of good family, *m.* The chief of a guild; an ant-hill. *n.* A group of from 5 to 15 stanzas forming one sentence.

कुलकंटक *m.* One who is a trouble to his family.

कुलकन्या (-कन्यका) *f.* A girl of high birth.

कुलकर *m.* The founder of a family.

कुलकलंक *m.* A disgrace to the family.

कुलगिरि (-पर्वत,-शैल) *m.* A principal mountain.

कुलज (-जात) *a.* Well-born; ancestral.

कुलट *m.* An adopted son.

कुलटा *f.* An unchaste woman.

कुलतस् *ind.* By birth.

कुलतंतु *m.* One who perpetuates a family.

कुलदीप (-क) *m.* Glory of a family.

कुलदेवता *f.* The guardian-deity of a family.

कुलधर्म *m.* A family custom.

कुलधारक *m.* A son.

कुलनंदन *a.* Gladdening or doing honour to a family.

कुलनाश *m.* Ruin of a family; an outcaste.

कुलपति *m.* The head of a family; a sage who teaches 10,000 pupils with free board and lodging.

कुलपांसुला *f.* An unchaste woman.

कुलपालि (-पालिका,-पाली) *f.* A chaste highborn woman.

कुलपुरुष *m.* An ancestor.

कुलभृत्या *f.* The nursing of a pregnant woman.

कुलंभर (-ल) *m.* A thief.

कुलमर्यादा *f.* Family honour

कुलवधू *f.* A woman of good family and character.

कुलसंख्या *f.* Family respectability.

कुलसेवक *m.* An excellent servant.

कुलस्त्री *f.* A woman of good family.

कुलस्थिति *f.* Antiquity or posterity of a family.

कुलाकुल *a.* Of mixed origin.

कुलांगना *f.* A respectable woman.

कुलांगार *m.* One ruining one's family.

कुलाचल, कुलाद्रि *m.* A principal mountain.

कुलान्वित *a.* Of noble birth.

कुलाय *m. n.* The nest of a bird; the body ; a place.

कुलायिका *f.* A bird-cage.

कुलाल *m.* A potter, a wild cock ; an owl.

कुलि *m.* A hand.

कुलिंग *m* A bird; a sparrow.

कुलि(ली)र *m. n.* A crab.

कुलि(ली)श *m. n* The thunderbolt of Indra.

कुली *f.* A wife's elder-sister

कुलीन *a.* Well-born.

कुलीनस *n.* Water.

कुल्माष *n.* Gruel.

कुलोद्वह *m.* The head of a family.

कुलोपदेश *m.* A family name.

कुल्य *a.* Well-born. *n.* A friendly inquiry after family affairs; a bone or flesh.

कल्या *f.* A virtuous woman; a canal; a ditch.

कुवल *n.* The water-lily; a pearl; water.

कुवलय *n.* The blue water-lily; the earth; (*m.* also.)

कुवलयिनी *f.* The lotus plant

कुवाद *a.* Detracting; low.

कुविं (पिं) द *m.* A weaver.

कुवेल *n.* A lotus.

कुश *m.* A kind of grass; name of the elder son of Ráma. *n.* Water; *a.* Wicked.

कुशल *a.* Right, good, auspicious, happy, skilful, clever. *n.* Welfare, happiness, ability.

कुशलप्रश्न *m.* Friendly inquiry after a person's health or welfare

कुशलिन् *a.* Happy, prosperous.

कुशस्थली *f.* The town of Dwárká.

कुशा *f.* A rope; a bridle.

कुशाग्रबुद्धि *a.* Having a sharp intellect.

कुशिक *a.* Squint-eyed. *m.* a plough-share.

कुशीद *m.* See कुसीद.

कुशीलव *m.* A bard, an actor a name of Válmíki.

कुशूल *m.* A granary, a fire made of chaff.

कुशेशय *n.* A lotus.

कुष् *vt.* 9. P To draw out, to test. With निस्-to extract.

कुषीद *m.* See कुसीद.

कुष्ठ *m. n.* A kind of leprosy.

कुष्ठारि *m.* Sulphur.

कुष्मल *a.* Cutting.

कुष्मांड (-क) *m.* A kind of pumpkin gourd; a false conception.

कुस् *vt.* 4. P To embrace.

कुसी (सि) द *m.* A money-lender; *n.* A loan.

कुसीदपथ *m.* Usury. [usurer.

कुसीदायी *f.* The wife of a

कुसीदिक (-न्) *m.* A usurer.

कुसुम *n* A flower, fruit; menstrual discharge.

कुसुमकार्मुक (-चाप, -धन्वन्, -शर) *m.* The god of Love.

कुसुमाकर *m.* A garden; a nosegay; the spring.

कुसुमास्त्र (or कुसुमायुध) *m.* The god of Love

कुसुमावतंसक *n.* A chaplet.

कुसुमासव *n.* Honey. [courses.
कुसुमवती *f.* A woman in her
कुसुमस्तबक *m.* A nosegay.
कुसुमाल *m* A thief.
कुसुंभ *m. n.* Safflower, the water-pot of an ascetic. *n.* Gold.
कुसूल *m.* A granary.
कुसृति *f.* Fraud, deceit.
कुस्तुभ *m.* An epithet of Vishṇu; the occan.
कुह *m.* Kubera; a rogue.
कुहक *m.* A cheat, a juggler.
कुहकचाकित *a.* Suspicious.
कुहकस्वन *m.* A cock.
कुहक *n.* (-का *f.*) Jugglery.
कुहन *m.* A mouse; a snake. *n.* A glass vessel.
कुहना (-निका) *f.* Hypocrisy.
कुहर *n.* A cavity, the ear; the throat; a hole.
कुहरित *n.* The cry of the Indian cuckoo; a sound.
कुहु(-हू) *f.* The new-moon day.
कुहूकंठ (-मुख, -रव, -शब्द) *m.* The Indian cuckoo.
कू *v.i.* 6. P. 9. U. To sound.
कू *f.* A female imp.
कूच *m.* The female breast.
कूचिका or कूची *f.* A small brush of hair, a key.
कूज् *v.i.* I P To coo, to warble. With परि, नि, or वि to coo, to make an indistinct noise.
कूज *m.* (-*n.*न) Cooing.
कूजित *n.* Cooing.
कूट *a.* False, steady; *m.* illusion; a fraud; puzzle; n. a horn; a corner, a summit; chief; a multitude; a plough-share.
कूटकार *m.* A rogue, a false witness.
कूटपालक *m.* A potter.
कूटपाश (-बंध) *m.* A trap.
कूटयंत्र *n.* A trap. [war.
कूटयुद्ध *n.* A treacherous
कूटशस् *ind.* In heaps.
कूटस्थ *a.* Standing at the top. *m.* the supreme soul.
कूटक *n.* Elevat on; a plough-share; fraud.
कूण् *vt.* 10. U To speak, *vi.* 10. A. to contract.
कूणिका *f.* The horn; the peg of a lute. [mast.
कूप *m.* A well, a hole, a
कूपकच्छप (-मण्डूक) *m.* An inexperienced person who never leaves home; a man of limited ideas.
कूपक *m.* A hole, a cave; a well; the mast; a funeral pile.
कूपांक (-ग) *m.* Horripilation.
कूपा (वा) र *m* The ocean.
कूपी *f.* A small well; a flask.
कूब (व) र *a.* Beautiful, hump-backed.
कूर्च *m. n.* A punch, a pea-

cock's feather; the hair between the eyebrows; beard; a brush; deceit; fraud; boasting.

कूर्चिका *f.* A painting brush or pencil; a key; a bud.

कूर्द् *vi* 1. U. To leap [knee.

कूर्पर *m.* The elbow; the

कूर्म *m.* A tortoise.

कूल *n.* A shore, a bank, a pond; the rear of an army; border; a heap.

कूलक *m.* An ant-hill.

कूलंकष *a.* Carrying or tearing away the bank. *m.* The current of a river.

कूलंकथा *f.* A river.

कूलहंडक,(-हुंडक) *m.* An eddy

कूष्मांड *m.* A kind of pumpkin gourd.

कूहा *f.* A fog, a mist.

कृ *vt.* 5 U To hurt. 8 U. To do, to prepare, to compose, to create, to tell, to obey, to make a sound, to appoint, to regard; आत्मसात् कृ to appropriate to one's self, भस्मी कृ to reduce to ashes; कालंकृ to die; चिरंकृ to delay; अंगीकृ to favour, to accept; to promise, अति-to exceed, to surpass; अधि-to be entitled, to have reference to, to overcome, to refrain from, अनु-[Paras.] to imitate, to be like. अप-to insult, to wrong; अपा-to remove to put aside, अभ्यंतरी कृ to initiate in; अलंकृ to adorn, आविस्-to show, उप-to serve, to oblige, to wait upon; to adorn, to perfect उपा-to deliver; to consecrate by hymns; तिरस्-to abuse, to revile, to conquer. दक्षिणा or प्रदक्षिणा-to walk round, दुस्-to act wrongly. धिक्-to reproach, to condemn. नमस्-to salute, नि-to injure; to wrong; निस्-to remove, to break, to frustrate, निरा-to make light of, to expel, to refute, to annihilate. न्यकृ-to insult, परा-(Paras.) to reject, परि-to surround; to refine; पुरस्-to place in front. प्र to commence, प्रति-to requite, to repay, to remedy, to retaliate, to restore, प्रमाणी-to meet out, to believe, प्रादुस्-to make manifest, प्रत्युप-to requite, to alter, to disfigure, to create : विप्र-to trouble, to affect, व्या-to make manifest, to explain; to tell, सम्-to commit, to perform purificatory ceremonies; समलं- to adorn, to polish, to refine. साची-to turn aside,

कृकवाकु *m.* A cock; a peacock; a lizard.

कृच्छ्र *m. n.* Trouble, danger, penance.

कृच्छ्रम् *ind.* Painfully.

कृत् *vt.* 6 P. To cut; with अव-to cut off, to divide, उत्-to tear out, नि-to cut, 7 P. To surround.

कृत् *a.* Doer, agent.

कृत *a.* Done *n.* Work, benefit, consequence, Name of the first of the four Yugas or ages of the world.

कृतान्त *m.* Fate, the god of Death; a proved doctrine.

कृतकृत्य *a.* One who has accomplished his object; contented.

कृतक्षण *a.* One who has got an opportunity.

कृतघ्न *a.* Ungrateful.

कृतज्ञ *a.* Grateful, correct in couduct.

कृतदास *m.* A hired servant.

कृतधी *a.* Prudent, learned.

कृतपूर्व *a.* Done formerly.

कृतप्रतिकृत *n.* Assault and counter-assault.

कृतफल *a.* Successful.

कृतबुद्धि *a.* Learned, wise.

कृतमंगल *a.* Blessed.

कृतम् *ind.* Enough, no more.

कृतक *a.* Done; artificial; adopted (as a son).

कृतमुख *a.* Learned, wise.

कृतयुग *n.* The first of the four Yugas or ages of the world.

कृतलक्षण *a.* Amiable; defined.

कृतवाप *m.* A penitent.

कृतविद्य *a.* Learned.

कृतवीर्य *a,* Powerful.

कृतवेदिन् *a.* Grateful.

कृतसंज्ञ *a.* Restored to consciousness; having presence of mind.

कृतहस्त (-हस्तक) *a.* Skilful.

कृतागम *a.* Advanced, proficient.

कृतात्मन् *a.* Self-controlled.

कृति *f.* Work; action.

कृतान्न *n.* Digested food; excretion.

कृतार्थ *a.* Successful; contented; clever.

कृतिन् *a.* Expert, pious; obedient; fortunate.

कृते (-न) *ind.* For the sake of.

कृत्ति *f.* Hide, bark of the birch tree.

कृत्तिवास, (-स्) *m.* S'iva.

कृत्तिका *f. pl.* The third of the lunar mansions.

कृत्तिकातनय (-पुत्र, -सुत) *m.* Name of Kârtikeya.

कृत्तिकाभव *m.* The moon.

कृत्नु *a.* Skilful. *m.* An artist.

कृत्य *a.* Proper; practicable. *n.* Duty; cause; work.

कृत्या *f.* Action, magic; a female deity to whom sacrifices are offered for destructive purposes.

कृत्रिम *a.* Artificial; adopted.

कृत्रिमपुत्र (-क) *m.* A doll.

कृत्स्न *a.* All whole.

कृंतन *n.* Cutting.

कृपण *a.* Pitiable. *m.* A miser.

कृपणधी (-बुद्धि) *a.* Little-minded.

कृपा *f.* Pity, compassion.

कृपाण *m.* A sword, a knife.

कृपाणिका *f.* A dagger, a knife.

कृपागी *f.* A pair of scissors; a dagger.

कृपालु *a.* Merciful, compassionate.

कृपीट *n* Forest; water.

कृमि *m.* A worm, an ass.

कृमिज (-जग्ध) *n.* Aloewood.

कृमिजा *f.* Lac.

कृमिण(-ल) *a.* Having worms.

कृमिला *f.* A fruitful woman.

कृश् *vi.* 4. P. To become lean.

कृश *a.* Lean, poor.

कृशला *f* Hair.

कृशानु *m.* Fire.

कृशाश्विन् *m.* An actor.

कृष् *vt.* I. P To draw, to tear, to attract, to subdue to plough, to obtain; अप-to take away, to diminish अव-to draw away from. आ-to pull, to bend, उत्-to draw up, to enhance, नि-to sink down, निस्-to draw out, परि-to drag. प्र-to draw away, ro lead, विप्र-to remove. संनि-to make near. *vt.* 6 A. to plough.

कृषक *m.* A farmer; an ox.

कृषाण, **कृषिक** *m* A ploughman, a husbandman.

कृषि *f.* Agriculture.

कृषीवल *m.* A farmer.

कृष्ट *a.* Drawn, attracted; ploughed (*pp.* of कृष्).

कृष्टि *m.* A learned man.

कृष्ण *a.* Black, dark-blue; wicked, evil. *m.* The black antelope; a crow; the Indian cuckoo; the dark half of a lunar month; the Kali age; the son of Vasudeva and Devakî; Name of Vyása, or of Arjuna; antimony; *n.* the black part of the eye; black pepper.

कृष्णग्रीव *m.* Śiva.

कृष्णदेह *m.* A bee.

कृष्णधन *n.* Money acquired by foul means.

कृष्णद्वैपायन *m.* Vyása.

कृष्णपक्ष *m.* The dark half of a lunar month.

कृष्णमृग *m.* The black antelope.

कृष्णलोह *m.* The loadstone.

कृष्णवर्त्मन् *m.* Fire; Ráhu; a low man.

कृष्णशार (-सार) *m.* The spotted antelope.

कृष्णा *f.* Name of द्रौपदी.

कृष्णागरु *m.* A kind of sandal wood.

कृष्णाजिन *n.* Skin of the black antelope.

कृष्णाध्वन् *m.* Fire.

कृष्णायस् (-स)*n.* Crude iron.

कृष्णार्चिस् *m.* Fire.

कृष्णिका *f.* Black mustard.

कृष्णिमन् *m.* Blackness.

कृष्णी *f.* A dark night.

कॄ *vt.* 6P. (*pp.* कीर्ण) to scatter, with अप or अव-to to scatter, अपा-to repudiate. आ-to spread round; उद्-to throw up; to dig out; to engrave; to surround, to deliver, to scatter, प्रति-to injure, वि-to throw about, विनि-to abandon, सम्-to mix, समुद्-to pierce, *vt.* 9. U. to injure.

कॄत् *vt.* 10. U. (*pp.* कीर्तित) To name, to praise.

कॢप् *vi.* 1.A To be fit for, to accomplish; to occur; to to be ready. With अव-to accomplish, उप-to be ready प्र-to happen; to be successful. वि-to be doubtful. *Caus.* (कल्पयति-ते) With आ-to adorn, प्र-to prepare to sketch; परि-to prepare; to decide वि-to doubt. सम्-to intend; to resolve; समुप-to prepare.

कॢप्त *a.* Prepared, thought of; produced; arranged; cut.

कॢप्ति *f.* Accomplishment invention, arranging.

कॢप्तिक *a.* Bought, purchased.

केकय *m. pl.* The name of a country and its people.

केकर *a.* Squint-eyed.

केका *f.* The cry of a peacock.

केकावल, केकिक (-न्) *m.* A peacock.

केत *m.* A house; a banner.

केतक (-की *f.*) Name of a plant, a banner.

केतन *n.* A house; summons, a spot, a flag, a sign, an indispensable act.

केतित *a* Called, inhabited.

केतु *m.* Brightness, a flag, a leader, eminent person, a comet, a meteor, a sign.

केतुग्रह *m.* The descending node.

केतुभ *m.* A cloud.

केतुयष्टि *f.* A flag-staff.

केदार *m.* A meadow; a basin for water; a mountain.

केदारखंड *n.* A small dyke.

केंद्र *n.* The centre of a circle; distance of a planet from the first point of its orbit in the 4th 7th, or 10th degree.

केयूर *m. n.* An armlet.
केलास *m.* A crystal.
केलि *m. f.* Play, armorous sport. *f.* The earth.
केलिग्रह (-निकेतन, -मंदिर, -सदन) *n.* A pleasure-house.
केलिसुख *m.* A joke, fun, pastime.
केली *f* Play, amorous sport.
केवल *a.* Peculiar; sole; pure; alone; whole absolute.
केवलतस् *ind.* Only, simply, wholly, purely. [wholly.
केवलम् *ind.* Only, merely;
केवलम्.अपि Not only but.
केवलात्मन् *a.* One whose essence is absolute unity.
केवलिन् *a.* Alone, only
केश *m.* Hair, a ray of light.
केशकर्मन् *n.* Dressing the hair
केशकलाप *m.* A mass of hair.
केशाकेशी *ind.* Pulling each other's hair.
केशगर्भ *m.* A braid of hair.
केशग्रह *m.* (-ण *n*) Pulling the hair. [a barber.
केशच्छिद् *m.* A hair-dresser,
केशपक्ष (-पाश, -हस्त) *m.* Much (or ornamented) hair.
केशभूमि *f.* That part of the body where hair grows.
केक्षप्रसाधनी *f.* (-मार्जक, -मार्जन *n.*) A comb.
केशट *m.* A goat; a bug.
केशव *m.* Name of Vishnu or Krishna.
केशिक *a.* Having fine or luxuriant hair.
केशिन् *m.* A lion; name of a Rákshasa.
केस (श) र *m. n.* The mane; the filament of a flower.
केस (श) रिन् *m.* A lion, a horse; the best.
कै *vi.* 1. P. To sound.
कैटभ *m.* Name of a demon killed by Vishnu.
कैतव *n.* Gambling; falsehood, deceit, a rogue, a gambler. [device.
कैतवप्रयोग *m.* A trick, a
कैरव *m.* A gambler, a cheat, an enemy. *n.* The white lotus.
कैरविन् *m.* The moon.
कैरवी *f.* Moonlight.
कैलास *m.* Name of a mountain and residence of Śiva.
कैवर्त (-क) *m.* A fisherman.
कैवल्य *n.* Exclusiveness; individuality; final emancipation or Moksha.
कैशोर *n.* Youth, an age below fifteen.
कोक *m.* A wolf, the ruddy goose, a frog.
कोकनद *n.* The red lotus.
कोकिल *m.* (-ला *f.*) The Indian cuckoo. [tree.
कोकिलोत्सव *m.* The mango-
कोंक (-ण) *m. pl.* The hilly

strip of land between the Sahyádri and the ocean.

कोजागर *m* Name of a festival held on the full moon night in the month of A's'vina.

कोट *m*. A fort; a hut.

कोटर *m. n.* The hollow of a tree.

कोटि(-टी) *f*. The extremity, the highest point, excellence, the horns of the moon, a crore, the side of a right-angled triangle, a class. [tives.

कोटिद्वय *n*. Two alterna-

कोटिशस् *ind*. In multitudes

कोटीर *m*. A crown; matted hair.

कोट्ट *m*. A fort.

कोट्टार *m*. A fortified town.

कोण *m*. A corner, the bow of a lute, the planet Mars or Saturn.

कोदंड *m. n.* A bow; *m*. An eyebrow.

कोद्रव *m*. A species of grain eaten by the poor.

कोप *m*. Passion, anger, morbid irritation.

कोपपद *n*. Pretended wrath.

कोपिन् *a*. Angry.

कोमल *a*. Tender, agreeable, beautiful.

कोयष्टि (-क) *m*. The lapwing.

कोरक *m. n.* A bud.

कोरित *a*. Budded, pounded.

कोल *m* A hog, a boat; the breast; the lap; an embrace.

कोलाहल *m. n* An uproar.

कोविद *a*. Experienced, learned; proficient.

कोश (-ष) *m. n.* A bud; a sheath; a cup, a box, a store-room; a treasury, wealth, a dictionary; the cocoon of a silk-worm; the womb; an egg; a globe.

कोशनायक (-पाल) *m*. A treasurer, a minister of finance.

को(कौ)शलिक *n*. A bribe.

कोशागार *m. n.* A treasury.

कोशाधिपति *m*. A treasurer.

कोशाध्यक्ष *m*. A treasurer.

कोशि(षि)न् *m*. The mango tree.

कोष्ठ *m*. The belly, store-room, the shell.

कोष्ठक *m*. A granary; *n*. A water trough.

कोष्ठपाल *m*. A constable; a storekeeper.

कोष्ठाग्नि *m*. The digestive faculty.

कोष्ण *a*. Tepid, lukewarm.

कोस (श) ला *f*. The city of Ayodhyà.

कौक्ष *a.* Tied to the sides, abdominal. [tar.

कौक्षेयक *m.* A sword, scimi-

कौट *a.* Independent, domestic, fraudulent.

कौटिलिक *m.* A hunter; a black-smith.

कौटिल्य *m.* An epithet of Chánakya. *n.* Crookedness; fraud.

कौटुंब *n.* Family relationship.

कौटुंबिक *a.* Constituting a family. *m.* The father.

कौणप *m.* A goblin, a demon.

कौतुक *n.* Desire, eagerness, curiosity, gaiety.

कौतुकतोरण *m. n* A triumphal arch.

कौतूहल (-ल्य) *n.* Desire, curiosity, vehemence.

कौंतिक *m.* A lancer.

कौंतेय *m.* A son of Kuntî.

कौपीन *n.* A privity, a small piece of cloth worn over the privities.

कौमार *a.* Juvenile, youthful, soft, tender, childhood.

कौमारक *n.* Boyhood youth.

कौमारभृत्य *n.* The rearing and education of children. [girls.

कौमारिक *m.* A father of

कौमुदी *f.* Moonlight.

कौमुदीपति *m.* The moon.

कौमुदीवृक्ष *m.* Stand of a lamp

कौरव(-व्य) *m.* A descendant of Kurus.

कौल *a.* Ancestral; wellborn *m.* A Śâkta. [tic.

कौलिक *m.* A weaver; a here-

कौलीन *m.* A scandal, bad conduct.

कौलीन्य *n.* High birth.

कौश *a.* Silken.

कौशल (-ल्य) *n.* Well-being; skilfulness.

कौशलिक *n.* A bribe.

कौशलिका, कौशली *f.* A present.

कौशल्या *f.* Mother of Ràma.

कौशांबी *f.* Name of an ancient city.

कौशिक *m.* An epithet of Indra or विश्वामित्र; an owl; an ichneumon.

कौशे (षे) य *n.* Silk cloth.

कौसीद्य *n.* Sloth; usury.

कौस्तुभ *m.* A celebrated gem worn by Vishnu.

क्रकच *m.* A saw.

क्रतु *m.* A sacrifice.

क्रथ् *vi.* I. P. To injure.

क्रथन *n.* A slaughter.

क्रथनक *m.* A camel.

क्रद् *vi.* or *vt.* I. P. To cry.

क्रन्द् *vt.* 10 U. To call out.

क्रम् *vt.* 1. U. 4. P. (*p.p.* क्रांत To walk, to step, to jump, to excel, with अति-to cross, to transgress, to surpass; to neglect. अधि-

to ascend. अध्या-to occupy. अनु-to follow; to begin; अन्वा-to visit one after another. अप-to leave, अभि-to approach, अव-to withdraw. आ-to seize, to begin, (Atm.) to come up उद्-to go up, उप-to approach, (Atm.) to commence, निस्-to go away, परा-(Atm.) to display spirit, to attack, परि-to walk about, प्र-(Atm.) to begin, to walk on, प्रति-to return. वि-(Atm.) to walk along or through, to overcome, व्याति-to transgress, to pass (time). सम्-to meet together; to traverse, to occupy.

क्रम *n.* A course, a step, order, manner; preparation

क्रमतस् *ind.* Successively.

क्रमभंग *m.* Irregularity.

क्रमशस् *ind.* Gradually.

क्रमक *a.* Orderly.

क्रमिक *a.* Successive.

क्रमु(-क) *m.* Betel-nut tree.

क्रमेल, (-क) *m.* A camel.

क्रय *m.* Buying, purchasing.

क्रयारोह *n.* A market, a fair.

क्रयलेख्य *n.* A deed of sale.

क्रयविक्रय *m. du.* trade, buying and selling. [chaser.

क्रयिक *m.* A trader, a pur-

क्रय्य *a.* A thing offered for sale in the market.

क्रव्य *n.* Raw flesh.

क्रव्याद्, (क्रव्याद) *a.* Eating raw flesh. *m.* A demon.

क्रांति *f.* A step, the ecliptic.

क्रांतिकक्ष *m.* (-मंडल,-वृत्त *n.*) The ecliptic.

क्रांतिपात *m.* The equinoctial points or nodes of the ecliptic.

क्रांतिवलय *m.* The ecliptic; the tropical zone.

क्रिमि *m.* A worm; an insect.

क्रिया *f.* An act, execution, labour, practice; knowledge; offering oblations to the deceased ancestors.

क्रियान्वित *a.* Practising ritual or observances.

क्रियापवर्ग *m.* Execution of a task, absolution.

क्रियाभ्युपगम *m.* Special agreement.

क्रियाकलाप *m.* The body of ceremonies.

क्रियानिर्देश *m.* Evidence.

क्रियापद *n.* A verb.

क्रियापर *a.* Diligent in the performance of one's duty.

क्रियालोप *m.* Omission or discontinuance of any of the essential ceremonies of the Hindu religion.

क्रियावत् *a.* An actual performer.

क्रियावश *m.* Necessity.

क्रियावादिन् *m.* A plaintiff, a complainant.

क्रियाविधि *m.* A rule of action.

क्रियाविशेषण *n.* An adverb; a predicative adjective.

क्रियासंक्रांति *f.* Teaching.

क्रियासमभिहार *m.* The repetition of any act.

क्री *vt.* 9 U. To buy, to exchange; with आ-to buy. निस् to buy off, परि-(Atm) to buy, to repay, sell (Atm).

क्रीड् *vi.* 1 P To play, to amuse oneself With सम-(Atm.) to play, (Paras.) to make noise.

क्रीड *m.* Sport, joke.

क्रीडनक *m. n.* क्रीडनीय *n.* क्रीडनीयक *n.* A plaything.

क्रीडा *f.* Sport, jest, joke.

क्रीडाकोप *m.* Feigned anger.

क्रीडानारी *f.* A prostitute.

क्रीडाशैल *m.* An artificial hill as a pleasure resort.

क्रुध् *vi.* 4 P To be angry; प्रति-to be angry in return; सम्-to get angry with.

क्रुध *f.* Anger.

क्रुश् *vt.* or *vi.* 1 P To cry, to weep. With अनु-to pity, अभि-to bewail. आ-to cry, to abuse, परि-to lament. प्रत्या-to revile in turn. वि-to call aloud, व्या-to lament.

क्रूर *a.* Cruel, hard-hearted. hard, terrible, disagreeable. *n.* A wound; slauhgter.

क्रेतृ *m.* A purchaser.

क्रोड *m.* A hog; the hollow of a tree; the middle part.

क्रोड *n.* (-डा *f.*) The breast, an interior cavity.

क्रोडपत्र *n.* Marginal writing; a supplement.

क्रोडीकरण *n.* Embracing.

क्रोडीमुख *m.* A rhinoceros.

क्रोध *m.* Anger.

क्रोधन *a.* Passionate, angry.

क्रोधालु *a.* Passionate, insolent.

क्रोश *m.* A cry, a shout, a noise; a distance equal to $\frac{1}{4}$th of a *Yojana*, or $2\frac{1}{2}$ miles.

क्रोष्टु *m.* (-ष्ट्री *fem.*) A jackal.

क्रौंच *m.* A curlew, a heron, name of a mountain.

क्रौर्य *n.* Cruelty.

क्लंद् 1. P To lament. 4. A To be confused.

क्लम् *vi.* 1. 4. P (*pp.* क्लांत) To be fatigued, to be depressed वि-to be fatigued.

क्लम, (-थ) *m.* Fatigue, exhaustion.

क्लांत *a.* Fatigued, faded.

क्लांति *f.* Fatigue.

क्लिद् *vi* 4. P (*pp.* क्लिन्न) To become wet.

क्लिश् *vt.* or *vi.* 4. A. To suffer, to torment, *vt.* 9. P. to distress.

क्लिष्ट *a.* Tormented; distressed.

क्लिष्टि *f.* Affliction, anguish.

क्लीब (-व) *a.* Impotent.

क्लेद *m.* Moisture, pain.

क्लेश *m.* Pain, suffering, anger.

क्लेशक्षम *a.* Capable of enduring trouble.

क्लैब्य, (-व्य) *n.* Impotence, cowardice.

क्लोम *n.* The lungs.

क्व *ind.* Whither, where.

क्वचित् In some places.

क्वण् *vi.* I. P. To hum, to tinkle.

क्वथ् *vt.* I. P. To boil.

क्वथ (क्वाथ) *m.* A decoction.

क्वापि *ind.* Somewhere, sometimes.

क्वाचित्क *a.* Rare, uncommon.

क्ष *m.* Destruction, lightning; a field; a farmer; a name of Narasinha.

क्षण (-नु) *vt.* 8. U. (*pp.* क्षत) To hurt, to break.

क्षण *m. n.* An instant, leisure, an opportunity, joy, the centre, the middle

क्षणद *m.* An astrologer.

क्षणदा *f.* Night, turmeric.

क्षणदाकर *m.* The moon.

क्षणदाचर *m.* A fiend.

क्षणद्युति, (-प्रकाशा, -प्रभा) *f.* Lightning.

क्षणभंगुर *a* Transient.

क्षणतु *m.* A wound, a sore.

क्षणन *n.* Injuring, killing.

क्षणिक *a.* Momentary.

क्षणिका *f.* Lightning.

क्षणिनी *f.* Night.

क्षत *a.* Wounded, hurt, injured, bitten (*pp.* of क्षण्); a wound.

क्षतज *n.* Blood, pus, matter.

क्षतयोनि *f.* A woman who is no longer a virgin.

क्षतवृत्ति *f.* Destitution.

क्षति *f.* Injury, loss.

क्षतृ *m.* Attendant, charioteer; the son of a female slave.

क्षत्र *m. n.* Dominion, supremacy, a kshatriya.

क्षत्रधर्म *m.* Bravery.

क्षत्रप *m.* A governor.

क्षत्रबंधु *m.* A vile Kshatriya.

क्षत्रविद्या *f.* Military science.

क्षत्रिय *m.* A member of the military caste.

क्षत्रिया, (-यका or -यिका) A Kshatriya woman.

क्षत्रियाणी *f.* A woman of the Kshatriya caste.

क्षत्रियी *f.* The wife of a Kshatriya.

क्षंतृ *a.* Patient, forbearing.

क्षप् *vi.* 1. U. To fast, To send.

क्षपण, (-क) *m.* A Bauddha mendicant.

क्षपणी *f.* An oar; a net.

क्षपा *f.* A night, turmeric.

क्षपाट *m.* A demon, a goblin.

क्षपाकर (-नाथ) *m.* The moon.

क्षपाचर *m.* A demon.

क्षम् *vt.* 1. A. 4 P. To suffer, to forgive, to be able.

क्षम *a.* Patient, competent, favourable, suitable.

क्षमा *f.* Forbearance; earth.

क्षमितृ (-त्री *f.*) } *a.* Patient,
क्षमिन् (-नी *f.*) } forgiving.

क्षय *m.* An abode; decline.

क्षयिन् *a.* Diminishing, consumptive. *m.* The moon.

क्षयिष्णु *a.* Wasting, fragile.

क्षर् *vt.* or *vi.* 1. P. To flow, to have no effect; with वि-to dissolve.

क्षर *a.* Perishable. *m.* A cloud. *n.* Water; ignorance.

क्षरण *n.* The act of oozing

क्षरिन् *m.* The rainy season.

क्षल् *vt.* 10 U. To wash. With प्र-to wash.

क्षात्र *a.* Belonging to the military tribe.

क्षांत *a.* Patient.

क्षांता *f.* The earth.

क्षांति *f* Patience.

क्षांतु *a.* Patient, forbearing.

क्षाम *a.* Scorched, weak, emaciated, little.

क्षार *a.* Corrosive. *m.* Essence; any corrosive or acid substance; glass; a rogue, *n.* Black salt; water.

क्षारक *m.* Alkali; a cage.

क्षारिका *f.* Hunger.

क्षारित *a.* Distilled from saline matter; falsely accused.

क्षालन *n.* Washing.

क्षालित *a.* Washed, cleaned.

क्षि *vi.* or *vt.* 1 P (*pp.* क्षित or क्षीण) To decay, to rule, *vt.* 5, 9, P. To destroy, to kill. With अप-to decay; परि-प्रसम् to decay.

क्षिति *f.* The earth; an abode.

क्षितिकण *m.* Dust.

क्षितिकंप *m.* An earthquake.

क्षितिक्षित A king, a prince.

क्षितिज *m.* A tree; an earthworm; the planet Mars; *n.* The horizon. [wife.

क्षितिजा *f.* Sîtá, Ráma's

क्षितिधर (-भृत्) *m.* A mountain.

क्षितिनाथ (-प, -पति, -पाल, -भुज्, -रक्षिन्) *m.* A sovereign.

क्षितिरंध्र *n.* A ditch.

क्षितिरुह् *m.* A tree

क्षितिवर्धन *m.* A corpse.

क्षिप् *vt.* 6 U. (only P. when preceded by अधि, प्रति and अति); 4. P. To throw, to reject, to insult; with अधि-to offend, अव-to cast down, to slander, आ-to hit, to throw off, to neglect, to object to (as an argument); उद्-to throw

up, उप-to cast on, to insult; नि-to entrust, to encamp; परि-to surround, to embrace, पर्या-to collect, प्र-to throw at, to interpolate; वि-to divert; to distract. सम्-to abridge.
क्षिपा *f.* Night.
क्षिपणी(-णि) *f.* An oar; a net;
क्षिप्त *a.* Thrown, disregarded.
क्षिप्त-चित्त *a.* Absent-minded.
क्षिप्र *a.* (*Comp.* क्षेपीयस्; *Super.* क्षेपिष्ठ) Quick, speedy.
क्षिप्रम् *ind.* Quickly.
क्षिया *f.* Loss, destruction.
क्षिव् 4 P. To vomit.
क्षी 1 U. To kill; to hurt.
क्षीण *a.* Thin, slender; weak.
क्षीब(-व) *a.* Excited, drunk.
क्षीर *m.n.* Milk; juice or sap of plants.
क्षीरकंठ *m.* A young child.
क्षीरद्रुम *m.* The as'vattha tree.
क्षीरनीर *n.* An embrace.
क्षीरसार *m.* Butter.
क्षीरशर *m.* The skim of milk.
क्षीराद *m.* A sucking child.
क्षीराब्धि *m.* The ocean of milk.
क्षीराब्धिज *m.* The moon; a pearl; nectar. [shmî.
क्षीराब्धिजा (-तनया) *f.* Lak-
क्षीरोद *m.* The sea of milk.
क्षु *vi.* 2. P. To sneeze, to cough.
क्षुण्ण *a.* Beaten; practised.
क्षुत *f.* (-त *n.*-ता *f.*) A sneeze.
क्षुद् *vt.* 7. U. To trample upon.
क्षुद्र *a.* (*Comp.* क्षोदीयस्, *Super.* क्षोदिष्ठ;) Minute, little, mean, poor, miserly.
क्षुद्रल *a.* Minute, small.
क्षुद्रा *f.* A bee, a fly, a prostitute, a quarrelsome woman.
क्षुध *vi.* 4. P. To be hungry.
क्षुध् (-धा) *f.* Hunger.
क्षुधालु, क्षुधित *a.* Hungry.
क्षुभ् *vt.* 1. A. 4. 9. P (*pp.* क्षुभित, क्षुब्ध) To shake. With प्र, वि or सम्-to tremble, to be agitated.
क्षुभित *a.* See under क्षुभ्.
क्षुब्ध *a.* Agitated, disturbed; afraid.
क्षुर् *vt.* 6. P. To cut.
क्षुर *m.* A razor, an arrow.
क्षुरप्र *m.* An arrow with a sharp head, a barber.
क्षुरिका or क्षुरी *f.* A knife, a dagger.
क्षुरिन् *m* A barber.
क्षुल्ल *a.* Small, little.
क्षुल्लतात *m.* The younger brother of a father.
क्षुल्लक *a.* Little, poor; wicked, young.
क्षेत्र *n.* A field, a place, a place of pilgrimage; a place of origin; the body; the mind, a wife.

क्षेत्रकर *m.* A cultivator.

क्षेत्रगणित *n.* Geometry.

क्षेत्रगत *a.* Geometrical.

क्षेत्रज *m.* The offspring of the wife by a kinsman duly appointed to raise up issue to the husband.

क्षेत्रजात *a.* Begotten on the wife of another.

क्षेत्रज्ञ *a.* Clever. *m.* The soul, the supreme soul, a libertine.

क्षेत्रफल *n.* The area (in mathe.)

क्षेत्रविद् *a.* Possessing spiritual knowledge.

क्षेत्राजीव *m.* A cultivator.

क्षेत्रिक *m.* A farmer.

क्षेत्रिन् An agriculturist, a husband; the supreme soul.

क्षेत्रिय *a.* Incurable.

क्षेप *m.* Tossing, delay, insult, abuse, pride.

क्षेपक *a. m.* A spurious or interpolated passage.

क्षेपणि *f.* An oar; a net for fishing.

क्षेम *a.* Good, beneficial, prosperous, happy. *m. n.* Safety, peace, happiness, well-being, protection, final beatitude

क्षेम (मं) कर *a.* Propitious.

क्षै *vi.* 1. P (*pp.* क्षात) To wane.

क्षैण्य *n.* Destruction; slenderness.

क्षोड *m.* The post to which an elephant is fastened.

क्षोणि-(णी) *f.* The earth; number 'one' (in mathe.)

क्षोत्त *m.* Pounding, grinding; dust.

क्षोदक्षम *a.* Standing to scrutiny or investigation.

क्षोदिमन् *m.* Minuteness.

क्षोभ *m.* Agitation, emotion.

क्षोभण *n.* Agitating, disturbing.

क्षौणि (-णी) *f.* *See* क्षोणी.

क्षौणी-प्राचीर *m.* The ocean.

क्षौणीभुज (-पति) *m.* A king.

क्षौद्र *n.* Honey, water.

क्षौद्रज, (क्षौद्रेय) *n.* Wax.

क्षौम *m. n* Silken cloth.

क्षौर *n.* Shaving.

क्षौरिक *m.* A barber.

क्ष्णु *vt.* 2. P. (With सम् A) To whet, to sharpen.

क्ष्मा *f.* The earth, [king

क्ष्माप, (-पति,-भृत,-सुज्) *m.* A

क्ष्माभृत् *m.* A mountain.

क्ष्विद् *vi.* 4. P (*pp.* क्ष्विण्ण or क्ष्वेदित) To hum. With प्र-to murmur.

क्ष्वेड *m.* Sound, poison.

क्ष्वेडीत *n.* The roaring of a lion.

क्ष्वेला *f.* Play, jest, joke.

ख

ख *m.* The sun. *n.* The sky, heaven; a hole; an organ of sense; a city; a dot; a wound; happiness, pleasure; tale; Brahman (*n.*).-**उल्क** *m.* a meteor; a planet.

खग *m.* A bird, air, the sun; a planet, a grasshopper, a deity; an arrow.

खगस्थान *n.* The hollow of a tree; a bird's nest.

खगंगा *f.* The milky way.

खगम *m.* A bird. [sphere.

खगोल *m.* The celestial

खगोलविद्या *f.* Astronomy.

खचमस *m.* The moon.

खचर (**खेचर**) *m.* A bird; a demon; the sun; the wind; a cloud.

खचित *a.* Fastened, studded.

खज् *vi.* 1. P. To churn, to limp.

खजल *n.* Dew, rain, frost.

खजाक *m.* A bird.

खजिका *f.* A ladle, a spoon.

खज्योतिस् *m.* A fire-fly.

खंज *a.* Lame, crippled.

खंजन, (-**ना**,-**निका** *f.*) *m.* A species of the wag-tail. *n.* Going lamely.

खट *m.* Phlegm; a blind well; a hatchet; a plough; grass

खटिनी, (**खटी**) *f.* Chalk.

खट्टन *m.* A dwarf.

खट्टा *f.* A bedstead.

खट्टि *m. f.* A bier. [er.

खट्टिक *m.* A butcher; a fowl-

खट्वा *f.* A cot; a swing.

खट्वांग *m.* A club or staff with a skull at the top considered as the weapon of S'iva and carried by ascetics and yogins.

खड् *vt* 1. A (*pp.* **खंडित**) To break.

खडिका, **खडी** *f.* Chalk.

खड्ग *m.* A sword, the horn of a rhinoceros; a rhinoceros. *n* Iron.

खड्गिक *m.* A swordsman.

खड्गिन् *a.* Armed with a sword.

खंड *m. n.* A break; a piece, a chapter; a multitude, an assemblage. *m.* Candied sugar.

खंडकथा *f.* A short tale.

खंडकाव्य *n.* A small poem.

खंडधारा *f.* Scissors.

खंडपरशु (-**र्शु**) *m.* S'iva.

खंडपाल *m.* A confectioner.

खंडविकार *m.* Sugar.

खंडशर्करा *f.* Candied sugar.

खंडशस् *ind.* Bit by bit.

खंडशीला *f.* A loose woman.

खंडक *m. n.* A fragment.

खंडन *n.* Breaking; cutting, injuring, interrupting,

deceiving; refuting; rebellion, opposition.

खंडल *m. n.* A piece.

खंडिता *f.* A woman whose husband or lover has been guilty of infidelity.

खंडिनी *f.* The earth.

खतमाल *m.* A cloud; smoke.

खदिर *m.* Name of a tree.

खद्योत *m.* A fire-fly, the sun

खद्योतन *m.* The sun.

खधूप *m.* A rocket

खन् *vt.* I. U (*pp.* **खात**) To dig up. With अभि-to dig, उद्-to dig out, नि-to dig, परि-to dig round.

खनक *m.* A miner; a housebreaker; a rat; a mine.

खनि (-नी) *f.* A mine.

खनित्र *n.* A spade.

खपराग *m.* Darkness.

खपुष्प *n.* Anything impossible.

खभ *m.* A planet.

खमणि *m.* the Sun.

खमीलन *n.* Sleepiness, weariness.

खसिंधु *m.* The moon.

खस्तनी *f.* The earth.

खर *a.* Hard, acid; dense; hurtful, cruel. *m.* An ass, a mule; a heron; a crow; name of a demon.

खरदंड (-नाल) *n.* A lotus.

खरी *f.* A she-ass.

खरु *a.* White; foolish; cruel *m.* A horse; a tooth; pride.

खर्जन *n.* Scratching.

खर्जिका *f.* A venereal disease.

खर्जु *m.* The date tree.

खर्जू *f.* Itching.

खर्जूर *m.* The date tree.

खर्जूरी *f.* A date tree.

खर्पर *m.* A thief; a beggar's bowl; the skull; an umbrella; a piece of a broken jar.

खर्ब (-र्व) *a.* Mutilated, low, sharp. *m. n.* A large number.

खल् *vi.* 1. P. To move.

खल *m.n.* A threshing floor, earth, place, sediment. *m.* A villain.

खलपू *m. f.* A sweeper.

खलि (-ली) *f.* An oil-cake.

खलु *ind.* Indeed; pray!

खलेधानी(-वाली) *f.* The post of a threshing floor.

खल्ल *m.* A mortar.

खल्लिका *f.* A frying pan.

खल्लि (ल्ली) **ट** *a.* Bald-headed

खल्वाट *a.* Bald.

खसूचि *m. f.* An expression of reproach (at the end of a compound).

खसखस *m.* Poppy.

खाट *m.* (**खाटा, खाटिका, खाटी** *f.*) A bier.

खांडव *m.* Sugar-candy. *n.* Name of a forest burnt by *Agni*.

खांडिक,(खांडविक) *m.* A confectioner.

खात *a.* Dug up, torn. *a.* An excavation; a ditch.

खातक *m.* A digger.

खात्र *n.* A spade.

खाद् *vt.* 1. P. To eat.

खादक *m.* A debtor.

खादन *m.* A tooth.

खादुक *a.* Mischievous.

खाद्य *n.* Food, victuals.

खान *n.* Digging; injury.

खानि *f.* A mine.

खानिल *m.* A house-breaker.

खार *m.* A measure of grain.

खार्वा *f.* The *Treta* age.

खिंखिर *m.* A fox.

खिद् *vi.* 6. P. (*pp.* खिन्न) To strike. *vt.* or *vi.* 4, 7. A. To be depressed. With परि-to be distressed.

खिदिर *m.* An ascetic.

खिन्न *a.* Distressed.

खिल *m. n.* A piece of waste or uncultivated land; a supplement in general.

खिलीकृ 5, 8 U. To devastate, to make powerless; to be blocked up.

खुर *m.* A hoof, a razor; the foot of a bedstead.

खुल्ल *a.* Small, little.

खुल्लतात *m.* A father's younger brother.

खेचरी *f.* A semi-divine female able to fly; an epithet of Durgá

खेट *m.* A village.

खेटिन *m.* A libertine.

खेद *m.* Lassitude, exhaustion, pain.

खेल् *vt.* or *vi.* 1. P. To shake.

खेल *a.* Sportive.

खेलन *n.* Shaking; play, pastime.

खेला(-ली) *f.* Sport, play.

खोड (-र or ल) *a.* Lame.

खोलक *m.* A helmet; an ant-hill.

ख्या *vt.* or *vi.* 2 P. To tell. With अभि-to be known. आ-to tell, to call, परि or प्र-to be well-known. प्रत्या-to decline, to surpass, वि-to be famous. व्या-to explain, to name, सम्-to enumerate.

ख्याति *f.* Renown; a name.

ख्यापन *n.* Declaring, celebrating.

ग

ग *a.* Going. *m* A Gandharva; Ganes'a.

गगन (-ण) *n.* The sky, a cypher.

गगनकुसुम (-पुष्प) *n.* Any unreal thing, an impossibility.

गगनांगना *f.* A celestial nymph.

गगनेचर *m.* A bird; a planet; a heavenly spirit.

गंगा *f.* The river Ganges.

गंगाधर *m.* An epithet of Śiva

गंगापुत्र *m.* Bhîshma; Kárti-keya; a man of a mixed and vile caste, whose business is to remove dead bodies. A Bràh-mana who conducts pilgrims to the Ganges.

गंगालहरी *f.* Name of a well-known poem by Jagan-nath Pandita.

गंग(-गा or गि) का *f.* Ganges.

गच्छ *m.* A tree. [confused.

गज् *vi.* I. P To roar, to be

गज *m.* An elephant, a parti-cular measure of length.

गजगति *f.* A stately gait like that of an elephant.

गजगामिनी *f.* A woman with a stately elephant like gait.

गजदान *n.* The liquid exud-ing from the temples of an elephant.

गजनासा *f.* The trunk of an elephant.

गजमोटन *m.* A lion.

गजसाह्वय *n.* Hastinâpur.

गजस्नान *n.* Vain or unpro-ductive efforts resembling the ablution of elephants.

गंज *m.* A mine; a treasury; a cow-house; a grain mart.

गंजन *n.* Putting to shame.

गंजा,(गंजिका) *f.* A tavern.

गजानन,(गजास्य, गजमुख, &c) *m.* God Ganes'a.

गड् *vt.* 1 P. To draw.

गड *m.* A screen, a ditch.

गडु *a.* Crooked. *m.* A hump on the back; a water-pot; any useless object.[bent.

गडुर (-ल) *a.* Hump-backed,

गडेर *m.* A cloud.

गडोल *m.* A mouthful.

गण् *vt.* 10. U. To count, to class with; to add up; to compute; to regard as; to attribute to, to care for. With अधि-to praise; to enumerate अव-to dis-regard. परि-to count over; to consider, प्र-to calculate वि-to number, to dis-regard

गण *m.* A flock, a collection, a series of followers, a company.

गणकृत्वस् *ind.* For a number of times.

गणछंदस् *n.* A metre meas-ured by feet.

गणदेवता *f. pl.* Groups of particular deities.

गणद्रव्य *n.* Public property. common stock.

गणनाथ, (-नायक) *m.* S'iva or Ganes'a.

गणनायिका *f.* Durgâ.

गणप (-पति) *m.* A name of Ganes'a or S'iva. [bosom.

गणपीठक *n.* The breast, the

गणभोजन *n.* Eating in common.

गणरात्र *n.* A series of nights.

गणशस् *ind.* In troops, by classes.

गणक *a.* Bought for a large sum. *m.* An arithmetician, an astrologer.

गणकी *f.* The wife of an astrologer.

गणन *n.* Calculation: considering; enumerating.

गणना *f.* See **गणन**.

गणाधिप *m.* See **गणप** above.

गणिका *f.* A harlot.

गणित *n.* Reckoning, mathematics, a sum in general. [cian.

गणितिन् *m.* A mathemati

गणेरुका *f.* A procuress.

गणेश *m.* God Ganes'a.

गंड *m.* The cheek, whole side of the face including the temple; an elephant's temple; a bubble; a boil.

गंडकुसुम *n.* Rut, ichor.

गंडग्राम *m.* Any large village.

गंडदेश (-प्रदेश) *m.* The cheek.

गडफलक *n.* A broad cheek.

गंडभित्ति *f.* An expansive cheek.

गंडमाल *m.* (**-माला** *f.*) Inflammation of the glands of the neck.

गंडमूर्ख *a.* Very stupid.

गंडाशिला *f.* Any large rock.

गंडस्थल *n.* (**-स्थली** *f.*) The cheek, the temples of an elephant.

गंडक *m.* A rhinoceros; an obstacle; a knot; a boil.

गंडकी *f.* The name of a river

गंडिका *f.* A pebble; a beverage. [pion.

गंडीर *m.* A hero, a cham-

गंडु *m.* *f.* A pillow; a joint.

गंडूप *m.* (**-पा** *f.*) A mouthful.

गत *a.* Gone, dead, being in, connected with. *n.* motion, gait, an event.

गतप्रभ *a.* Bereft of splendour.

गतभर्तृका *f.* A widow; a woman whose husband is abroad. [age.

गतवयस्क *a.* Advanced in

गतानुगतिका *a.* Blindly following a custom or precedent.

गतायुस् *a.* Very old.

गतार्तवा *f.* A woman past child-bearing.

गति *f.* Gait, motion, scope, entrance, condition, expedient, procession; origin, knowledge, fate, a stage of life; refuge.

गत्वर *a.* Moving, transient.

गद् *vt.* 1. P. To speak; with नि-to declare.

गद *m.* Speech, disease.

गदा *f.* A mace, a club.

गदाधर *m.* Vishnu.

गद्गद *a.* Faltering. *m. n.* Indistinct utterance.

गद्य *n.* Prose composition.

गंतृ *a.* Going. [ask.

गंध् *vt.* 10. A. To injure, to

गंध *m.* Smell, the first member, a perfume, sulphur; pounded sandalwood; connection, arrogance; a small quantity. *n.* Smell.

गंधगज (-इभ,-द्विप,-हस्तिन्) *m.* The scent-elephant, an elephant of the best kind.

गंधकारिका *f.* A female servant whose business is to prepare perfumes.

गंधकेलिका (-चेलिका) *f.* Musk.

गंधज्ञा *f.* The nose. [nose.

गंधनालिका (-नाली) *f.* The

गंधमातृ *f.* The earth.

गंधमादन *m.* A large black bee; sulphur. *m. n.* Name of a mountain.

गंधवती *f.* The earth; wine; Satyavati, mother of Vyasa; a kind of jasmine.

गंधवह् *m.* The wind.

गंधवाह *m.* The wind; the musk-deer.

गंधसार *m.* Sandal.

गंधक *m.* Sulphur.

गंधन *n.* Perseverance; hurting, manifestation; hint.

गंधर्व *m.* A celestial musician, a horse; the soul after death and previous to its being born again; a singer, the black cuckoo.

गंधर्वविद्या *f.* The science of music.

गंधर्वविवाह *m.* A form of marriage; a love marriage.

गंधार *m. pl.* The name of a country and its rulers.

गंधाली *f.* A wasp. [ed.

गंधालु *a.* Fragrant, perfum-

गंधाष्टक *n.* A mixture of eight fragrant substances.

गंधिक *a.* Having the smell of. *m.* A seller of perfumes.

गभस्ति *m. f.* A ray of light, *m.* The sun. *f* The wife of *Agni*.

गभीर *a.* Deep, thick.

गभीरिका *f.* A deep sounding drum.

गम् *vt.* or *vi.* 1. P. (*pp.* गत To go, to elapse, to be the subject of; to have sexual intercourse with. With अति to pass away. अधि-to obtain, to go to, to accomplish, to understand अध्या-to find. अनु-to follow, to imitate, to visit. अप-go away from. अभि-to meet; अभ्या-to arrive, to come to. अभ्युद्-to advance, अभ्युप-to accept; अव-to know, to guess; आ-to come, उद्-to rise up, to go up, to originate, to be well-known, उप-to attain, to undergo, to acquire, to consent to; उपा-to approach, to obtain; नि-to obtain, निस्-to depart from, to remove. परा-to pervade, to return. परि-to walk round, to surround; to obtain; to know, to understand, पर्या-to finish, to subdue. प्र-to advance. प्रति-to return. प्रत्या-to come back. प्रत्युद्-to advance towards as a mark of respect, वि-to disappear, to pass away, विनिस्-to vanish, विप्र-to separate. सम् (Atm.) to meet, समधि-to approach; to study; to acquire, समव-to know completely. समुपा-to befall. Caus. (गमयति-ते) to lead, to explain; to signify; to pass (as time). With अव-to tell, आ-to bring, to teach; वि-to pass (as time). सम्-to bring together.

गम *a.* Going to, reaching, touching, *m.* March, a road; inconsiderateness, superficiality.

गमक *a.* Indicative of.

गमन *n.* Going, gait, march of an assailant; cohabitation.

गम्य *a.* Accessible, intelligible, fit for sexual intercourse; implied; suitable, curable.

गंभीर *a.* See गभीर *m.* A lotus; a citron.

गर *a.* Swallowing. *m.* A beverage; sickness, swallowing. *m. n* Poison.

गरण *n.* Swallowing.

गरभ *m.* See गर्भ.

गरल *m. n.* Poison.

गरा *f.* Swallowing.

गरिमन् *m.* Weight, importance, worth, one of the eight *siddhis.*

गरिष्ठ *a.* Heaviest; most important, &c. (Super. of गुरु.)

गरीयस् *a.* (Compar. of गुरु.)

गरुड (-ल) *m.* King of birds and the vehicle of Vishnu.

गरुत् *m* The wing of a bird.

गरुत्मत् *m.* Garuda; a bird.

गर्ग *m.* Name of a sage.

गर्गर *m*. A whirlpool.
गर्गरी *f* A churn.
गर्ज् *vi*. P. To thunder, to roar. With अनु to echo, प्रति-to roar at, to oppose.
गर्ज *m*. The roaring of elephants; the thunder.
गर्जन *n*. Sound, roaring, passion, war.
गर्त *m*. *n*. A hollow.
गर्ता *f*. A hole, a ditch.
गर्द् *vi*. 1.P.10. U.To sound.
गर्दभ *m*. An ass, smell.
गर्ध *m*. Greediness.
गर्धन, गर्धित *a*. Covetous.
गर्धिन् *a*. Desirous, greedy.
गर्भ *m*. The womb, belly, an embryo, the time of conception, a child; the interior; a hole; food; fire.
गर्भांक (गर्भैक) *m*. An interlude during an act.
गर्भकोश, (-ष) *m*. Uterus.
गर्भच्युति *f*. Delivery; miscarriage.
गर्भतृप्त *a*. Contented as regards food or issue.
गर्भदास *m*. A slave by birth.
गर्भधारण *n*.(-णा *f*.) Jestation.
गर्भपात *m*. Miscarriage after the fourth month of pregnancy.
गर्भयोषा *f*. A pregnant woman.
गर्भरूप (-रूपक) *m*. A child.
गर्भव्याकरण *n*. The formation of the embryo.
गर्भशय्या *f*. The uterus.
गर्भागार *n*. Uterus; a lying-in-chamber; the sanctuary of a temple.
गर्भाधान *n*. Impregnation; name of a purificatory ceremony.
गर्भावेक्षण *n*. Midwifery.
गर्भाशय *m*. Uterus; womb.
गर्भास्राव *m*. Miscarriage.
गर्भिणी *f*. A pregnant woman or animal.
गर्व् *vt*. 1. P. To be proud.
गर्व *m*. Pride, arrogance.
गर्वाट *m*. A watchman.
गर्ह् *vt*. 1. 10 A. to blame; with वि-to blame.
गर्हण *n*. (-णा *f*.) Censure, blame.
गर्हा *f*. Abuse, censure.
गर्ह्य *a*. Blameable.
गल् I. *vi*. 1. P To drop, to drop down, to disappear; with निस्-to ooze out, पर्या-to drop down, वि-to drop down; to disappear. *vt*. 1. P To swallow. *vt*. 10 A. To filter.
गल *m*. The throat, the neck.
गलगंड *m*. Goitre.
गलग्रह *m* (-ण *n*.) Throtting.
गलचर्मन् *n*. The gullet.
गलमेखला *f*. A necklace.
गलवार्त *a*. Healthy.

गलव्रत *m.* A peacock.

गलस्तनी (गलेस्तनी) *f.* A she-goat.

गलहस्त *m.* Seizing by the throat. [neck.

गलक *m.* The throat, the

गलन *n.* Oozing, melting.

गलंती A small water-jar with a hole in the bottom.

गलित *a.* Dropped, melted; loose; lost, impaired.

गलितकुष्ठ *n.* Advanced and incurable leprosy when the fingers and toes fall off.

गल्भ् *vi.* 1. A To be bold, with प्र-to be bold.

गल्भ *a.* Bold, confident.

गल्ल *m.* The cheek.

गल्ह् *vt.* 1. A To blame.

गवाक्ष *m.* An air-hole; a round window.

गवाक्षजाल *n.* A lattice.

गवादन *n.* (-नी *f.*) A posture.

गविनी *f.* A herd of cows.

गव्य *a.* Consisting of or proper for cattle or kine; produce of a cow (as milk). *n.* A multitude of cows.

गव्या *f.* A herd of cows.

गव्यूत *n.* (-ति *f.*) A distance of nearly two miles.

गवेरुक *n.* Red chalk.

गवेष् *vt.* 10. A to seek.

गवेष् *m.* Search, inquiry.

गवेषण *n.* (-णा *f.*) Search.

गह् *vt.* or *vi.* 10. U To be thick.

गहन *a.* Deep, thick, impenetrable;inexplicable, distressing.*n.* A forest, a hiding place; a pave; pain.

गह्वर *a.* Deep, *n.* An abyss, a thicket a cave a riddle; hypocricy. *m* A bower.

गह्वरी *f.* A cave a cavern.

गा *f.* A song, a verse.

गांग *a.* Belonging to the Ganges. *m.* Bhishma, Kartikeya.

गांगायनि(गांगेय)*m.*Bhîshma. Kartikeya.

गाजर *n.* A carrot.

गाढ*a.*Deeply entered;close, thick, strong. [much.

गाढम् *ind.* Closely, fast,

गाढमुष्टि *a.* Avaricious.

गाणपत *a.* Relating to Ganes'a.

गाणपत्य *m.* A worshipper of Ganes'a.

गांडिव (गांडीव) *m* *n.* The bow presented by Agni to Arjuna.

गांडीविन् *m.* Arjuna.

गातागतिक *a.* Caused by going and coming.

गातानुगतिक*a.* Caused by following or imitating custom or precedent.

गातु *m.* A song; a singer.

गातृ *m.* A singer.

गात्र *n*. The body, a limb.

गाथ *m*. A song, singing.

गाथ(थि)क *m*. A musician.

गाथा *f*. A verse; a Prakrit dialect.

गाथिका *f*. A song, a verse.

गाध् *vt*.or *vi*. 1.A To stand, to set out, to seek, to compile, to string together.

गाध *a*. Fordable. shallow.

गाधेय *m*. Viśvâmitra.

गान *n*. Singing, a song.

गांधर्व *a*.Relating or belonging to Gandharvas. *m*. A singer; one of the eight forms of marriage (a love marriage); a horse. *n*. Music.

गांधार *m*. The third of the seven primary notes of music; the modern Kandâhâr.

गांधारि *m*. Śakuni.

गांधारी *f*. Duryodhana's mother.

गांधारेय *m*. Duryodhana.

गांधिक *m*. A perfumer; a clerk. *n*. Perfumes.

गामिन् *a*. (Used at the end of compounds) Going, relating to, leading to.

गांभीर्य *n*. Depth.

गायक *m*. A singer. [hymn.

गायत्र *m*. *n*. A song, a

गायत्री *f*. A vedic metre; Name of a sacred verse repeated by every Brâhmana at his morning and evening devotion.

गायन *m*. A singer. *n*. Singing.

गारित्र *n*. Rice, corn.

गारुड *a*.Relating to Garuda. *m*. *n*. Gold; a charm.

गारुडिक *m*. A charmer.

गार्दभ *a*. Asinine.

गार्द्ध्य *n*. Greediness.

गार्ध्र *a*. Derived from a vulture. *m*. Greediness.

गार्भ (**गार्भिक**) *a*. Uterine.

गार्हपत *n*. The position and dignity of a householder.

गार्हपत्य *m*. One of the three sacred fires maintained by a householder.

गार्हस्थ्य *n*. The order or estate of a householder; the five daily *yajnas* of a householder.

गालन *n*. Straining fluids.

गालि *f*. A curse, abuse.

गाह् *vt*. 1. A (*pp*. **गाढ, गाहित**) To dive into, to range, to be absorbed in; to entertain; to agitate; to destroy. With **अव** or **उप**-to break in. **वि**-to bathe in, to pervade; **सम्**-to enter. [rior.

गाह *m*. Diving into, inte-

गिर् *f*. Speech, language, invocation, the goddess of learning.

गीःपति (गीर्पति, गीष्पति) *m.* Brihaspati; a learned man.

गीर्बाण (गीर्वाण) *m.* A god, a deity.

गिरा *f.* Speech, voice.

गिरि *a* Venerable, *m.* A mountain, an honorific title given to Sannyásins.

गिरिकाण *m.* A blind or one-eyed man.

गिरिजा *f.* A name of Pàrvat; the hill plantain; a pebble; the Ganges.

गिरिद्वार *n.* A mountain pass.

गिरिणितंब, (-नितंब, -प्रस्ताप) *m.* The declivity of a mountain.

गिरिप्रस्थ *m.* The table-land of a mountain.

गिरिसानु *n.* Table-land.

गिरिसार *m.* Iron; tin.

गिरीश *m.* The Himálaya mountain; S'iva

गिल् *vt.* 6 P. To swallow.

गिल *a.* Swallowing.

गिलग्राह *m.* A crocodile.

गीत *n.* Singing, a song.

गीतक *n.* A song.

गीता *f.* Sacred writings in verse, in the form of a dialogue and containing an exposition of certain religious doctrines. A term specially applied to the Bhagavadgítá.

गीति *f.* A song, name of a metre.

गीतिका *f.* A short song.

गीर्ण *a.* Swallowed.

गीर्त्ति *f.* Praise; fame.

गुच्छ, (-क) *m.* A bunch of flowers, the plumage of a peacock; necklace of pearls.

गुच्छपत्र *m.* The palm tree.

गुज् *vi.* 1. P. (*pp.* **गुजित** or **गुंजित**) To hum, to buzz.

गुंज *m.* Humming; a nosegay. [low.

गुंजन, (गुंजित) *n* Sounding

गुंजा *f.* A small shrub bearing a red black berry; a low murmuring sound; a small weight; reflection.

गुटिका, (गुटी) *f.* A pill; a pebble, the cocoon of the silk-worm; a pearl.

गुड *m.* Treacle, molasses, a globe, a mouthful.

गुडशर्करा *f.* Refined sugar.

गुडक *m.* A ball.

गुडाकेश *m.* Arjuna, S'iva.

गुडेर *m.* A ball, a mouthful.

गुण् *vt.* 10. U. To invite; to multiply.

गुण *m.* A thread, a bowstring, a sinew; a secondary element; a quality, property, virtue, an adjective, excess, an organ of sense; chord of an arc; the substitution of **ए, ओ, अर्** and **अल्** for **इ, उ, ऋ,**

and ऌ (short or long); repetition, multiplication; proper course of action (in politics); efficacy.

गुणक *m.* A calculator; a multiplier (in mathe.)

गुणकर्मन् *n.* An unessential or secondary action.

गुणकार *a.* Profitable.

गुणगृह्य *a.* Appreciative.

गुणग्रहण *n.* Appreciation of merit.

गुणग्राहक, (-ग्राहिन्) *a.* One who appreciates good qualities.

गुणज्ञ *a.* Appreciative.

गुणधर्म *m.* The virtue or duty incidental to the possession of certain qualities.

गुणन *n.* Multiplication; enumeration.

गुणनी *f.* Studying.

गुणनिका *f.* Study; repeated reading; dancing; the prologue to a drama; a garland, a cypher, (in mathe.)

गुणप्रकर्ष *m.* Great merit.

गुणलक्षण *n.* Mark indicative of an internal property

गुणवचन,(-वाचक)*m.* An adjective.

गुणिका *f.* A tumor, a swelling.

गुणित *a.* Multiplied; collected.

गुणिन् *a.* Principal; endowed with merits; auspicious.

गुंठ् *vt.* 10. U.(*pp.* गुंठित) To enclose with अव-to veil.

गुंठन *n.* Concealing, smearing.

गुंडक *m.* Dust.

गुण्य *a.* Endowed with virtues; to be multiplied.

गुत्स, (-क) *m.* See गुच्छ.

गुद् *vi.* 1 A. To play.

गुद *n.* The anus.

गुदग्रह, (-स्तंभ) *m.* Constipation.

गुध् *vt.* 4 P. To cover, to cloth. *vt.* 9. P. To be angry. *vi.* 1. A To play.

गुप् I *vt.* 1. P. (*pp.* गोपायित or गुप्त; *pres.* गोपायति) To protect, to conceal. *vt.* or *vi.* 1 A(*pres.* जुगुप्सते,गोपते) To censure, to conceal. *vi.* 4 To be confused or disturbed. *vt.* or *vi.* 10 U. To shine; to speak, to declare.

गुप्त *a.* Protected, hidden, *m.* An appellation peculiar to a Vaiśya.

गुप्तम् *ind.* Privately.

गुप्तगति (-चर) *m.* A spy.

गुप्ति *f.* Protection, concealing a hole in the ground, a fortification, a prison.

गुफ्, गुंफ् *vt.* 6.P. (*pp.* गुंफित) To string together, to compose.

गुंफ *m.* Tying, composing; a bracelet; a whisker.

गुंफना *f.* Good composition.

गुर् *vi.* 6. A. (*pp.* गूर्ण) To make an effort or exertion *vt.* 4. A. to injure.

गुरण *n.* Effort, perseverance.

गुरु *a.* (comp गरीयस्, super. गरिष्ठ) Heavy, great, difficult, excessive, best, dear, venerable, haughty. *m.* A father, a respectable person, an elderly relative, a teacher, chief; Brihaspati, the planet Jupiter, an epithet of Drona; Pushya.

गुरुकार *m.* Worship.

गुरुक्रम *m.* Traditional instruction.

गुरुतल्प (-तल्पग, -तल्पिन्) *m.* A violator of his preceptor's bed.

गुरुता *f.* (-त्व *n.*) Weight; dignity.

गुरुदक्षिणा *f.* Fee given to a spiritual preceptor.

गुरुलाघव *n.* Relative importance or value.

गुरुवासर *m.* Thursday.

गुर्विणी, गुर्वी *f.* A pregnant woman.

गुल्फ *m.* The ankle.

गुल्म *m.n.* A thicket, a bush; a troop of soldiers; the spleen. A police station; a wharf of stairs. (Mar. घाट)

गुह् *vt.* 1. U. (*pp.* गूढ; pres. गूहति-ते) To cover, to conceal. With उप to embrace, नि to hide; to conceal.

गुह *m.* Kârtikeya; a horse.

गुहा *f.* A cave, a pit; the heart; hiding, concealing.

गुहाशय *m.* A mouse; the supreme soul.

गुहिन *n.* A wood, a thicket.

गुहेर *m.* A guardian; a black-smith.

गुह्य *a.* Secret, solitary, mysterious. *m.* Hypocricy; a tortoise. *n.* A secret, an organ of generation.

गुह्यक *m.* An attendant of Kubera and guardian of his treasures.

गुह्यदीपक *m.* The fire-fly.

गू *f.* Dirt; ordure.

गूढ *a.* Concealed.

गूढज *m.* A son born secretly of a woman when her husband is absent, the real father being unknown.

गूढपुरुष *m.* A spy.

गूढात्मन् *m.* The supreme soul.

गृ *vt.* 1. P. To covet.

गृज् *vi.* 1. P (*pres.* गृंजति or गर्जति) To sound.

गृध् *vt.* 4. P. To covet.

गृधु *a.* Lustful.

गृध्नु *a.* Greedy.

गृध्य *n.* (-ध्या *f.*) Desire, greediness.

गृध्र *a.* Greedy, *m.n.* A vulture

गृध्रकूट *m.* Name of a mountain near Râjagriha.

गृध्रपति (-राज) *m.* Jatâyu.

गृष्टि *f.* A young cow.

गृह *n.* A house, a wife, the inhabitants of a house; a sign of the zodiac; a name. *m. pl.* A house.

गृहकरण (-कर्मन्, -कार्य) *n.* Household affairs.

गृहच्छिद्र *n.* A family secret.

गृहजालिका *f.* Deceit, disguise. [rant, stupid.

गृहज्ञानिन्, गृहेज्ञानिन् *m.* Igno-

गृहतटी *f.* A terrace in front of the house.

गृहनीड *m.* A sparrow.

गृहपति *m.* A householder; an adviser; a sacrificer.

गृहपाल *m.* A dog.

गृहभंग *m.* One who is driven from his house; breaking into a house; ruin of a family.

गृहभूमि *f.* The site of a house.

गृहभेदिन् *a.* Prying into domestic affairs; causing family quarrels.

गृहमणि *m.* A lamp.

गृहमेध *m.* A householder; a domestic sacrifice.

गृहमेधिन् *m* A house-holder.

गृहयाय्य *m.* A householder.

गृहस्थ *m* A house-holder.

गृहस्थाश्रम *m.* See गृहाश्रम.

गृहाक्ष *n.* A loop- hole. [er.

गृहायानिक *m.* A house-hold-

गृहार्थ *m.* House-hold affairs. [house-holder.

गृहाश्रम *m.* The order of a

गृहिणी *f.* A house-wife.

गृहिन् *m.* A house-holder.

गृहीत *a.* Taken, accepted.

गृह्य *a.* To be attracted or pleased; domestic; situated outside of. [city.

गृह्या *f.* A village near a

गॄ *vi.* 9. P. (*pp.* गूर्ण; *pres.* गृणाति) To proclaim, to speak, to praise; with अनु- to encourage. *vt.* 6. P(*pres.* गिरति, गिलति) To swallow, अव (Atm.) to eat, उद्-to vomit, नि-to swallow, सम्-to swallow; (Atm.) to promise, समुद् to eject; to cry aloud. *vt.* 10. A. (*pres.* गारयते) to relate.

गेय *a.* Singing. *n.* A song.

गेष् *vt.* 1. A(*pp.* गेष्ण) To seek.

गेह *n.* A house.

गेहिन् *a.* See गृहिन्.

गेहिनी *f.* A wife.

गेहेक्ष्वेडिन् *a.* A coward.

गेहेदाहिन् *a.* A coward.

गेहेमेहिन् *a.* Indolent.

गेहेव्याड *m.* A braggart.

गेहेशूर *m.* A carpet-knight.

गै *vt.* 1. P. (*pp.* गीत; *pres.* गायति) To sing, to relate, अव-to censure, उद् to sing aloud, उप-to sing near, परि-to describe, वि-to censure.

गैर(-रिक)*a.* Mountain-born.

गो *m. f.* Cattle; produce of a cow; the stars; the thunderbolt; the sky; a ray of light; a diamond. *f.* A bow; the earth; a mother; speech; a quarter of the compass; water (*pl.*); the eye; an arrow. *m.* A bull; the hair of the body; an organ of sense; the sign Taurus of the zodiac; the sun; the number 'nine' an arrow.

गोकिल (-कील) *m.* A plough.

गोकुल *n.* A herd of kine; name of a town where Krishna was brought [up.

गोकृत *n.* Cowdung.

गोग्रंथि *m.* Dried cow-dung; a cow-house.

गोग्रास *m.* Offering a morsel of grass to a cow.

गोचर *a.* Grazed over by cattle; frequented; within the range of; moving on the earth; accessible. *m.* Pasturage, district, power, control; the horizon.

गोचारक *m.* A cowherd.

गोत्र *n.* A cowpen; lineage; a name; a multitude; forest; a road; wealth; an umbrella. *m.* A mountain.

गोत्रज *a.* A near relation.

गोत्रपट *m.* A genealogical table; *a.* pedigree.

गोत्रभिद् *m.* Indra.

गोदंत *n.* A yellow orpiment.

गोदा (-वरी) *f.* The river Godávarî.

गोदान *n.* The gift of a cow; the ceremony of tonsure.

गोधन *n.* A herd of cows.

गोधर *m.* A mountain.

गोधुम (-धूम) *m.* Wheat, the orange.

गोधूलि *m.* Evening twi- [light.

गोध्र *m.* A mountain.

गोप *m.* A cowherd, a king.

गोपाल *m.* A cowherd, a king Krishna.

गोपुर *n.* A town-gate; the ornamental gateway of a temple.

गोपुरीष *n.* Cow-dung.

गोप्रचार *m.* Pasturage.

गोप्रवेश *m.* Evening twilight.

गोभृत् *m.* A mountain.

गोमंडल *n.* The globe.

गोमय *m. n.* Cowdung.

गोमायु *m.* A jackal.

गोमुख *m. n.* A kind of musical instrument, a crocodile, a hole of a particular shape in a wall made by thieves.

गोमुखी *f.* A cloth-bag containing a rosary

गोमूढ *n.* A stupid person.

गोमूत्र *n*. Cow's urine.
गोमेद *m*. A kind of gem.
गोरक्ष *m* A cowherd.
गोरस *m*.Cow's milk; curds.
गोरोचना *f*.A bright yellow pigment prepared from the urine or bile of a cow.
गोलोमी *f*. A prostitute.
गोवर्धन *m*.A celebrated hill in the country about Mathurá.
गोविंद *m*. A cow-keeper; Krishna; Brihaspati.
गोविसर्ग *m*. Daybreak.
गोवीर्य *n*. The price received for milk.
गोवृंदारक *m*. An excellent bull or cow.
गोव्रज *m*. A herd of cows.
गोसर्ग *m*. The time.
गोस्तना (-स्तनी) *f*. A bunch of grapes.
गोस्वामिन् *m*. An owner of cows; a religious mendicant;an honorary title affixed to proper names.
गोणी *f*. A sack; a measure of capacity. [Gotama.
गोतमी *f*. Ahalyá, wife of
गोधा *f*. The alligator.
गोधि *m*. The forehead.
गोधिका *f*.A kind of lizard.
गोप *m*. Guarding concealment; abuse; agitation; light.
गोपायन *n*. Protecting.
गोपायित *a*. Protected.
गोप्तृ *a*. A protector.*m*. An epithet of Vishnu.
गोप्य*m*.The son of a female slave.
गोरण *n*. Energy.
गोर्द *n*. Brain.
गोल (-क) A ball, the celestial or terrestrial globe;a widow's bastard; a conjunction of six planets.
गोला *f*. A wooden ball;red arsenic; ink. [assemble.
गोष्ठ् *vt*. I A. (गोष्ठते) To
गोष्ठ *m*. *n*. A cowhouse. *m*. An assembly; God S'iva.
गोष्ठि (-ष्ठी) *f*. An assembly, conversation, relatives requiring maintenance, a multitude.
गोष्ठपंडित *a*. A vain boaster.
गोहिर *n*. The wheel.
गोह्य *a*. Secret.
गौड *m*. Name of a country; a particular sub-division of Bráhmanas.
गौडा *f*.Spirit distilled from molasses; one of the styles of poetic composition.
गौण *a*. Subordinate, unessential, figurative.
गौण्य *n*. Subordination.
गौर *a*. White, yellowish, brilliant.*n*.Saffron;gold.
गौरव *n*. Weight, import-

ance, dignity, cumbrousness, respect; depth of meaning, length of a syllable (in prosody).

गौरवित *a.* Highly esteemed.

गौरिका *f.* A virgin.

गौरिल *m.* White mustard; dust of iron.

गौरी *f.* A name of Pârvatî; a young girl eight years old; a woman with a white or yellowish complexion; the earth; turmeric; a yellow dye (called गोरोचना); the wife of Varuna.

गौरीकांत (-नाथ) *m.* Śiva.

गौरीगुरु *m.* The Himâlayas.

ग्मा *f.* The earth.

ग्रथ् *vi.* 1. A. (pres. ग्रंथते) To be crooked or wicked.

ग्रथन *n.* Coagulation, stringing together; composing.

ग्रथित *a.* strung together; composed.

ग्रथ्न *m.* A cluster, a bunch.

ग्रंथ् *vt.* 9. P, 10. U (*pp.* ग्रथित *pres* ग्रथ्नाति, ग्रंथयति-ते) To fasten, to compose, with उद्-to untie, to tie up.

ग्रंथ *m.* Binding, composition, a book, wealth, a verse consisting of 32 syllables written in the Anushtubh metre.

ग्रंथकार (-कृत्) *m.* An author.

ग्रंथकुटी (-कुटी) *f.* A library.

ग्रंथविस्तर (-विस्तार) *m.* Voluminousness.

ग्रंथसंधि *m.* A section or chapter of a work.

ग्रंथन *n.* See ग्रथन.

ग्रंथि *m.* A knot, joint; distortion; falsehood; wealth.

ग्रंथिबंधन *n.* Tying together the garments of the bride and the bridegroom at the marriage ceremony.

ग्रंथिहर *m.* A minister.

ग्रंथिक *m.* An astrologer.

ग्रंथिन् *m.* One who reads books, bookish.

ग्रंथिल *a.* Knotted, knotty.

ग्रस् *vt.* 1. A. To swallow; to seize; to eclipse, to destroy; सम्-to destroy, 1. P., 10. U To eat, to devour.

ग्रसन *n.* Swallowing, a partial eclipse of the sun or moon.

ग्रस्त *a.* Eaten, seized; eclipsed.

ग्रस्तास्त *n.* The setting of the sun or moon while eclipsed.

ग्रस्तोदय *m.* Rising of the sun or moon while eclipsed.

ग्रह् *vt.* 9. U. (*pp.* गृहीत; *desid.* जिघृक्षति) To seize, to receive, to attract, to persuade, to satisfy, to possess as by a spirit, to assume, to buy, to learn, to wear, to mention, to perceive. अनु-to favour, अनुसम्-to salute humbly. अप-to tear off. अभि-to seize, forcibly. अव-to oppose आ-to persist in. उद्-to raise; to deposit. उप-to provide, to support, नि-to curb, to close (as the eyes), to apprehend. to punish. परि-to embrace; to assume; to hold; to curb, to stretch forth; प्रति-to take, to accept, to oppose, to take in marriage, to obey, वि-to quarrel, सम्-to collect, to receive kindly; to unstring a bow. *vt*. 1. P. 10-U. To take, to receive.

ग्रह *m*. Grasp, stealing, robbing, receipt; an eclipse; a planet; a crocodile; separating, perception; perseverance; design; favour.

ग्रहदशा *f*. The aspect of a planet. [punishment.

ग्रहनिग्रह *m. du*. Favour and

ग्रहनेमि *m*. The moon.

ग्रहपति *m*. The sun; the moon.

ग्रहपीडन *n*. (-पीडा *f*.) Oppression caused by a planet; an eclipse. [of planets.

ग्रहयुति *f*. The conjunction

ग्रहविप्र *m*. An astrologer.

ग्रहण *n*. Acceptance, putting on; an eclipse; the hand; an organ of sense; mentioning; comprehension, echo. [star.

ग्रहाधार (-श्रय) *m*. The polar

ग्रहणि (-णी) *f*. Diarrhœa, dysentery.

ग्रहिल *a*. Stiff, unyielding.

ग्रहीतृ *a*. A taker, perceiver, a debtor.

ग्राम *m*. A village, a collection, a scale in music.

ग्रामकुक्कुट *m*. The domestic cock.

ग्रामकूट *m*. The noblest man in a village; a S'ûdra.

ग्रामगृह्य *a*. Being outside a village. [course.

ग्रामचर्या *f*. Sexual inter-

ग्रामचैत्य *m*. A sacred figtree of a village.

ग्रामजाल *n*. A number of villages, a district.

ग्रामणी *m*. The leader of a village or community; a barber, a whore. [ter.

ग्रामतक्ष *m*. A village carpen-

ग्राममुख *m*. A market.

ग्राममृग (-सिंह) *m*. A dog.

ग्रामिक *a*. Rude. rustic. *m*. The headman of a village.

ग्रामीण *m*. A villager, a dog, a crow; a hog.

ग्रामेय *a.* Village-born.
ग्रामेयी *f.* A prostitute.
ग्राम्य *a.* Rustic, tame, cultivated, vulgar.
ग्राम्याश्व *m.* An ass.
ग्रावन् *m.* A stone, a mountain, a cloud.
ग्रास *m.* Mouthful, food, the part of the sun or moon eclipsed.
ग्राह *a.* Seizing *m.* A crocodile, a prisoner; knowledge; importunity; determination; belief.
ग्राहक *a.* One who receives; a hawk.
ग्रीवा *f.* The neck.
ग्रीष्म *a.* Hot. *m.* The summer heat.
ग्रैव, ग्रैवेय *a.* Belonging to the neck. *n.* A necklace; a chain worn round the neck of an elephant.
ग्रैष्मक *a.* Sown in summer.
ग्लपन *n.* Withering; exhaustion.
ग्लस् *vt.* 1. A. to eat.
ग्लह *m.* A dice-player; a stake, gambling.
ग्लान *a.* Languid, exhausted.
ग्लानि *f.* Exhaustion, weakness; decline.
ग्लुच् *vt.* 1. P. (*pp.* ग्लुक्त) To go, to steal.
ग्लै *vi.* (pp. ग्लान; *pres* ग्लायति; caus. ग्लपयति or ग्लापयति) To dislike to be languid, to fade away, to decline. [phor.
ग्लौ *m.* The moon; cam-

घ

घ *a.* (Used only as the last member of compounds) Killing, *m.* A pitcher.
घट् *vi.* 1. A. To be busy with, to reach, to happen; with प्र-to commence, वि-to be disunited, to break down, सम्-to be united, to unite, to put-on, to shape, to effect, to impel; *vi.* or *vt.* 10. U. to kill, to collect. उद्-to open to reveal, 10. U. (*pres.* घण्टयति-ते) To speak.
घट *m.* A a pitcher, the sign *Aquarius* (कुंभ) of the zodiac.
घटज, (-योनी,-संभव) *m.* The sage अगस्त्य. [udder.
घटोध्नी *f.* A cow with a full
घटकर्पर *m.* The name of a poet; a piece of a broken jar.
घटकार (-कृत्) *m.* A potter.
घटदासी *f.* A procuress.
घटक *a.* Accomplishing. *m.* A match-maker; a constituent; a genealogist.
घटन *n.* घटना *f.* Effort, occurrence. [an assembly.
घटा *f.* Effort, a collection,

घटाटोप *m*. A covering for a carriage.

घटिक *m*. A waterman. *n*. The hip.

घटिका, घटी *f*. A small vessel of clay; a measure of time equal to24 minutes.

घटिंघम *m*. A potter. [erful.

घटिंधय *a*.Drinking a pitch-

घटियंत्र *n*. An Indian contrivance for raising water; a clock or watch.

घटोद्भव *m*. The sage अगस्त्य.

घट्ट *vt*.1. A to shake, to rub. *vt*.10.U to disturb. With अव-to open, परि to strike, वि-to strike, to rub, to open (as a door). सम्-to rub, to strike; to gather.

घट्ट *m*. A *Ghaut* a landing place; a toll-station.

घट्टकुटी *f*. A toll-station.

घट्टना *f*. Shaking, means of livelihood.

घंटा *f*. A bell, a gong.

घंटापथ *m*. The chief road.

घण्टिका *f*. A small bell.

घण्ड *m*. A bee.

घन *a*. Compact solid, fully developed; excessive; auspicious. *m*. A cloud, a mace; the body; the cube of a number (in mathe); a multitude. *n*. A symbol, gong; iron; tin; bark.

घनगोलक *m*. Alloy of gold and silver.

घननाभि *m*. Smoke.

घनपदवी *f*.(-वर्त्मन् *n*.)The sky.

घनफल *n*. The solid or cubical contents of a body.

घनमूल *n*. Cube-root (in mathe.).

घनरस *m*.Extract, decoction

घनवाल्लिका (-वल्ली) *f*. Lightning.

घनवाहन *m*. S'iva; Indra.

घनसार *m*. Camphor, mercury; water. [season.

घनाकर, घनागम *m*.The rainy

घनांबु *n*. Rain.

घनाश्रय *m*. The atmosphere.

घनोत्पल *m*. Hail-stone.

घनाघन *m*. Indra; a showering cloud.

घरट्ट *m*. A grinding stone.

घर्घर *a*. Indistinct gurgling noise. [sweat.

घर्म *m*. Heat, the hot season;

घर्मान्त *m*.The rainy season.

घर्मांबु or **घर्मांभस्** *n* Sweat.

घर्मांशु *m*. The sun.

घर्ष, *m*. (-ण *n*.) Rubbing.

घस् *vt*. 1. P. (a defective verb) To eat.

घस्मर *a*. Voracious.

घस्र *a*. Hurtful, *m* A day.

घात *m*.A blow destruction, an arrow; the product of a sum in multiplication.

घातचंद्र *m*. The moon when

in an inauspicious lunar mansion. [lunar day.

घाततिथि *f.* An inauspicious

घातनक्षत्र *n.* An inauspicious constellation.

घातवार *m.* An inauspicious day of the week. [derer.

घातक(-न) *a.* A killer, a mur-

घातुक *a.* Killing, cruel.

घात्य *a.* Proper to be killed.

घास *m.* Food; grass.

घु *vi.* I. A. To sound.

घुट् *vt.* 1. A. To return; to exchange *vt.* 6. P. to retaliate.

घुट *m.* (घुटी *f.*, घुटिक *m.*) The ankle. [take.

घुण् *vi.* 1. A, 6. P. To roll, to

घुण *m.* A kind of insect.

घुणाक्षर *n.* An incision in wood or in the leaf of a book made by an insect.

घुणाक्षरन्याय *m.* A maxim for any chance occurrence.

घुर् *vi.* 6. P. To grunt.

घुरी *f.* The nostrils of a hog.

घुर्घुर *m.* Guinea-worm; growling.

घुष् *vt.* 1. P. 10 U. (*pp.* घुषित or घुष्ट). To proclaim; with आ-to announce; to weep. उद्-to proclaim.

घूक *m.* An owl.

घूर्ण् *vi.* 6. U. To whirl.

घूर्ण *a.* Moving to and fro.

घूर्णवायु *m.* The whirl-wind.

घूर्णन *n* (ना *f.*) or **घूर्णि** *f.* Whirling round.

घृ *vt.* 1. P To sprinkle. 10. U. To cover. [shine.

घृण् *vi.* 8. P. (*pp.* घृण्ण) To

घृण *m* Heat; sunshine; a day.

घृणा *f.* Compasion, reproach.

घृणालु *a.* Compassionate.

घृणि *m.* Heat, sunshine; a wave. *n.* Water.

घृत *n.* Ghee, butter; water.

घृतकुल्या *f.* A stream of ghee.

घृतदीधिति *m.* Fire.

घृताची *a.* Greasy; *n. f.* Night; Name of Saraswatî; also of an *apsaras.*

घृष् *vt.* 1. P. (*pp.* घृष्ट) To rub, to strike against, to crush, to rival. With उद्-to scratch, सम्-to rival.

घृष्टि *m.* A hog. *f.* Grinding, rubbing; emulation.

घोटी or **घोटिका** *f.* A mare.

घोण(न)स *m.* A sort of reptile.

घोणा *f.* The nose.

घोणिन् *m.* A hog.

घोंट, (-क) *m* A horse.

घोर *a.* Terrific, violent. *n.* Horror. poison. *m* S'iva.

घोरा *f* A night

घोष *m.* Noise, the thundering of clouds; a proclamation;a herdsman;a hamlet, a Kâyastha.

घोषण n. (-णा f.) Proclamation.

घोषवती f. A lute.

घ्न a. Killing, destroying.

घ्रा vt 1. P (pp घ्रात or घ्राण: pres. जिघ्रति) To smell.

घ्राण p.p.Smelt. n The act of smelling;odour; nose.

घ्राति f. The nose; smell.

च.

च ind. And, alone, moreover,as well as;never the less, yet, certainly; if. m. The moon;a tortoise; a thief.

चक् vt. 1. To be satisfied; to resist.

चकास् vt. 2. U. To shine. With वि-to shine.

चकित a. Trembling; fearful; timid, startled.

चकोर m. A kind of bird.

चक्र n.The wheel of a carriage, a potter's wheel, a disc, an oil-mill; a ring; a form of military array; a circle;a cycle;the horizon;a multitude;an arm; a province,a section of a book; sovereignty; a whirlpool. m. The ruddy goose.

चक्रक a. Circular.

चक्रगति f.Revolution.

चक्रग्रहण n. (-णी f.) A rampart.

चक्रधर m.Vishnu; a sovereign or governor; a snake.

चक्रनेमि f. The circumference of a wheel.

चक्रपाणि m. Vishnu.

चक्रवा (वा) ल m. n. A ring; a multitude; horizon.

चक्रभेदिनी f. The night.

चक्रभ्रम (चक्रभ्रमी f.) A turner's lathe.

चक्रवर्तिन् m. An emperor.

चक्रवाक m.The ruddy goose

चक्रवृद्धि f. Compound interest.

चक्रांग m.A gander having a curved neck;the ruddy goose; a carriage.

चक्राट m. A juggler;a rogue; a particular coin, a Dinára

चक्रायुध m.Vishnu.

चक्रावर्त m.A whirling motion.

चक्ष् vt. 2. A. (pres.चष्टे) To see,to speak,to abandon.

चक्षस् m.A teacher;Brihaspati. n. Radiance; sight.

चक्षुःश्रवस् m. A serpent.

चक्षुस् n. The eye ; vision.

चक्षूराग m Redness in the eyes;love as expressed by an exchange of glances.

चक्षुष्य a. Good-looking.

चंकुर m A tree, a carriage.

चंक्रमण n. Running

चंच् vt. 1 P To leap, to dangle.

चंचरिन् (-रीक) *m.* The large black bee.

चंचल *a.* Moving, fickle. *m.* The wind; a lover. [mî.

चंचला *f* Lightning; Laksh-

चंचु *a.* Celebrated, clever. *m.* A deer. *f.* A beak.

चंचुपुट *m. n.* The bill of a bird when shut.

चंचुभृत् (-मत्) *m.* A bird.

चंचुर *a.* Clever, expert.

चंचू *f.* A beak.

चट् *vt.* 1. P To break. *vt.* 10. U. To kill; with उद्-to kill, to terrify; to remove.

चटक *m.* A sparrow.

चटु *m. n.* Flattering discourse. *m.* The belly.

चटुल *a.* Trembling, unsteady.

चटुला *f.* Lightning.

चण *a.* Renowned.

चणक *m.* The chick-pea.

चंड *a.* Fierce, passionate, active, pungent. *n.* Heat, passion.

चंडांशु *m.* The sun.

चंडा (-डी) *f* Durgá, a passionate lady.

चंडीश्वर *m.* S'iva.

चंडाल *a.* Wicked. *m.* The lowest and most despised of the mixed tribes.

चंडिका *f.* A name of Durgâ.

चंडिमन् *m.* Passion, heat.

चंडिल *m* A barber.

चतुर *a.* (nom. *pl.* चत्वार *m.* चतस्रः *f.* चत्वारि *n.*) Four.

चतुरंग *a.* Consisting of four members. *n.* An entire army consisting of foot, horse, elephants and chariots; a sort of chess.

चतुरंत *a.* Bordered on all sides. [four.

चतुरशीति *a.* or *f.* Eighty-

चतुरस्र *a.* Quadrangular; symmetrical. *m.* A square.

चतुरानन *m.* Brahman (*m.*).

चतुष्कर्ण *a.* Heard by two persons only.

चतुष्कोण *a* Quadrangular; *m.* A square. [ruple.

चतुर्गुण *a.* Fourfold, quad-

चतुश्चत्वारिंश *a.* Forty-fourth

चतुर्थक *m.* An intermittent fever returning every four days.

चतुर्थभाज् *a.* Receiving a fourth part of all income from the subjects as a king

चतुर्थी *f.* The fourth day of a lunar fortnight; the dative case in grammar.

चतुर्दशी *f.* The fourteenth day of a lunar fortnight.

चतुर्दिशम् *ind.* On all sides.

चतुर्धा *ind.* In four ways, fourfold [human life.

चतुर्भद्र *n.* The four ends of

चतुर्भुज *a.* Quadrangular. *m.* Vishnu. *n.* A square.

चतुर्वर्ग *m*. The four ends of hnman life (पुरुषार्थ.)

चतुर्वर्ण *m*. The four castes of the Hindus. [fourfold.

चतुर्विध *a*. Of four kinds,

चतुर्वेद *a*. Familiar with the four *Vedas*.

चतुर्व्यूह *n*. Medical science.

चतुःपंच(चतुष्पंच) *a*. Four or five.

चतुःपथ (चतुष्पथ) *m*. *n*. A place where four roads meet; a crossway.

चतुःशाली *f*. A quadrangle enclosed by four buildings.

चतुष्पद *m*. A quadruped.

चतुष्पदी *f*. A stanza of four lines.

चतुष्पाठी *f*. A school in which the four *Vedas* are repeated.

चतुष्पाद् *m*. A quadruped; a judicial proceeding.

चतुष्क *a*. Consisting of four. *n*. A quadrangular courtyard. [tain.

चतुष्की *f*. A mosquito-cur-

चतुष्टय *n*. A group of four.

चत्वर *n*. A quadrangular place.

चत्वारिंशत *f*. Forty.

चंदन *m*. *n*. Sandal. [moon.

चंदिर *m*. An elephant; the

चंद्र *m*. The moon the eye in a peacock's tail; camphor; water; gold.

चंद्रक *m*. The moon; the eye in a peacock's tail; a finger-nail

चंद्रकांत *m*. The moon-gem. *m*. *n*. The white water-lily. *n*. Sandalwood.

चंद्रकला *f*. A digit of the moon. [light.

चंद्रकांता *f*. A night; moon-

चंद्रचूड(-मौलि,-शेखर,-चूडामणि) *m*. An epithet of S'iva.

चंद्रमस् *m*. The moon.

चंद्ररेखा(-लेखा) *f*. The streak of the moon.

चंद्रवंश *m*. The lunar race of kings. [ing nasality.

चंद्रबिंब *m*. The sign express-

चंद्रशाला (-शालिका) *f*. An apartment on the top of a house; moonlight.

चंद्रहास *m*. A glittering sword.

चंद्रिका *f*. Moonlight; illumination; elucidation.

चप् *vt*. 10. U. To grind, to pound *vt*. 1. P To console *vt*. 10. U (*pres*. चंपयति-ते) To go, to move.

चपल *a*. Trembling, rash; unsteady, swif .

चपला *f* Lightning; a disloyal wife; a spirituou. liquor; Lakshmí; tongue.

चपेट *m*.(टा,-टिका *f*.) A blow with the open hand.

चम् *vt*. 1. P. (*pp*. चांत; with

आ *pres.* आचामति) To sip; with आ-to sip, to remove.

चमत्करण *n.* **चमत्कार** *m.* **चमत्कृति** *f.* Admiration, show, poetical charm.

चमर *m.* A kind of deer. *m. n.* A chowrie.

चमरी *f.* The female Chamara.

चमू *f.* An army; a division of an army consisting of 729 elephants, 729 cars, 2187 horses and 3645 foot.

चमूरु *m.* A kind of deer.

चंपक *m.* A tree bearing yellow fragrant flowers, or its flower.

चंपकमाला *f.* Name of a neck-ornament worn by women; a kind of a metre.

चंपकावती (**चंपा, चंपावती**) *f.* Capital of the Angas. (modern Bhâgalpur).

चंपू *f.* A kind of elaborate and artificial composition.

चय् *vt.* 1. A. To move.

चय *m.* An assemblage, a heap, a mound of earth, a rampart; the gate of a fort; a stool; gathering flowers, &c.

चयन *n.* The act of collecting(especially flowers, &c)

चर् *vt.* 1. P. To go, to act towards, to live, to practise, to graze. With अति to transgress, to offend, अनु-to follow. अन्वा-to imitate. अप-to disregard, अभि-to deceive, आ-to wander over or about; to behave towards. उद्-to originate, to pronounce, to ascend,(Atm)to transgress, उप-to serve, to treat medically. दुस्-to deceive, परि-to serve, to nurse, प्र-to stalk; to spread, to prevail. वि-to wander about; to perform. व्यभि-to be faithless, सम्-(Par. and Atm.) to move, to walk about, to perform.

चर *a.* Moving, shaking; moveable, animate, formerly (when used as an affix). *m.* A spy; a cowrie.

चरक *m.* A spy; a wandering mendicant.

चरण *m. n.* A foot, a pillar, the single line of a stanza. A school of any of the Vedas; a quarter. *n.* Moving, wandering; performance, conduct of life; accomplishment; eating.

चरणग्रंथि *m.* (-**पर्वन्** *n.*) The ankle.

चरणन्यास *m.* A footstep.

चरम *a.* Last, outermost, western, least.

चरमम् *ind.* At last.

चरित *n.* Practice, behaviour, life.

चरितार्थ *a.* Successful, contented.

चरित्र *n.* Behaviour, per formance, observance; nature;biography; duty.

चरिष्णु *a.* Moveable, active.

चरु *m.* Rice, barley and pulse boiled for presentation to the gods and the manes.

चर्च् *vt.* 10. U. to study. *vi.* 6. P To abuse, to discuss.

चर्चा, चर्चिका *f.* Study, discussion; smearing the body with unguents.

चर्पट *m.* The open palm of the hand with the fingers extended. [flour.

चर्पटी *f.* A thin cake of

चर्म *n.* A shield. [shield.

चर्मन् *n.* Skin; leather; a

चर्मकार (-कारिन्)*m.* A shoemaker.

चर्मचित्रक*n.* White leprosy.

चर्मज *n.* Hair; blood. [bal.

चर्मण्वती *f.* The river Cham-

चर्मतरंग *m.* A wrinkle.

चर्मदंड *m.* (-नालिका *f.*) A whip.

चर्मपादुका *f.* A leather shoe.

चर्मप्रसेवक *m.* (-प्रसेविका *f.*) A bellows.

चर्ममय *a.* Leathern.

चर्मयष्टि *f.* A whip.

चर्मवसन *m.* S'iva. [maker.

चर्मरु (चमार) *m.* A shoe-

चर्या *f.* Moving; behaviour, practice, usage.

चर्व् *vt.* 1. P. 10. U. To eat, to chew, to relish. [ing.

चर्वण*n.*(-णा *f.*) Eating, tast-

चर्वितचर्वण*n.* Vain and profitless reiteration.

चल् *vi.* 1. P. To stir, to go, to be disturbed, to swerve; उद्-to fly from, to set out, प्र-to tremble. वि-to be agitated, to move, to proceed.*vi.* 6.P. 1 o sport *vt* 10. U. To foster.

चल *a.* Shaking, loose, unsteady. *m.* Agitation, wind; quic-ksilver.

चलाचल*a.*Fickle, unsteady. *m.* A crow. [Motion.

चलन *m.* A foot; a deer. *n.*

चला *f.* Lakshmî.

चलु *m.* A mouthful.

चलुक *m.* A handful.

चष् *vt.* 1. U.To eat. *vt.* 1. P To kill. [honey.

चषक *m. n.* A wine-glass;

चाकचक्य *n.* Brilliancy.

चाक्र *a.* Circular; relating to a wheel.

चाक्रिक *a.* See **चाक्र.** *m.* A potter; an oilmaker; a coachman.

चाक्षुष *a.* Optical; visible.*n.* Knowledge dependent on vision. [dence.

चाक्षुषज्ञान *n.* Ocular evi-

चांचल्य *n.* Unsteadiness, quick motion, transitoriness.

चाट *m.* A cheat. [flattery.

चाटु *m.n.* Pleasing words,

चाटुकार *a.* Speaking sweetly

चाटुबटु *m.* A buffoon. [ulous

चाटुलोल *a.* Elegantly trem-

चाणक्य *m.* Name of a celebrated writer on civil polity.

चातक *m.* Name of a bird which is supposed to live only on rain-drops.

चातुर *a.* Relating to four; clever, flattering.

चातुरिक *m* A charioteer.

चातुरी *f.* Dexterity, skill.

चातुर्थक(-र्थिक) *n.* Occurring every fourth day.

चातुर्दश *n.* A demon.

चातुर्मास्य *n.* Name of the sacrifice performed every four months.

चातुर्य *n.* Dexterity, skill.

चातुर्वर्ण्य *n.* The four original castes of the Hindus. [sion.

चातुर्विध्य *n.* Fourfold divi-

चांद्र *a.* Lunar.

चांद्रमस *a.* Lunar. *n.* The constellation मृगशिरस्.

चांद्रमास *m.* A lunar month.

चांद्रायण *n.* A religious observance regulated by the waxing and waning of the moon.

चांद्री *f.* Moon-light.

चाप *m. n.* A bow; an arc of a circle; the ninth sign of the zodiac.

चापल (-ल्य) *n.* Quick motion; a rash act.

चामर *m. n.* A *chowrie.*

चामरिन् *m.* A horse.

चामीकर *n.* Gold.

चामुंडा *f.* Durgâ.

चार *m.* A spy, motion, performing, walking, prison.

चारक *m.* A spy; a herdsman; an associate; a groom; a prison.

चारचक्षुस् (-ईक्षण) *m.* A statesman or king who employs spies.

चारचंचु *a.* Graceful in gait.

चारण *m* A wanderer, a dancer, a celestial singer; a reader of scriptures; a spy [ant.

चारिका *f.* A female attend-

चारितार्थ्य *n* Attainment of an object; successfulness.

चारित्र *n.* Conduct, reputation, hereditary observance, temperament.

चारित्र्य *n.* Moral conduct.

चारु *a.* Agreeable, dear.

चारुव्रता *f.* A female who fasts for a whole month.

चार्म (चार्मिक) *a.* Leathern.

चार्मिण *n.* A number of men armed with shields.

चार्वाक *m.* Name of an old atheistic philosopher.

चार्वी *f.* A beautiful woman; moonlight; intelligence, lustre; wife of Kubera. [house.

चाल *m.* The roof of a

चालन *n.* (-नी *f.*) A sieve.

चाष (-स) *m.* The blue jay.

चि *vt.* 5. U. To collect, to cover. With अप-to diminish, अव-to gather, आ to spread, उद्-to gather, उप-to increase, to spread over, निस्- to determine, परि-to practise, to acquire, प्र-to collect, to increase, वि-to gather, to search for. विनिस्-to determine, सम्-to accumulate, to place; समुद्-to collect. *Pass.* (चीयते) To increase, to prosper. With अप-to decrease. उप-to grow, प्र-to grow *vt.* 10. U. To gather.

चिकित्सक *m.* A physician.

चिकित्सा *f.* Administering medicine. medical treatment, therapeutics.

चिकिल *m.* Mud, a slough.

चिकीर्षक *a.* Desirous of doing.

चिकीर्षा *f.* Desire of doing.

चिकीर्षित *a.* Design, intention. [ing.

चिकीर्षु *a.* Desirious of do-

चिकु (कू) र *a.* Moving, unsteady, rash. *m.* The hair of the head; a mountain; a reptile.

चिक्कण *a.* Smooth; glossy; slippery; greasy. [ness.

चिक्लीद *n.* Moisture, fresh-

चिंचा *f.* The tamarind tree, or its fruit.

चिच्छक्ति *f.* Intellectual capacity.

चित् *vt.* 1. P. 10 A. To perceive, to know; *vi.* 10. U. To think, to remember, to discover. With अनु-to ponder over, परि-to think, to remember, to discover, वि-to think, to ponder over, to intend, to regard, to discover.. सम्-to consider.

चित *f.* Perception, the mind, life, Brahman(*n.*)

चित् *ind.* A particle added to किम् (*pron*) and its derivatives imparts to them an indefinite sense.

चित *a.* Covered; gathered, obtained. *n.* A building.

चिता (चितिका) *f.* Funeral pile.

चिति *f.* A pile, gathering, a multitude.

चित्त *a.* Perceived; *n* Mind, thought, attention, desire, intellect, reason.

चित्तचारिन् *a.* Acting according to the wish of another.

चित्तज (-जन्मन्,-भू,-योनि) *m.* Love, passion; the god of love.

चित्तनिर्वृति *f.* Contentment.

चित्तभेद *m.* Inconsistency.

चित्तवत् *a.* Reasonable; kind-hearted. [ness, insanity.

चित्तविप्लव (-विभ्रम) *m.* Mad-

चित्तविश्लेष *m.* Breach of friendship.

चित्तवृत्ति *f.* Inclination, mental vision.

चित्तवैकल्य *n.* Distraction.

चित्तहारिन् *a.* Fascinating.

चित्य *n.* The place at which a corpse is burnt.

चित्या *f.* A funeral pile.

चित्र *a.* Bright; variegated, amusing; wonderful. *m.* The variegated colour. *n.* A picture; a wonder; a sectarial mark on the forehead; the sky; a spot; the white leprosy; the last of the three divisions of poetry.

चित्रक *m.* A painter; a tiger *n.* A sectarial mark on the forehead.

चित्रकथालाप *m.* Telling charming stories. [actor.

चित्रकर *m.* A painter; an

चित्रकर्मन् *n.* An extraordinary act; ornamenting; painting. *m.* A magician; a painter.

चित्रकाय *m.* A tiger.

चित्रकार *m.* A painter.

चित्रकूट *m.* Name of a hill and district near Prayága.

चित्रग (-गत) *a.* Painted.

चित्रगुप्त *m.* One of the beings in Yama's world recording the vice and virtues of mankind.

चित्रजल्प *m.* A random talk.

चित्रपट (-पट्ट) *m.* A painting, a picture. [painting.

चित्रफलक *n.* A tablet for

चित्रबर्ह *m.* A peacock.

चित्रभानु *m.* Fire; the sun.

चित्रम *ind.* Oh! what a wonder!

चित्रमेखल *m.* A peacock.

चित्रयोधिन् *m.* Arjuna.

चित्ररथ *m.* The sun; name of a Gandharva king.

चित्रल *a.* Variegated.

चित्रविचित्र *a.* Variously coloured. [ing.

चित्रविद्या *f* The art of paint-

चित्रशाला *f.* A painter's studio.

चित्रा *f.* Name of the fourteenth lunar mansion.

चित्राकृति *f.* A portrait

चित्रारंभ *m.* Tha outline of a picture.

चित्रिणी *f.* A woman of a particular class.

चित्रित *a* Variegated.

चित्रिन् *a.* Wonderful; variegated.

चित्स्वरूप *n.* The supreme soul

चिदात्मन् *m.* The thinking faculty; the supreme spirit.

चिदाभास *m.* The soul not freed from impurities.

चिद्घन *m.* The supreme spirit.

चिद्रूप *a* Intelligent; amiable.

चिंतन *n.* (-ना *f.*) Thinking; anxious thought.

चिंता *f.* Thought [anxiety.

चिंतापर *a.* Thoughtful, anxious.

चिंतामणि *m.* The philosopher's stone.

चिंतावेश्मन् *n.* A council-hall.

चिंतित *a.* Thought, devised.

चिंतिति (-या) *f.* Consideration.

चिंत्य *a.* To be thought over.

चिन्मय *a.* Spiritual [gence.

चिन्मात्र *n.* Pure intelligence.

चिप(पि)ट *a.* Flat-nosed.

चिबु (बु) क *n.* The chin

चिर *a.* Lasting a long time, long-standing. *n.* A long time.

चिरकार (-कारिका -कारिन्, -क्रिय *a.*) Acting slowly, dilatory.

चिरकाल *m.* A long time.

चिरकालिक (-कालीन) *a.* Of long standing, old.

चिरजीविन् *a.* L ng-lived.

चिरंजीव *a.* Long lived. *m.* An epithet of seven persons who are considered to be deathless.

चिरंतन *a* Of long standing.

चिल्ल *vi.* 1. P To become loose.

चिह्न *n.* Mark, sign, a sign of the zodiac, aim; direction.

चिह्नित *a.* Marked, known; [branded.

चीत्कार *m.* An onomatopoetic word; the cry of the ass or elephant.

चीन *m.* Name of a country (modern China.)

चीनांशुक, (चीनवासस्) *n.* Silken cloth.

चीर *n* A rag, a bark; a garment in general.

चीरवासस् *a.* Clothed in bark; dressed in tatters.

चीर्ण *a.* Studied; performed; divided.

चीवर *n.* A garment; the dress of a Buddhist mendicant

चीवरिन् *m.* A Buddhist or Jaina mendicant

चुक्रा *f* The tamarind tree.

चुक्रिमन् *m* Sourness.

चुचु (चू) क *m.n* The nipple of the breast.

चुंचु *a.* Celebrated, renowned.

चुत् *vi.* 1. P To ooze.

चुद् *vt* 10 U To send, to inspire;with **परि**-to push on,to impel. **प्र**-to impel, to drive, to direct, to throw.

चुप् *vi* 1 P. To creep.

चुबुक *n.* The chin.

चुंब् *vt.*1. P, 10. U (*pp.***चुंबित**) To kiss,to touch softly; with **परि**-to kiss.

चुंब *m.* (-**बा** *f.*) A kiss.

चुंबक *n* A kisser; a rogue; a libertine, a loadstone.

चुंबन *n* Kissing,attraction.

चुर् *vt.* 10. U To steal.

चुरा *f.* Theft. [handful.

चुलुक *m* Deep mud; a

चुलुकिन् *m.* A porpoise.

चुलुंप् *vt.* 1. P. To swing, to agitate With **उद्**-to swing; to agitate.

चुल्ल् 1 P. To sport.

चुल्लि (-**ल्ली**) *f.* A fire-place.

चुस्त *n.* Fried meat.

चूचु (**चू**) **क,** *n.* The nipple of a breast.

चूडा *f* The hair on the forehead; the ceremony of tonsure; the crest of a cock or peacock; top; a well.

चूडाकरण (–**कर्मन्**) *n.* The ceremony of tonsure.

चूडापाश *m.*A mass of hair.

चूडामणि*m.* (-**रत्न** *n.*) A jewel worn on the top of the hed; best, excellent.

चूडार (-**ल**) *a.* Crested.

चूत *m.* The mango tree.

चूर्ण् *vt.* 10, U. To pulverise; to crush. With **सम्**-to bruise, to crush.

चूर्ण *m. n.* Powder; dust, pounded sandal.

चूर्णक *n.* A fragrant powder; a style of prose composition not abounding in compounds.

चूर्णकुंतल *m.* Curly hair.

चूर्णखंड *n.* Gravel.

चूर्णि (-**र्णी**) *f.* Powder.

चूर्णिका *f.* A style of prose-composition.

चूल *m.* Hair. [crest.

चूला *f.* An upper room; a

चूलिका *f* The crest of a peacock.

चूष् *vi.* 1. P. to suck.

चूष्य *n.*Any article of food that is to be sucked.

चेकितान *m.* S'iva; name of a king. [slave.

चेट (-**ड**) *m.* A servant, a

चेट(ड)क *m.* A servant; a paramour. [slave.

चेटि(डि) का *f.* A female

चेत् *ind.* If, although, provided that.

चेतन *a.* Animate, living. *m.* A sentient being; soul,

mind. [ness; the mind.
चेतना f. Life, conscious-
चेतोजन्मन्, चेतोभव, चेतोभू m. Passion; the god of love.
चेतोमत् a. Living, sentient.
चेतोविकार m. Emotion.
चेय a. To be gathered.
चेल n. A garment; wicked.
चेलिका f. A bodice.
चेष्ट् vi. or vi. 1. A To be endowed with life. With वि-to move to stir, to act.
चेष्टन n. Motion, effort.
चेष्टा f. Emotion; jesture; effort; action
चेष्टानिरूपण n. Observing a person's actions [our.
चेष्टित n Motion, behavi-
चैतन्य n. Spirit, life, the supreme spirit.
चैत्य m. n. A pile of stones forming a boundary; a tomb-stone; a temple.
चैत्यतरु (-द्रुम,-वृक्ष) m A fig-tree standing on a sacred spot.
चैत्र m. Name of a lunar month.
चैत्ररथ (-श्य) n Name of the garden of Kubera.
चैद्य m. A name of Śis'upála.
चैल n. Garment.
चोक्ष a Pure honest clever.
चोटी f A petticoat.
चोडm. A bodice. a precept.
चोदनाf. Inspiration, citing;
चोदित a. Urged on, inspired.
चोद्य n. A question; an objection; wonder. [ber.
चो (चौ) र m A thief, a rob-
चो (चौ) रिका f. Theft.
चोल m. (-ली) f. A bodice.
चोष m. Sucking.
चोष्य n. See चूष्य.
चौर्यn. Theft secrecy. [tion,
च्यवन n. Motion; d priva-
च्यु vi. 1 A To drop down, to swerve from, to be deprived of; with परि or प्र- to proceed from; to swerve; to drop down.
च्युत vi. 1. P To drop, to flow, to fall down.
च्युत a. Dropped down; lost.
च्युतात्मन् a. Evil-minded.
च्युति f. A fall; deviation; deprivation. anus.
च्यूत m. The mango tree.

छ.

छग (-ल, -लक) m. A goat.
छटा f. Mass, number, lustre, a streak.
छटाभा f. Lightning.
छत्र m. A mushroom. n. an umbrella. [emperor.
छत्रपति m. A sovereign; an-
छत्रभंग m Loss of dominion deposition.
छत्रा f.(-क n.) A mushroom.
छत्वर m. A house; a bower.

छद् *vt*. 1, 10. U.(*pp*. छन्न or छादित) To cover, to spread anything as a cover; to conceal; with अव (or आ उप,परि,प्र,प्रति. सम्)-to cover, to conceal. उद्-to uncover. *vt*. 10. U (*pres*. छंदयति-ते) To cover; to please; to persuade. With उप to present any one (acc.) with anything (inst.); to coax.

छद *m*. (-न n.) A covering; a wing, a sheath. [fraud.

छद्मन् *n*. A disguise, a plea,

छद्मतापस *m*. A religious hypocrite. [guise.

छद्मरूपेण *ind*. Under dis-

छद्मवेशिन् *m*. A cheat. [ful.

छद्मिन् *a*. Fraudulent, deceit-

छंद *m*. Wish, fancy; whim.

छंदस् *n*. Wish, free will, intention; fraud; the *Vedas*; prosody.

छंदोग *m*. A student of the *Sâmaveda*.

छंदोभंग *m* A violation of the laws of prosody.

छन्न *a*. Covered; concealed.

छर्द् *vt*. 10. U. (*pp*. छर्दित) To vomit.

छर्द *m*. (-न n.), छर्दि (का) *f*., छर्दिस् *f*. } Vomiting; sickness.

छल *m*. Fraud, delusion, pretext; guise; knavery; wickedness; a fallacy.

छलन *n*. (-ना *f*.) Deceiving.

छलिन *m*. A cheat, a swindler.

छवि *f*. Skin, colour, light.

छाग, (-ल) *m*. A goat. [thin.

छात *a*. (*pp*. of छो) Divided,

छात्र *m*. A pupil. [comb.

छात्रक *n*. Honey in the

छात्रगंड *m*. An indifferent student of poetry.

छाद *n*. A thatch a roof.

छादन *n*. A cover, a screen

छादित *a*. See छन्न.

छाद्मिक *m*. A rogue.

छांदस *a*. Vedic, metrical. *m*. A Bráhmana learned in the *Vedas*.

छाया *f*. Shade, shadow, a reflection, hallucination, lustre, light, complexion, beauty, protection; a line; darkness, bribe.

छायांक *m*. The moon.

छायाग्रह *m*. A mirror.

छायातनय (-सुत) *m*. Saturn.

छायातरु *m*. A large umbrageous tree.

छायापथ *m*. The galaxy.

छायाभृत् *m*. The moon.

छायायंत्र *n*. A sun-dial.

छि *f*. Abuse, reproach.

छित्ति *f*. Cutting. [lent.

छित्वर *a*. Hostile; fraudu-

छिद् *vt*. 7 U. (*pp*. छिन्न) To

cut, to pierce, to divide. With अव-to cut off, to distinguish, आ-to cut, to remove, to exclude, to snatch, to disregard, उत् to extirpate, to interrupt, परि-to mutilate; to divide, to define, to cut to pieces; with प्र to draw, वि-to divide, to break off, सम्- to divide; to remove.

छिदि *f.* An axe; Indra's thunderbolt.

छिदिर *m.* An axe; a sword; fire; a rope.

छिदुर *a.* Broken; hostile.

छिद्र *a.* Pierced, *n.* A hole, rent, defect, weak side.

छिद्रात्मन् *a.* One whe exposes his weak points to attack.

छिद्रानुसंधानिन्, छिद्रानुसारिन्, छिद्रान्वेषिन् *a.* Seeking the weak points of another.

छिद्रान्तर *m.* A cane, reed.

छिद्रित *a.* Containing holes.

छिन्न *a.* Cut, torn, destroyed.

छिन्नभिन्न *a.* Cut up through and through; destroyed.

छिन्नसंशय *a.* Free from doubt, confirmed.

छिन्ना *f.* A whore, harlot.

छुछुंदर *m.* The musk rat.

छुर् *vt.* 1. P. To cut, to engrave. *vt.* 6. P. To cover, to envelop. With वि to anoint, to envelop.

छुरी, छुरिका छूरी *f.* A knife.

छेक *a.* Lame.

छेकानुप्रास *m.* A kind of alliteration.

छेकापन्हुति *f.* Name of a figure of speech.

छेकोक्ति *f.* Insinuation, double entendre; hint.

छेद *m.* Fraction; a section, dissipating, destruction a divisor.

छेदन *n.* A section, destruction, cutting.

छेदि *m.* A carpenter.

छो *vt.* 4. P (*pp.* छात or छित *pres.* छ्यति; caus. छाययति) To cut, to reap.

छोरण *n.* Abandoning.

ज

ज *a.* (At the end of compounds) Born from or in, growing in; victorious; swift. *m* A father; production, birth; poison; an imp; a conqueror.

जक्ष् *vt.* 2. P. (*pp.* जक्षित or जग्ध;) To eat.

जक्षण *n.* (जक्षि *f.*) Eating.

जगत् *a.* Moveable, *m.* Wind. *n.* The world.

जगती *f.* The earth, people, a cow; a kind of metre

जगदंबा(जगदंबिका) *f.* Durgâ.
जगदात्मन् *m.* The supreme spirit.
जगदाधार *m.* Time; air; wind.
जग्ध *a.* Eaten.
जग्धि *f.* Eating; food.
जगन्निवास *m.* The supreme deity; Vishnu.
जग्मि *m* Wind.
जघन *n.* The hip and the loins; rear-guard.
जघनचपला *f.* A libidinous woman. [vile.
जघन्य *a.* Hindmost, last.
जघन्य *m* A s'ûdra. [brother.
जघन्यज *m.* A younger
जघ्नि *m.* A weapon.
जघ्नु *a.* Striking, killing.
जंगम *a.* Living, moveable.
जंगमेतर *a.* Immoveable.
जंगल *n* A desert; a forest.
जंगाल *m.* A land mark.
जंघा *f.* Leg from the ankle to the knee. [runner.
जंघाकार, (-कारिक) *m.* A
जंघाल, जंघिल *a.* Rapid.
जटा *f.* Matted hair. [Si'va.
जटाधर (-चीर, -टंक, -टीर) *m.*
जटाजूट *m.* A mass of twisted hair.
जटाल *a.* Wearing a coil of twisted hair.
जटि(-टी) *f.* The Indian fig-free; matted hair; assemblage.
जटिन् *a.* Having twisted hair. *m.* S'iva.
जटिल *a.* Wearing twisted hair, complicated. *m.* A lion; a goat.
जठर *a.* Hard, *m.* *n.* The stomach, the womb; the interior.
जठराग्नि *m.* The gastric juice.
जठरामय *m.* Dropsy.
जड *a.* Cold, paralysed apathetic, stupid; dumb; stupefying.
जडता *f.* Dullness, stupidity.
जडिमन् *m.* Frigidity; stupidity; apathy.
जतु *n.* Lac; red resin.
जतुक *n.* (-का *f.*) Lac.
जत्रु *n.* The collar bone.
जन् *vt.* 4. A (pp. जात pres. जायते) To be born, to become. With अनु-to be born afterwards, अभि–to be born, to be turned into; उप(प्र, वि, or सम्) -to grow, to arise. [world.
जन *m* A person, people,
जनातिग *a.* Extraordinary.
जनचक्षुस् *n.* The sun.
जनता *f.* A community, mankind, birth.
जनपद *m.* A community, a nation, people, kingdom, mankind, the country (opp. the town.)

जनपदिन् *m.* The ruler.
जनप्रवाद *m.* Rumour.
जनमर्यादा *f.* Established custom or usage. [favour.
जनरंजन *n.* Courting popular
जनरव *m.* Rumour, calumny.
जनव्यवहार *m.* Popular usage.
जनश्रुति *f.* Rumour, report.
जनसंबाध *a.* Densely crowded with people.
जनस्थान *n.* Name of a part of the Dandaká forest (modern Nasik.)
जनक *a.* Generating, causing, *m.* A father; name of a famous king of Videha.
जनन *n.* Birth; life, race, origin, appearance
जननि *f.* A mother; birth.
जननी *f.* A mother; mercy.
जनयितृ *m.* A father.
जनयित्री *f.* A mother.
जना *f.* Birth.
जनि (-नी), जनीका *f* Birth, a woman; a mother; a daughter-in-law; a wife.
जनित *a.* Produced, created.
जनितृ *m* A father.
जनित्री *f.* A mother.
जनु (-नू) *f.* Birth. [life.
जनुस् *n.* Birth, duration of
जंतु *m* A creature, the soul.
जन्म *n.* Birth.
जन्मन् *n* Birth, life.
जन्मकुंडली *f.* A table in a horoscope showing the positions of different planets at the time of birth.
जन्मनक्षत्र *n.* The natal star.
जन्मनामन् *n* The name received on the 12th day after birth. [horoscope
जन्मपत्र *n.* (-पत्रिका *f.*) A
जन्मप्रतिष्ठा *f.* A birth-place.
जन्मभ *n.* The natal star.
जन्मभाज् *m.* A creature.
जन्मभाषा *f.* Mother-tongue.
जन्मयोग *m.* A horoscope.
जन्मलग्न *n.* The natal zodiacal sign.
जन्मशोधन *n.* Discharging the obl gation derived from birth.
जन्मसाफल्य *n.* Attainment of the end of existence.
जन्मांतर *n.* Another life.
जन्माष्टमी *f.* The eighth day of the dark fortnight of S'rávana, the birth day of Krishna.
जन्य *a.* To be born, occasioned by belonging to a family; vulgar. *m.* A father; the body; a rumour. *n.* Creation; an effect, a market, battle, censure.
जन्या *f.* The friend of a mother; a bride's maid; pleasure; affection.
जन्यु *m* Birth; a creature, fire; the creator.

जप् *vt.* 1. P. To mutter. With उप-to whisper, to rouse to rebellion.
जप *m*. A muttered prayer.
जपमाला *f*. A rosary.
जपा *f*. The China rose.
जप्य *m*. *n*. A muttered prayer.
जम् *vt*. 1. P. To eat.
जमन *n*. The same as जेमन.
जंपती *m*. *du*. Man and wife.
जंबाल *m*. Mud; moss.
जंबालिनी *f*. A river.
जंबीर *m*. The citron tree.
जंबु (-बू) *f*. The rose apple.
जंबुखंड (-द्वीप) *m*. Name of a continent.
जंबु (बू) क *m*. A jackal.
जंबूल *m*. A kind of tree.
जंभ *m*. The jaws, a tooth.
जंभका, जंभा, जंभिका, *f*. A yawn.
जय *m*. Conquest, son of Indra, Yudhishthira; attendant of Vishnu; Arjuna.
जयस्तंभ *m*. A trophy, a column commemorative of victory.
जयंती *f*. A flag.
जयिन् *a*. Victorious.
जय्य *a*. Conquerable.
जरठ *a*. Old, decayed; hard.
जरण *a*. Old, infirm.
जरत् *a*. Aged.
जरती *f*. An old woman.
जरद्गव *m*. An old ox.
जरा *f*. Old age.
जराजीर्ण *a*. Old through age.
जरायणि, जरासंध *m*. Name of a king.
जरायु *n*. The slough of a serpent; the womb.
जरित (-त्) *a* Old.
जर्जर (जर्जरित or जर्जरीक) *a*. Old, shattered, dull.
जल *n*. Water.
जलक्रिया *f*. A Offering libations of water to the manes of the deceased.
जलचर, जलेचर *a*. Aquatic.
जलचारिन् *m*. An aquatic animal, fish.
जलज *m*. A fish; moss; the moon; *m*. *n*. The conch-shell, *n*. A lotus
जलतरंग *m*. A wave; a metal cup filled with water producing harmonic notes.
जलताडन *n*. Any useless occupation.
जलत्रास *m* Hydrophobia.
जलद *m* A cloud, camphor.
जलदेवता *f*. A water- nymph.
जलद्रोणी *f*. A bucket.
जलधर *m* A cloud, the ocean.
जलधि *m*. The ocean; a hundred billions.
जलधिज *m*. The moon.
जलधिजा *f*. Lakshmî.
जलनिधि (-पति) *m*. The ocean
जलनिर्गम *m*. Drain.

जलपटल *n.* A cloud.
जलप्रपात *m.* A water-fall.
जलप्रदान *n.* See **जलांजली**.
जलप्रांत *m.* Bank of a river.
जलप्राय *n.* A country abounding with water.
जलप्लावन *n.* A deluge.
जलबालिका *f.* Lightning.
जलबिंब *m. n.* A bubble.
जलबिल्व *n.* A pond.
जलभृत *m.* A cloud.
जलमार्ग *m.* A drain, a canal.
जलमुच् *m.* A cloud.
जलयंत्र *n.* A fountain.
जलयात्रा *f.* A voyage.
जलयान *n* A ship.
जलरंड (-रुंड) *m.* A whirlpool; a drop of water; a snake.
जलरस *m.* Sea-salt.
जलराशि *m.* The ocean.
जलरुह् (-रुह) *n.* A lotus.
जललता *f.* A wave, a billow.
जलवाह *m.* A cloud.
जलवाहनी *f.* An aqueduct.
जलशय, (-शयन,-शायिन्) *m.* Vishnu.
जलशूकर *m.* A crocodile.
जलशोष *m.* Drought.
जलाका, जलालुका, जलिका, जलुका जलूका, *f.* A leech.
जलाजीव *m.* A fisherman.
जलांचल *m.* Spring.
जलांजलि *m.* Water presented to the deceased.
जलाटनी *f.* Leech.
जलात्यय *m.* Autumn.
जलाधिप *m.* Varuna.
जलार्णव *m.* Rainy season, the ocean of sweet water.
जलार्थिन् *a.* Thirsty.
जलावतार *m.* A landing place.
जलाधार *m.* A pond.
जलाशय } **जलाश्रय** } *m.* A pond.
जलेज *n.* A lotus.
जलेन्धन *n.* Sub-marine fire.
जलेशय *m.* Vishnu; fish.
जलोच्छ्वास *m.* A rain; overflow of a river.
जलोदर *n.* Dropsy.
जलोद्भव *a.* Aquatic.
जलौकस *m.* (**-स्** *m.*) A leech.
जल्प् *vt.* 1· P. To speak, to prattle, **सम्**·to converse.
जल्प *m.* Talk, debate.
जल्पक *a.* Talkative.
जल्पित *n.* Talk; gossip.
जव *a.* Swift. *m.* Speed.
जवन *a.* Quick.
जवनिका, जवनी *f.* A curtain.
जवाधिक *m.* A courser.
जवानिल *m.* A hurricane.
जष् *vt.* 1. U To hurt.
जहत् *a.* Abandoning.
जह्नु *m.* Name of a king.
जागर *m.* Wakefulness.
जागरण *n.* **जागरा** *f.* Watchfulness.
जागरितृ, जागरूक *a.* Wakeful; vigilant.

जागर्ति, जागर्या, *f.* Wakefulness.

जागृ *vi.* 2 P. To be awake.

जांगल *a.* Rural.

जांगुल *n.* Poison, venom.

जांगुलि, जांगुलिक *m.* A dealer in antedotes.

जाड्य *n.* Coldness, apathy.

जात *a.* Produced; caused. *m.* A son. *n.* A creature; a child; origin; a class.

जातकर्मन् *n.* A ceremony performed at the birth of a child. [confidence.

जातप्रत्यय *a.* Inspired with

जातमात्र *a.* Just born.

जातरूप *a.* Beautiful. *n.* Gold.

जातवेदस् *m.* Agni; fire.

जातक *a.* Born. *m.* A mendicant; name of a ceremony.

जाति *f.* Birth, family, caste, class, notes of music.

जातिब्राह्मण *m.* An ignorant Brâhmana.

जातिभ्रष्ट *a.* Out-caste. [istic.

जातिलक्षण *n.* A character-

जातिवाचक *a.* Generic.

जातिसंपन्न *a.* High-born.

जातु *ind.* Ever, at all some time, some day.

जातुधान *m.* A demon.

जातुष *a.* Made of lac sticky.

जात्य *a.* Of the same family; well-born, beautiful.

जानपद *m.* A country a rus-

जानि See जाया [tic.

जानु *m. n.* Knee.

जानुदघ्न *a.* Up to the knees.

जाप *m.* Muttered prayer.

जाबाल *m.* A goat-herd.

जामदग्न्य *m.* Paras'uráma.

जामा *f.* A daughter. [lord.

जामातृ *m.* A son-in-law, a

जामि *f.* A sister, a daughter; a daughter-in-law.

जामित्र *n.* The seventh zodiacal sign from the natal one.

जामेय *m.* A sister's son.

जांबव *n.* The fruit of the jambu tree; gold.

जांबीर (-ल) *n* A citron.

जांबूनद *n.* Gold; dhatura plant.

जाया *f.* A wife.

जायापती *m. du.* Husband and wife. [duing.

जायिन् *a.* Conquering, sub-

जायु *m.* Medicine, drug.

जार *m.* A paramour, a love.

जारज (-जन्मन्, -जात) *a.* A bastard.

जारिणी *f.* An adulteress.

जाल *n.* A snare; a cobweb; a coat of mail, a window, a collection; magic; illusion; an unblown flower.

जालकर्मन् *n.* Fishing.

जालक *n.* A net; a multitude, a window; a nest; an unblown flower; illusion; a particular ornament worn in the hair.

जालकिन् *m.* A cloud.
जालकिनी *f.* An ewe.
जालाक्ष *m.* A loop-hole.
जालिक *m.* A fisherman; a fowler, a spider; a rogue.
जालिका *f.* A net; a chain-armour; a spider, a leech: a veil; a window; iron.
जालम *a.* Cruel, rash.
जाल्मक *a.* Despised, base.
जाबन्य *n.* Speed swiftness.
जाह्नवी *f.* The river Ganges.
जि *vt.* or *vi.* 1 P (but with the prepositions वि and परा Atm.) To conquer, to surpass. With अधि-to subjugate, निस्-to conquer, to win, परा-to defeat, to lose, to be overcome by, वि-to conquer, to win, to be pre-eminent.
जिगत्नु *m.* Breath, life.
जिगीषा *f.* Desire of conquering; rivalry; eminence; exertion. [quering.
जिगीषु *a.* Desirous of con-
जिघत्सा *f* Hunger.
जिघत्सु *a.* Hungry.
जिघांसा *f.* Desire of killing.
जिघांसु *a.* Desirous of killing. *m.* An enemy.
जिघृक्षा *f.* Desire of taking.
जिघ्र *a.* Guessing.
जिज्ञासा *f.* Curiosity. [ous
जिज्ञासु *a.* Inquisitive, curi-

जित् *a.* (at the end of compound only) Vanquishing.
जित *a.* Conquered, surpassed, won.
जिताक्षर *a.* Reading readily.
जितात्मन् *a.* Self-subdued.
जिति *f.* Victory.
जितेंद्रिय *a.* One who has subdued his senses.
जित्वर *a.* Victorious.
जिन *a.* Victorious. *m.* A generic term for a chief *Bauddha* or *Jaina* saint.
जिष्णु *a.* Victorious. *m.* The sun; Indra; Vishnu; Arjuna.
जिह्म *a.* Oblique, tortuous, dishonest, slow, dim, dark. *n.* Falsehood.
जिह्मग *m.* A snake.
जिह्व *m.* The tongue.
जिह्वल *a.* Voracious.
जिह्वा *f* The tongue; a flame.
जिह्वाप *m.* A dog; a tiger; a cat; a bear.
जिह्वालौल्य *n.* Greediness.
जीन *a.* Old, *n.* A leather bag.
जीमूत *m.* A cloud Indra.
जीमूतवाहन *m.* Indra. [gested.
जीर्ण *a.* Old, decayed, di-
जीर्णोद्धार *m.* Repairs [den.
जीर्णोद्यान *n* A neglected gar-
जीर्णि *f.* Old age
जीव् *vi.* 1. P To live, to re-

vive. With अति-to surpass in living, अनु-to imitate the life of, to serve, to survive आ-to get a living, from (with an acc.). उद्-to revive, उप-to maintain oneself by.

जीव *a.* Living, existing. *m.* The principle of life, personal soul, life, a creature, livelihood; Karna;

जीवगृह (-मंदिर) *n.* The body, soul. [alive.

जीवग्राह *m.* A prisoner taken

जीवमातृका *f.* The seven mothers (*i. e.* female deities).

जीवक *m.* A living being; a servant; a *Buddhist* mendicant; an usurer; a snake-catcher.

जीवत् *a.* Living.

जीवन्मुक्त *m.* A man purified by knowledge of Brahman (*n.*) and freed from future birth and all ceremonial rites while yet living.

जीवन्मुक्ति *f.* Final liberation in the present state of life.

जीवथ *m.* Life, a tortoise, a peacock; a cloud.

जीवन *a.* Enlivening. *m.* A living being; wind; a son. *n.* Vitality, water, livelihood. [medicament.

जीवंत *m.* Life, a drug, a

जीवंतिक *m.* A fowler.

जीवा *f.* Water; the earth; a bow-string the chord of an arc; means of living.

जीवातु *m. n* Victuals, life.

जीवात्मन् *m.* The individual soul. [medicine).

जीवादान *n.* Bleeding (in

जीवाधान *n.* Preservation of life.

जीवाधार *m.* The heart.

जीवोत्सर्ग *m.* Suicide.

जीविका *f.* Livelihood.

जीवित *a.* Living, alive, returned to life; animated. *n.* Life, livelihood

जीविन् *a.* Living. [hood.

जीव्या *f.* Means of liveli-

जुगुप्सन *n.* **जुगुप्सा** *f.* Censure, aversion, disgust.

जुष् *vt.* or *vi.* 6. A. To be pleased or satisfied; to visit; 10 U. to think.

जुष् *a.* (generally at the end of compounds) Visiting, taking, liking.

जुष्ट *a* Gratified [phere.

जू *f.* Speed; the atmos-

जूट *m.* Matted hair.

जूति *f.* Speed, velocity.

जूर्ति *f.* Fever.

जृ *vt.* 1. P To humiliate

जृभ्, जृंभ् *vt.* 1. A. To recoil, to increase. With उद्-to rise, to yawn, to open, to spread, समुद्- to endeavour.

जृंभ, *m.* *n.* जृंभण *n.* जृंभा *f.* जृंभिका *f.* Yawning, blossoming.

जॄ *vi.* 4. 9, P. 10. U. (*pp.* जीर्ण) To grow old, to be digested; to perish.

जेतृ *m.* A conqueror.

जेमन *n.* Eating, dinner.

जेत्र *a.* Victorious.

जैन *m.* A believer in *Jaina* doctrines.

जैमिनि *m.* A celebrated sage and philosopher.

जोटिंग *m* S'iva.

जोष *n.* Happiness, pleasure.

जोषम् *ind.* With ease; silently.

जोषा, जोषित् *f.* A woman.

ज्ञ *a.* Knowing, *m.* A wise man, the sentient soul; the planet Mercury; the planet Mars.

ज्ञपित, ज्ञप्त *a.* Made known.

ज्ञप्ति *f.* Understanding; making known.

ज्ञा *vt.* 9 U. To know, to investigate, to recognize. With अनु-to permit, to promise, to acknowledge. अप-(Atm)to conceal, अभि-to know, to regard. अव-to disregard, आ, परि, वि-to know, प्रति-(Atm.) to promise, सम् (Atm.) to recognize; to agree together, *Caus.* (ज्ञापयति or ज्ञपयति) to inform, to announce; (Atm.) to request, to ask. With आ-to command, to give leave, वि-to request to speak.

ज्ञात *a.* Known.

ज्ञाति *m.* A father; the agnatic relatives.

ज्ञातिभाव *m.* Relationship.

ज्ञातिभेद *m.* Disunion among relatives.

ज्ञातेय *n.* Relation ship.

ज्ञातृ *n.* A wise man; an acquaintance; a surety.

ज्ञान *n* Knowledge, sacred knowledge; consciousness, sense; learning.

ज्ञानकांड *m.* That inner portion of the *Veda* which treats knowledge of the supreme spirit.

ज्ञानचक्षुस् *n.* Intellectual vision.

ज्ञानतस् *ind.* Knowingly.

ज्ञानयोग *m* Contemplation as the means of attaining the supreme spirit.

ज्ञानशास्त्र *n.* Astrology.

ज्ञानानुत्पात *m.* Ignorance.

ज्ञानापोह *m.* Forgetfulness.

ज्ञानिन् *a* Intelligent, wise. *m.* An astrologer, a sage.

ज्ञापक *m.* A teacher,

commander. *n.* A suggestive rule.

ज्ञापन *n.* Announcement; indication.

ज्ञीप्सा *f.* The desire of knowing.

ज्ञेय *a.* Perceptible.

ज्या *vi.* 2. P. (*pp.* जिन; *pres.* जिनाति) To become old.

ज्या *f.* A bow-string; the earth; a mother; the chord of an arc.

ज्यानि *f.* Old age; a river.

ज्यायस् *a.* (*comp.* of प्रशस्य and वृद्ध) Superior, more worthy, larger.

ज्येष्ठ *a.* (*super.* of प्रशस्य and वृद्ध) Most excellent, pre-eminent, eldest. *m.* Elder brother.

ज्येष्ठतात *m.* A father's elder brother.

ज्येष्ठवर्ण *m.* A Brâhmana.

ज्येष्ठा *f.* An elder sister; the eighteenth lunar mansion; the middle finger; a house-lizard.

ज्यैष्ठ्य *n.* Seniority.

ज्यो *vt.* 1.A. (*pres.* ज्यवते) To advise; to observe any religious obligation.

ज्योतिष *a.* Astronomical, astrological. *m.* An astronomer or astrologer *n.* Astronomy or astrology.

ज्योतिषी *f.* ज्योतिष्क *m.* A planet.

ज्योतिस् *m.* Fire, the sun. *n.* Light, brightness, the supreme spirit; lightning; the faculty of seeing; a heavenly body.

ज्योतिर्गण *m.* The heavenly bodies collectively.

ज्योतिश्चक्र *n.* The zodiac.

ज्योतिर्ज्ञ *m.* An astronomer or astrologer.

ज्योतिर्मंडल *n.* The stellar sphere.

ज्योतिर्मय *a.* Starry, consisting of stars.

ज्योतिष्मत् *a.* Illuminated, bright. *m.* The Sun.

ज्योतिष्मति *f.* The night illuminated by stars; peaceful state of mind (in *Yoga* phil.).

ज्योतीरथ *m* The polar star.

ज्योतिर्विद् *m.* An astronomer or astrologer.

ज्योतिर्विद्या *f.* जोतिःशास्त्र *n.* Astronomy or astrology.

ज्योतिष्टोम *m.* A Soma sacrifice.

ज्योत्स्ना *f.* Moonlight.

ज्योत्स्नी *f.* A moon-light night.

ज्यौतिषिक *m.* An astronomer or astrologer

ज्रि 9. P. 10 P. To grow old; 1 P. to conquer.

ज्वर *m.* Fever, mental pain.

ज्वरांकुश *m.* A febrifuge.

ज्वल् *vi.* 1. P To burn, to glow. With उद्–To kindle.

ज्वलन *a.* Flaming, *m.* Fire.

ज्वाल *m.* (-ला *f.*) Light, torch.

ज्वालजिह्व *m* Fire.
ज्वालमुखिन् *m*. A volcano.
ज्वालिन् *m*. Śiva.

झ

झ *m*. Wind, jingling; Brihaspati.
झगझगाय् *vi*. (*denom. pres.* झगझगायते) A. To flash
झंकार *m* झंकृत *n* A low murmuring sound. [ges
झंकारिणी *f*. The river Gan-
झंझन *n*. A rattling or jingling sound. [ing sound.
झंझा *f*. A hurricane, a clang-
झंझावात (-अनिल, -मरुत्) *m*. Wind with rain, a storm.
झटिति *ind* Quickly, at once
झणझण *n*. (-णा *f*.)Jingling.
झण (न) त्कार *m*. Jingling.
झंप *m*.(-पा *f*.) A spring, a jump. [an ape.
झंपाक (-रु) *m*. A monkey,
झर *m*. (-रा, -री *f*) A cascade, a spring.
झर्झरा *f* A whore [ing drops.
झलज्झला *f*. The noise of fall-
झला *f*. A girl, sunshine.
झल्ल *m*. A prize-fighter.
झल्लक *n*. (-की, -री *f*.) Cymbals.
झल्लिका *f*. Dirt, light.
झष *m*. A fish, heat, *n*. A forest.
झषकेतन (-केतु,-ध्वज) *m*. The god of love.
झषांक *m*. God of love.
झांकृत *n*. A rattling sound.
झांट *m*. An arbour, a thicket.
झिल्लि (-ल्ली, -ल्लिका) *f*. A cricket, light.

ट.

टंक् *vi*.10. U (pp. टंकित *pres.* टंकयति-ते) To bind; with उद्-to search.
टंक *m*. (-क *n*.) A hatchet, a sword; anger; a stamped coin.
टंकणक्षार *m*. Borax.
टंकशाला *f*. A mint.
टंका (-गा) *f*. The leg.
टंकार *m*. The twang of a bow-string; a cry.
टंग *m*. *n*. A spade, hatchet.
टंगण *m*. *n*. Borax.
टिक् *vt*.1. A To go to move.
टिटि (ट्टि) भ, (-क) *m*. A kind of bird. [ment.
टिप्पणी (-नी) *f*. A gloss; com-
टीक् *vt*.1. A To move, to go.
टीका *f*. A commentary.
डुंडुक *a*. Small, little; cruel.

ठ.

ठक्कुर *m* An idol, an honorific title.
ठार *m*. Hoar-frost.
ठालिनी *f*. A girdle.

ड

डमर *m.* Riot. *n.* Running away through fear.

डमरु *m. n.* A sort of small drum.

डंब् *vt.* 10. U (*pres.* डंबयति -ते) To throw. With वि- to imitate, to ridicule.

डंबर *a.* Famous. *m.* An assemblage.

डंभ् *vt.* 10. U To collect.

डयन *n.* Flight. [imp

डाकिनी *f.* A kind of female

डामर *a.* Terrific, beautiful.

डालिम *m.* Pomegranate.

डिंगर *m.* A servant, a rogue. [drum.

डिंडिम *m.* A kind of small

डिंडी(डि)र *m.* Foam.

डिम *m.* One of the ten kinds of drama.

डिंब *m.* Affray, a young child; a ball.

डिंभ, (-क) *m.* A young child, any young animal; a fool.

डी *vi* 1, 4. A (*pp.* डीन) To fly. With उद्, or प्र, प्रोद्- to fly up.

डीन *n.* The flight.

डुंडुभ *m.* A species of snakes not poisonous.

डोम *m.* A man of a very low caste. Also डोंब.

ढ

ढक्का *f.* A large drum.

ढुंढि *m.* God Ganes'a.

ढोल *m.* A large drum.

ढौक् *vt.* 1. A To approach; with उप- to offer.

ढौकन *n.* A present, a bribe.

त

तकिल *a.* Fraudulent, crafty.

तक्र *n.* Butter-milk.

तक्राट *m.* A churning stick.

तक्ष् *vt.* 1.5. P (*pp.* तष्ट) To cut. With सम्- to chisel; to wound.

तक्षक *m.* A carpenter, a name of the divine architect, the chief actor in the prelude of a drama (सूत्रधार); the name of a principal serpent.

तक्षन् *m.* A carpenter.

तंग् *vi.* 1. P. To go.

तंचू *vt.* 1.7. P To contract.

तट *m.* (-टा *f*) A slope, horizon. *m. n.* A field.

तटस्थ *a.* Indifferent, neutral.

तटाक *m. n.* A pond.

तटिनी *f.* A river.

तटी *f.* The same as तट.

तड् *vt* or *vi.* 10. U (*pp.* ताडित) To beat to strike.

तडग *m.* A pond

तडाग (-क) *m.* A pond.

तडित् *f.* Lightning.

तंड् *vt.* 1. A. (*pp.* **तंडित** *pres.* **तंडते**) To strike.

तंडुल *m. n.* Grain after thrashing, winnowing and unhusking. [gruel.

तण्डुलोत्थ, (-क) *n.* Rice-

तत *a.* Spread.

ततस् *ind.* Thence, there, thereupon; therefore; beyond that, further.

ततस्ततस् Here and there, what next. [forward

ततःप्रभृति From that time

ततःकिम् 'What matters it.'

ततस्त्य *a.* Coming from that.

तति *pron.* (Declined only in the plural; nom. and acc. **तति**) So many, a series, a number.

तत्कालम् (-**क्षणम्**) *ind.* Instantly. [out wages.

तत्क्रिय *a.* Working with-

तत्त्व (-**त्व**) *n.* True state, truth, essential nature; the mind, an element.

तत्त्वज्ञ (**विद्**) *a.* A philosopher.

तत्त्वतस् *ind.* Truly.

तत्त्वाभियोग *m.* A positive charge.

तत्त्वार्थ *m.* Truth.

तत्पर *a* Inferior; eagerly engaged in that.

तत्परायण *a.* Solely attached to that.

तत्पुरुष *m.* The supreme spirit; a class of compounds.

ततपूर्व *a.* Happening for the first time, prior.

तत्र *ind.* There, then, for that, even then, nevertheless.

तत्र तत्र Here and there.

तत्रत्य *a.* Belonging to that place

तत्रभवत् *pron.* His honour.

तथा *ind.* In that manner, so also, as well as, surely as.

तथापि *ind.* Even, then, yet.

तथा च *ind.* And likewise.

तथा हि *ind.* For instance.

तथागत *a.* Of such a quality; *m.* an epithet of Buddha.

तथात्व *n.* True nature.

तथाभूत *a.* Of such a nature.

तथाविध *a.* Of such a sort.

तथाविधम् *ind.* Thus, likewise.

तथैव *ind.* Just so, exactly so.

तथ्य *a.* True, genuine. *n.* Truth, reality

तद् *pron.* (nom. *sing.* **सः** *m.* **सा** *f.* and **तत्** *n.*) He, she, it; that. *ind.* Thither; then, in that case; consequently.

तदनंतरम् *ind.* Immediately after that.

तदनु *ind.* After that.

तदवधि *ind* So far.

तदा *ind.* Then.

तदात्व *n.* The present time.

तदासुख *a.* Commenced.

तदानीम् *ind.* Then.

तदानींतन *a.* Belonging to that time. [her or that.

तदीय *a.* Belonging to him,

तद्गत *a* Intent on that, belonging to that.

तद्धन *a.* Miserly.

तद्धित *n.* A derivative noun.

तन्मय *a.* Become one with that.

तन्मात्र *n.* Only a trifle; a subtle and primary element (in phil.)

तद्वत् *ind* Equally.

तन् *vt.* 8. U (pp. तत) To spread, to perform (as a sacrifice), to bestow, to compose, to bend (as a bow); to weave. With अव-to cover; to descend. आ–to stretch, to make; to spread. प्र–to spread to perform (as a sacrifice), to exhibit, वि–to cover, to spread; to stretch (as a bow), to form, सम्- to continue. *vt.* 1. P, 10. U. To confide, to aid; with वि-to spread.

तनय *m.* A son.

तनया *f.* A daughter.

तनिमन् *m.* Thinness.

तनु *a.* Thin, small, delicate, trifling *f.* The body, a form.

तनुकूप *m.* A pore of the skin.

तनुज *m.* A son.

तनुजा *f.* A daughter.

तनुत्याग *a.* Niggardly. [being.

तनुभृत् *m.* A living or human

तनुरस *m.* Perspiration.

तनुरुह् (-ह) *n.* The hair of the body.

तनुल *a.* Expanded.

तनुस् *n.* The body.

तनू *f.* The body.

तनूनप *n.* Clarified butter.

तनूनपात् *m.* Fire.

तनूरुह *m.* A son; *n.* the hair.

तन्वंगी *f* A delicate woman.

तंतिपाल *m.* Guardian of the cows.

तंतु *m.* A thread, a wire, a cob-web, a filament, a fibre, offspring, a shark.

तंतुक *m.* The mustard seed.

तंतुकाष्ठ *n.* A piece of wood used by weavers for cleaning thread.

तंतुकीट *m.* A silkworm.

तंतुनाभ *m.* A spider.

तंतुवाद्य *n.* A stringed musical instrument.

तंतुवाप *m.* A weaver; a loom.

तंतु (त्र) वाय *m.* A spider; a weaver.

तंतुविग्रहा *f.* A plantain.

तंत्र *n.* A loom; a thread; posterity; an uninterrupted series; principal doctrine; a scientific work; a chapter; a religious treatise teaching magical and mystical formularies for the worship of the deities or the attainment of supreme power; a drug; ordeal; the right way of doing anything; royal retinue; authority; an army; dependence (as in **स्वतंत्र** or **परतंत्र**), heap, wealth.

तंत्रि (-त्री) *f.* Cord, the wire of a lute; sinew.

तंद्रा *f.* Lassitude, sluggishness.

तंद्रालु *a.* Tired, sleepy.

तंद्रि (-द्री) *f.* Sleepiness.

तन्वी *f.* A thin and delicate woman.

तप् *vt.* or *vi.* 4 A. To trouble, to be powerful. With **अनु**-to grieve. *vi* or *vt.* 1 U. To shine, to heat, to suffer pain, to undergo penance; to repent; **उद्**-to burn. **निस्**-to purify **परि** to burn. **पश्चात्**-to repent. **वि**-to shine **सम्**-to heat, to be sorry, to repent *vt.* 10 U. To heat

तप *a.* Burning, distressing. *m.* Heat, the sun; the hot season; penance.

तपती *f.* The river Tâpti.

तपन *m.* The sun. the hot season; the sun-stone.

तपनी *f.* The river Godàvari.

तपनीय *n.* Gold purified with fire.

तपस् *n.* Heat; pain; penance, merit; special duty of any particular caste; one of the seven worlds. *m.* The month of Màgha.

तपश्चरण *n.* **तपश्चर्या** *f.* The practice of penance.

तपोधन *m.* An ascetic, a devotee.

तपोनिधि *m.* An eminently pious man, an ascetic.

तपोनुभाव *m.* The influence of religious penance.

तपोराशि *m.* An ascetic.

तप्त *a.* Heated, melted; afflicted; practised (as penance).

तपःस्थली *f.* A seat of religious austerity; a name of Benáres

तपस *m.* The sun; the moon; a bird.

तपस्य *vi.* To practise penance.

तपस्य *m.* The month of Fálguna; Arjuna.

तपस्या *f.* Religious austerity.

तपस्विन् *a.* Practising religious austerities; helpless.

तम् *vi*. 4. P. (*pp*. तांत; *pres* ताम्यति) To choke, to be distressed in body or mind, उद्-to be impatient.

तम *n*. Darkness; *m*. Ráhu.

तमस् *n*. Darkness, illusion, error, ignorance, grief, sorrow; sin. *m*. *n*. Ráhu.

तमस *m*. Darkness; a well.

तमस्कांड *m*. Great darkness.

तमस्विनी or **तमा** *f*. A night.

तमि (-मी) *f*. Dark night.

तमिस्र *a*. Dark; *n*. darkness, illusion; anger.

तमिस्रा *f*. A dark night

तमोगुण *m* Darkness or ignorance.

तमोपह, तमोरि, *m*. The sun, the moon.

तमोमणि *m*. A fire-fly.

तमोमय *m*. Ràhu.

तमोविकार *m* Disease, sickness.

तमोहन्, तमोहर *m*. The sun; the moon.

तय् *vt*. 1. To go, to protest.

तर *m*. Passage; freight; a ferry-boat.

तरक्ष (-क्षु) *m*. A hyena.

तरंग *m*. A wave; a section of a book.

तरंगिणी *f*. A river.

तरंगित *a*. Having waves; tremulous.

तरण *m*. A boat; heaven. *n*. Crossing over; conquering, coming; an oar.

तरणि *m*. The sun; a ray of light; a boat.

तरणी *f*. A float, a boat.

तरंड *m*. *n*. A boat, a oar.

तरंडी, तरत, तरंती *f*. A boat.

तरंत *m*. The ocean.

तरपण्य *n*. Freight.

तरल *a* Trembling, unsteady, splendid, liquid, wanton. *m*. The central gem of a necklace; bottom.

तरवारि *m*. A sword.

तरस् *n*. Speed, strength, a bank, float.

तरस *n*. Meat, flesh.

तरस्थान *n*. A wharf.

तरस्विन् *a*. Swift; powerful, strong. *m*. A courier, a hero, air, wind; Garuda.

तरि (-री) *f*. A boat, a box.

तरिक or **तरिकिन्** *m*. A ferry man.

तरिका *f*. (-त्र *n*., -त्री *f*. -णी *f*.) A boat.

तरु *m*. A tree.

तरुखंड (-षंड) *m*. *n*. An assemblage of trees

तरुण *a*. Newly born, new; youthfnl.

तरुणी *f*. A youthful woman.

तरुराज *m*. The *ta'la* tree.

तरुरुहा *f*. A parasitical plant

तरुशायिन् *m*. A bird.

तर्क् *vt*. or *vi*. 10. U. To guess, to infer, to think of. With प्र-to suppose, वि-to guess, to believe.

तर्क *m*. Supposition, conjecture, discussion, doubt; the science of logic.

तर्कविद्या *f.* Logic. [gician.

तर्कक *m.* A petitioner; a lo-

तर्कु *m.* A spindle.

तर्क्ष्य *m.* Nitre, saltpetre.

तर्ज् *vt.* 10. P. To threaten, to censure [ing

तर्जन *n.* (-ना *f.*) Threaten-

तर्जनी *f.* The forefinger.

तर्ण, तर्णक *m.* A calf.

तर्णि *m.* Raft; the sun.

तर्द् *vt.* 1. P To kill.

तर्पण *n.* Satisfaction, presenting libations of water to the manes of the deceased ancestors.

तर्ष *m.* Thirst; desire; the

तर्षण *n.* Thirst. [ocean.

तर्षित or **तर्षुल** *a.* Thirsty.

तर्हि *ind.* Then, in that case.

तल *m. n.* A surface, the palm of the hand or the sole of the foot; the forearm; a slap with the hand; lowness; bottom. *m.* The hilt of a sword. *n.* Origin. [tom.

तलतस् *ind.* From the bot-

तलनाल *m* Chapping of the hands.

तलप्रहार *m.* A slap.

तलातल *n* The fourth of the seven infernal regions.

तलित *n.* Fried meat.

तलिन *a.* Thin, clear, lying at the bottom. *n.* A bed.

तलिम *n.* A pavement; a bed; a sword; an awning.

तलुन *a.* Young.

तल्क *n.* A forest.

तल्प *m. n.* A couch, a sofa, a wife, the seat of a carriage; a turret.

तल्पक *m.* A servant whose business is to make beds.

तल्लज *m.* Excellence.

ताल्लिका *f.* A key.

तल्ली *f.* A youthful woman.

तष्ट (*pp.* of **तक्ष्**) *a.* Cut, fashioned.

तष्टृ *m.* A carpenter; the architect of gods.

तस्कर *m.* A thief, (at the end of a compound) anything bad or contemptible. [man.

तस्करी *f.* A passionate wo-

तस्थु *a.* Stationary, immoveable. [ference.

ताटस्थ्य *n.* Proximity; indif-

ताड *m.* A blow, noise; a mountain [richa.

ताडकेय *m.* The demon **Má-**

ताडन *n.* Beating.

ताडनी *f.* A whip [palm.

ताडि (-डी) *f.* A kind of

तांडव *m. n.* Dancing, the frantic dance of S'iva.

तात *m*. A father; a term of endearment applied to persons of inferior position; a term of reverence applied to elders.

तातल *m*. A disease.

ताति *m*. Offspring. *f*. Continuity. [immediate

तात्कालिक *a*. Simultaneous;

तात्त्विक *a*. Real, essential.

तात्पर्य *n*. Aim, purport; the intention of the speaker.

तादात्म्य *n*. Identity, unity.

तादृक्ष (-श,-श्‌) *a*. Such-like; ordinary; low.

तान *m*. A thread, a fibre; a protracted tone (in music). *n*. Expanse, an object of sense.

तानव *n*. Thinness.

तांतव *n*. Spinning, weaving; a web: a woven cloth.

तांत्रिक *a*. Relating to the *tantras*. *m*. A follower of *tantra* doctrines.

ताप *m*. Heat, pain, fever, misery, distress.

तापत्रय *n*. The three kinds of miseries to which human beings are subject.

तापन *m*. The sun; the hot season; the sun-stone; burning; distressing.

तापस *a*. Relating to religious penance. *m*. A hermit.

तापस्य *n*. Asceticism.

तापी *f*. The river Tápi or Yamuná. [butter.

तामर *n*. Water; clarified

तामरस *n*. The red lotus; gold; copper.

तामरसी *f*. A lotus pond.

तामस *a*. Dark; ignorant; vicious. *m*. A malignant person; a snake; an owl. *n*. Darkness.

तामसिक *a*. Dark [Durgá.

तामसी *f*. A dark night, sleep;

तामिस्र *m*. A division of hell.

तांबूल *n*. The areca nut, the leaf of piper-betel together with the areca nut and other spices generally chewed after meals.

तांबूलिक *m*. A seller of betel.

तांबूली *f*. The betel-plant.

ताम्र *a*. Red, copper.

ताम्रकार (-कुट्ट) *m*. A brazier.

ताम्रगर्भ *n*. Sulphate of cop-

ताम्रचूड *m*. A cock. [per.

ताम्रपट्ट *m*. (-पत्र *n*.) A copper plate.

ताम्रपर्णी *f*. Name of a river rising in Málawá.

ताम्राक्ष *m*. A crow; the Indian cuckoo.

ताम्रिक *a*. Made of copper, coppery. *m*. A copper-smith.

ताय् *vt.* 1. To spread, to preserve. With वि to spread, to create.

तार *a.* High, deep, shrill, radiant,excellent.*m.*The bank of a river;the clearness of a pearl *m. n.* A star or planet; *n.* the pupil of the eye.

तारक *m.* A pilot,name of a demon killed by Kárti-keya *m n.*A float. *n.* The pupil of the eye.

तारका *f.* A star; a meteor; the pupil of the eye.

तारकिणी *f.* A night during which stars are visible.

तारकित *a.* Starry.

तारण *m.*A boat, *n.* Crossing; rescuing.

तारणि(-णी) *f.* A float,a raft.

तारतम्य *n.* Gradation, distinction.

तारल *m.*A libidinous man.

तारवायु *m.* A whistling breeze.

तारस्वर *a.*Having a loud or shrill sound.

तारा *f.* A star, a planet;the pupil of the eye;a pearl.

तारापथ *m* The firmament.

तारामंडल *n.* The starry region, the zodic.

ताराधिप, तारापीड, तारापति, *m.* The moon.

तारिक *n.* Fare, freight.

तारुण्य *n* Youth.

तारेय *m.* The planet Mercury; Angada, son of Váli.

तार्किक *m.*A logician.

तार्क्ष्य *m.* Garuda; Aruna; a car; a horse, a snake; a bird.

तार्तीय *a.* The third.

तार्तीयीक *a.* The third.

ताल *m.*The palmyra tree; a banner formed of the palm;clapping the hands together, beating time (in music); the palm of the hand; a lock.*n.* The nut of the palmyra tree; yellow orpiment

तालबद्ध (-शुद्ध) *a.* Measured, regulated by musical time

तालवृंत *n.* A fan.

तालव्य *a.* Palatal.

तालिक *m.* The open palm of the hand; clapping the hands.

तालिका *f.* Clapping the hands.

तालित *n.* Coloured cloth; a string.

ताली *f.* Tadi liquor; a key.

तालु *n.* The palate.

तालुर *m.* A whirlpool.

तालूषक *n.* The palate.

तावक (-कीन) *a.* Thy, thine.

तावत् *a.* So much, so many, so great, all so long as, before, no sooner than, first, in the meanwhile, surely, completely, just, now, with respect to.

तावतिक or तावत्क *a.* Worth so much. [times.

तावत्कृत्वस् *ind.* So many

तावन्मात्र *a.* Just so much.

तिक्त *a.* Bitter, pungent, fragrant.

तिग्म *a.* Sharp, violent; hot; pungent.

तिज् *vt.* 1. A (*pres.* तितिक्षते) To endure, *vt.* 10. U (*pres.* तेजयाते-ते) To sharpen. With उद्-to instigate.

तितिक्षा *f.* Endurance, resignation. [ing.

तितिक्षु *a.* Patient, forbear-

तितिर or तित्तिर *m.* The francoline partridge.

तित्तिरी *m* The francoline partridge; name of a sage.

तिथि *m.f.* A lunar day.

तिथिक्षय *m.* The day of the new moon; the day on which a *tithi* begins and ends between two sunrises.

तिथिपत्री *f.* An almanac.

तिथिप्रणी *m.* The moon.

तिथिवृद्धि *f.* A *tithi* completed under two sunrises.

तिम् *vi.* 1. P. To be wet or damp. *vi.* 4. P. To make wet or damp [of whale.

तिमि *m.* The ocean; a kind

तिमिंगिल *m.* A kind of fish which swallows a *timi*.

तिमित *a.* Motionless, wet.

तिमिर *a.* Dark. *m. n.* Darkness, blindness; iron-rust.

तिरश्ची *f.* The female of any animal other than man.

तिरश्चीन *a.* Oblique, irregular.

तिरस् *ind.* Crookedly, invisibly, across; indirectly.

तिरस्करिणी, *f.* A curtain.

तिरस्कार *m.* or तिरस्क्रिया *f.* Concealment, abuse, contempt. [demned; covered.

तिरस्कृत *a.* Disergarded, con-

तिरोधान *n.* Disappearance, a covering. [ance.

तिरोभाव *m.* Disappear-

तिरोहित *a.* Vanished, concealed.

तिर्यक् *ind.* Obliquely.

तिर्यक्स्रोतम् *m.* The animal world.

तिर्यगयन *m* The annual revolution of the sun.

तिर्यग्जात (-योनि) *f.* The brute kind.

तिर्यच् *a.* (तिरश्ची or तिर्यंची *f*) Oblique, horizontal; curved *m. n.* Any animal other than man.

तिल *m.* The sesamum plant or its seed; a mole.

तिलकालक *a.* A mole.

तिलतंडुलक *n*. An embrace.
तिलंतुद *m*. An oilman.
तिलशस् *ind*. In small pieces.
तिलक *m*. *n*. A mark of sandal wood, &c on the forehead; the best (generally at the end of compounds). *n*. The lungs.
तिलोत्तमा *f*. Name of a heavenly nymph.
तिलोदक *n*. Water with sesamum seed offered to the dead as an oblation.
तिष्य *m*. The constellation named पुष्य; The *Kaliyuga*
तीक्ष्ण *a*. Sharp, harsh, injurious keen; intelligent; zealous, devoted.
तीक्ष्णकंद *m*. The onion.
तीक्ष्णदंष्ट्र *m*. A tiger.
तीक्ष्णधार *m*. A sword.
तीक्ष्णरश्मि *m*. The sun
तीक्ष्णलोह *n* Steel.
तीक्ष्णायस *n*. Steel. [gin.
तीर *n*.A shore, a bank,mar-
तीर्ण *a*. Crossed, surpassed.
तीर्थ *n* A road; a ford; a holy place;an expedient; a teacher source, a sacrifice; a minister; advice, a worthy person; a school of philosophy.
तीर्थ (तीर्थं) कर *m*. A Jaina *Arhat* or saint.
तीर्थराज *m*.A name of Prayága (modern Allahabad). [res.
तीर्थराजि (-राजी) *f*. Bena-
तीर्थवाक *m*. The hair of the head.
तीर्थविधि *m*. Rites observed at a place of pilgrimage.
तीर्थिक *m* A pilgrim. [ter.
तीवर *m*. The ocean; a hun-
तीव्र *a*. Severe, violent, hot, excessive; horrible, violently, sharply, excessively.
तु *ind*. But, on the contrary, on the other hand, as to, as for, as regards, and now, on one's part.
तुंग *a*. High, prominent, chief, passionate. *m*. A mountain. [rut.
तुंगभद्र *m*. An elephant in
तुंगी *f*. Night; turmeric.
तुंगीश *m*. The moon; S'iva; Krishna.
तुच्छ *a*.Empty,light; small, abandoned. *n*. Chaff.
तुण् *vt*. 6. P. To curve.
तुंड *n*. Mouth, face; the trunk of an elephant; point of an instrument.
तुंडि *m*. Face, mouth; a beak. *f*. The navel.
तुंडिन् *m*. The bull of S'iva.
तुंडिल *a*. Talkative.
तुद् *vt*. 6. U. (*pp*. तुन्न) To vex, to pain; to wound.

Caus. (तोदयति-ते). With प्र–to press.

तुंद *n.* A protuberant belly.

तुंदकूपिका(-कूपी) *f.* The cavity of the navel.

तुंदपरि-मार्ज्, (-मृज्, -मृज) *a.* Lazy, sluggish.

तुंदवत् *a.* Corpulent, fat.

तुंदिक (-त. -न्, -भ, -ल,) *a.* Corpulent.

तुन्न *a.* Wounded.

तुन्नवाय *m.* A tailor.

तुभ् *vt.* 4. 9. P. To hurt.

तुमुल (-र) *a.* Tumultuous, excited, confused.

तुंब *m.* A kind of gourd.

तुंबर *m.* Name of a *Gandharva.*

तुंबा (-बि, -बी) *f.* A kind of gourd.

तुंबु (ब) **रु** *m* The name of a *Gandharva.*

तुरग *m.* A horse, the mind.

तुरगब्रह्मचर्य *n.* Forced celibacy.

तुरगिन् *m.* A horseman.

तुरगी *f.* A mare.

तुरंग *m* A horse. *n.* The mind.

तुरंगवक्त्र (-वदन) *m.* A *Kinnara.*

तुरंगम *m.* A horse.

तुरंगी *f.* A mare.

तुरायण *n.* Non-attachment to any object or pursuit.

तुरासाह् *m.* (nom-*sing.* तुराषाट्-ड्) Indra.

तुरी *f.* A shuttle.

तुरीय (तुर्य) *a.* The fourth. *n.* A quarter.

तुल् *vt.* or *vi.* 1. P. 10 U. To raise, to weigh, to suspect, to examine, to compare, to liken, to support, to be unbearable. With -उद् to support.

तुलन *n.* Lifting; weighing; comparing.

तुलना *f.* Comparison; lifting, weighing; examining.

तुलसी *f.* A kind of shrub.

तुला *f.* A balance, measure, the seventh sign of the zodiac, resemblance.

तुलादान *n.* The gift to a Bráhmana of as much gold or silver as equals the weight of one's body.

तुलाधर (-धार) *m.* A trader.

तुल्य *a.* Well matched, similar fit for; same.

तुल्यदर्शन *a.* Regarding with indifferent eyes.

तुल्ययोगिता *f.* A figure of speech.

तुल्यशस् *ind.* In equal parts.

तुवर (तूवर) *a.* Astringent.

तुष् *vi.* 4. P. To be contented; with परि or सम्- to be satisfied.

तुष *m.* The husk or chaff of grain.

तुषार *a.* Cold. *m.* Frost, snow, dew; spray.

तुषारपर्वत (-अद्रि, -गिरि) *m.* The Himalayas.

तुष्ट *a.* Pleased, satisfied.

तुष्टि *f.* Satisfaction, pleasure.

तुस *m.* See तुष.

तुहिन *a.* See तुषार.

तुहिनशर्करा *f.* Ice.

तूण *vt.* 10. U. To contract. *vt.* 10. A. To fill up.

तूण *m.* (तूणी *f.* तूणीर *m. n.*) A quiver.

तूबर *m.* A beardless man.

तूर् *vt.* or *vi.* 4. A. To make haste ; to hurt.

तूर्ण *a* Quick. *n.* Rapidity.

तूर्णम् *ind.* Quickly, speedily.

तूर्य *m.n.* A kind of musical instrument.

तूल *m. n.* (-क *n*) Cotton. *n.* The sky, air.

तूला or तूली The wick of a lamp.

तूलिका *f.* A painter's brush, a pencil.

तूष्णीक *a.* Silent.

तूष्णीम् *ind.* Silently.

तूष्णींभाव *m.* Silence ; taciturnity.

तृंह् 6. P. To kill.

तृंहण *n.* Hurting, killing.

तृण *n.* Grass, straw ; a worthless thing.

तृणजलूका (or जलायुका) *f.* A cater-pillar.

तृणप्राय *a* Worthless.

तृणावर्त *f.* A whirl-wind.

तृतीय *a.* The third.

तृतीयक *m.* A fever returning every third day.

तृतीयप्रकृति *m. f.* A eunuch.

तृतीया *f.* The third day of a lunar fortnight; the instrumental case (in gram.).

तृद् *vt.* 1. P. 7. U(*pp.* तृण्ण) To split, to disregard.

तृप् *vt* or *vi.* 4 5 6, P. To please; become satisfied, to satisfy. *vt.* 1. P. 10 U. To kindle

तृप्त *a.* Satisfied

तृप्ति *f.* Satisfaction, contentment.

तृष् *vt.* 4 P. To be thirsty; to wish excessively.

तृष् *f.* Thirst, strong desire.

तृषार्त *a.* Suffering from thirst.

तृषाह *n.* Water.

तृषित *n.* Thirsty, greedy.

तृष्णज् *a.* Covetous, greedy.

तृष्णा *f.* Thirst, strong desire.

तृष्णालु *a* Very thirsty.

तृह् *vt.* 7. P. 10. U. To hurt.

तॄ *vi.* 1. P. (*pp.* तीर्ण) To cross over, to swim, to attain, to escape from; अति-to overcome, अव-to descend, to overcome; उद् -to rise from, to overcome. निस(प्र. सम)-to get over, to cross वि-to cross over, to give, व्यति-to overcome. *Causal*. With अव-to bend, प्र-to cheat.

तेजन *m*. A bamboo. *n*. Sharpening, polishing.

तेजस् *n*. Heat light, beauty, dignity, power; spirit, essence; gold; fire; bile.

तेजस्विन् *a*. Brilliant, powerful, noble; haughty.

तेजित *a*. Sharpened excited.

तेजोभंग *m*. Discouragement, disgrace, humiliation.

तेजोमय *a*. Brilliant.

तेजोमंडल *n*. A halo of light.

तेमन *n*. Whetting, sauce.

तैजस *a* Consisting of light, bright, passionate.

तैतिक्ष *a*. Patient

तैति (त्ति) र *m*. A partridge.

तैल *n*. Oil.

तैलिक (-न) *m*. An oil-man.

तैलिनी *f*. The wick of a lamp.

तैष *m*. The month of पौष.

तोक *n*. A child

तोडन *n*. Splitting; injuring.

तोद *m*. Pain, anguish.

तोमर *m*. *n*. An iron club.

तोय *n*. Water.

तोयकर्मन् *n*. Ablutions of the body with water; libations of water to the deceased.

तोयडिंब (-डिंभ) *m*. Hail.

तोयद(-धर -मुच्) *m*. A cloud.

तोयद *n*. Ghee.

तोयधि (-निधि,-राज् -राशि) *m*. The ocean.

तोययंत्र *n*. An artificial water jet.

तोयाधार (-आशय) *m*. A water-reservoir.

तोयालय *m*. An ocean.

तोरण *m n*. An arch, a portal. *n*. The neck.

तोल *m*. *n*. Weight, a *tola*.

तोष *m*., (-ण *n*.) Satisfaction.

तौर्य *n* The sound of musical instruments.

तौर्यत्रिक *n*. The union of song, dance and instrumental music.

तौल *n*. A balance.

त्यक्त *a*. Abandoned, surrendered.

त्यज् *vt*. 1. P. (*pp* त्यक्त) To abandon, to avoid, to disregard; with परि-to except, to abandon; to resign सम्-to abandon.

त्याग *m*. Leaving, separation, gift, donation, generosity excretion.

त्यागिन् *m*. Donor.

त्रप् *vi* 1. A. To be ashamed, to be embarrassed With अप-to turn away through shame.

त्रपा *f*. Bashfulness, modesty, a libidinous woman; fame, celebrity.

त्रपिष्ठ *a*. (super. of तृप्त) Highly satisfied.

त्रपीयस् (*comp r*. of तृप्त) *a*. More satisfied.

त्रय *a.* Triple.

त्रयस् (*nom.* pl. *m.* of त्रि) Three. *n.* A triad.

त्रयी *f* The three *Vedas* collectively; a triad, intellect.

त्रयीतनु *m.* The sun; Śiva.

त्रस् *vi.* 1. P. To tremble, to fear. with वि or सम्—to be frightened. *vt.* 10 U. To go; to seize; to oppose.

त्रस *a.* Moveable.

त्रसरेणु *m.* An atom, the mole of dust that is seen moving in a sunbeam.

त्रसुर, त्रस्नु *a.* Fearful, timid.

त्रस्त *a.* Frightened, timid.

त्राण *a.* Protected *n.* Protection, shelter, help.

त्रात *a.* Preserved (*pp.* of त्रै).

त्रास *a.* Moveable; frightening. *m.* Fear; terror, alarm.

त्रासन *a.* or *n.* Terrifying.

त्रि *num.* (nom *pl. m.* त्रयः, *f.* तिस्रः, *n.* त्रीणि) Three.

त्रिक *a.* Triple. *n.* A triad.

त्रिकर्मन् *n* The three chief duties of a Bráhmana.

त्रिकाय *m* A name of Buddha. The past, present and future.

त्रिकालज्ञ (-दर्शिन्) *a.* Omniscient.

त्रिकोण *n.* A triangle.

त्रिगत *a.* Tripled; done in three ways.

त्रिगर्ता *f.* A lascivious woman.

त्रिगुण *a.* Threefold, triple.

त्रिगुणा *f. Mâyá* or illusion

त्रिचतुर *a.pl.* Three or four

त्रिजीवा (-ज्या) *f* A radius.

त्रितय *n.* A triad.

त्रिदंडिन् *m.* A peculiar order of Sanyâsins.

त्रिदश *m.* A god.

त्रिदिव *n.* The heaven, sky, happiness.

त्रिदोष *n.* Disorder of the three humours of the body.

त्रिधा *ind.* In three ways or parts.

त्रिधारा *f.* The Ganges.

त्रिणयन, (-नयन, नेत्र, -लोचन) *m.* S'iva.

त्रिपथ *n* The three paths collectively; a place, where three roads meet.

त्रिपथगा *f.* The Ganges.

त्रिपद *n.* (-पादिका *f.*) A tripod.

त्रिपदी *f.* The girth of an elephant; the *Gâyatrî* metre; a tripod;

त्रिपाद *a.* Consisting of three-fourths. *m.* The वामन अवतार of Vishnu.

त्रिपुट *a.* Triangular; *m.* An arrow; the palm of the hand; a cubit; a bank.

त्रिपुटक *m.* A triangle.

त्रिपुंड्र *n.* A mark on the forehead consisting of three lines of ashes.

त्रिपुर *n.* The three cities of gold, silver and iron

erected by the demon Maya and burnt down by S'iva. *m*. Name of a demon.

त्रिपौरुष *a*. Extending over three generations.

त्रिभुज *n*. A triangle.

त्रिमार्गा *f*. The Ganges.

त्रिमूर्ति *m*. The united form of Brahman (*m*), Vishnu and Mahes'a.

त्रियामा *f*. Night.

त्रियोनि *f*. A lawsuit.

त्रिलिंग *a*. An adjective.

त्रिलोकी *f*. The universe.

त्रिवर्ग *m*. The three ends of life, *viz*. धर्म, अर्थ and काम.

त्रिवारम् *ind*. Three times.

त्रिविक्रम *m*. Vishnu.

त्रिविध *a*. three-fold.

त्रिविष्टप, (-पिष्टप) *n*. Heaven.

त्रिवेणि (वेणी) *f*. The place where the rivers Yamuná and Sarasvatî join the Ganges.

त्रिशिख *n*. A trident, crown.

त्रिशूल *n*. A trident.

त्रिस्थली *f*. The three sacred places, *viz* काशी, प्रयाग and गया.

त्रिस्रोतस् *f*. The Ganges.

त्रिंशक *a* Consisting of or bought for thirty.

त्रिंशति *f*. Thirty.

त्रिस् *ind*. Thrice, three times.

त्रुट् *vi*. 4. 6. P. To tear.

त्रुटि (-टी) *f*. An atom; a very minute space of time equal to $\frac{1}{4}$ of a *kshana*; doubt, loss.

त्रेता *f*. A triad, the three sacred fires; the second of the four *yugas* of the Hindus.

त्रेधा *ind*. In three ways.

त्रै *vt*. 1. A. (*pp*. त्रात, त्राण) To pro ect.

त्रैकालिक *a*. Relating to the past, present and future.

त्रैकाल्य *n*. The past, present and future.

त्रैगुण्य *n*. Triplicity; the three gunas or properties (सत्व, रजस् and तमस्).

त्रैमातुर *m*. Lakshmana or Ganes'a.

त्रैमासिक *a*. Quarterly.

त्रैराशिक *n*. The rule of three.

त्रैलोक्य *n*. The three worlds.

त्रैविष्टप (-पेय) *m*. A god.

त्रोटक *n*. A species of drama.

त्रोटि *f*. A bill, a beak.

त्र्यक्ष, (-क) *m* God S'iva.

त्र्यक्षर *m*. The mystic syllable ओम् which contains three letters.

त्र्यंबक, (त्रियंबक) *m*. God S'iva.

त्वक्कंडुर *m*. A sore.

त्वक्ष् *vt*. 1. P. (*pp*. त्वष्ट) To pare, to hew.

त्वक्सुगंध *m*. An orange.

त्वग् *vt*. 1. P. (*pres*. त्वंगति)

To move; to gallop.

त्वगंकुर *m*. Horripilation.

त्वगिंद्रिय *n*. The organ of touch.

त्वंकार *m*. Thouing, addressing disrepectfully.

त्वच् *f*. Skin, bark, touch.

त्वचा *f*. See त्वच्.

त्वदीय *a*. Thy, your.

त्वाद्विध *a*. Like you.

त्वर् *vt*. 1. A. To hurry.

त्वरा (-रि) *f*. Haste, speed.

त्वरित *a*. Quick, speedy. *n*. Despatch, haste.

त्वरितम् *ind*. Quickly, fast.

त्वष्टृ *m*. A carpenter, Vis'vakarman

त्वादृश् (-श) *a*. Similar to thee.

त्विष् *vt*. 1. U. To shine.

त्विष् *f*. Light, splendour, beauty;authority desire; custom, speech.

त्विषांपति, त्विषामीश *m*. The sun.

थ

थ *m*. A mountain. *n*. Protection.

थुड् *vt*. 6. P. To cover.

थुत्कार (थूत्कार or थूत्कृत) *m*. The sound थुत made in spitting.

थुर्व् *vt*. 1. P To hurt.

थैथै *ind*. The imitative sound of a musical instrument.

द

द *a*. (At the end of compounds only) Giving. *m*. A gift; a mountain. *n*. A wife.

दंश् *vt*. 1. P. (*pp*. दष्ट) or 10 A. To bite, to sting. With उप-to eat; सम्-to bite, to stick.

दंश *m*. Biting, stinging, a fault,an armour, a tooth.

दंशक *m*. A dog; a gadfly.

दंशिन् *m*. See दंशक.

दंशी *f*. A small gadfly.

दंष्ट्रा *f* A large tooth, a tusk, a fang

दंष्ट्रायुध *m*. A wild boar.

दंष्ट्राल *a*. Having large tusks.

दंष्ट्रिका *f*. See दंष्ट्रा

दंष्ट्रिन् *m*. A boar; a snake.

दक्ष *a*. Competent, clever, suitable; careful honest *m*. The father of Párvatî in her former birth.

दक्षकन्या (-जा, -तनया) *f*. Párvatî; any lunar mansion.

दक्षसुत *m*. A god.

दक्षिण *a*. Competent, right (*opp*. to वाम); southern; honest, agreeable; liberal, subm ssive; *m*. The right hand; Vishnu; a lover who is equally courteous to several mistresses.

दक्षिणपश्चात् *ind.* To the south-west. [ern.

दक्षिणपश्चिम *a.* South-west-

दक्षिणपश्चिमा *f.* The south-west. [south-east.

दक्षिणपूर्वा (-प्राची) *f.* The

दक्षिणस्थ A charioteer.

दक्षिणा *ind.* To the south. *f.* A present or gift to Bráhmanas.

दक्षिणाचल *m.* The Malaya.

दक्षिणापथ *m.* The Deccan.

दक्षिणायन *n.* The winter solstice.

दक्षिणार्ध *m.* The right hand.

दक्षिणावर्त *n.* Turned towards the right or south.

दक्षिणीय (दक्षिण्य or दाक्षिण्य) *m.* A Brahmana fit for a sacrificial fee.

दक्षिणेतर *a* Right, northern.

दक्षिणेतरा *f.* The North.

दक्षिणेन *ind.* On the right side of; on the south of.

दक्षिणोत्तरवृत्त *n.* The meridian line.

दग्ध *a.* Burnt, tortured, insipid; inauspicious; a term of abuse.

दघ्न *a.* A termination affixed to nouns to denote 'reaching to', 'as high as'.

दंड् *vt.* 10. U. To fine, to punish.

दंड *m.* *n.* A stick, the sceptre of a king; the trunk of an elephant; stalk, the handle, the oar, a measure of length equal to four hands; an army, a control, punishment; Yama; Vishnu; S'iva.

दण्डक *m* (-का *f.*) A district in the Deccan.

दण्डग्रहण *n.* Becoming a mendicant. [king.

दण्डधर, (-धार) *m.* Yama; a

दण्डनायक *m.* A judge, the chief police officer; a general.

दण्डनीति *f.* Polity, ethics.

दण्डनेत्र *m.* A king.

दण्डप *m.* A king.

दण्डपाणि *m.* Yama.

दण्डपाल (-पालक) *m.* The chief magistrate; a porter.

दण्डपांशुल *m.* A porter.

दण्डप्रमाण *m.* Bowing without bending the body.

दण्डभृत् *m.* A porter, Yama.

दण्डमाथ *m.* The highway.

दण्डयात्रा *m.* A solemn procession; warlike expedition.

दण्डयाम *m.* Yama; the sage Agastya; a day. [officer.

दण्डवाहिन् *m.* A police-

दण्डविधि *m.* Criminal law.

दण्डव्यूह *m.* A particular military array.

दण्डशास्त्र *n.* Criminal law.
दण्डहस्त *m.* A doorkeeper. Yama.
दण्डाजिन *n.* Hypocricy.
दंडादंडि *ind.*(Fighting)with sticks and staves.
दंडिक A staff-bearer.
दंडिका *f.* A stick; a line; a necklace.
दंडिन् *m.* A *Sannya'sin*; a door-keeper; Yama; a king; name of a poet.
दत् *m.* Tooth.
दत्त *a* (*pp.* of दा) Given, assigned; stretched forth. *m.*One of the twelve kinds of sons in Hindu law; the God दत्तात्रेय. *n.* A gift.
दत्तक *m.* An adopted son.
दत्तहस्त *a.* Supported.
दत्तात्रेय *m.* Name of a God.
दत्ति *f.* Donation; oblation.
दत्त्रिम *m.* An adopted son.
दद् *vt.* 1 A. To give.
दद *a.* Giving.
ददन *n.* Gift, donation.
दध् *vt.*1 A.To hold, to give.
दधि *n* Coagulated milk, a garment.
दधिचार *m.* A churning [stick.
दधिज *n.* Fresh butter.
दधिमंड *m.* (-वारि *n.*) Whey.
दधिसार, (-स्नेह) *m.* Fresh butter.
दनु *f.* Mother of the Dá- [navas.
दनुज (-संभव, -सूनु) *m.* A demon.
दंत *m.* A tooth, elephant's tusk, ivory; the point of an arrow; peak; a bower.
दंतक *m.* A peak, shelf projecting from a wall.
दंतग्राहिन् *a* Injuring the teeth.
दंतच्छद *m.* The lip.
दंतजात *a.* (A child) that is teething.
दंतधावन *n.* Washing the teeth; a tooth-brush.
दंतपत्र *n* An ear ornament.
दंतपवन *n* A tooth-brush.
दंतबीज (-वीज -बीजक,-वीजक) *m.*The pomegranate tree.
दंतमूल, (-वल्क) *n.* Gums.
दंतमूलीय *m. pl.* The dental letters.
दंतवस्त्र (-वासस्) *n.* The lip.
दंतवीणा *f.*A kind of musical instrument; chattering of the teeth.
दंतशठ *a.*Sour,acid.
दंतशाण *m.* A kind of tooth- [powder.
दंतशूल *m. n.* Toothache.
दंतादंति *ind:* Biting one another
दंतावल *m.* An elephant.
दंतिन् *m.* An elephant.
दंतुर *a.* Having long or projecting teeth, notched, undulatory.
दंत्य *m.* A letter of the dental [class.

दंदशूक *a.* Venomous. *m.* A demon, a snake.

दभ्र *a.*Little. *m.* The ocean.

दम् *vt.* or *vi.* 4. P. (*pp.*दमित or दांत) To be tamed, to subdue.

दम *m.* Punishment, self-command. [punishment.

दमथ(थु) *m.* Self restraint;

दमन *a* Subduing, tranquil. *n.* Subjugation; self-restraint.

दमयितृ *m.* A chastiser.

दंपती *m. du.*Man and wife.

दंभ् *vt.* 5. P. (*pp* दब्ध) To injure, to go, to deceive. *vt.* 10. U. To send.

दंभ *m.*,(-न*n.*)Deceit, hypocrisy; roguery;arrogance.

दांभिन् *m.* A hypocrite.

दम्य *a.* To be trained or subdued.

दय् *vt.* 1.A.To pity, to protect, to love, to move;to give. [sion.

दया *f.* Sympathy, compas-

दयालु *a.* Compassionate.

दयित *a.* Beloved.*m.* A husband, a lover.

दयिता *f.*A wife,a mistress.

दर *m. n.* A cave, a conch-shell. *m.* Fear. *ind.* A little.

दरण *n.*Breaking,splitting.

दरणि *m.* (-णी *f.*) An eddy; a current.

दरद *m.* Fear, terror.

दरि(-री) *f* A cave, a valley.

दरिद्र *a.*Poor, distressed.

दरिद्रा *vi.* 2. P. To be poor, to be sparse.

दर्दर *m.*A mountain.

दर्दरीक *m.*A frog; a cloud.

दर्दुर *m.* A frog, a cloud, a mountain. [rosy.

दर्द्रु (-द्रू) *m* A kind of lep-

दर्प *m.* Pride, insolence, vanity, sulkiness; heat; musk.

दर्पक *m.*The god of love.

दर्पण *m.* A mirror *n* The eye; kindling.

दर्पित(-न्)*a* Proud, arrogant.

दर्भ *m.* A kind of sacred grass.

दर्भट *n.* A retired room.

दर्व *m.* A demon; killing.

दर्वट *m.* A police officer.

दर्विका *f.* A ladle, a spoon.

दर्वी (-र्वि) *f* A ladle, a spoon; the expanded hood of a snake.

दर्श *m.* Sight, appearance; the day of the new moon. (अमावास्या); a sacrificial rite performed on the day of the new moon.

दर्शक*a.*Showing.*m.*A door-keeper; a skilful man.

दर्शन *n.*Looking,sight, eye, mirror, examination;becoming visible; exhibition; a visit; colour; a dream, judgment, religious knowledge, virtue;

a doctrine; a system of philosophy.

दर्शनपथ *m.* The range of sight. [some.

दर्शनीय *a.* Visible, hand-

दर्शयितृ *m.* A warder.

दर्शिन् *a.* (at the end of compounds) Seeing, knowing.

दल् *vt.* or *vt.* 1. P. To burst open, to expand; with वि- to break; to dig.

दल *m.n.* A piece, a degree, a half, a scabbard; a petal a leaf, the blade of any weapon; a heap.

दलन *n.* Bursting.

दलप *m.* A weapon; gold.

दलभ *m* A wheel; fraud.

दलाढक *m.* Foam; a ditch.

दलित *a.* Expanded.

दव *m.* A Wood, a forest conflagration; fever.

दविष्ठ *a.* Most distant (Super of दूर).

दवीयस् *a.* More distant (*Compar.* of दूर). [of ten.

दशक *a* Tenfold, *n* A group

दशकंठ (-कंधर,-ग्रीव) *m.* Râva-

दशगुण *a.* Tenfold. [na.

दशत् (-ति) *f.* A group of ten, a decade.

दशतय *a* Tenfold. [or ways.

दशधा *ind.* In ten parts.

दशन् *num.* (*pl.*) Ten.

दशन *m.n.* A tooth; biting. *m.* The peak of a mountain. *n.* An armour.

दशम *a.* The tenth.

दशमी *f.* The tenth day of a lunar fortnight; the tenth decade of the human life.

दशमुख (-आनन,-आस्य,-वक्त्र, -वदन) *m.* Rávana.

दशवाजिन् *m.* The moon.

दशहरा *f.* The Ganges; a festival in honour of the Ganges or of Durgá.

दशा *f.* The fringe of any garment, the wick of a lamp, age, a stage, circumstances, fate; understanding.

दशाश्व *m.* The moon. [stung

दष्ट *a.* (*pp.* of दंश्) Bitten;

दस्यु *m.* A demon, an outcaste, a robber.

दस्र *a.* Cruel, destructive. *m. du.* The twin physicians of the gods. *m.* An ass; a robber. *n* The cold season; the lunar mansion *As'vini.*

दह् *vt.* 1.P. (*pp.* दग्ध; *desid.* दिधक्षति) To burn, to pain; with निस् (परि, प्र, सम्)-to burn, to torment.

दह *m.* Fire.

दहन *a.* Burning, destructive. *m.* Fire; a bad man. *n.* Burning

दहनकेतन *m.* Smoke.

दहनसारथि *m.* Wind.

दहनोल्का *f.* A fire-brand.

दहर *a.* Small, thin; young *m.* A child, a rat.

दा *vt.* 1. P. (*pp.* दत्त; *pres* यच्छति) To give. *vt.* 2 P. To cut, *vt.* 3. U. To give. With आ-(Atm.) to take, to exact, to perceive उपा-(Atm.) to acquire, to carry परि- to deliver. प्र-to give, प्रति-to recompense, to exchange. व्या-to open, संप्र-to bestow, to bequeath.

दाक्षायणी *f.* Any one of the 27 lunar mansions; Name of Aditi mother of the gods; Párvatî.

दाक्षिण *a.* Relating to a sacrificial gift or to the south

दाक्षिणात्य *a.* Southern. *m.* A southerner; a Deccani.

दाक्षिणिक *a.* Connected with a sacrificial gift.

दाक्षिण्य *n.* Politeness, kindness; honesty; talent

दाक्ष्य *n* Cleverness, integrity.

दाघ *m.* Burning.

दाडक *m.* A tooth; a tusk.

दाडि (लि) म *m.*,(-मा *f.*) The pomegranate tree, *n.* its fruit.

दाडिंब *m.* See दाडिम

दाढा *f.* A large tooth; a multitude, wish.

दाढिका *f.* The beard.

दांडिक *m.* A chastiser.

दात *a.* Divided; cleaned.

दाति *f.* Giving; cutting

दातृ *a.* Giving. *m* A donor, a creditor a teacher.

दात्यूह *m.* The gallinule, the *châtaka* bird; a water-crow; a cloud

दात्र *n.* An instrument of cutting.

दाद *m.* A gift, a donation.

दान् *vt.* 1. U. To make straight; to cut.

दान *n* Charity, bribery; a gift, rut of an elephant; dividing; purification.

दानक *n.* A mean gift.

दानधर्म *m.* Alms-giving.

दानपति *m.* An exceedingly munificent man.

दानपत्र *n.* A deed of gifts.

दानपात्र *n.* Fit to recieve gifts.

दानप्रतिभाव्य *n.* Security for payment of a debt.

दानव *m.* A demon.

दानवारि *m* A god; Vishnu.

दानवीर (-शूर, -शौंड) *m.* An exceedingly liberal man.

दानवेय *m.* See दानव.

दांत (*pp.* of दम) *a.* Named, resigned.

दांति *f.* Self-restraint.

दांतिक *a.* Made of ivory.

दापित *a.* Fined, adjudged.

दामन् *n.* A string, a garland, a line.

दामनी *f.* A foot-rope.

दामिनी *f.* Lightning.

दांपत्य *n.* Matrimony.

दांभिक *a.* Deceitful, hypocritical; proud.

दामोदर *m.* Krishna.

दाय *m.* A gift, nuptial present, a share, inheritance, loss; irony; place; a son.

दायभाग *m.* Partition.

दायक *a.* Giving.

दायाद *m.* An heir; a son.

दायादा (-दी) *f.* An heiress.

दायाद्य *n.* Inheritance.

दार *m.* A rent, a ploughed field. *m pl.* (though singular in sense) A wife.

दारकर्मन् *n.* (-क्रिया *f.*) Marriage. [child.

दारक *a.* Breaking. *m.* A

दारग्रह (-उपसंग्रह, -परिग्राह *m.* -ग्रहण *n.*) Marriage.

दारण *n.* Splitting, opening.

दारद *m.* Quicksilver; the ocean *m.n.* Vermilion.

दारिका *f.* A daughter, a harlot.

दारित *a.* Torn, divided.

दारिद्र्य *n.* Poverty.

दारी *f* A cleft.

दारु *m.* A munificent man; an artist *n.* Wood, timber; a lever, the brass.

दारुका *f* A wooden puppet.

दारुगर्भा (-पुत्रिका, -पुत्री) *f.* A wooden puppet.

दारुण *a.* Hard, cruel, terrible. *m.* The sentiment of horror.

दारुमय *a.* Wooden.

दार्ढ्य *n.* Hardness, corroboration.

दार्भ *a* Made of *darbha* [grass.

दार्व *a.* Wooden.

दार्वट *n* A council-house.

दार्शनिक *m.* One versed in the philosophical sys- [tems.

दार्षद *a.* Mineral.

दार्ष्टांतिक *a.* Illustrative.

दाव *m.* See दव.

दावाग्नि, (दावानल) *m.* A forest conflagration.

दाश *m.* A fisherman.

दाशरथ (-थि) *m.* Son of Das'aratha.

दाशेर *m* The son of a fisherman; a camel.

दास *m.* A slave, a servant, a fisherman, a S'ûdra.

दासस्यकुल *n.* The mob.

दासी *f* A female servant or slave; a harlot.

दासेय (-र) *m* The son of a female slave; a Śûdra.

दास्य *n.* Slavery, service.

दास्याःपुत्र (दास्याःसुत) *m.* An abusive term.

दाह *m.* Burning, conflagration, glowing redness (as of the sky); feverish heat.

दाहसर *m.*(-सरस्,-स्थल *n.*) A place where dead bodies are burnt.

दाहक *a.* Burning, inflamma tory. *m.* Fire. [ing.

दाहन *n.* Burning, cauteriz-

दाहात्मक *a* Combustible

दाह्य *a.* Combustible.

दिक्कर *m.* A youth. [ful girl.

दिक्करिका, दिक्करी *f.* A youth-

दिक्करिन्,दिग्गज, दिग्दंतिन्,दिग्वारण *m.* Any of the eight elephants presiding over the eight quarters.

दिक्चक्र *n.* The horizon;the whole world.

दिगंत *m.* Remote distance.

दिगंतर *n.* A distant country; space.

दिगंबर *a.* Stark naked. *m.* A mendicant, S'iva; darkness.

दिगंश *m.* The ecliptic.

दिग्जय,दिग्विजय *m* The conquest of various countries in all directions.

दिग्दर्शन *n.* A general survey. [above.

दिङ्नाग *m.* See **दिक्करिन्**

दिग्भाग *m.* A point, a direction.

दिग्मंडल *n.* See **दिक्चक्र.**

दिङ्मात्र *n.* Mere indication.

दिग्वस्त्र See **दिगंबर.**

दिग्ध (*pp.* **दिह्**) Smeared, anointed.

दिंडी, (-र) *m.* A kind of musical instrument.

दित *a.* Cut, divided

दिति *f.* Cutting, liberality; name of the mother of the Ràkshasas.

दितिज (-तनय) *m* Rákshasa.

दित्य *m.* A demon.

दित्सा *f.* Desire of giving.

दिदृक्षा *f.* Desire of seeing.

दिदृक्षु *a.* Desirous of seeing.

दिधिषु *m.* The second husband of a woman twice married. *f.* A virgin widow re-married.

दिधि (धी) षू *f.* A woman twice married; an unmarried elder sister having a married younger sister.

दिधिषूपति *m.* A man who has sexual intercourse with the widow of his brother.

दिन *m. n.* A day.

दिनकर (-कृत्) *m.* The sun.

दिनचर्या *f.* Daily occupation.

दिनज्योतिस् *n.* Sunshine.

दिनप (-पति,-बंधु,-मणि,-मयूख *m.*, -रत्न *n.*) The sun.

दिनमुख *n.* The morning.

दिनागम (-आदि, आरंभ) *m.* The morning.

दिनांड *n.* Darkness.

दिनार्ध *m.* Noon.

दिनिका *f.* A day's wages.

दिलीर *n.* A mushroom.

दिव् *vt.* or *vi* 4. P. (*pp.* द्यूत or द्यून; *pres.* दीव्यति; *desid.* दुद्यूषति, दिदेविषति) To shine; to throw, to gamble, to trifle with, to sell; to praise; to rejoice; *vt.* 1. P. 10. U. (*pres.* देवति, देवयति-ते) to pain, *vi.* 10. A (*pres.* देवयते) To suffer pain; with परि-to lament, to suffer pain.

दिव् *f.* (nom. *sing.* द्यौः) The heaven, the sky; a day.

दिवस्पति *m.* Indra.

दिवस्पृथिव्यौ *f. du.* Heaven and earth.

दिविज *m.* A god.

दिविष्ट, दिविस्थ, दिविषद्, दिविसद् *m.* A god. [A god.

दिवोकस्, दिवौकस्, दिवौकस *m.*

दिव *n.* Heaven, the sky; a day; a forest.

दिवस *m.n.* A day.

दिवसमुख *n.* Day-break.

दिवसविगम *m.* Evening, sunset.

दिवा *ind.* By day.

दिवाकर *m.* The sun; a crow; the sun-flower.

दिवाकीर्ति *m.* A man of low caste; a barber; an owl.

दिवाटन *m.* A crow.

दिवांध *m.* An owl

दिवातन *a.* Belonging to the day. [night.

दिवानिशम् *ind.* Day and

दिवाप्रदीप *m.* An obscure man. [a thief.

दिवाभीत (-भीति) *m.* An owl,

दिवारात्रम् *ind.* Day and night.

दिवावसु *m.* The sun.

दिवाशय *a.* Sleeping at day.

दिवास्वप्न (-स्वाप) *m.* Sleep during day-time.

दिव्य *a.* Divine, supernatural, wonderful; beautiful. *m.* A superhuman being. *n.* Divinity; an ordeal; the sky; an oath.

दिव्यचक्षुस् *n.* Supernatural vision. *a* One possessing such vision; blind.

दिव्यदृश् *m.* An astrologer.

दिव्यप्रश्न *m.* Augury.

दिव्यरत्न *n.* The philosopher's. stone.

दिव्यसरित् *f.* The Ganges.

दिव्यांशु *m.* The sun

दिव्योदक *n.* Rainwater.

दिश् *vt.* 6. U (*pp.* दिष्ट) To produce, to point out, to assign, to grant, to allow. With अति to extend the application of; अप-to say, to pretend, to refer to, आ-to order, to point out, to instruct, to prescribe. उद्-to allude to, to aim at, to denote, to teach, उप-to advise, to prescribe, to refer to, to announce, निस्-to point out, to predict; to give; to make mention of; प्र-to assign,to grant; प्रत्या-to repulse, to reject, to defeat, व्यप-to name falsely,to pretend; सम्-to give, to direct, to send as a messenger.

दिश् *f.* Direction, indication, method, point of view, order, a tooth-bite.

दिशा *f.* Direction, region.

दिष्ट *a.* Shown, described, settled. *n.* Fate, order. *m.* Time.

दिष्टांत *m.* Death.

दिष्टि *f.* Direction, rule, a kind of measure; fate, happiness, joy.

दिष्ट्या *ind.* Fortunately.

दिह् *vt.* 2. U (*pp.* दिग्ध;*pres.* देग्धि, दिग्धे) To anoint, to soil. With सम्-to doubt, to mistake for.

दी *vi.* 1. (*pp.* दीन)To perish.

दीक्ष् *vi.* 4. A. (*pp.* दीक्षित) To consecrate, to dedicate, to initiate, to invest with the sacred thread.

दीक्षक *m.* A spiri ual guide.

दीक्षण *n.* Initiation.

दीक्षा *f.* Consecration, investiture with the sacred thread, a ceremony.

दीक्षित *a.* Initiated, consecrated; prepared for. *m.* An appellation affixed to the name of a person who or whose ancestors may have performed the *jyotishtoma* sacrifice.

दीधिति *f.* A ray of light.

दीधितिमत् *m* The sun.

दीधी *vi.* 2. A. To shine, to appear.

दीन *a.*Poor, wretched;ruined, melancholy; timid *m.* A man in distress.

दीनार *m.* A particular gold coin.

दीप् *vi.* 4. A. To shine to burn, to be illustrious.

दीप *m.* A light, a lamp.

दीपालि (दीपावली *f.* दीपोत्सव) *m.* Nocturnal illumination; lamp festival.

दीपकालिका *f.* The flame of a lamp.

दीपकीट्ट *n.* Lamp-black.

दीपकूपी (-खोरी) *f.* The wick of a lamp.

दीपध्वज *m.* Lamp-black.

दीपपादप (-वृक्ष) *m.* A lamp-stick, a lamp-stand.

दीपभाजन *n.* A lamp [tion.

दीपमाला *f.* An illumina-

दीपशत्रु *m.* A moth.

दीपशिखा *f.* The flame of a lamp. [illumination.

दीपशृंखला *f.* A row of lights;

दीपक *a.* (दीपिका *f*) Kindling; illustrating; exciting. *m.* A light, a lamp, a falcon; Kámadeva (also दीप्यक). *n*. Saffron; a particular figure of speech.

दीपन *n*. Kindling, promoting digestion; stimulating.

दीपान्विता *f*. The day of the new moon.

दीपिका *f*. A light, a torch.

दीपित *a*. Illuminated.

दीप्त *a*. Kindled; illuminated; *m*. A lion. *n*. Gold.

दीप्ति *f*. Brightness, lustre; extreme loveliness.

दीप्र *a*. Shining. *m*. Fire.

दीर्घ *a*. Long, deep (as a sigh), urgent.

दीर्घम् *ind*. Deeply, for a long time.

दीर्घकाय *a*. Tall.

दीर्घगति (-ग्रीव, -घाटिक, -जंघ) *m*. A camel.

दीर्घजिह्व *m*. A snake, a serpent.

दीर्घनिद्रा *f*. Long sleep; death.

दीर्घपत्र *m* The palm tree.

दीर्घपृष्ठ *m*. A snake

दीर्घमारुत *m*. An elephant.

दीर्घरद *m*. A hog.

दीर्घरसन *m*. A snake.

दीर्घरोमन् *m*. A bear.

दीर्घसूत्र (-सूत्रिन्) *a*. Slow, dilatory.

दीर्घाध्वग *m*. A messenger.

दीर्घाहन *m*. Summer (ग्रीष्म).

दीर्घिका *f*. A long lake.

दीर्ण *a*. Torn, frightened.

दु *vt*. or *vt*. 5. P To burn, to afflict.

दुःख *a*. Painful. *n*. Pain, difficulty.

दुःखग्राम *m*. Worldly life.

दुःखछिन्न *a*. Tough, distressed.

दुःखभाज् *a*. Unhappy.

दुकूल *n*. A silk garment.

दुग्ध (*pp*. of दुह) *n* Milk; the milky juice.

दुग्धतालीय *n*. Cream.

दुघ *a*. (generally at the end of a compound) yielding.

दुघा *f*. Milch cow.

दुंडुभ *m*. See डुंडुभ.

दुड्डुम *m*. A green onion.

दुंदु *m*. A kind of drum.

दुंदुभ *m*. (-भि *m*. *f*.) A large kettledrum.

दुर् *ind*. (A substitute of दुस् before words beginning with vowels or soft consonants). Bad.

दुरतिक्रम *a*. Unconquerable, insurmountable.

दुरत्यय *a*. Difficult to be overcome.

दुराधिगम *a*. Unattainable, difficult to be understood.

दुरधिष्ठित *a*. Badly managed.

दुरध्यवसाय *m*. A foolish undertaking.

दुरंत *a*. Infinite, unhappy.

दुरन्वय *a*. Difficult to be carried out or comprehended.

दुरवगम *a*. Incomprehensible.

दुरवग्रह *a.* Difficult to be restrained.
दुराक्रमण *n.* Unfair attack; difficult approach.
दुरागम *m.* Illegal gain.
दुराग्रह *m.* Foolish obstinacy.
दुराचार *a.* Ill-behaved. *m.* Ill conduct.
दुरात्मन् *a.* Base *m.* Rascal.
दुराधर्ष *a.* Dangerous.
दुराप *a.* Difficult to be obtained.
दुरालाप *m.* Curse, abusive language.
दुरालोक *a.* Dazzling.
दुराशा *f.* Hoping against hope.
दुरासद *a.* Unequalled, unconquerable.
दुरित *n.* Difficulty, evil, sin.
दुरुक्ति *f.* Offensive speech.
दुरुत्तर *a.* Unanswerable.
दुरूह *a.* Abstruse.
दुर्ग *m. n.* A citadel, difficulty.
दुर्गति *f.* Misfortune, hell.
दुर्गम *a.* Inaccessible, difficult to understand.
दुर्गा *f.* Párvatî.
दुर्गत *a.* Unfortunate, distressed; poor.
दुर्घट *a.* Difficult; impossible.
दुर्जन *a. m.* A bad man, a villain.
दुर्जर *a.* Ever youthful; indigestible.
दुर्जात *a.* Wretched; false; *n.* Difficulty.
दुर्णय (-नय) *m.* Bad conduct; injustice.
दुर्दांत *n.* Intractable, insolent. *m.* A calf; a quarrel.
दुर्दिन *n.* A cloudy day.
दुर्दैव *n.* Misfortune.
दुर्धर *a.* Irresistible.
दुर्धी *f.* Stupid, silly.
दुर्निमित *a.* Carelessly put to the ground.
दुर्नीत *n.* Misconduct.
दुर्बल *a.* Weak; scanty.
दुर्भग *a.* Unfortunate.
दुर्भगा *f.* An ill-tempered woman.
दुर्भाग्य *n.* Ill luck.
दुर्भिक्ष *n.* Famine, want.
दुर्मद *a.* Drunken, ferocious.
दुर्मनस् *a.* Discouraged, melancholy.
दुर्मल्लिका (-मल्ली) *f.* A farce.
दुर्मुख *a.* Ugly, abusive.
दुर्मेधस् *a.* Silly. *m.* A dunce.
दुर्ललित *a.* Ill-bred, fondled. *n.* Waywardness.
दुर्लेख्य *n.* A forged document.
दुर्वच *a.* Indescribable. *n.* Abuse.
दुर्वाच्य *a.* Harsh. *n.* Ill fame.
दुर्वाद *m.* Slander, calumny.
दुर्वार, (-ण) *a.* Irresistible.
दुर्वासना *f.* Evil propensity.
दुर्विदग्ध *a.* Stupid, silly; foolishly puffed up.

दुर्विध *a.* Mean, wicked; poor, silly. [haved.

दुर्विनीत *a.* Wicked, ill-be-

दुर्विपाक *m.* Bad result.

दुर्विलसित *n.* Rudeness [Vile.

दुर्वृत्त *n.* Misconduct. *a.*

दुरादेश *m.* A gamester; a stake. *n.* Gambling.

दुल् *vt.* 10. U. To shake to and fro.

दुश्चर *a.* Inaccessible.

दुश्चरित *n.* Misbehaviour.

दुष् *vi.* 4 P. To be corrupted, to sin; with प्र-to be corrupted. *Caus.* To deprave; to find fault with. With प्र, सम्–to censure, to violate.

दुष्कर *a.* Difficult, arduous. *n.* A difficult task, atmosphere.

दुष्कर्मन् *n.* Sin, crime. [deed.

दुष्कृत *n.* दुष्कृति *f.* Sin, mis-

दुष्ट *a.* Damaged; depraved; wicked; guilty; defective.

दुष्टि *f.* Corruption, depravity.

दुष्टर (दुस्तर) *a.* Difficult to be crossed, invincible.

दुस् *ind.* A prefix meaning 'evil, bad, wicked, hard, inferior, &c.'

दुस्सम *a.* Uneven, adverse.

दुःसमम *ind.* Ill, wickedly.

दुःस्थ (दुस्थ, दुःस्थित, दुस्थित) *a.* Distressed, unsteady; ignorant; foolish.

दुःस्थम्, दुस्थस् *ind.* Badly, ill.

दुह् *vt.* 2. U. (*pp.* दुग्ध) To milk, to squeeze out; to yield, to grant; to enjoy.

दुहितृ *f.* A daughter.

दू *vt.* or *vi.* 4. A (*pp.* दून) To suffer pain, to be sorry.

दूत (–क) *m.* A messenger.

दूतिका, दूती *f.* A female messenger, a go-between. [message.

दूत्य *n.* An embassy; a

दून *a.* Pained.

दूर *a* (*Comp.* दवीयस्, *super.* दविष्ठ) Distant. *n.* Distance. [far away.

दूरतस् *ind.* From a distance,

दूरदर्शन *m.* A vulture; a learned man.

दूरदर्शिन् *a.* Prudent; *m.* A vulture; a prophet.

दूरदृष्टि *f.* Foresight.

दूरभाज् *a.* Distant. [highly.

दूरम् *ind.* Far away,

दूरवर्तिन् *a.* Far removed.

दूरसंस्थ *a.* Remote, away.

दूरारूढ *a.* Far advanced, intense; vehement.

दूरीकृ *vt.* To separate; to surpass.

दूरीभू *vi.* To be away from.

दूरेण *ind.* From afar, by far.

दूर्वा *f.* Sacred grass.

दूष *a.* (at the end of a compound) Polluting.

दूषक *a.* Polluting, sinful.
दूषण *n.* Violation, blame, censure, objection, fault, sin. *m.* Name of a Râkshasa killed by Ráma.
दूषित *a.* Corrupted, injured; demoralized; censured; falsely accused.
दूष्य *a.* Corruptible; *n.* pus; matter, evil; poison
दृ *vt.* 6. A To honour. [ened.
दृंहित *a.* Grown; Strength-
दृक *n.* A hole, an opening.
दृक्पथ *m.* The range of sight.
दृक्पात *m.* A look, a glance.
दृक्प्रिया *f.* Beauty, splen-
दृग्गोचर *a.* Visible. [dour.
दृग्जल *a.* Tears.
दृग्ज्या *f.* The sine of the zenith-distance.
दृग्लंबन *n.* Vertical parallax.
दृग्वृत्त *n.* A vertical circle.
दृढ *a.* Fixed, tough; durable; sure; steady, established. [sively.
दृढम् *ind.* Firmly; exces-
दृप् *vt.* 1. P. 10. U To light *vi.* 4. P. To be glad; to be arrogant.
दृप्त *a.* Proud, mad. [ful.
दृप्र *a* Proud, strong, power-
दृश् *vt.* 1. P. To see, to wait upon, to know; with उद्-to expect, सम्-to see well. *Caus.* (दर्शयति-ते) to show, to prove, to adduce. With अनु (आ, उप, नि, प्र, or सम्)-to show, to prove.
दृश् *f.* The eye, sight, knowledge. *a* Looking like.
दृशद् *f.* A stone. [river.
दृशद्वती *f.* Name of a
दृशा *f.* The eye.
दृशान *m.* A spiritual teacher. *n.* Light. [tra.
दृशि(-शी) *f.* The eye; a Sás-
दृश्य *a.* Visible, beautiful.
दृश्वन् *a.* Conversant with.
दृषद् *f.* A rock, a stone.
दृष्ट *a.* (*pp.* of दृश्) Seen; known. *n.* Perception.
दृष्टांत *m. n.* An example; a figure of speech; a science. eye intellect, view.
दृष्टि *f.* Sight, knowledge
दृष्टिगोचर *a.* Visible. [sight.
दृष्टिपथ *m.* The range of
दृष्टिपात *m.* A look.
दृष्टिमत् *a.* Wise.
दृष्टिविक्षेप *m.* A side-glance.
दृष्टिविद्या *f.* Optics. [glance.
दृष्टिविभ्रम *m.* An amorous
दृह् *vt.* 1. P. To be fixed, to prosper.
दॄ *vt.* or *vi.* 4. 9. P. (*pp.* दीर्ण;) To burst asunder; with वि-to divide.
दे *vt.* 1. A. (*pp.* दात) To protect; te cherish.
देदीप्यमान *a.* Blazing.
देय *a.* To be given or restored; proper for a gift.

देव् *vt* 1. A. To gamble; to lament; with परि–to lament.

देव *a*. Divine. *m*. A deity; a Brâhmana; a king

देवकन्या *f*. A nymph.

देवकर्मन् (-कार्य) *n*. A religious rite.

देवकी *f*. Mother of Krishna.

देवकुसुम *n*. Cloves.

देवगृही *f*. Sarasvatî. [gods.

देवचर्या *f*. Worship of the

देवता *f*. Divinity; a god.

देवदत्त *m*. Name of the conch-shell of Arjuna.

देवदारु *m*. *n*. A pine tree.

देवदासी *f*. A courtezan employed as a dancer in a

देवदीप *m*. The eye.[temple.

देवदूत *m*. An angel.

देवदेव *m*. Brahman (*m*.); S'iva; Vishnu.

देवद्रोणि *f*. A procession with idols. [ing a deity.

देवद्र्यंच् *a*. (*f*. -द्रीचि) Ador-

देवर् *m* The younger brother of a husband.

देवन *m*. A die. *n*. Lustre, beauty; gambling; a garden; a lotus; emulation; business.

देवनागरी *f*. Name of the character in which Sanskrit is usually written.

देवनिकाय *m*. Paradise.

देवपथ (-वर्त्मन्) *m*. Heaven.

देवपुर(-पुरी *f*.) Amarâvatî.

देवप्रश्न *m*. Fortune-telling.

देवभूय *n*. Divinity, godhead.

देवमणि *m*. The jewel called कौस्तुभ; the sun.

देवमातृक *a*. Watered by the clouds only.

देवयज्ञ *m*. A sacrifice to the superior gods by oblations to fire

देवयुग *n*. The Krita age.

देवयोनि *m*. A demi-god.

देवयोषा *f*. A nymph.

देवर्षि *m*. A divine sage;

देवराज् (-राज) *m*. Indra.

देववाहन *n*. Agni.

देवव्रत *n*. Religious observance; Bhi'shma; Kartikeya. [sal of gods.

देवसात् *ind*. To the dispo-

देवस्व *n*. Religious endowment.

देवांगना *f* An apsaras.

देवानांप्रिय *m*.A goat; a fool.

देवांधस, देवान्न *n*. Ambrocia.

देवायतन(-आलय)*n*. A temple.

देवायुध *n*. A rain bow.

देवावास *m* Heaven; temple

देविक (-ल) *a*. Divine

देवी *f*. A goddess; Durgâ; Sarasvatî; Savitrî; a queen. [Sumeru.

देवौकस् *n*. The mountain

देश *m.* A place, a country, an institute; department.

देशक *m.* A ruler, an instructor; a guide.

देशना *f.* Direction, instruction.

देशाचार *m.* A local custom.

देशातिथि *m.* A foreigner.

देशिक *a.* Local. *m.* A spiritual teacher; a traveller; a guide.

देशिनी *f.* The fore-finger.

देशी *f.* The dialect of a country.

देशीय *a.* Provincial; inhabiting any country; an affix meaning 'about', 'almost.'

देश्य *a.* Local, provincial; native; genuine. *m.* An eye-witness; an inhabitant. *n.* The thing to be proved (पूर्वपक्ष).

देह *m.n* The body.

देहगत *a.* Incarnate, embodied.

देहज *m.* A son.

देहजा *f.* A daughter.

देहधारण *n.* Living, life.

देहधि *m.* A wing

देहधुष् *m.* Air, wind.

देहबंध *m.* Bodily frame.

देहभृत् *m.* A living being.

देहंभर *a.* Gluttonous.

देहयात्रा *f.* Death; food.

देहवायु *m.* A vital air.

देहसार *m.* Marrow.

देहलि *m.* (-ली *f.*) The threshold.

देहलीदीपन्याय *m.* A maxim indicating something serviceable in a double capacity.

देहात्मवाद *m.* Materialism.

देहात्मवादिन् *m.* A materialist.

देहिन् *m.* A living being, the soul.

देहिनी *f.* The earth.

दै *vt.* or *vi.* 1. P. (*pp.* दात) To purify. With अव–to whiten.

दैतेय (दैत्य) *m.* A demon.

दैन, दैनंदिन, दैनिक *a.* Diurnal, daily.

दैर्घ्य (-र्घ) *n.* Length.

दैन्य (-न) *n.* Poverty, miserable state; grief; meanness.

दैव *a.* Divine. *m.* One of the eight forms of marriage. *n.* Destiny.

दैवगति *f.* The course of fate.

दैवतस् *ind.* Perchance.

दैवदुर्विपाक *m.* Unpropitiousness of fate.

दैवयोग *m.* Fortuitous combination, chance.

दैववश *m. n.* The power of destiny.

दैवत(-क) *a.* Divine. *n* A god.

दैवत्य *a.* Sacred to a deity.

दैविक *a* Divine. *n.* An inevitable accident

दैविन् *m.* An astrologer.

दैव्य *a.* Divine. *n.* Fortune.
दैशिक *a.* Local; national. *m.* A teacher; a guide.
दैष्टिक *a.* Predestined. *m.* A fatalist.
दैहिक *a.* Corporeal.
दैह्य *a.* Bodily. *m.* The soul.
दो *vt.* 4. P. (*pp.* दित; *pres.* द्यति) To cut.
दोग्धृ *m.* A cowherd; a panegyrist.
दोग्ध्र *m.* A calf.
दोग्ध्री *f.* A cow which yields milk; a wet nurse.
दोर *m.* A rope.
दोल *m.* Swinging, name of a festival.
दोला (-लिका) *f.* A litter, a swing.
दोलाधिरूढ *a.* Disquieted; uncertain, irresolute (*fig*).
दोष *m.* Fault, badness, evil; detrimental effect; disorder of the humours of the body, error.
दोषग्राहिन् *a.* Malicious.
दोषज्ञ *a.* A physician; a learned man.
दोषण *n.* Accusation.
दोषन् *m.n.* An arm.
दोषल *a.* Faulty, corrupt.
दोषस् *f.* Night.
दोषा *ind.* At night. *f.* the arm; the night.
दोषातिलक *m.* A lamp.
दोषातन *a.* Nocturnal.
दोषारोप *m.* Accusation,
दोषिक *a.* Faulty. *m.* Sickness.
दोषिन् *a.* Impure, defective.
दोषैकदृश् *a.* Fault-finding.
दोस् *m.n.* The fore arm, the arm; a side of a triangle.
दोर्ग्रह *a.* Strong, powerful.
दोर्ज्या *a.* The sine of the base.
दोर्दंड *m.* The arm.
दोर्मूल *n* The arm-pit.
दोःशिखर *n.* The shoulder.
दोस्थ *m* Servant, play.
दोह *m.* Milking, milk.
दोहद *m. n.* The longing of a pregnant woman, pregnancy.
दोहदलक्षण *n.* The fœtus.
दोहन *a.* Milking.
दोहनी *f.* A milk pail.
दोहल *m.* The same as दोहद.
दौत्य *n.* Message, mission.
दौरात्म्य *n.* Wickedness.
दौर्गत्य *n.* Poverty, distress.
दौर्गन्ध्य *n.* Bad smell.
दौर्जन्य *n.* Wickedness.
दौर्जीवित्य *n.* A miserable life.
दौर्बल्य (-ल) *n.* Impotency.
दौर्भाग्य *n.* Ill-luck.
दौर्भ्रात्र *n* A quarrel between brothers.
दौर्मनस्य *n.* Evil disposition, affliction.
दौर्मंत्र्य *n.* Evil advice.
दौर्हार्द *n.* Enmity.
दौर्हद, दौर्हृद *n.* Enmity; pregnancy; desire.
दौर्हृदय *n.* Enmity.
दौःशील्य *n.* Bad temper.

दौवारिक *m.* A doorkeeper.
दौहित्र (-त्री *f.*) *m.* A daughter's son.[daughter's son
दौहित्रायण *m.* The son of a
द्यावापृथिव्यौ(द्यावाभूमी) *f.du.* Heaven and earth.
द्यु *vt.* 2 P. (*pres.* द्यौति) To attack.
द्यु *n.*A day; the sky.*m.*Fire.
द्युपति *m.* The sun; Indra.
द्युमणि *m.* The sun.
द्युलोक *m.* Heaven.
द्युवास *m.* A god. [planet.
द्युषद्, (-सद्) *m.* A deity; a
द्युत् *vi.* 1 A. To shine.
द्युति *f.* Splendour, beauty, light, dignity.
द्युम्न *n.* Splendour, strength.
द्युवन् *m.* The sun.
द्यूत *m. n.* Play, gambling,
द्यूतकर (-कार,-कृत्) *m.* A gambler. [despise.
द्यै *vt.* 1. P. (*pres.* द्यायति) To
द्यो *f.* (nom. *sing.* द्यौः) Heaven; the sky.
द्योभूमि *m.* A bird.
द्योत *m.* Light. [ing
द्योतक *a.* Shining; explain-
द्योतन *m.* A lamp. *n.* Explanation.
द्योतिस् *n.* Light, a star.
द्रढिमन् *m.* Firmness, heaviness; assertion.
द्रम् *vt.* 1. P. To run about.
द्रव *a.* Running(as a horse), wet, liquid. *m.* Flight; play, amusement; speed, fluidity; juice.
द्रवंती *f.* A river.
द्रविण *n.* Property, gold, thing, strength, valour.
द्रव्य *n.* Substance, wealth, a fit object; modesty; a wager.
द्रष्टव्य *a.* Beautiful.
द्रष्टृ *m.* A seer, a judge
द्रा *vt.* 2. P. (*pp.* द्राण) To run, to sleep. With नि- to sleep, वि-to retreat.
द्राक् *ind.* Immediately.
द्राक्षा *f.* Vine, grape.
द्राघय् *vt.* To lengthen.
द्राघिमन् *m.* Length; a degree of longitude.
द्राघीयस् *a.* Longer (*comp.* of दीर्घ). [of दीर्घ)
द्राघिष्ठ *a.* Longest (*super.*
द्राण *a.* Flown, sleepy.
द्राप *m.* Mud, sky.
द्राव *m.* Flight, speed.
द्रावक *m.* A flux to assist diffusion of metals, a thief, a libertine. *n.* Wax.
द्रावण *n.* Putting to flight; distilling.
द्राविड *m.* A Dravidian.
द्रु *vt.* or *vi.* 1 P. To flow, to retreat, to attack. With अनु-to follow, अभि or उप-to attack, प्र,

प्रति or वि-to run.

द्रु m. n. Wood.

द्रुणा f. A bow string.

द्रुणि (-णी) f. A small tortoise.

द्रुत a. Quick, run away, dissolved. m. A scorpion; a tree; a cat. [ately.

द्रुतम् ind. Quickly, immedi-

द्रुतविलंबित n. Name of a metre. [away.

द्रुति f. Melting, running

द्रुपद m. Name of a king.

द्रुपदात्मजा f. Draupadî.

द्रुम m. A tree.

द्रुह् vt. 4.P. To bear malice; with अभि-to do injury to.

द्रुह् a. Injuring. f. Injury,

द्रुह m. A son; a lake.

द्रोण m. A lake, a cloud, a raven, a tree, the preceptor of the Kauravas and Pândavas. n. A tub.

द्रोणि (-णी) f. A bucket, a water-reservoir; a measure of capacity, a valley.

द्रोह m. Injury, malice, treachery; rebellion.

द्रोहाट m. A religious impostor.

द्रौणायन or द्रौणि (-नि) m. A'svatthâman.

द्वंद्व n. A pair, a fortress; a secret, strife; duel; doubt. m. Name of a compound in Sanskrit Grammar. [discord.

द्वंद्वभाव m. Antagonism,

द्वंद्वयुद्ध n. A duel, a single combat. [in pairs.

द्वंद्वशस् ind. Two by two;

द्वय a. Double, of two kinds. n. Untruthfulness.

द्वयवादिन् a. Insincere.

द्वार् f. A door, an expedient.

द्वार n. A door, medium.

द्वारकपाट (-पट्ट) m. n. The leaf or panel of a door.

द्वारगोप (-नायक, -प, -पाल, -पालक) m. A door-keeper, a porter.

द्वारपिंडी f. The threshold.

द्वारयंत्र n. A lock, a bolt.

द्वारवती, द्वारावती f. Dwarka.

द्वार (रि) का f. See द्वारवती above. ['through'.

द्वारा ind. By means of,

द्वाःस्थ, द्वास्थ, द्वाःस्थित, द्वास्थित m. A door-keeper, a porter. [keeper.

द्वारिक (-न्) m. A door-

द्वि num (nom. du. द्वौ m., द्वे f., द्वे n.) Two, both.

द्व्यामुषायण, द्व्यामुष्यायण m. An adopted son who remains heir to his natural father.

द्विक *a.* Twofold, the second; two per cent.
द्विगु *m.* One of the four compounds (in gram.)
द्विगुण *a.* Double.
द्विज *m.* (twice born) A man of any of the first three castes of the Hindus; any oviparous animal; a tooth.
द्विजन्मन् (-जाति) *m.* See द्विज.
द्विजपति (-राज) *m.* The Moon or Garuda.
द्विजप्रपा *f.* A trench or basin for water; a trough.
द्विजिव्ह *m.* A snake; a talebearer. [a couple.
द्वितय *a.* Two-fold; *n.* A pair;
द्वितीय *a* Second. *m.* A son.
द्वितीयक *a.* Second.
द्वितीय *f.* The second day of a lunar fortnight; a wife; the accusative case (in gram.)
द्वित्र *a. pl.* Two or three.
द्वित्व *n.* A pair; duality.
द्विदंडि *ind.* Stick against stick. [two parts.
द्विध (-धा) *ind.* Divided into
द्विप *m.* An elephant.
द्विपथ *n.* A cross-way.
द्विपदिका (-पदी) *f.* A kind of Prákrit metre.
द्विपाद *m.* A biped.

द्विभुज *m.* An angle.
द्विरद *m.* An elephant.
द्विराप *m.* An elephant.
द्विरुक्ति *f.* Repetition, uselessness.
द्विरेफ *m.* A large black bee.
द्विर्भाव *m.* द्विर्वचन *n.* Reduplication.
द्विवाहिका *f.* A swing.
द्विविध *a.* Of two kinds.
द्विशस् *ind.* Two by two.
द्विशीर्ष *m.* *Agni* (Fire).
द्विष् *at.* 2. U. To hate. [my.
द्विष *a.* Hostile, *m.* An enemy.
द्विषत् *m.* An enemy.
द्विष्ट *a.* Hostile.
द्विस् *ind.* Twice.
द्विहन् *m.* An elephant.
द्वीप *m. n.* An island.
द्वीपवती The earth.
द्वीपिन् *m.* A tiger.
द्वेधा *ind.* In two parts.
द्वेष *m.* Dislike, enmity.
द्वेषण *n.* An enmity.
द्वेष्य *a.* Hateful.
द्वैगुण्य *n.* Double amount.
द्वैत *n.* Duality; name of a forest.
द्वैध *a.* Twofold, *n.* Duality, disunion, doubt, double-dealing.
द्वैधीकृत *a.* Embarassed.
द्वैधीभाव *m.* Duplicity, difference; doubt; one of the six military tactics.

द्वैपक्ष *n.* Two parties.
द्वैपायन *m.* Vyàsa. [mothers.
द्वैमातुर *m.* Having two
द्वैमातृक *a.* Nourished by rain and rivers.
द्वैरथ *m.* An adversary.
द्वैराज्य *n.* A dominion divided between two kings.
द्वैवार्षिक *a.* Biennial.
द्वैविध्य *n.* Duality, diversity.

ध

ध *m.* A Bràhmana; Kubera; virtue. *n.* Wealth.
धक्क् *vt.* 10. U. To destroy.
धट *m.* A balance.
धटिका, धटी *f.* Old cloth.
धटिन् *m.* S'iva.
धण् *vi.* I. P. To sound.
धत्तूर, (-क) *m.* The white thorn-apple.
धन् *vi.* 1. P. To sound.
धन *n.* Wealth; a match; surplus; an affirmative quantity.
धनक *m.* Avarice.
धनजात *n.* All kinds of valuable possessions.
धनंजय *m.* Fire; Arjuna
धनद *m.* A liberal man; Kubera.
धनदायिन् *m* Fire.
धनपति (-पाल) *m.* A treasurer; Kubera.
धनमूल *n.* Principal, capital.
धनाया *f.* Avarice.
धनिक *m.* A wealthy man; a creditor; a husband.
धनिका *f.* A virtuous woman.
धनिन् *a.* Rich.
धनिष्ठ *a.* Very rich.
धनिष्ठा *f.* Name of the twentythird lunar mansion.
धनी, (-का) *f.* A young girl.
धनु *m.* A bow.
धनुर्धर, धनुर्भृत् *m.* An archer.
धनुर्मार्ग *m.* A curve.
धनुर्विद्या *f.* The science of archery.
धनुर्वृक्ष *m.* A bamboo.
धनुर्वेद *m.* An upaveda treating of archery.
धनुष् *n.* A bow, a measure of length, an arc of a circle; a sign of the zodiac.
धनुःकांड *n.* A bow and arrow.
धनू *f.* A bow. [an atheist.
धन्य *a.* Wealthy; blessed,
धन्यवाद *m.* Thanks, praise,
धन्या *f.* A nurse.
धन्वन् *m. n.* A desert. [gods.
धन्वंतरि *m.* Physician of the
धन्विन् Armed; *m.* An archer; Arjuna; S'iva; Vishnu.
धम *a.* Blowing, melting. *m.* The moon; Krishna, Yama.
धमक *m* A blacksmith.

धमन *a.* Blowing; cruel.

धमनि(-नी) *f.* A reed; a pipe; a vein; throat.

धम्मिल (-ल्ल) *m.* The braided hair of a woman.

धय *a.* Drinking, sucking.

धर *a.* Holding, containing, possessed of. *m.* A mountain, a frivolous man.

धरण *m.* The side of a mountain; the world; the sun; the female breast; *n.* Holding, supporting.

धरणि(-णी) *f.* The earth; a beam; a vein.

धरणीधर (-धृत) *m.* S'esha; mountain; a tortoise; a king.

धरा *f.* The earth; a vein.

धरात्मज *m.* Mars.

धराधर *m.* See **धरणीधर.**

धरापुत्र, (-सूनु *m.* **)** The planet Mars.

धरित्री *f.* The earth, the soil.

धर्म *m.* Law, custom, piety, duty, justice, merit, character, a peculiarity, the soul, the god of death, the eldest of the Pandavas.

धर्मकाय (-केतु) *m.* Buddha.

धर्मकोष (-श) *m* Body of laws. [plain near Delhi.

धर्मक्षेत्र *n. Bharatavarsha*; a

धर्मचर्या *f.* Performance of duty. [wife.

धर्मचारिणी *f.* A virtuous

धर्मज *m.* A legitimate son; Yudhishthira.

धर्मजिज्ञासा *f.* Inquiry into the right course of conduct. [ously.

धर्मतस् *ind.* Rightly, virtu-

धर्मध्वज (-ध्वजिन्) *a.* A religious hypocrite.

धर्मपत्नी *f.* A lawful wife.

धर्मपर *a.* Pious, righteous.

धर्ममहामात्र *m.* A minister in charge of religious affairs. [righteous.

धर्मयु *a.* Virtuous, pious,

धर्मलोप *m.* Irreligion.

धर्मवासर *m.* The day of the full moon. [tue or piety.

धर्मवृद्ध *a.* Advanced in vir-

धर्मशाला *f.* A tribunal; a charitable institution.

धर्मशासन (-शास्त्र) *n.* A code of laws.

धर्मशील *a.* Virtuous, pious.

धर्माचार्य *m.* A religious preceptor.

धर्माधिकरण *n.* Administration of laws. *m.* A judge.

धर्माधिकरणिक(-न्) *m* A judge.

धर्माधिष्ठान *n.* A court of justice.

धर्माध्यक्ष *m.* A judge. [duct.

धर्मानुष्ठान *n.* Virtuous con-

धर्मारण्य *n.* A sacred grove.

धर्मासन *n.* The judgment seat.

धर्मिन् *a.* Virtuous, religi-

ous; endowed with properties. [tial.
धर्मोत्तर *a.* Just and impar-
धर्म्य *a.* Lawful, just, religious.
धर्ष *m.* Boldness, insult; impudence; impatience.
धर्षक *m.* A seducer, an actor [above.
धर्षण *n.* (-णा *f.*) See धर्ष
धर्षणि (-णी), **धर्षिणी** *f.* A harlot.
धर्षित *n.* Pride; impatience.
धव *m.* A husband; a master; a cheat.
धवल *a.* White, pure.
धवलगिरि *m.* The highest peak of the Himâlayas.
धवलिमन् *m.* Whiteness.
धा *vt.* 3. U. (*pp.* हित) To put, to grant, to confer, to produce, to put on, to bear up, to take, to undergo. With अतिसम्-to deceive; अंतर्-to cover; अनुसम्-to search to collect. अपि (sometimes changed into पि)-to cover, to bar; अभि-to speak; अभ्या-to throw under. अभिसम्-to aim at, to deceive, to make friendship with. अव-to give attention आ-(Atm.) to put, to direct towards, to bear, to create, to take; आविस्–to manifest. उप-to place under, in, or on; to employ; उपा-to put on; to create. तिरस्-(Atm.)-to hide, to disappear, नि-to place, to conceal, to deposit; परि-to put on, to surround; पुरस्-to put at the head of, प्रणि-to lay down, to set, to extend. प्रवि-to do, to divide, प्रतिवि-to despatch, to retaliate, वि-to do, to accomplish, to command, to shape, to appoint, व्यव-to intervene, श्रद्-to believe, सम्-to join, to fix upon, to inflict, समा-to put, to compose, to satisfy. संनि-to draw near.
धाटी *f.* Assault.
धातु *m.* An element, a secretion, a humour, a metal, a verbal root, the soul.
धातुक्रिया *f.* Metallurgy.
धातुपाठ *m.* A list of roots.
धातृ *m.* A creator, an author; a supporter; the creator of the world.
धात्री *f.* A nurse, a foster-mother; the earth [seat
धान *n.* A receptacle, a
धाना *f. pl.* Fried barley or rice [seat.
धानी *f.* A receptacle, a
धानुष्क *m.* An archer.
धान्य *n.* Grain, corn.
धान्यकल्क *n.* Chaff.
धान्यकोश *m.* (-कोष्ठक) *n.* A granary.

धान्यराज *m.* Barley.
धामन् *n.* A house, the members of a family; light; splendour, strength. glory. [धमनी.
धामनिका or **धामनी** *f.* See
धार *m.* Vishnu; a sudden and violent shower of rain; snow; hail; debt; a limit.
धारक *m.* A vessel, a debtor.
धारण *n.* Possession; keeping in the memory; indebtedness.
धारणक *m.* A debtor.
धारणा *f.* Good memory; steady abstraction of the mind; firmness; settled rule; intellect; propriety.
धारणी *f.* A vein; a row.
धारयित्री *f.* The earth.
धारा *f.* A stream; a shower, the margin, the sharp edge; a wheel; fence; the excellence; fame.
धारागृह *n.* A bath room.
धारांग *m.* A sword.
धारायंत्र *n.* A fountain.
धारावर्ष (-संपात) *m. n.* A hard unceasing shower.
धारावाहिन् *a.* Incessant.
धाराश्रु *n.* Flood of tears.
धारिन् *a.* Carrying, holding.
धारिणी *f.* The earth [cow.
धारोष्ण *a.* Warm from a
धार्मिक *a.* Righteous, virtuous; just.
धार्ष्ट्य *n.* Violence, arrogance.
धाव् *vi.* 1. P. To flow, to run, *vt.* 1. U (pp. धावित or धौत) To rub, to wash; with निस्–to wash off.
धावक *m.* A washerman.
धावन *n.* Running, attack, purifying; rubbing.
धावल्य *n.* Whiteness.
धि *vt.* 6. P. To possess; with सम्–to make peace with.
धि *m.* (at the end of compounds) Any receptacle.
धिक् *ind.* Fie! Shame!
धिक्कारक्रिया *f.* Reproach, contempt, disregard.
धिक्पारुष्य *n.* Abuse, reproach.
धिग्दंड *m.* Reprimand.
धिन्व् *vt.* 5. P. To delight.
धिप्सु *a.* Desiring to deceive.
धिषणा *f.* Speech; praise; intellect; the earth.
धिष्ण्य *m.* A place for the sacrificial fire; S'ukra, the preceptor of the demons; Venus; strength. *n.* A seat, a meteor, fire.
धी *f.* Intellect, the mind, thought, prayer.
धीत *a.* Drunk, propitiated.
धीति *f.* Drinking, thought.
धीमत् *a.* Wise, intelligent.
धीमंत्रिन् (-सचिव) *m.* A councillor or counsel.

धीर *a.* Wise, intelligent, steady, brave, calm, loud, solemn.

धीरम् *ind.* Firmly, steadily.

धीरता *f.* Fortitude.

धीरोदात्त *a.* Brave and noble minded.

धीरोद्धत *a.* Brave but haughty.

धीवर *m.* A fisherman.

धीवरी *f.* A fishermans' wife; a fish-basket.

धु *vt.* or *vi.* 5. U. See धू.

धुक्ष् *vi.* 1. A. To be kindled. With सम्-to be excited.

धुत *a.* Abandoned; shaken.

धुनी (-नि) *f.* A river.

धुर् *f.* (nom. *sing.* धूः) A yoke, the pole of a carriage, a burden, the top.

धूर्गत *a.* Fore-most.

धूर्जटि *m.* An epithet of Śiva.

धूर्धर or धुरंधर *a.* Chief, pre-eminent, *m.* A beast of burden; a leader.

धुरा *f.* A burden, a load.

धुरीण (-य) *a.* Charged with important duties. *m.* A leader.

धुर्य *a.* Foremost.

धुस्तु (स्तुर) र *m.* See धत्तूर.

धू *vt.* 1. U, 5. U, 6. P, 9. U. 10. U. (*pp.* धूत or धून) To shake, to remove, to hurt; with अव-to disregard, to shake off; उद् to raise, to shake off; निस्-to expel, to disregard; वि-to shake.

धूतपाप *a.* Who has shaken off his sins.

धूप् *vt.* or *vi.* 1. P. (*pp.* धूपायित) To heat; 10. U. To fumigate.

धूप *m.* Incense.

धूपन *n.* Fumigation; incense.

धूम *m.* Smoke, vapour, mist, a meteor; eructation.

धूमकेतन (-केतु) *m.* Fire, a comet, a falling star.

धूमज *m.* A cloud

धूमध्वज *m.* Fire.

धूमयोनि *m.* A cloud.

धूमल *a.* Smoke-coloured.

धूमिका *f.* Vapour, fog, mist.

धूम्र *a.* Smoke-coloured. *n.* Sin, vice.

धूम्रक *m.* A camel.

धूम्रलोहित *a.* Dark-red. *m.* S'iva.

धूर्त *a.* Cunning, mischievous, *m.* A rogue.

धूर्तक *m.* A jackal.

धूर्वी *f.* The forepart or pole of a carriage.

धूलि (-ली) *m. f.* Dust; powder.

धूलिका *f.* Fog, mist.

धूसर *a.* Grey, *m.* A donkey; a camel; a pigeon.

धृ *vt.* or *vi.* 1. U, 6. A. To be, *vt.* 10. U. To hold, to bear, to support, to curb; to suffer, to wear, to assign, to owe. With अव-to determine; to know. उद्-to save, to draw out. निस्-to determine accurately, वि-to seize, to wear, to maintain. सम्-to curb; to retain in the mind. समुद्-to pull up by the roots, to deliver. संप्र-to consider, to ascertain.

धृतात्मन् *a.* Firm-minded.

धृति *f.* Firmness, fortitude; satisfaction, pleasure.

धृत्वन् *m.* Brahman, (*m.*) Sky; ocean, Vishnu; virtue.

धृष् *vt.* or *vi.* 1. P. To be compact; to hurt, *vt.* 1. P, 10 U. To offend, to insult, to assail, *vi.* or *vt.* 5. P. To behold, to brave, *vt.* 10. A. to attack.

धृष्ट *a.* Bold, confident; impudent, profligate.

धृष्णज् *a.* Bold, shameless.

धृष्णि *m.* A ray of light.

धृष्णु *a.* Impudent.

धे *vt.* 1. P. (*pp.* धीत) To suck, to draw away.

धेन *m.* The ocean; a large river.

धेनु *f.* A cow, the female of a species.

धेनुका *f.* A milch-cow.

धैनुक *n.* A herd of cows.

धैर्य *n.* Firmness, courage, strength; calmness; patience; boldness.

धैवत *m.* The sixth of the seven primary notes of the gamut (in music).

धैवत्य *n.* Cleverness.

धोरण *n.* A vehicle.

धोरणि (-णी) *f.* An uninterrupted series, tradition.

धोरित *n.* Injuring, motion.

धौत *a.* Washed, purified, white, bright. *n.* Silver.

धौम्र *m.* Greyness.

धौरेय *a.* Fit for a burden. *m.* A beast of burden.

धौर्तक, धौर्तिक, धौर्त्य, } *n.* Fraud, dishonesty.

ध्मा *vt.* or *vi.* 1. P. To exhale, to blow; to throw away. With आ-to blow (as a wind instrument). उप-to excite by blowing, निस्-to blow out of some thing. प्र-to blow (as a wind-instrument). वि-to disperse.

ध्माकार *m.* A black-smith.

ध्मांक्ष *m.* See ध्वांक्ष.

ध्मात *a.* Blown, excited; puffed up.

ध्मापित *a.* Reduced to ashes.
ध्यात *a.* Thought of.
ध्यान *n.* Meditation, divine intuition. [tation.
ध्यानयोग *m.* Profound medi-
ध्यानस्थ *a.* Absorbed in meditation.
ध्यानिक *a.* Sought or obtained by pious contemplation.
ध्याम *a.* Unclean, dirty.
ध्यामन् *m.* Measure; light.
ध्यै *vi.* 1. P (*pp.* ध्यात) to meditate, to recollect. With अनु-to think of, अप-to disregard. अभि-to desire. अव-to disregard. नि-to remember. निस्-to think of.
ध्रुव *a.* Firm; permanent, *m.* The polar star, a post; epoch, a celebrated boy-devotee. *n.* The sky.
ध्रुव, (-क) The introductory stanza of a song.
ध्वंस् *vt.* or *vi.* 1 A.(*pp.* ध्वस्त) To perish; with प्र-to perish. वि-to be dispersed.
ध्वंस *m.*, (-न *n.*) Loss, ruin.
ध्वज *m.* *n* A flag; *m.* a mark; an attribute; the organ of generation.
ध्वजप्रहरण *m.* Air, wind.
ध्वजिन् *m.* A standard-bearer; a chariot; a mountain; a snake; a peacock; a horse; a Bráhmana.
ध्वजिनी *f.* An army.
ध्वजीकरण *n.* Raising a standard. [thunder.
ध्वन् *vi.* 1. P. To sound, to
ध्वन *m.* Sound, tune, hum.
ध्वनन *n.* Sounding; implying (as a meaning).
ध्वनि *m.* Sound, tone, a word; allusion.
ध्वनिग्रह *m.* The ear.
ध्वनिनाला *f.* Trumpet; a lute; a pipe.
ध्वस्ति *f.* Destruction.
ध्वांक्ष *m.* A crow; a beggar; an impudent fellow.
ध्वान *m.* Sound.
ध्वांत *n.* Darkness.

न.

न *ind.* Not, no, nor, neither.
नकिंचन *a.* Very poor.
नकुट *n.* The nose.
नकुल *m.* An ichneumon; the fourth Pandava prince. [at night.
नक्त *n.* Night; eating only
नक्तक *m.* Dirty cloth.
नक्तभोजन *n.* Supper.
नक्तमुखा *f.* Evening. [night.
नक्तम् *ind.* At night; by
नक्तंचर *m.* A demon, a thief.
नक्तंदिन *n.* Night and day.
नक्र *m.* A crocodile.

नक्रा *f.* The nose.

नक्षत्र *n.* A star, a lunar mansion, a pearl.

नक्षत्र (-नाथ,-प,-पति,-राज) *m.* The moon.

नक्षत्रनेमी *m.* The moon; the pole-star; Vishnu.

नक्षत्रपाठक *m.* An astrologer.

नक्षत्रमाला *f.* A group of stars; a necklace.

नक्षत्रयोग *m.* The conjunction of the moon with the lunar mansions.

नक्षत्रवर्त्मन् *n.* The sky.

नक्षत्रविद्या *f.* Astronomy or astrology.

नक्षत्रसूचक *m.* A bad astrologer.

नक्षत्रिन् *m.* The moon.

नख *m. n.* A nail, a claw.

नखकुट्ट *m.* A barber.

नखनिकृंतन or नखरंजनी *f.* A pair of nail-scissors.

नखपद *n.* (-व्रण *m.*) A nail-mark, a scratch.

नखर *m. n.* A finger-nail, a claw.

नखायुध *m.* A tiger, a lion.

नखाशिन् *m.* An owl.

नखिन् *m.* A lion; a tiger.

नग *m.* A mountain, a tree; the sun; a serpent.

नगजा (-नंदिनी) *f.* Pârvatî.

नगभिद् *m.* An axe; Indra.

नगर *n.* A town.

नगरप्रांत *m.* A suburb.

नगरमार्ग *m.* A principal road.

नगरी *f.* See नगर.

नगाधिप, नगाधिराज *m.* The Himâlayas.

नगौकस् *m.* A bird.

नग्न *a.* Naked, desolate, bare. *m.* A Buddhist or Jaina mendicant.

नग्नक *a.* Naked. *m.* A Jaina mendicant of the *digambara* sect; a bard.

नग्नका, नग्ना, नाग्निका *f.* A naked, shameless woman; a girl before menstruation or about ten years old.

नंग *m.* A lover, a paramour.

नचिकेतस् *m.* *Agni.*

नट् *vi.* 1. P. To dance; to act. Caus (नाटयति-ते) To represent; imitate; to fall; to shine.

नट *m.* A dancer, an actor.

नटन *n.* Dance; dramatic representation.

नटवर *m.* The *Sûtradha'ra* of a drama.

नटांतिका *f* Shame.

नटी *f* An actress; a courtezan.

नटेश्वर *m.* Siva.

नट्या *f.* A company of actors

नत *a.* Bent, depressed; curved. *n.* The distance of any planet from the meridian.

नतांगी *f.* A woman.

नति *f.* Curvature; a bow; parallax in latitude.

नद् *vi.* 1. P. To sound, to speack, to be glad. With उद्-to roar;-नि, प्र or वि-to sound; with अभि to congratulate upon, to praise, आ-to be glad, प्रति-to bless.

नद *m.* A great river; the ocean.

नदी *f.* A river.

नदीद्रोह *m.* Freight, fare.

नदीन (-कांत) *m.* The ocean.

नदीमातृक *a.* Watered by rivers, experienced, clever.

नद्ध *a.* Fastend, interwoven. *n.* A tie, a knot.

ननंदृ, ननांदृ *f.* A husband's sister.

ननु *ind.* Certainly, surely, please, pray, why!

नंद *m.* Happiness, Vishnu; name of the foster-father of Krishna; name of nine brother-kings of *Pa'taliputra* murdered by the machinations of Chânakya.

नंदक *a.* Rejoicing. *m.* A frog; the sword of Vishnu, a sword.

नंदथु *m.* Happiness, pleasure.

नंदन *a.* Delighting. *m.* A son; a frog; Vishnu; Śiva; The garden of Indra.

नंदा *f.* Joy; wealth, a husband's sister.

नंदि, (-क) *m. f.* Joy, name of an attendant of S'iva.

नंदिन् *a.* Happy, gladdening. *m.* A son; the door-keeper of S'iva.

नंदिनी *f.* A daughter; a husband's sister; a didine cow owned by Vasishtha.

नपुंस् (-स) *m.* A eunuch.

नपुंसक *m. n.* A eunuch; *n.* the neuter gender.

नप्तृ *m.* A grandson.

नप्त्री *f.* A grand-daughter.

नभ *m.* The month of S'ravana. *n.* The sky.

नभश्चर *m.* A demigod; a bird.

नभस् *n.* The sky, atmosphere, a cloud. *m.* The rainy season; the nose, smell; name of the month of Sra'vana.

नभस *m.* The sky; the rainy season; the ocean.

नभस्य *m.* Name of the month of *Bhâdrapada*.

नभस्वत् *m.* Air, wind.

नभःसद् *m.* A god.

नभःस्थली *f.* The sky.

नभोगज *m.* A cloud.

नभोदुह *m.* A cloud.

नभोदृष्टि *a.* Blind; looking up to heaven.

नभोद्वीप, नभोधूम *m.* A cloud.

नभोमणि *m.* The sun.

नभोमंडल *n.* The firmament.

नभोरजस् *n.* Darkness.

नभोरेणु *f.* Fog, mist.

नभोलय *m.* Smoke.

नभोलिह् *a.* Lofty, towering.

नभ्राज् *m.* A dark cloud.

नम् *vt.* or *vi.* 1 U. (*pp.* नत) To bow to, to sink, to bend; with अभ्युद्–to rise, अव–to bend, to go down. उद्-to rise. उप-to happen, to offer, to approach. परि-to stop, to bend down, to be changed into, to grow old, to be digested (as food). प्र-to bow to, to prostrate. वि-to bend one self. विपरि-to change for worse. सम् to subject oneself to.

नमत *a.* Bent; curved.

नमन *n.* Bow, obeisance.

नमस् *ind* Salutation.

नमस *a.* Favourable.

नमसित, नमस्यित *a.* Revered.

नमस्कार *m.* or **नमस्कृति** *f.* Reverential salutation.

नमस्य *vt.* (*denom. pres.* नमस्यति) To pay homage to.

नमस्य *a.* Venerable, humble.

नमुचि *m.* Name of a demon slain by Indra; the god of love.

नमोगुरु *m.* A spiritual teacher.

नमोवाकम् *ind.* Making obeisance to.

नम्र *a.* Bowing, inclined, humble. [tect.

नय् *vt.* 1. A. To go; to protect.

नय *m.* Leading, conduct, principle; method; opinion; a philosophical system.

नयन *n.* Conducting, the eye.

नर *m.* A person; a male; the supreme spirit; Arjuna.

नरक *m. n.* Hell.

नरपुंगव *m.* Best of men.

नरमानिका (-मानिनी, -मालिनी) *f.* An amazon.

नरयंत्र *n.* Sun-dial.

नरशृंग *n.* An impossibility, a non-entity.

नरसिंह or **नरहरि** *m.* Vishnu in his fourth incarnation.

नरस्कंध *m* A multitude or body of men.

नरी *f.* A woman.

नर्त *m.* Dancing; a dance.

नर्तक *m.* A dancer; an actor; a bard; an elephant; a peacock.

नर्तकी *f.* A female dancer, an actress; a female elephant; a pea-hen.

नर्तन *m.* A dancer. *n.* A dance. [to move.

नर्द् *vt.* or *vi.* 1. P. To roar,

नर्द *a* Bellowing, roaring.

नर्दित *m.* A die. *n.* Sound.

नर्मठ *m.* A jester; a rake.

नर्मदा *f.* Name of a river.

नर्मद्युति *a.* Cheerful, merry.

नर्मन् *n.* Amorous sport, jest, humour.

नर्मसचिव (-सुहृद्) *m.* An associate of the amusements of a prince.

नल *m.* A kind of reed; name of a celebrated king of the *Nishadhas*; a monkey chief. *n.* A lotus.

नलिन *m.* The Indian crane *n.* A lotus flower; the Indigo plant; water.

नलिनी *f.* A lotus plant.

नव *a.* New, fresh. *m.* A crow.

नवक *n.* A group of nine.

नवकारिका (-कालिका) *f.* A woman newly married.

नवकृत्वस् *ind.* Nine-times.

नवच्छिद्र (-द्वार) The body.

नवत *a.* The ninetieth.

नवति *f.* Ninety. [brush.

नवतिका *f.* Ninety;a paint-

नवनी *f.* (-नीत *n.*) Fresh butter.

नवन् *num.* (*pl.*) Nine.

नवम *a.* The ninth.

नवमल्लिका (-मालिका) *f.* A kind of jasmine.

नवमी *f.* The ninth day of a lunar fortnight.

नवरात्र *n.* The first nine days of the month of *Âs'vina* held sacred to Durgá.

नवीन *a* New, fresh.

नवोढा *f.* A newly married woman, a bride.

नव्य *a.* Recent, modern.

नश् *vt.*4. P. To be lost, to perish, to escape.

नश् *f.* नश *m.* नशन *n.* Detruction.

नश्वर *a.* Perishable.

नष्ट *pp.* Lost.

नष्टाग्निसूत्र *n.* Body, plunder.

नष्टचेतन (-चेष्ट,-संज्ञ) *a.* Unconscious. [struction.

नष्टचेष्टता *f.* Universal de-

नस् *f.* The nose.

नसा *f.* The nose.

नस्य *n.* The hairs in the nose.

नस्या *f.* The nose; the string through the nose of an animal.

नह् *vt.* 4. U. (*pp.* नद्ध) To tie, to bind togethsr, to dress, to arm oneself; with अप-to untie; अपि (sometimes changed to पि)-to fasten;to cover, to put on; उद्-to tie up, to bind up: परि to surround; सम्-to tie, to arm.

न हि *ind.* Surely not, by no means.

ना *ind.* No, not.

नाक *m.* Heaven, the firmament.

नाकिन् *m.* A god.

नाकु *m.* An ant-hill; a mountain.

नाक्षत्र *a.* Stellar.

नाग *m.* The cobra; an elephant; a semi-divine being having a human face with the tail of a shark; a cruel person; any pre-eminent person; a cloud; the number 'seven'. *n.* Tin; lead.

नागपंचमी *f.* A festival on the fifth day in the light half of *Śrâvana.*

नागपाश *m.* A lasso used in war.

नागभूषण *m.* Śiva.

नागमंडलिक *m.* A snake-catcher.

नागर *a.* Town-born, polite, clever. *m.* A citizen.

नागर (रि)क *a.* Town-bred; polite. *m.* A citizen; the chief of the police; an artist; a thief.

नागरी *f.* The Bálbodha character; a shrewd clever woman.

नागर्य *n.* Shrewdness.

नागलोक *m.* One of the regions below the earth called *Pâtâla.*

नागसाह्वय *n.* Hastinápura.

नाचिकेत *m.* Fire.

नाट *m.* Dancing; the *Karnátaka* country.

नाटक *n.* A drama. *m.* An actor.

नाटकीय *a.* Dramatic.

नाटिका *f.* A short or light comedy.

नाट्य *n.* A dancing; dramatic representation. *m.* An actor.

नाट्यशाला *f.* A theatre.

नाट्यशास्त्र *n.* Dramaturgy.

नाट्याचार्य *m.* A dancing master.

नाडि(-डी,-डिका) *f.* The tubular stalk of any plant; an artery; the pulse; a measure of time.

नाडिं(डीं)धम *m.* A goldsmith.

नाडिमंडल *n.* The celestial equator.

नाडीपरिक्षा *f.* Feeling the pulse.

नाणक *n.* A coin.

नातिचर *a.* Of no long duration.

नातिदूर *a.* Not very distant.

नातिवाद *m.* Avoiding opprobrious language.

नाथ *m.* A protector; a husband.

नाद *m* A sound.

नादेय *a.* River-born.

नाना *ind.* In different places; variously; distinctly. *a.*

various, different, diverse.

नानाकारम् *ind* Having done variously.

नानान्यय *a.* Of different kinds, manifold.

नानांद्र *m.* A husband's sister's son.

नांत *a.* Endless.

नांतरीयक *a.* Inseparable.

नांत्र *n.* Praise, eulogy.

नांदी *f.* Joy; praise of a deity; a benedictory verse.

नांदीपट *m.* The lid or cover of a well.

नांदीमुख (-श्राद्ध) *n.* A *S'râddha* to the manes.

नापित *m.* A barber.

नापित्य *n.* The trade of a barber.

नाभि *m. f.* The navel, a cavity. *m.* The nave of a wheel; the centre.

नाभिज (-जन्मन्,-भू) *m.* Brahman (*m.*)

नाभिल *a.* Relating to or coming from a navel.

नाभील *n.* The cavity of the navel; pain.

नाभ्य *a.* Relating to the navel.

नाम *ind.* Namely, indeed, perhaps, granting, it may be that.

नामकरण (-कर्मन्) *n.* The ceremony of naming a child.

नामग्रह *m.*, (-ण *n.*) Addressing by name.

नामग्राहम् *ind.* Mentioning by name.

नामधारक *a.* Only in name.

नामधेय *n.* A name, a title.

नामन् *n.* Name; a noun.

नाममुद्रा *f.* A seal ring.

नामवर्जित *a.* Nameless, stupid.

नामवाचक *a.* A proper name.

नामशेष *a.* Dead, deceased.

नामानुशासन *n.* A dictionary.

नामापराध *m.* Calling names.

नामि *m.* Vishnu.

नामित *a.* Bent, bent down.

नाय *m.* A leader, policy, means, expedient.

नायक *m.* A guide, a leader, a general, a hero in a piece of poetic composition.

नायिका *f.* A mistress; a wife; the heroine in a piece of poetic composition.

नार *m.* Water. *n.* An assemblage of men

नारक *a.* Hellish, infernal.

नारकिक, **नारकिन्**, **नारकीय**, *m.* An inhabitant of hell. *a.* Hellish.

नारा *f. pl.* Water.

नाराच *m.* An iron arrow, an arrow, a water-elephant.

नाराचिका, **नाराची** *f.* A goldsmith's scales.

नारायण *m.* Nāme of an ancient sage; Vishnu.

नारायणि *f.* Lakshmi, the goddess of wealth; the goddess Durgá.

नारिकेर (-ल) *m.*
नारिकेलि (-ली) *f.* } The same as नालिकेर.

नारी *f.* A woman.

नारीतरंगक *m.* A libertine.

नार्यंग *m.* The orange tree.

नाल *m. n.* A hallow stalk especially that of a lotus. *m.* A canal.

नालंबी *f.* The lute of Śiva.

नाला (नालि, नालिका) *f.* A stalk especially that of the lotus; a tube.

नालि *f.* Any tubular vessel of the body; a hollow stalk; a drain.

नालिकेर *m.*
नालिकेलि (-ली) *f.* } A cocoanut.

नाली *f.* A canal.

नालीक *m.* An arrow; a lotus; the fibrous stalk of a lotus.

नालीकिनी *f.* A multitude of lotus flowers.

नाविक *m.* A pilot, a passenger on board a ship.

नाविन् *m.* A boatman.

नाव्य *a.* Accessible by a boat or ship; praiseworthy. *n.* Novelty.

नाश *m.* Destruction, misfortune; abandonment, retreat.

नाशन *n.* Death, destruction, removal.

नाशिन् *a.* Destructive; perishable.

नासा *f.* The nose, the trunk of an elephant.

नासापुट *m. n.* A nostril.

नासिका *f.* See नासा.

नासिकंधम *a.* Snoring.

नासिकंधय *a.* Drinking through the nose.

नासिक्य *a.* Nasal.

नास्ति *ind.* Non-existence.

नास्तिक *m.* One who denies the divine authority of the Vedas, or a future life, or the existence of a creator of the universe.

नास्तिक्य *n.* Infidelity.

नास्तिवाद *m.* A theism.

नास्य *n.* A nose-cord.

नाह *m.* Confinement.

नाहुष (-षि) *m.* King Yayáti.

नि *ind.* As a prefix to verbs and nouns it implies 'lowness, inclusion, fulness, order, continuance, skill, proximity, restraint, resort, cessation, wrong, doubt, affirmation, &c.'

निःश्रयणी
निःश्रेणी } *f.* A ladder, a staircase.

निःश्रेयस *n*. Final beatitude; knowledge of the supreme spirit; happiness.

निःश्वास } निश्श्वास } *m*. Expiration; a sigh.

निःसरण *n*. Going out the outlet; death; expedient; final beatitude.

निःसह *a*. Impatient; powerless, unnerved; unbearable. [plus.

निःस्रव *m*. Remainder, surplus.

निःस्राव *m*. Expense. [mity.

निकट *a*. Near. *m. n*. Proximity.

निकटे *ind*. Near, at hand.

निकर *m*. A multitude; essence; a suitable gift; a treasure

निकर्तन *n*. Cutting.

निकर्षण *n*. An open space.

निकष (-स) *m*. The touch-stone; a streak of gold made on it a whet-stone.

निकषग्रावन् (-उपल) *m*. A touch-stone; a whet-stone.

निकषा *ind*. Near; betwixt.

निकषात्मज *m*. A demon.

निकाम *a*. Abundant

निकामम् *ind*. To one's satisfaction; exceedingly.

निकाय *m*. A class, a multitude; a congregation; a house; the body; aim; the supreme being.

निकाय्य *m*. A dwelling.

निकार *m*. Winnowing corn; slaughter; insult; malice; opposition. [ter.

निकारण *n*. Killing, slaughter.

निकाश (स) *m*. Appearance; proximity; likeness.

निकाष *m*. Scratching, rubbing.

निकुंज *m n*. A bower.

निकुरं (रुं) ब *n*. A flock.

निकृत *a*. Humbled; insulted; deceived; wicked.

निकृति *f*. Baseness; fraud; humiliation; removal.

निकृंतन *n*. Destruction.

निकृष्ट *a* Low; outcast.

निकेत *m*. A house.

निकेतन *m*. Onion. *n*. A house, an abode.

निकोचन *n*. Contraction.

निक्क (क्का) ण *m*. A musical sound.

निक्षिप्त *a*. Thrown down; rejected; pawned.

निक्षेप *m*. Casting upon, an open deposit. [burying.

निखनन *n*. Digging in, burying.

निखर्व *a*. Dwarfish. *n*. A billion. [burried.

निखात *a*. Dug up; fixed; burried.

निखिल *a*. Complate, entire.

निगड *a*. Fettered. *m. n*. A fetter, a shackle.

निगडित *a*. Fettered.

निग(गा)द m. Audible recitation of prayers; speech.

निगदित a. Speech, discourse.

निगम m. The Veda; a treatise explanatory of the Vedas; a root (as the source of a word); a sacred precept; logic; certainty, a market, traffic; a road.

निगमन n. Quotation of words from the Vedas; the conclusion in a syllogism.

निग (गा) र m Swallowing, devouring.

निगरण n. Swallowing, absorbing. m The throat.

निगीर्ण a Swallowed, completely absorbed.

निगूढ a Private, secret.

निगूहन n. Hiding, concealing.

निग्रंथन n. Killing, destroying.

निग्रह m. Restraint, subjection, seizing, imprisonment; removing punishment; dislike; a flaw in an argument; a handle; a limit.

निग्रहण a. Suppression; capture; punishment.

निग्राह m. An imprecation.

निघ a. As high as broad. m. A ball: sin.

निघंटु m. A vocabulary of Vedic words explained by Yaska.

निघर्ष m., (-ण n.) Friction.

निघात m. A blow, a stroke.

निघाति m. An iron club.

निघुष्ट n. Sound, noise.

निघ्न a. Dependant.

निचय m. Collection, certainty.

निचाय m A heap.

निचित a Covered, overspread, full of, raised up.

निचुल m. A kind of reed; a cover.

निचुलक n. A breast-plate.

निचोल m. A cover, a veil.

निचोलक m. A jacket, a bodice.

निज् vt. or vi. 3. U. (pp. निक्त) To wash, to purify; to nourish With अव-to wash, निस्-to clean.

निज a. Innate, peculiar; own perpetual

निञ्ज् vt. 2. A To wash; with प्र-to wash.

निटल n. The forehead.

निट(टि)लाक्ष m. S'iva.

निडीन n. The downward flight of a bird.

नितंब m. The buttocks, the ridge or side of a mountain, the shoulder.

नितंबबिंब n. Round hips.

नितंबिनी f. A woman with large and handsome hips.

नितराम् *ind.* Completely, extremely, continually, at all events.

नितल *n.* One of the seven divisions of the lower regions. [cessive.

नितांत *a.* Extraordinary, ex-

नितांतम् *ind.* Exceedingly.

नित्य *a.* Continual, constant, regular, fixed. necessary, ordinary. *m.* The ocean.

नित्यकर्मन् (-कृत्य *n.*, -क्रिया *f.*) A daily rite.

नित्यगति *m.* Air, wind.

नित्यदा *ind.* Always, perpetually.

नित्यनैमित्तिक *n.* Any rite or ceremony constantly performed.

नित्यप्रलय *m.* Sleep.

नित्यशस् *ind.* Always, constantly.

नित्यसमास *m.* A compound whose component parts cannot be used separately to convey its meaning.

निदर्शक *a.* Seeing, pointing out.

निदर्शन *n.* View, vision; showing; evidence; an illustration; a sign; a scheme; a precept.

निदर्शना *f.* A figure of speech.

निदाघ *m.* Heat, the hot season, perspiration.

निदाघकर *m.* The sun.

निदान *n.* A rope, a first cause, end, purity, pathology, diagnosis.

निदिग्ध *a.* Increased.

निदिध्यास *m.*, (-न *n.*) Profound and repeated meditation.

निदेश *m* Order, instruction, speech, conversation; neighbourhood.

निदेशिनी *f.* A quarter.

निद्रा *f.* Sleep.

निद्राण *a.* Sleepy.

निद्रालु *a.* Sleepy.

निद्रावृक्ष *m.* Darkness.

निद्रित *a.* Asleep.

निधन *a.* Poor, indigent *m.* *n.* End; *n.* family, race.

निधान *n.* A receptacle; treasure; store.

निधि *m.* Abode, receptacle, a store-house, a treasure, the ocean. [ing.

निधुवन *n.* Agitation, trembl-

निध्यान Beholding, sight.

निध्वान *m* Sound.

निनंक्षु Wishing to die.

निन (ना) द *m.* Sound, noise, humming.

निनयन *n.* Performance.

निंद् *vt.* 1. (*pp.* निंदित) To censure, to ridicule.

निंदक *a.* Blaming, abusing.

निंदा *f.* Blame, censure, defamation, injury.

निंदास्तुति *f.* Covert praise.
निंद्य *a.* Blamable, forbidden.
निप *m. n.* A water-jar.
निप (पा) ठ *m.* Study.
निपतन *n.* Falling down.
निपत्या *f.* Slippery ground; a battle-field.
निपात *m.* Falling down, attacking, hurling, death, accidental occurrence, irregularity, an indeclinable (in gram.), an irregular form of a word.
निपान *a.* Drinking off; a pool, a puddle.
निपीडन *n.* Squeezing, pressing; injuring. [hurt.
निपीडना *f.* Oppression,
निपुण *a.* Clever, shrewd, conversant with, kindly or friendly, sharp, perfect. [tally accurately.
निपुणम् *ind.* Skilfully; to-
निबंध *m.* Attachment; a literary composition; a fetter; an assignment of money &c. for support.
निबंधन *n.* The act of fastening; restraining, bond; a receptacle; support, cause; syntax, a composition, grant.
निबंधनी *f.* A bond, a fetter.
निब (व) र्हण *n.* Destruction.
निबिड *a.* Dense, thick.
निभ *a.* (At the end of compounds) Resembling; *m. n.* light, manifestation; disguise.
निभालन *n.* Seeing, sight.
निभूत *n.* Quite, frightened.
निभृत *a.* Secret, immovable; modest, lonely, silent.
निभृतम् *ind.* Privately, secretly, silently.
निमग्न *a.* Plunged, sunk, overwhelmed.
निमज्जथु *m.* The act of diving; sleeping.
निमज्जन *n.* Bathing, diving.
निमंत्रण *n.* Invitation; a summons.
निमय *m.* Barter, exchange.
निमान *m.* Measure; price.
निमि *m.* Twinkling.
निमित्त *n.* A mark, a sign, a target, an omen, motive; apparent cause, pretext.
निमित्तकारण *n.* (-हेतु *m.*) An instrumental or efficient cause.
निमित्तार्थ *m.* The infinitive mood.
निमिष *m.* Winking; a moment; the shutting (of flowers).
निमीलन *n* Winking, death; total eclipse.
निमीला } **निमीलिका** } *f.* Conniving at anything; fraud, pretence.

निम्रूल *a.* Down to the root.
निमेष *m.* See **निमिष.**
निम्न *a* Deep, low. *n.* A gap, depth ; a slope, a depression.
निम्नगत *n.* A low place.
निम्नगा *f.* A river. [fruits.
निंब *m.* A tree with bitter
निम्लुक्ति *f.* **निम्लोच** *m.* Sunset.
नियत *a.* Restrained; subdued, temperate; attentive; constant, inevitable; definite. [tainly.
नियतम् *ind.* Always, cer-
नियति *f.* Restraint; destiny; a religious duty, self-restraint.[governor.
नियंतृ *m.* A charioteer; a
नियंत्रण *n.*(-**णा** *f.*) Checking, restraint, restricting, guiding.
नियंत्रित *a.* Curbed, guided.
नियम *m.* Restraint, rule, restriction, certainty, agreement, promise; any self imposed religious observance, a poetic convention.
नियमन *n.* Restriction, limitation; a precept.
नियमनिष्ठा *f.* Rigid observance of prescribed rites.
नियमपत्र *n.* A written agreement.
नियमस्थिति *f.*Steady observance of religious obligations.
नियाम *m.* Restraint; a religious vow.
नियामक *a.* Restraining, guiding. *m.* A sailor, a charioteer. [ed.
नियुक्त *a.*Directed, appoint-
नियुक्ति *f.* Injunction, appointment, office.
नियुत *n.* A million; ten thousand crores.
नियुद्ध *n.* Close fight.
नियोग *m.* Employment, commission, charge, occupation, effort, necessity. A particular practice in ancient times.
नियोग्य *m.* A lord, a master. [an officer.
नियोज्य *m.* A functionary,
नियोद्धृ *m.* A cock
निर् *ind.* Same as **निस्.**
निरक्ष *m.* The place of no latitude (in astronomy).
निरंकुश *a.* Uncontrolled.
निरंजन *a.* Free from falsehood; simple. *m.* S'iva.
निरत *a.* Engaged or interested in; devoted to; delighted; ceased.
निरति *f.*Strong attachment.
निरतिशय *a.* Unsurpassed.
निरत्यय *a.* Secure, disinterested, quite successful.

निरनुक्रोश *a.* Pitiless.

निरंतर *a.* Constant, close dense; faithful.

निरंतरम् *ind.* Continually; tightly, immediately.

निरन्वय *a.* Childless; unconnected out of sight, unattended. [on.

निरपेक्ष *a.* Not depending

निरंबु *a.* Destitute of water.

निरय *m.* Hell.

निरर्गल *a.* Unimpeded.

निरर्थ *a.* Poor meaningless, vain, purposeless.

निरवग्रह *a.* Unrestrained, free, independent.

निरवद्य *a.* Faultless, unexceptionable. [plete.

निरवशेष *a.* Whole, com-

निरवशेषेण *ind.* Completely.

निरशन *n.* Fasting.

निरंश *a.* Whole.

निरस *a.* Tasteless, dry.

निरसन *n.* Expulsion, contradiction, extirpation.

निरस्त *a.* Cast away, repudiated, discharged, removed *n.* Rapid utterance.

निरहम् *a.* Free from self-conceit.

निराकरण *n.* Obstruction, contradiction, refutation, contempt.

निराकरिष्णु *a* Repudiating, expelling, obstructive.

निराकुल *a.* Full of; distressed.

निराकृति, निराक्रिया *f.* Repudiation rejection; refusal; obstruction.

निराग *a.* Dispassionate.

निरादिष्ट *a.* Paid off (as a debt.).

निरामय *a.* Healthy; infallible; *m. n* health.

निरालंब *a.* Friendless, alone.

निराश *a.* Hopeless.

निरास *m.* Expulsion, vomitting; refutation.

निरिश (-ष) *n.* A ploughshare.

निरीक्षण *n.* निरीक्षा *f.* A look; consideration, hope.

निरीह *a.* Desireless, indifferent.

निरुक्त *a.* Explanation; one of the six *Vedângas.*

निरुक्ति *f.* Etymological interpretation of words.

निरुत्सुक *a.* Extremely anxious.

निरुद्ध *a.* Obstructed.

निरुपधि *a* Guileless, honest.

निरुपपत्ति *a.* Unsuitable.

निरुपम *a.* Peerless, matchless.

निरूढ *a.* Conventional, accep ed; unmarried.

निरूढि *f.* Confirmation; long practice, close familiarity.

निरूपण *n.* (-णा *f.*) Form, sight; investigation, definition.

निरूपित *a.* Seen, appointed.
निरूह *m.* Logic, certainty.
निरोध *m*, (-न *n.*) Confinement, imprisonment, restraint, destruction; aversion.
निर्ऋति *f.* Decay, calamity, curse.
निर्गुण *a.* Stringless; bad, worthless. *m.* The supreme spirit
निर्ग्रंथ *m.* An idiot, a gambler. A devotee.
निर्ग्रंथिक *m.* A Jaina mendicant.
निर्गम *m.* An outlet.
निर्घट *n.* A free market.
निर्घृण *a.* Merciless, immodest.
निर्घोष *m.* A loud noise.
निर्जन *a.* Desolate. *n.* A desert.
निर्जर *a.* Young, imperishable. *m.* A deity, *n.* nectar.
निर्झर *m. n.* A spring.
निर्झरिन् *m.* A mountain.
निर्झरिणी, निर्झरी *f.* A river, a torrent.
निर्णय *m.* Removal; decision, inference; investigation; verdict (in law).
निर्णायन *n.* Making certain.
निर्णिक्त *a.* Washed, cleaned.
निर्णेक *m.* Washing, ablution; expiation.
निर्णेजन *n.* Ablution; expiation.
निर्णोद *m.* Removal, banishment.
निर्दट *a.* Unkind, envious; useless; violent.
निर्दर (-री) *m.* A cave.
निर्दलन *n.* Splitting.
निर्दहन *n.* Burning.
निर्दातृ *m.* A donor; a husbandman.
निर्दारित *a.* Torn, rent.
निर्दिग्ध *a.* Anointed, corpulent, stout.
निर्दिष्ट *a.* Specified, described; declared; ascertained.
निर्देश *m.* Order; instruction; declaring; specifying; special mention; ascertainment; proximity.
निर्द्वंद्व *a.* Indifferent.
निर्धार *m.*, (-ण *n.*) Determining, ascertainment.
निर्धारित *a.* Determined.
निर्धूत *n.* Shaken off, deserted, deprived of.
निर्धौत *a.* Washed off, bright.
निर्बंध *m.* Persistence, obstinacy; importunity, contest.
निर्बर्हण *n.* The same as निबर्हण.
निर्बुद्धि *a.* Ignorant, foolish.
निर्भट *a.* Hard, firm.
निर्भर्त्सन *n.* Threat, reproach, malignity.
निर्भर *a.* Excessive, ardent. *n.* Excess.
निर्भरम् *ind.* Excessively.

निर्भृति *a.* Without wages.

निर्भेद *m.* A rent.

निर्मक्षिक *a.* Private, lonely.

निर्मक्षिकम् *ind.* Lonely, private.

निर्म (र्मं) थ *m.*, (-न *n.*) Rubbing, churning.

निर्मम *a.* Disinterested.

निर्माण *n.* Measuring, production, manufacture, composition, form.

निर्माणा *f.* Propriety.

निर्माल्य *n.* Purity, faded flowers; remains in general.

निर्मिति *f.* Production, formation.

निर्मुक्त *a.* Liberated.

निर्मूलन *n* Eradication.

निर्मृष्ट *a.* Wiped off.

निर्मोक *m.* Setting free; a hide, the slough, mail.

निर्मोक्ष *m.* Liberation.

निर्मोचन *n.* Deliverance.

निर्याण *n.* Exit, departure; disappearance; death; final beatutide.

निर्यातन *n.* Returning, payment of a debt; donation; revenge, slaughter.

निर्याति *f.* Exit, death.

निर्याम *m.* A sailor, pilot.

निर्यास *m. n.* Exudation of trees or plants; gum, decoction.

निर्यूह *m.* A pinnacle, a crest; a door, decoction.

निर्लुंचन *n.* Pulling out, tearing.

निर्लुंठन *n.* Plundering.

निर्लेप *a.* Sinless.

निर्वचन *n.* A proverb; etymology; a vocabulary, an index.

निर्वपण *n.* Presentation of funeral offerings to the Manes; gift.

निर्वर्णन *n.* Seeing, sight.

निर्वर्तक *a.* Completing, accomplishing.

निर्वर्तन *n.* Accomplishment; completion.

निर्वहण *n.* End, completion.

निर्वाण *a.* Blown out, lost, dead, calmed, plunged. *n.* Extinction, disappearance; dissolution, death, eternal bliss, highest felicity; cessation; union, the bathing of an elephant.

निर्वाणभूयिष्ट *a.* Almost vanished or departed.

निर्वाद *m.* Blame, decision.

निर्वाप *m.* The same as **निर्वपण**.

निर्वापण *n.* A funeral oblation; gift; extinguishing; alleviation; slaughter; refreshing.

निर्वास *m.*, (-न *n.*) Expulsion, slaughter.

निर्वाह *m*. Completion, perseverance, describing; sufficiency.

निर्विकल्प (-क) *a*. Not admitting an alternative.

निर्विकार *a*. Unchangable.

निर्विचेष्ट *a*. Motionless.

निर्विवाद *a*. Undisputed.

निर्विशेष *a*. Without distinction, indiscriminate; *m*. Absence of difference.

निर्विशेषम्, निर्विशेषेण *ind*. Indifferently, equally.

निर्विष्ट *a*. Enjoyed; obtained as wages married.

निर्वृत्ति *f*. Accomplishment.

निर्वेद *m*. Disgust, despondency, humiliation.

निर्वेश *m*. Wages, enjoyment; expiation; marriage; fainting.

निर्व्यंजन *a*. Straight forward.

निर्व्यथन *n* Extreme pain; a hole.

निर्व्यलीक *a*. Not offending; sincere; genuine.

निर्व्याज *a*. Candid, honest. plain. [plainly.

निर्व्याजम् *ind*. Honestly,

निर्विण्ण *a*. Despondent.

निर्वृत *a*. Satisfied; secure; ceased.

निर्वृति *f*. Satisfaction; repose; final emancipation; accomplishment.

निर्वृत्त *a*. Accomplished.

निर्व्यूढ *a*. Finished, developed; vindicated; deserted. [top.

निर्व्यूढि *f*. Completion; the

निर्व्यूह *m*. A turret; a crest; a door.

निर्हार *m*. Extracting; removal; private hoard, evacuation of the natural excrements of the body.

निर्हारिन् *a*. Fragrant.

निर्हृति *f*. Removal.

निर्ह्राद *m* A sound.

निलय *m* A hiding place, a den, a nest; house; disappearance

निलयन *m*. A place of refuge; a dwelling.

निलिंप *m*. A god.

निलिंपा (-पिका) *f*. A cow.

निलीन *a*. Involved, destroyed, changed.

निवचने *ind*. Not speaking.

निवपन *n*. Scattering, sowing an offering to the Manes.

निवरा *f*. A virgin.

निवर्तक *v*. Returning, stopping, expelling.

निवर्तन *n*. Returning, ceasing, inactivity; repenting.

निवसति *f*. Residence, house.

निवसथ *m*. A village. [ment.

निवसन *n*. A house, a gar-

निवह *m.* A multitude.

निवात *a.* Sheltered from the wind, calm, safe. *m.* An asylum, a coat of mail.

निवाप *m.* Seed, an offering at the *śrâddha*; a gift.

निवार *m.*,(-ण *n.*) Preventing.

निवास *m.* Living, house, resting place, dress.

निवासन *n.* Residing, sojourn. [thick, dense.

निवि (चि) ड *a.* Close; fast,

निविरीस *a.* Compact, close.

निर्विशेष *a.* Alike.

निविष्ट *a.* Seated, intent upon; initiated.

निवीत *n.* Wearing the sacred thread round the neck like a garland. *m. n.* A veil, a mantle.

निवृत *a.* Surrounded. *m. n.* A veil, a mantle. [ing.

निवृति *f.* Covering; enclos-

निवृत्त *a.* Returned, departed, refrained from; abstracted from this world; completed; quiet.

निवृत्ति *f.* Return, disappearance, suspension, aversion, inactivity, separation from the world; beatitude.

निवेदन *n.* Announcement; delivering, representation; oblation; dedication.

निवेद्य *n.* Offering food to an idol.

निवेश *m.* Entrance; encampment; a house; marriage; copy; military array; decoration.

निवेशन *n.* Entrance; a house; a camp; a town.

निवेष्ट *m.* A cover.

निवेष्टन *a.* Covering.

निश् *f.* (This word has no forms for the first five forms) Night; turmeric.

निशमन *n.* Sight; hearing.

निश (शा) रण *n.* Killing.

निशा *f.* Night, turmeric.

निशाकर *m.* The moon.

निशाचर *a.* Moving about by night. *m.* A fiend, an owl; a snake; a thief.

निशाचरी *f.* A woman going to her love at night by appointment; a harlot.

निशाचर्मन् *m.* Darkness.

निशाजल *n.* Dew, frost.

निशाट *m.*, (-न *n.*) An owl; a ghost; a demon.

निशात *a.* Sharpened.

निशादर्शिन् *m.* An owl.

निशान *a.* Sharpening.

निशानिशम् *ind.* Every night.

निशांत *a.* Quiet. *n.* A house.

निशाम *m.* Observing.

निशामन *n.* Sight; hearing, reflection; a shadow.

निशामृग *m.* A jackal.
निशावन *m.* Hemp. [goblin.
निशाविहार *m.* A demon, a
निशित *a.* Sharpened.
निशीथ *m.* Midnight.
निशीथिनी निशीथ्या *f.* Night.
निशुंभ *m.* Name of a demon.
निशुंभन *n.* Killing, slaughter. [resolution.
निश्चय *m.* Ascertainment,
निश्चल *a.* Immovable.
निश्चला *f.* The earth.
निश्चायक *a.* Decisive.
निश्चित *a.* Ascertained, *n.* Certainty, decision.
निश्चितम् *ind.* Positively, decidedly. [determination.
निश्चिति *f.* Ascertainment,
निश्रम *m.* Continued practice.
निश्रयणी } *f.* A ladder,
निश्रेणि (-णी) } a staircase.
निश्वास *m.* Inspiration, inhaling sighing.
निःशब्द *a.* Inaudible.
निःशम *m* Anxiety.
निःशरण *a.* Helpless.
निःशलाक *a* Lonely.
निःश्रेयस *a.* The best. *n.* Absolution; happiness.
निषंग *m.* Attachment, union; a quiver, a sword.
निषण्ण *a.* Seated, supported; distressed.
निषण्णक *n* A seat. [love.
निषद्वर *m.* Mud, the god of
निषद्वरी *f.* Night.
निषाद *m.* Name of a wild aboriginal tribe; *Chandála*; the last or seventh note of the Hindu gamut.
निषादित *a.* Afflicted.
निषिक्त *a.* Sprinkled upon.
निषिद्ध *a.* Forbidden.
निषिद्धि *f.* Prohibition. [ter.
निषूदन *n.* Killing, slaugh-
निषेक *m.* Sprinkling, effusion, impregnation; dirty water.
निषेध *m.* Warding off, denial; rule, exception.
निषेवक *a.* Practising, frequenting, fond of.
निषेवण *n.* } Service; wor-
निषेवा *f.* } ship; practice.
निष्क *m* *n.* A practicular golden coin.
निष्कर्ष *m.* Extraction; the main point.
निष्कास (-श) *m.* Exit; a portico; daybreak.
निष्कासित *a.* Expelled.
निष्कुट *m.* A pleasure-grove, a field; the harem of a king.
निष्कुल *a.* Alone.
निष्कुषित *a.* Torn off.
निष्कुह *m.* See **निष्कुट**.
निष्कूज *a.* Silent.
निष्कूट *a.* Honest.
निष्कृत *n.* Expiation.

निष्कृति *f.* Expiation, compensation, removal; cure

निष्कोप *m.*, (-ण *n.*) Extirpating.

निष्क्रम *m.* Exit; a particular ceremony.

निष्क्रय *m.* Redemption, price, wages; reward; barter.

निष्क्राथ *m.* Decoction.

निष्टपन *n.* Burning.

निष्ठ *a.* Being in or on, depending on, relating to; devoted to.

निष्ठा *f.* Position, basis, steadiness, devotion; skill, faith, conclusion, accomplishment, death, certainty, distress.

निष्ठान *n.* Sauce, condiment.

निष्ठी (ष्ठे) व *m. n.* } Spiting out.
निष्ठी (ष्ठे) वन *n.* }
निष्ठीवित *n.* }

निष्ठुर *a.* Hard, severe, cruel.

निष्ठ्युत *pp.* Spit out; thrown [out

निष्ठ्यूति *f.* Spitting out.

निष्णात *a.* Clever, expert, perfect.

निष्पतन *n.* Rushing out.

निष्पत्ति *f.* Birth.

निष्पन्न *pp.* Born, effected.

निष्पादन *n.* Accomplishing.

निष्पीडित *a.* Squeezed.

निष्पेष *m.*, (-ण *n.*) Rubbing together, grinding, striking.

निष्प्रकारक *a.* Absolute.

निष्प्रचार *a.* Concentrated.

निष्प्रतिकार, निष्प्रतीकार, निष्प्रतिक्रिय *a.* Incurable, unobstructed.

निष्प्रतिघ *a.* Unhindered.

निष्प्रतिद्वंद्व *a.* Matchless.

निष्प्रतिभ *a.* Dull stupid.

निष्प्रतिभान *a.* Cowardly.

निष्प्रतीप *a.* Looking straight forward; unconcerned.

निष्प्रत्यूह *a.* Unobstructed.

निष्प्रपंच *a.* Honest.

निष्प्रभ, निःप्रभ *a.* Powerless, gloomy, dark.

निसर्ग *m.* A grant; evacuation; creation; nature; relinquishing.

निसर्गतः *a.* Naturally.

निसर्गज (-सिद्ध) *a.* Innate, natural.

निसार *m.* A multitude.

निसूदन *a.* Killing; *n.* slaughter.

निसृष्ट *a.* Delivered, abandoned; permitted; middle.

निसृष्टार्थ *m.* An agent; an [ambassador.

निस्तनी *f.* A pill.

निस्तरण *n.* Crossing over; release, an expedient.

निस्तर्हण *n.* Killing

निस्तल *a.* Round; bottomless.

निस्तार *m.* Crossing over;

release, rescue, final emancipation; aquittance.

निस्तीर्ण *a.* Saved.

निस्पंद *m.* Trembling, motion. [a stream.

निस्यं(ष्यं)द *m* A discharge,

निस्राव *m.* A stream.

निस्व(स्वा)न *m.* Noise, voice.

निःसंशयम् *ind.* Doubtlessly.

निःसंग *a.* Indifferent.

निःसंधि *a.* Compact.

निःसंपात *a.* Blocked up; *m.* thick darkness.

निःसंबाध *a.* Spacious.

निःसार *a.* Worthless.

निःस्पं (ष्पं) द *a.* Motion-less.

निःस्पृह *a.* Indifferent.

निःस्व *a.* Indigent, poor.

निहत *a.* Struck down, slain. [ter.

निहनन *n.* Killing, slaugh-

निहव *m.* Invocation.

निहार *m.* See नीहार.

निहित *a.* Laid, situated.

निहिंसन *n.* Killing, slaughter.

निहीन *a.* Low, vile.

निह्नव *m.* Denial, secrecy, doubt, wickedness; expiation; excuse.

निह्नुति *f.* Denial, secrecy.

नी *vt.* 1. U. To lead, to carry, to marry; to ascertain, to decide, to trace, (A.) to instruct; with अनु to conciliate, to please, to supplicate; अप to lead away, to plunder; to remove, to extract. अभि-to act, to quote; अभिवि-to instruct well. आ-to bring, to produce; उद्-(Atm.) to raise उप-to raise, to offer; (in the Atm.) to invest with the sacred thread, to hire; (Atm.) नि-to take near or towards, उपा-to lead, to bend. निस्-to investigate, परि-to lead round, to marry, to investigate, प्र-to offer, to perform, to teach, to write, प्रति-to carry back, वि-to remove; to educate, to tame, to appease, to present, to spend, to pay. सम्-to restore; to guide, समा-to join.

नी *m.* (at the end of a compound) A leader, a guide.

नीच *a.* Low, short.

नीचकैस् *ind.* See नीचैस्.

नीचगा *f.* A river.

नीचभोज्य *m.* Onion.

नीचैस् *ind.* (often used adjectively) Low, humbly, softly.

नीड *m. n.* A bird's nest; a couch; a den.

नीडक (-ज) *m*. A bird.

नीत *a*. Led; obtained; well-behaved.

नीति *f*. Guidance, conduct, acquisition; support; policy, politics, ethics.

नीप *m*. The foot of a mountain; the *kadamba* tree.

नीर *n*. Water, juice.

नीरज *n*. Lotus, a pearl.

नीरद *m*. A cloud.

नीरधि (-निधि) *m*. The ocean.

नीराजन *n*. (-ना *f*.) Lustration of arms; waving lights before an idol.

नील *a*. Dark-blue. *m*. The dark-blue colour; the sapphire; name of a monkey chief.

नीलक *n*. Black salt; blue vitriol.

नीलकंठ *m*. A peacock; Śiva, a blue-necked jay; a sparrow; a bee.

नीलग्रीव *m*. Śiva.

नीलमणि *m*. The sapphire.

नीललोहित *m*. S'iva.

नीलिका (-नी) *f*. The indigo plant.

नीलिमन् *m*. Blue colour.

नीली *f* The indigo plant.

नीवर *m*. Trade, a religious mendicant; mud.

नीवाक *m*. Famine, scarcity.

नीवार *m*. Rice growing wild.

नीवि (-वी) *f*. The knot of a wearing garment; capital; a stake.

नीवृत *m*. Kingdom.

नीशार *m*. A blanket; a mosquito-curtain.

नीहार *m*. Fog, mist.

नु *ind*. Whether-or; indeed.

नु *vt*. 2. P. To praise; to cry.

नुति *f*. Praise, reverence.

नुद् *vt*. 6. U. (*pp*. नुत्त or नुन्न) To push, to incite, to remove, to throw. With अप-to drive away. निस्-to reject. प्र-to drive off, नि-to strike; to play (on a musical instrument). सम्-to collect, to find. (*Causal*) With वि-to dispel, to spend (as time); to amuse.

नूतन, नूत्न *a*. New, fresh, young; strange.

नूनम् *ind*. Probably, surely.

नूपुर *m*. *n*. An anklet.

नृ *m*. A person, mankind.

नृप *m*. A king, a sovereign.

नृपति (-पाल) *m*. A king.

नृयज्ञ *m*. Hospitality.

नृशृंग *n*. An impossibility.

नृसिंह *m*. An eminent man; Vishnu in his fourth incarnation.

नृसोम *m*. An illustrious man.

नृत् *vi*. 4 P. To dance, to represent on the stage.

With उप or प्र-to dance; प्रति-to mock by dancing in return.

नृति *f*. Dancing; dance.

नृत्य *n*. Dancing, acting.

नृशंस *a*. Malicious, wicked.

नेजक *m*. A washermen.

नेजन *n*. Washing.

नेतृ *m*. A leader, a judge.

नेत्र *n*. Leading, the eye, the root of a tree; a carriage.

नेत्रकोष *m*. The eyeball.

नेत्रच्छद् *m*. The eyelid.

नेत्ररंजन *n*. Collyrium.[eyes.

नेत्रस्तंभ *m*. Rigidity of the

नेत्रांजन *n*. Collyrium.

नेत्रांबु or नेत्रांभस् *n*. Tears.

नेत्रामय *m*. Opthalmia.

नेत्री *f*. A river; a vein; Lakshmi; a female leader.

नेत्रोत्सव *m*. A pleasing or beautiful object

नेदिष्ठ *a*. (*super*. of अंतिक) Nearest, next.

नेदीयस् *a*. (*compar*. of अंतिक) Nearer.

नेपथ्य *n*. Decoration; dress; the part of the stage behind the curtain.

नेपालिका *f*. Red arsenic.

नेम *m*. A part; a season; enclosure, fraud, evening.

नेमि(-मी) *f*. The circumference; a thunderbolt, the earth.

नेष्टु *m*. A clod of earth.

नैकटिक *a*. Near, contiguous.

नैकट्य *n*. Proximity.

नैकषेय *m*. A demon.

नैकृतिक *a*. Dishonest, low.

नैगम *a*. Relating to the Veda. *m*. An interpreter of the sacred writing; an *Upanishad*; an expedient; a citizen, a merchant.

नैघंटुक *n*. The glossary of Vedic words commented upon by Yáska [ty.

नैत्य *n*. Eternity, perpetui-

नैत्य (त्यि) क *a*. Regularly recurring, obligatory.

नैदान *m*. An etymologist.

नैदानिक *m*. A pathologist.

नैदेशिक *m*. A servant.

नैपुण (-ण्य) *n*. Dexterity; a delicate matter; completeness. [ty.

नैभृत्य *n*. Modesty, humili-

नैमय *m*. A trader.

नैमित्तिक *a* Unusual, occasional. *m*. An astrologer. *n*. An effect.

नैमिष *a*. Momentary. *n*. Name of a sacred forest.

नैमेय *m*. Barter, exchange.

नैयत्य *n*. Restraint.

नैयमिक *a*. Regular.

नैयायिक *m*. A logician.

नैरंतर्य *n*. Continuity.

नैरपेक्ष्य *n*. Disregard.

नैरर्थ्य *n.* Senselessness.

नैराश्य *n.* Hopelessness, despair.

नैरुक्त *m.* A philologist.

नैर्ऋत *m.* A demon.

नैर्ऋती *f.* Durgá; the south-west.

नैर्गुण्य *n.* Absence, of qualities, want of excellence.

नैर्घृण्य *n.* Cruelty.

नैबिड्य *n.* Compactness.

नैवेद्य *n.* An offering of eatables presented to a deity.

नैश or **नैशिक** *a.* Nocturnal.

नैश्चल्य *n.* Fixedness.

नैश्चित्य *n.* Determination.

नैःश्रेयस, नैःश्रेयसिक *a.* Leading to happiness or final beatitude.

नैष्कर्म्य *n.* Idleness, inactivity; the salvation obtained by abstraction.

नैष्ठिक *a.* Final, constant, perfect; vowing perpetual abstinence and chastity. *m.* A perpetual religious student (op. to **उपकुर्वाण.**)

नैष्ठुर्य *n.* Cruelty, harshness.

नैष्ठ्य *n.* Constancy, firmness.

नैसर्गिक *a.* Natural, innate.

नैस्त्रिंशिक *m.* A swordsman.

नैःस्व (स्व्य) *n.* Poverty.

नो *ind.* Not, no.

नो चेत् *ind.* If not.

नोदन *n.* Impelling.

नोधा *ind.* Ninefold.

नौ *f.* A ship, a boat, a navy.

नौका *f.* A small boat.

नौकादंड *m.* An oar, a paddle.

नौतार्य *a.* Navigable.

नौदंड *m.* An oar.

नौयान *n* Navigation.

नौवाह *m.* A steersman.

न्यक् *ind.* Adverb prefixed to **कृ** or **भू** in the sense of 'humiliation or contempt.'

न्यक्करण *n.* **न्यक्कार** *m.* Humiliation, contempt.

न्यग्भाव *m.* Humiliation.

न्यग्रोध *m.* The Indian fig-tree; a fathom measured by the arms extended.

न्यग्रोधपरिमंडला *f.* An excellent woman.

न्यक्ष *a.* Low, *m.* A buffalo; an epithet of Paras'uráma. *n.* The whole.

न्यंच् *a.* Going downwards, lazy; short; whole.

न्यंचन *n.* A curve.

न्यय *m.* Destruction. [up.

न्यसन *n.* Depositing; giving

न्यस्त *a.* Cast down.

न्याद *m.* Eating.

न्याय *m.* Method, manner, rule, virtue, justice, judgment; policy, good government, a universal rule (in gram.); analogy, a popular maxim, a proverbial illustration; a system of Hindu philosophy founded by Gautama; logic; a Vedic accent.

न्यायशास्त्र *n*. Logic. [iour

न्यायसारिणी *f*. Right behav-

न्याय्य *a*. Just, equitable, suitable, usual, customary.

न्यास *m*. Placing, deposit, a pledge, entrusting, painting, stamp, abandoning, seizing(with the claws); mental assignment of the various parts of the body to several deities. [gee.

न्यासधारिन् *m*. A mortga-

न्यासिन् *m*. A *Sannyasin*.

न्युब्ज *a*. Turned downwards, crooked convex.

न्यून *a*. Inferior, deficient, less, defective, wicked.

न्यूनम् *ind*. Less.

प

प *a*. (At the end of compounds) Drinking, protecting. *m*. Air, a leaf.

पक्ति *f*. Cooking‘ digestion, ripening.

पक्तृ *m*. Fire.

पक्त्रिम *a*. Ripe, mature.

पक्व *a*. Cooked, digested; burned, ripe.

पक्वान्न *n*. Cooked food.

पक्वाशय *m*. The stomach.

पक्ष् *vt*. 1. P. 10 U. To take, to accept.

पक्ष *m*. A fortnight, wing, a party, a feather, the flank, an alternative, a point under discussion, a bird; an army; a limb of the body; a wall; an idea.

पक्षक *m*. A side-door; a partisan.

पक्षज *m*. The moon.

पक्षति *f*. The root of a wing; the first day of a lunar fortnight.

पक्षपात *m* Partiality; partisanship; desire.

पक्षपातिन् *a*. Partial.

पक्षपाद *m*. An *exparte* statement, expression of opinion.

पक्षपालि *m*. A private door.

पक्षवाहन *m*. A bird. [side.

पक्षहत *a*. Paralysed on one

पक्षहर *m*. A bird.

पक्षाघात *m*.Paralysis of one side; refutation of an argument.

पक्षांत *m* The day of the new or full moon.

पक्षालु *m*. A bird.

पक्षिणी *f*. A female bird; a night with the two days enclosing it.

पक्षिन् *m.* A bird; Siva; an arrow. [ary.

पक्षिशाला *f.* A nest, an aviary.

पक्ष्मन् *n.* An eyelash; the filament of a flower; a wing.

पक्ष्मल *a.* Having beautiful eyelashes, hairy.

पक्ष्य *m.* A partisan, a follower. [sin.

पंक *m. n.* Mud, a slough; sin.

पंकग्राह *m.* A crocodile.

पंकज *n.* A lotus.

पंकज (जन्मन्) *m.* Brahman (*m.*).

पंकिल *a.* Muddy. *m.* A boat.

पंकेज *n.* A lotus.

पंकेरुह् (-रुह) *n.* A lotus.

पंकेशय *a.* Dwelling in mud.

पंक्ति *f.* A row, a series, a group, the earth, fame.

पंक्तिपावन *m.* A respectable Bráhmana who imparts sanctity to the dining party or who is learned in the Vedas.

पंगु *a.* Crippled.

पंगुल *a.* Lame, crippled.

पच् *vi.* or *vi.* 1. P (*pp.* पक्व) To cook, to bake, to digest, to develop. With परि or वि-to mature, to digest, *vt.* 1 A. To make clear. *vt.* 10 U. To spread.

पचत *m.* The sun, fire.

पचन *a.* Cooking, maturing. *m.* Fire.

पचि *m.* Fire.

पज्झटिका *f.* A small bell.

पंचक *a.* Bought with five; consisting of five. *m. n.* An aggregate of five.

पंचक्रोशि *f.* A distance of five *kos'a*.

पंचगव्य *n.* Five products of the cow (collectively).

पंचगु *a.* Bought with five cows.

पंचजन *m.* Man, mankind *m. pl.* The five classes of beings, *viz*, gods, men, *gandharvas* serpents and *pitris*. [buffoon.

पंचजनीन *m.* A mimic, a buffoon.

पंचद् *f.* A pentad.

पंचतय *a.* Five fold. *n.* A pentad.

पंचता (-त्वं *n.*) Five-fold state; the five elements collectively.

पंचतंत्र *n.* A well-known Sanskrit work.

पंचत्वं गम To separate into the five elements, *i. e.* to die.

पंचदशि *f.* The fifteenth day of a lunar fortnight.

पंचन् *num.* (always *pl*; nom. and acc. पंच) Five.

पंचनद *m* The country of five rivers (the Punjab).

पंचबाण, पंचशर *m.* An epithet of the god of love.

पंचम *a.* The fifth; clever; brilliant. *m.* The fifth note of the Hindu musical scale.

पंचमी *f.* The fifth day of a lunar fortnight; the ablative case (in gram).

पंचयाम *m.* A day.

पंचराशिक *n.* The rule of five.

पंचलक्षण *n.* A Puràna.

पंचवटी *f.* The five fig trees, name of a part of the *Dandaka* forest where the Godávari rises.

पंचवर्षदेशीय *a.* Nearly five years old.

पंचवर्षीय *a.* Five years old.

पंचविंशति *f.* Twentyfive.

पंचशाख *m.* The hand; an elephant.

पंचशिख *m.* A lion.

पंचष *a pl* Five or six.

पंचसूना *f.* The five things by which animal life may be accidentally destroyed.

पंचहायन *a.* Five years old.

पंचांग *a.* Having five parts. *m.* A turtle, a horse. *n.* A calender, an almanac.

पंचानन, पंचास्य, पंचमुख, *m.* An epithet of Śiva; a lion.

पंचामृत *n.* An aggregate of five sweet things.

पंचार्चिस् *m.* The planet Mercury.

पंचावस्थ *m.* A corpse.

पंचाविक *n.* The five products of the sheep.

पंचाह *m.* A period of five days.

पंचालिका *f.* A doll, a puppet.

पंचाली *f.* A doll, a puppet; a kind of song.

पंचाशति *f.* Fifty. [fifty.

पंचाशिका *f.* A collection of

पंचेषु *m.* The god of love.

पंचोष्मन् *m. pl.* The five digestive fires.

पंजर *n.* A cage. *m. n.* A skeleton. *m.* The body, the *Kaliyuga.*

पंजिका *f.* A running commentary; a journal.

पद् *vt.* 1. P To go. (*Causal*) To split, to pierce, to tear out; 10 U. to clothe.

पट *m. n.* A garment, a veil; a tablet. *n.* A roof.

पटकार *m.* A weaver; a painter.

पटकुटी *f.* (-मंडप *m.*, -वाप *m.*, -वेश्मन् *n.*) A tent.

पटच्चर *m.* A thief.

पटत्क *m.* A thief.

पटल *n.* A roof, a thatch, a veil, a coating; a basket;

a mass, a multitude, retinue. A tree. *m. n.* A chapter of a book.

पटला *f.* A heap.

पटवास *m.* A tent.

पटह *m.* A kettle-drum, uproar of the battle.

पटालुका *f.* A leech. [tain.

पटि (-टी) *f.* Cloth, the cur-

पटिक्षेप *m.* Tossing aside the curtain of the stage.

पटिमन् *m.* Cleverness, acidity; harshness.

पटीर *m.* Sandal wood; a ball. *n.* Catechu; the belly; a sieve; a field.

पटु *a.* Clever, skilful, sharp, healthy; cruel; cunning; eloquent; expanded.

पटोलक *m.* An oyster.

पट्ट *m.n.* A slab, a plate, a royal edict; a diadem; a grinding stone; a town; a throne; a shield; an upper garment, a stool; silk; a bandage.

पट्टदेवी (-महिषी, -राज्ञी) *f.* The principal queen.

पट्टन *n.* (-नी *f.*) A city.

पट्टवस्त्र (-वासस्) *a.* Attired in colored cloth. [queen.

पट्टार्हा *f.* The principal

पट्टिका *f.* A table, a document; a piece of cloth.

पट्टि (ट्टी) श (स) *m.* A spear with a sharp edge.

पट्टोलिका *f.* A title-deed.

पठ् *vt.* 1. P. To read, to recite, to study, to quote; to describe. *Caus.* With परि-to teach.

पठन *n.* Reading.

पठि *f.* Reading, perusal.

पंड् *vi.* 1. A. (*pp.* पंडित *pres.* पंडते) To go, to move; *vt.* 10. U. to collect.

पण् *vt.* or *vi.* 1. A. To bargain, to bet, to praise. With वि-to sell.

पण *m.* A game played for a stake; a stipulation, wages, price; a coin equal in value to eight *cowries*; wealth; commodity for sale; a vendor; a shop.

पणग्रंथि *m.* A market.

पणन *n.* Betting; sale.

पणबंध *m.* An agreement.

पणव *m.* A sort of musical instrument.

पणाया *f.* Transaction, a market-place; gambling; praise. [miser.

पणि *f.* A market. *m.* A

पणित *a.* Transacted; betted.

पणितृ *m.* A trader.

पंड *m.* A eunuch.

पंडा *f.* Wisdom, learning.

पंडित *a.* Learned, clever; proficient. *m.* A scholar, incense; an expert.

पांडितंमन्य *a.* A pedant who thinks himself a *Pandita.*

पण्य *a.* Saleable. *n.* A commodity, business; price.

पण्ययोषित् (-विलासिनी, -स्त्री, -अंगना) *f.* A courtezan.

पण्यपाति *m.* A great merchant.

पण्यभूमि *f.* A warehouse.

पण्यवीथिका (-वीथी, -शाला) *f.* A market; a shop.

पण्याजिर *n.* A market.

पण्याजीव *m.* A trader.

पत् *vt.* or *vi.* 1. P. To fly, to descend, to alight, to sink, to throw oneself down, to fall, to occur, to be degraded, to fall upon. With अनु–to fly to; अभि-to fly near, अभ्युद्-to attack, आ-to rush in or on; to happen; to assail; उद्-to jump up, to rise, नि-to fall upon, to assault, to become fixed in, to happen, निस्-to issue from; परा-return, to arrive, परि-to hover about, to attack, to fall down; प्रणि-to salute, प्रोद्-to fly into, सम् to fly together, to attack, to happen.

पत *m.* Flight; alight.

पतग *m.* A bird.

पतंग *m.* A bird, the sun, grass-hopper. [hopper.

पतंगम *m.* A bird; a grass-

पतंगिका *f.* A small bird; a kind of small bee.

पतंगिन् *m.* A bird.

पतंचिका *f.* A bow string.

पतंजलि *m.* Name of a celebrated grammarian and philosopher.

पतत्र *m.* A wing.

पतत्रि *m.* A bird. [a horse.

पतत्रिन् *m.* A bird; an arrow;

पतद्ग्रह *m.* The reserve of an army.

पतद्भीरु *m.* A hawk.

पतन *n* Alighting, descending: setting; apostacy; decline.

पतनीय *n.* A degrading sin.

पतम (-स) *m.* The moon; a bird; a grass-hopper.

पतयालु *a.* Prone to fall.

पताका *f.* A flag, a flag-staff, a mark, an episode in a drama; auspiciousness.

पताकिक *a.* Having or carrying a banner. [bearer.

पताकिन् *m.* A flag; standard-

पताकिनी *f.* An army.

पति *m.* A master, a ruler, the president, a husband.

पतित *a.* Fallen, dropped; overthrown; degraded; fallen (morally).

पतिधर्म *m* Duty towards a husband

पतिव्रता *f.* A devoted and virtuous wife. [husband.

पतिव्रतात्व *n.* Fidelity to a

पत्तन *n.* A town, a city.

पत्ति *m.* A foot-soldier; a pedestrian; a hero. *f.* A small division of an army.

पत्तिकाय *m.* Infantry.

पत्तिन् *m.* A foot-soldier.

पत्तिसंहति *f.* A body of infantry.

पत्नी *f.* A wife.

पत्र *n.* The wing; a vehicle, the feather of an arrow, the leaf; paper, a letter, the blade of a weapon; painting the person, a knife.

पत्रक *n.* A leaf; painting figures on the body.

पत्रणा *f.* Painting figures on the body; feathering an arrow.

पत्रदारक *m.* A saw. [leaf.

पत्रनाडिका *f.* The fibre of a

पत्रपाल *m.* A large knife.

पत्रपाली *f.* A pair of scissors.

पत्रपुट *n.* A vessel of leaves.

पत्रपुष्पा *f.* The holy basil.

पत्रबाल (-वाल) *m.* An oar.

पत्रभंग *m.* (-भंगि, -भंगी *f.*) Drawing figures on the person, an ornament.

पत्ररथ *m.* A bird.

पत्ररेखा (-लेखा, -वल्लरी, -वल्लि, -वल्ली) *f.* See **पत्रभंग**.

पत्रवाह *m.* A bird, an arrow, a letter-carrier.

पत्रसूचि *f.* A thorn.

पत्रांजन *n.* Ink.

पत्रावलि *f.* Red chalk; a row of leaves; decorating the person with coloured substances.

पत्रिका *f.* A letter.

पत्रिन् *a.* Winged, having leaves. *m.* An arrow, a bird, a falcon; a tree; a mountain; a chariot.

पत्रिवाह *m.* A bird.

पत्सल *m.* A way, a road.

पथ *m.* A way, a road.

पथकल्पना *f.* Juggling tricks.

पथिक *m.* A traveller, a guide.

पथिन् *m.* (nom. पंथाः, -न्थौ, -न्थः, acc. *pl.* पथः) A path, a way, a journey, course, manner, a sect.

पथिल *m.* A wayfarer.

पथ्य *a.* Wholesome, beneficial, proper. *n.* Wholesome diet; welfare.

पद् *vt.* 10 A. To go, *vt.* 4. A (*pp.* पन्न) To attain, to observe; with अनु-to follow, to understand, अभि-to approach, to know as, to consider, to assist, to attack to take possession of, to assume, अभ्युप-to protect; to assent. आ-to go near, to go to, to fall into misfortune, to occur. उद्-to originate, to be born, to occur, (*causal*) to produce, to bring about, adequate for, to be obtained. निस्-to spring from; with प्र-to resort to, to take refuge, to arrive at a condition, to attain, to deal with, to allow, प्रति-to step upon, to get, to share, to resort to, to recover, to understand, to acknowledge, to regard, to perfrom, to undertake वि-to fall into a bad state, to be disabled; to die. सम्-to succeed, to be prosperous, to be completed, to become, to unite, to obtain, to bring about. समा-to take place; to attain to. *Caus.* With आ to lead to, to bring to subjection, to cause. उद्-to create; उप-to lead to; to present, to achieve, to give reasons for. निस्-to prepare, प्रति- to give, to prove, to consider. व्या-to kill. सम्-to prepare, to accomplish, to obtain, to strike a bargain.

पद् *m.* (This word has no forms for the first five forms.) A foot; a quarter.

पद *m. n.* A foot; a ray of light. *n.* Step; station; employment; an office; a foot; print; a rank; an object; a line of a stanza; an inflected word.

पदक *n.* A step. *m.* A necklace.

पदच्युत *a.* Dismissed from office.

पदन्यास *m.* Step, a footmark, position of the feet.

पदवि (-वी) *f.* Road, rank, place.

पदांगुष्ठ *m.* The great toe.

पदाजि (-ति, -त) *m.* A pedestrian; a foot-soldier.

पदातिन् *m.* A foot soldier.

पदानुग *m.* A follower.

पदानुशासन *n.* Grammar.

पदार्थ *m.* An object; meaning; a topic; a category.

पदिक *a.* Going on foot.

पद्धति, पद्धती *f.* A way, road.

पद्म *n.* A lotus, one thousand billions. *m.* An elephant; one of the nine treasures of Kubera.

पद्मखंड (-षंड) *n*. A multitude of lotuses.

पद्मज (-जात,-भव,-भू, -योनि, -संभव. *m*. An epithet of Brahman (*m*.).

पद्मनाभ (-भि) *m*. Vishnu.

पद्मबंध *m*, The artificial arrangement of words of a stanza in the figure of a lotus flower.

पद्मबंधु *m*. The sun; a bee.

पद्मराग *n*. A ruby.

पद्मा *f*. Lakshmi.

पद्माकर *m*. A pond.

पद्मालय *m*. Brahman (*m*.).

पद्मालया *f*. Lakshmi.

पद्मावती *f*. Lakshmi.

पद्मासन *m*. Brahman (*m*.)

पद्मिन् *m*. An elephant.

पद्मिनी *f*. The lotus plant,a cluster of lotuses; a female elephant; a fine woman.

पद्य *m*. A S'udra. *n*. A praise, stanza.

पद्या *f*. A way, a path.

पद्व *m*. The human world.

पन् *vt*. 1. U. (*pp*. पनायित or पनित) To praise.

पनस *m*. The bread-fruit

पंथक *a*. Produced in the way.

पन्न *p.p*. Fallen.

पन्नग *m*. A serpent.

पन्नगारि,पन्नगाशन *m*. Garuda.

पपि *m* The moon.

पपी *m*. The sun,the moon.

पपु *a*.Fostering,protecting.

पयश्चय *m*. A lake.

पयस् *n*. Water.

पयस्था *f*. Curds.

पयस्य *a*. Milky; watery.

पयस्वल *a*. Rich in milk.

पयस्विनी *f*. A river;a milch cow; a she-goat; night.

पयोगल *m*. Hail; Island.

पयोघन *n*. Hail.

पयोजन्मन् *m*. A cloud.

पयोद *m*. A cloud.

पयोधर *m*. A cloud; a woman's breast.

पयोधस् *m*. The ocean; a lake.

पयोधि *m*. The ocean.

पयोनिधि *m*. The ocean.

पयोमुच् *m*. A cloud.

पयोवाह *m*. A cloud.

पयोष्णी *f*. Name of a river.

पर *a*. Different, another, distant, highest, next, (with an abl.); exceeding, adverse;last;(at the end of a compound) solely devoted to. *m*. A foe, a stranger.*n*.The supreme spirit.

परकीय *a*.Belonging to another.

परग्रंथि *m*. A finger-joint.

परचक्र *n*. A hostile campaign.

परच्छंद *m*. The will of another.

परंज *n*. An oil mill.

परंजन (-य) *m*. Varuna.

परतंत्र *a*. Dependant, subservient.

परतस् *ind*. After, beyond, differently.

परत्र *ind*. Elsewhere,in another world,further on.

परपुष्ट*m*.The Indian cuckoo.

परपूर्वा *f* A woman who has had a former husband

परप्रेष्य*m*. A servant [spirit.

परब्रह्मन् *n*. The supreme

परभाग *m*. Excellence.

परभृत *m*. A crow.

परभृता *f*. The Indian cuckoo.

परम् *ind*. Beyond; over; otherwise; to the utmost.

परम *a*. Principal; chief; excellency; best; sufficient; pure.

परमगति *f*. Final beatitude.

परमम् *ind*. A particle expressing permission or assent.

परमहंस *m* An ascetic who has subdued all his senses.

परमाणु *m*. An atom.

परमान्न *m*. Rice boiled in milk.

परमार्थ *m*. The highest knowledge (about soul).

परमार्थतः *ind*. Truly; properly.

परमेष्ठ *a*. Supreme.[man(*m*.)

परमेष्ठ (-ष्ठिन्) *m*. Brah-

परंपर *a*. Successive, repeated.

परंपरा *f*.A succession; lineage; a collection.

परंपराक *n*. Killing an animal as a sacrifice.

परंपरीण *a*. Hereditary; traditional.

परवत् *a*. Dependent upon.

परवत्ता *f*.Subjection.[other.

परवश (-श्य) *a*. Subject to an-

परवाच्य *n*.A fault a defect.

परवाणि *m*.A judge; a year.

परवाद *m*. Objection; rumour. [alist.

परवादिन् *m*. A controversi-

परश *m*. The philospher's stone. [axe.

परशु *m*. A battle, a battle-

परशुधर *m*. Paras'urâma; Ganes'a. [axe.

परश्व (स्व) ध *m*. A battle-

परश्वस् *ind*. The day after tomorrow.

परस् *ind*. Beyond, further, on the other side of.

परःकृष्ण *a*. Extremely dark.

परस्तात् *ind*.Beyond, More than.

परस्पर *pron.* (Used in the singular only) One another, each other. *a.* Mutual.

परस्मैपद *n.* **परस्मैभाषा** *f.* One of the two modes or voices in which Sanskrit verbs are conjugated.

परा *ind.* Away, back, aside.

पराक *a.* Small; *m.* A kind of penance.

पराकरण *n.* Rejecting.

पराके *ind.* At a distance.

पराक्रम *m.* Heroism, valour, attempt; Vishnu.

पराक्रांत *a.* Strong; energetic.

पराग *m.* Dust, the pollen of a flower, fragrant powder, fame; sandal; an eclipse; self-will.

परांगव *m.* The ocean.

पराङ्मुख *a.* Averse from, unfavourable, regardless of.

पराच् *a.* Distant.

पराचीन *a.* Averse; disinclined.

पराचीनं *ind.* Beyond; more than.

पराजय *m.* Overpowering, defeat, loss.

पराजिष्णु *a.* Victorious.

परात्पर *m.* The supreme being.

परात्मन् *m.* The supreme spirit.

पराधि *m.* Hunting; extreme mental pain.

पराधीन *a.* Dependent.

परान (ण) सा *f.* Medical treatment.

परांतक *m* Śiva.

परापर *a.* Far and near; best and worst.

पराभव *m* Defeat, overthrow humiliation, contempt.

पराभूत *a.* Defeated.

पराभूति *f.* See **पराभव**.

परामर्श *m.* Seizing, attack; hindrance, consideration.

परामर्शन *n.* Remembrance.

परामृष्ट *a.* Touched; violated; judged; endured.

परायण *a.* Attached to.

परारि *ind.* The year before last.

परार्ध *n.* The highest of all numbers; the latter half.

परावर *a.* Far and near; higher and lower; all including.

परावर्त *m.* (-वृत्ति) *f.* Retreat; exchange.

पराशर *m.* Name of a sage.

परासन *n.* Killing, slaughter.

परासु *a.* Lifeless, dead.

परास्कंदिन् *m.* A thief.

परास्त *a.* Thrown away, rejected.

पराहत *a.* Repulsed; attacked.

पराह्न *m.* The afternoon.

परि (री) *ind.* Round about; in addition to; against; excessively; towards; severally; except. [tion.

परिकथा *f.* A work of fic-

परिकंप *m.* A great terror.

परिकर *m.* Retinue, a crowd, commencement; a girth, name of a figure of speech.

परिकर्तन *n.* Cutting.

परिकर्मन् *m.* A servant. *a.* Personal decoration.

परिकर्ष *m.*, (-ण *n.*) Dragging out; extraction.

परिकल्पना *f.* Invention.

परिकांक्षित *m.* A devotee.

परिकीर्ण *pp.* Scattered about; surrounded.

परिकीर्तन *n.* Proclaiming.

परिकूट *n.* A barrier.

परिकोप *m.* Great anger.

परिक्रम *m.* Roaming about.

परिक्रय *m.*, (-ण *n.*) Engaging for hire; barter.

परिक्रांति *f.* Revolution.

परिक्रिया *f.* Intrenching, attention.

परिक्लांत *a.* Exhausted.

परिक्लेद *m.* Dampness. [ship.

परिक्लेश *m.* Fatigue. Hard-

परिक्षय *m.* Decay, failure.

परिक्षाम *a.* Emaciated.

परिक्षालन *n.* Washing.

परिक्षिप्त *pp.* Scattered, encircled, abandoned.

परिक्षीण *pp* Exhausted.

परिक्षेप *m.* Encircling.

परिखा *f.*,(-त *n.*) A moat.

परिखेद *m.* Fatigue.

परिख्याति *f.* Fame.

परिगणन *n.* (-ना *f.*) Complete enumeration.

परिगत *a.* Surrounded, spread, known.

परिगलित *pp.* Dropped down; melted.

परिगर्हण *n.* Excessive blame.

परिगूढ *pp.* Very mysterious.

परिगृहीत *pp* Grasped, surrounded, accepted. [man.

परिगृह्या *f.* A married wo-

परिग्रह *m.* Taking, property, marriage, a wife, retinue, an eclipse, a claim, origin.

परिग्लान *pp.* Languid.

परिघ *m.* A bar; a pitcher; gate.

परिघट्टन *n.* Stirring up.

परिघात *m.*, (-न *n.*) Killing.

परिघोष *m.* Noise.

परिचय *m.* Accumulation, familiarity, practice.

परिचर, (-ण) *m.* A servant.

परिचरण *n.* Serving.

परिचर्या *f.* Attendance, worship.

परिचार *m.* Attendence.

परिचार (रि) क *m.* A servant.

परिचित *pp.* Accumulated; familiar with, learnt.

परिचिति *f.* Acquaintance.

परिच्छद् *f.* Paraphernalia.

परिच्छद *m.* A covering, a dress; paraphernalia.

परिच्छन्न *pp.* Covered; overlaid.

परिच्छित्ति *f.* Accurate definition; partition.

परिच्छिन्न *pp.* Divided; limited.

परिच्छेद *m.* Limit; section.

परिच्छेद्य *a.* Definable. [ly.

परिजन *m.*Attendants,fami-

परिजन्मन् *m.* The moon.

परिजल्पित *n.* A covert indication of one's own superiority by finding fault with one's master.

परिज्ञप्ति *f.* Conversation,recognition.

परिज्ञान *n.*Thorough knowledge. [bird in circles.

परिडीन *n.* The flight of a

परिणत *pp.*Ripe,full grown.

परिणति *f.*Bowing;maturity, transformation, result, end.

परिणद्ध *pp.* Broad; large.

परिणय *m.*,(-न *n.*) Marriage.

परि (री) णाम *m.*Alteration, digestion, result end.

परिणायक *m.* A leader; a husband. [ence,extent.

परि (री) णाह *m.* Circumfer-

परिणिष्ठा *f.*Perfect skill.

परिणीत *a.* Married.

परिणेतृ *m.* A husband.

परितर्पण *n.* Gratifying.

परि(री)ताप *m.*Extreme heat, pain.

परितुष्ट *a.* Completely satisfied.

परितुष्टि *f.* Contentment.

परितोष *m.* Contentment, approbation, delight.

परित्यक्त *a.* Abandoned;discharged.

परित्याग *m.* Abandonment, liberality, omission.

परित्राण *n.* Deliverance.

परित्रास *m.* Terror, fright, fear. [votion.

परिदान *n.* Exchange, de-

परि (री) दाह *m.* Burning, pain; anguish.

परिदेव *m.* Lamentation.

परिदेवन *n.* (-ना *f.*) Lamentation. [able.

परिद्यून *a* Sorrowful,miser-

परिधर्षण *n* Assault, illtreatment. [garment.

परि (री) धान *n.* Dressing, a

परिधानीय *n.* An undergarment.

परिधि *m.*A wall,a halo;the horizon; circumference.

परिधूसर *a.* Quite grey.

परिधेय *n.* An undergarment.

परिध्वंस *m.*Distress,failure; destruction. [tion.

परिनिर्वाण *n.* Final extinc-

परिनिवृत्ति *f.* Final liberation of the soul.

परिनिष्ठा *f.* Extreme limit; complete skill.

परिपक्व *a.* Quite ripe, fully digested.

परिपण *n.* Capital.

परिपणन *n.* Promise.

परिपणित *pp.* Pledged.

परिपंथ *m.* An enemy. [foe.

परिपंथिन् *a* Opposing. *m.* A

परि (री) पाक *m.* Ripening. perfection, digestion, fruit, skilfulness.

परिपाटल *a.* Pale red.

परिपाटि (-टी) *f.* Method.

परिपाठ *m.* Complete enumeration; detail.

परिपार्श्व *a.* Near.

परिपालन *n.* Protecting.

परिपीडन *n.* Squeezing, hurting. [shipping.

परिपूजन *n.* परिपूजा *f.* Wor-

परिपूत *pp.* Purified.

परिपूरण *n.* Filling.

परिपूर्ण *pp.* Full, complete, content. [ness.

परिपूर्ति *f.* Completion, ful-

परिपेलव *a.* Very delicate.

परिपोषण *f.* Furthering, nourishing.

परिप्रश्न *m.* Inquiry.

परिप्राप्ति *f.* Acquisition.

परिप्रेष्य *m.* A servant.

परिप्लव *a.* Floating; trembling. *m.* Inundation.

परिप्लुत *pp.* Flooded.

परिब (व) र्ह *m.*, (-ण *n.*) Retinue, furniture; property.

परिबाधा *f* Trouble.

परिबृं (वृं) हण *n.* Prosperity, supplement.

परिबृं [वृं] हित *pp.* Increased. *n.* The roar of an elephant.

परिभंग *m.* Shattering.

परिभर्त्सन *n.* Threatening.

परि [री] भ (भा) व *m.* Insult, humiliation, defect.

परिभाविन् *a.* Treating with contempt; surpassing.

परिभाषण *n.* Speaking, admonition; discourse.

परिभाषा *f* Speech; censure; a technical term, any general rule or definition.

परिभुक्त *pp.* Eaten, enjoyed.

परिभुग्न *a.* Bowed, bent

परिभूति *f.* Contempt, humiliation.

परिभोग *m.* Enjoyment illegal use of another's goods.

परिभ्रम *m.* Rambling discourse; error; delusion.

परिभ्रमण *n.* Wandering; revolving.

परिभ्रंश *m.* Escape, falling from. [ed; void of.

परिभ्रष्ट *a.* Fallen off, escap-

परिमंडल *a.* Circular. *n.* A a ball; a circle.

परिमंथर *a.* Extremely slow.
परिमंद *a.* Very dull, very little.
परिमर्द *m.*, (-**न***n.*) Rubbing; destruction.
परिमर्ष *m.* Envy, dislike.
परिमल *m.* Fragrance, copulation. [weight, value
परि (री) माण *n.* Measure,
परिमार्ग*m.*,(-**ण***n.*)Searching.
परिमार्जन *n.* Cleaning.
परिमित *pp.* Moderate. [ty.
परिमिति *f.* Measure, quanti-
परिमिलन *n.* Touch, contact.
परिमुखम्*ind.* About the face.
परिमुग्ध *a.* Lovely, very simple.
परिमृदित *pp.* Trodden.
परिमृष्ट *pp.* Washed, purified.
परिमेय *a.* Measurable.
परिमोक्ष *m* ,[-**ण***n.*] Destroying, deliverance.
परिमोष *m.* Theft. [ber.
परिमोषिन् *m.* A theif, a rob-
परिमोहन *n.* Fascinating.
परिम्लान *pp* Faded
परिरक्षण *n* **परिरक्षा** *f.* Frotec tion, keeping.
परिरथ्या *f.* A street. [brace.
परि [री] रंभ *m.*,[-**ण** *n.*] Em-
परिलघु *a.* Very light. [ed
परिलुप्त *pp.* Lost; interrupt-
परिलेख *m.* An outline, a sketch.
परिलोप*m* Injury; omission.
परिवत्सर *m.* A full year.
परिवर्जन *n* Abandonment.
परि [री] वर्त*m.*, (-**न***n.*) Revolution, repetition, change, exchange; retreat.
परिवर्तन् *a* Revolving.
परिवर्धन *n.* Growing.
परिवसथ *m.* A village.
परिवह *m* Name of the second of the seven courses of wind.
परि [री] वाद *m.* Reproach.
परिवादिन् *m.* An accuser, a plaintiff. [strings.
परिवादिनी *f.* A lute of seven
परि (री) वाप *m.* A reservoir, shaving furniture; retinue.
परिवापित *a.* Shaven.
परि (री) वार *m.* Retinue; a sheath.
परिवारण *n.* A cover; a retinue; warding off.
परिवारित *a.* Encompassed.
परिवास *m.* Residence.
परि (री) वाह *m* Inundation, a drain.
परिविद्ध *m.* Kubera.
परिविहार *m.* Walking for pleasure.
परिवीत *a.* Surrounded.
परिवृत *pp.* Surrounded, concealed; pervaded.
परिवृत्ति *f.* Revolution, termination; exchange, a figure of speech in rhetoric.

परिवृद्धि *f.* Growth, increase.
परिवेदन *n.* Complete knowledge; universal existence.
परिवेदना *f.* Shrewdness; foresight
परि (री) वेश (ष) *m.*,(-ण*n.*) A circle, the circumference, a halo, the disc, serving up meals.
परिवेष्टन *n.* A cover.
परिव्रज्या *f.* Strolling, religious austerity.
परिव्राज् (-ज), (-क) *m.* An ascetic who has renounced the world. [appendix.
परिशिष्ट *n.* A supplement, an
परिशीलन *n.* Intercourse, study.
परिशुद्धि *f.* Complete purification; acquittal.
परिशुष्क *a.* Completely dry.
परिशून्य *a.* Quite empty.
परि (री) शेष *m.* Remainder; supplement; conclusion.
परिशोध *m.*,(-न*n.*) Purifying.
परिशोष *m.* The act of being completely dry.
परिश्रम *m* Fatigue, trouble; labour; study. [lum.
परिश्रय *m.* A meeting, asy-
परिश्रांति *f.* Fatigue, exertion.
परिश्लेष *m.* An embrace.
परिषद् *f.* An assembly.
परिषद (-द्य) *m* A member of an assembly.

परिषेक *m.* (-चन*n.*) Sprinkling over, moistening.
परिष्क(ष्का) र *m.* Decoration.
परिष्क्रिया *f.* Decorating.
परिष्वक्त *a.* Embraced.
परिष्वंग *m.* An embrace.
परिस् *ind.* On all sides, towards.
परिसंख्या *f.* Enumeration, total; exclusion.
परिसंख्यात *a.* Enumereted.
परिसंख्यान *n.* Enumeration.
परिसमापन *n.* Finishing.
परिसमाप्ति *f.* Completing.
परिसमूहन *n.* Heaping up, sprinkling water round the sacrificial fire.
परिसर *m* Verge, neighbourhood, death; a rule.
परिसर्पण *n.* Creeping about, constantly moving.
परिसंवत्सर *m.* Whole year.
परिस्तरण *n.* A covering.
परिस्फुट *a.* Quite manifest.
परिस्यंद *m.* Oozing, stream, retinue, decoration of the hair with flowers. [rent.
परिस्रव *m.* A river, a tor-
परिस्राव *m.* Effluxion.
परिहत *a.* Loosened. [seizing.
परिहरण *n.* Abandoning,
परिहाणि (-नि) *f.* Loss decline.
परि (री) हार *m.* Abandonment, confutation omission, disrespect, a grant

परिहार्य *a.* To be avoided.
परि (री) हास *m.* Joking, mirth, merriment.
परिहृत *a.* Avoided, repelled, seized. [judge.
परीक्षक *m.* An examiner,
परीक्षण *n.* Examining.
परीक्षा *f.* Examination, test.
परीत *a.* Surrounded, expired, seized. [ing, haste.
परीप्सा *f.* Desire, of obtain-
परीष्टि *f.* Research, worship.
परुत *ind.* Last year.
परुष *a.* Hard, harsh, sharp.
परुस् *n.* A joint.
परेत *pp.* Dead. *m.* A ghost.
परेतराज् *m.* God of death.
परेद्यवि, परेद्युस् *ind.* The other day.
परेश *m.* Brahman (*m.*)
परोक्ष *a.* Invisible, absent. *m.* An ascetic. *n.* Absence. [one's back.
परोक्षम् , परोक्षे *ind.* Behind
परोक्षमन्मथ *a.* Inexperienced in love-matters.
परोपकार *m.* Charity.
परोपजाप *m.* Causing dissension among enemies.
परोष्णि(-ष्णी) *f.* A cock-roach.
पर्जन्य *m.* Rain; a cloud.
पर्ण् *vt.* 10. U. To make green.
पर्ण *n.* A wing; the feather of an arrow; a leaf.
पर्णकुटिका, पर्णकुटी *f.* A hut made of leaves. [ance.
पर्णकृच्छ्र *m.* A kind of pen-
पर्णखंड *m.* A tree without apparent blossoms. *n.* A collection of leaves.
पर्णमुच् *m.* The winter.
पर्णरुह् *m* The spring(वसंत).
पर्णल *a.* Full of leaves.
पर्णवाटिका *f.* Spices of the areca-nut and other spices rolled up in betal leaves.
पर्णशाला *f.* See पर्णकुटिका.
पर्णसि *m.* A lotus.
पर्णिन् *m.* A tree.
पर्णिल *a* See पर्णल.
पर्द् *vi.* 1. A. To break wind.
पर्यक् *ind.* Round about.
पर्य (ल्यं) क *m.* A bed, a sofa.
पर्यटन *n.* Wandering about, peregrination.
पर्यंत *a.* Bounded, adjoining. *m.* Circumferece; extremity, end, flank.
पर्यंतिका *f.* Depravity.
पर्यय *m.* Revolution, lapse, confusion, neglect of duty. [clean.
पर्यवदात *a.* Quite pure or
पर्यवरोध *m.* Obstruction.
पर्यवसान *n.* End.
पर्यवसित *pp.* Finished, lost.
पर्यवस्था *f.*,(-न *n.*)Opposition.
पर्यश्रु *a.* Shedding tears.
पर्यस्त *a.* Surrouuded, upset; laid aside.

पर्याकुल *a.* Turbid; confused.
पर्याण *n.* A saddle.
पर्याप्त *a.* Obtained, completed; whole; adequate.
पर्याप्तम् *ind* Readily; satisfactorily, fully.
पर्याप्ति *f.* Acquisition; end, sufficiency; satisfaction.
पर्याय *m.* Course, lapse, succession, method, manner, a synonym, opportunity, preparation; a figure of speech in rhetoric. [random.
पर्यायेण *ind.* In turn; at
पर्याली *ind.* A particle expressing harm or injury.
पर्यालोचन *n* (-ना *f.*) Circumspection, deliberation.
पर्यावर्त *m.*, (-न *n.*) Return.
पर्याविल *a.* Very turbid.
पर्यास *m* End, revolution.
पर्युक्षण *n.* Sprinkling round without uttering any *mantras.* [ous, anxious.
पर्युत्सुक *a.* Sorrowful, desir-
पर्युदस्त *a.* Excluded, prohibited.
पर्युदास *m.* An exception, a prohibitive rule.
पर्युपस्थान *n.* Serving. [esy.
पर्युपासन *n* Worship, court
पर्युप्ति *f.* Sowing. [tion.
पर्युषण *n.* Worship, adora-
पर्युषित *a.* Stale, stupid.
पर्येषण *n* (-णा *f.*) Investigation, worship.
पर्येष्टि *f.* Search, inquiry.
पर्वक *n.* The knee-joint.
पर्वणी *f.* The full-moon-day, a festival. [rock.
पर्वत *m.* A mountain, a
पर्वतजा *f.* A river.
पर्वताशय *m.* A cloud. [fy.
पर्वतीकृ *v.* 8. U. To magni-
पर्वतीय *a.* Hilly.
पर्वधि *m.* The moon.
पर्वन् *n.* Joint, a limb, a portion, a chapter, a festival, an opportunity, the day of the new moon.
पर्शु *m.* A weapon; an axe.
पर्शुका *f.* A rib.
पर्षद् *f.* An assembly.
पल् 1 P. To move.
पल *m.* Straw. *n.* Flesh, weight equal to four *karshas*; a moment.
पलंकट *a.* Bashful, timid.
पलंकष *m.* A goblin.
पलल *m.* A demon. *n.* Flesh.
पलाग्नि *m* Bile.
पलांग *m.* A tortoise.
पलांडु *m.* *n.* An onion.
पलाद, पलाशन *m.* A demon.
पलायन *n.* Flight, escape.
पलायित *pp.* Fled.
पलाल *m.* *n.* Straw, husk.

पलाश *m.* Name of a tree.
पलित *a.* Grey old.
पल्ययन *n.* A saddle; a rein.
पल्ल *m.* A large granary.
पल्लव *m. n.* A sprout, a bud, expansion; a bracelet, love.
पल्लव (वि) क *m.* A libertine.
पल्लि (-ल्ली) *f.* A hut, a small village. [house-lizard.
पल्लिका *f.* A small village; a
पल्वल *n.* A small pool.
पव *m.* Wind; purification.
पवन *m.* Air, wind. *n* A sieve; water.
पवनात्मज *m.* Fire. Hanuman or Bhîma.
पवनाश *m.* A serpent.
पवमान *m.* Air, wind.
पवाका *f.* A whirlwind.
पवि *m.* The thunderbolt of Indra.
पवित *a.* Purified.
पवित्र *a.* Holy; pure; a ring of *kusa* grass. *n.* The sacred thread.
पवित्रक *n.* Thread of which nets are made.
पशव्य *a.* Fit for cattle.
पशु *m.* Cattle, a beast.
पशुक्रिया, पशुचर्या *f.* Copulation.
पशुनाथ *m.* An epithet of S'iva. [S'iva.
पशुपति *m.* A herdsman.;
पशुमारम् *ind.* According to the manner of slaughtering cattle.
पश्चात् *ind.* From behind, after, subsequently, at last, westward.
पश्चार्ध *m.* The latter half.
पश्चात्कृत *a.* Put into the shade. [remorse.
पश्चात्ताप *m.* Repentance,
पश्चिम *a.* Western, hindmost.
पश्चिमा *f.* The west.
पश्चिमेन *ind.* Behind, after.
पश्यतोहर *m.* A robber.
पश्यंती *f.* A harlot, a particular sound.
पा *vt.* 1. P. (*pp.* पीत) To drink, to feast on. With अनु-to drink after, आ-to drink up; नि-to drink; *vt.* 2. P. To protect, to rule. *Caus.* (पालयति-ते) to protect, to govern, to await; with परि-to preserve to nourish; to rule, to wait for; with प्रति-to protect, to obey, to await.
पा *a.* (at the end of a compound) Drinking, keeping. [contemptible.
पांस (श) न *a.* Disgracing,
पांस (श) व *a.* Consisting of dust.
पांसु (-शु) *m.* Dust, dung.
पांसुकुली *f.* A high road.

पांसुकूल *n.* A dust-heap.
पांसुचामर *m.* A tent; praise.
पांसु (शु) र *m.* A gadfly.
पांसु (शु) ल *a.* Covered with dust; sullied. *m.* A libertine.
पांसु (शु) ला *f.* A licentious woman; the earth.
पाक *a.* Small; mature; honest; ignorant. *m.* Cooking, digestion; result; maturity; perfect development; a domestic fire; corn, fruit, greyness of hair. [Indra.
पाकशासन *m.* An epithet of
पाकल *m.* Fire; wind.
पाकातीसार *m.* Chronic dysentery.
पाकिम *a.* Cooked; ripened.
पाकु, (-क) *m.* A Cook.
पाक्ष *a.* Belonging to a lunar fortnight; relating to a party.
पाक्षिक *a.* Fortnightly; favouring a party; optional.
पाखंड *m.* A heretic.
पागल *a.* Mad.
पांक्तेय *a.* Fit to sit in the same row at a dinner.
पाचक *m.* A Cook. Fire. *n.* Bile.
पाचन *n.* Cooking; penance.
पांचजन्य *m.* Name of the conch of Krishna.
पांचदश *a.* Relating to the fifteenth day of a month. [the five elements.
पांचभौतिक *a.* Composed of
पांचवार्षिक *a.* Five years old.
पांचालिका *f.* A doll.
पांचाली *f.* Draupadî, the wife of the Pândavas; a puppet; a particular style of composition.
पाटक *m.* A splitter. [ber.
पाटच्चर *m.* A thief, a rob-
पाटन *n.* Splitting, breaking. [trumpet flower.
पाटल *a.* Pale-red. *m.* The
पाटला *f.* See पाटल; Durgá.
पाटालिक *m.* A pupil.
पाटव *n.* Sharpness.
पाटविक *a.* Clever, cunning.
पाटित *pp.* Torn, pierced.
पाटी *f.* Arithmetic.
पाटीर *m.* Sandal, a field.
पाठ *m.* Recitation, study; the text of a book.
पाठक *m.* A teacher.
पाठच्छेद *m.* A pause
पाठन *n.* Teaching. [lege.
पाठशाला *f.* A school, a col-
पाठित *a.* Taught.
पाठीन *m.* A public reader of mythological books.
पाण *m.* Trade, a trader; a contract; praise; the hand.
पाण्णि *m.* The hand.

पाणिगृहीतृ (-ग्राह) *m.* A bridegroom.

पाणिग्रह *m.*, (-ण *n.*) Marriage.

पाणिघ *m.* A drummer; a handicraftsman.

पाणिज *m.* A finger-nail

पाणिनि *m.* Great grammarian.

पाणिनीय *a.* Relating to Pánini.

पाणिंधम (-य) *a.* Blowing through the hands.

पाणिपीडन *n.* (-बंध *m.*) Marriage.

पाणिरुह् (-ह) *m.* A finger-nail.

पाणीकरण *n.* Marriage.

पांडर *a.* Whitish.

पांडव *m.* A descendant of Pându.

पांडवेय *m.* See पांडव.

पांडित्य *n.* Scholarship.

पांडु *a.* White, pale *m.* Name of the father of the Pándavas.

पांडुर *a* Whitish pale.

पांडुराग *m.* Whiteness, pallor.

पांडुरिमन् *m.* Paleness.

पांडुरोग *m.* Jaundice.

पांडुलेख *m* A draft.

पात *a.* Protected; *n.* flight; fall; occurrence; an attack.

पातक *m.* *n.* Sin.

पातंगि *m.* Saturn; Yama; Karna, Sugrîva.

पातंजल *a.* Composed by Patanjali.

पातन *n.* Causing to fall, humbling.

पाताल *n.* The lower world, a hole.

पातित *a.* Cast down, overthrown.

पातित्य *n.* Loss of caste or position.

पातिन् *a.* Falling, discharging.

पात्र *n.* A cup, a vessel, bed or current of a river; a receptacle; a worthy person; dramatis personœ.

पात्रिक *a.* Fit, adequate *n.* A vessel.

पात्रिय } पाड्य } *a.* Worthy to partake of a meal.

पात्रेबहुल, पात्रेसमित *a.* Parasitical.

पाथ *m.* Fire; the sun. *n.* Water.

पाथस् *n.* Water; food; air.

पाथेय *n.* Provisions for a journey; the sign *Virgo* of the zodiac.(कन्याराशि).

पाथोज *n.* A lotus.

पाद् *f.* A shoe.

पाद *m.* The foot, a ray of light.

पादक्षेप *m.* Foot-step.

पादग्रंथि *m.* The ankle.

पादचतुर *m.* A slanderer.

पादचार *m.* Going on foot.

पादचारिन् *m.* A pedestrian.
पादज *m.* A S'udra.
पादत्र *m.* (-त्रा *f.* -त्राण *n.*) A shoe.
पादप *m.* A plant, a tree.
पादपालिका *f.* An anklet.
पादपूरण *n.* An expletive.
पादप्रहार *m* A kick.
पादबंधन *n.* A fetter.
पादमुद्रा *f.* A foot-print.
पादमूल *n.* The sole.
पादरथी *f.* A shoe.
पादशाखा *f.* A toe.
पादसेवन *n.*(-सेवा *f.*)Service.
पादविक *m.* A traveller.
पादात(-त)*m.* A foot-soldier.
पादाति *m.* A foot-soldier.
पादांतरे *ind.* Close to.
पादालिंदि *f.* A boat.
पादिक *a.*(*f.*-की) Amounting to a quarter or fourth.
पादिन *m.* A fourth part.
पादुक *a.* (-का or की) Going on foot.
पादुका *f.* A wooden shoe.
पादोदक *n.* Water hallowed by washing sacred feet.
पाद्य *n.* Water for washing the feet.[sharpening.
पान *n.* Drinking; a drink;
पानक *n.* A drink, a beverage.
पानागार *m.* *n.* A tavern.
पानगोष्ठिका (-गोष्ठी) *f.* A drinking party.
पानविभ्रम *m.* Intoxication.
पानिक *m.* A vendor of spirituous liquors.
पानीय *n.* Water; a drink.
पांथ *m.* A traveller.
पाप *a* Vicious, sinful, low, inauspicious. *n* Sin; vice; evil. *m.* A wretch.
पापग्रह *m.* A planet of malignant aspect.
पापभाज् *a.* Sinful.
पापयोनि *f.* Birth in an inferior condition.
पापात्मन् *a.* Wicked.
पापिन् *a.* Sinful, wicked.
पापिष्ठ *a.* Extremely wicked.
पापीयस् *a.* More wicked.
पाप्मन् *m.* Crime, wickedness. Sin. [low, stupid.
पामर *a.* Poor, wicked,
पायस *a.* Made of water or milk. *m.* *n.* Rice boiled in milk.
पायिक *m.* A foot soldier.
पार *m.* *n.* The opposite bank of a river; extremity, the opposite side, the end of limit; quicksilver. *n.* The fullest extent, totality.
पारक्य *a.* Alien, hostile.
पारग *n.* Profoundly learned.
पारग्रामिक *a.* Alien, hostile.
पारज *m.* Gold.
पारजायिक *m.* An adulterer.

पारटीन *m*. A stone, a rock.
पारण *a*. Carrying across; saving *m*. A cloud; satisfaction. *n*. Accomplishing; reading through; eating after a fast.
पारणा *f*. Eating after a fast.
पारत *m*. Quick-silver.
पारतंत्र्य *n*. Dependence.
पारत्रिक *a*. Belonging to the next world.
पारत्र्य *n*. Reward in a future state.
पारद *m*. Quick-silver.
पारदर्शक *a*. Transparent.
पारदारिक *m*. An adulterer.
पारदार्य *n*. Adultery.
पारदृश्वन् *a*. Wise; knowing thoroughly.
पारदेशिक *m*. A foreigner.
पारदेश्य *m*. A foreigner.
पारभृत *n*. A present.
पारमार्थिक *a*. Relating to spiritual knowledge; real.
पारमिक *a*. Supreme.
पारमित *a*. Transcendant.
पारमेष्ठ्य *n*. Supremacy, royal insignia.
पारंपरीण *a*. Hereditary.
पारंपरीय *a*. Traditional.
पारंपर्य *n* Hereditary succession; tradition; intermediation.
पारयिष्णु *a*. Able to accomplish anything
पारलौकिक *a*. Relating to the next world
पारवत *m* A pigeon.
पारवश्य *n*. Dependence.
पारशव *m* Iron; a bastard.
पारस *a*. Persian.
पारसिक *m*. Persia.
पारसी *f*. The Persian language.
पारस्त्रैणेय *m*. An adulterine, a bastard.
पारापत *m*. A pigeon.
पारापा (वा) र *n*. Both banks of a river. *m*. A sea.
पारायण *n*. Perusal.
पारायणिक *m*. A lecturer; a reader of sacred books.
पारावत *m*. A pigeon, a monkey; a mountain.
पारावारीण *a*. One who goes to both sides.
पाराशर (-र्य) *m*. Vyása, son of Parásara.
पारिखेय *a*. Surrounded by a ditch.
पारिजात, (-क) *m*. The coral tree.
पारितोषिक *n*. A reward.
पारिध्वजिक *m*. A standard-bearer.
पारिंद्र *m*. A lion.
पारिपंथिक *m*. A robber.
पारिपाट्य *n*. Mode, method.
पारिपार्श्व *n*. Retinue.
पारिपार्श्वक *m*. A servant.
पारिपार्श्विका *f*. A chamber-maid.

पारिप्लव a. Unsteady. m. A boat.

पारिबर्ह m. A wedding present.

पारिभाव्य n. Bail, security.

पारिभाषिक a. Technical.

पारिमांडल्य n. An atom.

पारिमुख n. Presence.

पारिमुखिक a. Present.

पारिव्राजक } n. Asceticism.
पारिव्राज्य

पारिशील n. The remainder.

पारिषद m. A person present at an assembly; a king's companion.

पारिहार्य m. A bracelet.

पारिहास्य n. Jest, joke, fun.

पारीण a. Being on the opposite side; completely versed in.

पारीणह्य n. Household furniture.

पारुष्य n. Harshness, roughness, abuse, violence.

पार्ण a. Relating to leaves.

पार्थ m. Yudhishtira, Bhîma and Arjuna (but especially Arjuna).

पार्थक्य n. Separateness.

पार्थव n. Greatness.

पार्थसारथि m Krishna.

पार्थिव a. Earthen, princely, terrestrial. m. A king.

पार्थिवी f. Sîtá, wife of Râma.

पार्यंतिक a. Final, conclusive.

पार्वण n. Presenting oblations to all the Manes at a *parvan*.

पार्वत a. Relating to a mountain.

पार्वती f. Durgá, daughter of the Himālaya.

पार्वतीय m. A mountaineer.

पार्श्व m. n. The side.

पार्श्वक m. A swindler.

पार्श्वग m. An attendant.

पार्श्वचर m. An attendant.

पार्श्वतस् ind. By the side.

पार्श्वद m. An attendant.

पार्श्वम् ind. Near to, towards.

पार्श्ववर्तिन् a. Attending.

पार्श्वस्थ m. A companion.

पार्श्विक m. A partisan, a juggler.

पार्श्वे inn. Near, at the side.

पार्षती f. Draupadî; Durgâ.

पार्षद् f. An assembly.

पार्षद m. A companion.

पार्षद्य m. A member of an assembly.

पार्ष्णि m, f. The heel, the back, a kick. f. Kuntî, wife of Pându.

पार्ष्णिग्रह m. A follower.

पार्ष्णिग्राह m. An enemy in the rear; an ally.

पाल m. A protector.

पालक m. A guardian, a sovereign; a groom.

पालन n. Guarding, fostering.

पालयितृ m. A protector.

पालाश a. Belonging to the *Palâs'a* tree; green.

पालि (-ली) *f*. The tip of the ear; a margin; a row, a mark; a louse. Name of a language. [sharp edge.
पालिका *f*. The tip of the ear;
पावक *m*. Fire.
पावकि *m*. Kártikeya.
पावन *a*. Purifying, holy. *m*. Fire. *n*. Penance.
पाश *m*. A snare, a dice.
पाशक्रीडा *f*. Gambling.
पाशधर (-भृत्, -पाणि) *m*. Varuna.
पाशबंध *n*. A noose, a halter.
पाशक *m*. A die, dice.
पाशव *n*. A flock, a herd.
पाशुपतास्त्र *n*. Name of a missile.
पाश्चात्य *a*. Hinder; western.
पाषंड *m*. see पाखंड.
पाषंडक } पाषंडिन् } *m*. A heretic.
पाषाण *m*. A stone.
पि *vt*. 6 P. To go.
पिक *m*. The Indian cuckoo.
पिकबांधव *m*. The spring.
पिकबंधु (-राग, -वल्लभ) *m*. The mango tree.
पिकानंद *m*. The Spring.
पिंग *a* Reddish brown.
पिंगल *a*. Reddish brown *m*. Fire; a monkey; an ichneumon; name of a sage.
पिंगलाक्ष *m*. Śiva.
पिंगला *f*. A kind of an owl; name of a courtezan.
पिंगा *f*. Turmeric, saffron.
पिचंडक *m*. A glutton.
पिचिंडिल *a*. Corpulent.
पिचु *m* Cotton.
पिचुल *m*. Cotton; water-crow.
पिच्छ *m*. A tail.
पिच्छल *a*. Slimy, slippery.
पिच्छा *f*. A multitude, a row.
पिच्छिल *a*. Slippery.
पिंज *m*. The moon.
पिंजर *a*. Gold-coloured. *n*. Gold; a cage; a skeleton.
पिंजरक *n*. Orpiment.
पिंजल *a*. Panic-stricken.
पिंजाल *n*. Gold.
पिंजूष *m*. The box of the ear.
पिटक *m*. *n*. A box.
पिठर, (-क) *m*. *n*. A pot.
पिंड *a*. Solid. *m*. *n*. A ball, especially one offered to the Manes; livelihood, flesh; the body.
पिंडक *m*. *n*. A lump.
पिंडपात *m*. Collecting or giving alms.
पिंडपातिक *m*. One who lives on alms.
पिंडभूति *f* Livelihood.
पिंडलोप *m*. Interruption in offering the funeral cakes.
पिंडसंबंध *m*. Relationship.

पिंडल *m.* A bridge.
पिंडस *m.* A beggar.
पिंडात *m.* Incense.
पिंडाभ्र *n.* Hail.
पिंडायस *n.* Steel.
पिंडार *m.* A religious mendicant; cowherd.
पिंडाशन, पिंडाश, पिंडाशक, पिंडाशिन् *m.* A beggar.
पिंडि (-डी) *f.* The nave of a wheel; the calf of the leg.
पिंडिन् *m* A beggar.
पिंडीर *a.* Sapless, dry. *m.* The pomegranate tree.
पिंडीशूर *m.* A braggart.
पिंडोदकाक्रिया *f.* An oblation of cakes and water to the deceased.
पितामह *m.* A paternal grandfather; Brahman(*m.*)
पितृ *m.* A father. *m. du.* Parents. *m. pl.* Forefathers.
पितृकानन *n.* A cemetery.
पितृतर्पण *n* An oblation to the Manes
पितृतिथि *f.* (-दिन *n.*) The day of the new moon.
पितृदाय *m.* (-द्रव्य *n.*) Patrimony.
पितृपक्ष *m* The paternal side; the second half of the month of *Bhâdrapada.*
पितुःपुत्र *m.* The son of an illustrious father.
पितृसंनिभ *a.* Fatherly.
पितृस्थान (-स्थानीय) *n.* A guardian.
पितृहत्या *f.* Parricide.
पितृहन् *m.* A parricide.
पितृक *a.* Paternal, ancestral.
पितृव्य *m.* A paternal uncle.
पित्त *n.* Bile.
पित्तल *a.* Billious. *n.* Brass.
पित्र्य *a.* Ancestral *m.* The elder brother.
पित्र्या *f.* The day of the new moon.
पिधान *n.* Covering.
पिधानक *n.* A sheath.
पिधायक *a.* Concealing.
पिनद्ध *a.* Fastened, penetrated.
पिनाक *m. n.* The bow of Śiva; a trident.
पिनाकिन् *m.* Śiva.
पिपासा *f.* Thirst.
पिपासित (-तु) *a.* Thirsty.
पिपासु *a.* Thirsty.
पिपील *m.* (-ला *f.*) An ant.
पिपीलक *m.* A large black ant.
पिपीलिका *f.* A female ant.
पिप्पल *m.* The holy fig tree.
पिप्पलि(-ली) *f.* Long pepper.
पिप्लु *m.* A mark, a mole
पिल् *v.t.* 10. U. To throw.
पिशंग *a.* Reddish
पिशाच *m.* A fiend.
पिशाचभाषा *f.* One of the lowest *prâkrit* dialects.

पिशाचिका *f.* A female imp; excessive attachment.

पिशाची *f.* see **पिशाचिका.**

पिशित *n.* Flesh.

पिशित (-आशन, -आश, -आशिन्-भुज्)*m.* A demon.

पिशुन *a.* Slanderous; cruel, stupid. *m.* A traitor, a slanderer.

पिष् *vt.* 7. P. To grind, to injure; with. **निस्** -to bruise

पिष्टपेष *m.*, (–ण *n.*) Vain repetition.

पिस् *vi.* I. P. To go; 10 U. To be strong; to dwell.

पिहित *a.* Shut, covered.

पी *vt.* 4. A. To drink.

पीठ *n.* A seat, a pedestal.

पीठिका *f.* A bench; a festival; a section of a book.

पीड् *vt.* 10. U. To squeeze, to harass, to oppose. With **उद्**–to press out of, **उप**–to harass, **नि**–to squeeze, to harass. **निस्**–to press out, **परि, प्र** or **सम्** to press.

पीडक *m.* An oppressor.

पीडन *n.* Pressing; espousing;oppressing;an eclipse.

पीडा *f.* Pain, damage, violation; pity.

पीडित *a.*Harassed, eclipsed.

पीत *a.* Drunk, yellow. *n.* Gold.

पीतल *a* Yellow. *n.* Brass.

पीति *m.* A horse. *f.* Drinking.

पीतु, (-थ) *m.* The sun. Fire

पीथि *m.* A horse.

पीन *a.* Fleshy; round, plump.

पीनस् *m.* Cough.

पीनोध्नी *f.* A cow with swelled udders.

पीयूष *m.* *n.* Nectar.

पीलु *m.* An atom; an elephant; a flower.

पीवन् *a.* (*f.* **पीवरि**) Fat, strong. *m.* Wind.

पीवर *a.* Fat, stout.

पीवरी *f.* A young woman; a cow.

पीवा *f.* Water.

पुंस् *m.* A man, a male.

पुंसवन *n.* A religious ceremony held on a woman's perceiving the first signs of a living conception.

पुंसानुज *a.* having an elder brother.

पुंस्त्व *n.* Virility, the masculine gender (in gram.)

पुंख *m. n.* The feathered part of an arrow, a heron.

पुंग *m. n.* A heap.

पुंगव *m.* A bull; the best.

पुच्छ *m n.* A tail; the end.

पुच्छकंटक *m.* A scorpion.

पुच्छटि (-टी) *f.* Cracking the fingers.

पुच्छिन् *m*. A cock.

पुंज *m*. A heap, a collection.

पुंजि *f*. A heap, a quantity.

पुंजित *a*. Heaped together.

पुट् *vt*. 6 U. To embrace, to bind togetter, to shine; to speak.

पुट *m*. *n*. A pocket; a cup made of a leaf, cavity, a cover. *m*. A casket.

पुटकिनी *f*. A lotus.

पुटग्रीव *m*. A jar.

पुटपाक *m*. A method of preparing drugs.

पुटित *a*. Rubbed, ground.

पुंड *m*. A mark, a sign.

पुंडरीक *m*. A white lotus flower; *m.n.N.*of an elephant; southeast quarter.

पुंडरीकाक्ष *m*. Vishnu.

पुंड्र, (-क) *m*. A white lotus; a mark on the forehead.

पुण्य *a*. Holy, meritorious, favourable, beautiful, solemn. *n*. Merit, virtue,

पुण्यकीर्ति *a*. Famous, celebrated.

पुण्यकृत् *a*. Meritorious.

पुण्यक्षेत्र *n*. The holy land of A'ryâvarta.

पुण्यजन *m*. A demon, a *yaksha*.

पुण्यजनेश्वर *m*. Kubera.

पुण्यभाज् *a*. Blessed, meritorious.

पुण्यभूमि *f*. The holy land A'ryávarta.

पुण्यलोक *m*. Heaven, paradise.

पुण्यशील *a*. Pious, righteous.

पुण्यश्लोक *a*. Of good fame.

पुण्याहवाचन *n*. Repeating 'this is an auspicious day' three times at the commencement of most religious rites.

पुत्तल *m*. (-ली *f*.) An idol.

पुत्तलक *m*. -लिका *f*.) see पुत्तल.

पुत्र *m*. A son; a dear child; anything little of its kind.

पुत्रक *m* A little son, a term of endearment, a doll; a rogue.

पुत्रका, पुत्रिका, पुत्री } *f*. A daughter; a puppet, anything little of its kind.

पुत्रकाम *a*. Desirous of sons.

पुत्रकृतक *m*. Adopted as a son.

पुत्रपौत्रीण *a*. Transmitted from son to son, hereditary.

पुत्रवत् (-वल) *a*. Having a son or sons.

पुत्रि (त्री) य or पुत्र्य *a*. Filial.

पुत्रेष्टि, (-का) *f*. A sacrifice

performed for obtaining a son.

पुङ्गल *a.* Beautiful.

पुनर् *ind.* Again, back, but, on the other hand; besides.

पुनरपि *ind.* Even, again, on the other hand.

पुनरावृत्ति *f.* Repetition; return.

पुनरुक्ति *f.* Repetition; tautology.

पुनरुत्थान *n.* Resurrection.

पुनरुपगम *m.* Return.

पुनःपुनः *ind.* Repeatedly.

पुनर्जन्मन् *n.* Metempsychosis.

पुनर्णव (-नव) *m.* A finger-nail.

पुनर्भव *m.* Transmigration.

पुनर्भाव *m.* New birth.

पुनर्भू *f.* A virgin widow remarried.

पुनर्वसु *m.* (usually du.) The 7th lunar mansion consisting of four stars.

पुनर्विवाह *m.* Second marriage.

पुंनाग *m.* White nutmeg; a distinguished man.

पुप्फुस *m.* The lungs.

पुमपत्य *n.* A male off-spring.

पुमर्थ *m.* An object of human life.

पुंयोग *m.* Cohabitation with men.

पुंश्चली *f.* A harlot.

पुर् *f.* A town, a fortress, a rampart.

पुर *n.* A town, a fortress. the body, brothel.

पुरग *a.* Favourably inclined.

पुरजित् (-द्विष, -भिद्) *m.* S'iva.

पुरतस् *ind.* Before, in front, afterwards.

पुरंदर *m.* Indra; S'iva; Agni; thief.

पुरंध्रि (-ध्री) *f.* An elderly married woman.

पुरश्चरण *n.* Repetition of the name of a deity accompanied by burnt offerings.

पुरस् *ind.* Before, in front, in the presence of, in the east.

पुरस्करण *n* Deference, preference.

पुरस्कृत *a.* Placed in front, adopted, honoured.

पुरस्क्रिया *f.* A preparatory rite showing respect.

पुरस्तात् *ind.* In front, of, before, previously, in the east

पुरःसर *a.* Moving in front. *m.* A servant; a leader.

पुरा *ind.* Formerly; hitherto; at first.

पुराकथा *f.* An old legend.

पुराकल्प *m.* A former creation

पुराण *a.* Ancient, old. *n.* Any legendary tale; the whole body of Hindu mythology.

पुराणपुरुष *m.* Vishnu.

पुरातन *a.* Old, worn out.

पुराविद् *n.* Acquainted with the past. [dary event.

पुरावृत्त *n.* History; a legen-

पुरि *f.* A city; a river.

पुरी *f.* A city, a stronghold, the body.

पुरीष *n.* Feces, ordure.

पुरीषण *m.* Feces, ordure. *n.* Evacuation by stool.

पुरु *a.* Much, abundant. *m.* The pollen of a flower. A son of Yayáti.

पुरुष *m.* Mankind; a man, an official, a measure of length; the soul; the supreme being; the pupil of the eye; a person (in gram.)

पुरुषक *n.* Standing on two feet like a man.

पुरुषकार *m.* Manly act, human exertion, virility.

पुरुषता *f.* (-त्व *n.*) Virility, manliness.

पुरुषव्याघ्र (-शार्दूल, -सिंह) *m.* A distinguished or eminent man.

पुरुषसूक्त *n.* The 90th hymn of the tenth Mandala of the Rigveda.

पुरुषायित *n.* Manly conduct.

पुरुषार्थ *m.* Any one of the four principal objects of human existence.

पुरुषोत्तम *m.* Vishnu.

पुरोग, पुरोगम, पुरोगामिन् *a.* Leading; chief.

पुरोट्टि *m.* The current of a river.

पुरोडाश् (-श) *m.* An oblation; a sacrificial cake of ground rice.

पुरोधस् *m.* A family priest.

पुरोधान *n.* Priestly ministration.

पुरोधिका *f.* A favourite wife.

पुरोभाग *m.* The front part. *a.* Fault-finding.

पुरोभागिन् *a.* Officious.

पुरोहित *a. m.* A family priest. [dwell.

पुर्व् *vt.* 1. P, To fill; to

पुलक *m.* Horripilation.

पुलकित (-न) *a.* Having the hairs of the body erect.

पुलस्ति (-स्त्य) *m.* Name of a sage.

पुलह *m.* Name of a sage.

पुलाक *m. n.* A lump of boiled rice; abridgment.

पुलिन *m. n.* A sand-bank, a small island.

पुलिंद, (-क) *m.* A savage.

पुलिरिक *m.* A snake.

पुलोमजा *f.* Sáchî, wife of Indra.

पुलोमन् *m.* Name of a demon.

पुल्लिंग *a.* Masculine. *n.* Manhood.

पुष् *vt. vi.* 4 P, 9 P. To nourish; to bring up; to support; to enjoy. *vt.* 10 U. To maintain.

पुष्कर *n.* A blue lotus; water; name of a place of pilgrimage. *m.* A lake; the sun; a cloud of a particular class.

पुष्करिणी *f.* A female elephant; the lotus plant; a lake. [did.

पुष्कल *a.* Much; full; splen-

पुष्कलक *m.* The musk-deer.

पुष्ट *pp.* Nourished; perfect.

पुष्टि *f.* Nourishment, growth; fatness. [blow.

पुष्प् *vt* 4 P. To open, to

पुष्प *n.* A flower; the menstrual flow. [of Kubera.

पुष्पक *m.* A flower; the car

पुष्पकेतु (-चाप,-धनुस्,-धन्वन्, -ध्वज,-बाण) *m.* The God of love.

पुष्पंधय *m.* A bee.

पुष्पमास *m.* The spring.

पुष्परजस् *n.* The pollen.

पुष्पराग (-राज) *m.* A topaz.

पुष्परेणु *m.* The pollen.

पुष्पलिक्ष (-लिह्) *m.* A bee.

पुष्पवती *f.* A woman in her courses. [flower-garden.

पुष्पवाटिका (-वाटी) *f.* A

पुष्पशर (-शरासन,-सायक) *m.* The god of love

22

पुष्पसार(-स्वेद) *m.* The honey.

पुष्पागम *m.* The spring.

पुष्पायुध *m.* The god of love.

पुष्पासव *m.* Honey.

पुष्पिका *f.* The concluding words of a chapter.

पुष्पिणी *f.* See पुष्पवती.

पुष्पित *a.* Flowery.

पुष्पिता *f.* See पुष्पवती.

पुष्य *m.* The *Kali* age; the month *Pausha*; the eighth constellation.

पुस्तक *m. n.* A book; a manuscript.

पू *vt.* 1. A. 4 A. 9 U. To purify; to clean.

पूग *m.* A heap, nature. *n.* An areca nut.

पूज् *vt.* 10 U. To adore.

पूजक *a.* Worshipping.

पूजन *n.* Worshipping.

पूजा *f.* Worship, honour.

पूजित *a.* Venerable.

पूज्य *a.* Venerable.

पूण् *vt.* 10 U. To accumulate.

पूत *a.* Cleaned. *n.* Truth.

पूतना *f.* N. of a female demon. [tion.

पूति *a.* Putrid. *f.* Purifica-

पूतिक *a.* Stinking; foul.

पून *pp.* Destroyed.

पूय *m.n.* Pus. [to satisfy.

पूर् *vt.* 4 A. 10 U. To fill;

पूर *m.* Supply; a flood.

पूरक *a.* Filling up. *m.* The multiplier.

पूरण *a.* Completing. *m.* A bridge. *n.* Multiplication.

पूरुष *m.* See **पुरुष.** [norous.

पूर्ण *pp.* Full of; whole; so-

पूर्णपात्र *m.* A present.

पूर्णमासी *f.* The day of the full moon.

पूर्णांक *m.* An integer.

पूर्णिमा, पूर्णिमासी *f.* See **पूर्णमासी.**

पूर्त *a.* Full; covered. *n.* Fulfilment.

पूर्ति *f.* Filling; satisfaction.

पूर्व *a.* Foremost; eastern, old. *m.* A fore-father.

पूर्वक *a.* Preceding.

पूर्वकल्प *m.* Former times.

पूर्वकालिक, पूर्वकालीन *a.* Ancient. [point.

पूर्वकोटि *f.* The starting

पूर्वज *a.* First born; ancient. *m.* An elder brother; an ancestor. [front of.

पूर्वतस् *ind.* In the east; in

पूर्वत्र *ind.* In the preceding part.

पूर्वद्युस् *ind.* On a former day.

पूर्वपक्ष *m.* The first half of a lunar month; the first part of an argument.

पूर्वम् *ind.* Formerly; beforehand.

पूर्वमीमांसा *f.* An inquiry into the ritual portion of the Veda.

पूर्वरंग *m.* A prologue.

पूर्वसंध्या *f.* Day-break; dawn.

पूर्वाषाढा *f.* The twentieth luuar constellation.

पूर्विन् (-णी) *a.* Ancient.

पूल् *vt.* 1 P. 10 U. To gather.

पूषन् *m.* The sun.

पृ *vi.* 6 A. To be busy; with **व्या-** to engage in; to appoint. 3 P. (*p.p.* **पूर्ण**) To protect; to fill; *vt.* 10 U. To accomplish; 5 P. To delight. [Property.

पृक्त *a.* Mixed, touched. *n.*

पृक्ति *f.* Touch, contact.

पृक्थ *n.* Property, wealth.

पृच् *vi.* 2 A. (*p. p.* **पृक्ण**) To come in contact with; *vt.* 7 P. (*p.p.* **पृक्त**) To unite; 1 P. 10 U. To hinder.

पृच्छक *m.* An inquirer.

पृच्छन *n.* Asking.

पृच्छा *f.* An inquiry.

पृत्, पृतना *f.* An army.

पृथक् *ind.* Separately; except. [fool.

पृथग्जन *m.* A low man; a

पृथग्भाव *m.* Separateness; individuality.

पृथवी *f.* The earth.

पृथा *f.* Name of Kuntî.

पृथिवी *f.* The earth.

पृथु *a.* Wide numerous, important. [flattened.

पृथुक *m.* Rice parched and

पृथुल *a*. Broad, large.
पृथ्वी *f*. The earth. N. of a metre. [light.
पृष्णि *a*. Short. *f*. A ray of
पृषत् *n*. A drop.
पृषतांपाति *n*. The wind.
पृषत्क *m*. An arrow.
पृषंति *m*. A drop of water.
पृषोदर *m*. Air, wind.
पृष्ट *pp*. Asked; sprinkled.
पृष्टि *f*. Inquiry. [face.
पृष्ठ *n*. The back; the sur-
पृष्ठक *n*. The back. [ly.
पृष्ठतस् *ind*. Behind, secret-
पृष्ठमांसाद् *a*. A slanderer.
पृष्ठमांसादन *n*. Back-biting.
पृष्णि *f*. The heel.
पॄ *vt*. 3 P., 9 P. To fill, to blow; to satisfy.
पेचक *m*. An owl. [phant.
पेचकिन्, पेचल *m*. An ele-
पेट *m*. *n*. A bag; a chest.
पेटक *m*. *n*. A basket.
पेटिका, पेटी *f*. A basket.
पेय *n*. A drink.
पेयूष *n*. Nectar.
पेल् *vt*. *vi*. 1 P. 10 U. To shake.
पेलव *a*. Delicate.
पेशल *a*. Tender, charming.
पेष *m*. Grinding. [ing.
पेषण *n*. Grinding; pound-
पेषणि (-णी) *f*. A mill-stone.
पै *vi*. 1 P. To dry.
पैंजूष *m*. The ear.

पैतामह *a*. Relating to a paternal grand-father.
पैतृक *a*. Ancestral.
पैत्त, पैत्तिक *a*. Bilious.
पैत्र *a*. Ancestral. [lity.
पैशल्य *n*. Mildness; affabi-
पैशाच *a*. Infernal. *m*. One of the eight forms of marriage.
पैशाचिक *a*. Demoniacal.
पैशाची *f*. A prâkrit dialect.
पैशुन (-न्य) *n*. Back-biting; roguery.
पैष्ट, पैष्टिक *a*. Made of flour.
पोगंड *a*. Young. *n*. Boyhood.
पोटलिका, (-ली) *f*. A bundle.
पोटा *f*. An amazon.
पोत, पोतक *m*. The young of any animal.
पोष *m*. Increase, plenty.
पोषण *n*. Nourishing.
पोष्य *a*. Dependent.
पोष्यपुत्र *m*. An adopted son.
पौंड्र *m*. N. of a country; the conch-shell of Bhîma.
पौत्र *m*. A son's son.
पौत्री *f*. A son's daughter.
पौनःपुनिक *a*. Frequently repeated [petition.
पौनःपुन्य *n* Frequent re-
पौनरुक्त (-क्त्य) *n*. Repetition
पौनर्भव *m*. The son of a remarried widow.
पौर *m*. A citizen.

पौरस्त्य *a.* Eastern.

पौराणिक *a.* Ancient. *m.* A mythologist.

पौरुष *a.* Manly. *n* Manliness, heroism.

पौरुषेय *a.* Made by man.

पौरुष्य *n.* Manliness, courage. [finding.

पौरोभाग्य *n.* Ill-luck; fault-

पौरोहित्य *n.* The office of a family priest.

पौर्णमी, पौर्णिमा, पौर्णिमासी, *f.* A day of the full moon.

पौर्व *a.* Relating to the past or the east.

पौर्वापर्य *n.* The context.

पौर्विक *a.* Previous, ancestral.

पौलस्त्य *m.* Râvana; Kubera.

पौलोमी *f.* Śachî (wife of Indra.) [month.

पौष *m.* Name of a lunar

पौष्टिक *a.* Nutritive.

पौष्प *a.* Floral.

प्याय *vi.* 1 A. (*pp* प्यान or पीन) To grow.

प्यायन *n.* Growth.

प्यै *vi.* 1 A. (*pp* पीन) To grow.

प्र *ind.* Forward; prefixed to nouns it means excellent, intense, excessive, complete

प्रकट *a.* Manifest.

प्रकटन *n.* Manifesting.

प्रकंप *m.* Wind; *n.* excessive motion.

प्रकर *m.* A heap; assistance.

प्रकरण *n.* Subject, chapter, opportunity; a kind of dramatic composition.

प्रकारिका, प्रकरी *f.* An interlude. [lence, length.

प्रकर्ष *m.* Intensity, excel-

प्रकर्षेण *ind.* Exceedingly, eminently.

प्रकल्पना *f.* Settlement.

प्रकल्पित *a.* Made; settled.

प्रकांड, प्रकांडक *m. n.* The trunk of a tree; any thing excellent of its kind.

प्रकाम *a.* Much. *m.* Desire.

प्रकामम् *ind.* Willingly; exceedingly. [property.

प्रकार *m.* Kind, manner,

प्रकाश *a.* Manifest, bright, famous. *m.* Light, fame, display.

प्रकाशक *a.* Brilliant; renowned. [publishing.

प्रकाशन *a.* Illuminating;

प्रकाशम् *ind.* Openly, aloud.

प्रकाशनारी *f.* A prostitute.

प्रकाशित *pp.* Illuminated; published.

प्रकिरण *n.* Scattering.

प्रकीर्ण, (-क) *a.* Scattered about, confused, miscellaneous.

प्रकीर्तन *n.* Proclaiming; praising. [fame.

प्रकीर्ति *f.* Declaration, praise,

प्रकुपित *a.* Enraged; stimulated.

प्रकृत *a.* Commenced, under consideration.

प्रकृति *f.* Nature; constitution; original form; the crude form of a word; the female organ of generation. (Plu.) A king's ministers; subject of a king.

प्रकृतिस्थ *a.* In the natural condition.

प्रकृष्ट *a.* Lengthy, excellent.

प्रकोष्ठ *m.* The wrist; a court in a house.

प्रक्रम *m.* A step; beginning; method; leisure.

प्रक्रांत *a.* Commenced; in hand; valourous.

प्रक्रिया *f.* Manner; high position; a chapter; etymological formation.

प्रक्लिन्न *pp.* Moist.

प्रक्षय *m.* Ruin. [ing.

प्रक्षालन *n.* Washing; clean-

प्रक्षालित *a.* Washed. [ous.

प्रक्षिप्त *a.* Thrown at; spuri-

प्रक्षीण *pp.* Decayed.

प्रक्षुण्ण *pp* Crushed.

प्रक्षेप *m.* A throw; an interpolation; a deposit.

प्रक्षोभण *n.* Exciting.

प्रखर *a.* Very sharp or hard.

प्रख्य *a.* Distinct.

प्रख्या *f.* Fame, similarity.

प्रख्यात *pp.* Renowned.

प्रख्याति *f.* Celebrity, fame.

प्रगमन *n.* Advance.

प्रगल्भ *a.* Bold, eloquent, spirited, mature.

प्रगल्भा *f.* A bold woman.

प्रगाढ *a.* Much, hard.

प्रगाढम् *ind.* Exceedingly; firmly. [excellent.

प्रगुण *a.* Clever, honest,

प्रगृहीत *a.* Accepted. [ing.

प्रगे *ind.* Early in the morn-

प्रगोपन *n.* Protection.

प्रग्रह *m.* A rein; an eclipse.

प्रग्राह *m.* A string; a rein.

प्रघस *a.* Voracious.

प्रघात *m.* Killing; a battle.

प्रघुण, प्रघूर्ण *m.* A guest.

प्रघोष *m.* A loud sound.

प्रचंड *a.* Terrible, intolerable.

प्रच (चा) य *m.* A multitude.

प्रचर *m.* A road; a custom.

प्रचल *a.* Shaking, customary.

प्रचार *m.* Wandering; a path; manifestation; use, custom; conduct.

प्रचालन *n.* Stirring. [with.

प्रचुर *a.* Abundant, replete

प्रचेतस् *m.* Varuna.

प्रचोदन *n.* Instigating; a rule.

प्रच्छ् *vt*. 6 P. (*p.p*.**पृष्ट**) To ask; with **आ** (Atm.)-to take leave of.

प्रच्छद *m*.A cover. [quiry.

प्रच्छन *n*. **प्रच्छना** *f*. An in-

प्रच्छन्न *pp*. Covered, secret.

प्रच्छन्नम् *ind*. Secretly.

प्रच्छादन *n*. A covering.

प्रच्छाय *n*. Thick shade; a shadowy place.

प्रच्छिल *a*. Dry.

प्रच्यव *m*.Ruin; growth.

प्रच्युत *pp*. Fallen, degraded.

प्रच्युति *f*. Ruin, loss.

प्रजन *m*. Impregnation.

प्रजनन *n* Procreation, birth.

प्रजल्प *m*.Prattle, gossip.

प्रजल्पन *n*. Talking.

प्रजविन् *a*.Rapid.[mankind.

प्रजा *f*. Offspring; subjects;

प्रजागर *m* Sleeplessness.

प्रजाति *f*. Procreation, delivery.

प्रजापति *m*. The creator (Brahmá); the sun; a king.

प्रजीवन *n*. Livelihood.

प्रजुष्ट *a*. Attached to.

प्रज्ञ *a*. Wise,learned. [trine.

प्रज्ञप्ति *f*. Agreement, doc-

प्रज्ञा *f*. Understanding; wisdom; judgment

प्रज्ञाचक्षुस् *a*. Blind. *m*. Dhritaráshtra.

प्रज्ञात *pp* Known, famous.

प्रज्ञान *n*. Intelligence; a mark.

प्रज्ञिन्(-**ल**) *a*.Wise, prudent.

प्रज्वलन *n*. Blazing.

प्रज्वलित *a*. Blazing.

प्रडीन *n*. Flight.

प्रणत *a*. Bending; humble.

प्रणति *f*.Obeisance,courtesy.

प्रणदन *n*. Sounding.

प्रणय *m*. Love, friendship, request, trust, familiarity.

प्रणयकलह *m*. A lover's quarrel.

प्रणयकोप *m*. The feigned anger of a coquette towards her lover.[posing.

प्रणयन *n*. Bringing; com-

प्रणयिन् *a*. Beloved, kind. *m*. A favourite, a lover, a petitioner.

प्रणयिनी *f*. A mistress.

प्रणव *m*. The mystic syllable (*om*.)

प्रणाद *m*. A loud noise.

प्रणाम *m*. Prostration, salutation.

प्रणायक *m*. A leader.

प्रणाय्य *a*. Beloved.

प्रणाल *m* **प्रणालिका** *f*.**प्रणाली** *f*. A channel; a series.

प्रणाश *m*. Loss.

प्रणाशन *n*. Destruction.

प्रणिधान *n*. Effort;use; profound religious meditation. [tention; a spy.

प्रणिधि *m*. Solicitation, at-

प्रणिनाद *m* A deep sound.

प्रणिपात *m.* Obeisance; a bow.

प्रणिहित *a.* Stretched forth; entrusted.

प्रणीत *a.* Delivered, executed, composed.

प्रणेतृ *m.* A leader, teacher, author.

प्रणेजन *n.* Washing, bathing.

प्रणेय *a.* Submissive.

प्रतति *f.* Extension; a creeper.

प्रतन *a.* Ancient, old.

प्रतनु *a.* Very thin; delicate. puny, insignificant.

प्रतपन *n.* Warming.

प्रतप्त *a.* Heated; tortured.

प्रतर्क *m.* Conjecture.

प्रतल *n.* One of the seven divisions of the lower world.

प्रतान *m.* A shoot; extension.

प्रताप *m.* Heat, radiance, splendour, majesty, zeal, valour.

प्रतापिन् *a.* Glorious, powerful.

प्रतार *m.*, (-ण *n.*) Deceit, fraud.

प्रतारक *m.* A cheat.

प्रतारणा *f.* Fraud, hypocrisy.

प्रति *ind.* Towards, again, against, opposite, by the side of, concerning, severally, at each.

प्रतिकण्ठम् *ind.* One by one.

प्रतिकर *m.* Requital; compensation.

प्रतिकर्मन् *n.* Requital; remedy; toilet.

प्रतिकाय *m.* An image; a mark.

प्रति (ती) कार *m.* Retaliation; rem·dy; prevention.

प्रति (ती) काश *a.* Resembl·ing. *m.* Appearance.

प्रतिकूप *m* A moat.

प्रतिकूल *a.* Unfavourable; disagreeable.

प्रतिकूलम् *ind.* Inversely.

प्रतिकृति *f.* Revenge; image.

प्रतिक्षेप *m.* Rejection; contest.

प्रतिख्याति *f.* Renown.

प्रतिगमन *n.* Returning.

प्रतिगृहीत *a.* Accepted.

प्रतिग्रह *m.* Right of accepting gifts; a favour; a gift.

प्रतिग्रहण *n.* Marrying.

प्रतिघ *m.* Opposition; a combat.

प्रतिघात *m.* Opposition; a blow.

प्रतिच्छदन *n.* A cover.

प्रतिच्छंद *m.* A likeness.

प्रतिच्छन्न *pp.* Covered.

प्रतिच्छाया *f.* A picture; a reflection.

प्रतिच्छेद *m.* Resistance.

प्रतिजल्प *m* A reply.

प्रतिजागर *m.* Watchfulness.

प्रतिज्ञा *f.* Admission; promise; a vow; assertion; a plaint.

प्रतिज्ञात *pp.* Promised.

प्रतिज्ञान *n.* An agreement.

प्रतिदान *n.* Restoration; exchange.

प्रतिद्वंद्व *m.* An opponent.

प्रतिधावन *n.* An attack.

प्रतिध्वनि *m.* An echo.

प्रतिध्वस्त *a.* Downcast.

प्रतिनंदन *n.* Greeting.

प्रतिनव *a.* New, young, fresh.

प्रतिनिधि *m.* A representative or image.

प्रतिनियम *m.* A general rule.

प्रतिनिविष्ट *a.* Obstinate.

प्रतिपक्ष (-क्षिन्) *m.* An opponent; a foe.

प्रतिपत्ति *f.* Knowledge; gain; admission; resolution; tendency; procedure; method; fame; respectful behaviour; assent.

प्रतिपद् *f.* The first day of lunar fortnight. [above.

प्रतिपदा (-दी) *f.* See प्रतिपद्

प्रतिपन्न *a.* Undertaken; gained; known; admitted; proved.

प्रतिपादन *n.* Gift; proving, practice.

प्रतिपालन *n.* Protecting.

प्रतिपीडन *n.* Oppressing.

प्रतिपूजन *n.* Mutual obei-

प्रतिपूरण *n.* Filling up. [sance.

प्रतिपु(पू) रुप *m.* A substitute; a deputy.

प्रतिफल *m.*, (-न *n.*) An image.

प्रतिबंध *m.* Obstacle; opposition; siege; connection. [ful.

प्रतिबल *a.* Equally power-

प्रतिबिंब *m. n.* A reflection; image.

प्रतिबिंबन *n.* Correspondence; comparison.

प्रतिबुद्धि *n.* Hostile intention.

प्रतिबोध *m.* Waking; knowledge; reason.

प्रतिभय *a.* Terrible.

प्रतिभा *f.* An appearance; splendour; intellect; genius; audacity.

प्रतिभाग *m.* A share.

प्रतिभान *n.* Light; intellect.

प्रतिभाव *m.* Corresponding disposition.

प्रतिभाषा *f.* An answer.

प्रतिभास *m.* Sudden perception; illusion.

प्रतिभू *m.* A bail.

प्रतिभोग *m.* Enjoyment.

प्रतिमा *f.* An image; a reflection; a measure; a symbol.

प्रतिमान *n.* A model; part of an elephant's head. [tion.

प्रतिमोक्ष *m.*, (-ण *n.*) Libera-

प्रतिमोचन *n.* Loosening, retaliation; liberation.

प्रतियत्न *m.* Desire; making

captive; revenge;favour; preparation.

प्रतियोग *m.* Opposition; an antidote.

प्रतिरव *m.* A quarrel.

प्रतिरुद्ध *a.* Obstructed.

प्रतिरूप *a.* Corresponding.

प्रतिरोध *m.* Hindrance; siege; theft; abuse.

प्रतिलोम *a* Inverted; contrary to caste; low, perverse.

प्रतिवसथ *m.* A village

प्रतिवस्तु *n.* An equivalent.

प्रतिवाद *m.* A rejoinder.

प्रतिवादिन् *m.* A defendant.

प्रतिवार *m.*, (-ण *n*) Keeping back.

प्रतिवार्ता *f.* Account; news.

प्रतिवासिन् *a.* Dwelling near.

प्रतिविधान *n.* Counteracting.

प्रतिविशिष्ट *a.* Most excellent.

प्रतिवेश *m.* A neighbour.

प्रतिवेशिन् *m.* A neighbour.

प्रतिशब्द *m.* An echo.

प्रतिशम *m.* Cessation.

प्रतिशयन *n.* Lying down without food.

प्रतिशासन *n.* A rival authority.

प्रतिश्रय *m.* A shelter; a house; help; promise.

प्रतिश्रव *m.* Assent; promise

प्रतिश्रवण *n.* Listening to; agreeing

प्रतिश्रुति *f.* A promise; reverberation.

प्रतिषेध *m.* Expulsion; prohibition; denial; exception.

प्रतिष्क *m.* A spy; a messenger.

प्रतिष्टंभ *m.* Opposition.

प्रतिष्ठा *f.* Position; a residence; stability; foundation; a support; fame.

प्रतिष्ठान *n.* Foundation, site.

प्रतिष्ठित *a.* Fixed, valued, settled, endowed, famous.

प्रतिसर *a.* Dependent. *m* A cord; ornament; a guard; a bracelet; a garland; the rear.

प्रतिसंहत *pp.* Withdrawn.

प्रतिसंहार *m.* Withdrawing; comprehension.

प्रतिसंक्रम *m.* Reflection; reabsorption.

प्रतिसंख्या *f.* Consciousness.

प्रतिसंधान *n* Period of transition; a remedy; praise.

प्रतिसंधि *m.* Reunion; period of transition.

प्रतिस्पर्धा *f.* Rivalry.

प्रतिस्पर्धिन् *m.* A rival.

प्रतिहत *a.* Overthrown repelled, obstructed, hated.

प्रतिहनन *a.* Returning a blow.

प्रति (ती°) हर *m.* A porter; a door-keeper.

प्रतिहारक *m.* A juggler.
प्रतिहारण *n.* Entrance.
प्रतिहारभूमि *f.* A threshold.
प्रतिहिंसा *f.* Revenge.
प्रतीक *a.* Reverse. *m.* A limb.
प्रतीक्षण *n.* } Consideration;
प्रतीक्षा *f.* } expectation.
प्रतीची *f.* The west.
प्रतीचीन *a.* Western; future.
प्रतीच्य *a.* Western.
प्रतीत *a.* Famous; known as; past; learned; pleased.
प्रतीति *f.* Knowledge; conviction; fame.
प्रतीप *a.* Inverted; obstinate; contrary.
प्रतीपम् *ind.* Against
प्रतीर *n.* A shore, a bank.
प्रतीहारी *f.* A female door-keeper.
प्रतुष्टि *f.* Gratification.
प्रतूर्ण *a.* Speedy.
प्रतोद *m.* A goad; a whip.
प्रतोली *f.* A street.
प्रतोष *m.* Gratification.
प्रत्न *a.* Old. [erly, against.
प्रत्यक् *ind.* Opposite; form-
प्रत्यक्ष *a.* Present, visible.
प्रत्यक्षम् *ind.* In the presence of; immediately.
प्रत्यक्षप्रमाण *n.* Ocular proof.
प्रत्यक्षिन् *m.* An eye-witness.
प्रत्यग्र *a.* Fresh. [ern.
प्रत्यच् *a.* Subsequent; west-
प्रत्यंचित *a.* Worshipped, honoured.
प्रत्यनीक *n.* Hostility.

प्रत्यंत *a.* Contiguous. *m.* A border or bordering country.
प्रत्यपकार *m.* Retaliation.
प्रत्यभिज्ञात *a.* Recognised.
प्रत्यय *m.* Belief; certainty; notion; an instrument; fame; practice; knowledge.
प्रत्यर्थ *a.* Useful. *n.* A reply.
प्रत्यर्थक *m.* An opponent.
प्रत्यर्थिन् *a.* Hostile *m.* An enemy; a match; a defendant.
प्रत्यर्पण *n.* Restoring.
प्रत्यवाय *m.* Decrease; opposition; sin. [ing after.
प्रत्यवेक्षण *n.* प्रत्यवेक्षा *f.* Look-
प्रत्यहम् *ind.* Every day.
प्रत्याकार *m.* A scabbard.
प्रत्याघात *m.* A reaction.
प्रत्याचार *m.* Suitable behaviour.
प्रत्यात्मन् *ind.* Singly.
प्रत्यादेश *m* Command; refusal; reproach.
प्रत्यापत्ति *f.* Return; indifference to worldly objects.
प्रत्यायन *n.* Marrying.
प्रत्यावर्तन *n* Returning.
प्रत्याशा *f.* Hope.
प्रत्याश्वास *m.* Respiration; consolation.
प्रत्यासत्ति *f.* Close contact.

प्रत्यासन्न *a.* Near; proximate.

प्रत्याहार *m.* Withholding; retreat; restraining the organs of sense (in Yoga phil.)

प्रत्युक्ति *f.* reply.

प्रत्युच्चार *m.* Repetition.

प्रत्युत्क्रम *m.* } Preparations
प्रत्युत्क्रांति *f.* } for war.

प्रत्युत्पन्न *a.* Ready; regenerated. [bold.

प्रत्युत्पन्नमति *a.* Ready-witted;

प्रत्युद्यम *m.* Counteracting.

प्रत्युपपन्न *a.* See प्रत्युत्पन्न.

प्रत्युलूक *m.* A crow.

प्रत्युष *m.*
प्रत्युषस् *n.*
प्रत्यूष *m. n.*
प्रत्यूषस् *n.*
} Morning; dawn.

प्रत्यूह *a.* Impediment.

प्रथ् *vi.* 1 A. To increase; to become famous; to appear. 10 U. To proclaim; to show; to spread. [est.

प्रथम *a.* First, chief, earli-

प्रथमतः or प्रथमम् *ind.* At first; newly; before; immediately. [case.

प्रथमा *f.* The nominative

प्रथा *f.* Fame. [ous.

प्रथित *a.* Published; fam-

प्रथिमन् *m.* Extension; greatness. [Largest.

प्रथिष्ठ (Super. of पृथु) *a.*

प्रथीयस् (Comp. of पृथु) *a.* Larger.

प्रथु *a.* Wide. [flattend.

प्रथुक *m.* Rice parched and

प्रद (at the end of compouds) *a.* Giving.

प्रदक्षिण *a.* Moving to the right; respectful; auspicious.

प्रदक्षिणक्रिया *f.* Turning the right side towards one as a mark of respect.

प्रदक्षिणम् *ind.* From left to right; in the southern direcction.

प्रदर *m.* A fracture.

प्रदर्प *m.* Pride. [an example.

प्रदर्शन *n.* Look, displying;

प्रदातृ *m.* A donor; Indra.

प्रदान *n.* Granting; a gift.

प्रदाय *m.* A present. [tion.

प्रदीप *m.* A light; elucida-

प्रदीप्त *pp.* Illuminated; excited.

प्रदीप्ति *f.* Lustre; splendour.

प्रदेश *m.* A place; a country; decision.

प्रदेशन *n.* Advice; a gift.

प्रदेशिनी *f.* A fore-finger.

प्रदोष *a.* Bad. *m.* A fault; sin; violation; disorder; night-fall. [king.

प्रद्योत *m.* Light. Name of a

प्रद्योतन *m.* The sun.

प्रद्रव or प्रद्राव *m.* Retreat.

प्रधन *n.* War; spoil; destruction.

प्रधर्ष *m.* प्रधर्षण *n.* प्रधर्षणा *f.* Attack; ill-treatment.

प्रधर्षित *a.* Attacked; haughty.

प्रधान *a.* Chief, best, predominant. *m.* A minister of a king; a courtier. *n.* The primary germ. [off.

प्रधावन *m.* Air. *n.* Washing

प्रधी *f.* A great intelligence.

प्रधृष्ट *a.* Proud.

प्रध्वंस *m.* Utter destruction.

प्रनप्तृ *m.* A great grandson.

प्रना (णा) यक *a.* Destitute of a leader. [succession.

प्रना (णा) ली *f.* A channel;

प्रपंच *m.* Display; development; copiousness: explanation; phenomenon; fraud; the visible world.

प्रपंचन *n.* Diffusion; exposition. [tion, fall.

प्रपतन *n.* Death; destruc-

प्रपन्न *a.* Possessed of; distressed; suppliant.

प्रपा *f.* A well.

प्रपाक *m.* Ripening.

प्रपाठक *m.* A chapter.

प्रपात *m.* Departure; a fall; a sudden attack; a bank; discharge; a spring.

प्रपितामह *m.* A paternal great-grand-father; Krishna; the Supreme Spirit.

प्रपितामही *f.* A paternal great-grand-mother.

प्रपितृव्य *m.* A paternal grand-uncle.

प्रपीत (-न) *a.* Swollen.

प्रपूरण *n.* Filling up; satisfying. [son.

प्रपौत्र *m.* A great-grand-

प्रपौत्री *f.* A great grand-daughter. [cheerful.

प्रफुल्ल *a.* Blooming; smiling;

प्रबंध *m.* A bond, a series, continuance; a connected discourse; a literary composition.

प्रबर्ह *a.* Most excellent.

प्रबल *a.* Mighty, violent; excessive. [a coral.

प्रबा (वा) ल *m. n.* A sprout;

प्रबाहु *m.* The fore-arm.

प्रबाहुकम् *ind.* On high; at the same time.

प्रबुद्ध *a.* Awakened; wise.

प्रबोध *m.* Awaking, vigilance; wisdom.

प्रभंजन *m.* Wind.

प्रभव *m* Birth, origin, source, strength; the creator.

प्रभविष्णु *m.* A lord; Vishnu.

प्रभा *f.* Light, splendour, Durgà. [moon; fire.

प्रभाकर *m.* The sun; the

प्रभाग *m* Division.

प्रभात *n.* Dawn; day-break.

प्रभान *n.* Light, splendour

प्रभाव *m.* Lustre, glory, power, extension, magnanimity.

प्रभावक, प्रभावन *a.* Prominent.

प्रभावना *f.* Disclosing. [ty.

प्रभास *m.* Splendour; beauty.

प्रभास्वर *a* Brilliant. [ed.

प्रभिन्न *a.* Severed; expanded.

प्रभु *a* Mighty, able, abundant, eternal. *m.* A lord, owner; Vishnu; Indra.

प्रभुता *f.* (–त्व *n.*) Supremacy; authority. [abundant.

प्रभूत *a* Sprung from; high; abundant.

प्रभूति *f.* Source; power

प्रभूष्णु *a.* Able; powerful.

प्रभृति *f.* Beginning. *ind.* From, since. [tion.

प्रभेद *m* Difference; distinction.

प्रमत्त *a.* Intoxicated, mad, negligent, wanton.

प्रमथ *m.* A horse. [ter.

प्रमथन *n.* Hurting; slaughter.

प्रमथित *a.* Trampled.

प्रमद *a.* Intoxicated, careless. *m.* Joy; pleasure.

प्रमदा *f.* A young handsome woman; a woman.

प्रमद्वर *a.* Careless.

प्रमनस् *a.* Delighted [ed.

प्रमन्यु *a.* Enraged; distressed.

प्रमय *m.* Death. [Vishnu.

प्रमर्दन *n.* Crushing ; *m.* Vishnu.

प्रमा *f.* Conciousness; correct knowledge.

प्रमाण *n.* A measure, exetnt, limit, evidence, authority.

प्रमाणज्ञ *m.* A logician.

प्रमातामह *m.* A maternal great-grant-father.

प्रमातामही *f.* A maternal great-grant-mother.

प्रमाथ *m.* Agitating, excessive pain, destruction.

प्रमाथिन् *a.* Torturing.

प्रमाद *m.* Intoxication, carelessness, blunder.

प्रमार्जन *n* Wiping off.

प्रमित *a.* Measured; few; known; proved.

प्रमिति *f.* Measurement; true knowledge. analogy.

प्रमीढ *a.* Thick; compact.

प्रमीत *a.* Dead.

प्रमीति *f* Death, destruction.

प्रमीला *f.* Lassitude.

प्रमुक्त *a.* Liberated.

प्रमुक्तकंठम् *ind.* Bitterly.

प्रमुख *a.* Facing, chief, respectable, headed by. *m.* A respectable man. *n.* Mouth; the present time.

प्रमुखतस् or प्रमुखे *ind.* In front of. [ing.

प्रमुग्ध *a.* Extermely charming.

प्रमुद् *f.* Exterme joy. [ed.

प्रमूढ *a.* Foolish; bewildered.

प्रमृष्ट *a.* Washed off; bright.

प्रमेय *a.* Measurable. *n.* A theorem.

प्रमेह *m* A urinary disease.

प्रमोद *m* Joy; a perfume.

प्रमोह *m.* Stupefaction.

प्रयत *a.* Restrained; holy.

प्रयत्न *m.* Effort; labour.

प्रयत्नतः, प्रयत्नेन *ind.* Diligently, scarcely.

प्रयाग *m.* Name of a town (modern Allahabad) at the confluence of the Gangâ and Yamunâ.

प्रयाण *n.* Journey; progress; attack; departure; beginning; death.

प्रयात *a.* Advanced; dead.

प्रयाम *m.* Restraining; scarcity; length. [difficulty.

प्रयास *m.* Effort; labour;

प्रयुक्त *a.* Yoked; appointed; applied; abstracted; endowed with; lent; thick.

प्रयुक्ति *f.* Use; application; instigation; motive.

प्रयुत *n.* A million.

प्रयुत्सु *m.* A warrior.

प्रयुद्ध *n.* War, battle.

प्रयोक्तृ *a.* An author; agent; executor.

प्रयोग *m.* Use; application; general usage, exhibition; usury; experiment; beginning; result.

प्रयोजक *m.* Author, founder, money-lender.

प्रयोजन *n.* Use; need; aim; cause; profit.

प्रयोज्य *a.* To be used.

प्ररूढ *a.* Full-grown.

प्ररूढि *f.* Growth; increase.

प्ररोचन *n.* Stimulating; approval; explanation.

प्ररोह *m.* A sprout; an offspring.

प्ररोहण *m.* A bud, a shoot.

प्रलपन }
प्रलपित } *n.* Talking nonsense.

प्रलब्ध *a.* Decieved.

प्रलंब *a.* Hanging, slow. *m.* A branch.

प्रलंबन *n.* Hanging down.

प्रलंबित *a.* Pendulous.

प्रलंभ *m.* Obtaining; deceiving.

प्रलय *m.* Universal destruction; death; swoon.

प्रलव *m.* A fragment.

प्रलाप *m.* Talk; lamentation; talking non sense.

प्रलीन *a.* Melted.

प्रलेप *m.* An ointment.

प्रलेह *m.* A kind of broth.

प्रलोभ *m.* Cupidity; allurement. [ed.

प्रलोल *a.* Extremely agitat-

प्रवग, प्रवंग, प्रवंगम *m.* A monkey. [position.

प्रवचन *n.* Declaration; ex-

प्रवण *a.* Inclined.

प्रवप *a.* Very fat.

प्रवयस् *a.* Aged, old.

प्रवर *a.* Chief, best *m.* A call, a race, a cover.

प्रवर्तक *m.* Originator.

प्रवर्तन *n.* Prompting, action, conduct, happening.

प्रवर्धन *n*. Increasing.
प्रवर्ष *m*. Heavy rain.
प्रवसन *n*. Going on a journey.
प्रवह *m*. Stream; wind.
प्रवाच् *a*. Eloquent.
प्रवाचन *n*. Proclamation.
प्रवात *m*. A current of air.
प्रवाद *m*. Discourse, rumour, a fable, mutual defiance.
प्रवार *m*., (-क *n*.) A cover.
प्रवारण *n*. Opposition; prohibition.
प्रवास *m*. Foreign residence, a temporary sojourn.
प्रवासन *n*. Exile; slaughter.
प्रवासिन् *m*. A traveller.
प्रवाह *m*. A stream, an uninterrupted series; course of events.
प्रवाहि f. Sand.
प्रविकीर्ण *a*. Scattered.
प्रविचय *m*. Examination.
प्रविभाग *m*. A part. [rare.
प्रविरल *a*. Isolated; very
प्रविलय *m*. Complete dissolution.
प्रविवाद *m*. Dispute.
प्रविविक्त *a*. Detached, quite solitary. [gaged in.
प्रविष्ट *a*. Entered into; en-
प्रविस्त (स्ता) र *m*. Expanse, circumference.
प्रवीण *a*. Skilled in.
प्रवीर *a*. Excellent.
प्रवृत्त *a*. Begun, fixed, round. *n*. An action.
प्रवृत्ति *f*. Origin, flow, appearance, commencement, tendency, conduct, news, fate, sense.
प्रवृत्तिमार्ग *m*. Wordly life.
प्रवृद्धि *f*. Increase; prosperity; promotion.
प्रवेग *m*. Great speed.
प्रवेदन *n*. Announcing.
प्रवेप *m*., (-क *m*.); प्रवेपथु *m*. प्रवेपन *n*. Trembling.
प्रवेश *m*. Entrance, access; income; close application.
प्रवेशक *m*. An interlude.
प्रवेशन *n*. Entrance, gate.
प्रवेष्ट *m*. An arm.
प्रव्यक्त *a*. Apparent.
प्रव्यक्ति *f*. Manifestation.
प्रव्रजन *n*. Going abroad; becoming a recluse.
प्रव्रजित *m*. An ascetic; a Bráhmana.
प्रव्रज्या *f*. Migration, a mendicant's life. [cetic.
प्रव्राज् *m*. प्रव्राजक *m*. An as-
प्रव्राजन *n*. Banishment.
प्रशम *m*. Calmness, appeasement, extinction.
प्रशमन *n*. Pacification; peace. [guished.
प्रशमित *a*. Composed, extin-
प्रशंसन *n*. Praising. [fame.
प्रशंसा *f*. Praise, description,

प्रशंसित *a.* Praised.
प्रशस्त *a.* Commendable.
प्रशस्ति *f.* Praise; a small poem written in praise; excellence, guidance.
प्रशस्य *a* Excellent; praiseworthy. [dead.
प्रशांत *a.* Composed, ended,
प्रशांति *f.* Quite, rest, extinguishing.
प्रशाम *m.* Calm, quenching.
प्रशासन *n.* Government.
प्रशास्तृ *m.* A king, an adviser. [pupil.
प्रशिष्य *m.* The pupil of a
प्रशुद्धि *f.* Clearness; purity.
प्रश्न *m.* A question; an inquiry, a subject of controversy.
प्रश्रथ *m.* Laxity. [modesty.
प्रश्रय *m*, (-ण *n.*) Respect,
प्रश्रित *a.* Civil, courteous.
प्रश्लिष्ट *a.* Twisted; reasonable.
प्रश्लेप *m.* Close contact.
प्रश्वास *m.* Breath [front.
प्रष्ठ *a.* Chief, standing in
प्रसक्त *a.* Attached to, constant.
प्रसक्ति *f.* Devotion; application; union; energy; conclusion; a topic; gain. [number.
प्रसंख्या *f.* Sum; total
प्रसंख्यान *m.* Payment. *n.* Enumeration; fame, deep meditation.
प्रसंग *m.* Attachment, intercourse, occupation, a subject; an occasion, an inference. [dentally.
प्रसंगेन, प्रसंगतः *ind.* Inci-
प्रसत्ति *f.* Clearness; purity; favour.
प्रसंधान *n.* Combination.
प्रसन्न *a.* Clear, transparent, pleased, gracious, plain, correct, tranquil.
प्रसभ *m.* Force, violence.
प्रसभम् *ind.* Exceedingly; forcibly.
प्रसमीक्षा *f.* Judgment.
प्रसर *m.* Free motion, diffusion, extent, a stream, a group, war, ruin.
प्रसरण *n.* Streaming forth; amiability. [directions.
प्रसर्पण *n.* Spreading in all
प्रसव *m.* Generation, childbirth, progeny, source, flower, fruit, a current, help. [chamber.
प्रसवगृह *n.* A lying-in-
प्रसवस्थली *f.* A mother.
प्रसवन *n.* Fecundity.
प्रसवितृ *m.* A father.
प्रसवित्री *f.* A mother.
प्रसव्य *a.* Contrary. [ingly.
प्रसह्य *ind.* Forcibly; exceed-
प्रसाद *m.* Favour; good tem-

per; composure; calmness; clearness. Food offered to idols, or its remnant; welfare.

प्रसादन *a.* Purifying. *m.* Propitiation. [ship.

प्रसादना *f* Service, wor-

प्रसाधक *a.* Accomplishing. *m.* A valet-de chamber.

प्रसाधन *m. n.* A comb. *n.* A decoration.

प्रसाधनी *f.* A comb

प्रसाधिका *f.* A lady's maid.

प्रसार *m.* Spreading; extension; diffusion.

प्रसारण *n.* Diffusing, change of a semi-vowel into a vowel (in gram.)

प्रसित *a.* Bound, devoted to, desirous.

प्रसिति *f.* A net, a tie.

प्रसिद्ध *a.* Famous, adorned.

प्रसिद्धि *f.* Fame, success, decoration.

प्रसुप्त *a.* Asleep. [lysis.

प्रसुप्ति *f.* Sleepiness; para-

प्रसू *a.* Bearing. *f.* A mother.

प्रसूत *a.* Begotten.

प्रसूति *f.* Delivery, generation, offspring.

प्रसूति or **प्रसूतिका** *f.* A woman recently delivered.

प्रसून *a.* Produced. *n* A flower, fruit. [modest.

प्रसृत *a.* Extended, swift,

प्रसृति *f.* Progress, a handful.

प्रसृष्ट *a.* Hurt. [ing.

प्रसेक *m.* Discharge: ooz-

प्रस्कंदिका *f.* Dysentery.

प्रस्तर *m.* A flat surface; a couch; a stone, a gem.

प्रस्तरण *n.* **प्रस्तारणा** *f.* A bed, couch. [a thicket.

प्रस्तार *m.* Spreading, a bed,

प्रस्ताव *m.* Beginning, introduction, allusion, a topic, proper time.

प्रस्तावना *f.* Praise, beginning, introduction.

प्रस्तावेन *ind.* Incidentally; suitably.

प्रस्तुत *a.* Praised, commenced, done, proposed, desired, ready. *n.* A matter in hand.

प्रस्थ *a.* Going to; firm. *m. n.* A level; a table-land; a particular measure.

प्रस्थान *n.* Departure; death; method. [proving.

प्रस्थापन *n.* Despatching;

प्रस्थापित *a.* Despatched; proved.

प्रस्थायिन् *a.* Travelling.

प्रस्थित *a.* Departed [ney.

प्रस्थिति *f* A march; jour-

प्रस्नव *m.* A current. [son.

प्रस्नुषा *f.* Wife of a grand-

प्रस्फुट *a.* Blown; clear.

प्रस्फुरित *a.* Vibrating.

प्रस्फोटन *n.* Expanding; making manifest; beating.

प्रस्यंद *m.* Gum.

प्रस्यंदन *n.* Trickling forth.

प्रस्रव, प्रस्राव *m.* Oozing out; a flow.

प्रस्रवण *n.* Oozing; a spring.

प्रस्वन *m.* A loud noise.

प्रस्वाप *m.* Sleep; a dream.

प्रस्वापन *n.* Inducing sleep.

प्रस्वेद *m* Excessive perspiration.

प्रहणन *n.* Killing.

प्रहत *a.* Wounded, killed, defeated, spread, accomplished.

प्रहर *m.* A period of three hours.

प्रहरण *n.* Striking, removing; war; a weapon.

प्रहरिन् *m.* A watchman.

प्रहर्ष *m.* Exultation.

प्रहर्षण *n.* Enrapturing.

प्रहर्षणि *f.* Turmeric; name of a metre.

प्रहसन *n.* Violent laughter, ridicule, satire, farce.

प्रहासित *n.* A laughter, mirth.

प्रहार *m.* A stroke, a thrust.

प्रहारण *n.* A desirable gift.

प्रहास *m.* Violent laughter, ridicule, irony, an actor.

प्रहित *a.* Extended, despatched, suitable.

प्रहीण *a.* Abandoned. *n* Loss.

प्रहृत *a.* Struck. *n.* A blow.

प्रहृष्ट *a.* Delighted.

प्रहेलक *n.* A riddle.

प्रहेला *f.* Loose behaviour.

प्रहेलि, (-का) *f.* A poetic riddle.

प्रन्हा (ह्ला) द *m.* Joy; son of हिरण्यकशिपु.

प्रन्हादन *n.* Gladdening.

प्रह्व *a* Sloping, stooping, humble.

प्रांशु *a.* High. *m.* A tall man.

प्राक् *ind.* Already, before, in the east, in front, as far as, at dawn.

प्राकट्य *n.* Publicity, notoriety.

प्राक्तन *a.* Ancient; former.

प्राकरणिक *a.* Relevant to the matter in hand.

प्राकर्षिक *a.* Entitled to preference.

प्राकाम्य *n.* Freedom of will.

प्राकार *m.* A fence, wall.

प्राकाश्य *n.* Publicity; fame.

प्राकृत *a.* Original, natural, usual, vulgar, unimportant, vernacular. *m.* A low man. *n.* A vernacular dialect.

प्राखर्य *n.* Strictness, sharpness, ardour.

प्रागल्भ्य *n* Boldness, pride, skill, development, appearance, eloquence, rank.

प्रागार *m.* A house.

प्राग्ज्योतिष *m.* Name of a

country(modern Assam).

प्राग्भार *m.* The peak of a mountain; the forepart; a heap.

प्राग्भाव *m.* Previous existence; superiority.

प्राग्र *n.* The highest point.

प्राग्रसर *a.* Foremost, first.

प्राघात *m.* War, battle.

प्राघुण, प्राघुणक, प्राघुणिक, प्राघूर्णक, प्राघूर्णिक *m.* A guest, a visitor. [yard.

प्रांगण *n.* A court, a court-

प्राच् *a.* Foremost; eastern, prior. *m.* (*pl.*) Eastern people.

प्राची *f.* The East.

प्राचीन *a.* Eastern, previous, old. *m. n.* A wall.

प्राचीनबर्हिस् *m.* Indra.

प्राचीनम् *ind.* In front; before. [thread.

प्राचीनावीत *n.* The sacred

प्राचीपति *m.* Indra.

प्राचीमूल *n.* The eastern horizon. [wall.

प्राचीर *m.* An enclosure;

प्राचुर्य *n.* Abundance, plenty.

प्राचेतस *m.* Manu; Daksha; Válmîki. [old.

प्राच्य *a.* Eastern, prior,

प्राच्यक *a.* Eastern.

प्राच्छ् *a.* Inquiring.

प्राजक *m.* A charioteer.

प्राजन *m. n.* A whip.

प्राजापत्य *m.* One of the eight forms of marriage.

प्राज्ञ *a.* Intellectual. *m.* A learned man.

प्राज्ञा *f.* Understanding.

प्राज्ञी *f.* Wife of a learned man; a learned woman.

प्राज्य *a.* Abundant; great.

प्रांजल *a.* Honest; sincere.

प्रांजलि *a.* Folding hands in supplication. [लि above.

प्रांजलिक, प्रांजलिन्–See प्रांज-

प्राड्विवाक *m.* A judge.

प्राण् 2 P. To breathe.

प्राण *m.* Breath; vitality; life; wind; energy; spirit; a beloved thing; inspiration; digestion, power.

प्राणन *m.* The throat. *n.* Respiration. [band.

प्राणनाथ (-पति) *m.* A hus-

प्राणंती *f.* Hunger.

प्राणमय *a.* Living.

प्राणमयकोश *m.* The vesture of the vital airs.

प्राणवत् *a.* Living, powerful.

प्राणाद *a.* Fatal. [breath.

प्राणायाम *m.* Restraining the

प्राणिजात *n.* A whole class of animals.

प्राणिन् *m.* A living being.

प्राणीत्य *n* Debt. [early.

प्रातर् *ind.* At day-break;

प्रातःकर्म (-कार्य, -कृत्य) *n.* A morning duty.

प्रातराश *m.* Morning meal.
प्रातस्तन *a.* Matutinal.
प्रातस्तराम् *ind.* Very early in the morning.
प्रातस्त्य *a.* Matutinal.
प्रातस्त्रिवर्गा, प्रातस्त्रियामा *f.* The Ganges.
प्रातिकूलिक *a.* Unfavourable.
प्रातिकूल्य *n.* Opposition.
प्रातिजनीन *a.* Suitable against an adversary.
प्रातिपदिक *n.* The crude form of a substantive
प्रातिभ *a.* Relating to divination or genius.
प्रातिभाव्य *n.* Suretiship. [lity.
प्रातिलोम्य *n.* Invertion, hosti-
प्रातिवेशिक, प्रातिवेश्मक, प्रातिवेश्य, प्रातिवेश्यक *m.* A neighbour.
प्रातिस्विक *a.* Peculiar, own.
प्रातीतिक *a.* Mental.
प्रातीपिक *a.* Contrary.
प्रात्ययिक *a.* Trusted.
प्रात्याह्निक *a* Daily.
प्राथमिक *a.* Primary, first.
प्राथम्य *n.* Priority. [ly.
प्रादुस् *ind.* Visibly, evident-
प्रादुर्भाव *m.* Arising; appearance.
प्रादेश *m.* Place, spot.
प्राधानिक *a.* Most eminent.
प्राधान्य *n* Pre-eminence.
प्राध्व *a.* Distant, bent.
प्राध्वम् *ind.* Favourably.
प्रांत *m.n.* Border, extremity, point. [shade.
प्रांतर *m.* A road without
प्रापक *a.* Leading to. [ment.
प्रापण *n.* Reaching; attain-
प्राप्त *a.* Attained, won, suffered, present, proper.
प्राप्तकाल *a.* Opportune [fit.
प्राप्तरूप *a.* Beautiful; wise;
प्राप्तव्य *a* Fit, attainable.
प्राप्तव्यवहार *m.* A man who has come of age.
प्राप्ति *f.* Acquisition, guess, range, share collection.
प्राप्य *a.* Attainable; fit.
प्राबल्य *n.* Powerfulness, ascendancy.
प्राबोधिक *m.* Dawn.
प्राभातिक *a.* Relating to the morning.
प्राभृत *n.* A present.
प्रामाणिक *a.* Founded on authority. *m.* A logician.
प्रामाण्य *n.* Proof, genuineness.
प्रामादिक *a* Faulty; wrong.
प्राय *m* Seeking death by starvation; majority, excess; (at the end of comp.) generally, nearly, like.
प्रायशस् *ind.* Generally.
प्रायश्चित्त *n.* प्रायश्चित्ति *f.* Atonement. [ally.
प्रायस् *ind.* Mostly, gener-
प्रायिक *a.* Common.

प्रायेण *ind*. In all probability; mostly.

प्रारब्ध *a*. Begun. *n*. An undertaking; fate.

प्रारब्धि *f*. Beginning.

प्रारंभ *m*.Beginning; enterprise.

प्रारोह *m*. A shoot.

प्रार्थना *f*. A request; desire.

प्रार्थनीय *a*. To be desired.

प्रार्थयितृ *m*.A suitor,beggar.

प्रार्थित *a*. Desired.

प्रार्थिन् *a*.Begging,desiring.

प्रालंब *a*. Pendant. *m*. A garland.

प्रालेय *m*. Snow.

प्रावरण *n*. प्रावार or प्रावारक *m*.An upper garment.

प्रावीण्य *n*. Skilfulness.

प्रावृत *a*.Enclosed.*m*.A veil.

प्रावृति *f*. An enclosure.

प्रावृष् *f* प्रावृष *m*. or प्रावृषा *f*. The rainy season.

प्रावृषेण्य *a*. Relating to the rainy season.

प्राश *m*.प्राशन *n*.Eating; food.

प्राशस्त्य *n*. Excellence.

प्राश्निक *m* An arbitrator.

प्रास *m*.A missile. [vant.

प्रासंगिक *a*.Incidental, relevant.

प्रासाद *m*. A palace

प्रासादतल *n*.The flat roof of a palace.

प्रासादपृष्ठ *m*. A balcony on the top of a palace.

प्रास्ताविक *a*. Introductory; opportune.

प्राह्ण *m*.The forenoon.

प्राह्णेतराम् , प्राह्णेतमाम् *ind*. Very early in the morning.

प्रिय *a*.Dear,agreeable fond, expensive, usual. *m*. A lover. *n* A favour.

प्रियंगु *m*. *f*. Name of a creeper. [news.

प्रियदर्शन *a* Lovely.

प्रिया *f*. A wife; mistress; news.

प्री *vi* 4 A. or 9 U. To be pleased.

प्रीण *a*. Pleased.

प्रीणन *n*. Pleasing. [kind.

प्रीत *pp*. Pleased, happy, kind.

प्रीति *f*. Pleasure, favour, love.

प्रु *vt*. I. A. To go.

प्रुष् *vt*. I. P. To burn. 9 P. To become wet.

प्रुष्ट *a*. Burnt.

प्रेक्षक *m*. A spectator.

प्रेक्षण *n*. View, sight, eye.

प्रेक्षणीय *a*. Beautiful.

प्रेक्षा *f*. Sight, intellect, deliberation. [theatre.

प्रेक्षागार or प्रेक्षागृह *n*. A theatre.

प्रेङ्खा *f*. A swing,dancing.

प्रेत *a*. Dead. *m*. The spirit.

प्रेतकर्मन् *n*.(-कृत्य *n* ,-कृत्या *f*.) Funeral rites.

प्रेतगृह (-वन) *n*. A cemetery.

प्रेतराज *m*. Yama.

प्रेत्थ *ind.* In the next world.
प्रेप्सु *a.* Longing for.
प्रेमन् *m* *n.* Love, sport.
प्रेयस् *a.* Dearer.
प्रेयसी *f.* A wife, a mistress.
प्रेरक *a.* Urging. [sending.
प्रेरण *n* प्रेरणा *f.* Impulse;
प्रेरित *pp.* Impelled [send.
प्रेष् 1 U. To go. *vt* 1,4,P. To
प्रेषित *a.* Sent.
प्रेष्ठ *a.* Dearest.
प्रेष्य *m.* A servant [ness.
प्रैष *m.* Order, sorrow, mad-
प्रोक्त *a.* Spoken.
प्रोक्षण *n.* Sprinkling; killing animals at a sacrifice.
प्रोच्छ्रित *a.* High.
प्रोज्झित *pp.* Forsaken.
प्रोड्डीन *pp.* Flown away.
प्रोत *a.* (*pp.* of वे with प्र) Sewn, extended, lengthwise, tied, pierced.
प्रोत्साह *m.* Zeal, stimulus.
प्रोत्साहन *n.* Stimulating
प्रोथ् *vi.* 1 U. To be full; to be equal.
प्रोथ Fixed; *m.* The nostrils of a horse; the hip.
प्रोषित *a.* Living abroad
प्रोषितभर्तृका *f.* A woman whose husband is abroad.
प्रोष्ठ *m.* A bull.
प्रोढ *a.* Full-grown, adult; thick, bold, strong.
प्रौढि *f.* Full development; greatness, boldness, enterprise.
प्लक्ष *m.* Indian fig-tree; one of the seven continents of the world; a side-door.
प्लव *a.* Swimming. *m.* A boat, a frog, a monkey, a slope. [monkey.
प्लवग or प्लवंग, (-म) *m.* A
प्लवन *n.* A deluge. [ened.
प्लावित *a.* Overflowed, moist-
प्लीहा *f.* The spleen.
प्लु *vi.* I A. To float; to jump; with अभि-to overflow; अव-to jump; आ-to bathe; उप-to assault, to harass. [*n.* A jump.
प्लुत *a.* Floating; protracted.
प्लुति *f.* A jump; protraction.
प्लुष् *vi.* I 4 P. To burn.
प्लुष्ट *a.* Burnt
प्सा *vt.* 2 P. To devour.
प्सान *n.* Eating, food.

फ.

फक्किका *f.* A thesis.
फट *m.* फटा *f.* The expanded hood of a serpent.
फण् *vi.* 1 P. To go.
फण *m.* फणा *f.* See फट.
फणिन् *m.* The hooded serpent.
फणिफेन *m.* Opium.
फल् *vi.* 1 P. To split, to go. *vt.* P. To bear fruit.

फल *n.* A fruit, result, reward, a deed, an object, profit; offspring, a gift, a board, a product, a plough-share.

फलक *m.* A board, a shield, a flat surface.

फलतः *ind.* Really.

फलन *n.* Fructifying.

फलिन् *a.* Bearing fruit.

फलिन *a.* Fruitful.

फल्गु *a.* Unsubstantial. *f.* Name of a river.

फल्गुन, फाल्गुन *m.* Name of a month. [stellation.

फल्गुनी *f.* Name of a constellation.

फाल *n.* A ploughshare.

फाल्गुन *m.* Name of a month; Arjuna.

फिरंगिन् *m.* A European.

फुत्कार, फूत्कार *m.* Hissing.

फुप्फुस *m. n.* The lungs.

फुल्ल् *vi.* 1 P. To open.

फुल्ल *a.* Blown, expanded.

फेन(-ण), फेणक *m.* Foam.

फेनिल *a.* Foamy; frothy.

फेरव *m.* A jackal; a demon.

फेरु *m.* A jackal.

फेल *n.* फेला *f.* फेलिका *f.* फेली *f.* Remnants of food.

ब

बंहिमन् *m.* Abundance; multitude. [abundant.

बंहिष्ठ *a.* Very great, very abundant.

बंहीयस् *a.* (comp. of बहुल) Much, more. [a rogue.

बक *m.* The Indian crane; a rogue.

बकव्रत *n.* Hypocrisy.

बटु *m.* A boy, a youth.

बत *ind.* Expressing pity, regret, joy, wonder.

बदर *n.* The jujube fruit.

बदरिका, बदरी *f.* The jujube tree or its fruit.

बद्ध *pp.* Tied, confined, cherished. [ed.

बद्धपरिकर *a.* Ready, prepared.

बद्धमुष्टि *a.* Close-fisted.

बद्धमूल *a.* Deeply rooted.

बद्धराग *a.* Impassioned.

बधिर *a.* Deaf.

बधिरिमन् *m.* Deafness.

बंदिन् *m.* A bard, a prisoner.

बंदी *f.* Confinement.

बंध् *vt.* 9 P. To bind; to fix; to attract; to wear; to compose; with अनु-to be attached to; to follow; with आ-to form; उद्-to tie; नि—to fasten; to build; निस्—to press; परि—to stop; प्रति—to tie; to encase; to obstruct; to shut out; सम्-to unite; to attach.

बंध *m.* A bond, a hair-bond, confinement, arranging, union, agreement, result, border, body, display.

बंधक *m*. A binder; a tie, a bank, a deposit, a ravisher, a promise.

बंधन *n*. A bond, captivity, a prison, a sinew.

बंधु *m*. A relative, a brother, a friend; a husband.

बंधु (धू) र *a* Fluctuating; uneven handsome.

बंधुल *a*. Bent; attractive. *m*. A bastard.

बंध्य *a*. Unproductive.

बंध्या *f*. A barren woman.

बभ्रु *a*. Brown.

बंभर *m* A bee. [fool.

बर्बर *m*. A non-Aryan; a

बर्ह् *vt*. I. A. To hurt; to give; with नि-to destroy.

बर्ह *m.n*. The tail of a bird.

बर्हि *m*. Fire.

बर्हिण *m*. A peacock.

बर्हिन् *m*. A peacock.

बर्हिस् *m*. Fire; light. *n*. Water. [a sprout.

बल *n*. Power, figure, army,

बलक्ष *a*. White.

बलचक्र *n* Supremacy; an army. [battle.

बलज *n*. A field; a grain;

बलद *m*. An ox.

बलद्विष् *m*. Indra.

बलभद्र *m*. A strong man.

बलभृत् *a*. Strong.

बलवत *ind*. Forcibly; in a high degree.

बलाक *m*. A crane. [tress.

बलाका *f*. A crane; a mis-

बलात्कार *m*. Violence; injustice.

बलाबल *n*. Comparative strength or weakness.

बलाह *n*. Water.

बलाहक *m*. A cloud; a crane.

बलि *m*. An oblation, a gift; worship; a tax; name of a demon. *f*. A wrinkle.

बलिन् *a*. Strong.

बलिन *a*. Wrinkled.

बलिभ *a*. Wrinkled.

बलिभुज् *m*. A crow.

बलिमन् *m*. Power.

बलिमंदिर *n*. The infernal regions.

बलिवर्द *m*. A bull

बलिष्ठ *a*. Most powerful.

बलिष्णु *a*. Despised.

बलिहरण *n*. An offering of oblation to all creatures.

बलीयस् *a*. More powerful.

बलीवर्द *m*. A bull; an ox.

बल्लव *m*. A Cowherd; a cook.

बहल *a*. Much; thick; hard.

बहिस् *ind*. Out of doors; outside. [circumstance.

बहिरुपाधि *m*. An external

बहिश्चर *a*. External; outward.

बहु *a*. (Comp. भूयस्; super. भूयिष्ठ) Much; frequent.

बहुक *m*. The sun.

बहुकर *a.* Diligent.
बहुकरी *f.* A broom. [ing.
बहुकालीन *a.* Of long-stand-
बहुतिथ *a.* Much.
बहुधा *ind.* Variously.
बहुमति *f.* Great value.
बहुल *a.* Abundant, thick, full. *m.* The dark half of a month. *n.* The sky.
बहुला *f.* A cow.
बहुविध *a.* Manifold diverse.
बहुव्रीहि *m.* Name of a compound in Sanskrit grammar.
बहुशस् *ind.* Frequently.
बाढ *a.* (Comp. साधीयस्, super. साधिष्ठ) Firm.
बाढम् *ind.* Certainly.
बाण *m* An arrow, aim; name of a demon; name of a Sanskrit poet.
बाणिनी *f.* A drunken woman.
बादरायण (-णि) *m.* Vyâsa
बादरायणसंबंध *m* An imaginary relation.
बाध *vt* I. A. To torment, to resist, to remove; with अभि–to inquire; आ–to vex; प्र–to avert; सम्–to troubla. [tion.
बाध *m* Pain, hurt; opposi-
बाधक *a* Troubling.
बाधना *f.* Pain.
बाधा *f.* Pain, annoyance, opposition.

24

बाधित *a.* Oppressed.
बाधिर्य *n.* Deafness.
बांधव *m.* A relation; a brother; a friend.
बांधव्य *n.* Consanguinity.
बाभ्रवी *f* Durgā.
बाल *a.* Young; new; unwise. *m.* A child, a fool; a hair. [A child.
बालक *a.* Young; unwise. *m.*
बालखिल्य *m.* A class of divine personages of extremely small stature.
बालतंत्र *n* Midwifery.
बालव्यजन *n.* A *Chowrie.*
बाला *f.* A girl, a young woman. [ring.
बालिका *f* A girl; an ear-
बालिमन् *m.* Boyhood.
बालिश *a.* Childish; foolish.
बालिश्य *n* Youth; folly.
बाली *f* An ear ring.
बालुका *f.* Sand.
बाल्य *n* Childhood. [iron.
बाष्प *m. n.* A tear, vapour,
बाह *m.* The arm.
बाहाबाहवि *ind.* Hand in hand.
बाहु *m.* The arm; the base of a right-angled triangle.
बाहुक *m.* A monkey.
बाहुज *m.* A Kshatriya.
बाहुपाश *m.* An embrace.
बाहुमूल *n.* An armpit.
बाहुयुद्ध *n.* A personal encounter.

बाहुल *m.* Fire, the month of कार्तिक.

बाहुलग्रीव *m.* A pea-cock.

बाहुल्य *n.* Multiplicity; plenty.

बाह्य *a.* Outward, foreign.

बिडाल,(-क) *m.* A cat.

बिंदु *m.* A drop; a point.

बिभित्सा *f.* A desire to break.

बिंब *m. n.* The disc of the sun or moon; a disc; a shadow, an image. *n.* A kind of fruit.

बिंबित *a.* Reflected.

बिल् *vt.* 6 P., 10 U. To split.

बिल *m.* A hole, a pit.

बिलंगम *m.* A snake.

बिल्व *m.* A kind of tree.

बिस *n.* The fibrous stalk of a lotus.

बिसतंतु *m.* The lotus fibre.

बिसनाभि *f.* The lotus plant.

बिसल *n.* A sprout.

बीज *n.* Seed, grain; origin, semen virile; the divine truth.

बीजगणित *n.* Algebra.

बीजमन्त्र *m.* The mystic syllable with which a *mantra* begins.

बीजल *a.* Full of seed.

बीभत्स *a.* Disgusting, envious, savage. *m.* Disgust; Arjuna.

बीभत्सु *m* Arjuna.

बुक्क *m. n.* The heart.

बुद्ध *a.* Wise, awakened. *m.* A wise man; the ninth incarnation of Vishnu.

बुद्धि *f.* Perception, intellect, knowledge, judgment, opinion, idea, intention.

बुद्धिपूर्व *a.* Intentional.

बुद्धिपूर्वम्, बुद्धिपुरःसरम् } *ind.* Intentionally.

बुद्धिमत्ता *f.* Wisdom.

बुद्धिशालिन् *a.* Intelligent.

बुद्ध्या *ind.* Intentionally.

बुद्बुद *m.* A bubble.

बुध् *vt. vi.* I. U. 4 A. To know, to mark, to consider, to awake; with अनु, अव, नि, सम्-to know; उद्, प्र, प्रति–to awake.

बुध *a.* Wise, intelligent. *m.* A wise man; a god; Mercury.

बुधदिन *n.* (-वार,-वासर *m.*) Wednesday.

बुधिल *a.* Learned.

बुभुक्षा *f.* Hunger.

बुभुक्षित *a.* Hungry.

बुभुक्षु *a.* Hungry; desirous of worldly enjoyment.

बुभूषा *f.* Desire of becoming.

बुभूषु *a.* Desirous of becoming.

बुलि *f.* Fear.

बुष *n.* Chaff; refuse.

बृंहित *n*. The roaring of an elephant.

बृह् *vi*. 1 P. To grow; with उद्-to raise up.

बृहत् *a*. Large, wide, ample, powerful, high. *n*. The supreme spirit.

बृहति *f*. A large lute; the part of the body between the breast and the back-bone.

बृहन्नट, बृहन्नल *m*. बृहन्नला *f*. Name assumed by Arjuna.

बृहस्पति *m*. The preceptor of the gods; Jupiter.

बृहस्पतिवार *m*. Thursday.

बैडाल *a*. Relating to a cat.

बैडालव्रत *n*. Concealing one's malice under the garb of piety.

बोध *m*. Perception, wisdom, instruction. [spy.

बोधक *a*. Instructing. *m*. A

बोधन *n*. Instruction, awkening, signifying. *m*. The planet Mercury.

बोधि *m*. Perfect knowldge.

बोधिसत्त्व *m*. One who has attained perfect wisdom.

बौद्ध *m*. A follower of Buddha.

बौधायन *m*. Name of a sage.

ब्रह्म *n*. The supreme spirit.

ब्रह्मन् *n*. The supreme spirit; a hymn; the Vedas; the sacred syllable *om*; the Brâhmana class; religious penance; chastity; final beatitude; theology, wealth, food. *m*. The creator, a Brâhmana; the sun.

ब्रह्मगोल *m*. The universe.

ब्रह्मघोष *m*. The recital of the Veda.

ब्रह्मचर्य *n*. Life of celibacy.

ब्रह्मचारिन् *m*. A religious student; a celibate.

ब्रह्मज्ञान *n*. Divine knowledge.

ब्रह्मण्य *m*. Vishnu; Saturn.

ब्रह्मतत्त्व *n*. True knowledge of the supreme spirit.

ब्रह्मत्व *n*. Absorption into the supreme spirit.

ब्रह्मनिर्वाण *n*. See ब्रह्मत्व.

ब्रह्मबंधु *m*. A contemptuous Brâhmana. [ble *om*.

ब्रह्मबीज *n*. The mystic sylla-

ब्रह्मभूति *f*. Twilight.

ब्रह्मभूयस् *n*. See ब्रह्मत्व.

ब्रह्मयज्ञ *m*. One of the five daily *Yajnas* to be performed by a Brâhmana.

ब्रह्मयोग *m*. Cultivation of spiritual knowledge.

ब्रह्मरंध्र *n*. An aperture in the crown of the head.

ब्रह्मलिखित *n*. The destiny.

ब्रह्मवर्चस् (-स) *m*. Eminence in sacred knowledge.

ब्रह्मवादिन् *m*. An expounder of the Vedas or the Vedánta philosophy.

ब्रह्मसत्र *n*. Recital of the Vedas.

ब्रह्मसूत्र *n*. The sacred thread.

ब्रह्मस्व *n*. The property of a Brâhamna.

ब्रह्महृदय *m n*. Name of a star.

ब्रह्मांड *n*. The Universe.

ब्रह्मार्पण *n*. The offering of sacred knowledge.

ब्रह्मास्त्र *n*. A kind of missile.

ब्रह्मानंद *m*. The rapture of absorption into the supreme spirit.

ब्राह्म *a*. Relating to Brâhmana; holy. *m*. A form of marriage.

ब्राह्ममुहूर्त *m*. The early part of the day.

ब्राह्मण *m*. A man of the priestly class among Hindus. *n*. A particular portion of the Veda.

ब्राह्मणक *m*. A vile Brâhmana.

ब्राह्मणब्रुव *m*. A Brâhmana only in name.

ब्राह्मणी *f*. A woman of the Brâhmana caste.

ब्राह्मण्य *m*. A multitude of Brâhmanas.

ब्राह्मी *f*. The goddess of speech

ब्रू *vt*. 2 U. To speak; to call; with प्रति-to answer.

भ

भ *m*. Venus, error. *n*. A star, a bee.

भक्त *a*. Divided; devoted to. *m*. A votary. *n*. A share, food, boiled rice.

भक्तदास *m*. A slave who receives only his meals as a return for his services.

भक्तवत्सल *a*. Kind to devotees.

भक्ति *f*. Partition, devotion; faith; service, texture.

भक्तिभाज् *v*. Devout, loyal.

भक्तिमार्ग *m*. Devotion to God as the way to salvation.

भक्तियोग *m* Loyal devotion.

भक्तिरस *m*. Sense of devotion.

भक्तिराग *m*. Affection

भक्तिमत् *a*. Devout, pious.

भक्तृ *a*. Devoutly attached.

भक्ष् *vt*. 10 U. To eat.

भक्षक *a*. One who eats.

भक्षण *n*. Eating.

भक्षणीय *a*. Eatable.

भक्षित *a*. Eaten. *n*. Food

भक्ष्य *n*. Food.

भग *m*. The sun, the moon, luck, prosperity, beauty, fame love, virtue, desire, effort, final beatitude, strength.

भगदेव *m*. A libertine.

भगंदर *m*. A fistula in the anus.

भगवत् *a*. Glorious, divine. *m*. A deity. [did.

भगिन् *a*. Prosperous; splen-

भगिनी *f*. A sister, a woman.

भागिनीय *m*. A sister's son.

भगीरथ *m*. Name of a king.

भगीरथप्रयत्न *m*. A herculean effort.

भग्न *a*. Broken; defeated.

भग्नी *f*. A sister.

भक्ति *f*. Breaking; a fracture.

भंग *m*. Spliting; a break; a division, a piece, failure, rejection, a wave, fraud, a canal.

भंगा *f*. Hemp.

भंगिन् *a*. Fragile, perishable.

भंगिमन् *m*. A breach, perversity, deceit.

भंगी *f*. A breach; a division, a wave a current, a crooked path, irony, fraud, a step, modesty.

भंगुर *a*. Fragile, bent.

भचक्र *n*. The zodiac.

भज् *vt*. 1 U. To divide, to resort to, to enjoy, to choose, to be attached to; with वि-to divide; संवि-to admit to a share.

भजक *m*. A worshipper.

भजन *n*. Worship.

भजमान *a*. Right, proper.

भंज् *vt*. 7 P. To break; to frustrate. [moving.

भंजन *n*. Destroying; re-

भट्ट *m*. A soldier.

भट्ट *m*. A tittle of respect; a learned man.

भट्टारक *a*. Venerable.

भट्टिनी *f*. A queen not crowned; a woman of high rank.

भण् *vt*. I. P. To speak.

भणन *n*., भणित *n*., भणिति *f*. Talk, conversation.

भंड *m*. A jester; an actor.

भंडि (-डी) *f*. A wave.

भंडिल *n*. Fortunate.

भदंत *m*. A term of respect.

भद्र *a*. Auspicious, able, dear, chief. *n*. Prosperity.

भद्रा *f*. A cow; name of the 2nd, 7th & 12th days of a lunar fortnight.

भद्रासन *n*. A throne.

भय *n*. Fear, danger *m*. A disease. [fearful.

भय (यं) कर *a*. Terrifying;

भयप्रद *a*. Terrible.

भयातुर, भयार्त *a*. Alarmed.

भयानक *a*. Terrible. *n*. A terror.

भयावह *a*. Dangerous.

भर *m.* A burden; theft; a multitude; excess.

भरण *n.* Maintaining; hire; nutriment; wages.

भरणी *f.* Name of a constellation. [an ox.

भरंड *m.* A master, a king,

भरण्य *n.* Wages.

भरत *m.*Name of a king. N. of a sage; one of the brothers of Ráma.

भरतखंड *n.* Name of a part of India.

भरतवर्ष *n.* India.

भरतवाक्य *n.*The final benediction or chorus.

भरित *a.* Nourished, full of.

भर्ग *m.* Śiva; Brahman (*m.*);

भर्जन *n.* Roasting.

भर्तृ *m.*A husband; lord.

भर्तृदारक *m.*A crown prince.

भर्तृदारिका *f.* A princess.

भर्तृहरि *m.* Name of a well-known author.

भर्त्स् *vt.* 10 U. To abuse; with निस्-to reproach.

भर्त्सन *n.*, भर्त्सना *f*, भर्त्सित *n.* Threat; reproach.

भर्मन् *n.* Support, wages.

भल् *vt.* 10 A. To see; with नि-to see. [missile.

भल्ल *m.* भल्ली *f.* A kind of

भल्लु (ल्लू) क *m.* A bear

भव *m.* Existence; world; life origin; prosperity; Śiva.

भवत् *a.* Being, present; a term of respect (Your honour).

भवदीय *a.* Your honour's.

भवन *n.* Existence, birth, nature, house, a field.

भवंत *m.*, भवंति *f.* The present time.

भवंती *f.* A virtuous wife.

भवभूति *m.* Name of a famous poet.

भवादृक्ष, भवादृश्, भवादृश *a.* One like you

भवानी *f.* Parvatî.

भवाब्धि, भवार्णव, भवसमुद्र, भवसिंधु *m.* The ocean of worldly existence.

भवितव्य *n.* What is destined to happen.

भवितव्यता *f* Destiny.

भविष्य, भविष्यत् *a.* Future *n.* Futurity.

भव्य *a* Existing; future; suitable, good happy. *n.* Existence, future time, result, prosperity.

भसित *n.* Ashes.

भस्मन् *n.* Holy ashes.

भस्मरोग *m.* A kind of disease. [ashes.

भस्मसात् कृ To reduce to

भा *vi.* 2 P. To shine, to seem, to be; with अभि, आ, निस्, प्र, प्रति, वि, व्यति -to shine.

भा *f.* Lustre, shadow.
भाक्त *a.* Dependent, inferior.
भाग *m.* A part, a quarter, division, place.
भागधेय *n* A share, destiny, property. *m.* A tax.
भागवत *m.* A devotee of Vishnu; name of a Purána. [ing interest.
भागिक *a.* Fractional; bear-
भागिन् *n.* Sharing in; lucky.
भागिनेय *m.* A sister's son.
भागिनेयी *f.* A sister's daughter.
भागीरथी *f.* The Ganges.
भाग्य *n.* Luck, happiness.
भाग्ययोग *m.* The accession of good luck
भाग्यवत् *a.* Fortunate.
भाग्यवशात् *ind.* Fortunately.
भाज् *vt.* 10 U. To divide; with सं,वि-to admit to a share.
भाज् *a.* (at the end of a comp.) Entitled to; sharing
भाजक *m.* A divisor.
भाजन *n.* Division, a vessel, a deserving person.
भाज्य *n* A portion; the dividend (in Mathe.)
भाण *m.* A kind of dramatic composition.
भांड *n.* A vessel, a tool.
भांडागार *m. n.* A treasury.
भांडार *n.* A store-house.
भांडारिन् *m.* The keeper of a store-house.
भाति *f.* Light, knowledge.
भाद्र, भाद्रपद *m.* Name of a lunar month.
भान *n.* Light, knowledge.
भानु *m.* Light, the sun.
भानुमत् *a.* Luminous; handsome. *m.* The sun.
भामा *f.* A passionate woman. [woman.
भामिनी *f.* A handsome
भार *m.* A burden, excess, labour.
भारत *m.* A descendant of Bharata; a native of India. *n.* India.
भारती *f.* Speech.
भारद्वाज *m.* Drona; Agastya; Planet Mars; a sky lark.
भारयष्टि *f.* A peg; a pole.
भारवाह *m.* A porter. [den.
भारवाहन *m.* A beast of bur-
भार्गव *m.* Śukra; name of Parashuráma.
भार्या *f.* Wife.
भाल *n.* The forehead.
भालचंद्र *m.* Śiva, Ganesha.
भालपट्ट *m. n.* The forehead.
भाललोचन *m.* Śiva.
भालु *m.* The sun. [The bear.
भालु (लू) क, भाल्लु (ल्लू) क *m.*
भाव *m.* State, existence, manner, temper, sentiment, love, inclination of mind; opinion, con-

templation, soul, thing, conduct; the world, intention; a learned man.

भावक *m.* Sentiment.

भावगंभीरम् *ind.* Gravely.

भावज *m.* God of love.

भावन *m.* An efficient cause. *n.* Imagination, reflection, perception; proof.

भावना *f.* See भावन.

भावमिश्र *m.* A man of consequence.

भावरूप *a.* Real, actual.

भाववाचक *n.* An abstract noun. [two emotions.

भावसंधि *m.* Co-existence of

भावसर्ग *m.* The intellectual creation. [tached.

भावस्निग्ध *a.* Sincerely at-

भाविक *a.* Natural, real, sentimental.

भाविन् *a.* Future.

भाविनी *f.* A noble woman.

भावुक *a.* Happy. *m.* A sister's husband. *n* Welfare.

भाव्य *n.* Futurity.

भाष् *vt.* 1 A. To speak; with अप-to abuse; अभि-to address; आ-to address; परि-to speak conventionally; प्रति-to reply, to call; वि-to lay down optionally; सम्-to converse.

भाषण *n* Speech.

भाषा *f.* Speech, language, a vernacular dialect.

भाषांतर *n.* Translation.

भाषिका *f.* Speech, language.

भाषित *n.* Speech, language.

भाष्य *n.* A commentary.

भाष्यकर (-कार, -कृत्) *m.* A commentator.

भास् *vi.* 1 A. To shine.

भास् *m.* Light, a reflection, glory, desire.

भास *m.* Lustre, brightness. Name of a poet.

भासु *m.* The sun.

भासुर *a.* Shining; terrible.

भास्कर *m.* The sun.

भास्वर *a.* Brilliant. *m.* The sun; a day.

भिक्ष् *vt. vi.* 1 A. To beg.

भिक्षण *f.* Begging.

भिक्षा *f.* Begging. [alms.

भिक्षावृत्ति *f.* Living on

भिक्षु *m.* A beggar.

भिक्षुक *m.* A beggar; a mendicant.

भित्त *n.* A part, a wall.

भित्ति *f.* A wall, a piece, a defect. [tion.

भित्तिका *f.* A wall; a parti-

भिद् *vt.* 1 P. To divide; *vt.* 7 U. To break; to open; to change, to become loose; to interrupt; to betray; with उद् to grow; निस्-to tear up; to flow;

प्रति-to censure.
भिदुर *a.* Brittle; mixed
भिद्य *m.* A rushing river.
भिंद् (दि) पाल *m.* A small javeline; a sling.
भिन्न *a.* Broken, different.
भिन्नार्थ *a.* Intelligible.
भिल्ल *m.* N. of a wild tribe.
भिषज् *m.* A physician.
भी *vi.* 3 P. To fear.
भी *f.* Fear, alarm. [of.
भीत *a.* Frightened; afraid
भीति *f.* Fear, terror.
भीम *a.* Terrible. *m* N. of the second Pândava.
भीमनाद *m.* A lion. [dava.
भीमसेन *m.*N. of second Pân-
भीरु *a.* Timid, afraid of.
भीलु (ल्लू) क *m* A bear.
भीषण *a.* Formidable.
भीषा *f.* Terror.
भीष्म *a.* Terrible.
भुक्त *pp.* Eaten, enjoyed.
भुक्ति *f.* Enjoyment; food, eating.
भुग्न *a.* Bent, bowed
भुज् *vt.* 6 P. To bend; 7 U. To eat, to enjoy, to govern, to suffer.
भुज *m* The arm, hand, a side of a figure.
भुजग *m.* A snake. [mour.
भुजंग *m.* A snake; a para-
भुजंगम *m.* A serpent; Râhu.
भुजा *f.* The arm; hand.
भुवन *m.* Mankind; world.
भुवर्, भुवस् *ind.* The atmosphere, ether.
भुविस् *m.* The ocean.
भू *vi* 1 P. To be, to arise, to live, to remain; *vt.* 1 U. To obtain; *vt.* 10 A. To attain; to regard as; (*causal* भावयति-ते) To bring into existence; to cherish; to exhibit; to know; to prove; with उद् to produce; वि-to contemplate; सम् to consider; to honour.
भू *a.* (At the end of a comp.) Springing from.
भू *f.* The earth, ground, lane, place, subject.
भूकंप *m* An earth-quake.
भूगोल *m* A terrestrial globe
भूगोलविद्या *f.* Geography.
भूचक्र *n.* The equator.
भूत *a.* Past. *m.* A son; S'iva. *n.* A creature, a living being, a ghost, an element; the past, welfare, the number 'five'.
भूतकाल *m.* The preterite tense; past time.
भूतगण *m.* A class of demons.
भूतग्राम *m.* The aggregate of living beings; the body.
भूतदया *f.* Universal benevolence.

भूतनाथ *m.* S'iva.
भूतपूर्व *a.* Prior.
भूतपूर्वम् *ind.* Formerly. [nu.
भूतभावन *m.* Brahmá; Vish-
भूतविज्ञान *n.* (-विद्या *f.*) Demonology. [session.
भूतसंचार *m.* Demoniac pos-
भूतसंप्लव *m* Universal deluge.
भूतात्मन् *m.* The individual soul. [demon.
भूतार्त *a.* Possessed by
भूतार्थ *m.* Reality. [session.
भूतावेश *m.* Demoniac pos-
भूति *f.* Birth, existence; majesty; ashes; riches; welfare; decoration of elephants. [state.
भूतिकाम *m.* A minister of
भूतिकील *m.* A hole; a cellar.
भूमन् *m.* Abundance.
भूमि *f.* The earth; land; posture; a character; subject; degree.
भूमिकंप *m.* An earth-quake.
भूमिका *f.* Earth; step; a character in a play; a preface.
भूमिज *m.* The planet Mars.
भूमिदेव *m* A Brâhmana.
भूमिनाथ (-प,-पति,-पाल,-भुज्) *m.* A king.
भूमिलाभ *m.* Death.
भूमिवर्धन *m.n.* A dead body.
भूमी *f.* See भूमि
भूम्रा *ind.* Abundantly.
भूय *n.* Becoming.
भूयस् *a.* More numerous or abundant; greater.
भूयस् *ind.* Exceedingly; again; moreover, repeatedly; for the most part.
भूयशस् *ind.* Again.
भूयिष्ठ *a.* Most numerous; nearly.
भूयिष्ठम् *ind.* Mostly.
भूर् *ind.* The first of the three mystical syllables uttered by Brâhmanas.
भूरि *a.* Much, great. *ind.* Exceedingly. [tree.
भूर्ज *m.* A species of birch
भूष् *vt.* 1 P. 10 U. To adorn.
भूषण *n.* An ornament.
भूषा *f.* Adorning; an ornament. [perity.
भूष्णु *a.* Being; desiring pros-
भृ *vt.* 1 U. 3 U. To bear; to nourish; to hold; to suffer; to bestow; to fill; with सम्-to collect; to prepare; to offer.
भृकुटि (-टी) *f.* Knitting of the eye-brows.
भृगु *m.* N. of a sage; Jamadagni; S'ukra; a cliff.
भृगुनंदन *m.* Parashurâma.
भृगुवार (-वासर) *m.* Friday.
भृंग *m.* A large black bee.
भृंगार *m. n.* A golden jar.
भृंगी *m.* N. of an attendant.

of S'iva. *f.* The female of the large black bee.

भृज् *vt.* 1 A. To fry.

भृत *a.* Borne, supported, full of. *m.* A hired servant.

भृति *f.* Nourishment; maintenance; wages.

भृत्य *m.* A servant, a minister.

भृत्यजन *m.* A dependant.

भृत्यता *f.* (-त्व *n*) Service.

भृत्यवर्ग *m.* The body of servants.

भृश् *vi.* 4 P. To fall down.

भृश *a.* Intense, strong.

भृशम् *ind.* Exceedingly.

भृष्ट *a.* Fried.

भॄ *vt.* 9 P. (*pp.* भूर्ण) To nourish; to reproach.

भेक *m.* A frog; a cloud.

भेकी *f.* A small frog (fem. of भेक).

भेद *m.* Interruption; breach; disturbance, change, disuniou; difference, variety.

भेदक *a.* Separating.

भेदन *n.* Splitting.

भेदिर, भेदुर *n.* A thunderbolt.

भेद्य *n.* A substantive.

भेर *m.* A kettle-drum.

भेरी *f.* A kettle-drum.

भेलक *m. n.* A boat.

भेषज *n.* A medicine.

भैक्ष *a. n.* Begging; alms.

भैक्ष्य *n.* Alms, charity.

भैरव *a.* Terrible. *m.* A form of Śiva.

भैरवी *f.* Durgâ; N. of a Râginî.

भैषज *n.* A drug, medicine.

भैषज्य *n.* A drug.

भोक्तृ *a.* Enjoying. *m.* A king; a lover.

भोग *m.* Eating; use; enjoyment; sexual enjoyment; rule; a banquet; profit; the body of a serpent; a snake.

भोगिन् *a.* Enjoying, rich. *m.* A serpent.

भोग्य *a.* To be enjoyed. *n.* Wealth.

भोग्या *f.* harlot.

भोज *m.* N. of a country; N. of a king of Mâlwâ.

भोजन *n.* Taking one's meals; eating food.

भोजनीय *n.* Food.

भोज्य *n.* Food; enjoyment.

भोस *ind.* A particle of addressing; O! Oh!

भौतिक *a.* Elemental; material. *n.* A pearl.

भौम *a.* Earthly.

भामवार (-वासर) *m.* Tuesday.

भौमिक, भौम्य *a.* Earthly.

भ्रंश् *vi.* 1 A. 4 P. To fall; to decline; to escape; with परि or वि-to go astray.

भ्रंश *m.* Falling off; overthrow; ruin; loss.

भ्रम् *vt., vi.* 1, 4 P. To wander, to circulate; to waver, to fall in error, to flicker; with उद् to be confused or mad; परि–to ramble; वि–to scatter; सम्–to err; to be confused.

भ्रम *m.* A whirpool; a potter's wheel; a circular motion; an error; confusion; delusion.

भ्रमण *n.* Wandering about; giddiness.

भ्रमर *m.* A large black bee, a libertine. *n.* Giddiness.

भ्रमि *f.* Revolving; a whirl-wind; an error.

भ्रष्ट *a.* Fallen off; ruined, lost; vicious.

भ्रस्ज् *vt.* 6 U. To fry.

भ्राज् *vi.* 1 A. To shine.

भ्राजथु *m* Brilliance.

भ्रातृ *m.* A brother; an intimate friend; a relative.

भ्रातृहत्या *f.* Fratricide.

भ्रातृव्य *m.* A nephew.

भ्रात्रीय, भ्रात्रेय *m.* A nephew.

भ्रात्र्य *n.* Brotherhood.

भ्रांत *a.* Mistaken; perplexed. *n.* Wandering; an error.

भ्रांति *f.* Revolution; delusion, perplexity; doubt.

भ्राम *m.* Delusion.

भ्राश्, भ्लाश् *vi.* 1, 4 A. To [shine

भ्रास्, भ्लास् *vi.* 1, 4 A. To shine.

भ्रू *f.* An eye-brow.

भ्रूकुटि (-टी) *f.* A frown; contraction of the eye-[brow.

भ्रूक्षेप *m.* See भ्रूकुटि.

भ्रूण *m.* An embryo, a child.

भ्रूभंग, भ्रूभेद *m.* See भ्रूकुटि.

भ्रूविक्षेप *m.* See भ्रूकुटि.

भ्रूहति, भ्रूहत्या *f.* Procuring abortion.

म

म *m.* Brahmà; Vishnu; S'iva; Yama; time. *n.* Water, happiness.

मकर *m.* A crocodile.

मकरकेतन (-केतु; -ध्वज; -केतुमत्) *m.* God of love.

मकरंद *m.* The honey of flowers.

मकरराशि *m.* The sign *Capri-*[*cornus.*

मकरसंक्रमण *n.* The passing of the sun into *Capricornus.*

मकरिन् *m.* An ocean.

मकुर *m.* A mirror.

मकुल *m.* A bud.

मक्ष *m.* Hypocrisy.

मक्षिका *f.* A fly.

मख *m.* A sacrifice; an ob-[lation.

मगध *m.* The South Behar.

मग्न *a.* Plunged; absorbed.

मघवत् *m.* Indra.

मघवन् *m* Indra.

मघा *f.* N. of the tenth lunar [mansion.

मघोनी *f.* Wife of Indra.
मंक्षु *ind.* Quickly.
मंगल *a.* Lucky. *m.* Mars. *n.* Bliss; festivity.
मंगलवार *m.* Tuesday.
मंगलसूत्र *n.* The marriage string worn by married women. [stanza.
मंगलाष्टक *n.* A benedictory.
मंगलाचरण *n.* An auspicious introduction.
मंगलीय, मंगल्य *a.* Auspicious.
मज्जन *n.* Sinking; ablution.
मज्जा *f.* The marrow.
मज्जूषा *f.* A basket.
मंच, मंचक *m.* A raised platform; a dais; a bed; a couch.
मंजरि (–री) *f.* A shoot; a cluster of blossoms.
मंजिका *f.* A courtezan.
मंजिमन् *m.* Beauty.
मंजीर (-ल) *m.n.* An anklet.
मंजु, (-ल) *a.* Lovely.
मंजूषा *f.* A box; a case.
मठ *m. n.* A monastery; a school; a temple.
मठी *f.* A cell; a cloister,
मणि *m.* A jewel, a magnet, the wrist.
मणिकर्णिका *f.* N. of a sacred pool in Benares.
मणिकार *m.* A jeweller.
मणिबंध *m.* The wrist.
मणिमत् *m.* The sun.

मंड् *vt.* 1 P. 10 U. To adorn.
मंडप *m.* An open hall; a pavilion. [ment.
मंडन *n.* Decorating; ornament.
मंडल *m.* A dog. *n.* A circle, a disc; a group; a district; horizon.
मंडलक *n.* A circle; a disc.
मंडा *f.* A spirituous liquor.
मंडूक *m.* A frog.
मंडूर *n.* Rust of iron.
मत *a.* Thought; honoured. *n.* Opinion, aim. [cloud.
मतंग *m.* An elephant; a
मतंगज *m.* An elephant.
मतल्लिका *f.* Anything excellent of its kind.
मति *f.* Understanding; reverence, opinion, wish.
मतिपूर्वकम् *ind* Knowingly.
मत्क *a.* Mine. *m.* A bug.
मत्कुण *m.* A bug; a buffalo.
मत्त *a.* Intoxicated; mad; furious; proud.
मत्स *m.* A fish.
मत्सर *a.* Envious *m.* Envy, jealousy; a mosquito.
मत्सरिन् *a.* Envious; greedy, wicked. [*m.* A fish.
मत्स्य *m.pl.* N. of a country.
मत्स्यबंधन *n.* An angle.
मथ् *vt.* 1 P. To churn; to kill.
मथन *n.* Churning killing, friction; injury.

मथि *f.* A churning stick.

मथिन् *m.* A churning stick.

मद् *vi.* 4 P. To be drunk or mad; with प्र-to swerve from; to err; सम्-to be glad.

मद *m.* Intoxication; madness; lust; rut; pride, joy, desire.

मदकल *a.* Furious. [lust.

मदन *m.* God of love; love;

मदनमोहन *m.* Krishna.

मदार *m.* A rogue; an elephant.

मदिर *a.* Intoxicating.

मदिरा *f.* Wine.

मदिराक्षी *f.* A woman with fascinating eyes.

मदिरागृह *n.* A tavern.

मदीय *a.* Mine.

मद्य *n.* Wine.

मद्यप *m.* A drunkard.

मद्र *m.* N. of a country (Madras). *n.* Joy.

मधु *a.* Pleasant. *m.* The spring. *n.* Honey; sugar; spirituous liquor.

मधुकर *m.* A large black bee; a lover.

मधुज *n.* Wax.

मधुप *m.* A bee.

मधुपर्क *m.* (A mixture of honey) An offering made to a respectable guest on his arrival.

मधुमक्षिका *f.* A bee.

मधुमेह *m.* Diabetes.

मधुलिह् (-लिह,-लेहिन्,-लोलुप) *m.* A bee.

मधुर *a.* Sweet; agreeable. *m.* Molasses. *n.* Poison.

मधुरम् *ind.* Sweetly.

मधुरिमन् *m.* Sweetness.

मधुवार *m. pl.* Drinking repeatedly. [tree.

मधूक *m.* A bee. N. of a

मधूच्छिष्ट *n* Wax.

मध्य *a.* Middle; neutral; just. *m. n.* The centre; the waist. *n.* Ten thousand billions.

मध्य (ध्यं) दिन *m.* Noon.

मध्यम *a.* Middle; moderate.

मध्यमा *f.* A woman arrived at puberty.

मध्यलोक *m.* The earth.

मध्यवर्तिन् *m.* A mediator.

मध्यवेला *f.* मध्यसमय *m.* Noon-tide.

मध्यस्थ *a.* Intermediate; impartial. *m.* An umpire; an arbitrator.

मध्व *m.* N. of an A'chárya.

मन् *vi.* 10 A. To be proud; *vt.* 4, 8 A. To think; with अनु-to permit; अभि-to approve; अव-to disregard; सम्-to think much of. [ence.

मनन *n.* Reflection; infer-

मनस् *n.* Mind, thought, wish.

मनसिज *m.* Love.
मनस्कांत *a.* Agreeable.
मनस्विन् *a.* Resolute, prudent.
मनाक् *ind.* A little.
मनीषा *f.* Desire.
मनीषिका *f.* Intelligence.
मनीषित *a.* Desired. *n.* Wish.
मनीषिन् *a.* Intelligent, wise. *m.* A learned man.
मनु *m.* N. of a sage.
मनुज *m.* A man.
मनुष्य *m.* A man.
मनोगत *n.* Wish, thought.
मनोजव *a.* Quick as thought.
मनोज्ञ *a.* Pleasing.
मनोनीत *a.* Chosen. [love.
मनोभव, मनोभू *m.* God of
मनोमय *a.* Mental.
मनोरंजन *n.* Entertainment.
मनोरथ *m.* Desired object.
मनोरम *a.* Charming. [air.
मनोराज्य *n.* A castle in the
मनोविकार *m.* An emotion.
मनोवृत्ति *f.* Disposition.
मनोहत *a.* Disappointed.
मनोहारिन् *a.* Fascinating.
मन्तु *m.* A fault; an offence.
मंत्र् *vt.* 10 A. To consult; to speak; with अनु or परि-to win over; अभि-to consecrate by *Mantras*; to speak; नि-to invite; सम्-to consult.
मंत्र *m.* A Vedic hymn; the Samhitá portion of the Veda; a sacred formula; counsel.
मंत्रजिव्ह *m.* Fire. [tion.
मंत्रण *n.* मंत्रणा *f.* Delibera-
मंत्रविद्या *f.* Magic. [state.
मंत्रि *m.* A minister of
मंत्रिन् *m.* A minister.
मंथ् *vt.* 9 P. To shake; to kill; to oppress; to churn.
मंथ(-न) *m.* A churning stick
मंथन *n.* Churning.
मंथनी *f.* A churning vessel.
मंथर *a.* Lazy, stupid; large. *m.* A churning stick; anger, a treasure.
मंथा *f.* A churning stick.
मंद *a.* Slow; silly, feeble.
मंदम् *ind.* Slowly, gently.
मंदाक *n.* A stream.
मंदाकिनी *f.* The Ganges.
मंदार, मंदारक, मंदारव, मंदारु *m.* The coral tree.
मंदिमन् *m.* Dullness.
मंदिर *n.* A palace, a temple.
मंदुरा *f.* A stable.
मंद्र *a.* Hollow. *m.* A drum.
मन्मथ *m.* The god of love.
मन्मन *m.* Confidential whispering.
मन्यु *m.* Anger, sorrow, Śiva.
मम *a.* My; mine.
ममता *f.* Self-interest; pride
ममत्व *n.* Pride; sense of ownership.

मय *a*. Consisting of.
मयूख *m*. A ray of light, a flame.
मयूर, (-क) *m*. A pea-cock.
मरकत *n*. An emerald.
मरण *n* Death [flowers.
मरंद, (-क) *m*. The juice of
मराल *m*. A goose; a cloud.
मरीचि *m*. *f*. A ray of light.
मरीचिमालिन् *m*. The sun.
मरीचिका *f*. Mirage.
मरीचिन् *m*. The sun.
मरु *m*. A desert.
मरुत् *m*. Wind; a god.
मरुत *m*. Wind; a god.
मरुस्थली *f*. A waste, desert.
मर्कट *m*. A monkey; a spider. [man.
मर्त, मर्त्य *a*. Mortal. *m*. A
मर्त्यलोक *m*. The earth.
मर्दन *n*. Shampooing.
मर्मन् *n*. A vital part of the body; a weak point; pith; a secret [secret.
मर्मभेद *m*. Disclosing the
मर्मर *a*. Rustling.
मर्मस्पृश् *a*. Sharp.
मर्यादा *f*. A limit; a bank; propriety of conduct.
मर्शन *n*. Examination.
मर्ष *m*., (-ण *n*.) Endurance.
मल *m*. *n*. Dirt, dust, sin.
मलपृष्ठ *n*. The outer page of a book. [month.
मलमास *m*. An intercalary
मलय *m*. N. of a mountain.
मलयज *n*. A sandal tree.
मलाशय *m*. The belly.
मलिन *a*. Dirty; sinful; black.
मलिना, मलिनी *f*. A woman during menstruation.
मलिनिमन् *m*. Impurity.
मलीमस *a*. Dirty; impure.
मल्ल *a*. Strong. *m*. A wrestler. [match.
मल्लक्रीडा *f*. A wrestling
मल्लशाला *f*. A gymnasium.
मल्लिका *f*. Arabian jasmine.
मल्लिकाक्ष *m*. A kind of goose.
मशक *m*. A mosquito.
मस् *vt*. *vi*. 4 P. To weigh.
मसि(-सी) *f*. Ink; lamp-black.
मसूरिका *f*. Small-pox.
मसृण *a*. Soft; sweet.
मस्करिन् *m*. An ascetic.
मस्ज् *vi*. 6 P. (*pp*. मग्न) To bathe; to sink; with उद्-to come out of; नि-to sink.
मस्तक *m*. *n*. The head; top.
मस्तिष्क *m*. *n*. The brain.
मस्तु *n*. Whey.
मस्तुलुंग *m*. *n*. The brain.
मह *m*. A sacrifice.
महत् *a*. Large; intense.
महती *f*. A lute.
महनीय *a* Worthy of honour.
महन्त *m*. The head of a monastery.

महर्लोक *m.* The fourth of the seven worlds.

महस् *m.* A sacrifice; a festival.

महाकाल *m.* Śiva.

महाक्ष *m.* Śiva.

महाजन *m.* The chief of a trade; the general populace.

महात्मन् *a.* Noble.

महादशा *f.* Influence of a predominant planet on a man's destiny.

महादेव *m.* S'iva.

महानस *m. n.* A kitchen.

महानिद्रा *f.* Death.

महानिशा *f.* Dead night.

महानुभाव *a.* Magnanimous.

महामाया *f* Durgâ; worldly illusion.

महालय *m.* A temple.

महाशय *a.* Magnanimous.

महिमन् *m.* Greatness; glory.

महिर *m.* The sun.

महिला *f.* A woman.

महिष *m.* A buffalo.

महिषी *f.* A she-buffalo; the chief queen.

मही *f.* The earth; cow.

महीक्षित *m.* A king.

महीधर *m.* A mountain.

महीनाथ(-पा,-पति,-पाल,-भुज्, -भृत्,-मघवन्,-महेंद्र) *m.* A king.

महीभृत् *m.* A mountain.

महीयस् *a.* Larger, mightier.

महोदय *m.* Final beatitude; prosperity; pride.

मा *vt. vi.* 2 P., 3 A., 4 A. To measure, to be contained; with अनु-to infer; उप-to compare with; निस्-to create; to settle; to compose; परि, प्र, सम्-to measure

मा *ind.* A prohibitive particle meaning 'no, not, lest'.

मांस *n.* Flesh.

मांसग्रंथि *f.* A gland.

मांसज (-तेजस्,-सार) *n.* Fat.

मांसपेशी *f.* A muscle.

मांसल *a.* Fleshy.

मांसहासा *f.* Skin.

मांसाद *a.* Flesh-eating.

मांसिक *m.* A butcher.

माक्षिक *n.* Honey.

मागधी *f.* N. of a Prákirt dialect; refined sugar.

माघ *m.* N. of a lunar month; name of an author.

माघवती *f.* The east

मांगलिक *a.* Auspicious.

मांगल्य *n.* Welfare; auspiciousness.

माच (-ठ) *m.* A road.

माणव, (-क) *m* A boy; a lad; a dwarf.

माणिक्य *n.* A ruby.

मांडलिक *m.* The ruler of a province.

मातंग *m.* An elephant; a *chándála.*

मातरिश्वन् *m.* Wind.

मातलि *m.* N. of Indra's charioteer.

माता *f.* A mother.

मातामह *m.* A maternal grand-father.

मातामही *f.* A maternal grand-mother

मातुल *m.* A maternal uncle.

मातुला, (-नी), मातुली *f.* The wife of a maternal uncle.

मातृ *f.* A mother; a cow; Durgá; earth; an elderly woman. [mother.

मातृक *a.* Coming from a

मातृका *f.* A mother, source, an alphabet.

मातृगामिन् *m.* One who has committed incest with his mother.

मात्र *a.* As much; only, the same. *n* A measure.

मात्रा *f.* A measure; money; a little; an atom; a syllabic foot, the upper limb of a Nâgarî character.

मात्सर, मात्सरिक *a.* Jealous.

मात्सर्य *n.* Envy, jealously.

माद *m.* Joy, drunkenness, pride.

मादक *a.* Intoxicating

मादृश्, मादृश *a.* Like me.

माधव *m.* The spring; the month of वैशाख; Indra. Krishna.

माधवी *f.* A sacred basil; a kind of spirituous liquor.

माधुकरी *f.* Alms obtained from different places.

माधुरी *f.* Sweetness.

माधुर्य *n.* Sweetness.

माध्यस्थ्य *n.* Neutrality; indifference. [चार्य.

माध्व *m.* A follower of मध्वा-

मान् *vt.* 1 A. To seek knowledge.

मान *m.* Honour, pride, indignation. *n.* Proof; a measure; dimension; likeness. [rod.

मानदंड *m.* A measuring

मानभंग *m.* Insult; humiliation

मानना *f.* Respect.

माननीय *a.* Respectable.

मानव *m.* A man.

मानवधर्मशास्त्र *n.* The institutes of Manu.

मानस *a.* Mental; implied. *n.* The mind; N. of a lake.

मानसिक *a.* Mental.

मानिन् *a.* Proud.

मानिनी *f.* A woman indignant towards her lover

मानुष *a.* Human. *m.* A man.

मानुष्य, (-क) *n.* Human nature; mankind.

मांत्रिक *m.* A sorcerer.

मांद्य *n.* Slowness; weakness.

मान्य *a*. Respectable.
मापन *n*. Measuring.
माम *a*. My, mine.
मामक *m*. A miser; a maternal uncle.
माया *f*. Deceit, illusion; diplomacy.
मायात्मक *a*. Illusory.
मायाद *m*. A crocodile.
मायाविन् *a*. Employing deceit.
मायिक *a*. Deceitful.
मार *m*. Slaughter; god of love; the devil. [al rite.
मारण *n*. Killing; a magic-
मारांक *a*. Displaying signs of love.
मारात्मक *a*. Murderous.
मारिष *m*. A venerable person.
मारुत *m*. Wind. [ma.
मारुति *m*. Hanuman; Bhî-
मार्ग् *vt*., 1 P, 10 U. To seek; to solicit; with परि -to look for.
मार्ग *m*. A way, method, inquiry, style.
मार्गण *m*. A beggar. *n*. Begging. [month.
मार्गशीर्ष *m*. N. of a lunar
मार्गस्थ *a*. Travelling.
मार्गिक *m*. A traveller, a hunter.
मार्ज् *vt*. 10 U. To clean.
मार्जन *n*. Cleaning.
मार्जनी *f*. A broom.
मार्जार, (-क) *m*. A cat.
मार्जारी *f*. A female cat.
मार्जिता *f*. Curds with sugar and spices (श्रीखंड).
मार्तंड *m*. The sun.
मार्तिक *a*. Made of clay.
मार्त्य *n*. Mortality.
मार्दव *n*. Tenderness.
माल *n*. A field; a rising ground [jasmine.
मालति (-ती) *f*. A kind of
मालव *m*. N. of a country (Málwâ).
माला *f*. A garland, a row, a streak; a group.
मालाकार *m*. A gardener.
मालिक *m*. A gardener; a florist. [row.
मालिका *f*. A garland, a
मालिन्य *n*. Impurity. [land.
माल्य *n*. A flower; a gar-
माष *m*. A kind of bean; a particular weight.
मास् or मास *m*. A month.
मासक *m*. A year.
मासिक, मासीन *a*. Monthly.
माहात्म्य *n*. Greatness; an account giving merits of particular deities &c.
माहाराज्य *n*. Sovereignty.
माहिष *a*. Coming from a buffalo.
माहिषिक *m*. A buffalo keeper, a paramour.
माहेंद्री *f*. The east.
मि *vt*. 5 U. To throw.
मित *a*. Measured; moderate.
मिति *f*. Measure; weight; proof. [friend.
मित्र *m*. The sun. *n*. A

मिथस् *ind.* Secretly; mutually. [twins.

मिथुन *n.* A pair; union;

मिथ्या *ind.* Falsely, improperly; in vain.

मिथ्यादृष्टि *n.* Atheism.

मिल् *vt. vi.* 6 U. To meet to join.

मिलन *n.* Meeting; contact.

मिश्र् *vt.* 10 U. To mix; to unite. [title of respect.

मिश्र *a.* Mixed, diverse *m.* A

मिश्रण *n.* A mixture.

मिष् *vt.* 1 P. To sprinkle; 6 P. to rival; to look on; with उद्-to open the eyes; नि-to shut the eyes.

मिष *m.* Rivalry. *n.* Pretext, fraud. [meat.

मिष्ट *a.* Sweet. *n.* Sweet-

मिहिका *f.* Mist; snow.

मिहिर *m.* The sun; the moon; wind.

मी *vi.* 4 A. To perish; 9 U. to hurt; 1 P. 10 U. To go.

मीन *m.* A fish. [love.

मीनकेतन *m.* The god of

मीमांसक *m.* An examiner; a followe rof the Mîmâmsá school of Indian philosophy.

मीमांसा *f.* Examination; a particular school of philosophy.

मील् *vt.* 1 P. To close the eyes; to wink; with उद्-to open the eyes; नि-to shut the eyes; सम्-to close.

मुकुट *n.* A crown; a peak.

मुकुंद *m.* Vishnu.

मुकुर *m.* A mirror; a bud.

मुकुल *m. n.* A bud.

मुक्त *a.* Liberated; loosened; granted; discharged.

मुक्तकच्छ *m.* A Buddhist.

मुक्तकर *a.* Liberal.

मुक्ता *f.* A pearl; a harlot.

मुक्तांबर *m.* A Jain ascetic.

मुक्ति *f.* Deliverance; abandonment; final liberation.

मुख *n.* The face, head, mouth; a direction; an opening; a top; beginning.

मुखबंध *m.*,(-न *n.*) A preface.

मुखर *a.* Talkative; resounding; abusive.

मुखरित *a.* Resonant.

मुखरी *f.* The bit of a bridle.

मुख्य *a* Chief; first. *m.* A leader.

मुग्ध *a.* Charming; stupid; simple; infatuated.

मुच् *vt.* 1 A. To deceive; 6 U. to liberate; to loosen; to grant; with आ-to put on; निस्-to free; परि, प्र, प्रति, वि-to release; सम्-to shed.

मुंज *m.* A sort of rush. N. of a king. [shave.

मुंड् *vt.* 1 P. To grind; to

मुंड *a.* Low, bald. *m.* A bald head; forehead. *n.* The head; iron.

मुंडक *m.* A barber; *n.* The head.

मुंडन *n.* Shaving the head.

मुंडिन् *m.* A barber.

मुद् *vt.* 10 U. To cleanse. *vi.* 1 A. To be glad; with अनु-to permit; आ-to be glad; to be fragrant; प्र-to be glad.

मुद् *f.* Joy; pleasure.

मुदा *f.* See मुद्.

मुदित *a.* Glad. *n.* Pleasure.

मुदिता *f.* Joy.

मुदिर *m.* A cloud.

मुदी *f.* Moon-light.

मुद्गर *m.* A hammer.

मुद्गल *n.* A species of grass.

मुद्रण *n.* Sealing.

मुद्रा *f.* A seal; a stamp; a coin; a medal; a badge.

मुद्रिका *f.* See मुद्रा.

मुधा *ind* In vain.

मुनि *m.* A sage; a recluse.

मुमुक्षा *f.* Desire of final emancipation.

मुमुक्षु *a.* Striving after final emancipation.

मुमूर्षा *f.* Desire of death.

मुमूर्षु *a.* Being on the point of death.

मुरज *m.* A kind of drum.

मुरजा *f.* A great drum.

मुरली *f.* A flute; a pipe.

मुर्च्छ् *vt. vi.* 1 P. To faint; to thicken; to become strong; with सम्-to be strong.

मुष् *vt.* 1 P. To kill; 4 P. to break; 9 P. to steal; to surpass, with परि-to rob.

मुषक *m.* A mouse.

मुष्क *m.* The scrotum; a thief; a heap.

मुष्टि *m. f.* मुष्टिका *f.* The fist; a handful; a hilt.

मुष्टिंधय *m.* A child.

मुष्टिबंध *m.* Clenching the fist; a handful.

मुसल *m.n.* A club; a pestle.

मुसलिन् *m.* Balaráma.

मुस्त् *vt.* 10 U. To accumulate. [grass.

मुस्त *m.n.* (-स्ता *f.*) A kind of

मुह् *vt.* 4 P. To faint; to err; with प्र-to be infatuated; वि-to be perplexed; सम्-to be foolish.

मुहिर *a.* Foolish.

मुहुर्भाषा *f.* Repetition.

मुहुर्मुहुस् *ind.* Over and over again.

मुहुस् *ind.* Repeatedly.

मुहूर्त, (-क) *m.* A moment; a period of 48 minutes.

मूक *a*. Dumb; silent.
मूकभाव *m*. Silence.
मूढ *a*. Perplexed, dull. *m*. A fool.
मूत्र *n*. Urine.
मूर्ख *a*. Foolish. *m*. A fool.
मूर्च्छन *n*. Fainting.
मूर्च्छना *f*. Fainting; modulation of sounds.
मूर्च्छा *f*. A swoon.
मूर्त *a*. Incarnate.
मूर्ति *f*. A body; manifestation; image.
मूर्तिमत् *a*. Incarnate.[front
मूर्धन् *m*. The head; top;
मुर्धज *m*. The hair (of the head). [lent.
मूर्धन्य *a*. Cerebral; excel-
मूल् *vi*. 1 U. To take root; *vt*. 10 U. to rear; with उद् or निस्-to root out.
मूल *n*. The root; bottom; origin; basis; capital; square root (in Mathe.); territory.
मूल्य *n* Value, price, gain.
मूष, मूषिक *m*. A rat.
मूषक *m*. A rat.
मूषकवाहन *m*. Ganeśa.
मूषा, मूषिका *f*. A crucible.
मृ *vi*. 6 A. To die.
मृग् *vt*. 4 P. 10 A To seek.
मृग *m*. An animal; a deer; a search. N. of a constellation.
मृगजल *n*. A mirage.
मृगतृष्णा *f*. A mirage.
मृगनाभि *m*. Musk; the musk-deer.
मृगमद *m*. Musk.
मृगराज *m*. A lion.
मृगलांछन *m*. The moon.
मृगलोचन *m*. The moon.
मृगवाहन *m*. Wind.
मृगशीर्ष *m*. *n*. N. of a constellation.
मृगणा *f*. Searching.
मृगया *f*.Hunting;the chase.
मृगयु *m*. A hunter.
मृगी *f*. A female deer.
मृज् *vt*.2 P.,10 U. To wipe; with अव-to rub; परि, प्र, वि, सम्-to wipe off.
मृजा *f*. Purity.
मृड *m*. Śiva.
मृडा, (-नी *f*.) Pārvatī.
मृणाल *m*.*n*.The fibrous root of a lotus. [stalk.
मृणालिका, मृणाली *f*.A lotus.
मृणालिनी *f*. A lotus plant; a number of lotuses.
मृणमय, (मृन्मय) *a*. Made of clay.
मृत *a*. Dead.
मृति *f*. Death.
मृत्तिका *f*. Clay, earth.
मृत्यु *m*. Death; Yama.
मृत्युंजय *m*. S'iva.
मृत्युलोक *m*. The earth.
मृत्सा, मृत्स्ना *f*. The earth.

मृद् *vt.* 9 P. To press; with उप-to kill.

मृद् *f.* Clay, earth.

मृदंग *m.* A kind of drum.

मृदु, (-ल) *a.* Soft; gentle.

मृध *m.* War, battle.

मृश् *vt.* 6 P. To touch; to consider.

मृष् *vt.* 1 P. To sprinkle; (Atm.) to suffer, 10 U. to forgive.

मृषा *ind.* Falsely; in vain.

मृषार्थक *n.* An absurdity.

मृषावाद *m.* A tie; irony.

मे *vt.* 1 A. To exchange.

मेखला *f.* A belt; a girdle; the slope of a mountain.

मेघ *m.* A cloud; a mass.

मेघगर्जना *f.* Thunder.

मेघडंबर *m.* Thunder. [jit.

मेघनाद *m.* Thunder; Indra-

मेघवर्त्मन् *n.* The atmosphere.

मेघवाहन *m.* Indra.

मेघस्तनित *n.* Thunder.

मेघागम *m.* The rainy season.

मेघाध्वन् *m.* The atmosphere.

मेघोदक *n.* Rain water.

मेचक *a.* Black. *m.* An eye on a pea-cock's tail; smoke, a cloud.

मेढ्र, (-क) *m.* A ram.

मेंढ, (-क) *m.* A ram.

मेद *m.* Fat.

मेदस् *n.* Fat.

मेदस्विन् *a.* Corpulent.

मेदिनी *f.* The earth; land.

मेदुर *a.* Fat; smooth; thick.

मेध *m.* A sacrifice.

मेधा *f.* Intelligence; retentive memory.

मेधाविन् *m.* A learned man.

मेध्य *a.* Fit for a sacrifice; pure. *m.* A goat. [*as.*

मेनका *f.* One of the *Apsaras*-

मेय *a.* Measurable.

मेरु *m.* N. of a mountain; the central bed in a rosary. [pany.

मेल *m.* Meeting; a com-

मेला *f.* Union; a company.

मेष *m.* A ram; the sign *Aries* of the Zodiac.

मेषपाल,(-क) *m.* A shepherd.

मेषिका, मेषी *f.* A ewe.

मेह *m.* Urine. [ship.

मैत्र *a.* Friendly *n.* Friend-

मैत्रक *n.* Friendship.

मैत्रावरुण (-णि) *m.* Vâlmîki; Agastya.

मैत्री *f.* Friendship; union.

मैत्रेय *a.* Friendly.

मैत्र्य *n.* Friendship.

मैथिली *f.* Sîtâ.

मैथुन *n.* Copulation; marriage; union. [rate.

मोक्ष् *vt.* 1 P. 10 U. To libe-

मोक्ष *m.* Liberation; release; delivery. [ful.

मोघ *a.* Aimless; unsuccess-

मोचन *n.* Liberating.

मोद *m.* Delight; fragrance.

मोदक *m. n.* A kind of sweetmeat.

मोष *m.* A theft; plundering; stolen property.

मोषक *m.* A thief.

मोषा *f.* Robbery; theft.

मोह *m.* Swoon; confusion; illusion; folly; wonder; pain.

मोहन *a.* Stupefying; puzzling *m.* S'iva. *n.* Temptation.

मोहनिद्रा *f.* Over-weening confidence.

मोहिनी *f.* Vishnu in the form of a fascinating woman.

मौक्तिक *n.* A pearl.

मौखर्य *n.* Talkativeness.

मौंज *a.* Made of *munja* grass.

मौंजि *f.* The girdle of a Bràhmana, made of a triple string of *munja* grass.

मौंजीबंधन *n.* Investiture with the sacred thread.

मौद्गलि *m.* A crow.

मौन *a.* Silence.

मौनिन् *a.* Silent. *m.* An ascetic.

मौर्ख्य *n.* Folly.

मौर्य *m.* N of a dynasty.

मौर्वी *f.* A bow string.

मौल *a.* Original; old.

मौलि *m.* The head.

मौली *f.* The earth.

मौल्य *n.* Price.

मौष्टिक *m.* A rogue.

मौसल *a.* Fought with clubs.

म्ना *vt.* 1 P. To repeat; to remember; to think; with आ -to proclaim.

म्रक्ष *m.* Hypocrisy.

म्रद् *vt.* 1 A. To pound.

म्रदिमन् *m.* Tenderness.

म्रुच् *vt.* 1. P To go.

म्लान *a.* Faded; feeble.

म्लानि *f.* Decay; weariness.

म्लिष्ट *a.* Indistinct.

म्लुंच् *vt.* 1 P. To go.

म्लेच्छ *m* A barbarian; an outcast.

म्लेच्छभाषा *f.* A foreign tongue.

म्लै *vt.* 1 P. To be fatigued; to be sad.

य

य *m.* Air, union; fame, light.

यकृत् *n.* The liver.

यक्ष् *vt.* 10 A. To honour; 1 P. to move.

यक्ष *m.* A demi-god.

यक्षराज् (-ज) *m.* Kubera.

यक्षिणी *f.* A female Yaksha.

यक्ष्म, (-न्) *m.* Pulmonary disease.

यक्ष्मग्रस्त *a.* Consumptive.

यज् *vt.* 1 P. To worship; to sacrifice; to give.

यजन *n.* A sacrifice.

यजमान *m.* A sacrificer; a host; the head of a family.

यजुस् *n.* A sacrificial prayer; the Yajurveda.

यज्ञ *m.* A sacrifice; worship.
यज्ञपुरुष *m.* Vishnu.
यज्ञभुज् *m.* A god.
यज्ञसूत्र *n.* Sacred thread.
यज्ञिय *n.* Sacred. *m.* A god; the Dwâpára Age.
यज्वन् *m.* A sacrificer.
यत् *vi.* 1 A. To attempt; to long for; to labour; to go.
यत *p. p.* Restrained.
यतन *n.* Exertion.
यत्न *m.* Effort; perseverance; care; difficulty. [many.
यतम *a.* Who or which of
यतर *a.* Who or which of the two.
यतस् *ind.* As, wherefore; because, ever since, on all sides.
यति *pron. a.* As many.
यति *f.* Restraint, a pause; *m.* An ascetic.
यतिन् *m.* An ascetic.
यत्कृते *ind.* Wherefore.
यत्र *ind.* Where, because, whenever.
यत्रत्य *a.* Of which place.
यथा *ind.* As, like, for instance; so that.
यथाकामम् *ind.* To the heart's content.
यथागत *a.* Foolish.
यथाजात *a.* Foolish.
यथानुपूर्वं (-र्व्य) *ind.* In regular order.
यथानुरूपम् *ind.* Properly.
यथायथम् *ind.* Properly.
यथार्थ *a.* True; real; proper.
यथावत् *ind.* Duly; rightly.
यद् *Pron.* Who, which, what. *ind.* Because, why, since.
यदा *ind.* When, if. [though.
यदि *ind.* If; provided that,
यदृच्छा *f.* Self-will; chance.
यद्वा *ind.* Whether.
यंतृ *m.* A governor, a charioteer.
यंत्र् *vt.* 10 U. To restrain.
यंत्र *n.* A tie; an instrument or machine; an amulet. [pain.
यंत्रणा *f.* A restraint; force;
यंत्रमार्ग *m.* A canal.
यम् *vt.* 1 P. To restrain; to give; with आ-to restrain; निरा-to contract; व्या-to fight, to exert; उद्-to rise, to offer, to study; अभ्युद्-to raise; समुद्-to incite, to lift up; उप-to marry; नि-to stop, to punish, to govern; विनि-punish; संनि-to subdue; प्रतिप्र-to restore; संप्र-to give; सम्-to constrain.
यम *m.* Self-control; a twin; the god of death. [twin.
यमक *m.* Rhyme. *m.* A
यमनिका *f.* A curtain.

यमल *a.* Twin.
यमुना *f.* N. of a river.
यर्हि *ind.* When, because, while.
यव *m.* Barley; a particular measure.
यवक्षार *m.* Salt-petre.
यवन *m.* A foreigner.
यवनिका or **यवनी** *f.* Wife of a Yavana; a curtain.
यवस *n.* Grass; fodder.
यवागू *f.* Sour gruel.
यविष्ठ *a.* (Super. of युवन्) Youngest.
यवीयस् *a.* (Comp. of युवन्) Younger.
यशस् *n.* Fame, glory.
यशस्कर *a.* Bringing glory.
यशस्य *a.* Famous.
यष्टि, (-का) *f.* A stick; a branch; a necklace.
यष्टिनिवास *m.* A pigeon-house.
यष्टी *f.* See यष्टि.
यस् *vi.* 4 P. To strive.
या *vt.* 2 P. To go; to obtain; to request; to attempt; with अति-to transgress; अधि-to escape; अनु-to follow; अभि-to approach; आ-to come, to obtain, to salute; उप-to attain, to salute; परि-to go round; प्र-to march on; प्रति-to return; प्रत्युद् to welcome; विनिस्-to pass away; सम्-to enter, to depart.
याग *m.* A sacrifice.
याच् *vt.* 1 U. To beg.
याचक *m.* A beggar.
याचन *n.* (-ना *f.*) A request.
याजक *m.* A sacrificer.
याज्ञिक *m* A sacrificer; a sacrificing priest.
याञ्चा *f.* Begging; entreaty.
यात *p.p.* Gone.
यातना *f.* Agony; requital.
यातयाम *a.* Stale; raw.
यातु *m.* A traveller. *n.* A demon.
यातुधान *m.* An evil spirit.
यातृ *f.* A husband's brother's wife.
यात्रा *f.* Journey; a march; a pilgrimage; a festival; subsistence; intercourse; a vehicle; a custom.
यात्रिक *n.* A march; provisions.
याथातथ्य *n.* Reality; truth.
याथार्थ्य *n.* Truth.
यादस् *n.* A sea-monster. *m.* The ocean.
यादृक्ष (-श्, -श) *a.* What like.
यान *n.* A journey; a carriage.
यापन *n.* (-ना *f.*) Expulsion cure; spending time; maintenance.

याप्य *a.* Low.

याम *m.* Restraint; a period of three hours; a watch.

यामवती *f.* Night.

यामिक *m.* A watchman.

यामिका (-नी) *f.* Night.

याम्य *a.* Southern.

याम्या *f.* The south; night.

याम्योत्तर *a.* Going from south to north.

यावत् *a.* As much;as large; *ind.* Just now; till; so long as, as soon as.

यावदर्थम् *ind.*In all senses.

यावन्मात्र *a.* As large;little.

यावन्मात्रम् *ind.* A little.

यु *vt.* 2 P. To join; 9 U. to bind; with व्यति-to mix.

युक्त *p.p.* Primitive; attentive; proper; yoked; skilful.

युक्तरूप *a.* Suitable; fit.

युक्ति *f.* Expedient; art; junction; propriety; probability; arrangement of words; sum.

युग *m.* *n.* A yoke. *n.* A pair; an age; a particular measure; life.

युगपद् *ind.* At the same time.

युगल, (-क) *n.* A pair.

युग्म *a.* Even. *n.* A pair.

युज् *vt.* 10 U To join; with नि-to appoint; *vi.* 4 A. To curb; 7 U. To join, to apply, to meditate; with अनु-(Atm); to ask; अभि-to attack, to claim; उद्-to endeavour; उप (Atm.)-to experience, to employ; नि (Atm)- to appoint; प्र (Atm.)- to order, to lend money, to grant, to move, to use, to perform; वि (Atm.)- to separate, to abandon; विनि-to expend, to apportion; सम्-to unite.

युतक *n.* A pair; union.

युति *f.* Union; addition; a conjunction.

युद्ध *n.* A war; opposition.

युध् *vi.*4 A. To fight. *f.* War.

युधान *m,* A soldier.

युयुत्सा *f.* Desire to fight.

युयुत्सु *a.*Hostile;ambitious.

युवति (-ती) *f.* A young woman.

युवन् *a.* Young.

युवराज *m.*A crown-prince.

युष्मद् *Pron.* You, thou.

यूक *m.* (-का *f.*) A louse.

यूति *f.* Union.

यूथ *n.* A herd.

यूथप *m.* The leader of a herd.

यूप *m.* A sacrificial post.

येन *ind.* Whereby, wherefore.

योक्त्र *n.* A chord.

योग *m.* Union; contact; conveyance; use; fraud; work; religious meditation, a rule; zeal; result.

योगक्षेम *m.* Welfare; property. [a constellation.

योगतारा *f.* The chief star in

योगधारणा *f.* Perseverance in devotion.

योगनिद्रा *f.* The sleep of Vishnu at the end of the world.

योगिन् *m.* An ascetic.

योगिनी *f.* A devotee; a female attendant on Durgâ.

योग्य *a.* Fit, useful.

योग्यता *f.* Propriety, ability.

योग्या *f.* Practice.

योजन *n.* A distance equal to 8 miles; application; abstraction of mind.

योजना *f* Union; a scheme.

योद्धृ *m.* A warrior.

योध *m.* A warrior; war.

योधसंराव *m.* A challenge.

योधिन् *m.* A warrior.

योनि *m.f.* Womb, origin; water.

योनी *f.* See योनि.

योषा *f.* A young woman.

योषित्, योषिता *f.* A woman, a girl. [ful.

यौगिक *a.* Derivative; use-

यौतक *n.* A nuptial gift.

यौतव *n.* A measure.

यौन *n.* Marriage.

यौवत *n.* An assemblage of young women; youth.

यौवन *n.* Youth; a number of young women.

यौष्माक, यौष्माकीण *a.* Your.

र

र *m.* Fire; love, speed.

रंह् *vt. vi.* 1 P., 10 U. To hasten; to speak.

रंहति *f.* Velocity, speed.

रंहस् *m.* Speed; violence.

रक्त *n.* Coloured, red, passionate, pleasant. *n.* Blood, saffron, copper.

रक्ति *f.* Charmingness; attachment.

रक्तिमन् *m.* Redness.

रक्ष् *vt.* 1 P. To protect; with अभि-to defend; प्र-to save.

रक्षक *m.* A guard.

रक्षण *n.* Preservation.

रक्षस् *n.* A demon.

रक्षा *f.* Preservation; a watch; ashes; an amulet.

रक्षागृह *n.* A lying-in-chamber.

रंक *a.* Low; miserable.

रंकु *m.* A deer.

रंग *m.* Colour; a theatre; an assembly; a field of battle.

रंगभूमि *f.* A stage.
रंगमंडप *m.* A theatre.
रंगशाला *f.* A theatre.
रच् *vt.* 10 U. To make; to compose; with वि-to arrange.
रचना *f.* Arrangement; performance; composition.
रजक *m.* A washerman.
रजका (-की) *f.* A washerwoman.
रजत *a.* White. *n.* Silver, a necklace; blood.
रजनि (-नी) *f.* Night.
रजस् *n.* Dust; a small particle; the second of three Gunas; passion; menstrual discharge.
रजस्वल *a.* Dusty.
रजस्वला *f.* A woman during her courses.
रज्जु *f.* A rope.
रंज् *vt. vi.* 1, 4 U. To colour; to be attached to; with अनु-to love; अप-to be discoloured; उप-to be eclipsed; to suffer; वि-to dislike.
रंजक *m.* A painter.
रंजन *n.* Colouring; pleasing.
रट् *vi.* 1 P. To shout.
रण् *vi.* 1 P. To sound.
रण *m. n.* A war; a sound.
रणरण, (-क) *m.* Regret for a lost object.
रणस्तंभ *m.* A monument of war.
रंडा *f.* A widow.
रत *a.* Devoted to; engaged in. *n.* Pleasure.
रति *f.* Pleasure; attachment; goddess of love.
रत्न *n.* A jewel; anything excellent.
रत्नसानु *m.* A mountain.
रत्नसू *f.* The earth.
रत्नाकर *m.* An ocean.
रथ *m.* A chariot.
रथांग *n.* A wheel. *m.* The ruddy goose.
रथिक (-न्), रथिन, रथिर *m.* A warrior fighting in a car.
रथ्या *f.* A high road.
रद *m.* A tooth.
रदच्छद *m.* A lip.
रध् *vt.* 4 P. To torment.
रंध्र *n.* A hole; a defect.
रभ् *vt.* 1 A. To begin; with परि-to embrace; सम्-to be enraged.
रभस *a.* Violent. *m.* Speed; rashness; regret, joy.
रम् *vi.* 1 A. To rest; to rejoice, to play; with उप-to cease; to die; वि-to stop; सम्-to rejoice.
रमण *a.* Pleasing. *m.* A lover. *n.* Sport; pleasure

रमणा (-णी) *f.* A charming woman; a mistress.

रमणीय *a*. Charming.

रमा *f.* Lakshmî; a wife.

रंभा *f.* A plantain tree. N. of an *apsaras*.

रम्य *a*. Delightful. [zeal.

रय *m*. A current; speed;

रल्लक *m*. An eye-lash.

रव *m*. A sound.

रवि *m*. The sun.

रविकांत *m*. The sun-stone.

रश (स) ना *f.* A rope; a girdle; the tongue. [ray.

रश्मि *m*. A rope; a rein; a

रश्मिमत् *m*. The sun.

रस् *vi.* 1 P. To cry; 10 U. to taste.

रस *m*. A juice; water; poison; mixture taste; desire; love; sentiment; an elixir.

रसज्ञ *m*. A poet, a critic; a physician. [tongue.

रसन *n*. Crying; taste;

रसना *f.* The tongue, a girdle.

रसा *f.* The hell; earth; tongue.

रसातल *n.* Hell.

रसाल *m*. A mango tree.

रसिक *a*. Tasteful; elegant, appreciative.

रसित *n*. Wine; a cry.

रसेंद्र *m*. Mercury.

रस्य *a*. Juicy. [abandon.

रह् *vt.* 1 P; 10 U. To

रहण *m*. Desertion.

रहस् *n*. Secrecy, a secret. *ind*. Secretly.

रहस्य *n*. A secret.

रहित *a*. Deprived of.

रा *vt.* 2 P. To give.

राका *f.* The full moon day or night.

राक्षस *m*. An evil spirit; one of the eight forms of marriage.

राक्षसी *f.* A female demon.

राग *m*. A colour, passion, a musical mode; pleasure; anger, beauty.

रागिणी *f.* A modification of a musical mode.

राज् *vi.* 1 U. To shine; (*causal*) with निस्-to wave lights.

राज् *m*. A king.

राजक *m*. A petty prince; a circle of princes.

राजन् *m*. King; Indra; moon; Yaksha

राजदण्ड *m*. Royal authority; a sceptre.

राजधानी *f.* The metropolis.

राजनीति *f.* Politics

राजन्य *m*. A kshatriya.

राजन्वत् *a* Governed by a just king. [street.

राजपथ (-मार्ग) *m*. A public

राजपुरुष *m*. A minister.

राजयक्ष्मन् *m*. Pulmonary consumption.

राजयोग *m*. A sign indicating future kingship; a

mode of religious meditation.

राजर्षि *m.* A royal sage

राजशासन *m.* King's edict.

राजस *a.* Possessing the quality named रजस्.

राजसूय *m.* A great sacrifice performed by a paramount monarch.

राजहंस *m.* A white goose.

राजि (-जी) *f.* A line.

राजीव *n.* A blue lotus.

राज्ञी *f.* A queen.

राज्य *n.* Sovereignty; kingdom; government.

राज्याभिषेक *m.* Coronation.

रात्रि(-त्री) *f.* Night; darkness.

रात्रि (त्रिं) चर *m.* A thief; a guard; a demon.

राद्ध *pp.* Propitiated; performed; successful.

राद्धांत *m.* A doctrine.

राद्धि *f.* Accomplishment; success.

राध् *vt.* 5 P. To propitiate; to effect; to kill; 4 P. to be favourable; with अप- or वि-to offend; to injure.

राधा *f.* Prosperity; lightning.

राधेय *m.* N. of Karna.

राम *a.* Delightful. *m.* The hero of the Rámáyana.

रामणीयक *a.* Lovely.

रामा *f.* A beautiful woman; a woman.

राव *m.* A cry, a sound.

रावण *m.* N. of a demon.

रावणि *m.* Indrajit, son of Rávana.

राशि *m.* A heap; a sign of the zodiac.

राशिचक्र *m. n.* The zodiac.

राशित्रय *n.* The rule of three.

राष्ट्र *n.* A nation; kingdom, people.

राष्ट्रिक *m.* A subject.

राष्ट्रिय *m.* A king; a queen's brother.

रास *m.* An uproar; a kind of dance.

रासभ *m.* An ass.

रासमण्डल *n.* Sportive dance.

राहु *m.* A demon supposed to swallow the moon; an eclipse.

रिक्त *p.p.* Divided; emptied. *n.* A vacuum.

रिक्थ *n.* Property; inheritance.

रिच् *vt.* 10 P. To divide; with आ-to move; to contract; 7 U. To empty, to purge; with अति, उद् or व्यति-to exceed.

रिपु *m.* An enemy.

रिष् *vt.* 1 P. To injure.

री *vi.* 4 A. To ooze. 9 U. To move; to kill.

रीति *f.* Manner; course; a line; style.

रु *vt.* 2 P. To cry.

रुक्म *a.* Bright. *n.* Gold.

रुग्ण (*pp.* of रुज्) *a.* Diseased.

रुच् *vi.* 1 A. To shine; to please; with वि-to shine. *f.* Light; beauty; colour.

रुचि *f.* Light, beauty, desire, taste, passion.

रुचिर *a.* Bright; pleasant.

रुज् *vt.* 6 P. To break; to pain.

रुज्, रुजा *f.* Fracture; pain; [disease.

रुण्ड *m. n.* A trunk.

रुत *n.* A cry; note of a bird.

रुतव्याज *m.* Mimicry.

रुद् *vi.* 2 P. To cry.

रुदन, रुदित *n.* Weeping.

रुद्ध *a.* Obstructed; besieged.

रुद्र *a.* Terrible. *m.* Śiva.

रुद्राक्ष *m.* A kind of tree or its berry.

रुद्राणी *f.* Pârvatî.

रुध् *vt.* 7 U. To stop; to hold; to shut; to besiege; to harass; with अनु-(4 A.) to comply with; to obey; to love; अव-to obstruct; to besiege; उप to restrain; to molest; नि-to obstruct; to oppose; सम्-to fetter.

रुधिर *n.* Blood. *m.* Mars.

रुरु *m.* A kind of deer.

रुष् *vt.* 1 P. To vex 4 U. To be angry.

रुष्, रुषा *f.* Anger.

रुह् *vi.* 1 P. To rise, to grow; with अधि-to ascend; अव-to descend; आ-to ascend; प्र-to grow; (*causal*)-to elevate to fix; with आ-to ascribe; to put; वि-to heal.

रूक्ष *a.* Rough; austere; dry.

रूढ *a.* Mounted; grown; traditional.

रूढि *f.* Rise, growth, fame, tradition, custom.

रूप् *vt.* 10 U. To gesticulate; with नि-to consider; to appoint; वि-to disfigure.

रूप *n.* Form, beauty, type, quality, colour, natural state.

रूपक *m.* A rupee. *n.* A sign; a figure of speech.

रे *ind.* A vocative particle.

रेख *m.* रेखा *f.* A line; fullness; drawing; a small portion.

रेचक *a.* Purgative. *m.* Exhalation; a syringe.

रेणु *m.* Dust; pollen of flowers.

रेतस् *n.* Semen virile.

रेफ *m.* A grating sound.

रेवा *f.* The river Narmadà.

रै *f.* Property.

रैवत, (-क) *m.* N. of a mountain near Dwârakā.

रोग *m.* A disease.

रोचक *m.* Hunger; a stimu-[lant.

रोचन *a.* Bright.

रोचना *f.* The bright sky; a kind of yellow pigment.

रोचिष्णु *a.* Shining.

रोचिस् *f.* Light, splendour.

रोदनं *n.* Weeping tears.

रोदस् *n.* रोदसी *f.* (dual) Heaven and earth.

रोध *m.* Obstruction; siege.

रोधस् *n* A bank; a dam.

रोपण *n* Planting.

रोमक *n.* The city of Rome; a Roman.

रोमन् *m.n.* The hair; down.

रोमंथ *m.* Ruminating. [hair.

रोमपुलक *m.* Bristling of the

रोमश *a.* Hairy. [hair.

रोमहर्ष *m.* Bristling of the

रोमहर्षण *a.* Causing shudder.

रोमांच *m.* Horripilation.

रोलंब *m.* A bee.

रोष *m.* Anger. [stone.

रोषण *a.* Angry. *m.* A touch-

रोह *m.* Rising; height.

रोहिणी *f.* A red cow; a young girl; lightning; mother of Balaráma; N. of a constellation.

रोहिणीपति *m.* The moon.

रोहित *a.* Red-coloured.

रोहिताश्व *m.* Fire.

रौद्र *a.* Violent; terrible. *m.* Wrath. *n.* Fierceness.

रौप्य *n.* Silver. [a hell.

रौरव *a.* Dreadful. *m* N. of

ल

ल *m.* Indra.

लक *n.* The forehead.

लक्तक *m.* Lac.

लक्ष् *vt.* 1 A. To see. 10 U. To mark; to signify; with उप-to characterise; to regard; सम्-to test; to know.

लक्ष *m. n.* One hundred thousand. *n.* A mark

लक्षण *n.* A sign; a quality; definition; designation; subject; cause; merit.

लक्षणा *f.* Aim; indirect application of a word.

लक्ष्मन् *n.* A sign; a spot.

लक्ष्मी *f.* Goddess of wealth; good fortune; royal power.

लक्ष्मीपति *m.* Vishnu; a king.

लक्ष्य *n.* An aim; a sign; the thing defined; one hundred thousand; a secondary meaning; pretence. [To touch.

लग् *vt. vi* 1 P. To go; 1 P.

लगुड (-र,-ल) *m.* A stick.

लग्न *n.* An auspicious moment; the point of contact; the rising of the sun. [significance.

लघिमन् *m.* Lightness; in-

लघिष्ठ *a.* Lightest.

लघीयस् *a.* Lighter.

लघु *a.* Light, small, swift.

लंका *f.* Capital of Rávaṇa.

लंघ् *vt. vi.* 1 U. To fast; to transgress; to dry.

लंघन *n.* Ascending; exceeding; fasting; going by leaps. [mark.

लंछ् *vt.* (लच्छति) 1 P. To

लज् *vi.* 1 A. To be ashamed. *vt.* 1 P. To blame. 10 U. To seem; to cover.

लज्जा *f.* Shame, modesty.

लज्जालु *a.* Bashful; modest.

लटक *m.* A rascal. [meat.

लड्डु, (-क) *m.* A sweat-

लता *f.* A creeper.

लतागृह *n.* A bower.

लताप्रतान *m.* The tendril of a creeper.

लतिका *f.* A small creeper

लप् *vt.* 1 P. To chatter; to whisper; with अनु-to repeat; अप- to conceal; आ- to converse; प्र -to speak wildly; वि -to lament; विप्र-to dispute; सम्-to converse.

लब्ध *a.* Obtained; perceived.

लब्धि *f.* Acquisition; gain; the quotient.

लभ् *vi.* 1 A. To get; to be able; to know; with आ-to touch; to offer as a sacrifice; उप-to obtain; to see; उपा-to taunt; विप्र-to deceive; to insult.

लभ्य *a.* Attainable; fit.

लंपट *a.* Covetous; dissolute;

लंफ *m.* A leap; jump.

लंब् *vt. vi.* 1 A. To hang down; to stretch out; to fall behind; to delay; with अव-to cling to; to depend on; to bear up; to take; आ-to rest upon; to support; उद्-to stand erect; वि-to stay; to delay.

लंब, (-क) *m.* A perpendicular, a pendulum.

लंबोदर *m.* Ganeśa. [covery.

लंभन *n.* Attainment; re-

लय *m.* Union; absorption; concentration; time (in music); habit.

लल् *vi.* 1 U. To sport. 10 U. To fondle; to desire.

ललना *f.* A woman.

ललाट *m.* The forehead.

ललाटतट *m* The slope of the forehead.

ललाटपट्ट *m* A tiara; the flat surface of the forehead. [An ornament.

ललाम *a.* Beautiful *m. n.*

ललामन् *n.* An ornament; anything best. [beauty.

ललित *a.* Elegant. *n.* Sport;

ललिता *f.* Durgá; a woman.

लव *m.* A small quantity; a drop; wool; a degree.

लवंग *m* The clove-plant, cloves.

लवंण *a*. Saline. *m*. A sea. *n*. Salt.

लवणांबुराशि *m* An ocean.

लवन *n*. Reaping; mowing.

लवम् *ind*. A little.

लवली *f*. A kind of creeper.

लशु (शू) न *m*. *n*. Garlic

लष् *vt*. 4 U. To wish; with अभि-to long for.

लस् *vi*. 1 P. To embrace; to shine; to arise; with उद्-to shine; to blow; परि-to glitter; वि-to play.

लसि (सी) का *f*. Saliva.

लस्ज् *vi*. 1 A. To be ashamed; with वि-to blush.

लहरि (-री) *f*. A wave.

ला *vt*. 2 P. To take; to give.

लाक्षणिक *a*. Characteristic.

लाक्षा *f*. A kind of red dye.

लाघव *n*. Littleness; quickness; activity; brevity; ease; contempt.

लांगल *n*. A plough.

लांगलिन् *m*. Balarâma.

लांगलीग्रह *m*. A ploughman

लांगलीषा *f*. The pole of a plough.

लांगु (गू) ल *n*. A tail.

लाज् *vt*. 1 P. To blame.

लाज *m*. *pl*. Parched grain.

लाजा *f*. *pl*. Parched grain.

लांछ् *vt*. 1 P. To mark.

लांछन *n*. A sign; a name; a stain; a spot.

लाभ *m*. Gain; knowledge.

लांपट्य *n*. Lewdness.

लालन *n*. Indulging; caressing. [devoted to.

लालस *a*. Ardently desirous;

लालसा *f*. Ardent desire.

लाला *f*. Saliva.

लालाटिक *a*. Dependent on destiny. [sure.

लालित *a*. Fondled. *n*. Plea-

लालित्य *n*. Grace, beauty.

लालिनी *f*. A wanton woman

लाव *a*. Cutting; killing.

लावक *m*. A cutter.

लावाणिक *a*. Beautiful.

लावण्य *n*. Saltness; charm.

लास *m*. Dancing.

लासिका *f*. A prostitute.

लास्य *n*. A dance.

लिख् *vt*. 6 P. To write; to scratch; to paint; to touch; with उद्-to scrape; to polish; प्रति-to reply; वि-to scratch, to delineate; to implant; समुद्-to strike. [writing.

लिखन *n*. A manuscript;

लिखित *n*. A composition; document.

लिंग् *vt*. P. 1 To go; to move; 10 U to paint.

लिंग *n*. A sign; gender; the male organ.

लिंगदेह *m*. (-शरीर *n*.) One of the five sheaths that encase the soul. [kindle.

लिप् *vt.* 6 U. To anoint; to

लिपि (-पी) *f.* Alphabet; a letter.

लिपिक (का) र *m.* A scribe; writer. [ing.

लिप्सा *f.* Desire of obtain-

लिप्सु *m.* Desirous to obtain.

लिंप *m.* Anointing.

लिह् *vt.* 1 P. (*p p.* लीढ) To lick; with उद्-to polish.

ली *vt* 1 P. (*p.p.* लीन) To melt. 4 A. To cling to; to lurk in; to vanish; with अभि-to cover; नि-to lie down; प्र-to be absorbed in; वि-to cling to; to perish; सम्-to cling to. 9 P. To melt.

लीन *a.* Absorbed; devoted to. [grace, disguise.

लीला *f.* Sport, manner,

लुच् *vt.* 1 P. To pluck.

लुट् *vt. vi.* 1, 4 P. To rob, to go; to roll on the ground, 1 A. To resist; 10 U. To speak.

लुठ् *vt.* 1 A. To resist. 1 P. To strike. 6 P. To roll on the ground.

लुड् *vt.* 1 P. To stir. 6 P. To cover.

लुंट् *vt.* 1 P., 10 U. To rob; to despise.

लुंटाक *a.* Stealing.

लुंठ् *vt. vi.* 1 P. To go; to agitate; to rob.

लुंठक *m.* A thief.

लुंठन *n.* Robbing.

लुप् *vi.* 4 P To be confused, to vanish; 6 U. To cut off; to rob; to suppress; with वि-to ruin.

लुप्त *pp.* Disappeared. [for.

लुब्ध *pp.* Covetous; longing

लुब्धक *m.* A hunter; libertine.

लुभ् *vt. vi.* 4 P. To covet; to go astray; (*causal*) with प्र or वि-to allure; to amuse. [about.

लुल् *vt. vi.* 1 P. To roll

लुलाय *m*, A buffalo.

ललित *a* Tremulous; elegant; languid.

लू *vt.* 9 U. (*p.p.* लून) To cut off; to destroy; with आ or विप्र-to pluck off.

लूतिका *f.* A spider.

लून *pp.* Cut off.

लूम *m.* A tail. [a god.

लेख *m.* A writing, a letter,

लेखक *m.* A writer; a painter.

लेखन *n.* Writing.

लेखनी *f.* A pen.

लेखा *f.* A line; a stroke; painting; border. [ing.

लेख्य *n.* A writing; paint-

लेप *m.* Anointing; plaster; impurity.

लेपन *m.* Incense. *n.* An ointment; plaster.

लेलिह, लेलिहान *m*. A snake.
लेश *m*. A particle.
लेष्टु *m*. A lump of earth.
लेह *m*. Licking; food
लोक् *vt*. 1 A. To see; with अव, आ-to look at.
लोक *m*. A world; people; a class; a region; usage; sight.
लोकपाल *m*. A king.
लोकप्रवाद *m*. Rumour.
लोकमर्यादा *f*. Established usage.
लोकयात्रा *f*. Worldly affairs; support of life. [world.
लोकसंग्रह *m*. Welfare of the
लोकालोक *m. du*. The visible and the invisible world. *m*.N. of a mythical mountain.
लोच् *vt*. 1 A. To see; *causal*-with आ-to know.
लोचन *n*. The eye.
लोडन *n*. Disturbing. [perty.
लोत्र (-प्त्र) *n*. Stolen pro-
लोप *m*. Loss; violation; omission.
लोभ *m*. Avarice, desire.
लोभन *n* Allurement.
लोम *n*. A tail.
लोमन् *n*. Hair.
लोमहर्ष *m*.,(-ण *n*.) Horripilation.
लोमश *a*. Hairy.
लोल *a*. Tremulous, restless, greedy, fickle.
लोलुप *a*. Ardently desiring.
लोलुपा *f*. Eager, desire.
लोष्ट *m. n*. A lump of earth.
लोह *m. n*. Iron, copper, gold.
लोहकांत *m*. A magnet.
लोहकार *m*. A blacksmith.
लोहित *a*. Red *m*. Red colour; a snake. *n*. War, copper, blood.
लोहिताक्ष *m*. A snake; Indian cuckoo; Vishnu.
लोहिताश्व *m*. Fire.
लौकिक *a*. Terrestrial; worldly; ordinary.
लौल्य *n*. Fickleness, passion.
लौहित्य *n*. Redness. [move.
ल्वी *vt*. 9. P. To go; to

व

व *m*. Air; Vishnu; Varuna. *ind*. Like.
वंश *m*. A bamboo; race; an assemblage. [race.
वंशकर *a*. Perpetuating a
वंशकृत *m*. The founder of a family.
वंशज *m*. Progeny.
वंशी *f*. A flute; an artery.
वंशीधर *m*. A flute-player; Krîshna. [scendant.
वंश्य *m*. An ancestor; a de-
वक्तव्य *n*. Censure; an aphorism.

वक्तृ *m*. An orator.
वक्त्र *n*. The mouth, face.
वक्र *a*. Crooked; indirect; ambiguous.
वक्रतुंड *m*. Ganeśa.
वक्रदृष्टि *a*. Envious.
वक्रदंष्ट्र *m*. A boar.
वक्रनासिक *m*. An owl.
वक्रपुच्छ (-च्छिक) *m*. A dog.
वक्रिमन् *m*. Curvature, ambiguity.
वक्रोक्ति *f*. Sarcasm.
वक्षस् *n*. The breast.
वक्षःस्थल *n*. The breast.
वगाह *m*.Bathing;ablution.
वंग *m*. *pl*. Bengal. *n*. Lead.
वच् *vt*. 2 P. To speak, to call, to announce; with अनु-to recite, निस्-to explain; प्रति-to answer.
वचन *n*. A speech; a sentence; a precept; the number (in Grammar.)
वचनीय *n*. Censure.
वचनेस्थित *a*. Obedient.
वचस् *n*. See वचन.
वचसांपति *m*. Brihaspati.
वज्र *m*. *n*.Indra's thunderbolt; a diamond.
वज्रधर (-पाणि, भृत्,-मुष्टि) *m*. Indra.
वज्रलेप *m*. A hard cement
वज्रसार *a*. Hard like diamond.
वज्रिन् *m*. Indra.
वंच् *vt*. 1 P. To go; 10 A. To deceive. [*a*.Crafty.
वंचक *m*.A rogue; a jackal.
वंचना *f*. Deceit, fraud.
वंचुक *a*. Fraudulent.
वंजुल *m*. The cane.
वट् *vt*. 1 P. To surround; 1 P., 10 U. To divide.
वट *m* The Indian fig-tree.
वटर *m*. A cock; a thief.
वटिका *f*. A pill.
वटी *f*. A rope; a pill.
वडु *m*. See बटु.
वडभी *f*. A turret.
वडवा *f*. A mare; a female slave;the nymph अश्विनी.
वडवानल*m*. Submarine fire.
वण् *vi*. 1 P. To sound.
वणिज् *m*. A merchant. *f*. Merchandise.
वणिज *m*. A merchant.
वणिज्य *n*. वणिज्या *f*. Trade, traffic.
वंटन *n*. Dividing.
वंठ *a*. Dwarfish. [crest.
वतंस *m*. An ear-ring; a
वत्स *m*. A calf; a child, a darling; a year *n*. The breast.
वत्सतरी *f*. A heifer.
वत्सर *m* A year. [ate.
वत्सल *a*. Loving; affection-
वद् *vt*. *vi* 1 P. To speak. (Atm) To shine;to toil; with अनु-to repeat, अप-

(Atm.) to hate; to revile; उप-to flatter; परि-to calumniate; प्र-to converse; to explain; विप्र-to disagree; वि-(Atm.) To dispute; विसम्-to be inconsistent with.

वदन *n.* Mouth; face; look

वदंती *f.* Speech.

वदान्य *a.* Liberal; eloquent.

वध् *vt.* 1 P. To kill.

वध *m.* Killing; a blow.

वधु, (-का) *f.* A daughter-in-law.

वधू *f.* A woman; a bride; a wife; a daughter-in-law.

वधूटी *f.* A young woman.

वध्या *f.* Murder.

वध्री *f.* A leather strap

वन् *vt. vi.* 1 P. To honour, 10 U. To sound; to hurt; 8 A. to beg.

वन *n.* A forest; a residence; water.

वनचर *m.* A forester; a wild animal.

वनमाला *f.* A garland reaching to the knees.

वनमालिन् *m.* Krishna.

वनमुच् *m.* A cloud.

वनराज *m.* The lion.

वनस्पति *m.* A tree.

वनि *f.* Wish.

वनिका *f.* A little wood.

वनिता *f.* A woman; a wife.

वनी *f.* A forest, a grove.

वनीपक,वनीयक *m.* A beggar.

वनेचर *m.* See वनचर.

वंद् *vt.* 1 A. To praise; to salute; with अभि to salute.

वंदन *n.* Obeisance.

वंदारु *a.* Praising; respectful. *m.* A bard.

वंदिन् *m.* A bard; a captive.

वंद्य *a.* Adorable.

वंध्या *f.* A childless woman.

वन्य *a.* Wild; savage.

वन्या *f.* A large forest; a flood.

वप् *vt.* 1 P. To sow; to shave; with आ-to scatter; नि-to scatter seed; to kill; निस्-to offer; प्रति-to fix. [seed.

वपन *n.* Shaving; sowing

वपा *f.* Marrow; fat.

वपुस् *n.* A body, form, beauty [nate.

वपुष्मत् *a.* Corporeal; incar-

वप्तृ *m.* A sower; a husband.

वप्र *m. n.* A mud-wall; the slope of a hill; the bank of a river; a ditch.

वप्रक्रीडा *f.* The butting against a bank.

वम् *vt.* 1 P. To vomit; to drop.

वमथु *m.* Vomitting.
वयन *n.* Weaving. [a crow.
वयस् *n.* Age, youth, a bird,
वयस्य *m.* A friend.
वयोधस् *m.* A young man.
व्रृ *vt.* 10 U To choose.
वर *a.* Excellent, better than. *m.* Desire, gift; a bridegroom. [goose.
वरटा (-टी) *f.* A wasp; a
वरण *m.* A wall, a camel, a tree. *n.* A covering; choice of a husband.
वरंड *m.* A multitude; a veranda; a long rod; a projecting wall.
वरतनु *f* An elegant woman.
वरदा *f.* A maiden; a girl.
वरम् *ind.* Rather, preferably.
वराक *a.* Miserable. *m.* A battle.
वरांग *n.* The head [cowrie.
वराट, (-क) *m.*, **वराटिका** *f.* A
वराह *m.* A boar, a bull, a cloud.
वरिमन् *m.* Excellence.
वरिवस्या *f.* Worship.
वरिष्ठ *a.* Best, greatest heaviest.
वरीयस् *a.* Better, greater.
वरी (**ली**) **वर्द** *m.* An ox.
वरुण *m.* N. of the deity presiding over the ocean; an ocean.
वरुणपाश *m.* A shark.
वरुणानी *f.* Varuna's wife.
वरूथ *n.* A shield; an armour.
वरूथिनी *f.* An army.
वरेण्य *a.* Chief; desirable.
वर्ग *m.* A class, a chapter, the square of a number.
वर्गशस् *ind* in groups.
वर्ग्य *m.* A colleague.
वर्चस् *n.* Light, shape, power, ordure.
वर्जन *n.* Exclusion; hurt.
वर्जम् *ind.* Excepting.
वर्ण् *vt.* 10 U. To describe; to paint, to spread; with अनु, उप-to expose, निस्-to look at.
वर्ण *m.* Colour, form, a covering, glory, a syllable, a caste, race, quality.
वर्णक *m.* An unguent.
वर्णतूलि (-तूलिका, -तूली) *f.* A paint brush.
वर्णन *n.* Description.
वर्णना *f.* Description, praise.
वर्णमातृ *f.* A pen.
वर्णमाला *f* The alphabet.
वर्णसंकर *m.* Confusion of caste through intermarriage.
वर्णिन् *m.* A writer, Brahmachârin. [woman.
वर्णिनी *f.* Turmeric; a
वर्तन *m.* A dwarf. *n.* Residence, livelihood; conduct

वर्तनी *f.* A road. [ing.
वर्तमान *a.* Present; revolv-
वार्ति (-र्ती) *f.* An unguent; a collyrium; the wick; a line. [the wick.
वार्तिका *f.* A paint-brush;
वर्तुल *a.* Circular. *n* A circle.
वर्त्मन् *n.* A road; a custom.
वर्त्मनि (-नी) *f.* A path.
वर्ध् *vt.* 10 U. To fill; to divide.
वर्ध *m.* Increase. [penter.
वर्धक (-किन्,-कि) *m.* A car-
वर्धन *n.* Growth; increase; educating.
वर्धनी *f.* A broom.
वर्धिष्णु *a.* Increasing.
वर्मन् *m.* An affix applied to the names of Kshatriyas. *n.* An armour.
वलय *n.* A bracelet, a circle.
वल्क.(-ल) *m. n.* The bark of a tree; a garment.
वल्ग् *vt.* 1 P. To gallop; to be pleased.
वल्गा *f.* A bridle.
वल्गु *a.* Beautiful.
वल्मीक *m. n.* An ant-hill.
वल्लकी *f.* An Indian lute.
वल्लभ *a.* Beloved. *m.* A lover; husband.
वल्लरी *f.* A creeper.
वल्लि (-ल्ली) *f.* A creeper.
वश् *vt.* 2 P. To wish; to shine.

वश *a.* Subdued; charmed. *m. n.* Wish, influence; submission.
वशग *a.* Obedient.
वशंवद *a.* Submissive.
वशा *f.* A wife, daughter, a female elephant
वशिक *a* Empty. [sage.
वशिन् *a.* Powerful. *m.* A
वश्य *a.* Tamed, obedient.
वश्यका,वश्या *f.* An obedient wife.
वषट्कार *m.* The formula used on offering an oblation to a deity.
वस् *vt.vi.* 4 P. To be straight. 10 U. To perfume; to cut, to kill; to take. 2 A To wear. 1 U. to dwell; to be; with उप to fast; आ, नि, परि, प्र, प्रति, सम्-to dwell.
वसति (-ती) *f.* A house; an abode.
वसन *n.* A garment, a house.
वसंत *m.* The vernal season (spring); dysentery; small-pox. [metre.
वसंततिलक *m. n.* N. of a
वसंतदूत *m.* (-दूती *f.*) The Indian cuckoo. [tree.
वसंतद्रु, (-म) *m.* The mango-
वसा *f.* Fat; brain.
वसु *n.* Wealth; a jewel; gold; water. *m.* A class

of demi-gods; Kubera; Śiva; Agni; a lake; the number 'eight'; a ray of light. [*f*. The earth.

वसुदा, वसुधा, वसुंधरा, वसुमती

वस्ति *f*. Dwelling.

वस्तु *n*. A thing; a reality; subject. [ally.

वस्तुतस् *ind*. Really, actu-

वस्त्र *n*. Garment, clothes.

वस्त्रपुत्रिका *f*. A doll.

वह् *vt*. 1 P. To bear; to carry; to flow; to blow; to marry; to take care of; to possess; with अप-to remove; आ-to cause; उद्-to raise; to wear; उप to bring about; नि-to support; निस्-to be finished; परि-to overflow; वि-to marry; सम्-to marry; to disply; *causal*-To go over; with अति-to lead; आ-to invoke; निस्-to perform; सम्-to press together.

वहन *n*. A conveyance; vehicle; a boat.

वहिवी *f*. A boat.

वह्नि *m*. Fire; digestion.

वा *ind*. Or, and, like, possibly.

वा *vt*. *vi*. 2 P. To blow; *causal*-with निस्-to extinguish.

वाक्पति *a*. Eloquent. *m*. Brihaspati.

वाक्य *n*. A sentence; a speech; a precept.

वाक्यपद्धति *f*. Style.

वाक्यप्रबंध *m*. A treatise.

वाक्यरचना *f*. (-विन्यास *m*.) Syntax.

वाक्यालाप *m*. Conversation.

वागुरा *f*. A net.

वागुरिक *m*. A hunter.

वाग्दान *n*. Betrothal.

वाग्दुष्ट *a*. Abusive.

वाङ्निश्चय *m* Affiance by word of mouth.

वाङ्मुख *n*. Commencement. of a speech.

वाग्याम *m*. A dumb man.

वाग्युद्ध *n*. A controversy.

वाग्विभव *m* Command over language.

वाच् *f*. Goddess of speech; speech, language, voice, a phrase.

वाचक *a*. Expressive of. *m*. A speaker; a reader.

वाचन *n*. Reading; declaration.

वाचनिक *a*. Verbal. [haspati.

वाचसांपति, वाचस्पति *m*. Bri-

वाचस्पत्य *n*. Eloquence, a harangue.

वाचंयम *a*. Silent.

वाचा *f*. Speech; a text; an oath.

वाचाट *a*. Talkative.

वाचाल *a*. Talkative. [sage.
वाचिक *a*. Oral. *n*. A mes-
वाच्य *a*. Blamable; attributive; expressed. *n*. Blame; expressed meaning of a word.
वाज *m*. A wing; a sound.
वाजसनेय *m*. N. of an author (याज्ञवल्क्य).
वाजिन् *m*. A horse; a bird.
वाजिशाला *f*. A stable.
वाजीकरण *n*. Excitement of amorous desire.
वांछ् *vt*. 1 P. To desire.
वांछा *f*. Desire.
वाट *m*. *n*. An enclosure; a garden; a road.
वाटिका *f*. The site of a house; a garden.
वाटी *f*. A house; a garden; a road. [fire.
वाडव *m*. The submarine
वाणिज *m*. A merchant.
वाणिज्य *n*. Trade.
वाणी *f*. The goddess of speech; speech; eloquence; praise; a composition.
वात *m*. Wind; gout.
वातायन *m*. A horse. *n*. A window.
वाति *m*. The sun, wind.
वातुल *a*. Mad. *m*. A whirlwind.
वातृ *m*. Wind.
वात्या *f*. A storm; a whirlwind.
वात्सल्य *n*. Affection towards a child.
वाद *m*. An assertion; discussion; a rumour.
वादग्रस्त *a*. Disputable; in dispute. [music.
वादन *n*. Instrumental
वादविवाद *m*. A debate.
वादि *a*. Learned. [ment.
वादित्र *n*. A musical instru-
वादिन् *m*. A disputant; a plaintiff. [ment.
वाद्य *n*. A musical instru-
वानप्रस्थ *m*. A hermit.
वानर *m*. A monkey.
वानीर *m*. A sort of cane.
वांत *a*. Vomitted.
वांति *f*. Vomitting.
वापिका *f*. A small tank.
वापी *f*. A well.
वाम *a*. Adverse; left; handsome; wicked. [low.
वामन *a*. Dwarfish; small;
वामलूर *m*. An ant-hill.
वामा *f*. A woman; Lakshmî; Saraswatî.
वामी *f*. A mare.
वाय *m*. Weaving.
वायक *m*. A weaver; a heap.
वायन *n*. Sweetmeat given to a Brâhmana.
वायवी *f*. North-west.
वायस *m*. A crow.

वायु *m*. Wind.

वायुजात (-तनय, -नंदन, -पुत्र, -सुत,-सूनु) *m*. Hanuman; Bhîma.

वायुसख (-सखि) *m*. Fire.

वार् *n*. Water.

वार *m*. A multitude;a day; turn; a gate; water.

वारंवारम् *ind*. Again and again.

वारण *m*. An elephant; an armour. *n*. Restraining; opposition.

वारनारी (-अंगना,-युवति,-योषित,-वाणी,-विलासिनी,-स्त्री) *f*. A harlot

वाराणसी *f*. Benares.

वाराही *f*. The earth. [tî.

वारि *n*. Water. *f*. Saraswa-

वारित्रा *f*. An umbrella.

वारिधर (-मसि,-मुच्,-र,-वाह, -वाहन) *m*. A cloud

वारी *f*. See वारि.

वारुणी *f* Wine; the west.

वार्त्त *n*. Health; welfare.

वार्त्ता *f*. News; agriculture

वार्त्तावह (-हर) *m*. A messenger.

वार्त्तायन *m*. A spy. [rule

वार्त्तिक *n*.A supplementary

वार्द्धक (-क्य) *n*. Old age.

वार्द्धुष्य *n*. Usury.

वार्य *n*. A blessing.

वार्षिक *a*. Annual.

वालुका *f*. Sand.

वावदूक *a*. Garrulous; eloquent.

वावृत्त *a*. Chosen.

वाश् *vt*. *vi*. 4 A. To howl.

वाशिता *f*. A female elephant.

वास् *vt*. 10 U. To perfume.

वास *m*. Perfume; residence; dress. [a box.

वासन *n* Perfuming;abode;

वासना *f*. Desire; fancy; ignorance.

वासंत (-तिक) *a*. Vernal.

वासंती *f*.A kind of jasmine.

वासर *m* A day.

वासव *a*.Belonging to Indra.

वासवि *m*. Arjuna.

वासस् *n*. A garment.

वासुकि *m*. N. of a serpant.

वासुदेव *m*. Krishna.

वास्तव (-विक) *a*. Real.

वास्तव्य *n*. Residence.

वास्तु *m*. *n*. A house.

वाह *m*. A burden;a porter; a horse. [man.

वाहक *m*.A porter, a horse-

वाहन *n* Bearing; a conveyance; a horse.

वाहिन् *m*. A chariot.

वाहिनी *f*. An army; a river.

विंश *a*. Twentieth.

विंशक *a*. Twenty.

विंशति *f*. A score, twenty.

विकच *a*. Blown; opened.

विकट *a*. Formidable;horrible large, beautiful. *n.* A boil.

विकत्थन *n.* Boasting; irony.

विकरण *n.* The inserted conjugational affix.

विकराल *a.* Very horrible

विकर्तन *m.* The sun

विकर्मन् *n.* Irrigation or prohibited conduct.

विकल *a.* Defective; agitated.

विकल्प *m* Doubt, hesitation, alternative, error, variety, device.

विकल्पन *n.* Indecision.

विकस *m.* The moon.

विकसित *a.* Expanded.

विकस्वर *a.* Expanding.

विकार *m.* Disease, emotion, excitement

विकारिन् *a* Susceptible of emotion

विकाल(-क) *m.* Evening twilight.

विकाश *m.* Manifestation, sky, expanding.

विकाशि (सि) न् *a.* Expanding.

विकास *m*, (-न *n.*) Expanding.

विकिर *m.* Scattered portion.

विकिरण *n.* Scattering; knowledge.

विकीर्ण *a.* Scattered; diffused

विकुर्वाण *a.* Cheerful.

विकूजन *n.* Cooing.

विकूणन *n.* A side-glance.

विकृत *a.* Changed; deformed; imperfect.

विकृति *f.* See विकार.

विक्रम *m.* Heroism, a step.

विक्रमण *n.* The stride of Vishnu.

विक्रय *m.* Sale.

विक्रयिक (-न्) *m* A vendor.

विक्रांत *a.* Valiant.

विक्रांति *f.* Heroism.

विक्रिया *f.* Change, passion, anger, vitiation.

विक्रीड *m.* A play-ground.

विक्रेय *a.* Saleable.

विक्रोशन *n.* Calling out.

विक्लव *a.* Excited; unsteady; grieved.

विक्लिन्न *a.* Decayed, old.

विक्षाव *m.* A sound.

विक्षिप्त *a.* Dispersed; bewildered.

विक्षेप *m.* Fear, confusion, refutation.

विक्षोभ *m* Agitation; alarm.

विखानस *m.* A hermit

विखुर *m.* A thief; a goblin.

विख्यात *a.* Famous, confessed.

विख्याति *f.* Fame.

विगणन *n.* Reckoning, considering.

विगत *a.* Departed.

विगम *m.* Departure; stoppage.

विगर्हण *n.* (-णा) *f.* Censure.

विगर्हित *a.* Condemned; bad.

विगाढ *a.* Deep.

विगाह *m.* Bathing.

विगीति *f*. Censure.
विगुण *a*. Worthless.
विगृहीत *a*. Separated.
विग्रह *m*. Expansion; body; quarrel;a part; analysis.
विघटन *n*. Ruin.
विघटन *n*. (-ना *f*.) Undoing.
विघस *m*. The residue of food eaten; food
विघात *m*. A blow; destruction; obstacle.
विघूर्णित *a*. Rolling.
विघृष्ट*a*.Rubbed excessively.
विघ्न *m*. Obstacle.
विच् *vt*. 3, 7 U. To deprive of,to divide; with वि-to describe; to remove.
विचक्षण *a*. Clever; able.
विचक्षुस् *a*. Blind.
विचय *m*. Search.
विचर्चिका *f*. Itch. [ceited.
विचल *a*. Unsteady, con-
विचार *m*. Deliberation; reason; doubt.
विचारणा *f*. Examination.
विचि (-ची) *f*. A wave.
विचिकित्सा *f*. Error, doubt.
विचिति *f*. Search.
विचित्र *a*. Variegated; various; wonderful.
विचेतन *a*. Senseless.
विचेष्टित *n*. Act; jesture.
विच्छ् *vt*. 6. P. To go. 10 U. To shine.
विच्छंद, (-क) *m*. A palace.
विच्छाय *n*. A.gem.
विच्छित्ति *f*.Cutting; boundary; absence. [space.
विच्छेद *m*. Interruption;
विच्युति *f*. Decay, failure, deviation.
विज् *vt*. 3 P. To separate; *vi*. 5 A., 7 P. To shake; with उद्-to. fear; to be disgusted.
विजन *a*. Lonely.
विजन्मन् *m*. A bastard.
विजय*m*.Conquest; Arjuna.
विजया *f*. Durgá; hemp.
विजर *n*. A stalk.
विजल्प *m*. Talk; speech.
विजाता *f*. A mother.
विजाति *f* Different kind.
विजातीय *a*. Dissimilar.
विजिगीषा *f*. Emulation; ambition. [conquer.
विजिगीषु *a*. Desirous to
विजित *a*. Subdued.
विजिति *f*. Conquest.
विजिह्म *a*. Crooked.
विजृंभण *n*. Yawning; sport.
विज्ञ *a*. Wise; learned.
विज्ञप्ति *f*. Respectful communication. [ness.
विज्ञान *n*. Knowledge; busi-
विज्ञापक *m*. An instructor.
विज्ञापन *n*. विज्ञापना *f*. See विज्ञप्ति.
विट*m*.A Paramour;a rogue;

a companion of dissolute persons. [tree.
विटप *m.* The branch of a
विटपिन् *m.* A tree.
विडंब *m.*, (-न *n.*), विडंबना *f.* Imitation, disguise, fraud, ridiculousness.
विडीन *n.* A flight of birds.
वितण्डा *f.* A frivolous argument.
वितत *a.* Extended, accomplished; large. [tity.
विततिं *f.* Extension; quan-
वितथ *a.* False, vain.
वितरण *n.* A gift. [guess.
वितर्क *m.* Reasoning, doubt,
वितल *n.* The second lower world.
वितान *a.* Empty; dull. *m.*n. Expansion; a canopy; a sacrifice; season.
वितानक *m.* *n.* An expanse; a heap; a canopy.
वितीर्ण *pp.* Crossed over, given; overcome.
वितुष्ट *a.* Displeased.
वित्त *a.* Discovered; gained. *n.* Wealth. [hood.
वित्ति *f.* Knowledge, liveli-
विद् *vt.* 2 P. To know, to consider; *vi.* 4 A. To be *vt.* 6 U. to find; to obtain; to marry; with अनु-to feel; 7 A. to know; 10 A. to tell; te live; *causal.* To inform; with आ-to communicate; to show; with नि-to tell; to present. [Knowledge
विद् *m.* A learned man. *f.*
विद *m.* A learned man.
विदग्ध *a.* Burnt up; digested; shrewd. *m.* A learned man. [(Berar).
विदर्भ *m.pl.* N. of a province
विदारण *m.* War. *n.* Splitting, killing.
विदारणा *f* War, battle.
विदित *a.* Known.
विदिश् *f.* An intermediate point of the compass.
विदिशा *f.* An intermediate point of the compass.
विदीर्ण *a.* Rent asunder.
विदुर *m.* A learned man; younger brother of Pándu.
विदून *a.* Distressed.
विदूर *a.* Distant.
विदूषक *m.* A jester.
विदूषण *n.* Abuse.
विदेश *m.* A foreign country.
विदेशीय *a.* Foreign.
विद्ध *a.* Pierced.
विद्या *f.* Learning.
विद्यार्थिन् *m.* A student.
विद्याधर *m.* A class of demigods. [thunderbolt.
विद्युत *f.* Lightning; a
विद्युद्दामन् *n.* A flash of zigzag lightning.

विद्युल्लता, विद्युल्लेखा *f.* A streak of lightning.

विद्योतन *n.* Illumination.

विद्रव *m.* Retreat; liquefaction. [liquid.

विद्रुत *a.* Fled; alarmed;

विद्रुम *m.* The coral tree.

विद्वस् *a.* Learned.

विद्विष् (-ष) *m.* An enemy.

विद्वेष *m.* Enmity.

विध *m.* A kind; manner.

विधवा *f.* A widow. [widow.

विधवावेदन *n.* Marrying a

विधा *f.* Manner, a kind.

विधातृ *m.* Brahmá.

विधान *n.* Arrangement; a rule; means. [ing.

विधायक *a.* Doing; enjoin-

विधि *m.* Brahmá; fate; method; a ceremony, practice, a sacred precept.

विधु *m.* The moon. [tion.

विधुति *f.* विधुनन *n.* Trepida

विधुंतुद *m.* Ráhu.

विधुर *a.* Destitute of. *m.* A widower; *n.* terror.

विधेय *n.* To be performed; governable. obedient. *n.* The predicate. [enmity.

विध्वंस *m.* Ruin, insult,

विध्वस्त *a.* Destroyed; tossed up.

विनत *a.* Humble.

विनति *f.* Humility; modesty

विनय *m.* Discipline; decorum; modesty.

विनयन *n.* Discipline.

विनशन *n.* Loss.

विना *ind.* Without, except.

विनायक *m.* God Ganes'a.

विनाश *m.*, (-न *n.*) Ruin.

विनिग्रह *m* Restraining.

विनिद्र *a.* Sleepless. [evil.

विनिपात *m.* A fall; ruin;

विनिमय *m.* Exchange; a deposit.

विनियोग *m.* Use; a task.

विनीत *a.* Disciplined; gentle.

विनोद *m.* Diversion; pleasure.

विन्यस्त *a.* Deposited.

विन्यास *m.* A deposit; a composition.

विपक्ष *a.* Adverse.

विपण *m.*, (-न *n.*) Sale.

विपणि *m.f.* (-णी *f.*) A market; trade.

विपणिन् *m.* A dealer.

विपत्ति *f.* Distress; death.

विपथ *m.* A wrong way.

विपद् (-दा) *f.* Calamity; death.

विपन्न *a.* Distressed.

विपरीत *a.* Inverted; wrong.

विपर्यय *m.* Inversion; change, absence; error, destruction. [conceived.

विपर्यस्त *a.* Inverted; mis-

विपर्याय *m.* See विपर्यय.

विपर्यास *m.* Reverse; error; interchange.

विपश्चित् *a.* Learned.

विपाक *m.* Ripeness; digestion; result

विपिन *n.* A forest.

विपुल *a.* Abundant

विपुला *f.* The earth

विप्र *m.* A Brâhmana.

विप्रकर्ष *m.* Distance.

विप्रकृति *f.* Injury; insult.

विप्रकृष्ट *a.* Protracted.

विप्रतिकार *m.* Contradiction; retaliation.

विप्रतिपत्ति *f.* Perplexity.

विप्रतिपन्न *a.* Confused.

विप्रतिषेध *m.* Conflict.

विप्रयुक्त *a* Separated.

विप्रयोग *m.* Disunion.

विप्रलब्ध *a.* Cheated.

विप्रलंभ *m.* Disunion; separation.

विप्रिय *a.* Unpleasant. *n.* Offence.

विप्रुष् *f.* A drop; a spot.

विप्रोषित *a.* Banished.

विप्लव *m.* Confusion; sin; loss; deluge, the rust (of a mirror).

विफल *a.* Fruitless.

विबुध *m.* A learned man; a god.

विबुधान *m.* A learned man.

विबोध *m.* Awakening; intelligence.

विभक्त *a.* Divided; isolated.

विभक्ति *f.* Separation; a case (in grammar).

विभंग *m.* A division; contraction; obstruction;

विभव *m.* Wealth; power.

विभा *f.* Light; beauty.

विभाकर *m.* The sun; fire.

विभाग *m.* A portion; share.

विभावन *n.* (-ना *f.*) Judgment.

विभावरी *f.* Night.

विभावसु *m.* The sun; the moon; fire.

विभाषा *f.* An alternative.

विभासा *f.* Light.

विभिन्न *a.* Different; mixed.

विभीषिका *f.* Terror.

विभु *a.* Mighty. *m.* The supreme being; a king.

विभूति *f.* Might; welfare; ashes; superhuman power; wealth.

विभूषण *n*, **विभूषा** *f.* An ornament.

विभ्रम *m.* Wandering; agitation; doubt; grace; amorous gesture.

विभ्राज् *a.* Shining.

विभ्रांति *f.* Confusion, error.

विमति *f.* Dissent.

विमन्यु *a.* Free from grief or anger.

विमनस्क *a.* Sad, depressed.

विमर्द *m.*, (-न *n.*, -ना *f.*) Crushing; destruction.

विमर्श *m.* Examination.

विमर्ष *m.* Displeasure; impatience.

विमल *a.* Pure; clear.

विमातृ *f.* A step-mother.

विमान *m. n.* Dishonour; a celestial car; a palace.

विमानना *f.* Disrespect.

विमार्ग *m.* A bad road; immorality

विमुक्त *a* Liberated.

विमुक्ति *f.* Final emancipation.

विमुख *a.* Averse; devoid of.

विमुग्ध *a.* Confused.

विमूढ *a.* Foolish.

विमोक्ष *m.* Final emancipation.

विमोचन *n.* Emancipation.

विमोहन *n.* Seduction.

वियत् *n.* The sky, atmosphere.

वियुक्त *a.* Separated.

वियोग *m.* Separation; absence.

विरक्त *a.* Free from worldly attachment.

विरंचि *m.* Brahmá.

विरत *a.* Stopped; desisting from.

विरति *f.* Cessation; indifference.

विरम *m.* Cessation; sunset.

विरल *a.* Rare; few.

विरलम् *ind.* Rarely.

विरस *a.* Tasteless.

विरह *m.* Separation; abandonment.

विराग *m.* Change of colour; disinclination.

विराज् *m.* Splendour; beauty.

विराजित *a.* Manifested; illuminated.

विराद्ध *a.* Opposed, offended.

विराध *m.* Opposition; vexation.

विराधन *n.* Injuring; pain.

विराम *m.* Cessation; end.

विराव *m.* Noise sound.

विरिंच, (-न), विरिंचि *m.* Brahmā.

विरुत *n.* Humming; din.

विरुद *m.* A panegyric.

विरुद्ध *a.* Contradictory; opposed.

विरूप *a.* Deformed.

विरूपाक्ष *m.* Śiva.

विरेचन *n.* A purgative.

विरोचन *m.* The sun; the moon; fire.

विरोध *m.* Opposition; calamity; obstacle; a siege.

विरोपण *n.* Healing

विलक्ष *a.* Ashamed; surprised.

विलक्षण *a.* Different; puzzled.

विलग्न *a.* Clinging to.

विलपित *n.* Lamentation.

विलंब *m.* Delay.

विलय *m.* Dissolution; end.

विलसन *n.* Dallying; sporting.

विलसित *n.* A flash; manifestation; sport.

विलाप *m.* Lamentation.

विलास *m.* Sport; wantonness; grace.

विलासिन् *m.* A voluptuary.

विलासिनी *f.* A coquettish woman.

विलिप्त *a.* Anointed.
विलीन *a.* Immersed in; vanished.
विलुलित *a.* Unsteady.
विलेप *m.* An unguent.
विलेपन *n.* An ointment.
विलोकन *n.* Sight; seeing.
विलोचन *n.* The eye.
विलोडन *n.* Churning.
विलोम *a.* Inverse; contrary.
विलोल *a.* Unsteady.
विवक्षित *a.* Meant.
विवर *n.* A hole.
विवरण *n.* Exposition.
विवर्ण *a.* Pale; low.
विवर्त *m.* Modification; unreal appearance; a heap.
विवर्तन *n.* Whirling.
विवश *a.* Uncontrolled; unconscious.
विवस्वत् *m.* The sun; a god.
विवाद *m.* A dispute.
विवार *m.* Expansion. [ment.
विवास *m.*, (-न *n.*) Banish-
विवाह *m.* Marriage.
विविक्त *a.* Solitary; pure.
विविग्न *a.* Very angry.
विविध *a.* Various.
विवृत *a.* Uncovered; explained. [planation.
विवृति *f.* Expansion; ex-
विवृत्ति *f.* Revolving.
विवृद्धि *f.* Growth. [sion.
विवेक *m.* Judgment; discus-
विश् *vt.* 6 P. To enter; with अभिनि to resort to; उप-to sit down; नि (Atm.)-to sit down, to be intent on, to marry, to enter; निस्-to enjoy. *Causal*-with नि-to draw; विनि-to put.
विश् *m.* A man.
विशंकट *a.* Great; strong.
विशद *a.* Clear; at ease.
विशय *m.* Doubt; refuge.
विशल्य *a.* Free from trouble.
विशसन *n.* Ruin. [asterism.
विशाखा *f.* N. of a lunar
विशांपति *m.* A king.
विशारण *n.* Killing. [mous.
विशारद *a.* Versed in; fa-
विशाल *a.* Large; great.
विशाला *f.* Ujjain.
विशिख *m.* An arrow.
विशिखा *f.* A spade; a needle.
विशित *a.* Sharp.
विशिष्ट *a.* Distinguished.
विशीर्ण *a.* Shattered.
विशुद्धि *f.* Purification.
विशृंखल *a.* Unchecked.
विशेष *m.* Distinction; peculiarity; a species.
विशेषण *n.* A distinguishing mark; an adjective.
विशेष्य *n.* A noun.
विश्र (श्रा) णन *n.* A gift.
विश्रब्ध *a.* Confidential; excessive.

विश्रम *m*. Rest; relaxation.
विश्रंभ *m*. Confidence; rest.
विश्रांति *f*. Rest.
विश्राम Rest; cessation; tranquility.
विश्राव *m*. A flow.
विश्रुत *a*. Renowned.
विश्रुति *f*. Fame.
विश्लथ *a*. Loose. [tion.
विश्लेष *m*. Disunion; separa-
विश्व *a*. All. *m. pl*. N. of a class of deities. *n*. The universe. [moon; fire.
विश्वपा *m*. The sun; the
विश्वंभरा *f*. The earth.
विश्वसनीय *a*. Trustworthy.
विश्वस्त *a*. Confident.
विश्वास *m*. Trust; faith.
विश्वासघात *m*. Treachery.
विश्वासभूमि *f*. A trustworthy person.
विष् *vt*. 1 P. To sprinkle; 1, 3 U. To pervade.
विष *n*. Poison; water.
विषधर (-भृत्, -दंतक, -आस्य, -आनन) *m*. A snake.
विषण्ण *pp*. Dejected.
विषम *a*. Uneven; irregular; adverse. *n*. A difficulty.
विषय *m*. An object; sensuality; scope, a place.
विषाण . *n*., **विषाणी** *f*. A horn. [spair; sorrow.
विषाद *m*. Dejection; de-
विषालु *a*. Poisonous.

विषुप (-व) *n*. The equinox.
विषूचिका *f*. Cholera.
विष्कंभ *m*. An obstacle; the bolt; a post; an interlude
विष्कंभक *m*. See विष्कंभ.
विष्टप *m*. *n*. A world.
विष्टंभ *m*. Obstruction.
विष्टर *m*. A seat.
विष्ठा *f*. Excrement.
विष्पंद *m*. Throbbing.
विष्व *a*. Injurious.
विष्वच् *a*. All pervading.
विसंगत *a*. Inconsistent.
विसर्ग *m*. Emission; a gift; evacuation; a hard aspiration.
विसर्जन *n*. Relinquishing.
विसंवाद *m*. Disagreement; deception.
विसार *n*. Expansion; fish.
विसृष्ट *a*. Discharged; granted; emanated.
विस्त (स्ता) र *m*. Expansion. abundance.
विस्तीर्ण *a*. Extended.
विस्फार *a*. Vibration.
विस्फुरित *a*. Enlarged.
विस्फूर्जथु *m*. Thundering.
विस्फोट *m*. (-टा, -टिका *f*.) A tumour.
विस्मय *m*. Wonder; pride; astonishment; doubt.
विस्मरण *n*. Forgetting.
विस्मापन *m*. Illusion.

विस्मृति *f*. Forgetfulness.

विस्रंसन *n*. Loosening.

विस्राव *m*., विस्रुति *f*. A flow.

विह (हं) ग *m*. A bird; a cloud; an arrow.

विहंगम *m*. A bird.

विहति *m*. A friend. *f*. Failure. [pleasure.

विहर *m*., (-ण *n*.) Pastime;

विहायस् (-स) *m*. *n*. The sky. *m*. A bird.

विहार *m*. Sport; a pleasure-ground; convent.

विहास *m*. Laughing gently.

विहित *a*. Done; fixed; proper.

विहीन *a*. Devoid of; low.

विह्वल *a*. Distressed.

वी *vt*. *vi*. 2 P. To go; to throw; to be born.

वीक्षण *n* (-णा *f*.), वीक्षा *f*. Sight; looking.

वीचि (-ची) *f*. A wave; delight; leisure.

वीज् *vt*. 1 A. To move. 10 U. To fan.

वीटि (-टी) *f*. A tie.

वीणा *f*. The Indian lute.

वीत *a*. Gone. *n*. Goading.

वीति *m*. A horse. *f*. Motion; light. [a market.

वीथि(-थी) *f*. A time; a road;

वीप्सा *f*. Repetition.

वीर *a*. Mighty. *m*. A hero.

वीरुध (-धा) *f*. A creeper; a branch.

वीर्य *n*. Strength; heroism; semen virile; lustre.

वृ *vt*. 1, 5, 9 U. To cover; to choose; with अप-to show; अपा-to open; आ-to conceal, to beg; निस्-to be satisfied; परि-to surround; प्र-to wear; वि-to disclose; सम्-to hide, to restrain; *causal*-to to prevent; with नि-avert; विनि-to oppose. *vt*. 10 U. To beg; to choose.

वृक *m*. A wolf; a jackal; a crow.

वृकोदर *m*. Bhîma.

वृक्ष *m*. A tree.

वृक्षखंड *m*. A grove.

वृक्षवाटिका (-वाटी) *f*. A garden; a grove.

वृच् *vt*. 7 P. To choose

वृज् *vt*. 7 P. To choose, to lose; to purify; *vt*. 2 A. To avoid; 1 P. 10 U. To give up; with आ-to bend.

वृजिन *n*. Sin.

वृत् *v*. *i*. 1 A. To be, to proceed, to happen, to do, to tend to; with अति-to overcome, to surpass, to slight; अनु-to follow, to seek; अप-to turn away from; अभि-to go to; आ-to come; उद्-to overflow; उप-to approach; नि-to return, to abstain from; परा-to turn back; परि-to change; प्र-to begin, to prevail, to set about; वि-to revolve; व्यप to turn back; सम्-to become; *Causal*-to turn, look after; with नि-to send back; निस् to finish; व्या-to exclude

वृति *f.* A request; a fence.

वृत्त *a.* Round. *n.* A circle; an event, occupation, behaviour, a metre

वृत्तांत *m* An event, news, a story.

वृत्ति *f.* The circumference, behaviour, profession, style, gloss.

वृथा *ind.* Uselessly, in vain, wrongly.

वृद्ध *a.* Old. *m.* An old man.

वृद्धि *f.* Increase, prosperity, the substitution of आ, ए, औ, आर् and आल् for अ, इ उ, ऋ and ऌ, short or long.

वृध् *vi.* 1 A. To grow.

वृंत *n.* The foot-stalk of a leaf or fruit.

वृंद *n.* A multitude.

वृंदा *f.* The holy basil.

वृंदार *a* Large, attractive.

वृंदारक *a.* Large; respectable. *m.* A god.

वृश्चिक *m.* A scorpion.

वृष् *vt. vi.* 1 P. To rain, to give.

वृष *m.* A bull.

वृषण *m.* The scrotum.

वृषध्वज *m.* S'iva.

वृषन् *m.* A bull; Indra.

वृषभ *m.* A bull, anything best of its kind.

वृषल *m.* A Shûdra.

वृषली *f.* An unmarried girl having menstruation.

वृषिन् *m.* A peacock.

वृष्टि *f.* Rain, a shower.

वृष्णि *a.* Heretical. *m.* Wind; Krishna.

वॄ *vt.* 9 U. To choose.

वे *vt.* 1 U. To weave, to [sew

वेग *m.* Speed, current, force.

वेगिनी *f* A river. [current.

वेणी *f.* Braided hair, a

वेणु *m.* A bamboo, a pipe.

वेतन *n.* Salary, livelihood.

वेतस *m.* (-सी *f.*) The cane.

वेताल *m.* A kind of ghost.

वेत्र *m.* The cane; A stick.

वेत्रधर (-धारक) *n.* A staff-bearer. [Scriptures.

वेद *m.* Knowledge, Hindu

वेदना *f.* Sensation, pain.

वेदांत *m.* A school of Hindu philosophy.

वेदि *m.* A learned man; *f.* an altar; a seal-ring.

वेदी *f.* An altar.

वेध *m.* Wounding, depth.

वेधस् *m.* Brahmâ, Śiva, Vishnu.

वेपृ 1. A. To shake.
वेपथु *n.* Tremor, trembling.
वेम *m.*, (-न् *m. n.*) A loom.
वेला *f.* Time, flow, sea-shore, boundary.
वेल्ल् *vt. vi.* 1 P. To move.
वेश (-ष) *m.* Dress, entrance, a hosue.
वेशनारी (-वनिता) *f.* A harlot.
वेश्मन् *n.* A house.
वेश्या *f.* A harlot.
वेश्यागमन *n.* Debauchery.
वेष्टन *n.* An envelope, a case, a fence, a turban.
वै *ind.* Used as an expletive.
वैकल्प *n.* Uncertainty.
वैकल्पिक *a.* Optional, doubtful.
वैकल्य *n.* A defect, agitation.
वैकाल *m.* Afternoon.
वैकुंठ *n* The heaven of Vishnu. [an ill omen.
वैकृत *a.* Hideous. *n.* Change,
वैकृत्य *n.* Change, misery.
वैक्लव्य *n.* Confusion, grief.
वैखरी *f.* Speech.
वैखानस *m.* A Vânaprastha.
वैगुण्य *n.* A defect.
वैचित्र्य *n.* Variety.
वैजयंतिका *f.* A banner.
वैजयंती *f.* A banner, a garland.
वैज्ञानिक *a.* Clever.
वैतनिक *m.* A hired labourer.
वैतरणा (-णी) *f.* The river in the hell. [cane-like.
वैतस *a.* Humble; yielding;
वैतान *a.* Sacred.
वैतालिक *m.* A bard.
वैदग्ध्य *n.* Skill, proficiency.
वैदिक *m.* A Brâhmana versed in the Vedas.
वैदेशिक *a.* Foreign.
वैदेहिक *m.* A merchant.
वैदेहि (-ही) *f* Sitâ. [sician.
वैद्य *m.* A learned man, phy-
वैद्यक *m.* Physician; *n.* the science of medicine.
वैद्युत *a.* Electric. [fulness.
वैधर्म्य Deference, unlaw-
वैधवेय *m.* The son of a widow.
वैधव्य *n.* Widowhood.
वैनतेय *m.* Garuda, Aruna.
वैपरीत्य *n.* Opposition, contrariety.
वैपुल्य *n.* Plenty. [wealth.
वैभव *n.* Greatness, power,
वैमनस्य *n.* Sadness, sickness.
वैमात्रेय *m.* A step-mother's son.
वैयर्थ्य *n.* Uselessness.
वैयाकरण *m.* A grammarian.
वैयात्य *n.* Boldness.
वैर *n.* Hostility.
वैरशुद्धि *f.* Revenge.
वैरागिन् *m.* An ascetic.
वैराग्य *n.* Dislike, asceticism.
वैरिन् *m.* An enemy.

वैरूप्य *n.* Deformity.
वैवस्वत *m.* The present or seventh Manu.
वैवाहिक *a.* Matrimonial.
वैशाख *m.* N. of a month; a churning stick.
वैशिष्ट्य *n.* Peculiarity.
वैशेषिक *a.* A system of Indian philosophy.
वैश्य *m.* A man of the third caste.
वैश्रवण *m.* Kubera; Râvana.
वैश्वदेव *m.* An offering made to Vishwadevas.
वैश्वानर *m.* Fire.
वैषम्य *n.* Inequality; injustice.
वैष्ट *n.* Wind; heaven; a world.
वैष्णव *m.* One of the Hindu sects.
वैहासिक *m.* A clown.
वौषट् *ind* An exclamation used in offering an oblation to gods or manes.
व्यक्त *a.* Manifest; wise.
व्यक्ति *f.* Manifestation; individuality; a person; origin; gender.
व्यग्र *a.* Bewildered; eagerly engaged in.
व्यंग *a.* Mutilated.
व्यंग्य *n.* Insinuation.
व्यज *m.*, (-न *n*) A fan.
व्यंजक *a.* Indicative.
व्यंजन *n.* A sign; a consonant; condiment.
व्यतिकर *m.* Mixture; an incident; a calamity; a garb.
व्यतिक्रम *m.* Violation, sin, contrariety.
व्यतिरिक्त *a.* Surpassing; withheld; separate.
व्यतिरेक *m.* Excellence; contrast; exclusion.
व्यतिषंग *m.* Junction; intermixture.
व्यति (ती) हार *m.* Exchange.
व्यतीत *a.* Past; disregarded.
व्यतीपात *m.* An ill omen; disrespect.
व्यत्यय *m.* Inversion; obstruction.
व्यत्यास *m.* Opposition; inverted order.
व्यथ् *vi.* 1 A. To be vexed; to dry.
व्यथा *f.* Pain; fear.
व्यध *vt.* 4 P. (*pp.* विद्ध) To hurt; to perforate.
व्यपगत *a.* Departed.
व्यपदेश *m.* Notice; race; fraud; a name; fame.
व्यपाकृति *f.* Denial.
व्यपाय *m* End.
व्यपाश्रय *m.* Having recourse to.
व्यपेक्षा *f.* Mutual regard.
व्यभि (भी) चार *m* Deviation; error; infidelity.
व्यभिचारिणी *f.* An adulteress.

व्ययं *a.* Perishable. *m.* Loss, decay, expenditure.

व्यर्थ *a.* Useless;unmeaning.

व्यलीक *a.* False; offensive. *m.* A libertine; *n.* pain; fault; falsehood.

व्यवच्छिन्न *a.* Interrupted

व्यवच्छेद *m.* A chapter; dissection; contrast.

व्यवधा *f.* A screen; partition.

व्यवधान *n.* Intervention; a screen; interval.

व्यवसाय *m.* Determination; effort; conduct; trade.

व्यवासित *a.* Settled; undertaken; cheated.

व्यवस्था *f.* Arrangement; fixity,statute;agreement.

व्यवस्थान *n.* Steadiness; determination.

व्यवास्थिति *f.* See व्यवस्थान.

व्यवहार *m.* Business; usage; a law-suit

व्यवाहित *a.* Interrupted, obstructed. [formance.

व्यवहृति *f.* Practice; per-

व्यष्टि *f.* An aggregate; individuality. [difficulty.

व्यसन *n.* A clamity; vice;

व्यस्त *a.* Dispersed; single; perplexed; upset. [ysis.

व्याकरण *n.* Grammar; anal-

व्याकार *m.* Deformity.

व्याकीर्ण *a.* Scattered.

व्याकुल *a.* Perplexed; busy.

व्याकृति *f.* Fraud.

व्याकृति *f.* Analysis; explanation.

व्याकोश (-ष) *a.* Blown.

व्याक्षेप *m.* Delay.

व्याख्या *f.* Comment;exposition; narration. [tion.

व्याख्यान *n.* Speech; exposi-

व्याघात *m.* A blow; obstacle.

व्याघ्र *m* A tiger; the best.

व्याज *m.* Deception; pretext.

व्याजस्तुति *f.* Irony.

व्याजोक्ति *f.* Insinuation.

व्याध *m.* A hunter.

व्याधि *m.* Disease.

व्यान *m.* One of the five vital airs.

व्यापक *a.* Pervading.

व्यापत्ति *f.* Misfortune.

व्यापन्न *a.* Ruined.

व्यापादन *n.* Ruin; malice.

व्यापादित *a.* Killed.

व्यापार *m.* Trade; occupation; effort.

व्यापृत *a.* Engaged in. [effort.

व्यापृति *f.* Employment,

व्याप्ति *f.* Pervasion.

व्यामोह *m.* Embarrassment.

व्यायाम *m.* Exercise, struggle.

व्याल *m.* A snake; a tiger; a rogue; a vicious elephant.

व्यालीन *a.* Thick.

व्यावहारिक *a.* Usual.

व्यावृति *f.* Exclusion.

व्यावृत्त *a.* Surrounded.

व्यावृत्ति *f.* Exclusion, exception; praise.

व्यास *m.* The diameter of a circle. N. of a sage.

व्यासंग *m.* Excessive attachment, diligent study.

व्याहरण *n.* Speech.

व्याहृत *a.* Obstructed.

व्याहार *m.* Voice, jest.

व्याहृति *f.* Speech; a mystic word; a statement.

व्युत्क्रम *m.* Inverted order.

व्युत्पत्ति *f.* Etymology, learning; origin.

व्युत्पन्न *a.* Learned.

व्युदास *m.* Rejection, indifference; killing. [broad.

व्यूढ *a.* Married; arrayed;

व्यूति *f.* Weaving.

व्यूह *m.* An army, a military array; a multitude.

व्योमन् *n* The sky; water.

व्योमकेशिन् *m.* Śiva.

व्योमगंगा *f.* The celestial Ganges.

व्रज् *vt.* 1 P. To go.

व्रज *m.* A flock; a cowpen; a road; a cloud.

व्रजांगना *f.* A cowherdess.

व्रण *m. n.* A sore. [votion.

व्रत *m.n.* A vow; a rite; de-

व्रतति (-ती) *f.* A creeper.

व्रतिन् *m.* An ascetic.

व्रश्च *vt.* 6 P. To cut.

व्रात *m.* A multitude.

व्रात्य *m.* A Bráhmana who has not undergone the thread ceremony.

व्रीड् *vt. vi.* 4 P. To be ashamed. [modesty.

व्रीड *m.* (-डा *f.*) Shame;

व्रीहि *m.* Rice.

श

श *m.* A cutter; *n.* happiness.

शंयु *a.* Happy.

शंस् *vt.* 1 P. To relate, to praise; with अभि-to curse; आ-(Atm.) to expect; to tell; प्र-to praise.

शक् *vi.* 5 P. *vt.* 4 U. To be able; to bear.

शक *m.* An era.

शकट *m. n.* A carriage.

शकटिका *f.* A toy-cart.

शकल *m. n.* A fragment.

शकार *m.* The brother of a king's concubine.

शकुन *n.* An omen; a bird.

शकुनि *m.* A bird, vulture.

शकुंत, (-क), शकुंति *m.* A bird.

शकुल *m.* A fish.

शकृत् *n.* Excrement.

शक्त *a.* Able; strong; clever.

शक्ति *f.* Ability; strength; a missile; a female deity.

शक्य *a.* Possible; directly expressed.

शक्र *m.* Indra; an owl.

शंक् *vt. vi.* 1 A. To doubt; with आ-to doubt; to expect.

शंकनीय *a.* Doubtful.

शंकर *a.* Propitious. *m.* S'iva.

शंका *f.* Doubt; impression.

शंकित *a.* Doubtful; suspicious; uncertain; weak.

शंकु *m.* A post; a nail; a shaft; a spear; a measuring rod; ten billions.

शंख *m.* A conch-shell; a hundred billions; a treasure of Kubera.

शंखध्म (-ध्मा) *m.* A shell-blower.

शंखिन् *m.* The ocean; Vishnu.

शंखिनी *f.* A particular class of women.

शचि (-ची) *f.* Indra's wife.

शटा *f.* The clotted hair of an ascetic.

शट् *vt. vi.* 1 P. To deceive; to hurt.

शठ *m.* A rogue; a fool.

शण *m.* Hemp.

शंड (-ढ) *m.* A eunuch; a bull.

शत *n.* A hundred; a large number.

शतकृत्वस् *ind.* A hundred times.

शतकोटि *m.* Indra's thunderbolt.

शतक्रतु *m.* Indra.

शतखंड *n.* Gold.

शतगुण *a.* A hundred-fold.

शतघ्नी *f.* A kind of missile.

शतपत्र *m.* A peacock.

शतयोनि *m.* Brahmá.

शतक *n.* A century.

शत्रु *m.* An enemy.

शत्रुंजय *m.* An elephant.

शत्वरी *f.* Night.

शद् *vi.* 1 P. To perish; to go.

शनकैस् *ind.* See शनैस्.

शनि *m.* Saturn; Saturday.

शनैश्चर *m.* Saturn.

शनैस् *ind.* Slowly; gradually; successively.

शप् *vt. vi.* 1, 4 U. To curse; to swear; to blame.

शप *m.* A curse.

शपत्र *n.* (-थ *m.*) A curse; an oath.

शफ *m. n.* A hoof; the root.

शफर *m.* (-री *f.*) A small fish.

शबर *m.* A barbarian.

शब्द् *vt.* 10 U. To sound; with प्र-to explain.

शब्द *m.* A sound; a word; verbal authority; title.

शब्दब्रह्मन् *n.* The Vedas.

शब्दवेधिन् *a.* Hitting an invisible mark on hearing its sound only.

शब्दसौष्ठव *n.* Elegance of diction.

शब्दाडंबर *m.* Verbosity; bombast.

शब्दालंकार *m.* Rhetorical use of words.

शम् *vt. vi.* 4 P. To be appeased; to end; with नि-to hear; सन्-to be allayed; उप, प्र-to allay.

शम् *ind.* Happily.

शम m. Calm; alleviation.
शमन a. Soothing.
शमि (-मी) f. N. of a tree.
शमीगर्भ m. Fire.
शंपा f. Lightning.
शंब a. Poor; happy.
शंबरारि m. Cupid.
शंबरी f. An illusion.
शंबल m. n. A bank.
शंबूक m. A conch; a snail.
शंभु m. S'iva.
शय a. Sleeping;
शयथ a. Sleeping. m. Death.
शयन a. Sleeping; a bed.
शयालु a. Sleepy.
शय्या f. A bed.
शर m. An arrow; a reed; hurt; n. water.
शरण n. Protection; a house.
शरण्य a. Helpless; helping. n. A refuge, protector.
शरद् f. The autumn.
शरदा f. Autumn; a year.
शरधि m. A quiver.
शरभ m. A fabulous animal; a young elephant; locust.
शरव्य n. A target. [arrow.
शरसंधान n. Aiming with an
शरासन n. A bow.
शरीर n. The body.
शरीरयष्टि f. A slender body.
शरीरयात्रा f. Maintenance.
श (शा) रीरिक m. The soul.
शर्करा f. Sugar; a stone.
शर्मन् n. Happiness; a house; a title of Brâhmanas.
शर्व m. S'iva; Vishnu.
शर्वरी f. A night.
शलभ m. A locust.
शलाका f. An arrow; a small stick; a shoot.
शल्य m. n. A spear; an arrow; a thorn.
शव m. n. A corpse.
शश m. A hare; spots on the moon.
शशधर m. The moon.
शशविषाण or शशशृंग n. An impossibility.
शशांक m. The moon.
शशाद m. A hawk.
शशिन् m. The moon.
शशिकला (-लेखा) f. The digit of the moon.
शशिभूषण (-भृत, -मौलि, -शेखर) m. S'iva.
शश्वत् ind. Eternally.
शष्कुली f. The orifice of the ear; a cake.
शष्प n. Young grass.
शस् vt. 1 P. To kill.
शस्ति f. Praise.
शस्त्र n. An arm; an instrument; repetition.
शस्त्री f. A knife.
शस्य n. Corn; merit.
शाक m. n. A vegetable.
शाकिनी f. A kind of female demon.
शाकुनिक m. A fowler.
शाक्त m. A worshipper of Sakti.

शाखा *f.* A branch; a part.
शाखामृग *m.* A monkey.
शाखिन् *m.* A tree
शाट *m.* (-टी *f*) A garment.
शाठ्य *n.* Villainy.
शाण *m.* A touch-stone.
शाणित *a.* Whetted; sharpened. [saw.
शाणी *f.* A whet-stone; a
शात Sharpened; weak.
शातमान *a.* Bought with a hundred.
शात्रव *a.* Hostile. *n.* Enmity.
शाद्वल *a.* Grassy; green.
शान *m.* A whet-stone.
शांत *a.* Calm.
शांतनव *m.* Bhîshma.
शांतम् *ind.* Heaven forbid; enough.
शांति *f.* Tranquility; rest; pacification; felicity.
शाप *m.* A curse; oath; abuse; an interdiction.
शार *a.* Variegated. [deer.
शारंग *m.* A peacock; a
शारद *a.* Autumnal; new.
शारदा *f.* Saraswatî; a lute.
शारदी *f.* The full-moon day in कार्तिक.
शारीर, शारीरक *a.* Bodily.
शार्ङ्ग *m.* A bow.
शार्ङ्गधन्वन् (-धर, -पाणि, -भृत) *m.* Vishnu.
शार्दूल *m.* A tiger; foremost.
शाल *m.* N. of a tree.
शालग्राम *m.* A sacred stone typical of Vishnu.
शालभंजिका *f.* A puppet.
शाला *f.* A house; a stable.
शालि *f.* Rice.
शालिन् *a.* Endowed with.
शालिनी *f.* A mistress of the house.
शालिवाहन *m.* N. of a king.
शालिहोत्र *m.* A veterinary surgeon.
शालीन *a.* Bashful; *m.* A house-holder.
शालूक (-र) *m.* A frog.
शाल्मल *m.* (-लि, -ली *f.*) *m.* N. of a tree; a division of the earth. [an animal.
शाव, (-क) *m.* The young of
शाश्वत (-तिक) *a.* Eternal.
शाश्वती *f.* The earth.
शास् *vt.* 2 P. To teach; to rule; with अनु-to punish; आ-to command; (Atm.) To confer a blessing on; to desire; प्र(Atm.)-to pray.
शासन *n.* An order; government; a precept; a deed.
शास्तृ *m.* A king; a teacher.
शास्त्र *n.* A science; a precept. [statement
शास्त्रार्थ *m.* A scriptural
शास्त्रिन् *m.* A learned man.
शास्त्रीय *a.* Scriptural; scientific.
शि *vt vi.* 5 U. To sharpen,
शिक्ष् *vt.* 1 A. To learn.

शिक्षक *m*. A teacher.
शिक्षण *n*. Learning; instruction. [modesty.
शिक्षा *f*.Study; instruction;
शिखंडिन् *m*. A peacock; an arrow; son of Drupada.
शिखर *m.n*. A peak; a top.
शिखरिणी *f*. A kind of dish; N. of a metre. [tree.
शिखरिन् *m*. A mountain; a
शिखा *f*. Top; a flame; a crest; a pigtail.
शिखिन् *m*. A peacock; fire; an arrow: a mountain, a Brâhmana; Ketu.
शिज् *vi*. 2 A. 10 U. To tinkle. [string.
शिंजा, शिंजिनी *f*. A bow-
शित *a*. Sharpened.
शिति *a*. White. [cock.
शितिकंठ *m*. Siva: a pea-
शिथिल *a*. Loose; weak.
शिपि *n*. Water.
शिपिविष्ट *a*. Bold. *m*. Śiva; a leper. [ing by Ujjain.
शिप्रा *f*.N.of of a river flow-
शिबिका *f*. A Palanquin
शिबिर *n*. A camp.
शिंबा,शिंबिका,शिंबी *f*.A pod.
शिरच्छेद *m*. Decapitation.
शिरस् *n*. The head; a peak; chief; front, van.
शिरसिज *m*. The hair of the head.
शिरस्त्र (-त्राण) *n*. A helmet.
शिरा *f*.A vessel of the body.
शिराल *a*. Sinewy.
शिरीष *m*. N. of a tree; *n*. its flower.
शिरोधरा,शिरोधि *f*.The neck.
शिरोमणी *m*. A jewel worn on the head; a title of respect. [head.
शिरोरुह *m*. The hair of the
शिला *f*. A stone; arsenic.
शिलींध्र *n*. A mushroom; a particular flower.
शिलीमुख *n*.An arrow;a bee.
शिल्प *n*. An art; skill.
शिल्पकर्मन् *n*. Handicraft.
शिल्पकार *m*. An artisan.
शिल्पशाला *f*. Workshop.
शिल्पिन् *m*. An artisan.
शिव *a*. Auspicious. *m*. The god Śiva; *n*. well-being.
शिवताति *a*. Propitious
शिवा *f*. Pârvatî; a jackal.
शिवानी *f*. Párvatî.
शिशिर *a*. Cold. *n*. Dew; winter. [*m*. The moon.
शिशिरकिरण (-अंशु, -दीधिति)
शिशिरात्यय *m*. The spring season.
शिशु, (-क) *m*. A child.
शिष्ट *a*. Remaining; tamed, educated; chief.
शिष्टाचार *m*. Good manners.
शिष्य *m*. A pupil
शी *iv*. 2 A. To Sleep; with अति-to surpass; सम्-to

doubt; अधि-to recline upon.

शीकर *m*. Spray.

शीघ्र *a*. Quick.

शीघ्रम् *ind*. Quickly.

शीत *a*. Cold; dull.

शीतभानु *m*. The moon.

शीतल *a*. Cold.

शीतला *f*. Small-pox.

शीन *a*. Thick. *m*. A dolt.

शीर्ण *a*. Withered; emaciated; shattered; dry.

शीर्ष *n*. The head.

शीर्षक *m*. Râhu. *n*. head; helmet; judgment.

शीर्षन् *n*. The head.

शील् *vt*. 1 P. 10 U. To honour; to study; to visit; to wear. [tion.

शील *n*. Character, inclina-

शीलन *n*. Study.

शुंशुमार *m*. A porpoise.

शुक *m*. A parrot. [oyster.

शुक्ति, (-का) *f*. A pearl-

शुक्र *m*. Venus; the preceptor of demons; *n*. semen virile; the essence.

शुक्रिय *a*. Seminal.

शुक्ल *a*. White. [cock.

शुक्लांग; शुक्लापांग *m*. A pea-

शुक्लिमन् *m*. Whiteness.

शुच् *vi*. 1 P. To bewail.

शुच् (-चा) *f*. Sorrow; distress. [The hot season.

शुचि *a*. Bright; holy. *m*.,

शुंठि (-ठी) *f*. Dry ginger

शुंड *m* शुंडा *f*. An elephant's proboscis.

शुद्ध *a*. Pure; chaste; bright.

शुद्धांत *m*. A harem.

शुद्धि *f*. Purification, cleanness, retaliation, correctness, lustre, correction.

शुद्धिपत्र *n*. A list of errata.

शुध् *vi*. 4 P. To become pure.

शुनि *m*. A dog.

शुनी *f*. A bitch.

शुन्य *a*. Empty.

शुभ् *vi*. 1 A. To look beautiful, to shine. [ful.

शुभ *a*. Auspicious, beauti-

शुभंकर *a*. Auspicious.

शुभंयु *a*. Fortunate. [man.

शुभांगी *f*. A beautiful wo-

शुभ्र *a*. White, bright.

शुल्क *m*. *n*. A present made to the bride-groom or the bride; a tax. [Copper.

शुल्व *m*. *n*. *f*. A rope. *n*.

शुश्रूषा *f*. Service.

शुष् *vi*. 4 P. To become dry.

शुष्क *a*. Dry, groundless, offensive.

शुष्म *m*. *n*. Fire; *n*. light.

शूकर *m*. A hog.

शूद्र *m*. A man of the fourth caste. [S'ûdra caste.

शूद्रा *f*. A woman of the

शूद्राणी, शूद्री *f*. Wife of a Sûdra.

शून्य *a.* Vacant, empty, lonely. *n.* A cipher.

शून्यवाद *m.* Atheism.

शूर *a.* Brave.

शूर्प *m. n.* A winnowing basket.

शूर्मिका, शूर्मी *f.* An anvil.

शूल *m. n.* A pike; acute pain.

शूलिन् *m.* A spear-man; Śiva.

शृगाल *m.* A jackal; a rogue.

शृंखल *m.n.*(-ला *f.*) A chain.

शृंग *n.* A horn; a peak; a mark; a lotus.

शृंगबेर *n.* Ginger.

शृंगार *m.* Love; sexual passion.

शृंगिन् *m.* A mountain; Śiva; Śiva's attendant.

शॄ *vt.* 9 P. To split; with वि-(passive) to fade.

शेखर *m.* A peak; a crest.

शेमुषी *f.* Intellect.

शेवधि *m.* A valuable treasure.

शेवल शेवाल, शैवल, शैवाल *m. n.* Green moss.

शेवलिंनी *f.* A river.

शेष *a.* Remaining. *m. n.* Residue. *m.* King of serpents; Balarâma.

शैत्य *n.* Cold.

शैथिल्य *n.* Laxity; slackness.

शैल *m.* A mountain.

शैली *f.* Style; conduct.

शैलूष *m.* An actor; a musician; a rogue.

शैलेय *a.* Mountainous. *m.* A lion. *n.* Benzoin.

शशव *n.* Childhood.

शो *vt.* 4 P. To sharpen.

शोक *m.* Sorrow, lamentation, deep anguish.

शोचन *n.* Sorrow, mourning.

शोचनीय *a.* Deplorable.

शोचिस् *n.* Light, a flame.

शोच्य *a.* Deplorable, low.

शोण *a.* Red. *m.* Name of a large river.

शोणित *n.* Blood. *a.* Red.

शोथ *m.* Swelling.

शोध *m.*, (-न *n.*) Correction; retaliation; acquittance.

शोधनी *f.* A broom.

शोभन *a.* Beautiful, virtuous.

शोभा *f.* Grace, lustre, ornament, grandeur, light.

शोष *m.* Dryness.

शोषण *n.* Absorption.

शौक्तिकेय, शौक्तेय *n.* A pearl.

शौच *n.* Purification.

शौटीर *a.* Proud.

शौटीर्य *n.* Pride.

शौंड *a.* Skilful, intoxicated.

शौंडिक (-न्) *m.* A distiller and seller of wines.

शौंडीर *a.* Proud.

शौनिक *m* A butcher.

शौर्य *n.* Valour, strength.

श्मशान *n.* A cemetery.

श्मशानवैराग्य *n.* Momentary despondency.

श्मश्रु *n.* The beard.
श्यान *a.* Thick, dry.
श्याम *a* Black. *m.* A cloud.
श्यामकर्ण *m.* A horse suitable for a horse-sacrifice
श्यामल *a.* Blackish.
श्यामा *f.* A dark woman; dark night; a cow.
श्यामाक *m.* A kind of grass.
श्यामिका *f.* Blackness, impurity. [brother.
श्याल, (-क) *m.* A wife's
श्येन *m.* A hawk.
श्यै *v. i.* 1 A. To go; to wither.
श्रद्धा *f.* Faith, respect, strong desire. [rous.
श्रद्धालु *a.* Faithful, desi-
श्रपण *n.* Boiling.
श्रम् *vi.* 4 P. To be weaired; with वि-to rest.
श्रम *m.* Labour, weariness.
श्रमण *m.* An ascetic.
श्रम्भ् *vi.* 1 A. To err; with वि-to confide in.
श्रय *m.* Shelter. [fame.
श्रव *m.* The ear; *n.* hearing;
श्रवण *n.* Hearing; the hypotenuse.
श्रवस् *n.* The ear.
श्राद्ध *a.* Faithful. *n.* A funeral ceremony performed at various times.
श्रान्त *a.* Fatigued; calmed.
श्रान्ति *f.* Fatigue.
श्राम *m.* Time; a month; a shed.
श्रावक *m.* A pupil.[month.
श्रावण *m.* N. of a lunar
श्रावणी *f.* A religious rite performed on the full-moon day in S'rávana.
श्राव्य *a.* Audible.
श्रि *vt.* 1 U. To have recourse to: with अधि-to ascend; आ to assume; उद्-to raise; सम्-to depend on; to get.
श्री *f.* Wealth; majesty; splendour; Lakshmî; intellect; fortune; colour.
श्रीखंड *m. n.* Sandal wood.
श्रीधर, श्रीपति *m.* Vishnu.
श्रीफल *n.* The Bilva fruit.
श्रीमत् *a.* Wealthy; famous.
श्रु *vt.* 1 P. 5 P. To hear; with आ-to promise; उप-to learn from; प्रति-to promise.
श्रुत *n.* Revelation; learning.
श्रुति *f.* Hearing, the ear; a report, the Vedas; an interval in music.
श्रुतिविषय *m.* Sound, the reach of the ear.
श्रेढी *f* A progression.
श्रेणि *m. f.* (णी *f.*) A line.
श्रेणिका *f.* A tent.
श्रेयस् *a.* Preferable. *n.* Virtue; happiness.

श्रेयस्कर *a.* Propitious.
श्रेष्ठ *a.* Oldest; excellent.
श्रेष्ठिन् *m.* The head of traders; a merchant.
श्रोणि (-णी) *f.* The buttocks; a row.
श्रोतस् *n.* A current.
श्रोतृ *m.* A hearer.
श्रोत्र *n.* The ear. [Vedas.
श्रोत्रिय *a.* Learned in the
श्रौत *n.* Vedic ritual. [fine.
श्लक्ष्ण *a.* Smooth; minute;
श्लघ् *vt. vi.* 1 A. To praise.
श्लथ् *vt. vi.* 10 U. To relax; to hurt.
श्लथ *a.* Loose.
श्लाघा *f.* Boast.
श्लाघ्य *a.* Praiseworthy.
श्लिष् *vt.* 1 P. To burn. 4 P. To embrace; with वि- to burst.
श्लेष *m.* Union; society; a figure of speech.
श्लेष्मन् *m.* The phlegmatic humour. [fame.
श्लोक *m.* A stanza; praise;
श्वन् *m.* A dog.
श्वपच्(-च), श्वपाक *m.* A chándàla. [slavery.
श्ववृत्ति *f.* Life of a dog;
श्वशुर *m.* Father-in-law.
श्वश्रू *f.* Mother-in-law.
श्वस् *vi.* 2 P. To breathe; with आ-to take courage; वि-to confide in; to be fearless; समा-to take heart.
श्वस् *ind.* To-morrow. [tion.
श्वसन *m.* Air. *n.* Respira-
श्वस्तन, श्वस्त्य *a.* Future.
श्वान *m.* A dog
श्वापद *m.* A beast of prey.
श्वि *vt. vi.* 1 P. (*pp.* शून) To swell; to move.
श्वित *a.* White.
श्वित्र *n.* White leprosy.
श्वेत *a.* White. [moon.
श्वेतवाहन *m.* Arjuna; the
श्वेता *f.* A cowrie.

ष

ष *m.* Loss; final beatitude.
षट्क *n.* An aggregate of six.
षंढ *m.* A eunuch.
षट्पद *m.* A bee.
षड्ज *m.* The first of the seven primary notes in music.
षष् *num.* (*pl.*) Six.
षष्टि *f.* Sixty.
षष्ठ *a.* Sixth.
षोडश *a.* Sixteenth.
षोढा *ind.* In six ways.
ष्ठिव् *vt. vi.* 1, 4 P. To spit.

स

स *ind.* With; same.
संयत् *m. f.* Battle; fight.
संयत *a.* Restrained.
संयत्त *a.* Ready.
संयम *m.*, (-न *n.*) Restraint.
संयात्रा *f.* A sea-voyage.
संयुक्त *a.* Joint. [ance-
संयोग *m.* Conjunction; alli.

संरब्ध *a.* Enraged; swelled.
संरंभ *m.* Anger; pride.
संराधन *n.* Propitiation.
संरुद्ध *a.* Checked; refused.
संलग्न *a.* Closely attached.
संलाप *m.* Conversation.
संवत् *ind.* A year.
संवत्सर *m.* A year.
संवर *m.* A bridge; *n.* concealment.
संवर्त *m.* Periodical dissolution.
संवर्तक *m.* Submarine fire; N. of a cloud.
संवलित *a.* Diversified.
संवसथ *m.* A village.
संवाद *m.* A dialogue.
संवार *m.* Covering; diminution.
संवाहन *n.* Shampooing.
संविग्न *a.* Distracted.
संवित्ति *f.* Perception; harmony.
संविद् *f.* Intellect; contract; war.
संविधा *f.* Arrangement.
संविधानक *n.* A Plot.
संविष्ट *a.* Sleeping.
संवृत *a.* Concealed.
संवृत्त *a.* Happened.
संवेग *m.* Agitation; haste.
संवेदन *n.* (-ना) *f.* Sensation.
संशय *m.* Doubt; difficulty.
संशयात्मन् *m.* A sceptic.
संशीति *f.* Doubt.
संशुद्धि *f.* **संशोधन** *n.* Thorough purification.
संश्रय *m.* Refuge.
संश्लिष्ट *a.* Pressed together.
संश्लेष *m.* Union.
संसक्त *a.* Attached to; confused.
संसद् *f.* An assembly.
संसर्ग *m.* Association.
संसार *m.* The world.
संसिद्धि *f.* Complete accomplishment.
संसृति *f.* Course, world.
संसृष्टि *f.* Union.
संस्कार *m.* Decoration; education; a ceremony.
संस्कृत *a.* Refined. *n.* The Sanskrit language.
संस्तर *m.* A couch; a bed.
संस्था *f.* An assembly; business.
संस्थान *n.* Position; a mark; a heap.
संस्थापन *n.* Establishment, regulation, confirmation.
संस्थित *a.* Contiguous.
संस्थिति *f.* Accumulation; abode.
संस्मृति *f.* Remembrance.
संहत *a.* United.
संहति *f.* Combination; bulk.
संहार *m.* Contraction; collection; end.
संहिता *f.* Collection.
संह्राति *f.* Contraction; loss.
सकर्मक *a.* Transitive.
सकल *a.* All, whole; full.
सकाम *a.* Lustful; satisfied.
सकाश *m.* Presence; vicinity.
सकाशात् *ind.* From; near.
सकृत् *ind.* Once, formerly.

सक्त *pp.* Devoted.
सक्ति *f.* Contact; attachment.
सखि *m.* A companion.
सखी *f.* A female companion.
सख्य *n.* Friendship.
सगोत्र *m.* A kinsman of the same family.
संकट *n.* A difficulty.
संकर *m.* Mixture; confusion.
संकलन *n.* (-ना *f.*) Addition; blending.
संकल्प *m.* Will, desire, resolve.
संकार *m.* Dust.
संकाश *a.* Like. *m.* Vicinity.
संकीर्ण *a.* Miscellaneous.
संकुचित *a.* Contracted.
संकुल *a.* Crowded. *n.* A crowd; a confused fight.
संकेत *m.* Agreement; appointment; sign.
संकोच *m.* Contraction.
संक्रम *m.* Transition. *n.* A bridge.
संक्रमण *n.* Concurrence; the sun's passage from one sign of the zodiac to another; progress.
संक्रांति *f.* See संक्रमण.
संक्राम *m.* Difficult progress.
संक्षय *m.* Utter ruin
संक्षेप *m.* An epitome; abridgment.
संक्षोभ *m.* Agitation; pride.
संख्य *n.* War, battle.
संख्या *f.* A number; reason; intellect; manner.
संख्यात *a.* Calculated.
संग *m.* A meeting; contact; company; worldly attachment; fight.
संगति *f.* Union; society; connection; knowledge.
संगम *m.* See संगति.
संगर *m.* Agreement; battle.
संगीत *m.* A chorus; singing accompanied with music and dancing.
संगीतशाला *f.* A concert-hall.
संगीति *f.* Concert; harmony.
संग्रह *m.* Accumulation; propitiation; conjunction; amount; summary.
संग्रहणी *f.* Dysentery.
संग्राम *m.* War, battle.
संग्राह *m.* The fist; seizing forcibly; the handle.
संघ *m.* Multitude, quantity.
संघट्टन *n.* (-ना *f*) Close contact; collision; meeting.
संघर्ष *m.* Friction, rivalry.
संघात *m.* Association; slaughter; phlegm.
सचिव *m.* A minister; companion.
सचेल *a.* Dressed.
सजाति, सजातीय *a.* Of the same kind, like.
सजुस् *m.* A companion.
सज्ज *a.* Ready.

सज्जा *f.* An armour; dress.
संचय *m.* A collection.
संचर *m.* A narrow passage.
संचरण *n.* Motion.
संचलन *n.* Shaking. [tress.
संचार *m.* A passage; dis-
संचारक *m.* A leader.
संचिति *f.* A collection.
संज् *vi.* 1 P. To cling to; with अनु-to associate; व्यति-to link together.
संजीवनी *f.* A kind of elixir.
संज्ञा *f.* Consciousness; sign; designation; knowledge.
सटा *f.* Matted hair; a mane.
सट्टक *n* A minor species of a drama.
संडीन *n.* A mode of flight.
सत् *a.* Being; real; good. *n.* Existence; truth. Brahman (*n.*)
सत्कार *m.* Hospitable treatment; reverence.
सतत *a.* Eternal.
सती *f.* A virtuous wife.
सतीर्थ *m.* A fellow student.
सत्ता *f.* Existence; reality.
सत्र *n.* A sacrificial session.
सत्त्व *m. n.* Existence, life; spirit, wealth; an animal. *n.* A noun; virtue, truth; courage; natural quality.
सत्य *a.* True. *n.* Truth; an oath; the first of the four Yugas.
सत्यसंध *a.* Veracious.
सत्या *f.* Veracity. [truth.
सत्यापन *n.* Observing the
सत्वर *a.* Speedy; quick.
सद् *vi.* 1 P. (*pp.* सन्न) To sit down; to perish; with अव-to faint; to perish; उप-to approach; प्र-to favour; to be clear.
सदन *n.* A house.
सदस् *n* Abode; assembly.
सदस्य *m.* A member of an assembly.
सदा *ind.* Always. [per.
सदृक्ष (-श,-श्) *a.* Like; pro-
सद्मन् *n.* A house; temple; water. [mediately.
सद्यस् *ind.* To-day, im-
सद्योजात *a.* Newly born.
सधर्मचारिणी, सधर्मिणी *f.* A wife legally married.
सना *ind.* Always.
सनात् *ind.* Always.
सनातन *a.* Eternal; permanent.
संतत *a.* Uninterrupted.
संतति *f.* Continuity; race; progeny; a heap.
संतर्पण *n.* Satisfying.
संतान *m. n.* See संतति.
संताप *m.* Heat; fire; pain; penance, passion.
संतोष *m.* Contentment.
संत्रास *m.* Fear. [herence.
संदर्भ *m.* Connection; co-
संदिग्ध *a.* Doubtful; obscure

संदिष्ट *n.* News.
संदीपन *n.* Exciting.
संदेश *m.* News; message; command.
संदेह *m.* Doubt. [titude.
संदोह *m.* Assemblage; mul-
संधा *f.* Promise; limit.
संधान *n.* Alliance; fixing.
संधि *m.* Uuion; peace, a joint; an interval. [tion.
संध्या *f.* Twilight; medita-
सन्नद्ध *a.* Harnessed; arrayed; prevalent.
सन्नाह *m.* Armour. [lation.
संनिकर्ष *m.* Proximity; re-
संनिधान *n.* **संनिधि** *f.* Proximity; appearance.
संनिपात *m.* Collision; mixture; a morbid state of three humours of the body producing fever
संनिभ *a.* Similar
संनिवेश *m.* A place; construction; a figure.
संनिहित *a.* Proximate; present.
संन्यास *m.* Abandonment of worldly attachment.
संन्यासिन् *m.* One who has given up all worldly affections.
सपत्न *m.* An enemy.
सपत्नी *f.* A co-wife.
सपदि *ind.* Instantly.
सपर्या *f.* Worship.

सपाद *a.* One and one fourth.
सपिंड *m.* A kinsman connected by blood. [dha.
सापिंडी *f.* A kind of S′rád-
सपीति *f.* Drinking in company. [seven things.
सप्तक *n.* An aggregate of
सप्ततंतु *m.* A sacrifice.
सप्तति *f.* Seventy.
सप्तन् *num.* Seven.
सप्तम *a.* Seventh.
सप्ति *m.* A yoke,a horse.
सफरी *f.* A small fish.
सफल *a.* Successful.
सबंधु *m.* A kinsman.
सभा *f.* An assembly.
सभाज् *vt.* 10 U. To serve; to congratulate.
सभाजन *n.* Courtesy; thanks; congratulation.
सभासद् *m.* Member of an assembly.
सभ्य *a.* Polite. *m.* A person of honourable parentage.
सम् *ind.* With, together, greatly. [like.
सम *a.* Even, equal, common,
समकालीन *a.* Contemporary.
समक्ष *a.* Visible.
समग्र *a.* Entire
समचतुर्भुज *m.* A rhombus.
समज्ञा *f.* Fame [sonable.
समंजस *a.* Proper, true, rea-
समता *f.* Equality.
समदर्शिन *a.* Impartial.

समंततस् *ind.* On all sides.
समन्वय *m.* Natural order; application; conjunction.
समभिव्याहार *m* Association; company; proximity.
समम् *ind.* With, together.
समय *m.* Time; oath; established custom; agreement; bargain; limit; sign; end; poetical conventionality. [near.
समया *ind.* In due time;
समर *m. n.* War, battle.
समर्थ *a.* Powerful; proper.
समर्थन *n.* Corroboration, allaying disputes.
समर्पण *n.* Delivering. [tion.
समवाय *m.* Union; collec-
समवायिन् *a.* Closely connected.
समष्टि *f.* An aggregate.
समस्त *a.* All.
समा *f.* Year. *ind.* With.
समाकुल *a.* Crowded; confused; full of. [ed.
समाख्यात *a.* Famed; count-
समागम *m.* Arrival; union; association.
समाघात *m.* Slaughter; war.
समाचार *m.* Report.
समाज *m.* An assembly.
समाजिक *m.* A spectator.
समाज्ञा *f.* Fame.
समाधान *n.* Contentment, contemplation; answering an objection; peace.
समाधि *m.* Deep meditation; silence; a collection.
समान *a.* Like, same; good.
समापत्ति *f.* Chance.
समापन *n.* Conclusion. [ed.
समापन्न *a.* Obtained; happen-
समाप्त *a.* Concluded.
समाप्ति *f.* Conclusion; perfection; reconciliation.
समाम्नाय *m.* A revelation; totality. [undertaking.
समारंभ *m.* Commencement;
समाराधन *n.* Gratification.
समारोह *m.* Ascending.
समावर्तन *n.* A pupil's return home after completing his study.
समावाय *m.* Association; number.
समास *m.* A compound; contraction; reconciliation. [cinctly.
समासेन, समासतः *ind.* Suc-
समाहार *m.* Collection
समाह्वय *m.* Fight; name.
समाह्वान *n.* A challenge
समित् *f.* War, battle.
समिति *f.* Assembly; battle.
समिध् *f.* Fuel for sacred fire. [milation.
समीकरण *n.* Equation; assi-
समीक्षा *f.* Investigation; essential nature.
समीचीन *a.* Right.
समीप *a.* Near.
समीर, (-ण) *m.* Air, wind.

समीहा *f.* Desire.
समुच्चय *m.* Collection.
समुत्थान *n.* Increase.
समुत्पत्ति *f.* Production.
समुत्सुक *a.* Sorrowful; agitated.
समुत्सेध *m.* Height; thickness.
समुद (दा) य *m.* Rise; number; effort; war.
समुद्भव *m.* Production; origin.
समुद्यम *m.* Effort.
समुद्र *m.* The sea.
समुद्वाह *m.* Marriage.
समुद्वेग *m.* Fear, alarm.
समुन्नति *f.* Elevation; dignity; prosperity.
समुपवेशन *n.* A building.
समूढ *a.* Collected; bent.
समूह *m.* Assemblage.
समूहन *n.* Collection; plenty.
समृद्ध *a.* Prosperous.
समृद्धि *f.* Prosperity; abundance.
संपत्ति *f.* Prosperity.
संपद् *f.* Wealth; prosperity; excellence.
संपन्न *a.* Endowed with; fortunate.
संपराय *m.* Conflict; a calamity.
संपर्क *m.* Mixture; contact.
संपा *f.* Lightning.
संपात *m.* Collection; alighting; concurrence.
संपादन *n.* Accomplishment.
संपुट *m.* Cavity; a casket.
संपूर्ण *a.* Whole.
संपृक्त *a.* Mixed; related.
संप्रति *ind.* Now; at present.
संप्रदान *n.* Gift
संप्रदाय *m.* Tradition; usage.
संप्रधारणा *f.* Deliberation.
संप्रयोग *m.* Union; contact.
संप्रसारण *n.* The substitution of इ, उ, ऋ, लृ, for य्, व्, र्, ल्, respectively.
संप्लव *m.* Inundation; ruin.
संबंध *m* Connection; fitness. friendship;
संबाध *m.* Pressure; difficulty.
संबुद्धि *f.* Perfect knowledge; the vocative case.
संबोधन *n.* Calling; the vocative case.
संभव *m.* Origin; posibility; agreement.
संभार *m.* Preparation; multitude.
संभावना *f.* Possibility; respect; fancy.
संभाषा *f.* Conversation; contract.
संभूति *f.* Combination; origin.
संभोग *m.* Enjoyment.
संभ्रम *m.* Confusion; error.
संमति *f.* Agreement; approval; regard.
संमर्द *m.* Friction; battle.
संमान *m.* Respect.
संमार्जन *n.* Sweeping.
संमार्जनी *f.* A broom
संमित *a.* Equal.
संमुख (-खीन) *a.* Facing; opposite

संमेलन *n*. Assembly; meeting.

संमोह *m*. Bewilderment; folly; fascination.

सम्यच् *a*. All, true. *ind*. Properly; together; wholly.

सम्राज् *m*. A paramount sovereign.

सर *n*. A lake. *m*. A string; an arrow.

सरघा *f*. A bee.

सरट *m*. A wind; a crow.

सरणि *f*. A way; arrangement; a straight line.

सरमा *f*. The bitch of gods.

सरल *a*. Straight; simple.

सरस् *n*. Water; a lake.

सरसिज, सरोज, सरोजन्मन्, सरोरुह, सरसिरुह *n*. A lotus; a lily.

सरस्वती *f*. The goddess of learning.

सरित् *f*. A river.

सरितांपति *m*. An ocean.

सरीसृप *m*. A snake.

सरोजिनी *f*. A pond abounding in lotuses.

सरोवर *m*. A lake.

सर्ग *m*. Creation; resolution; nature; a canto.

सर्प *m*. A snake.

सर्पण *n*. Creeping.

सर्पिस् *n*. Clarified butter.

सर्व *pron. a*. All, whole.

सर्वंकष *a*. All-destroying.

सर्वज्ञ *a*. Omniscient.

सर्वतोभद्र *m. n*. A house with four doors; the car of Vishnu.

सर्वतोभद्रा *f*. A dancing girl.

सर्वतोमुख *n*. Water; sky; *m*. Śiva; Brahman (*m*.).

सर्वत्र *ind*. Everywhere.

सर्वथा *ind*. In all ways; altogether; by all means

सर्वरी *f*. The night.

सर्व (र्वं) सहा *f*. The earth.

सर्षप *m*. Mustard.

सलिल *n*. Water.

सलोकता *f*. Residence in the same heaven with a particular deity.

सव *m*. A sacrifice.

सवन *m*. The moon; *n*. a sacrifice.

सविकल्प *a*. Optional.

सवितर्क *a*. Thoughtful.

सवितृ *a*. Producing. *m*. The sun.

सविभ्रम *a*. Sportive

सविमर्शम् *ind*. Thoughtfully.

सविशेष *a*. Peculiar; superior.

सविस्तर *a*. Detailed.

सव्य *a*. Right; backward.

सव्यपेक्ष *a*. Dependent on.

सव्यसाचिन् *m*. Arjuna.

सव्याज *a*. Pretended.

सव्येष्टृ *m*. A charioteer.

सश्रीक *a*. Prosperous; fortunate.

ससत्त्व *a*. Pregnant.

सस्ज् *vt.* 1 P. To become ready.

सस्य *n.* Corn.; weapon.

सह् *vt.* 1 A. To bear; to forbear; with उद्-to be able; to desire; प्र-to overpower; वि-to sustain. [With.

सह *a.* Able; patient. *ind.*

सहकार *m.* Co-operation; a mango tree.

सहगमन *m.* A woman's burning herself on the funeral pile of her husband.

सहचर *m.* A companion.

सहचार *m.* Harmony.

सहज *m.* A brother; natural disposition. [married.

सहधर्मिणी *f.* A wife legally

सहसा *ind.* Rashly, suddenly.

सहस्र *n.* A thousand.

सहस्रकर (-अंशु,-किरण,-धामन्-पाद) *m.* The sun.

सहस्रदृश् (-अक्ष, -नयन, -नेत्र) *m.* Indra; Vishnu.

सहा *f.* The earth

सहाय *m.* A companion, a patron. [help.

सहायता *f.* Companionship;

सहित *a.* Accompanied by.

सहिष्णु *a.* Patient.

सहृदय *m.* A man of taste. *a.* Kind; good-hearted.

सह्य *a.* Endurable. *m.* N. of a mountain.

सांवत्सरिक *a.* Annual.

सांसारिक *a.* Worldly.

साकम् *ind.* Simultaneously.

साकल्य *n.* Entirety.

साकूत *a.* Significant.

साक्षात् *ind.* Manifestly; actually; directly. [fest.

साक्षात्कार *m.* Making mani-

साक्षिन् *m.* A witness.

सागर *m.* The ocean.

साग्निक *m.* A house-holder maintaining a sacred fire.

सांकेतिक *a.* Conventional.

सांख्य *m.* N. of a system of Hindu philosophy.

सांग *a.* Complete.

साचि *ind.* Crookedly.

साटोप *a.* Proud; majestic.

सातत्य *n.* Continuity.

साति *f.* Gift; end.

सात्त्विक *a.* Virtuous, good.

साद *m.* Weariness; decay; stoppage, thinness; purity.

सादृश्य *n.* Resemblance.

साध् *vt.* 5 P. To accomplish; 4 P. to be accomplished; 10 P. to go.

साधक *a.* Skilful. *m.* A Yogin; a magician.

साधन *n.* Accomplishment; means; an instrument; killing; source; proof.

साधना *f.* Worship.

साधर्म्य *n.* Likeness, community. [mon; equal.

साधारण *a.* General; com-

साधिष्ठ *a* (Super. of साधु or बाढ) Best.

साधीयस् *a.* (Comp. of साधु or बाढ) Better, stronger.

साधु *a.* Good; fit; strong. *m.* A saint; a merchant. *ind.* Well, enough.

साध्य *a.* Practicable; attainable. *n.* An object to be gained; accomplishment.

साध्वस *n.* Terror; torpor.

साध्वी *f.* A chaste woman.

सानु *m. n.* A peak

सानुमत् *m.* A mountain.

सांत्व *m.*, (-न *n.*, -ना *f.*) Conciliation; appeasing.

सान्द्र *a.* Thick; stout; oily; abundant. [twilight.

सान्ध्य *a.* Relating to the

सान्निध्य *n.* Vicinity; presence.

सापत्न *m. pl.* Children of the different wives of the same husband. [rivalry

सापत्न्य *m.* An enemy; *n.*

साफल्य *n.* Fruitfulness.

सामग्री *f.* Materials; provision.

सामग्र्य *n.* Perfection,

सामंजस्य *n.* Fitness.

सामन् *n.* Conciliation, negotiation; a metrical hymn of the Sáma Veda.

सामन्त *m.* A neighbour; a tributary prince.

सामयिक *a.* Periodical.

सामर्थ्य *n.* Power; wealth.

सामाजिक *m.* A spectator.

सामानाधिकरण्य *n.* Common relationship.

सामान्य *a.* Common; alike.

सामि *ind.* Half.

सामीची *f.* Praise.

सामीप्य *n.* Vicinity.

सामुद्रिक *m.* A palmist; *n.* palmistry.

सांपराय *m. n* Conflict.

सांप्रतम् *ind.* Now; immediately; properly.

सांप्रदायिक *a.* Traditional.

साम्य *n.* Similarity; equality.

साम्राज्य *n.* Empire; universal sovereignty.

सायक *m.* An arrow.

सायन्तन *a.* Vespertine.

सायम् *ind.* In the evening.

सायुज्य *n.* Identification.

सार *m. n.* The essence; strength; worth. *m* Climax; summary.

सारंग *m.* Variegated colour; a lion; an elephant; the spotted deer.

सारणि (-णी) *f.* A canal.

सारथि *m.* A charioteer.

सारथ्य *n.* The office of a charioteer.

सारमेय *m.* A dog.

सारस *m.* The Indian crane.

सारस(श)न *n.* A girdle.

सारस्वत *n*. Speech, eloquence.
सारिका *f*. A kind of bird.
सारिन् *a* Resorting to.
सारूप्य *n*. Sameness.
सार्थ *a*. Significant. *m*. A caravan; a collection.
सार्थवाह *m*. The leader of a caravan ; a merchant.
सार्द्र *a*. Wet ; damp.
सार्वकालिक *a*. Everlasting.
सार्वजनिक, सार्वजनीन *a*. Public ; general.
सार्वभौम *m*. An emperor.
सावधान *a*. Attentive
सावधि *a*. Finite. [sacrifice.
सावन *m*. Conclusion of a
साविका *f*. A mid-wife.
सावित्री *f*. Párwatí; a celebrated verse of the Rigveda; a ray of light.
साशंस *a*. Hopeful.
साशंक *a*. Apprehensive.
साहचर्य *n*. Association.
साहस *n* Violence; daring.
साहासिक *a*. Bold, cruel.
साहायक *n*. Assistance.
साहाय्य *n*. Help.
साहित्य *n*. Society; a literary composition; materials; rhetoric; art of poetry.
साह्य *n*. Assistance.
सिंह *m*. A lion.
सिंहनाद *m*. A war-cry.
सिंहासन *m*. A throne.
सिंही *f*. A lioness.
सिकता *f*. Sand.
सिक्त *a*. Moistened.
सिक्थ *m*. Boiled rice.
सिच् *vt*. 6 U. To sprinkle.
सिंजित *n*. Tinkling.
सित *a*. White. *n*. Silver.
सिता *f*. Sugar.
सिति *a*. White; black.
सितिकंठ *m*. S'iva.
सिद्ध *a*. Acquired; established; proved; ready; cooked; well-versed. *m*. A sage.
सिद्धान्त *m*. The demonstrated conclusion; a proved fact.
सिद्धि *f*. Accomplishment ; proof ; truth; preparation ; success; superhuman power; readiness.
सिध् *vt*. *vi*. 1 P. To go; with अप-to remove ; नि-to remove ; to prohibit ; with प्रति-to contradict ; 4 P. To succeed; to be established; प्र, सम्-to be accomplished.
सिध्म, (-न्) *n*. Leprosy.
सिंदूर *n*. Red lead.
सिंधु *m*. The Indus, an ocean.
सिंधुर *m*. An elephant.
सिव् *vt*. 4 P. To sew.
सीकर *m*. Drizzle, a spray.
सीता *f*. A furrow, Ráma's wife.
सीमन् *f*. A boundary.

सीमन्त *m.* Separation of the hair on each side of the head; *m. n.* the head.

सीमन्तिनी *f.* A woman.

सीमंतोन्नयन *n.* A particular purificatory rite observed by women in their pregnancy.

सीमा *f.* Boundary; a land-mark; last degree.

सीर *m.* A plough.

सीवनी *f.* A needle.

सु *vt.* 1 U. To go; 1, 2 P. To possess power; 5 U. To sprinkle; with अभि- to mix; प्र-to beget.

सु *ind.* Good; well; much.

सुकर *a.* Easy to be done.

सुकुमार *a.* Very delicate.

सुकृत *n.* A virtuous act.

सुख *a.* Happy; easy; *n.* happiness, ease.

सुखम् *ind.* Happily; easily.

सुखावह *a.* Pleasant; comfortable.

सुगत *m.* Buddha.

सुगन्ध *m.* Fragrance.

सुचरित *n.* Good conduct.

सुजनता *f.* Goodness, benevolence; virtue.

सुत *m.* A son.

सुतराम् *ind.* Exceedingly; better.

सुता *f.* A daughter.

सुतिनी *f.* A mother.

सुदक्षिण *a.* Very sincere or liberal

सुदर्शन *m.* The discus of Vishnu.

सुदामन् *m.* A cloud; sea; one of Krishna's friends.

सुधा *f.* Nectar; water; juice; whitewash.

सुधांशु *m.* The moon.

सुधी *n.* A wise man.

सुन्दर *a.* Beautiful.

सुन्दरी *f.* A beautiful woman.

सुपर्ण *m.* Garuda.

सुप्त *a.* Sleeping.

सुप्ति *f.* Sleep.

सुप्रतिष्ठा *f.* Good position.

सुप्रभात *n.* The earliest dawn.

सुबोध *a.* Easily understood.

सुब्रह्मण्य *m.* Kárttikeya.

सुभग *a.* Pretty; happy; amiable; very fortunate.

सुभगा *f.* A favourite wife.

सुभाषित *n.* A witty saying; eloquence; learning.

सुभिक्ष *n.* Abundance of food

सुभ्रू *f.* A lovely woman.

सुमध्यमा *f.* A graceful woman.

सुमनस् *m.* A god; *f n.* a flower.

सुर *m.* A god.

सुरंगा *f.* A subterranean passage.

सुरत *n.* Amorous pleasure.

सुरतरु *m.* A tree of paradise.

सुरद्विष् *m.* A demon.

सुरधनुस् *n.* Rainbow.

सुरभि *a.* Fragrant; handsome. *m*. Fragrance; *f*. a cow; the earth.

सुरस *a*. Savoury; elegant.

सुरा *f*. Wine.

सुलभ *a*. Attainable; proper.

सुवर्ण *n*. Gold; money, *a*. beautiful.

सुवास *m*. An agreeable perfume.

सुवासिनी *f*. A woman married or unmarried residing in her father's house; a woman whose husband is alive.

सुविधम् *ind*. Easily.

सुविहित *a*. Well-arranged.

सुवृत्त *a*. Well-behaved.

सुवेल *a*. Tranquil; humble.

सुषमा *f*. Exquisite beauty.

सुषीम *a*. Cold.

सुषुप्ति *f*. Profound sleep; spiritual ignorance.

सुषुम्णा *f*. A particular artery of the body.

सुष्ठु *ind*. Well; very.

सुस्थ *a*. Healthy; happy; *n*. a happy condition.

सुहृद् *m*. A friend.

सू *vt*. 2, 4 A. To bring forth; 6 P. to excite.

सूकर *m*. A hog.

सूक्त *n*. A Vedic hymn.

सूक्ष्म *a*. Minute; sharp, exact.

सूक्ष्मदेह *m*. (**-शरीर** *n*.) The subtle body which is invested by the grosser material frame.

सूच् *vt*. 10 U. To pierce; to show; to suggest.

सूचक *a*. Indicative. *m*. A needle; a spy; a teacher.

सूचना *f*. Information; spying; teaching; a hint.

सूचि *f*. A needle; a sharp point; a military array.

सूचिक *m*. A tailor.

सूचिका *f*. A needle.

सूची *f*. See **सूचि**.

सूत *m*. A charioteer; a bard; the son of a Kshatriya by a Brhâmana woman.

सूतक *n*. Birth.

सूतिका *f*. A woman recently delivered.

सूति *f*. Birth; offspring; origin.

सूत्र *n*. A thread, a precept or aphorism.

सूत्रधार *m*. A stage-manager, a carpenter; an artisan.

सूद् *vt*. 1 A To hurt. 10 U. To incite; with-अभि or नि-to kill.

सूद *m*. Massacre, mud, a cook.

सूदकर्मन् *n*. Cookery.

सूदशाला *f*. A kitchen.

सूदन *a*. Destroying.

सून *a*. Born: empty.

सूना *f*. A slaughter-house.

सूनु *m*. A son.

सूनू *f*. A daughter.

सूनृत *a.* True, agreeable.
सूप *m.* Broth, a cook.
सूरि,(-न्) *m.* A learned man, a sage; the sun. [basket.
सूर्प *m. n.* A winnowing
सूर्य *m.* The sun.
सृ *vt. vi.* 1, 3 P. To bow; to blow; with अनु-to follow; अप-to retire; निस्-to slip; परि-to flow round; प्र-to spread; प्रति-to assassin; सम्-to obtain; *Causal*-to extend; with अप to withdraw; अभि-to meet; उद्-to drive away; प्र-to spread; प्रति-to replace; सम्-to cause to revolve.
सृक्क *n.* **सृक्कणी** *f.* **सृक्कन्** *n.* **सृक्क** *n.* **सृक्कणी** *f.* The corner of the mouth.
सृगाल *m.* A jackal.
सृज् *vt.* 6 P., 4 A. To let loose; to create; to apply; with अति to give; अव-to throw; उद्-to abandon; to give उप-to connect; to oppress; नि-to deliver; प्र-to injure; वि-to send; to throw; सम्-to mix.
सृणि (णी) का *f.* Saliva.
सृति *f.* A road.
सृप् *vt.* 1 P. To creep; with व्यति or परि-to move to and fro; अनु or समुप-to approach; अप-to deviate from; to espy; व्यप-to run away; उद्-to rise; वि-to sneak about; सम्-to flow; to move.
सृष्टि *f.* Creation; nature.
सेक *m.* Sprinkling.
सेचनी *f.* A bucket.
सेतु *m.* A mound; a causeway; a pass; a barrier.
सेदिवस् *a.* Setting.
सेना *f.* An army.
सेनानी (-पति) *m.* A commander of an army.
सेव् *vt.* 1 A. To serve; to enjoy; to inhabit; with उप-to practise; नि-to pursue; to employ; to enjoy; परि-to take.
सेवक *m.* A servant; a votary. [service.
सेवन *n.* Sewing; enjoying;
सेवनी *f.* A needle.
सेवा *f.* Service; use.
सैंह *a.* Belonging to a lion.
सैकत *a.* Sandy. *n.* A sandbank.
सैकतिक *a.* Wavering.
सैनापत्य *n.* The command of an army. [tinel.
सैनिक *m.* A soldier; a sen-
सैंधव *m.* A horse; *m. n.* rock-salt.
सैन्य *m.* A soldier. *n.* Army.
सैरंध्र (-ध्रि) *m.* A menial servant.

सैरं (रिं) ध्री *m.* A maid servant; Draupadî.

सैरिक *a.* Relating to a plough; *m.* A ploughman.

सैरिभ *m.* A buffalo.

सो *vt.* 4 P. To destroy; to finish; with अव-to fail; to finish; अध्यव-to -do; to be able; पर्यव-to endeavour; to resolve; to perish; व्यव-to accept; to strive: to wish; संवि-to decree.

सोढ *pp.* Endured.

सोत्क, सोत्कंठ *a.* Very eager.

सोत्प्रास *m.* Sarcasm.

सोत्सेध *a.* Lofty.

सोदर्य *m.* One's own brother.

सोपधि *a.* Fraudulent.

सोपप्लव *a.* Eclipsed.

सोपाधि (-क) *a.* Restricted by conditions; qualified.

सोपान *n.* Stairs; a ladder.

सोम *m.* Name of a plant or its juice; Kubera; Yama; S'iva; water; nectar; wind.

सोमपीति (थि) न् *m.* One drinking Soma.

सोमवंश *m.* The lunar dynasty.

सौकर्य *n.* Facility.

सौकुमार्य *n.* Delicacy.

सौख्य *n.* Pleasure.

सौगत(-तिक) *m.* A Buddhist.

सौगंध (-ध्य) *n.* Fragrance.

सौचि, (-क) *m.* A tailor.

सौजन्य *n.* Goodness, generosity.

सौदर्य *n.* Brotherhood.

सौदाम (मि) नी, (-म्नी) *f.* Lightning.

सौध *m.* A mansion.

सौनिक *m.* A butcher.

सौंदर्य *n.* Beauty; elegance,

सौपर्ण *n.* Dry ginger.

सौपर्णेय *m.* Garuda.

सौप्तिक *n.* A night attack.

सौभग *n.* Good luck; wealth.

सौभाग्य *n.* Auspiciousness; beauty; wifehood (as opp. to widowhood).

सौभाग्यवती *f.* A married and unwidowed woman.

सौभ्रात्र *n.* Good brotherhood.

सौमनस *a.* Pleasing. *n.* Benevolence.

सौमनस्य *n.* Pleasure.

सौमित्र (-त्रि) *m.* Lakshmana.

सौम्य *a.* Mild. *m.* Planet Mercury.

सौर *a.* Sacred to the sun; celestial.

सौरथ *m.* A hero.

सौरभ (-भ्य) *n.* Fragrance.

सौरभी (भेयी) *f.* A cow.

सौरमास *m.* Solar month.

सौराज्य *n.* Good government.

सौराष्ट्र *m.* N of a country (modern Kathiawar).

सौरिक *a.* Celestial. *m.* Saturn.

सौष्ठव *n.* Excellence. [ship.
सौहार्द (-र्द्य), सौहृद *n.* Friend-
स्कद् *vt. vi.* 1 A. To jump
स्कंद् *vt. vi.* 1 P. To jump; with अव- to assail; परि- to spring about.
स्कंद *m.* Kárttikeya.
स्कंदन *n.* Emission; effusion.
स्कंध *m.* The shoulder; a branch; a chapter; five objects of senses; war; a road.
स्कु *vt.* 5, 9 U. To jump.
स्खल् *vt.* 1 P. To stumble; to blunder; to lisp; with प्र-to jolt. [ing.
स्खलन *n.* Blunder; falter-
स्तन् *vi.* 1 P. 10 U. To sound; to sigh; to thunder; with नि-bewail.
स्तन *m.* The female breast.
स्तनंधय *m.* A suckling; an infant.
स्तनयित्नु *m* Thundering; a cloud; lightning.
स्तनांतर *n.* The heart
स्तनाभोग *m.* Fullness of the breast.
स्तन्य *n.* Mother's milk.
स्तबक *m.* A bunch.
स्तब्ध *a.* Hard; stopped.
स्तंब *m.* A clump of grass; a bush; insensibility.
स्तंबेरम *m.* An elephant.
स्तंभ् *vt. vi.* 1 A. 5, 9 P. To fix firmly; to stupefy; to stop; with अव-to bind; उद्-to uphold; नि-to stop; पर्यव-to surround; वि-to fix; सम्-to support; to stop; समव-to encourage.
स्तंभ *m.* A prop; a pillar; rigidity; suppressing.
स्तर *m.* A layer; a bed.
स्तरि (री) मन् *m.* A bed, a couch.
स्तव *m.*, (-न *n.*) Praise.
स्तिमित *a.* Wet; dull; paralyzed; gratified.
स्तु *vt.* 2 U. To praise.
स्तुति *f.* Praise.
स्तुत्य *a.* Laudable.
स्तूप *m.* A mound; a Buddhistic tope.
स्तृ *vt.* 5 P. To love; 5 U To spread; with अव-to cover; to fill; परि-to arrange; वि or सम्-to spread.
स्तृति *f.* Expansion.
स्तॄ 9 U. To cover.
स्तेन *m.* A thief.
स्तैन (-न्य) *n.* Theft.
स्तोक *a.* Little.
स्तोत्र *n.* Praise. [collection.
स्तोम *m.* Praise; sacrifice;
स्त्यान *n.* Thickness; bulk.
स्त्यै *vt.* 1 U. To spread.
स्त्री *f.* A woman; a wife.
स्त्रीजित *m.* A hen-pecked husband.

स्त्रैण *a.* Feminine. *n.* Womanhood.

स्थ *a.* Standing.

स्थपति *m.* A soverign; an architect.

स्थग् *vt.* 1 P. To hide.

स्थग *m.* A rogue.

स्थंडिल *n.* An altar.

स्थपुट *m.* An uneven place.

स्थल *n.* Place; topic.

स्थली *f.* Forest land.

स्थविर *m.* An old man.

स्थविष्ठ *a.* (Super. of स्थूल) Greatest.

स्थवीयस् *a.* (Comp. of स्थूल) Greater.

स्था *vt. vi.* 1 U. To stand; to exist; to perform; with अति–to exceed; अधि-to tread upon;to remain; to surpass; to govern; अनु-to obey; अव–to remain; आ-to turn to; उप-to serve; to stand opposite;उद्-to get up; अभ्युद्-to rise; व्युद् to incite; पर्युप-to surround;परिनि-to be skilled in; विप्र (Atm.) -to depart; संप्र (Atm.) -to depart; प्रति-to stand firm; संप्रति- to rest on; वि (Atm.) -to spread; सम् (Atm.) -to agree.

स्थाणु *a.* Firm. *m.* Śiva; a post; *m. n.* a branchless trunk of a tree.

स्थान *n.* Place; condition; rank; an object; indication.

स्थानक *n.* A position; a city; a division.

स्थानिक *a.* Local.

स्थाने *ind.* Appropriately.

स्थापत्य *n.* Architecture.

स्थापना *f.* Establishing.

स्थामन् *n.* Strength.

स्थायिन् *a.* Steady; enduring.

स्थायिभाव *m.* A lasting feeling.

स्थाली *f.* A cooking-pot.

स्थालीपुलाकन्याय *m.* Inference about the whole from that of a part.

स्थावर *a.* Stationary. *m.* A mountain.

स्थितप्रज्ञ *a.* Firm in judgment.

स्थिति *f.* Residence;natural state; stability; station; pause; propriety; consistency; settled order; boundary; rule.

स्थितिस्थापक *a.* Elastic.

स्थिर *a.* Firm; calm, steady.

स्थिरा *f.* The earth.

स्थूणा *f.* A pillar.

स्थूल *a.* Bulky; great; dull; rough.

स्थूलशरीर *n.* The material body.

स्थेमन् *m.* Firmness.

स्थैर्य *n.* Stability, resolution, patience.

स्थौल्य *n.* Bulkiness.

स्नपन *n.* Bathing.

स्ना *vi.* 2 P. To bathe; with नि-to be perfect.

स्नातक *m.* An initiated house holder.

स्नान *n.* Bathing; ablution.

स्नायु *m.* A muscle.

स्निग्ध *a.* Glossy; oily; kind; moist; thick. *m.* A friend.

स्निह् *vi. vt.* 4 P. To love.

स्नु *vi.* 2 P. To flow.

स्नुषा *f.* A daughter-in-law.

स्नेह *m.* Oil; moisture; love.

स्पंद् *vt.* 1 A To throb; with वि-to struggle.

स्पंद *m.* Vibration.

स्पर्ध् *vi.* 1 A. To rival; to [defy.

स्पर्धा *f.* Rivalry.

स्पर्श् *vt.* 10 A. To touch.

स्पर्श *m.* Touch; sensation; contact, conflict, disease, gift, consonants from क् to म्; a spy; sky; wind.

स्पश *m.* A spy.

स्पष्ट *a.* Evident.

स्पष्टम् *ind.* Openly; boldly.

स्पृश् *vt.* 6 P. To touch; to take; to wash.

स्पृह् *vt.* 10 U. To desire.

स्पृहणीय *a.* Enviable.

स्पृहा *f.* Desire; envy.

स्फटिक *m.* Crystal.

स्फल् *vi.* 1 P. To tremble; *causal*-with आ-to dash.

स्फार *a.* Large; expanded. *m.* Vibration; *n.* plenty.

स्फालन *n.* Friction.

स्फीत *a.* Swollen; abundant.

स्फीति *f.* Abundance; enlargement.

स्फुट् *vt. vi.* 10, 6 P. To burst; to blow

स्फुट *a.* Opened; manifest; well-known, bright; diffused; clear, white, loud.

स्फुर् *vi.* 6 P. To tremble; to start; to glitter; with अभि-to expand.

स्फुरण *n.* Trembling; flash-[ing.

स्फुलिंग *m. n.* (-गा *f.*) A spark of fire.

स्फूर्ति *f.* Vibration; display: inspiration; poetical genius.

स्फोट *m.* Bursting; disclosure; a boil.

स्म *ind.* A pleonatic parti-[cle.

स्मय *m.* Astonishment. *m.* pride.

स्मर *m.* God of love; love; [recollection.

स्मरण *m.* Remembrance; memory; tradition.

स्मरणपदवी *f.* Death.

स्मार *a.* Relating to love; *n.* recollection.

स्मारक *a.* Reminding. *n.* A memorial.

स्मार्त *a.* Memorial; written in the Smriti; domestic (as fire); name of a particular sect.

स्मि *vt.* 1 A. To smile; with वि-to be proud.

स्मित *n.* A smile.

स्मृ *vt. vi.* 5 P. To please; 1 P. To remember, to repeat; with अप or वि-to forget. [book

स्मृति *f.* Memory; a law

स्मृतिशेष *a.* Deceased.

स्मेर *a.* Smiling; blooming.

स्यद *m.* Speed.

स्यंद्, *vi* 1 A. To drop.

स्यंद, (-न) *m.* A chariot.

स्यंदिनी *f.* Saliva.

स्यमंतक *m.* The gem worn by Krishna.

स्यात् *ind.* Perhaps.

स्याद्वाद *m.* An assertion of probability.

स्यूत *a.* Sewn; woven.

स्रंस् *vi.* 1 A. To fall down.

स्रग्विन् *a.* Bearing a garland.

स्रग्धरा *f.* A kind of metre.

स्रज् *f.* A garland.

स्रंभ् *vt.* 1 A. To entrust; with वि-to confide.

स्रव *m.* Trickling, a drop.

स्रवती *f.* A river.

स्रष्टृ *m.* The creator.

स्रस्त *a.* Dropped; loosened.

स्रस्तर *m.* A sofa, bed.

स्राक् *ind.* Quickly.

स्रु *vt. vi.* 1 P. To drop.

स्रुति *f.* A stream; exudation.

स्रोत, (-स्) *n.* A stream.

स्रोतस्वती, स्रोतस्विनी *f.* A river.

स्व *pron. a.* Own; natural; *m.* One's self; a relative; the soul; *m. n.* wealth; the pulse or positive quantity.

स्वक, स्वकीय *a.* Own.

स्वगतम् *ind.* To oneself; aside (in drama).

स्वच्छ *a.* Pure.

स्वच्छंद *a.* Wanton.

स्वज् *vt.* 1 A. To embrace.

स्वतंत्र *a.* Independent.

स्वत्व *n.* Ownership.

स्वधा *f.* Self-will; food offered to the manes.

स्वन् *vi.* 1 P. To sound.

स्वप् *vi.* 2 P. To sleep.

स्वप्न *m.* Sleep; a dream.

स्वप्रकाश *a.* Self-evident.

स्वभाव *m.* Nature.

स्वभावसिद्ध *a.* Inborn.

स्वयम् *ind.* By one-self.

स्वयंभू *a.* Self-existent.[age.

स्वयंवर *m.* A choice marri-

स्वर् *ind.* Heaven.

स्वर *m.* Sound; a vowel; a Vedic accent. [scale.

स्वरग्राम *m.* The musical

स्वरूप *n.* Nature.

स्वर्ग *m.* Heaven.
स्वर्गिन् *m.* A deity.
स्वर्गीय *a.* Divine.
स्वर्ग्य *a.* Heavenly.
स्वर्ण *n.* Gold.
स्वर्णकार *m.* A gold-smith.
स्वर्भानु *m.* Ràhu.
स्वर्वधू, स्वर्वेश्या *f.* A heavenly nymph. [ficant.
स्वल्प *a.* Very few, insigni-
स्वशुर *m.* A father-in-law.
स्वसृ *f.* A sister.
स्वस्ति *ind.* Hail, adieu.
स्वस्तिक *m.* A mystical mark; the meeting of four roads.
स्वस्तिमुख *m.* A letter; a bard.
स्वस्तिवाचन (-वाचनक,-वाचनिक) *n.* A religious rite preparatory to any important observance.
स्वस्तिवाच्य *n.* Congratulation.
स्वस्थ *a.* Firm; contented; healthy; at ease. [son
स्वस्रीय,स्वस्रेय *m.* A sister's
स्वस्रीया,स्वस्रेयी *f.* A sister's daughter.
स्वागत *n.* A welcome.
स्वाच्छंद्य *n.* Independence.
स्वातंत्र्य *n.* Independence.
स्वाति (-ती) *f.* The fifteenth lunar asterism. [vour.
स्वाद *m.*, (-न *n.*) Taste, fla-
स्वादिमन् *m.* Sweetness.
स्वादिष्ट *a.* Very sweet.
स्वादु *a.* Sweet, pleasing.
स्वाधीन *a.* Self-dependent.
स्वाध्याय *m.* Sacred study.
स्वाप *m.* Sleep, a dream; paralysis; numbness.
स्वापतेय *n.* Prosperity.
स्वापद *m.* A wild beast.
स्वाभाविक *a.* Natural. *m.* A king; a religious man.
स्वामिन् *m.* A master.
स्वामिनी *f.* A mistress.
स्वाम्य *n.* Mastership.
स्वायत्त *a.* Depending on one's self.
स्वायंभुव *m.* The first Manu.
स्वारसिक *a.* Sweet. [priety.
स्वारस्य *n.* Excellence; pro-
स्वाराज्य *n.* The dominion of heaven.
स्वार्थ *m.* Self-interest.
स्वाल्प *a.* Little.
स्वास्थ्य *n.* Health; prosperity; self-reliance.
स्वाहा *f.* Wife of Agni. *ind.* An exclamation used in making an oblation to gods.
स्वित् *ind.* What ! Hey !
स्विद् *vi.* 4 P. To sweat.
स्वीकार *m.* Acceptance.
स्वीकृति *f.* Acceptance.
स्वीय *a.* Own.
स्वेद *m.* Perspiration; heat; free, gentle.

स्वैर *a.* Wanton; optional.
स्वैरम् *ind.* Of one's own accord, indistinctly.
स्वैरता *f.* Wilfulness. [talk.
स्वैरालाप *m.* Confidential
स्वैरिणी An adulteress.

ह *ind.* Verily; indeed.
हंस *m.* A swan; the individual soul; the sun; a horse. [particle.
हंजा (-जे) *ind.* A vocative
हट्ट *m* A market.
हट्टविलासिनी *f.* A harlot.
हठ *m.* Violence, oppression.
हठयोग *m.* A mode of Yoga difficult to practise.
हठात्, हठेन *ind.* Forcibly.
हंडिका, हंडी *f.* An earthen
हत *a.* Killed; miserable. [jar.
हतक *a.* Miserable
हति *f.* A defect.
हत्या *f.* Murder, slaughter.
हन् *vt.* 2 P. To kill; with अप-to lessen; अभि-to strike; आ (Atm) -to hit; उद्-to raise up; to become haughty; उप-to vex; नि-to strike; परा-to repulse; प्रति-to ward off; वि-to oppose; सम्-to unite.
हनु (-नू) *m. f.* The chin.
हनुमत् *m.* N. of a monkey-chief.
हन्त *ind.* Oh ! alas !
हन्तकारव *m.* An offering to be presented to a guest.
हम्बा, (-वर) *m.*, Lowing of kine.
हय *m.* A horse; Indra.
हयग्रीव *m.* Vishnu.
हयंकष *m.* A charioteer.
हयशाला *f.* A stable for horses.
हर *a.* Taking away. *m.* S'iva; fire; an ass.
हरण *n.* Carrying off; a gift.
हरि *a.* Green, brown. *m.* Vishnu; Indra; S'iva; Yama; the sun; fire; wind; a lion; a horse; a monkey. [paradise.
हरिचंदन *m. n.* A tree in
हरिण *a.* Pale. *m.* A deer.
हरिणक *m.* A deer.
हरिणी *f.* A female deer; a class of women; N. of a metre. [ish.
हरित् *a.* Greenish, yellow-
हरित *a* Green.
हरिताल *n.* Yellow orpiment.
हरिद्रा *f.* Turmeric.
हरिद्राराग *a.* Fickle in love.
हर्म्य *n.* A palace; a hearth.
हर्ष *m.* Joy. [Delighting.
हर्षण *a.* Pleasurable. *n.*
हल *n.* A plough.
हलभू(भृ)ति *f.* Agriculture.
हलभृत् (-धर) *m.* A ploughman; Balarâma.

हला *f.* A female friend; the earth. *ind.* A vocative particle. [poison.

हलाहल *m. n.* A deadly

हल्य *a.* Arable; ugly.

हव *m.* An oblation; prayer; a call; order; challenge.

हवन *n.* An oblation; offering an oblation.

हवनीय *n.* Clarified butter.

हविर्भुज् *m.* Fire.

हविष्य *n.* Clarified butter.

हविष्यान्न *n.* Food fit to be eaten during certain holidays.

हविस् *n.* An oblation.

हव्य *n.* An oblation.

हव्यकव्य *n.* Oblations to the gods and to the manes.

हव्यवाह् (-वाह,-वाहन) *m.* Fire.

हस् *vt. vi.* 1 P. To laugh; to open; to resemble; with उप, परि, प्र-to deride; वि-to smile.

हसित *n.* Laughter.

हस्त *m.* The hand, a particular measure; an elephant's trunk; abundance; a lunar mansion.

हस्तक *m.* A hand.

हस्तगत *a.* Secured.

हस्तदोष *m.* A slip of the hand.

हस्तवत् *a.* Skilful.

हस्ताग्र *n.* A finger.

हस्तामलक *n.* Anything completely grasped.

हस्ताहस्ति *ind.* Hand to hand.

हस्तिदंत *n.* Ivory; a radish.

हस्तिन् *m.* An elephant.

हस्तिनी *f.* A female elephant. A woman of a particular description.

हस्तिस्नान *n.* A useless occupation.

हस्तेकरण *n.* Marriage.

हा *ind.* Alas ! oh !

हा *vt.* 3 A. To go; to obtain; with उद्-to rise; to revive; to arise; to leave; with उप-to descend; सम्-to attend; 3 P. To abandon.

हाटक *n.* Gold.

हात्र *n.* Wages.

हानि *f.* Loss; decrease.

हायन *m. n.* A year.

हार *m.* A necklace; deprivation; war; a division.

हारक *m.* A thief.

हारि *a.* Captivating [ing.

हारिन् *a.* Robbing; captivat-

हारीत *m.* A rogue.

हार्द *n.* Affection; intention.

हार्य *a.* To be carried.

हाल *m.* A plough.

हालहली, हाला *f.* Wine.

हालाहल *n.* See हलाहल.

हाली *f.* A wife's younger sister.

हाव *m.* A blandishment.

हास *m*. Laughter; merriment.

हासक *m*. A buffoon.

हासिका *f*. Mirth. [ridicule.

हास्य *n*. Laughter; mirth;

हास्यपदवी *f*. Ridicule.

हास्यास्पद *n*. A laughing stock. [tion; uproar

हाहाकार *m*. Great lamenta

हि *ind* Because;surely,only

हि *vt*. 5 P. To send.

हिंस् *vt*. 1 P. 10 U. To hurt.

हिंसक *m*. A beast of prey.

हिंसा *f*. Injury; harm.

हिंसालु *a*. Hurtful.

हिंस्र *a*. Hurtful;terrible.*m*. A beast of prey.

हिक्का *f*. Hiccough.

हिंगु *m.n*. Asafœtida. [lion.

हिंगुल *m*. *n*. (-लि *m*.) Vermi-

हित *a*. Pleased; proper; wholesome *m*. A benefactor; *n*. the welfare.

हितवादिन् *m*. A friendly adviser.

हिंदोल, (-क) *m*., हिंदोला *f*. A swing.

हिम *a*.Cold.*m*. Winter; the moon; the Himalayas; *n*. frost; snow.

हिमकर *m*. The moon.

हिमकूट *m*. Winter; the Himalayas.

हिमगु (-दीधिति, -द्युति, -भास्, -रश्मि) *m*. The moon.

हिमागिरि(-अचल,-अद्रि,-आलय, -शैल) *m*. The Himálayas.

हिमानी *f*. A mass of snow.

हिरण्मय *a*. Golden. [virile.

हिरण्य *n*. Gold,silver,semen

हिरण्यगर्भ *m*. Brahman(*m*.), Vishnu, the soul invested by the subtile body.

हिरण्यबिंदु (-रेतस्) *m*. Fire.

हिल्लोल *m*. A wave; a whim.

हीन *a*. Destitute of; low.

हीर *m*. A snake. *n*. A diamond; a lion; a necklace.

हीरक *m*. A diamond.

ही, हिही *ind*. Ah ! [tion.

हु *vt*. 3 P. To offer an obla-

हुंकार *m*. हुंकृति *f*. Uttering the sound Hum; grunting.

हुड (-डु) *m*. A ram. lation.

हुत *a*. Sacrificed. *n* An ob-

हुतभुज्(-अशन,-आश)*m*.Fire.

हुति *f*. Offering oblations.

हुम् *ind*. An interjection of remembrance, reproach, or assent

हूण *m*. A barbarian.

हूति *f*. Inviting; challenging; a name. [dharva.

हूहू *m*. A kind of a Gan-

हृ *vt*. 1 U. To carry; with अनु-to imitate; अभ्यव-to eat; आ-to bring; उद्-to take out; to destroy;उदा-to illustrate; उप-to offer; निस्-to extract; परि-to abandon; प्र-to strike; वि-to remove; व्यव-to sue; व्या-to speak; सम्-to collect; to withdraw; to curb; to destroy.

ह्रणीया *f.* Censure.

ह्रति *f.* Seizure.

हृद् *n.* The chest; the heart.

हृदय *n.* The heart; the chest; essence; science.

हृदयंगम *a.* Thrilling; attractive; beloved.

हृदयस्थ *a.* Cherished in the heart.

हृद्गत *n.* Meaning; intention.

हृद्य *a.* Pleasant; cherished.

हृद्रोग *m.* Grief; love.

हृल्लेख *m.* Knowledge.

हृष् *i.* 1, 4 P. To rejoice; to stand erect.

हृषीक *n.* An organ of sense.

हृषीकेश *m.* Vishnu.

हृष्ट *a.* Pleased.

हृष्टि *f.* Delight, pride.

हे *ind.* A vocative particle.

हेक्का *f.* Hiccough.

हेठ *m.* Vexation, obstruction, injury.

हेड *m.* Disregard.

हेति *m.f.* A weapon; a ray of light; flame.

हेतु *m.* Object; motive; impulse; means; origin; logic.

हेतुमत् *n.* Effect.

हेत्वाभास *m.* A fallacy.

हेम *n.* Gold. *m.* Mercury.

हेमन् *n.* Gold.

हेमकर (-कर्तृ, -कार, -कारक) *m.* A gold-smith.

हेमज्वाल *m.* Fire.

हेमन्त *m.* The cold season.

हेममालिन् *m.* The sun.

हेमल *m.* A touch-stone.

हेय *a.* Fit to be abandoned.

हेरंब *m.* Ganes'a.

हेरिक *m.* A spy.

हेलना *f.* Insult; disregard.

हेलया Easily.

हेला *f.* Disrespect; dalliance.

हेलि *m.* The sun; *f.* dalliance.

हेवाक *m.* Engerness.

हेषा *f.* Neighing.

हैतुक *a.* Causal. *m.* Sceptic.

हैम *a.* Gold; golden.

हैमन *a.* Wintry; golden.

हैमवत *a.* Snowy.

हैयंगवीन *n.* Butter prepared on the previous day.

होतृ *m.* A priest; presiding at a sacrifice.

होत्र *n.* A sacrifice.

होत्री *a.* The offerer of oblations.

होम *m.* A sacrifice.

होमि *m.* Fire; clarified butter; water.

होरा *f.* The rising of a zodiacal sign.

होलाका, होलिका, होली *f.* The full-moon day in Phálguna or the festival celebrated on that and following days.

हृ *vt.* 2 A. To rob; to hide; with अप-to conceal.

ह्यस् *ind.* Yesterday.

ह्यस्तन *a.* Belonging to yesterday.

ह्रद *m.* A deep lake.

ह्रदग्रह *m.* A crocodile.

ह्रदिनी *f.* A river. [sound.

ह्रस् 1 P. To wane; to

ह्रस्व *a.* Short.

ह्राद *m.* Noise.

ह्रास *m.* Decline; sound.

ह्री *vi.* 3 P. To blush.

ह्री *f.* Shame, modesty.

ह्लाद् *vi.* 1 A. To be delighted.

ह्लादिनी *f.* Lightning.

ह्वान *n.* Calling; a cry.

ह्वे *vt. vi.* 1 U. To call; with आ (Atm.)-to challenge.